# CREATIVITY 29

editor
**David E. Carter**

art direction
  Suzanna M.W.
cover design
  Jenette Reed Williams
production, layout
  Graham Allen, Tania Lambert,
  Anthony B. Stephens,
  & Christa Carter

Creativity 29

First published in 2000 by HBI,
an imprint of HarperCollins Publishers
10 East 53rd Street
New York, NY 10022-5299

ISBN: 0688-17987-8

Distributed in the U.S. and Canada by
Watson-Guptill Publications
1515 Broadway
New York, NY 10036
Tel:   (800) 451-1741
       (732) 363-4511 in NJ, AK, HI
Fax:   (732) 363-0338

Distributed throughout the rest of the world by
HarperCollins International
10 East 53rd Street
New York, NY 10022-5299
Fax:   (212) 207-7654

©Copyright 2000 HBI and David E. Carter

All rights reserved. No part of this book may be reproduced in any form or by an electronic or mechanical means, including information storage and retrieval systems, without permission in writing from the copyright owners, except by a reviewer who may quote brief passages in a review.

All images in this book have been reproduced with the knowledge and prior consent of the individuals concerned. No responsibility is accepted by producer, publisher, or printer for any infringement of copyright or otherwise arising from the contents of this publication. Every effort has been made to ensure that credits accurately comply with information supplied.

Printed in Hong Kong by Everbest Printing Company through Four Colour Imports, Louisville, Kentucky.

# Introduction

This book marks some major changes in the *Creativity Annual*.

But to put those changes into perspective, let's look at a brief history of *Creativity*.

It was in 1972 that Don Barron, editor of *Art Direction* magazine, recognized the need for an advertising and design competition that was open to all—regardless of geography.

In 1972, *Creativity 1* was published and from that time forward, the *Creativity Annual* has been the book that has attracted work from the most diverse locations. In the 1970s and 1980s, that meant showing work from outside New York, Chicago and Los Angeles. Imagine: people back then were surprised to see great work from such places as Minneapolis, Boston, Atlanta, Richmond, and a lot of other places that were definitely not Madison Avenue.

As the 1990s saw the emergence of the global economy, *Creativity* once again led the way with international work being shown. In recent years, the *Creativity Annual* has had work from as many as 40 countries around the world. (Compare that with the other annuals: few of them have as many as 20 countries represented.)

Now that the *Creativity Annual* has spread the notion that "*Creativity* is everywhere," the changes we instituted have completed the goal of making the *Creativity Annual* an even more important source around the world. This year, we have a new publisher. HBI (Hearst Books International), a division of HarperCollins Publishers, gives us a much greater distribution all over the earth. When I recently asked them for a list of countries where they sell books, their answer was "how many countries are there?" HBI sells books virtually everywhere, and this will mean greatly expanded distribution for *Creativity*.

Another change this year is that the book has expanded from 320 pages to 384. The larger book means that each piece chosen can be seen in more detail. In addition, the paper and binding quality have been improved from previous volumes.

In summary, we are doing everything possible to make the *Creativity Annual* into an even better showcase for advertising and design.

This year's book showcases the best work from entries we received from 40 states in the USA and from 40 countries around the world. Less than 20% of the work submitted was chosen for publication. The Gold Medal Awards (noted in the book with a **C**) were given to fewer than 2% of the total entries.

Once again, the work included in Creativity 29 is truly world-class.

# CREATIVITY

## Table of Contents

| | |
|---|---|
| Consumer Ads, Full | 5 |
| Consumer Ads, Fractional | 21 |
| **Consumer Ads, Campaign** | **26** |
| **Trade Ads, Full** | **45** |
| Trade Ads, Fractional | 54 |
| Trade Ads, Campaign | 56 |
| **Posters** | **66** |
| **Billboards** | **94** |
| Annual Reports | 100 |
| Brochures | 122 |
| **Catalogs** | **152** |
| **Book Jackets** | **163** |
| Records, CDs, Video Packaging | 170 |
| Package Designs | 176 |
| **Calendars** | **202** |
| **Direct Mail Pieces** | **207** |
| T-Shirts | 217 |
| Promotional Pieces | 219 |
| **Trademarks/Logos** | **258** |
| **Letterheads/Stationery** | **278** |
| Corporate Identity Manuals | 292 |
| Signage, Environmental Graphics | 294 |
| **Editorial Designs** | **300** |
| **Magazine Covers** | **312** |
| Public Service Ads, Single | 320 |
| Public Service Ads, Campaign | 325 |
| **Creative Achievement for Art, Illustration** | **328** |
| **Creative Achievement for Photography** | **338** |
| Creative Achievement for Typography | 344 |
| Consumer TVc, Single | 345 |
| **Consumer TVc, Campaign** | **357** |
| **Corporate TVc, Single** | **362** |
| Corporate TVc, Campaign | 363 |
| Public Service TVc, Single | 364 |
| **Public Service TVc, Campaign** | **366** |
| **Show Openings, IDs, Titles** | **367** |
| Demo/Presentation Videos | 370 |
| Corporate Videos | 371 |
| **Web Site Designs** | **373** |
| **CD-ROMs** | **378** |
| Index | 380 |

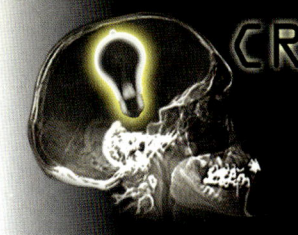

# CREATIVITY
## Consumer Ads Full

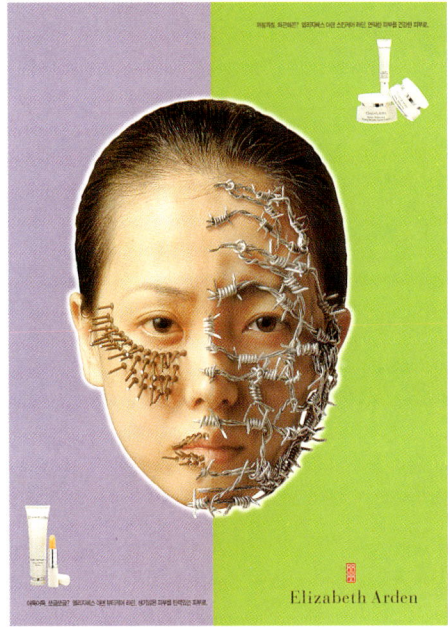

creative firm
 Young & Rubicam Mexico
 Mexico City, Mexico
creative director
 Enrique Laguardia
art director
 Mauricio Castillo
photographer
 Miguel Icaza
copywriter
 Enrique Laguardia
client
 Whitehall Robins

creative firm
 McCann-Erickson Korea Inc.
 Seoul, Korea
creative director
 Jeremy Perrott
art directors
 S.Y. Kim & S.T. Kim
copywriter
 W.H. Kim
client
 Elisabeth Arden

creative firm
 JMC/Y&R
 Caracas, Venezuela
creative people
 Mabel Ruiz & Ruben Perez
client
 El Universal

creative firm
 KPR
 New York (New York), USA
creative people
 Norene Oldfield, Nancy Richman, & Ted Whitby
client
 Janssen Pharmaceutica

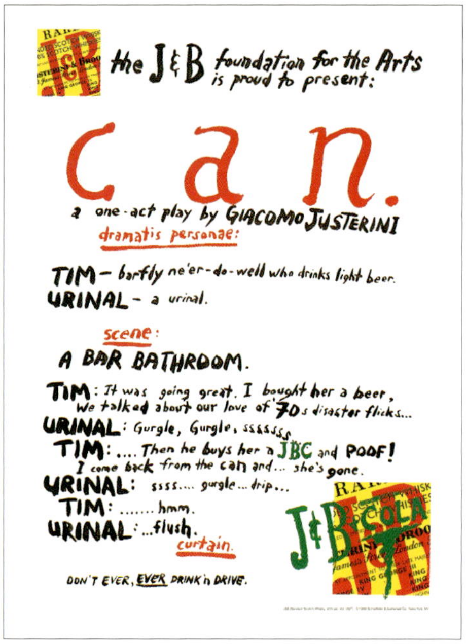

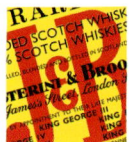

creative firm
  J. Walter Thompson/N.Y.
  New York (New York), USA
creative directors
  Michael Hart & J. J. Jordan
art directors, copywriters
  Rick Streed, Anders Carlsson,
  & Michael Hart
clients
  Schieffelin & Somerset Co./
  J&B Scotch

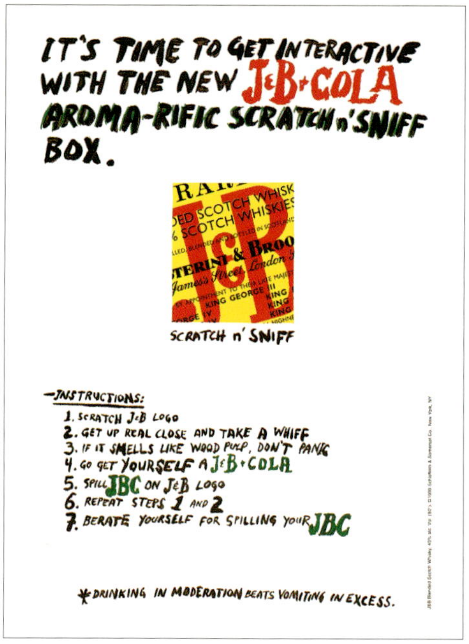

creative firm
  J. Walter Thompson/N.Y.
  New York (New York), USA
creative director
  J.J. Jordan
art directors, copywriters
  Rick Streed, Anders Carlsson,
  & Michael Hart
clients
  Schieffelin & Somerset Co./
  J&B Scotch

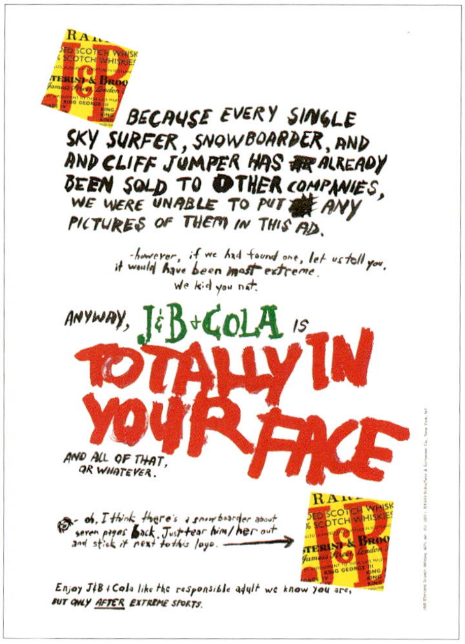

creative firm
  J. Walter Thompson/N.Y.
  New York (New York), USA
creative directors
  J.J. Jordan, Michael Hart
art directors, copywriters
  Rick Streed, Anders Carlsson,
  & Michael Hart
client
  Schieffelin & Somerset Co./
  J&B Scotch

creative firm
  bb communication inc.
  New York (New York), USA
creative people
  Chin-Chih Yang & Eric Feng
client
  APWM, Inc.

creative firm
  Morgan & Partners
  Jacksonville (Florida), USA
art director
  Bryan Co.
copywriter
  Kathy Bronson
client
  Swisher International

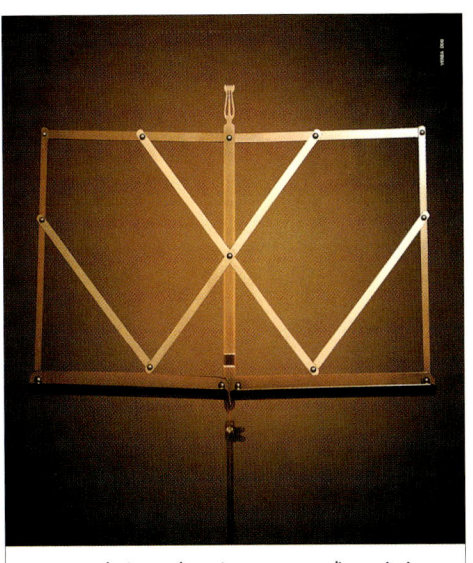

creative firm
Verba DDB
Milan, Italy
creative directors
Enrico Bonomini & Francesco Emiliani
artist
Umberto Mauri
copywriter
Dario Alesani
client
Autogerma

creative firm
The Zimmerman Agency
Tallahassee (Florida), USA
creative director
Doug Engel
art director
Rob Kerr
production
Emily Barrow
copywriter
Lee Gonzalez
client
Hotel Tverskaya

creative firm
Sawyer Riley Compton
Atlanta (Georgia), USA
creative directors
Bart Cleveland & Rob Hardison
art directors
Bart Cleveland & David Paprocki
photographer
Sally Gall
copywriters
Brett Compton, John Spalding,
Bart Cleveland, & David Paprocki
client
Ritz-Carlton

creative firm
Sawyer Riley Compton
Atlanta (Georgia), USA
creative directors
Bart Cleveland & Rob Hardison
art directors
Bart Cleveland,
Tammy Thorn Anderson,
& Rob Hardison
photographers
Larry Ladig & David Kiesgen
copywriters
Brett Compton, John Spalding,
& Bart Cleveland
client
Ritz-Carlton

creative firm
Sawyer Riley Compton
Atlanta (Georgia), USA
creative directors
Bart Cleveland
& Rob Hardison
art directors
Bart Cleveland
& Tammy Thorn Anderson
photographer
L. Charles Marrero
copywriters
Brett Compton, John Spalding,
& Bart Cleveland
client
Ritz-Carlton

creative firm
  Temerlin McClain
    Irving (Texas), USA
creative director
  Artie Megibben
art director
  Han Kim
photographer
  Bob Stevens
copywriter
  Tina Widner
client
  Subaru

creative firm
  Temerlin McClain
    Irving (Texas), USA
creative director
  Artie Megibben
art director
  Han Kim
photographer
  Bob Stevens
copywriter
  Jim Weber
client
  Subaru

creative firm
  Temerlin McClain
    Irving (Texas), USA
creative director
  Artie Megibben
art directors
  Michelle Courtad & Han Kim
photographer
  Bob Stevens
copywriter
  Tina Widner
client
  Subaru

creative firm
  Temerlin McClain
    Irving (Texas), USA
creative director
  Artie Megibben
art directors
  Michelle Courtad & Han Kim
photographer
  Bob Stevens
copywriter
  Melvin Strobbe
client
  Subaru

creative firm
  Fry Hammond Barr
    Orlando (Florida), USA
creative directors
  Tim Fisher & Tom Kane
art director
  Sean Brunson
production manager
  Chris Opsahl
copywriter
  Tom Kane
client
  Toyota Marine Sports

creative firm
  Sawyer Riley Compton
    Atlanta (Georgia), USA
creative director
  Bart Cleveland
art director
  Karl Madcharo
photographer
  Michelle Clement
copywriter
  Brett Compton
client
  James Hardie Building Products

creative firm
  Verba
    Milan, Italy
creative director, artist
  Stefano Longoni
copywriter
  Enrico Bonomini
client
  Autogerma

creative firm
  Verba
    Milan, Italy
creative director
  Francesco Emiliani & Stefano Longoni
artist
  Stefano Longoni
copywriter
  Francesco Emiliani
client
  Autogerma

creative firm
  Verba
    Milan, Italy
creative director
  Stefano Longoni
illustrator
  Marcello Porta
copywriter
  Francesca De Luca
client
  Autogerma

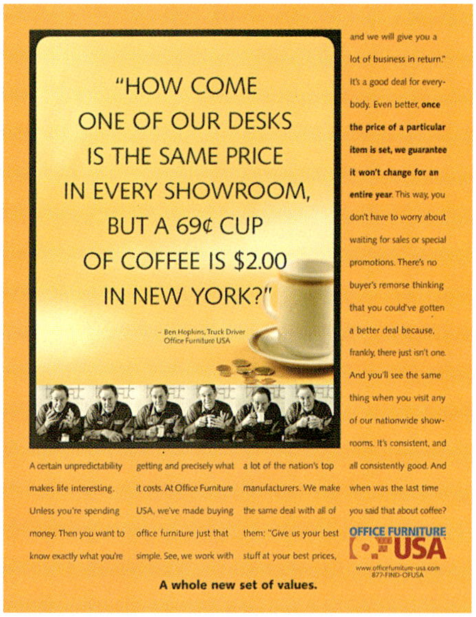

creative firm
  Cadmus Com
    Richmond (Virginia), USA
creative directors
  Kelly O'Keefe & Robyn Konieczny
art directors
  Cathy Oliver & J.B. Hopkins
photographers
  Marc Prpich & Thomas Daniel
copywriter
  Brian Fox
client
  Office Furniture USA

creative firm
  JWT Specialized
    Communications
    St. Louis
      Los Angeles (California), USA
creative director
  Tim Kidwell
art director
  Gene Kuehnle
production artist
  Kari Michelek
copywriter
  Rich Heend
client
  Federal Express

creative firm
  Ammirati Puris Lintas/Column
    Johannesburg, South Africa
creative director
  Rob McLennan
art directors
  Gavin Dexter & Michael Macneil
copywriter
  Dennis Platt
client
  Dell Computers

10

creative firm
  The Ungar Group
    Chicago (Illinois), USA
creative people
  Tom Ungar & Mark Ingraham
client
  Sanford

creative firm
  Ammirati Puris Lintas/Column
    Johannesburg, South Africa
creative director
  Rob McLennan
art director
  Gavin Dexter
copywriter
  Dennis Platt
client
  Dell Computers

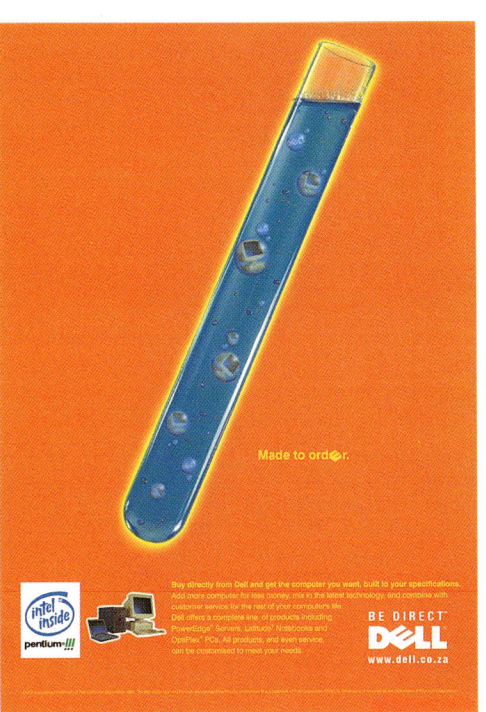

creative firm
  Ammirati Puris Lintas/Column
  Johannesburg, South Africa
creative director
  Rob McLennan
art directors
  Gavin Dexter & Michael Macneil
copywriter
  Dennis Platt
client
  Dell Computers

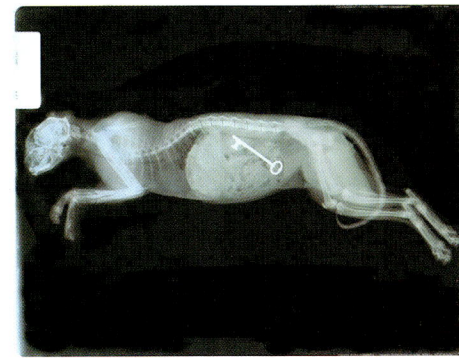

creative firm
  Bleecker & Sullivan
  New York (New York), USA
creative director
  Itzhak Beery
copywriter
  Sela Francis
client
  ASPCA

creative firm
  Sawyer Riley Compton
  Atlanta (Georgia), USA
creative director
  Bart Cleveland
art director
  Tammy Thorn Anderson
photographer
  Joe Lampi
copywriter
  John Spalding
client
  Mitsubishi Wireless
  Digital Cellular Phones

11

creative firm
  Alcone Marketing Group
  Irvine (California), USA
creative director, art director
  Luis Camano
copywriter
  Cameron Young
client
  Airtouch

creative firm
  Ammirati Puris Lintas/Column
  Johannesburg, South Africa
creative director
  Rob McLennan
art director
  Gavin Dexter
copywriter
  Dennis Platt
client
  Dell Computers

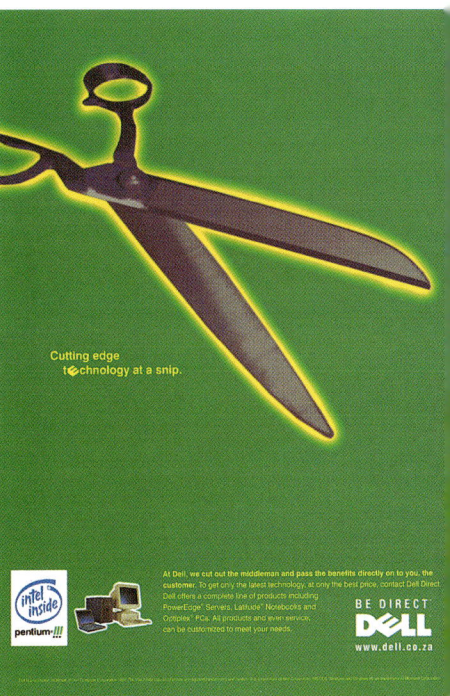

creative firm
  J. Walter Thompson
  Chicago (Illinois), USA
creative director
  Jeff York
art director
  Mark Westman
copywriter
  Greg Oreskovich
client
  CheezeWhiz

creative firm
  Young & Rubicam Mexico
  Mexico City (D.F.), Mexico
director of creative services
  Enrique Laguardia L.
creative directors
  Yuri Alvarado & Ignacio Zeleny
art director
  Walter Sendra
copywriter
  Ignacio Zeleny
client
  Danone de Mexico

creative firm
  J. Walter Thompson
  Chicago (Illinois), USA
creative director
  Jeff York
art director
  Mark Westman
copywriter
  Greg Oreskovich
client
  CheezWhiz

12

creative firm
  Chris Collins Studio
  New York (New York), USA
creative directors
  Chris Collins & Robin Gara
client
  Oneida

creative firm
  J. Walter Thompson
  Chicago (Illinois), USA
creative director
  Jeff York
art director
  Mark Westman
copywriter
  Greg Oreskovich
client
  CheezWhiz

creative firm
  Vogue Magazine
    New York (New York), USA
art director
  Nancy Arnold
designers
  Aloise Levesque
client
  Bacardi

creative firm
  Gauger & Silva Associates
    San Francisco (California), USA
creative people
  Isabelle Laporte & David Gauger
client
  Sunspire

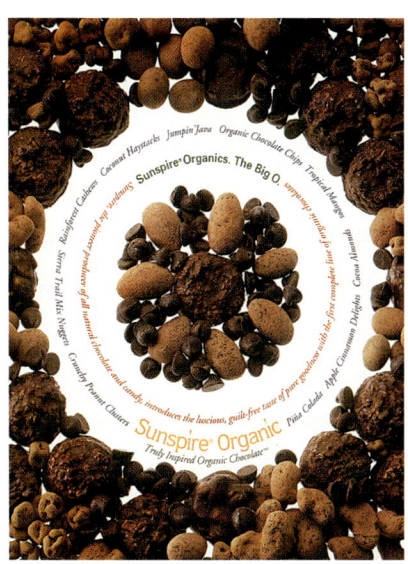

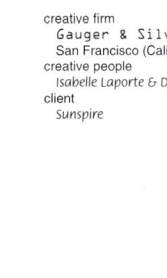
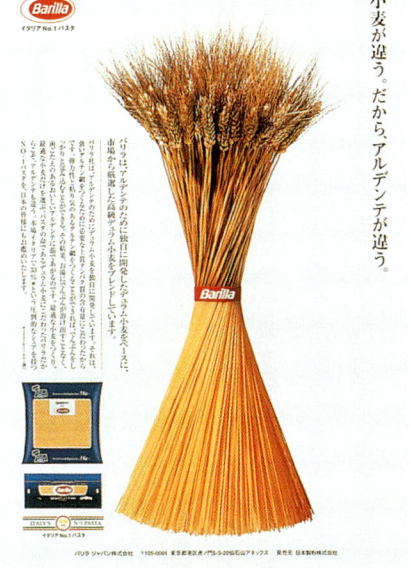

creative firm
  Grey Daiko Advertising Inc.
    Minato-ku (Tokyo), Japan
creative director
  Miyagawa Kanji
art director
  Arai Kouichi
photographer
  Mizuno Yasuo
copywriter
  Matsushima Chikako
client
  Barilla Japan

creative firm
  Gauger & Silva Associates
    San Francisco (California), USA
creative people
  Isabelle Laporte & David Gauger
client
  Imagine Foods

creative firm
  Design Guys
    Minneapolis (Minnesota), USA
creative people
  Steven Sikora & Anne Peterson
client
  Target Stores

creative firm
    L3 Advertising Inc.
        New York (New York), USA
creative people
    Nicholas Tsang & Charles Lui
client
    Chase

translation
    In the year of the rabbit, Chase wishes everyone a prosperous New Year.

creative firm
    Dymun Nelson & Company
        Pittsburgh (Pennsylvania), USA
creative directors
    John Dymun & Craig Otto
art director
    Diane Dugina
copywriter
    Terrence McClusky
client
    Pittsburgh Post-Gazette

creative firm
    Ogilvy & Mather Frankfurt
        Frankfurt, Germany
creative directors
    Bernd Lange & Gregor Seitz
art directors
    Gregor Seitz & Alexander Toskar
copywriter
    Bernd Lange
client
    American Express Int. Inc. Frankfurt

translation
    Don't worry. It's insured.

    New Service: Shop Garant.
    Everything you buy with your
    American Express Card is insured
    against theft and damage.

creative firm
    Ketchum Advertising
        Pittsburgh (Pennsylvania), USA
executive creative director
    Lee St. James
creative director, copywriter
    Jim Anderson
client
    Zippo Manufacturing Company

creative firm
    Ketchum Advertising
        Pittsburgh (Pennsylvania), USA
executive creative director
    Lee St. James
creative director, copywriter
    Jim Anderson
client
    Zippo Manufacturing Company

# The world is 10 years old.

It was born when the Wall fell in 1989. It's no surprise that the world's youngest economy — the global economy — is still finding its bearings.

The intricate checks and balances that stabilize economies are only incorporated with time. Many world markets are only recently freed, governed for the first time by the emotions of the people rather than the fists of the state.

From where we sit, none of this diminishes the promise offered a decade ago by the demise of the walled-off world. We're as convinced as ever that the coming years will be a disappointing time for pessimists.

The spread of free markets and democracy around the world is permitting more people everywhere to turn their aspirations into achievements. And technology, properly harnessed and liberally distributed, has the power to erase not just geographical borders but also human ones.

It seems to us that, for a 10-year-old, the world continues to hold great promise. In the meantime, no one ever said growing up is easy.

**Merrill Lynch**

creative firm
  J. Walter Thompson
  New York (New York), USA
creative director
  Bill Hamilton
art director
  John Morrison
copywriters
  Stuart Mickle & Michael Eilperin
client
  Merrill Lynch

creative firm
  Sawyer Riley Compton
  Atlanta (Georgia), USA
creative director
  Bart Cleveland
associate creative director
  Rob Hardison
art directors
  Bart Cleveland, Tammy Thorn Anderson,
  & Rob Hardison
photographers
  Larry Ladig & David Kiesgen
copywriters
  Brett Compton, John Spalding, & Bart Cleveland
client
  Ritz-Carlton

creative firm
  Ogilvy & Mather Frankfurt
  Frankfurt, Germany
creative director
  Bernd Lange & Gregor Seitz
art directors
  Gregor Seitz & Alexander Toskar
copywriter
  Bernd Lange
client
  American Express Int. Inc. Frankfurt

translation
  If your flight is delayed, we'll invite you for dinner.

  New Service: Travel Inconvenience
  Insurance. If a flight is delayed, American
  Express pays for any costs incurred on
  behalf of the delay like restaurants,
  hotel, and clothing.

15

creative firm
  Ketchum Advertising
  Pittsburgh (Pennsylvania), USA
executive creative director
  Lee St. James
creative director, copywriter
  Jim Anderson
client
  Zippo Manufacturing Company

creative firm
  Ketchum Advertising
  Pittsburgh (Pennsylvania), USA
executive creative director
  Lee St. James
creative director, copywriter
  Jim Anderson
client
  Zippo Manufacturing Company

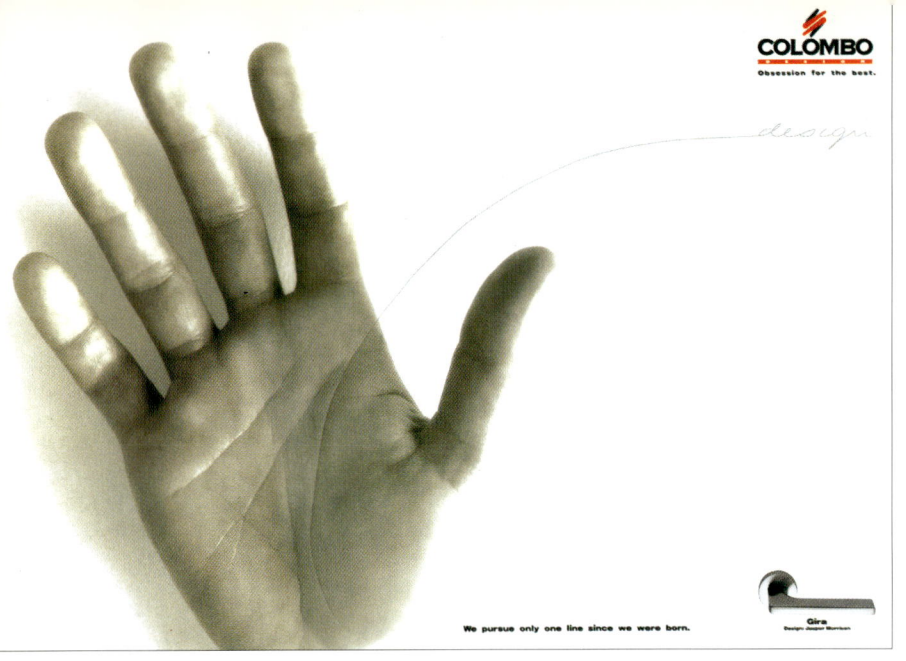

creative firm
 Verba
  Milan Italy
creative director, illustrator
 Stefano Longoni
copywriter
 Enrico Bonomini
client
 Colombo Design

creative firm
 Foley Sackett
  Minneapolis
  (Minnesota), USA
creative director
 Ron Sackett
art director
 Wayne Thompson
copywriter
 Jeff Schuller
client
 W.A. Lang

16

creative firm
 Fry Hammond Barr
  Orando (Florida), USA
creative directors
 Tim Fisher, Tom Kane
art director
 Sean Brunson
production manager
 Marie Shumilak
copywriter
 Tom Kane
client
 Kennedy Space Center Visitor Complex

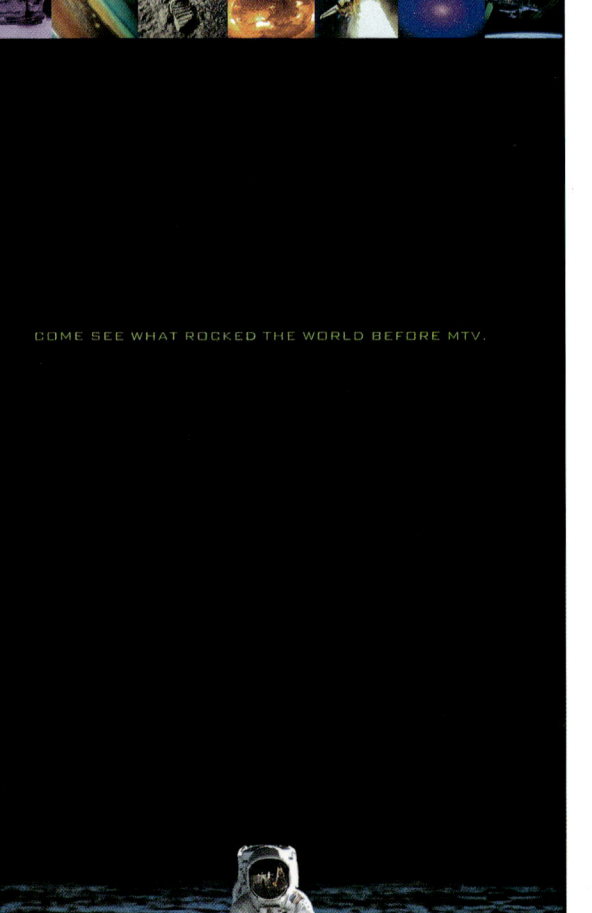

creative firm
 Paul Kaza Assoc.
  S. Burlington (Vermont), USA
art director, designer
 David Walker
photographer
 George A. Robinson
copywriter
 Paul Kaza
client
 Vermont Department
  of Tourism & Marketing

creative firm
 Nelson & Schmidt, Inc.
  Milwaukee (Wisconsin), USA
creative director
 Mark Gale
art director
 Brian Marconnet
photographer
 Ricco Photography
copywriter
 Bill Stadick
client
 "Clown Hall of Fame"

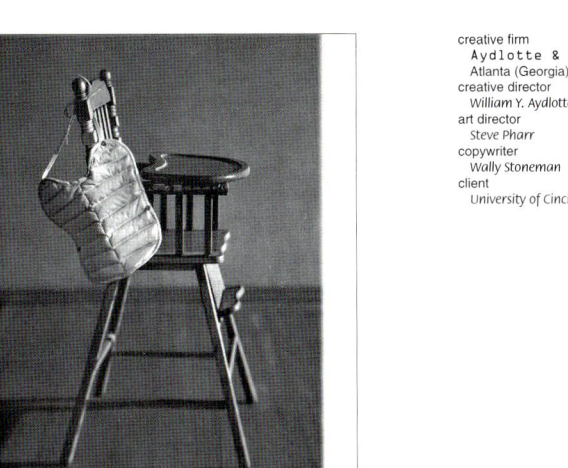

creative firm
    Aydlotte & Cartwright
    Atlanta (Georgia), USA
creative director
    William Y. Aydlotte
art director
    Steve Pharr
copywriter
    Wally Stoneman
client
    University of Cincinnati

creative firm
    Ketchum Advertising
    Pittsburgh, (Pennsylvania), USA
executive creative director
    Lee St. James
creative directors
    Bill Garrison, Jay Giesen
art director
    Jay Giesen
copywriter
    Bill Garrison
client
    Pittsburgh Pirates

17

creative firm
    Parham Santana Inc.
    New York (New York), USA
creative director
    William Snyder
design services
    Peter Aguanno (Rainbow Programming)
designer
    Liz Driesbach
client
    The Independent Film Channel

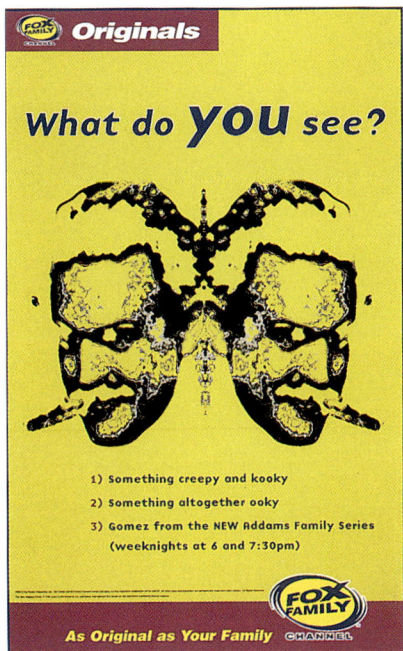

creative firm
    Foley Sackett
    Minneapolis (Minnesota), USA
creative director
    Ron Sackett
art director
    Wayne Thompson
copywriter
    Jeff Schuller
client
    W.A. Lang

creative firm
    The Sloan Group
    New York (New York), USA
creative directors
    Cliff Sloan & Wyndy Wilder
designer
    Lea Ann Hutter
client
    Fox Family Channel

creative firm
 FCB Singapore
 Singapore
creative director
 Chris Kyme
art directors
 Dali Meskam & Nick Tan
client
 Adidas Singapore

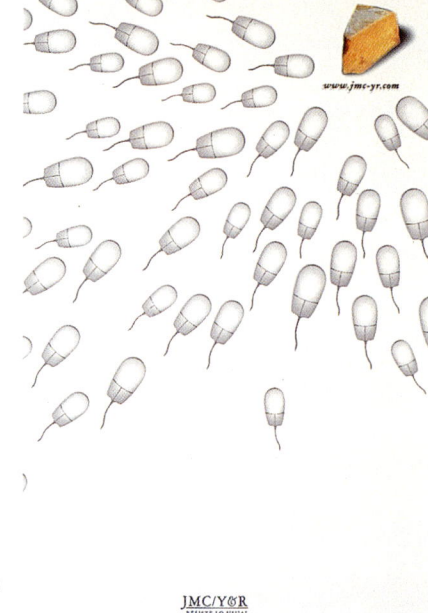

creative firm
 JMC/Y&R
 Caracas, Venezuela
creative people
 Mabel Ruiz & Ruben Ruiz
client
 JMC-Web Page

creative firm
 JMC/Y&R
 Caracas, Venezuela
creative people
 Mary Torres & Jose Navas
client
 Colgate Palmolive
translation
 Smile. Happy day, dentists.
 From Colgate.

18

creative firm
 JMC/Y&R
 Caracas, Venezuela
creative people
 Mariana Barnola, J. Mendez,
 & R. Natale
client
 Web Page Promotion—JMC/Y&R

translation
 There is a place with more
 passionate stories, where the
 action never stops, and the
 courage is fundamental.

 www.jmc-yr.com

 (Strategies that seduce, award-
 winning ads, highly fashioned
 work. Just to begin with. JMC/Y&R.
 Resist The Usual.)

creative firm
 KPR
 New York (New York), USA
creative people
 Mitch Siegel, David Adler,
 & Denise Bourcier
client
 3M Pharmaceuticals

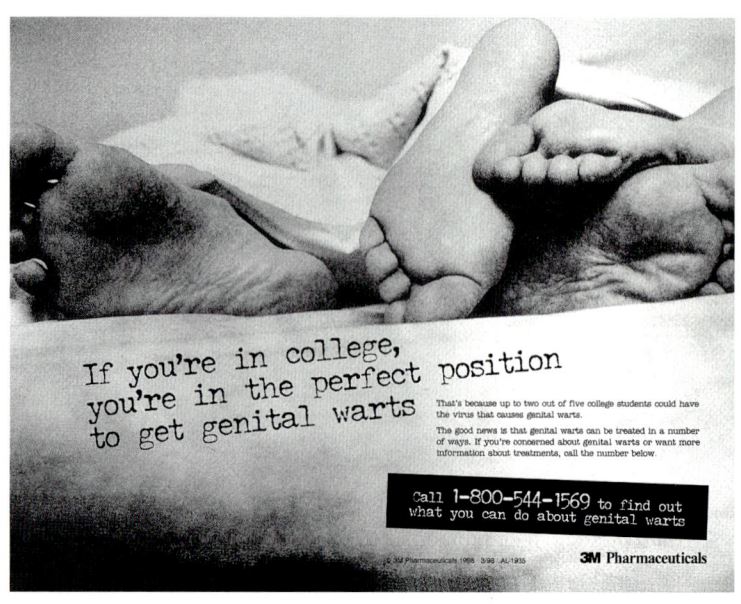

creative firm
 Saatchi & Saatchi Vietnam
  Ho Chi Minh City, Vietnam
creative people
 Paul Ewen, Mike Sands, & Le Duc Thang
client
 Procter & Gamble

translation
 The Vietnam National Hairstylist Competition. The National Hairstylist Competition is back and once again it's brought to you by Head & Shoulders and Phu Nu magazine. If you're a Vietnamese hairstylist, then there's a chance to aim for selection in Vietnam's most prestigious hairstylist competition. Entry forms available in this magazine.

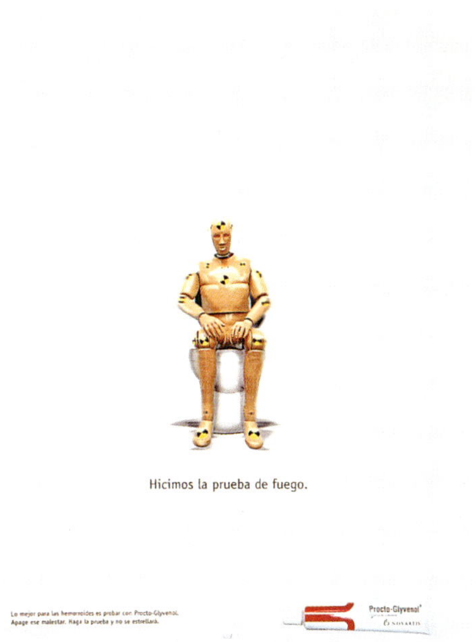

creative firm
 JMC/Y&R
  Caracas, Venezuela
creative people
 Exequiel Rodriguez
 & Adolfo Davila
client
 Novartis

translation
 We did the Fireproofing.

 The best way to treat hemorrhoids is to use Procto-Glyvenol. It will turn off the "fire sensation" you feel now.

creative firm
 JMC/Y&R
  Caracas, Venezuela
creative people
 Mariana Barnola,
 Roberto Natale, & J. Mendez
client
 JMC/Y&R

translation
 To create, create, create. Nobody does it as we do. JMC/Y&R. Resist the usual.

creative firm
 Young & Rubicam Mexico
  Mexico City, Mexico
creative director, copywriter
 Ignacio Zeleny
director of creative services
 Enrique Laguardia Longega
art director
 Walter Sendra
client
 Whitehall Robins

19

creative firm
 JMC/Y&R
  Caracas, Venezuela
creative people
 C. Lander, Exequiel Rodrigues,
 Johny R. & L. Bernardo
client
 United Airlines

translation
 You don't necessarily have to behave yourself everyday to guarantee your place in heaven.

 There will always be a special place in heaven for everybody in United Airlines. Heavenly services, heavenly attention on heavenly planes with the most heavenly advanced technology. If flying is part of your life, fly United.

creative firm
 The Imagination Company
  Bethel (Vermont), USA
creative director
 Jim Giberti
art director
 Mark Connolly
client
 FischerSkis U.S.

creative firm
 J. Walter Thompson
  New York (New York), USA
art directors
 D.J. Pierce & Young Seo
photographer
 Bob Scott
copywriter
 Scott Duchon
client
 Blades Board & Skate

20

creative firm
 J. Walter Thompson
  New York (New York), USA
art director
 D.J. Pierce
photographer
 Bob Scott
copywriter
 Scott Duchon
client
 Blades Board & Skate

creative firm
 J. Walter Thompson
  New York (New York), USA
art director
 D.J. Pierce
photographer
 Bob Scott
copywriter
 Scott Duchon
client
 Blades Board & Skate

creative firm
  JMC/Y&R
  Caracas, Venezuela
creative people
  Mabel Ruiz & Ruben Perez
client
  United Airlines

translation
  If we were only concerned with bringing and delivering our passengers, we would only be a courier.

  United Airlines. Rising.

creative firm
  JMC/Y&R
  Caracas, Venezuela
creative people
  Mabel Ruiz & Ruben Perez
client
  United Airlines

translation
  How about some extra sleeping time? Our second daily flight departs at 10:30 a.m.

  United Airlines. Rising.

creative firm
  JMC/Y&R
  Caracas, Venezuela
creative people
  Mabel Ruiz & Ruben Perez
client
  United Airlines

translation
  We've improved the size of the seats, leg room and your comfort in our 767-200 Boeings. So spread out as you never did before with all of our XXL services and XXL attention.

  United Airlines. Rising.

creative firm
  JMC/Y&R
  Caracas, Venezuela
creative director
  Mabel Ruiz & Ruben Perez
client
  United Airlines

translation
  Two daily flights to New York. If flying is part of your life, fly United.

  United Airlines. Rising.

21

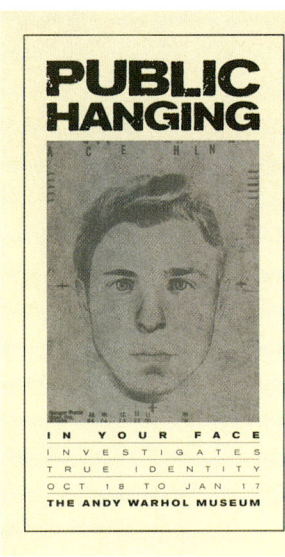

creative firm
 Dymun Nelson & Company
  Pittsburgh (Pennsylvania), USA
creative directors
 John Dymun & Craig Otto
art director, copywriter
 Craig Otto
electronic designer
 Robyn Riel
client
 The Andy Warhol Museum

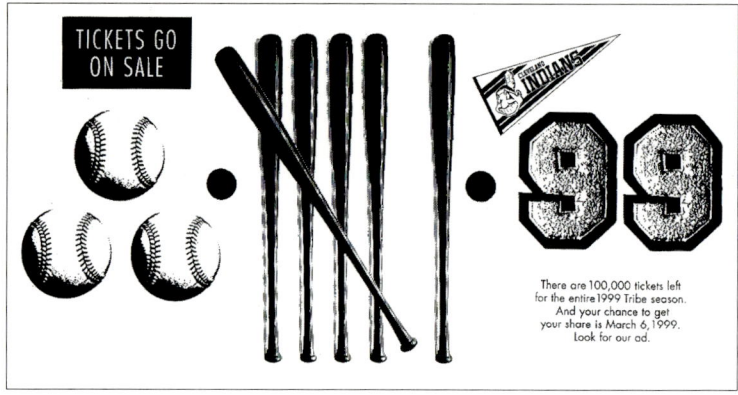

creative firm
 Bryan Nimeth
  Solon (Ohio), USA
art director, designer, artist
 Bryan Nimeth
copywriter
 Jim Sollisch
client
 Cleveland Baseball

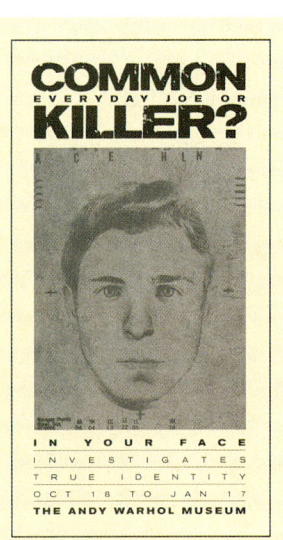

creative firm
 Dymun Nelson & Company
  Pittsburgh (Pennsylvania), USA
creative directors
 John Dymun & Craig Otto
art director, copywriter
 Craig Otto
electronic designer
 Robyn Riel
client
 The Andy Warhol Museum

creative firm
 Philadelphia 76ers
  Philadelphia (Pennsylvania), USA
creative people
 Mark Elmore, Gary Yealdhall,
 Dave Coskey, & Lara White
client
 Philadelphia 76ers

creative firm
 MARC Advertising
  Pittsburgh (Pennsylvania), USA
creative people
 Ed Fine, Tony Jaffe, Ron Sullivan,
 & Kris Knieriem, Eva Sullivan
client
 Carnegie Museum of Natural History

creative firm
　Cadmus Com
　　Richmond (Virginia), USA
creative director
　　Tony Platt
art director
　　Cathy Oliver
copywriter
　　Maryann Neary-Gill
client
　　Richmond Symphony

creative firm
　L3 Advertising Inc.
　　New York (New York) USA
creative people
　　Nicholas Tsang, Raymond Tam, & Julie Au
client
　　Bell Atlantic Yellow Pages

creative firm
　Dymun Nelson & Company
　　Pittsburgh, (Pennsylvania), USA
creative directors
　　John Dymun & Craig Otto
art director
　　Craig Otto
copywriters
　　Craig Otto & Sandy Stewart
client
　　Pittsburgh Post-Gazette

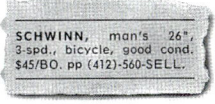

creative firm
　Dymun Nelson & Company
　　Pittsburgh, (Pennsylvania), USA
creative directors
　　John Dymun & Craig Otto
art director
　　Craig Otto
copywriters
　　Craig Otto & Sandy Stewart
client
　　Pittsburgh Post-Gazette

creative firm
　The Zimmerman Agency
　　Tallahassee (Florida), USA
creative director
　　Doug Engel
art director, copywriter
　　Rob Kerr
production
　　Emily Barrow
client
　　Mayfair House

23

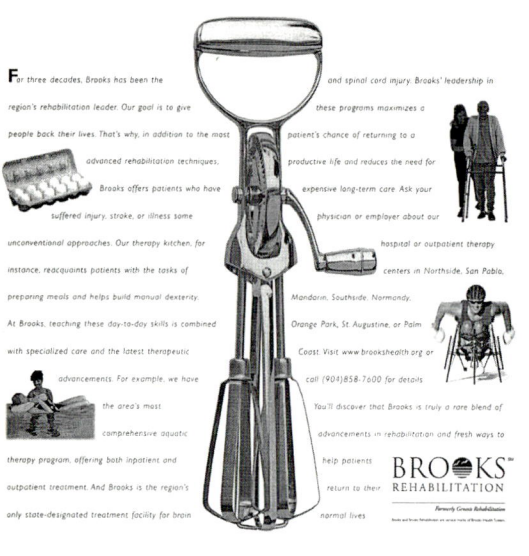

creative firm
Armando Testa-Rome Italy
Milan, Italy
photographer
Joe Oppedisano
c.a.d.
Claudio Antonacci
client
I.N.A. National Insurance

creative firm
Morgan & Partners
Jacksonville (Florida), USA
art directors
Tim Ryan & Steve Moran
production
Brian Thompson
copywriter
Bill Reishtein
client
Brooks Rehabilitation Hospital

creative firm
Fry Hammond Barr
Orlando (Florida), USA
executive creative director
Tim Fisher
art director
Sean Brunson
production manager
Chris Opsahl
copywriter
John Logan
client
Valencia Community College

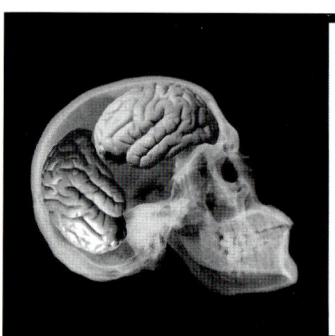

creative firm
Wray Ward Laseter Advertising
Charlotte (North Carolina), USA
creative director
Jennifer Appleby
producer
Sheila B. Dulin
copywriter
Tom Cocke
client
Gaston Health Care

creative firm
Dennis S. Juett & Associates Inc
Pasadena (California), USA
creative directors
Dennis S. Juett & Dennis Scott Juett
client
Huntington Memorial Hospital

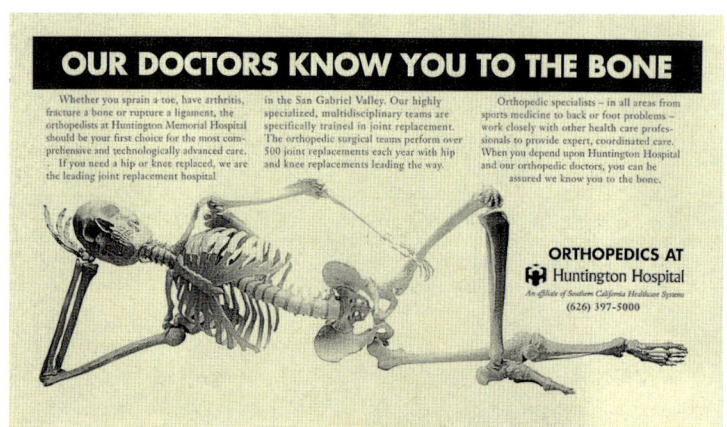

creative firm
  Hindustan Thompson Associates
  Mumbai, India
creative people
  HTA Team
client
  Hindustan Lever Ltd

creative firm
  RDW Group Inc
  Providence (Rhode Island), USA
creative people
  Anthony Gill
client
  Ross Simonds

creative firm
  Wray Ward Laseter
  Charlotte (North Carolina), USA
creative director
  Jennifer Appleby
art director
  Todd Kinley
production manager
  Elaine Boswell
copywriter
  Jim Stadler
client
  Junior League of Charlotte

creative firm
  McCann-Erickson
  New York (New York), USA
creative director
  Joyce King Thomas
art directors
  Michael Gambino
print production
  Robert Ford
copywriter
  Cheryl Chapman
client
  MasterCard

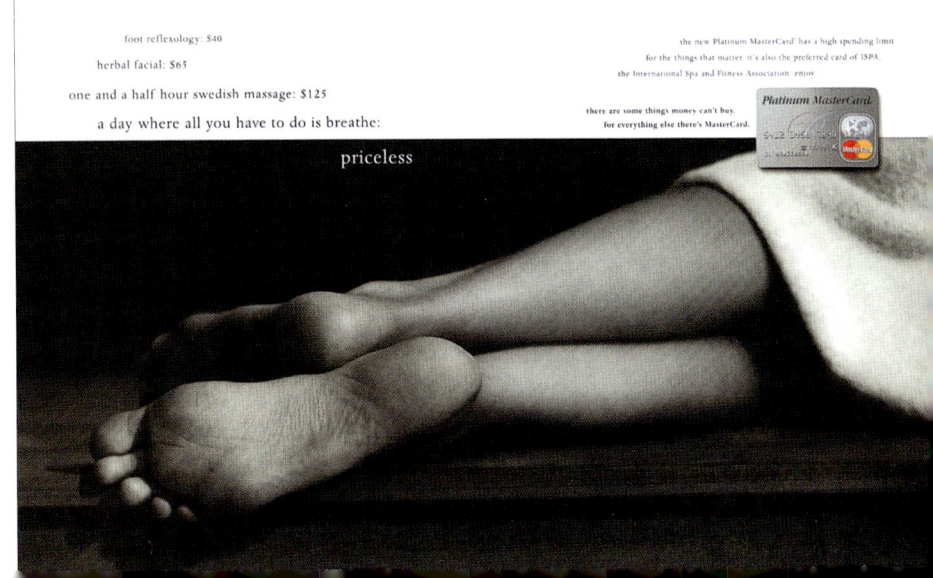

# CREATIVITY

## Consumer Ads Campaign

creative firm
  Gauger Silva & Associates
  San Francisco (California), USA
creative people
  Tony Molinero & David Gauger
client
  Dublin Ranch

Stocks. Bonds.
Commercial real estate.

FOCUS PROPERTIES, INC.
Sell. Sell. Buy.   Call 616.394.4500

Super model. Movie star.
Commercial Realtor.

It's an ugly job but someone has to do it.   FOCUS PROPERTIES, INC.   Call 616.394.4500

creative firm
  Fairly Painless Advertising
  Holland (Michigan), USA
creative directors
  Peter Bell & Cheryl Bell
art director
  Cheryl Bell
copywriters
  Peter Bell & Karen Lannin
client
  Focus Properties

# The world is 10 years old.

*It was born when the Wall fell in 1989. It's no surprise that the world's youngest economy — the global economy — is still finding its bearings.*

*The intricate checks and balances that stabilize economies are only incorporated with time. Many world markets are only recently freed, governed for the first time by the emotions of the people rather than the fists of the state.*

*From where we sit, none of this diminishes the promise offered a decade ago by the demise of the walled-off world. We're as convinced as ever that the coming years will be a disappointing time for pessimists.*

*The spread of free markets and democracy around the world is permitting more people everywhere to turn their aspirations into achievements. And technology, properly harnessed and liberally distributed, has the power to erase not just geographical borders but also human ones.*

*It seems to us that, for a 10-year-old, the world continues to hold great promise. In the meantime, no one ever said growing up is easy.*

**Merrill Lynch**

# Timing is nothing.

*For as long as there have been markets, investors have tried to time them — to predict the precise moment when a down market turns upward or the legs give out on a bull. Sometimes it's hubris, sometimes it's fear: watching their investments fall, even seasoned investors can lose faith in the markets and, in a moment of panic, sell.*

*A great number of investors succumbed to this urge a few weeks back — or hundreds of Dow points ago. Then, a big upswing was all but unthinkable. But as we've just seen, markets have an uncanny way of turning the unthinkable into the inevitable.*

*The best defense against rash action and its faithful companion, eternal regret, is the guidance of an objective advisor. To calm the emotions and remind an investor, especially in volatile times, that investing should be done from the neck up. To analyze market conditions and balance a portfolio accordingly. To encourage a long-term perspective. To take real market knowledge and apply it to unique situations. To distinguish opportunities from fads. And to offer the occasional reminder that timing may be everything, but only in comedy.*

**Merrill Lynch**

creative firm
  J. Walter Thompson
  New York (New York), USA
creative director
  Bill Hamilton
art director
  John Morrison
copywriter
  Stuart Mickle
client
  Merrill Lynch

26

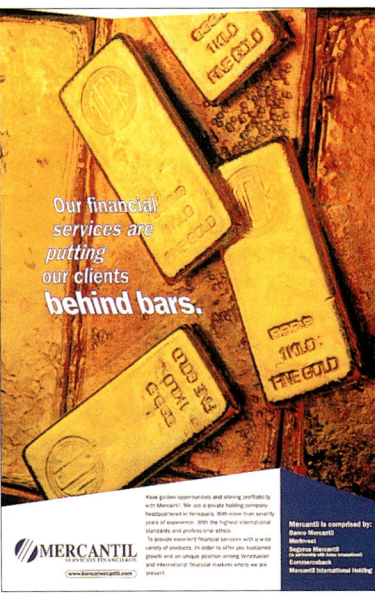

creative firm
   JMC/Y&R
   Caracas (Miranda), Venezuela
creative people
   Roberto Natale, Mariana Barnola, & J. Mendez
client
   Banco Mercantil

creative firm
   Wray Ward Laseter
   Charlotte (North Carolina), USA
creative director
   Jennifer Appleby
art director
   Shawn Kelley
production manager
   Elaine Boswell
copywriter
   Jim Stadler
client
   Dennis & Company

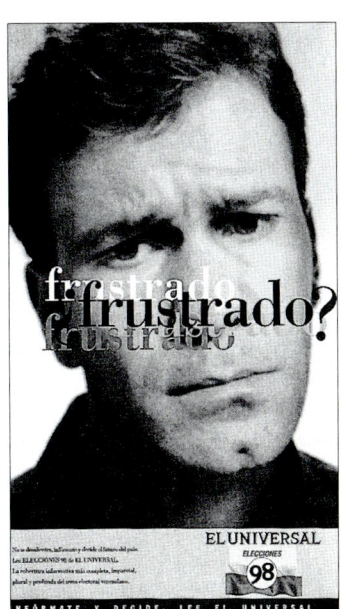

creative firm
   JMC/Y&R
   Caracas (Miranda), Venezuela
creative people
   Mabel Ruiz & Ruben Perez
client
   El Universal

translation
   Frustrated?
   Apathetic?
   When you have a wider and more objective vision of every candidate, it'll be easier to decide who to vote for. For you, for your country. Elections '98 will give you everyone's story. From many sides. Remember, more than change your attitude, you can change your country.

   El Universal
   Nothing convinces more than the truth.

creative firm
  JMC/Y&R
  Caracas (Miranda), Venezuela
creative people
  Carolina Lander, Johny R,
  Luis Bernado, & Exequiel R.
client
  United Airlines

translation
  Make a Wish.

creative firm
  Paul Kaza Assoc.
  S. Burlington (Vermont), USA
art director, designer
  David Walker
photographers
  Paul O. Boisvert, Alan Jakubek, & Alan Graham
copywriter
  Paul Kaza
client
  Vermont Department of Tourism & Marketing

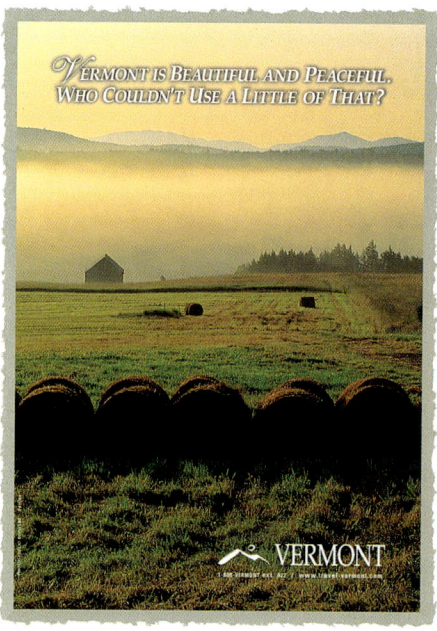
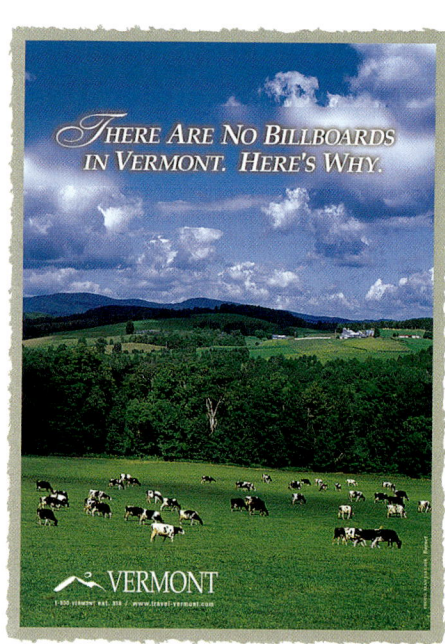

creative firm
  MARC Advertising
  Pittsburgh (Pennsylvania), USA
creative people
  Ed Fine, Tony Jaffe, Cathy Bowen,
  Kris Knieriem, & Jill Trimble
client
  Make A Wish Foundation

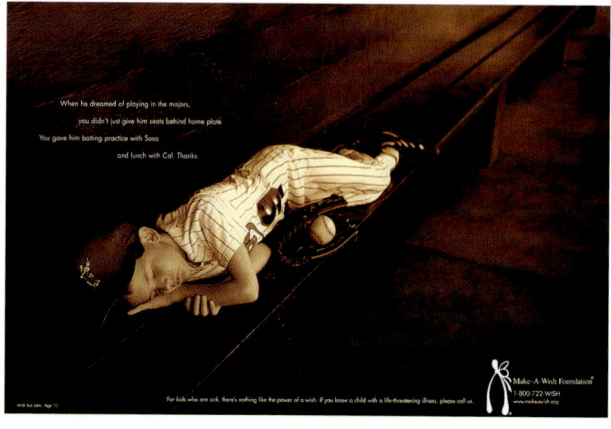

creative firm
  Sawyer Riley Compton
    Atlanta (Georgia), USA
creative directors
  Bart Cleveland & Rob Hardison
art directors
  Bart Cleveland, Tammy Thorn Anderson,
  & Rob Hardison
photographers
  Larry Ladig & David Kiesgen
copywriters
  Brett Compton, John Spalding,
  & Bart Cleveland
client
  Ritz-Carlton

creative firm
  Trikaya Grey Advertising India Ltd.
    Mumbai (Maharashtra), India
art director
  Kanad Banerjee
photographer
  Prabuddha Das Gupta
copywriter
  Alok Nanda
client
  Mauritius Tourism Information Service

creative firm
  Armstrong Graphics
    Minneapolis (Minnesota), USA
art director, designer
  Bruce Armstrong
client
  Henderson House B&B

creative firm
 egan/st. james
  Pittsburgh (Pennsylvania), USA
executive creative director
 Lee St. James
creative director, copywriter
 Jim Anderson
client
 Zippo Manufacturing Company

30

creative firm
 Verba
  Milan, Italy
creative director
 Enrico Bonomini
illustrators
 Marco Pupella &
 Marcello Porta
copywriter
 Sofia Ambrosini
client
 Campari

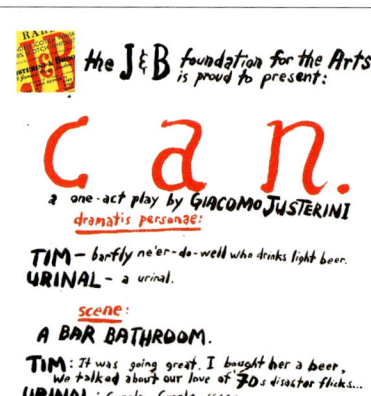

creative firm
 J. Walter Thompson/N.Y.
  New York (New York), USA
creative directors
 J.J. Jordan & Michael Hart
art directors, copywriters
 Rick Streed, Anders Carlsson, & Michael Hart
client
 Schieffelin & Somerset Co. J&B Scotch

creative firm
 Jones Studio Limited
  Staten Island (New York), USA
creative people
 Pui-Pui Li & Mikio Sekita
client
 Cassina USA

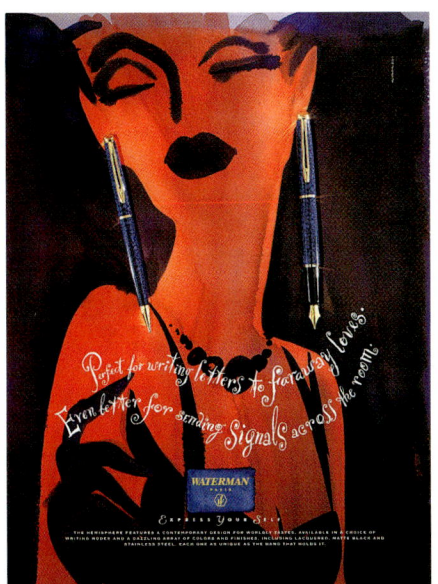
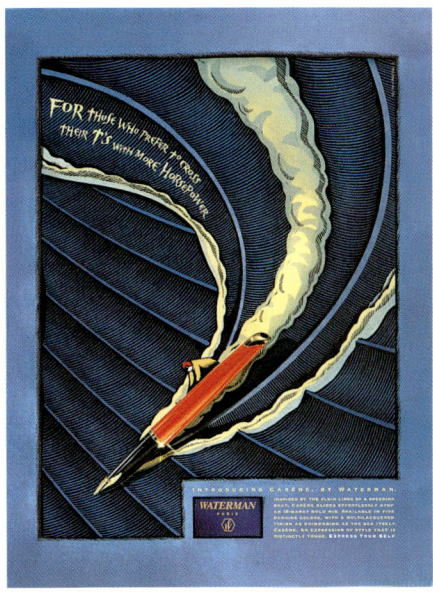

creative firm
 McCann-Erickson
  New York (New York), USA
creative directors
 Paul Behnen & Gib Marquardt
art director
 Paul Behnen
print producer
 Robert Ford
copywriter
 Ward Parker
client
 Waterman

creative firm
 Sawyer Riley Compton
  Atlanta (Georgia), USA
creative director
 Bart Cleveland
art director
 Karl Madcharo
photographer
 Michelle Clement
copywriter
 Brett Compton
client
 James Hardie Building Products

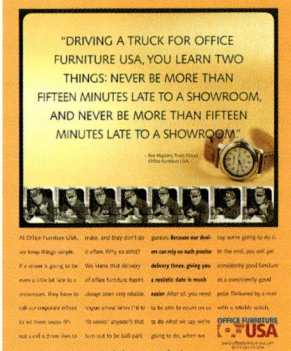

creative firm
   CadmusCom
   Richmond (Virginia), USA
creative directors
   Kelly O'Keefe & Robin Konieczny
art directors
   Cathy Oliver & J.B. Hopkins
photographers
   Marc Prpich & Thomas Daniel
copywriter
   Brian Fox
client
   Office Furniture USA

creative firm
   Wray Ward Laseter Advertising
   Charlotte (North Carolina), USA
creative director
   Jennifer Appleby
art director
   Shawn Kelley
production director
   Sheila B. Dulin
copywriter
   Tom Cock
client
   Gaston Health Care

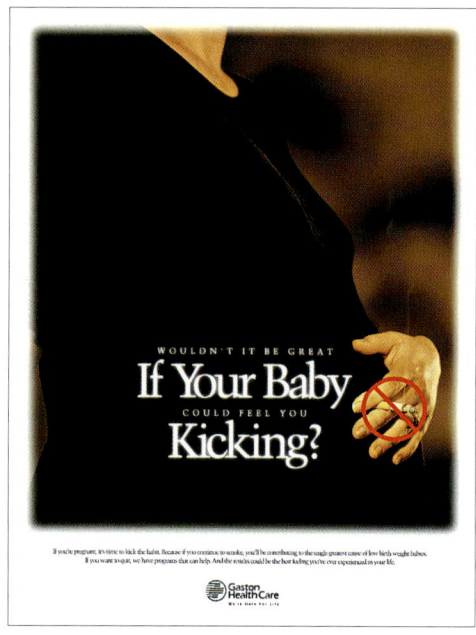

creative firm
   Wray Ward Laseter
   Charlotte (North Carolina), USA
creative director
   Jennifer Appleby
art director
   Todd Kinley
production director
   Sheila B. Dulin
copywriter
   Tom Cocke
client
   Mint Museum of Craft & Design

creative firm
  Campbell-Ewald Advertising
  Warren (Michigan), USA
creative people
  Bill Ludwig, Jim Millis, Nancy Wellinger,
  & Jason Henderson
client
  Onstar

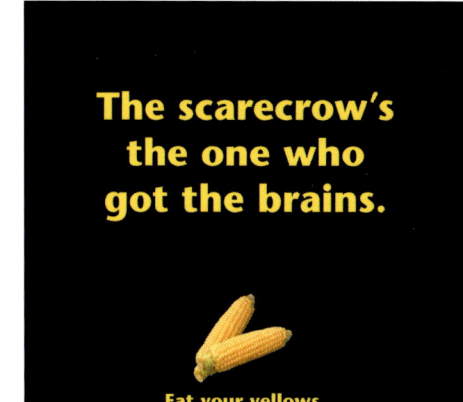

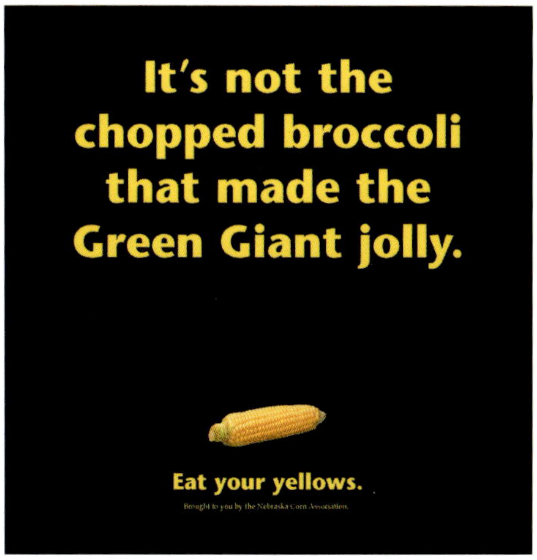

designer
  Kevin Botfeld
  Jacksonville (Florida), USA
art director
  Keri Nathan
copywriter
  Kevin Botfeld

creative firm
  Verba DDB
  Milan, Italy
creative directors
  Enrico Bonomini & Francesco Emiliani
illustrator
  Umberto Mauri
copywriter
  Dario Alesani
client
  Autogerma

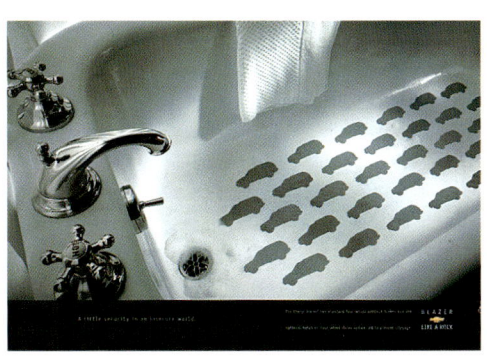

creative firm
  Campbell-Ewald Advertising
  Warren (Michigan), USA
creative directors
  Jim Gorman & Joe Putty
art director
  John Clarey
copywriter
  Jon Stewart
client
  Chevrolet

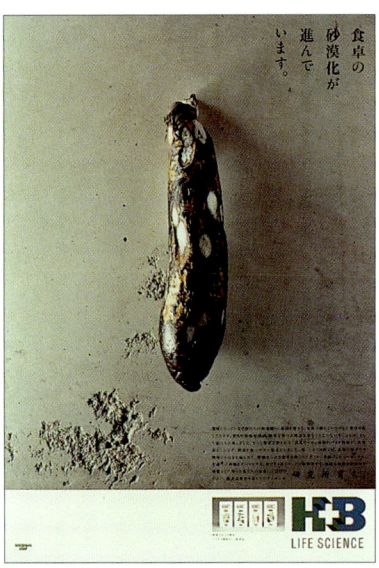

creative firm
  Nakatsuka Daisuke Inc.
  Tokyo, Japan
creative director, art director
  Daisuke Nakatsuka
designers
  Kanna Numajiri & Mayumi Inoue
photographer
  Shozo Nakamura
copywriter
  Tom Nakatsuka
client
  H+B Lifescience Co., Ltd.

translation
  Even the dining table is becoming a desert.

  Vegetables shouldn't be fertilizing your refrigerator.

  More and more, children disliking vegetables is becoming more of a problem. Perhaps one reason the family doesn't always eat together is so that there's less chance to eat vegetables. So we came up with the idea of making it easier to have more vegetables by using bio-technology to powderize foods without any loss of nutrition. Taste and smell are mild and by adding it to dishes, healthier meals are easliy made. The name is NUMIX, the latest product of H+B brand. It's a brand with a future, and it's from Hayashibara Bio-Chemical Laboratories. H+H Life Science.

creative firm
  Dieste & Partners Publicidad
  Dallas (Texas), USA
executive creative director
  Aldo Quevedo
art director
  Chris Sendra
copywriter
  Javier Guemes
client
  Mrs. Bairds

creative firm
  Ukulele Design Consultants Pte Ltd
  Singapore
design director
  Kim Chun-wei
designer
  Lee Shin Kee
copywriter
  Evelyn Teng
client
  McIlhenny Company

creative firm
  **The Miller Group**
    Towson (Maryland), USA
creative director
  *Jack Miller*
art director
  *Sara Lowery*
photographer
  *Dean Ray*
illustrator
  *Bob Lynch*
copywriter
  *Jennifer Stein*
client
  *Goetze's Candy Co.*

creative firm
  **Cramer-Krasselt**
    Milwaukee (Wisconsin), USA
creative director
  *Mike Bednar*
art director
  *Dan Koel*
copywriter
  *Adam Albrecht*
client
  *Reddi-Wip*

creative firm
  **J. Walter Thompson/N.Y.**
    New York (New York), USA
creative director, art director, copywriter
  *Alan Platt*
client
  *Kellogg's*

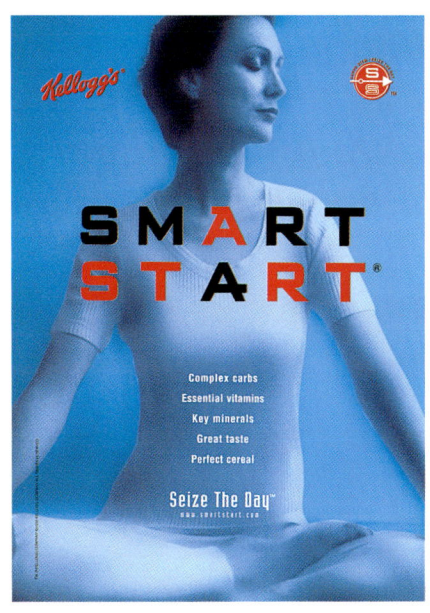

creative firm
  Fry Hammond Barr
  Orlando (Florida), USA
creative director
  Tim Fischer
art director
  Sean Brunson
production manager
  Stephanie Ruelke
copywriter
  John Logan
client
  Orlando Sentinel Interactive

creative firm
  Pisarkiewicz Mazur & Co., Inc.
  New York (New York), USA
creative director, designer
  Mary F. Pisarkiewicz
client
  Cybersmith, Inc.

creative firm
  Louis London
  St. Louis (Missouri), USA
art director
  Aaron Segall
copywriter
  Lori Jones
client
  Postnet.com

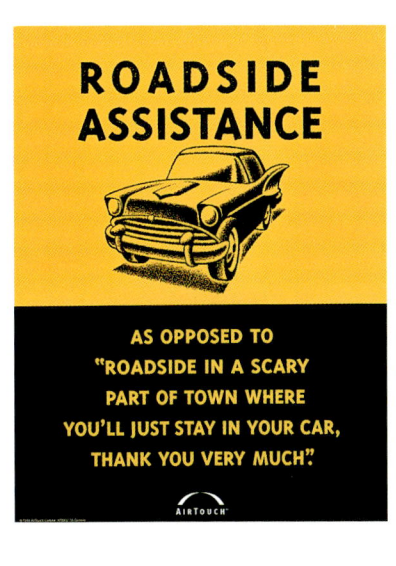

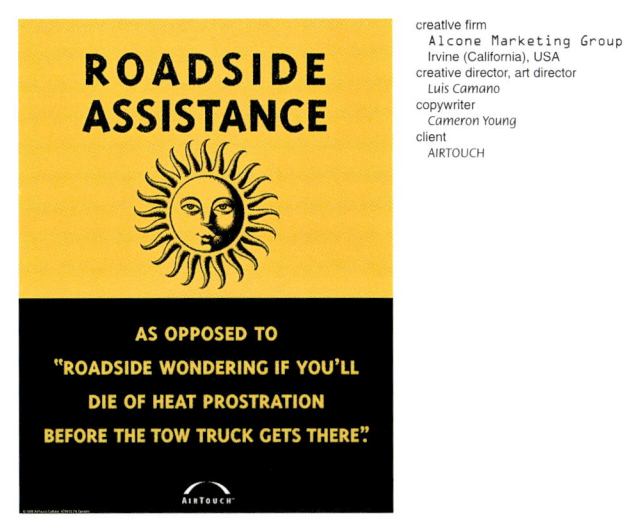

creative firm
  Alcone Marketing Group
  Irvine (California), USA
creative director, art director
  Luis Camano
copywriter
  Cameron Young
client
  AIRTOUCH

creative firm
  J. Walter Thompson
  Chicago (Illinois), USA
creative directors
  Jeff York & Doug Kamp
art director
  Eric Revels
copywriter
  Laura Keeler
client
  DELL

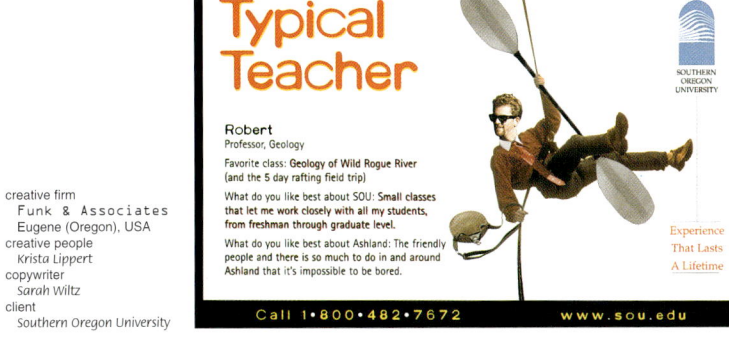

37

creative firm
  Funk & Associates
  Eugene (Oregon), USA
creative people
  Krista Lippert
copywriter
  Sarah Wiltz
client
  Southern Oregon University

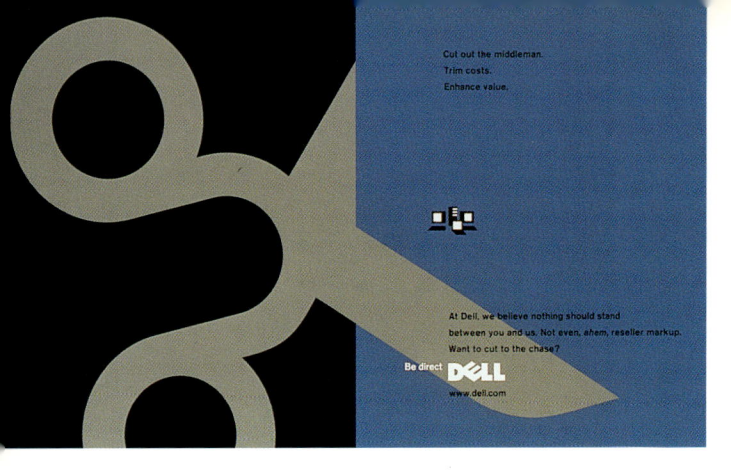

creative firms
    Design Machine Co.
    New York (New York), USA
    J. Walter Thompson
    Chicago (Illinois), USA
creative directors
    Jeff York & Doug Kamp
art director
    Eric Revels
creative people
    Alexander Gelman & Eric Revles
copywriter
    Laura Keeler
client
    DELL Computers

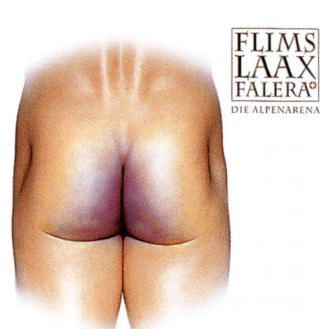

creative firm
    Advico Young & Rubicam
    Zurich (Gockhausen), Switzerland
creative director
    Hansjörg Zürcher
art director
    Dana Wirz
copywriter
    Peter Brönnimann
client
    Mountain Marketing

38

creative firm
    BGS DMB&B
    Milan, Italy
creative people
    BGS DMB&B
client
    Sara Lee/Champion

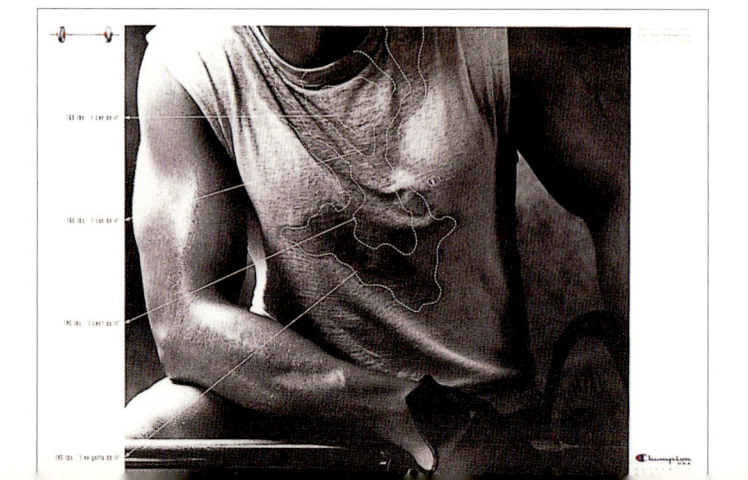

creative firm
 J. Walter Thompson/N.Y.
  New York (New York), USA
art director
 D.J. Pierce
photographer
 Bob Scott
copywriter
 Scott Duchon
client
 Blades Board & Skate

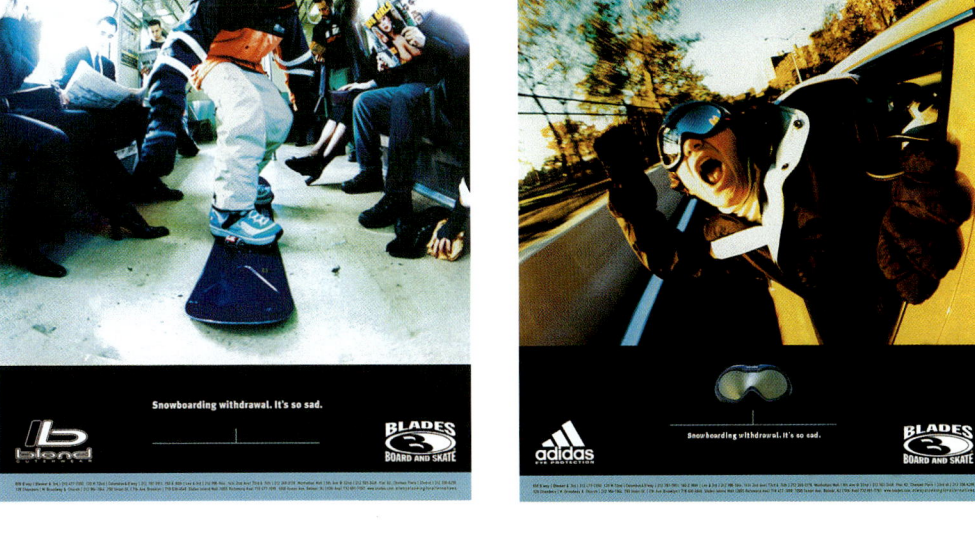

creative firm
 Verba DDB
  Milan, Italy
creative director, copywriter
 Enrico Bonomini
art director
 Andrea Maggioni
client
 Diadora

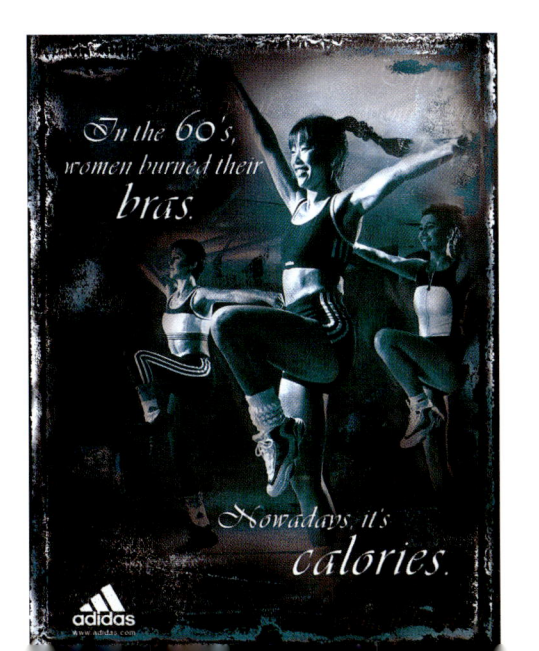

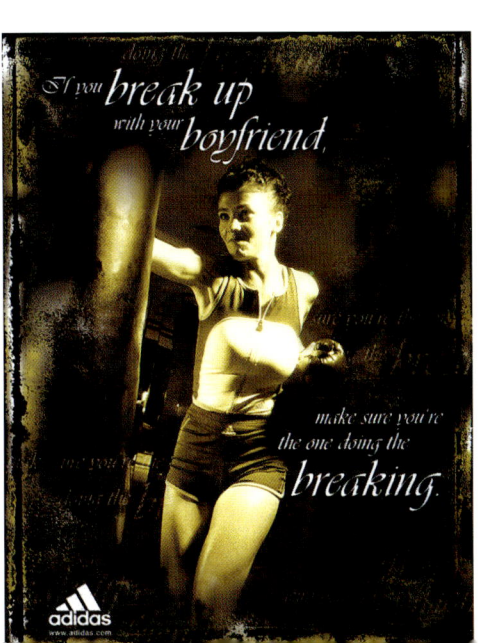

creative firm
 FCB Singapore
  Singapore
creative director
 Chris Kyrne
art directors
 Dali Meskam &
 Nick Tan
client
 Adidas Singapore

39

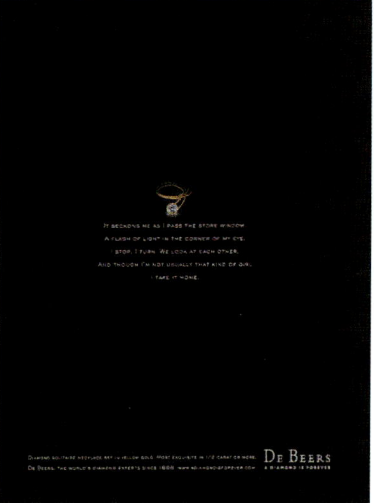

40

creative firm
  J. Walter Thompson/N.Y.
  New York (New York), USA
creative directors
  Ed Evangelista & Chris D'Rozario
art director
  Ed Avangelista
designer
  Phil Kelly
copywriters
  Chris D'Rozario & Anne Nodar
client
  DeBeers

creative firm
  J. Walter Thompson
  Chicago (Illinois), USA
creative director
  Jeff York
art director
  Mark Westman
copywriter
  Greg Oreskovich
client
  CheezWhiz

creative firm
  Grey Advertising
  New York (New York), USA
creative people
  Ron Castillo, Jan Egan, Kira Shalom,
  Jerry Saviola, Jayne Horowitz,
  Stephen DeAngelis, Heather Foster,
  Melissa McHugh, & Phil Bambino
client
  Jockey

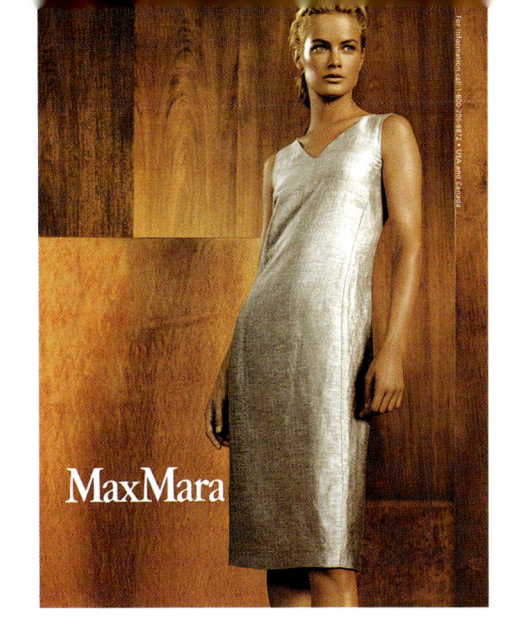

creative firm
  Dente & Cristina, Inc.
  New York (New York), USA
creative people
  Barbara Dente &
  Donna Cristina
client
  MaxMara

creative firm
  The Zimmerman Agency
  Tallahasee (Florida), USA
creative people
  Steve Baker, Lee Gonzalez,
  & Jeff Flassig
client
  Narcissus

creative firm
  Leslie Evans Design Associates
  Portland (Maine), USA
art director
  Leslie Evans
designers
  Leslie Evans & Teresa Otul Cummings
photographer
  Harry DeZitter
copywriter
  Liz Peavy
client
  Hathaway

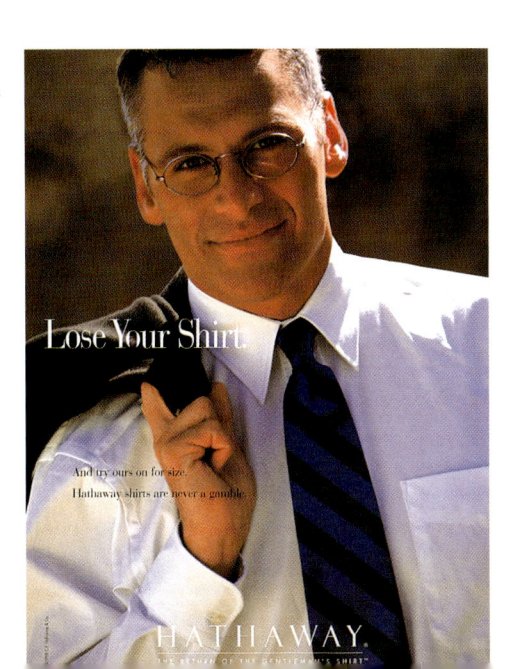

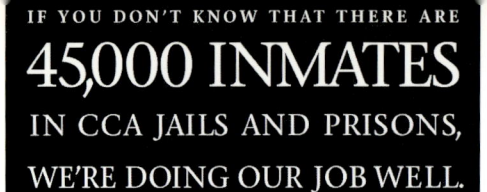

creative firm
  Dye, Van Mol & Lawrence
  Nashville (Tennessee), USA
creative director
  Chuck Creasy
art director
  Dale Addy
client
  CCA

creative firm
  Burkhardt & Hillman
  New York (New York), USA
creative people
  Patrick Hillman
client
  Tom's of Maine

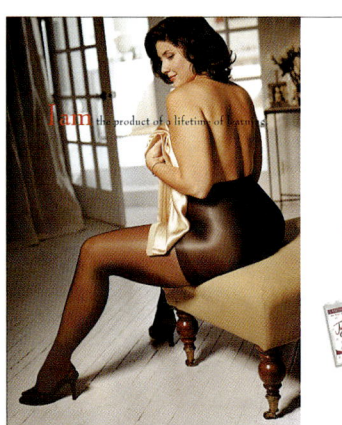

42

creative firm
  Temerlin McClain
  Irving (Texas), USA
creative director
  Glenn Ashley
art directors
  Janet Ferguson &
  Donna Lempert
designer
  Judy Zipkes
photographer
  Chris Sanders
copywriter
  Dee Leone
client
  Just My Size

creative firm
  Bozell Kamstra
  Pittsburgh (Pennsylvania), USA
art director
  Brian Bronaugh
print production
  Greg Hope
copywriter
  Mike Hoff
client
  Carnegie Science Center

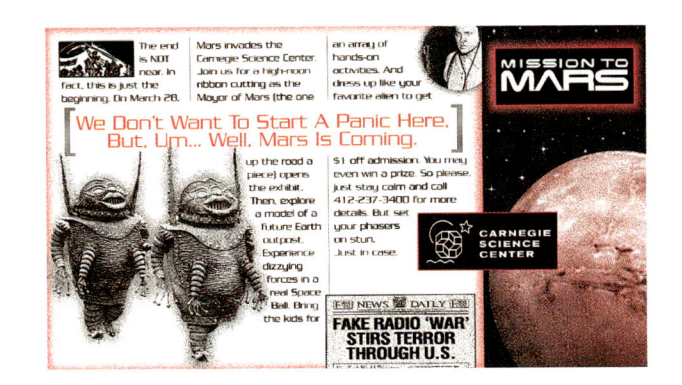

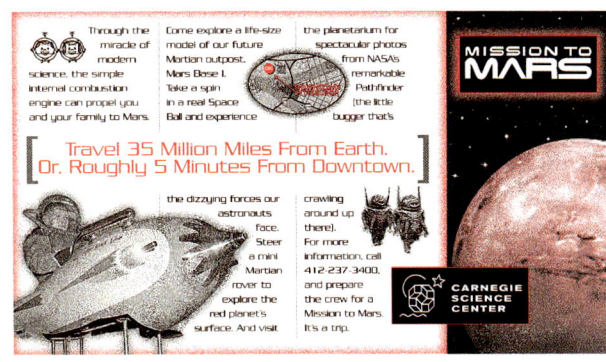

creative firm
  Wray Ward Laseter
  Charlotte (North Carolina), USA
creative director
  Jennifer Appleby
art director
  Todd Kinley
producer
  Sheila B. Dulin
copywriters
  Tom Cocke & Jim Stadler
client
  Mint Museum of Craft & Design

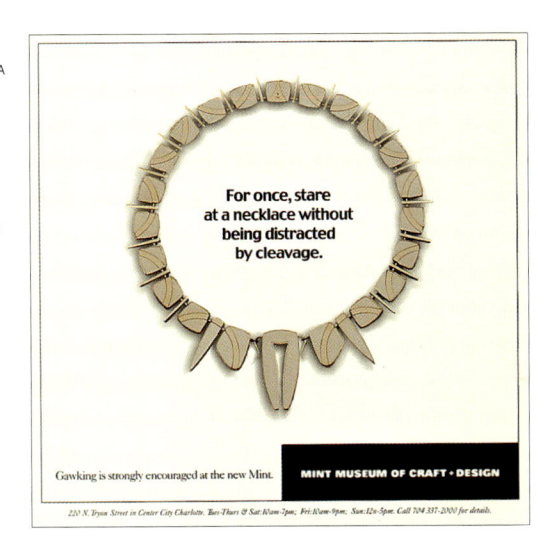

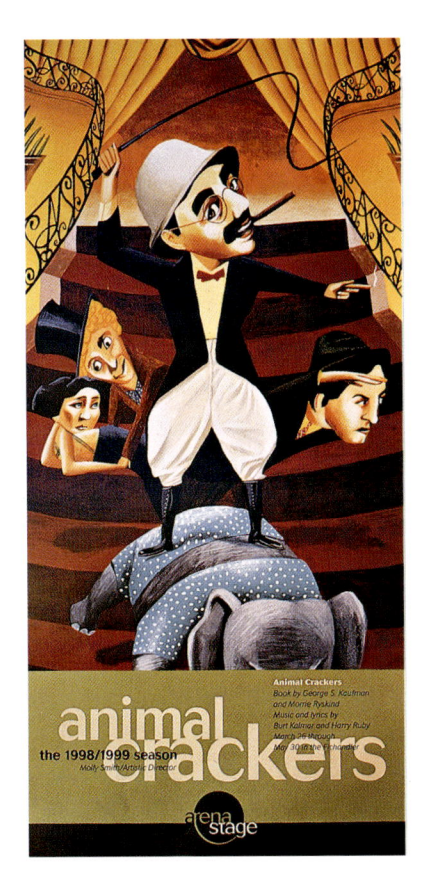

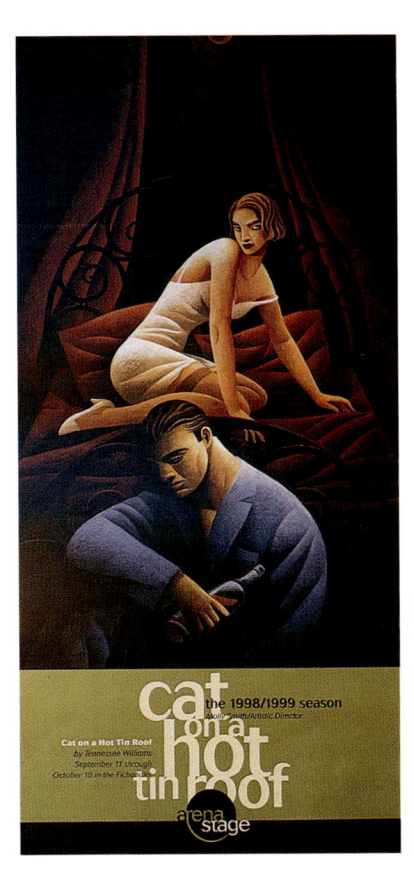

43

creative firm
  Mires Design
  San Diego (California) USA
art directors
  Scott Mires, Neill Archer Roan, & Laura Hull
designer
  Miguel Perez
illustrators
  Jody Hewgill & Mike Ulriksen
client
  Arena Stage

creative firm
  Wray Ward Laseter
  Charlotte (North Carolina), USA
creative director
  Jennifer Appleby
art director
  Shawn Kelley
production director
  Sheila B. Dulin
copywriter
  Jim Stadler
client
  Junior Achievement

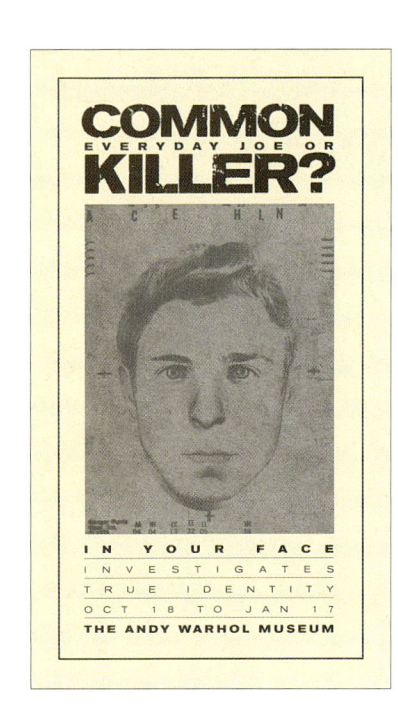

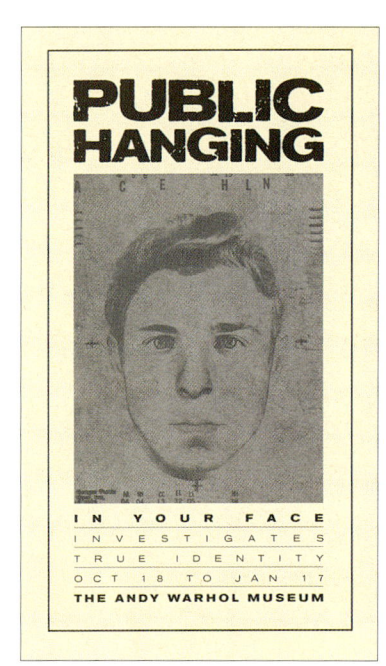

44

creative firm
  Dymum Nelson & Company
  Pittsburgh (Pennsylvania), USA
creative directors
  John Dymun & Craig Otto
art director, copywriter
  Craig Otto
designer
  Robyn Riel
client
  The Andy Warhol Museum

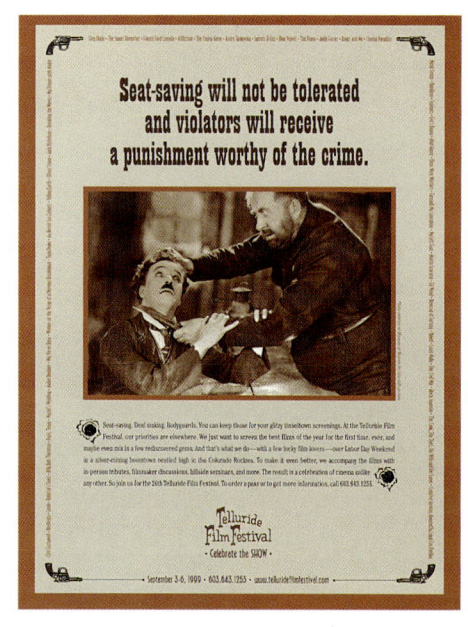

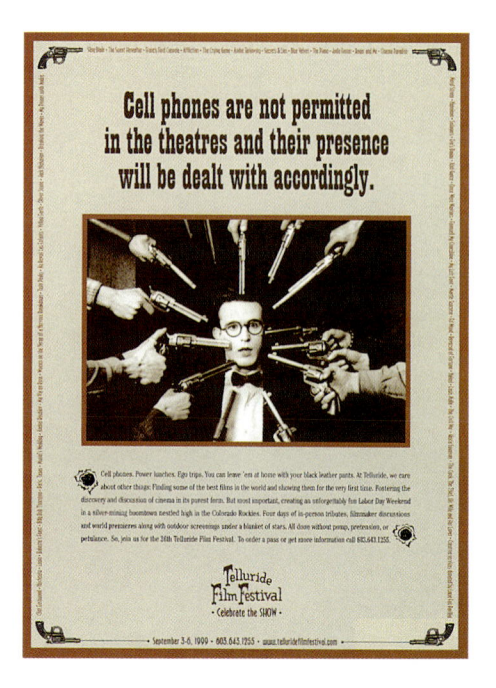

creative firm
  Lowe Fox Paulika
  New York (New York), USA
creative people
  Deb Hiller, Paula Cunyus, &
  Carol Fiorino
client
  Telluride Film Festival

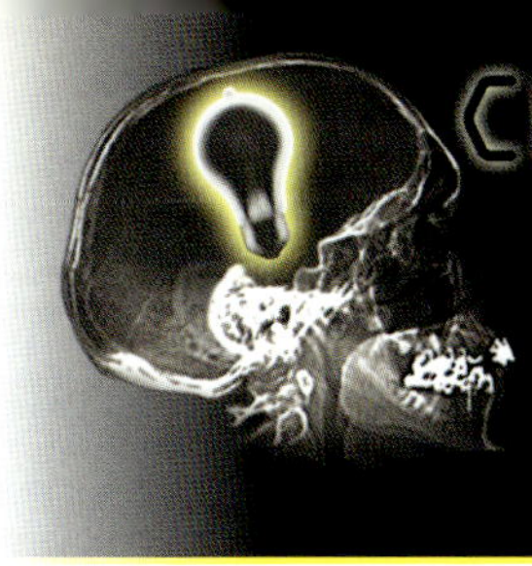

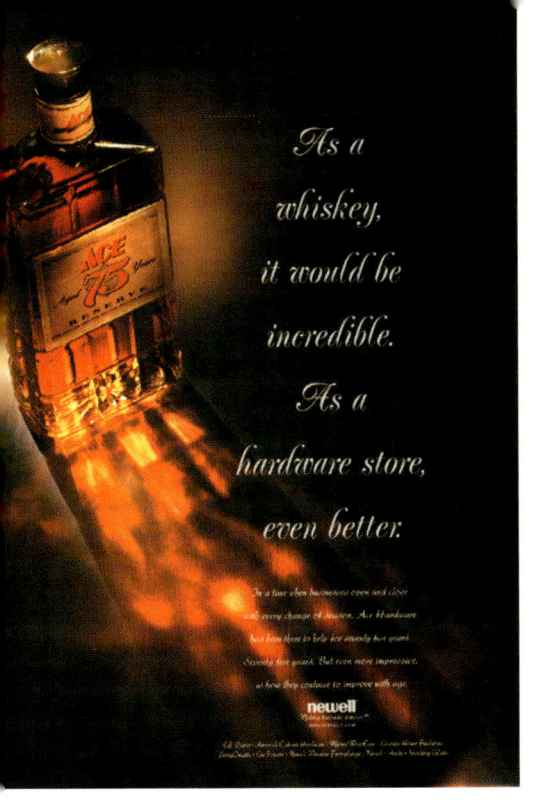

# CREATIVITY

## Trade Ads
## Full

creative firm
  The Ungar Group
    Chicago (Illinois), USA
creative people
  Tom Ungar &
  Mark Ingraham
client
  Newell Rubbermaid

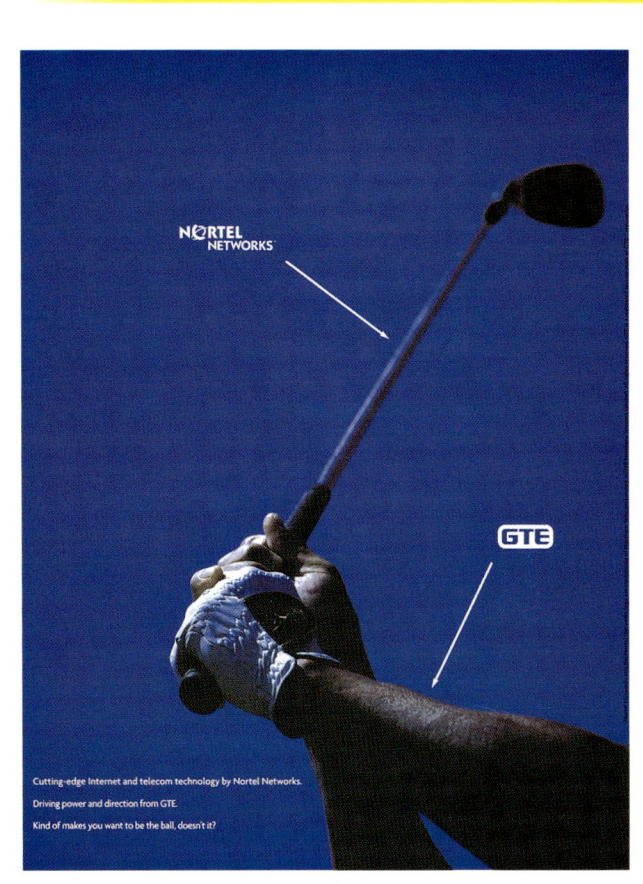

creative firm
  Aydlotte & Cartwright
    Atlanta (Georgia), USA
creative director
  William Y. Aydlotte
art director
  Allison Rooke
copywriter
  Wally Stoneman
client
  Yamaha Golf Cars

creative firm
  Termerlin McClain
    Irving (Texas), USA
creative director
  Vinny Minchillo
art director, copywriter
  Glen Day
client
  GTE

creative firm
  Sawyer Riley Compton
    Atlanta (Georgia), USA
creative director, art director
  Bart Cleveland
photographer
  David Kiesgen
copywriters
  Bart Cleveland &
  John Spalding
client
  Creative Circus

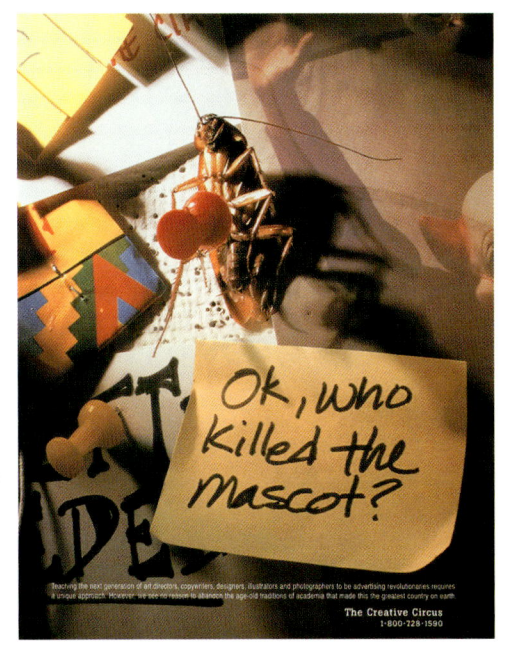

45

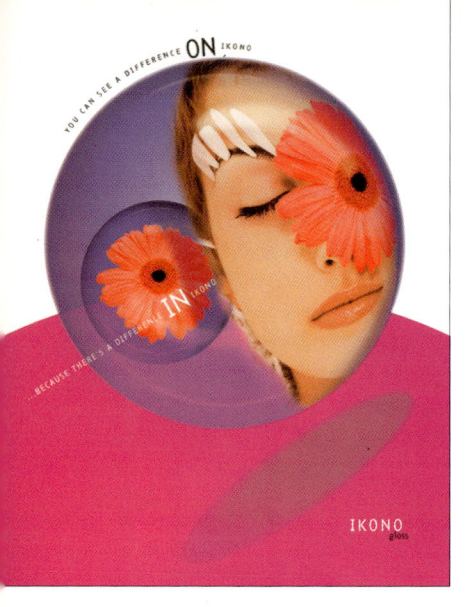

creative firm
 **The Frasier/ Bell Group**
 Horsham (Pennsylvania), USA
creative director
 Ted Bell
art director
 Bill Healey
designer
 Tom Brill
photographer
 Charles Bush
copywriter
 Margaret Frasier
client
 Zanders USA

creative firm
 **Sawyer Riley Compton**
 Atlanta (Georgia), USA
creative director
 Bart Cleveland
art directors
 Kevin Thoem &
 Tony Messano
illustrator
 Frederic Remington
copywriter
 Brett Compton
client
 Pony Express Delivery Service

46

creative firm
 **The Ungar Group**
 Chicago (Illinois), USA
creative people
 Tom Unger & Mike Franzese
client
 Edward Don & Company

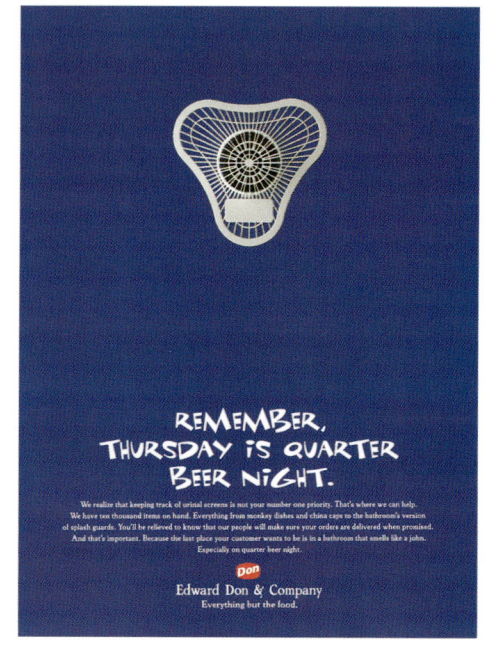

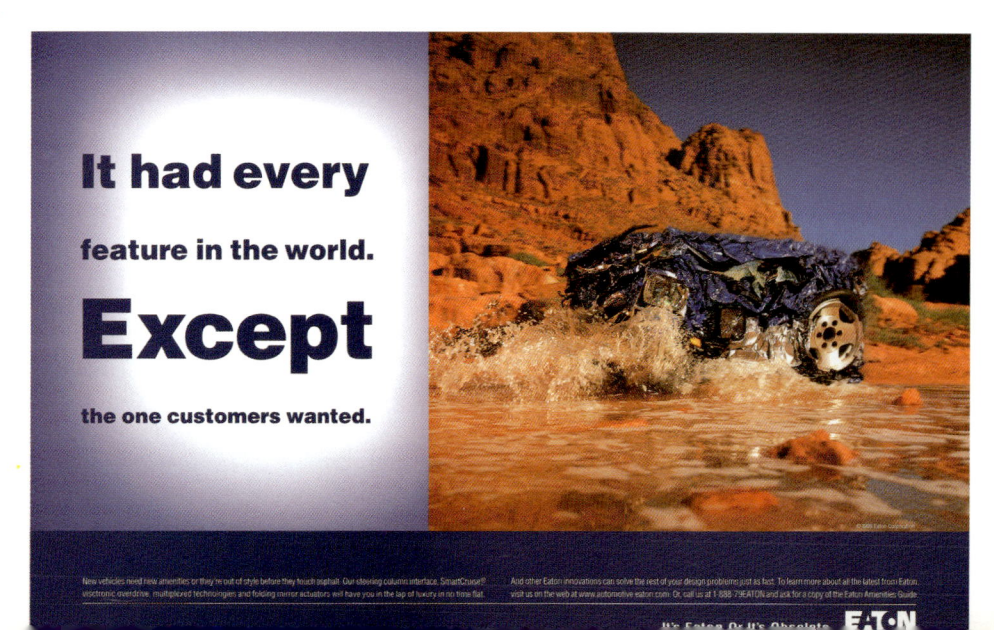

creative firm
 **Louis London**
 St. Louis (Missouri), USA
art director
 Mark Masterson
copywriters
 Doug Outman &
 Michelle Spencer
client
 Miller Brewing Company

creative firm
 **Sawyer Riley Compton**
 Atlanta (Georgia), USA
creative director
 Bart Cleveland
art director
 Kevin Thoem
photographer
 Rick Graves
copywriters
 Brett Compton &
 John Spalding
client
 Eaton Feature

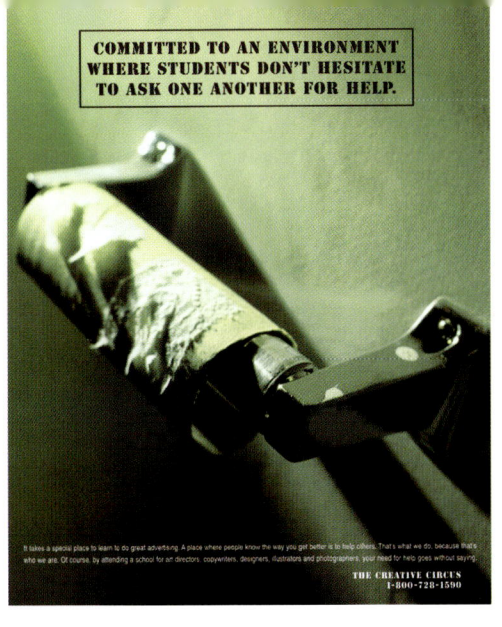

creative firm
 Sawyer Riley Compton
 Atlanta (Georgia), USA
creative director, art director
 Bart Cleveland
photographer
 David Kiesgen
copywriters
 Bart Cleveland &
 John Spalding
client
 Creative Circus

creative firm
 Cramer-Krasselt
 Milwaukee (Wisconsin), USA
creative director
 Pat Knapp
art director
 Dan Koel
copywriter
 Adam Albrecht
client
 CASE AG

47

creative firm
 Sawyer Riley Compton
 Atlanta (Georgia), USA
creative director
 Bart Cleveland
art director
 Kevin Thoem
photographer
 Rick Graves
copywriters
 Brett Compton &
 John Spalding
client
 Eaton Corporation

creative firm
 Sawyer Riley Compton
 Atlanta (Georgia), USA
creative director
 Bart Cleveland
art director
 Kevin Thoem
photographer
 Greg Slater
copywriter
 Brett Compton
client
 Delta Apparel

creative firm
 The Ungar Group
 Chicago (Illinois), USA
creative people
 Tom Ungar &
 Mark Ingraham
client
 Newell Rubbermaid

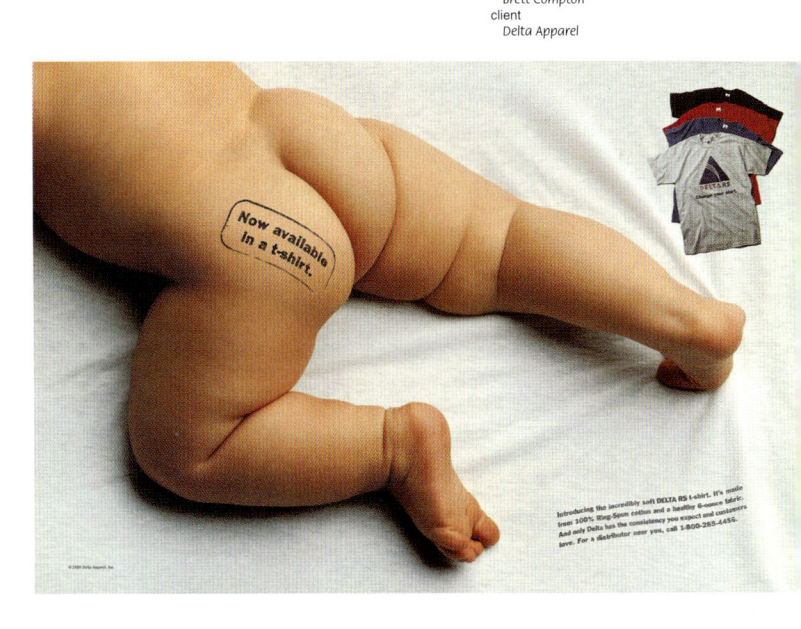

creative firm
 KPR
 New York (New York), USA
creative people
 John Dietz, Susana Padron, & Paul Weiss
client
 Pasteur Mérieux Connaught

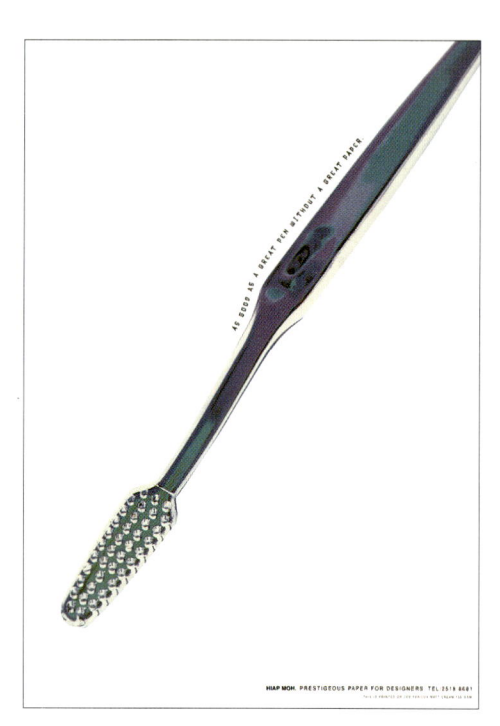

creative firm
 Gallery Ltd
 Hong Kong
creative people
 Benny Cheng, Giles Tse, & Kelvin Parker
client
 Hiap Moh (HK) Ltd

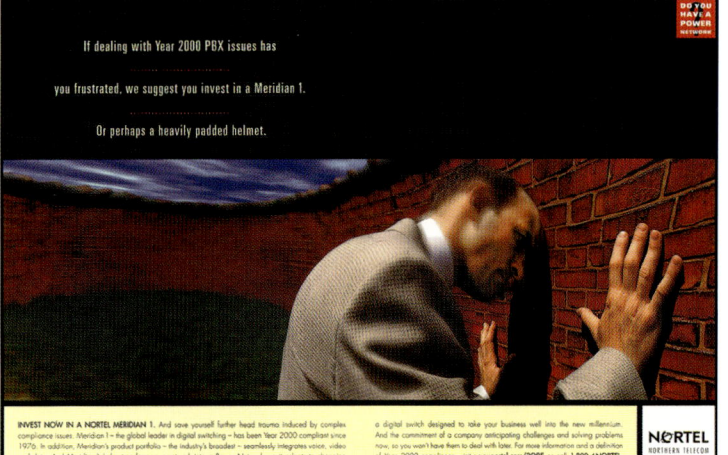

48

creative firm
 Temerlin McClain
 Irving (Texas), USA
creative directors
 Bill Oakley, Brad White, & Leigh Sander
art director
 Brad White
photographer
 Marc Hauser
copywriter
 Leigh Sander
client
 Nortel Networks

creative firm
 Fairly Painless Advertising
 Holland (Michigan), USA
creative director
 Peter Bell
art director
 Tom Crimp
designer
 Rick Vanderleek
copywriter
 Dick Holm
client
 Herman Miller

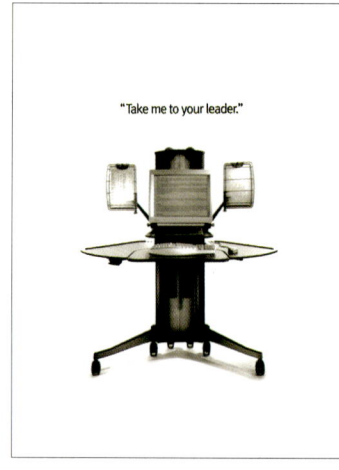

creative firm
 Stackig/TMP
 McLean (Virginia), USA
creative people
 Terry Wilson & Kenn Speicher
client
 BSI, Inc

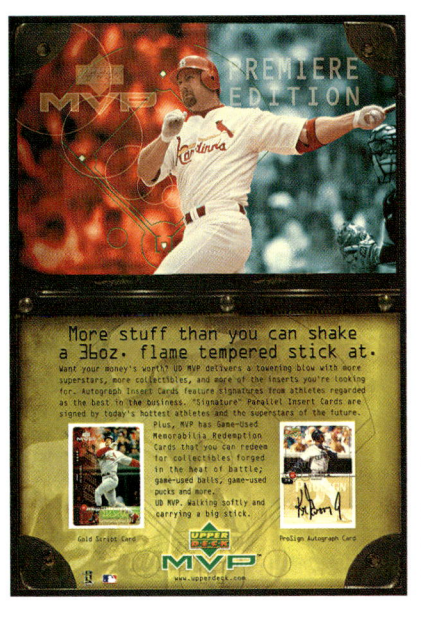

creative firm
 Louis London
  St. Louis (Missouri), USA
creative director
 David Bannecke
copywriter
 Steve Hunt
client
 The Upper Deck Company

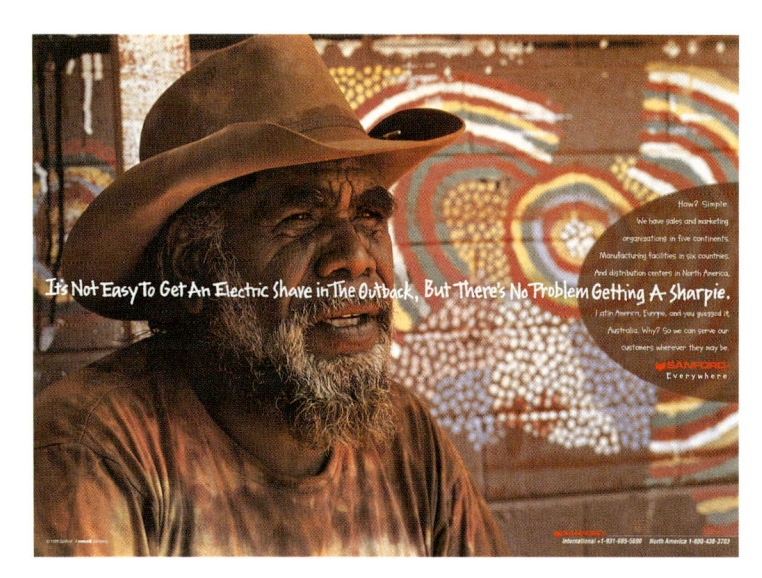

creative firm
 The Ungar Group
  Chicago (Illinois), USA
creative people
 Tom Ungar, Mark Ingraham, &
 Mete Moran
client
 Sanford

creative firm
 LaRowe Advertising
  Chicago (Illinois), USA
creative director
 Randy LaRowe
art director
 Denis Hagen
copywriter
 Gary Lande
client
 First Chicago NBD Bank

creative firm
 The Frasier/Bell Group
  Horsham (Pennsylvania), USA
creative director
 Ted Bell
art director
 Bill Healey
designer
 Tom Brill
copywriter
 Margaret Frasier
client
 Zanders USA

49

creative firm
 Sawyer Riley Compton
  Atlanta (Georgia), USA
creative director
 Bart Cleveland
art director
 Karl Madcharo
photographer
 Tom Smugala
copywriter
 Ried Cartwright
client
 Delta Apparel

creative firm
 Temerlin McClain
 Irving (Texas), USA
creative directors
 Bill Oakley, Brad White, &
 Leigh Sander
art director
 Brad White
photographer
 Robb Debenport
copywriter
 Leigh Sander
client
 Nortel Networks

creative firm
 The Ungar Group
 Chicago (Illinois), USA
creative people
 Tom Ungar &
 Mike Franzese
client
 Newell Rubbermaid

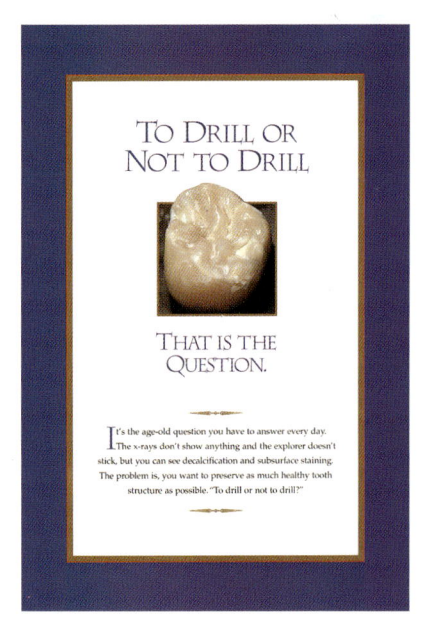

50

creative firm
 Catalyst Direct, Inc.
 Rochester (New York), USA
creative directors
 Meghan Labonge &
 Kevin Schroer
art director
 Jennifer Wagner
copywriter
 Meghan Labonge
client
 SS White

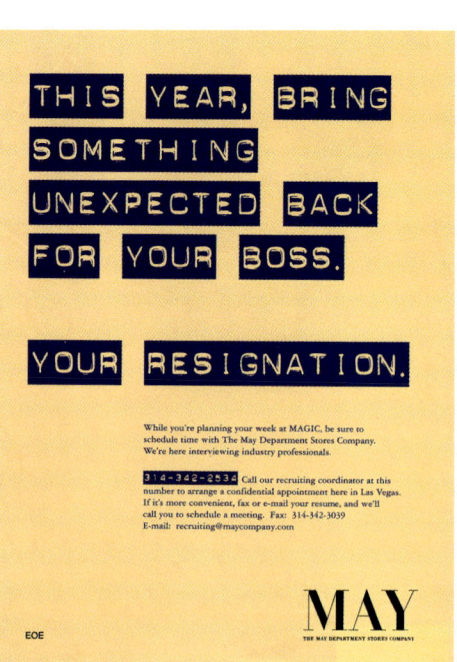

creative firm
 JGA, Inc.
 Southfield (Missouri), USA
creative people
 Tony Camilletti, Brian Eastman,
 & Mike Farris
client
 JGA, Inc.

creative firm
 JWT Specialized Communications
 Los Angeles (California), USA
creative director
 Tim Kidwell
art director, production artist
 Gene Kuehnle
copywriter
 Rich Heend
client
 May Department Stores Company

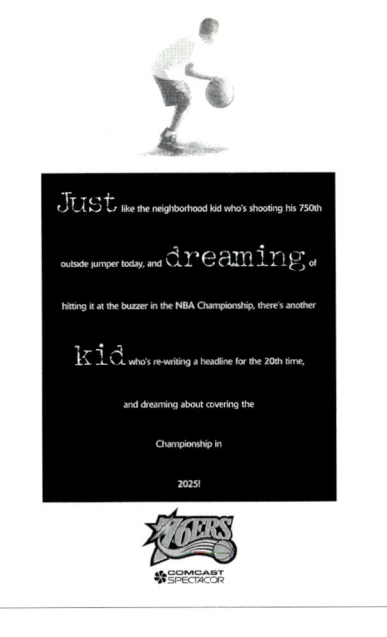

creative firm
 **Philadelphia 76ers**
  Philadelphia (Pennsylvania), USA
creative people
 Mark Elmore, Gary Yealdhall,
 Dave Coskey, & Lara White
client
 Philadelphia 76ers

50 Jahre
Ogilvy & Mather
Werbeagentur

creative firm
 **Ogilvy & Mather Frankfurt**
  Frankfurt, Germany
creative director, art director
 Gregor Seitz
client
 Ogilvy & Mather Frankfurt

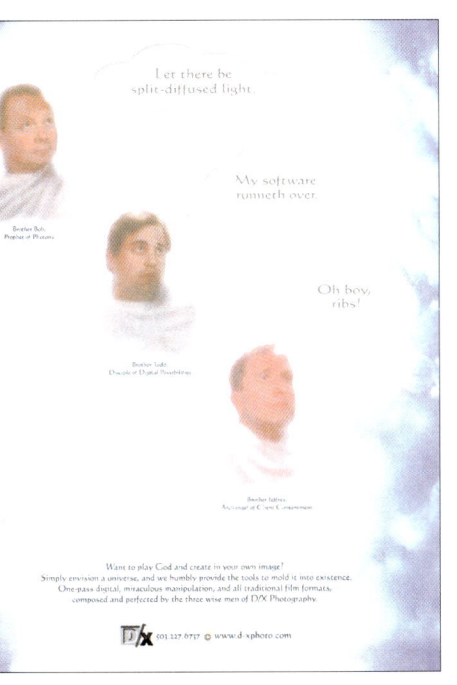

creative firm
 **Young & Roehr Group**
  Portland (Oregon), USA
creative director
 David Galluzzo
art director
 Barbara Baugwon
copywriter
 Anno Ballard
client
 DX Photography

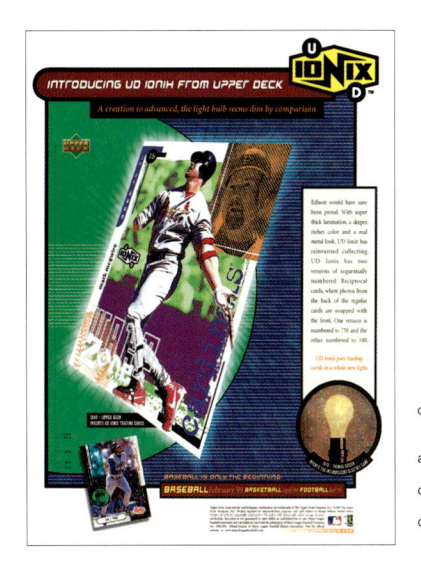

creative firm
 **Louis London**
  St. Louis (Missouri), USA
art director
 Aaron Segall
copywriter
 Doug Outman
client
 The Upper Deck Company

creative firm
 **Ambush Communication**
  New York (New York), USA
art director
 Keith Mastandrea
copywriter
 Tom Pastore
client
 Crain Communication, Inc.

creative firm
  Mike Salisbury Communications
    Venice (California), USA
creative people
  Mike Salisbury Communications
client
  Rollerblade

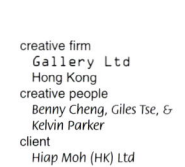

creative firm
  Gallery Ltd
    Hong Kong
creative people
  Benny Cheng, Giles Tse, &
  Kelvin Parker
client
  Hiap Moh (HK) Ltd

52

creative firm
  Sawyer Riley Compton
    Atlanta (Georgia), USA
creative director
  Bart Cleveland
art directors
  Kevin Thoem &
  Tony Messano
illustrator
  Frederic Remington
copywriter
  Brett Compton
client
  Pony Express Delivery Service

creative firm
  Sudler & Hennessey
    North Sydney (NSW), Australia
creative people
  Marlyn Docherty &
  Peter Ryan
client
  Pfizer Pty Ltd

creative firm
  Gauger & Silva Associates
   San Francisco (California), USA
creative people
  Bob Ankers, John Horvers, &
  David Gauger
client
  Tetra Pak

creative firm
  Heye & Partner
   Unterhaching, Germany
creative directors
  Peter Hirrlinger &
  Ralph Taukenberger
art director
  Oliver Oelkers
designer
  Jessica Menke
copywriter
  Doris Haider
client
  Tony Stone

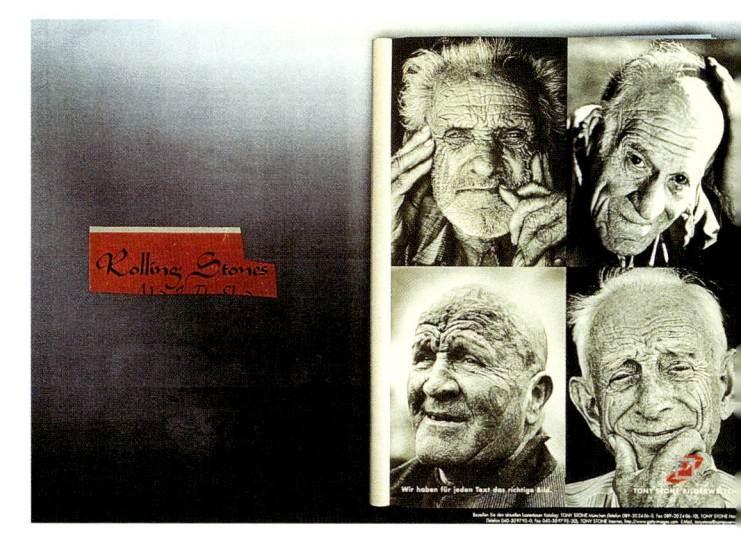

creative firm
  Gauger & Silva Associates
   San Francisco (California), USA
creative people
  Bob Ankers, John Horvers, &
  David Gauger
client
  Tetra Pak

53

creative firm
  JMC/Y&R
   Caracas (Miranda), Venezuela
creative people
  J.C. Ariza, Adriana Moreno, &
  J. Diaz
client
  Corporcion C. Carabobo

translation
  As you can see, the competition
  doesn't have much to show...

# CREATIVITY

## Trade Ads Fractional

---

**Hey Son, When Are You Going To Check Us Into That Nursing Home?**

Once again, your parents know what's best. This is no ordinary "rest home." As the originator of "luxury assisted-living," The Mann Houses set the highest standard for dignity and excellence. Call 404-250-9500 to arrange a personal tour with Charles H. Mann III, Chairman, or Debra Berry, VP/Administrator, or to receive a complimentary video tour. "Silver Tray Service." 5411–5413 Northland Dr., Atlanta 30342. The Mann Houses

creative firm
 Burkhardt & Hillman
 New York (New York), USA
creative director
 Ron Burkhardt
art director
 Rena Wong
copywriter
 Eddi Bainoute
client
 The Mann House

---

**How do you fit 2,000,000 products, 2,000 scientists and 16 manufacturing sites in the palm of your hand? Easy. Just click.**

www.sigma-aldrich.com. Now Sigma-Aldrich Fine Chemicals' custom manufacturing expertise is as close as your computer. Access our global network of scientific experts, state-of-the-art cGMP manufacturing and extensive product line. Or perform lightning-flash structure searches. Quite simply, it's the assistant you've always wanted.

SIGMA-ALDRICH
FINE CHEMICALS
www.sigma-aldrich.com

creative firm
 JWT Specialized
 Communications
 Los Angeles (California), USA
creative director
 Tim Kidwell
art director, production artist
 Gene Kuehnle
copywriter
 Rich Heend
client
 Sigma-Aldrich

---

54

---

**How adaptable should a pharmaceutical distributor be?**

At the Canadian Pharmaceutical Distribution Network, we can be as flexible as you want us to be. That means no separate service charges. No contracts. No minimum orders. What you will get is an adaptable pharmaceutical distribution service that offers you direct contact with a growing number of manufacturer members, fast and reliable delivery and no substitutions, unless you ask for them.

CPDN / RCDP
Find out more about the
Canadian Pharmaceutical Distribution Network
Phone 1-800-680-3839   Fax (905) 812-1477

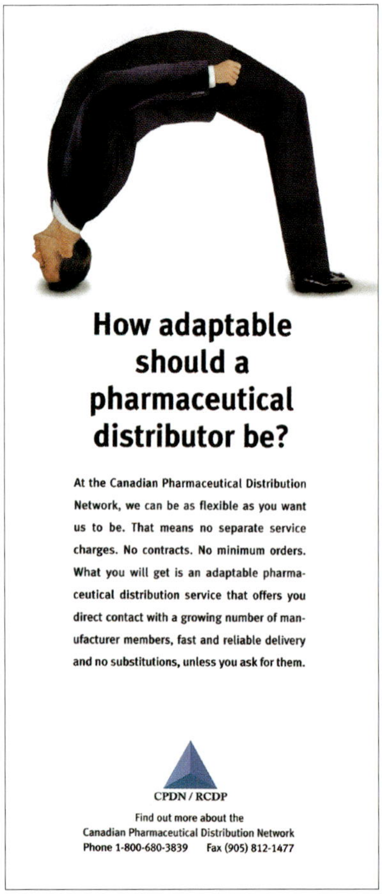

creative firm
 Wright Ideas, Inc.
 King City (Ontario), Canada
creative director, art director
 Rob Wright
photographer
 Ken Davies
copywriter
 Helen Nugent
client
 CPDN

---

**Sometimes advertising has to fly under the radar.**

GoCARD POSTCARD ADVERTISING — Unlike conventional media, GoCARDs are sought out, selected and enjoyed by Generation X-ers and thirty-somethings who often look askance at advertising. That's because GoCARDs are cool, usable, and best of all, free postcards. They're available in trendy restaurants and bars, as well as high-traffic health clubs and college campuses in eleven of the top U.S. markets. So fly in the face of convention, and call (212) 925-2420 for samples and a media kit.

creative firm
 Mires Design, Inc.
 San Diego (California), USA
art director
 John Ball
designers
 Gretchen Leary &
 Deborah Hom
client
 Go Card

---

**Pernas, pra que te quero?**

creative firm
 Oswaldo Mendes
 Belém (Pará), Brasil
creative people
 Oswaldo Mendes &
 Eduardo Reis
client
 O Liberal

A nova conta da Mendes é de dar água na boca da concorrência.

**Mendes**
Há 10 anos consecutivos, a melhor Agência do Norte.
Prêmio "The Hot Tops".

creative firm
  Oswaldo Mendes
  Belém (Pará), Brasil
creative people
  Oswaldo Mendes &
  Eduardo Reis
client
  Mendes Publicidade Ltda.

translation
  The New Account of Mendes makes
  the competitor's mouth water

## Os dois lados do ecoturismo no Pará. Ambos atraentes e gratificantes.

1. Não há, no Brasil, lugar algum mais virgem, mais exótico e bonito, mais adequado para o exercício do ecoturismo, do que o Estado do Pará. Nele convivem a floresta com os rios, lagos e igarapés, os sítios indígenas com os santuários ecológicos, as frutas de nomes esquisitos e sabores incríveis com a cozinha mais genuinamente brasileira, em meio a um delicioso clima equatorial, e junte-se a isso a reconhecida hospitalidade de um povo alegre e simpático.
Você escolhe entre a costa atlântica, a região do Baixo Amazonas, o Araguaia-Tocantins ou a Ilha do Marajó, a partir de Belém, a cidade mais portuguesa do Brasil.
Esse é o lado atraente e gratificante do ecoturismo no Pará, que você nunca vai esquecer e a que vai querer voltar sempre.
Volte correndo, que nós estamos de braços abertos à sua espera.

2. O outro lado do ecoturismo no Pará é do empreendedor, porque ainda há muito o que fazer para receber essa turma, e abrigá-la e levá-la às trilhas e percursos que vão desbravar tanta beleza e tantos caminhos novos.
Esse é o lado gratificante do nosso ecoturismo. O Pará está prontinho da silva para receber empreendedores talentosos que queiram aproveitar o seu potencial turístico, aproveitando, também, os incentivos fiscais, financeiros e de caráter infra-estrutural que a lei nº 5.943 garante aos novos empreendimentos.
E há, ainda, os incentivos fiscais da Amazônia geridos pela Sudam e pelo Banco da Amazônia.
Traga as suas idéias, que nós ajudamos com os incentivos, como acima está dito, e, juntos, podemos construir o melhor lugar do mundo para a prática do ecoturismo, o turismo com maior futuro em toda parte.
Não é gratificante, agora atraente?!

**GOVERNO DO PARÁ**

creative firm
  Oswaldo Mendes
  Belém (Pará), Brasil
creative people
  Oswaldo Mendes &
  Eduaro Reis
client
  Governo do Pará

translation
  Both sides of ecotourism in Pará. Both
  are attractive and gratifying

55

## Some men rely on verbal skills.

*Please, baby, please, please, please, please, please, please, please, please, please, please, please, please, please, please, please, please, please, please, please, please, please, please, please, please, please, please, please, please, please, please, please, please, please, please, please, please, please, please, please, please, please, please, please, please.*

## Some don't.

Make Valentine's a day you'll both remember.

# JEWELERS ON FIFTH
578 FIFTH AVENUE AT 47TH STREET 212.593.7171

creative firm
  Bleecker & Sullivan
  New York (New York), USA
creative director
  Itzhak Beery
copywriter
  Sela Francis
client
  Jewelers on Fifth

## Patience Is A Virtue
### [ For A Dog ]

We keep *rapid* in rapid prototyping.

• SLA • Actua • SLS • QuickCast • RTV Molding • Castings
• Standard and Flexible Resin • Keltool • Rapid Tooling
• Tinting • PRO-E⁵ and more.
**Seven days a week.**

**VISTA**
TECHNOLOGIES LLC

www.vistatek.com
(651) 653-0400 • Fax (651) 653-0900
4457 White Bear Pkwy, Suite D, White Bear Lake, MN 55110

creative firm
  Risdall Linnihan Advertising
  St. Paul (Minnesota), USA
art director
  Mark Arnold
copywriter
  Jenny Radack
client
  Vista Technologies

# FIBER'S GOOD FOR YOUR SYSTEM

**KMC Telecom. Roanoke**
Creative Solutions with a Hometown Touch.

To discover the business benefits of switching to KMC Telecom's FiberEdge network for local, toll, long distance, multimedia, and high-speed data services,
call Kim Stanley @ **540.982.8180**

visit our web site at www.kmctelecom.com

creative firm
  Emphasis Seven
  Communications, Inc.
  Chicago (Illinois), USA
designer
  Craig Niedermaier
copywriter
  Jim Briles
client
  KMC Telecom Inc.

# CREATIVITY

## Trade Ads Campaign

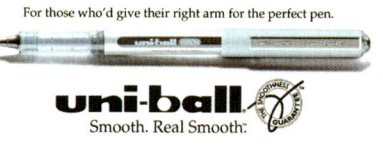

creative firm
  Louis London
  St. Louis (Missouri), USA
art director
  Joe Ortmeyer
copywriter
  Judy Milanovits
client
  Sanford

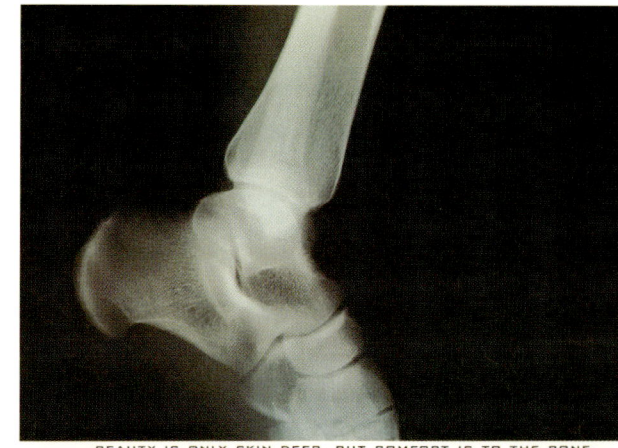

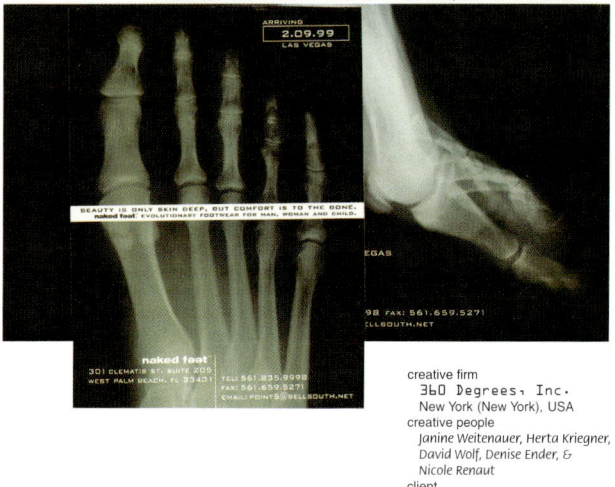

creative firm
  360 Degrees, Inc.
  New York (New York), USA
creative people
  Janine Weitenauer, Herta Kriegner, David Wolf, Denise Ender, & Nicole Renaut
client
  Utopia Marketing

creative firm
  The Ungar Group
  Chicago (Illinois), USA
creative people
  Tom Ungar, Mark Ingraham, & Mete Morgan
client
  Sanford

"Lisse, riche et satisfaisante?"

"Abair lióm rud éigin nach bhfuil fhios agam faoi."

creative firm
 The Ungar Group
 Chicago (Illinois), USA
creative people
 Tom Ungar &
 Mike Franzese
client
 American Hardware
 Maunfacturers Assn.

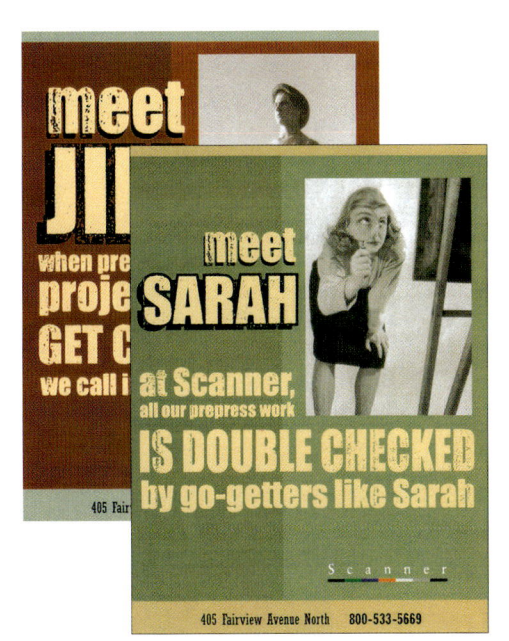

57

creative firm
 Belyea
 Seattle (Washington), USA
art director
 Patricia Belyea
designer
 Ron Lars Hansen
copywriter
 Liz Holland
client
 Scanner

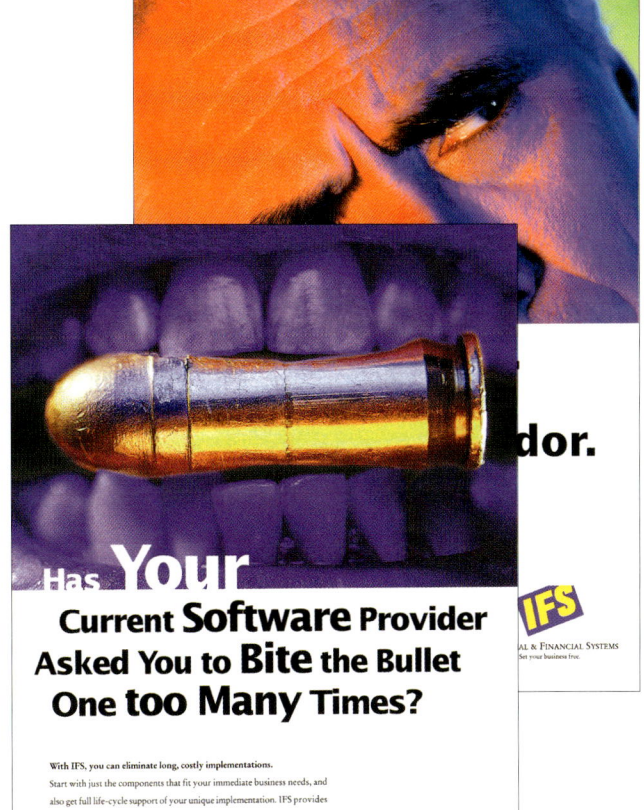

Has **Your** Current **Software** Provider Asked You to **Bite** the Bullet One **too Many** Times?

creative firm
 Tieken Design +
 Creative Services
 Phoenix (Arizona), USA
creative director, designer
 Fred E. Tieken
copywriters
 John Bridges, Fred E. Tieken, &
 Gail Smith Tieken
client
 IFS Industrial +
 Financial Systems

58

creative firm
 HBO
  New York (New York), USA
art director
 Venus R. Dennison
client
 Cinemax

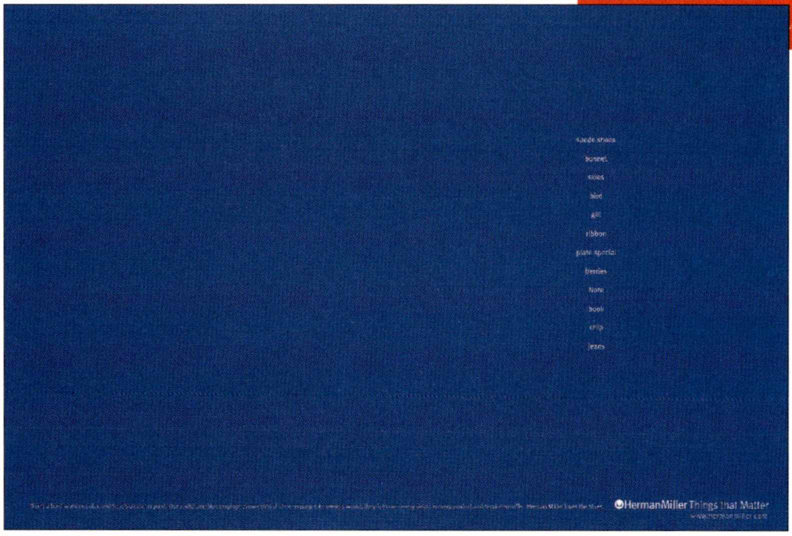

creative firm
 Fairly Painless Advertising
  Holland (Michigan), USA
creative director, copywriter
 Peter Bell
art director
 Tom Crimp
designer
 Rick Vanderleek
client
 Herman Miller

creative firm
 Young & Roehr Group
  Portland (Oregon), USA
creative director, copywriter
 Brian Mount
art director
 Martin Rupert
client
 Freightliner

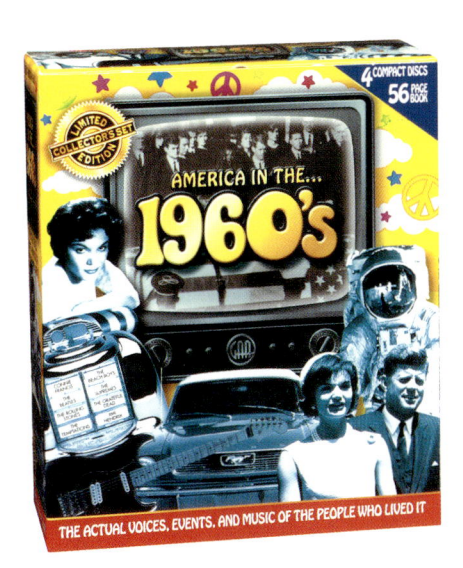

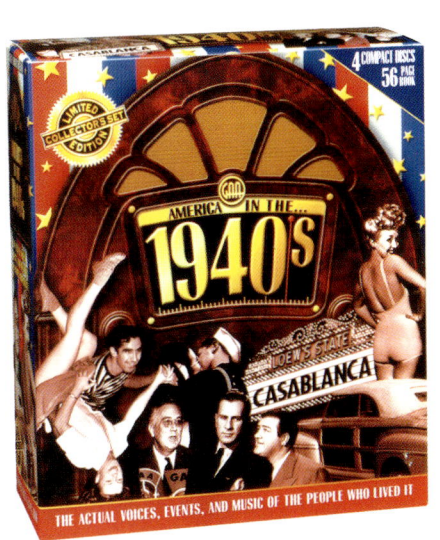

creative firm
 The Ungar Group
  Chicago (Illinois), USA
creative people
 Tom Ungar &
 Mike Franzese
client
 Newell Rubbermaid

creative firm
 Zunda Design Group
  South Norwalk (Conneticut), USA
creative people
 Charles Zunda &
 Todd Nickel
client
 Great American Audio

59

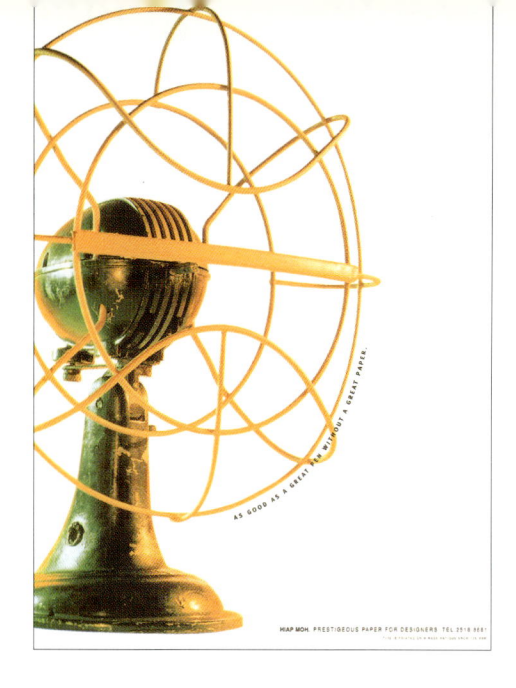

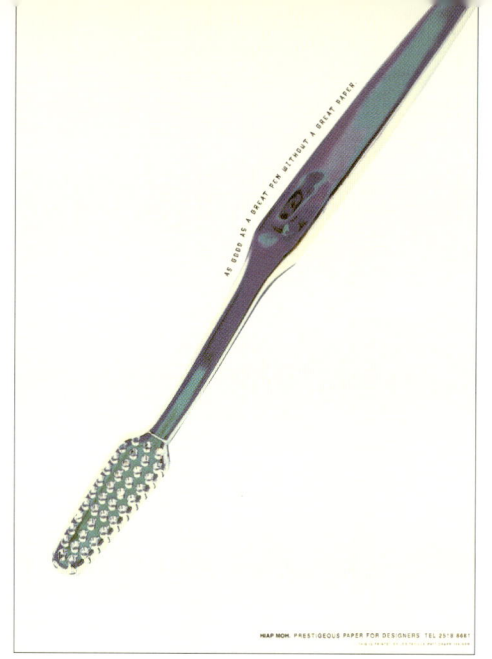

creative firm
   Gallery Ltd.
   Hong Kong, China
creative people
   Benny Cheng, Giles Tse, &
   Kelvin Parker
client
   Hiap Moh (HK) Ltd

creative firm
   The Signature Agency
   Raleigh (North Carolina), USA
creative people
   Robert Morrow & Anne Shelton
client
   Tobacco Associates, Inc..

60

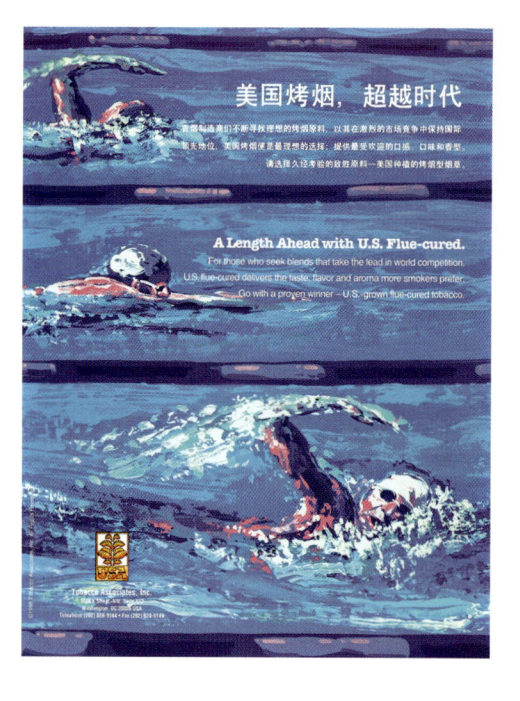

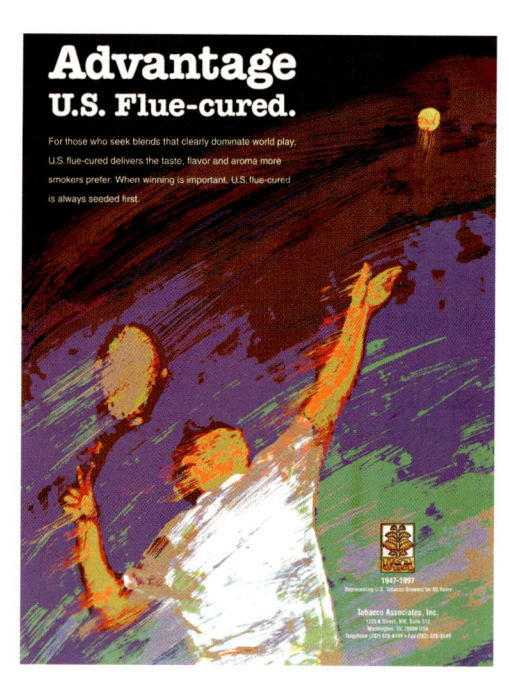

creative firm
   Young & Roehr Group
   Portland (Oregon), USA
creative directors
   David Galluzzo & Brian Mount
art director
   David Galluzzo
copywriter
   Brian Mount
client
   CFI

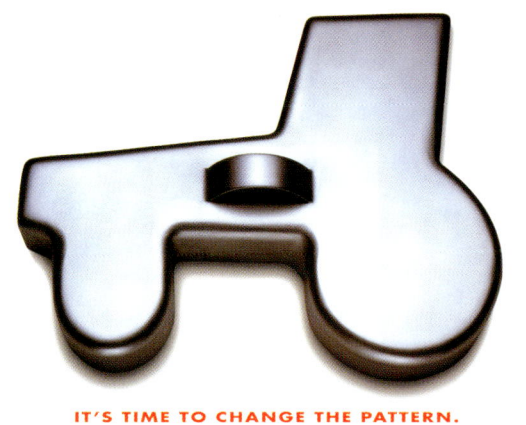

IT'S TIME TO CHANGE THE PATTERN.    IT'S TIME TO EXPAND THE BOUNDARIES.

creative firm
 Cramer-Krasselt
 Milwaukee (Wisconsin), USA
creative director
 Pat Knapp
art director
 Dan Koel
copywriter
 Adam Albrecht
client
 CASE AG

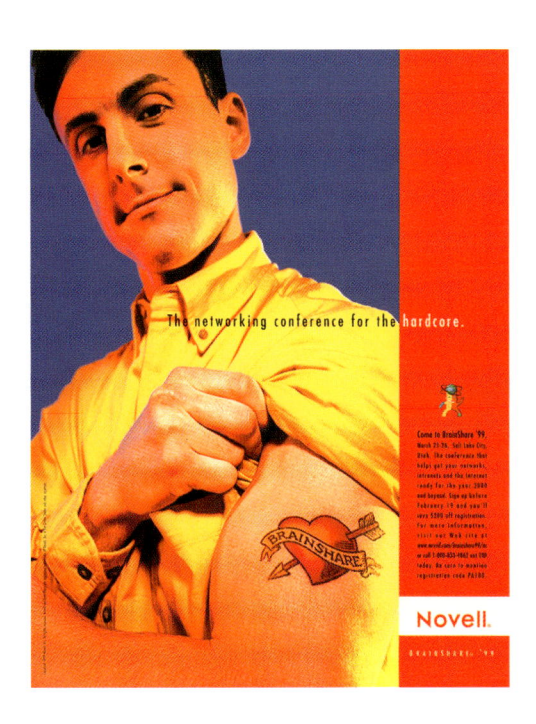

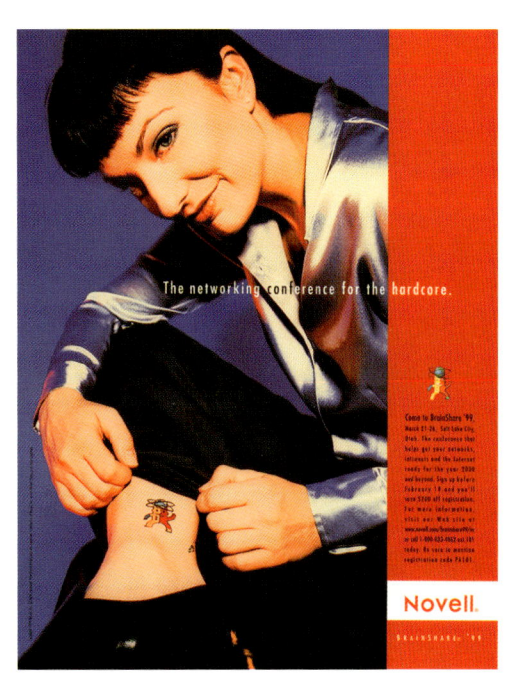

The networking conference for the hardcore.

61

creative firm
 Wunderman Cato Johnson
 San Francisco (California), USA
creative directors
 John Meyer & Steve Alfano
art director
 Shannon Brown
copywriter
 Ida Gamban
client
 Novell

creative firm
 Morgan & Partners
 Jacksonville (Florida), USA
art director
 Kenny Sink
production
 Brian Thompson
copywriter
 Kathy Bronson
client
 ACSYS Professional Staffing

ACSYS PROFESSIONAL STAFFING. NO MISMATCHES.

creative firm
  Propeller Communication AB
  Göteborg, Sweden
creative people
  Jörgen Forssling &
  Klas Ekstrand
client
  Stora Enso Nymölla AB

62

creative firm
  Cramer-Krasselt
  Milwaukee (Wisconsin), USA
creative director
  Pat Knapp
art director
  Jon Grider
copywriter
  Steve Bernfeld
client
  Johnson Controls

creative firm
  Gallery Ltd
  Hong Kong, China
creative people
  Benny Cheng &
  Kenneth Tung
client
  Miracle Printing Co. Ltd.

translation
  Only if there is a Miracle.

Is the meeting near at hand while you still lack the printed material? Just call Miracle Printing Digital Express to give you a great hand. Miracle performs miracles whenever time presses!

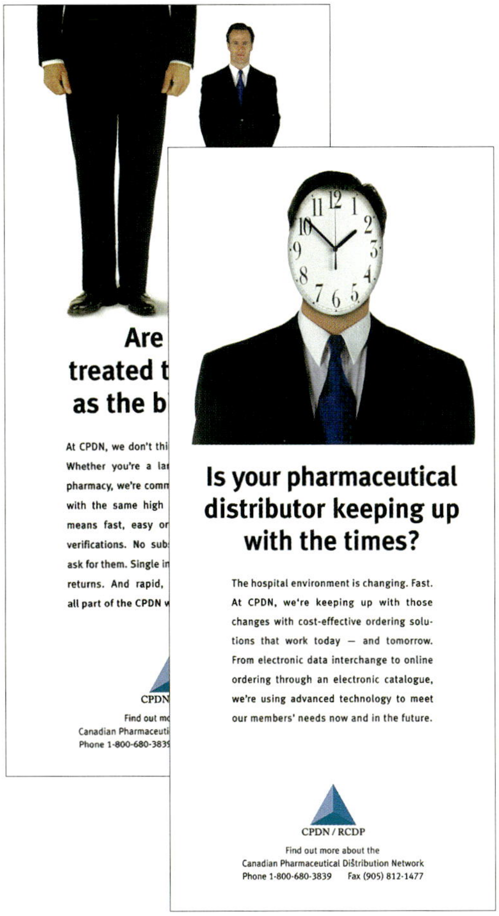

creative firm
 Wright Ideas Inc.
  King City (Ontario), Canada
creative director, art director
 Rob Wright
photographer
 Ken Davies
copywriter
 Helen Nugent
client
 CPDN

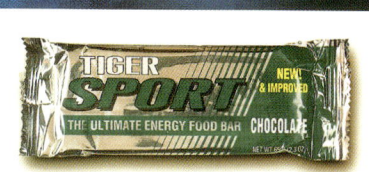

**Is your pharmaceutical distributor keeping up with the times?**

The hospital environment is changing. Fast. At CPDN, we're keeping up with those changes with cost-effective ordering solutions that work today — and tomorrow. From electronic data interchange to online ordering through an electronic catalogue, we're using advanced technology to meet our members' needs now and in the future.

CPDN / RCDP
Find out more about the
Canadian Pharmaceutical Distribution Network
Phone 1-800-680-3839   Fax (905) 812-1477

creative firm
 Bald & Beautiful
  Venice (California), USA
creative director
 Luis Camano
art director
 Carlos Musquez
copywriter
 Cameron Young
client
 Tiger Sport

creative firm
 Burkhardt & Hillman
  New York (New York), USA
creative people
 Rena Wong, Luke Scott, &
 Ron Burkhardt
client
 Outdoor Life Network

63

**WHILE OTHER NETWORKS ARE SHOWING RE-RUNS OF "HOGAN'S HEROES," WE'RE FIGHTING AN ENTIRELY DIFFERENT BATTLE.** Spending three weeks on the frigid Alaskan coastline, knee deep in petroleum, is no picnic. But for these volunteers, it's a small price to pay for keeping the oceans clean and sustaining the delicate web of life. And when they're not out helping the community, they're tuning in to Outdoor Life Network. The only network focused on conserving our natural resources and cleaning up our seas and rivers. Which is important to these folks. Frankly, it's important to everyone. So if you want to see a difference in your system's growth, and enhance your image in the community, carry the channel that makes a difference. Call in the East, 203-406-2500; in the West, 310-268-2100; or in the Midwest, 312-832-0808.

OLN
Outdoor Life Network
THE LEADER IN OUTDOOR ADVENTURE
www.GreatOutdoors.com

**WHILE SOME NETWORKS ARE RERUNNING "EIGHT IS ENOUGH," WE'VE GOT A FEW BILLION OTHER THINGS ON OUR MIND.** Like redwoods, firs and aspens to name a few. The clear-cutting in America has endangered some of our last remaining ancient forests, as well as the wildlife that lives there. So while we understand the entertainment value of sitcoms, we at Outdoor Life Network are more concerned with serious situations. Like providing compelling entertainment and information about conserving our natural resources and promoting responsible use of our public lands and natural parks. Which is important to everyone. So if you want to see a difference in your system's growth, and enhance your image in the community, carry the channel that makes a difference. Call in the East, 203-406-2500; in the West, 310-268-2100; or in the Midwest, 312-832-0808.

OLN
Outdoor Life Network
THE LEADER IN OUTDOOR ADVENTURE
www.GreatOutdoors.com

# THE CAPTIVE AUDIENCE,
### and other things that make a ratings giant.

creative firm
  Sawyer Riley Compton
  Atlanta (Georgia) USA
creative director
  Bart Cleveland
art directors
  Bart Cleveland, Kevin Thoem, &
  Rob Hardison
copywriters
  Bart Cleveland & John Spalding
client
  CNN Newsource

# VIEWERS AREN'T PROGRAMMED TO LIKE YOU.
### On second thought, that's exactly what happens.

64

# Metasys helps me regulate over 24 critical systems.
# Including my blood pressure.

creative firm
  Cramer-Krasselt
  Milwaukee (Wisconsin) USA
creative director
  Pat Knapp
art director
  Jon Grider
client
  Johnson Controls

creative firm
 Sawyer Riley Compton
  Atlanta (Georgia) USA
creative director
 Bart Cleveland
art director
 Kevin Thoem
photographer
 Rick Graves
copywriters
 Brett Compton & John Spalding
client
 Eaton Corporation

65

creative firm
 Sawyer Riley Compton
  Atlanta (Georgia), USA
creative director
 Bart Cleveland
art directors
 Kevin Thoem & Tony Messano
illustrator
 Frederic Remington
copywriter
 Brett Compton
client
 Pony Express Delivery Services

creative firm
 Mike Salisbury
  Venice (California), USA
creative people
 Mike Salisbury
client
 Levis

# CREATIVITY

## Posters

creative firm
  Fry Hammond Barr
  Orlando (Florida), USA
creative director
  Tim Fisher
art director
  Sean Brunson
production manager
  Chris Opsahl
copywriter
  John Logan
client
  Valencia Community College

creative firm
  Zebra Design
  Fairport (New York), USA
creative people
  James L. Selak
client
  Upstate Litho, Inc.

creative firm
  J. Sposato
  New York (New York), USA
art director
  Johnny Schumate
designer
  John Sposato
client
  The Sunday School Board

creative firm
  Design Club
  Tokyo, Japan
art director
  Akihiko Tsukamoto
illustrator
  Yenpitsu Nemoto
client
  Yamato Inc.

creative firm
  Batey Ads (Pte) Ltd
  Singapore
creative director, copywriter
  Gary Knight
art director
  Darren Hogan
photographer
  John Clang
client
  Singapore Anti - Narcotics Association

creative firm
  Ted Bertz Design
    Middletown (Connecticut), USA
designer
  Ted Bertz
illustrator
  Aleta Gudelski
client
  Durham Fair Association

creative firm
  Wendell Minor Design
    Washington (Connecticut), USA
art director
  David Kapp
designer, illustrator
  Wendell Minor
client
  University of Connecticut

creative firm
  Verba
    Milan, Italy
creative director, art
  Stefano Longoni
copywriter
  Enrico Bonomini
client
  Autogerma

creative firm
  Callahan and Company
    Baltimore (Maryland), USA
creative people
  Paula Sloane & Kate Cogswell
client
  Charles Village Community
  Benifits District

creative firm
  Batey Ads (Pte) ltd
    Singapore
creative director, copywriter
  Gary Knight
art directors
  Bobbi Gassy & Darren Hogan
photographer
  Shaun Pettigrew
client
  Ministry of Health

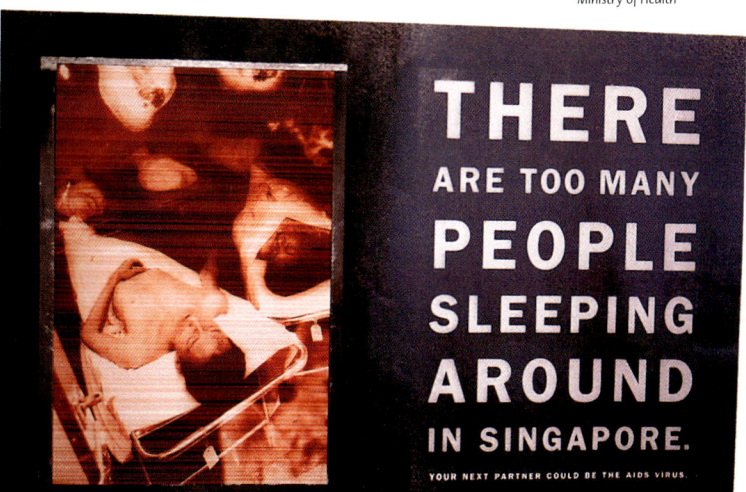

67

creative firm
 Blank-Robert
 Kent Wilson
 Washington (D.C.), USA
creative people
 Robert Kent Wilson &
 Suzanne Ultman
client
 Poetry-in-Motion

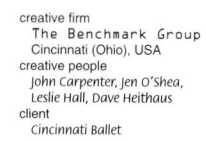

creative firm
 The Benchmark Group
 Cincinnati (Ohio), USA
creative people
 John Carpenter, Jen O'Shea,
 Leslie Hall, Dave Heithaus
client
 Cincinnati Ballet

creative firm
 Foley Sackett
 Minneapolis (Minnesota), USA
creative director
 Ron Sackett
art director
 Wayne Thompson
copywriter
 Jeff Schuller
client
 W.A Lang

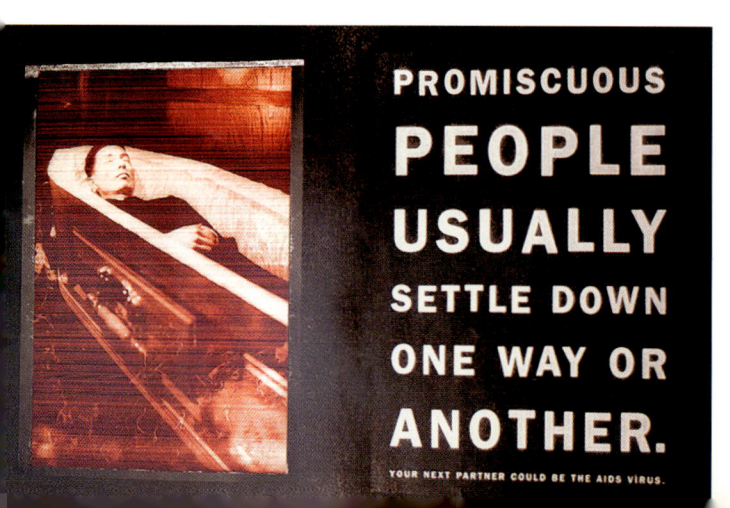

creative firm
 Concept CA-Studio JMV
 Miami (Florida), USA
creative people
 Armando Cardenas, Jose M. Vidaurre,
 Alberto Hernandez, & Humberto D'Ascoli
client
 Cedesa

creative firm
 Batey Ads (Pte) Ltd
 Singapore
creative director, copywriter
 Gary Knight
art directors
 Bobbi Gassy & Darren Hogan
photographer
 Shaun Pettigrew
client
 Ministry of Health

creative firm
  Wet Paper Bag
  Graphic Design
    Forth Worth (Texas), USA
art director, designer, copywriter
  Lewis Glaser
client
  Wet Paper BagGraphic Design

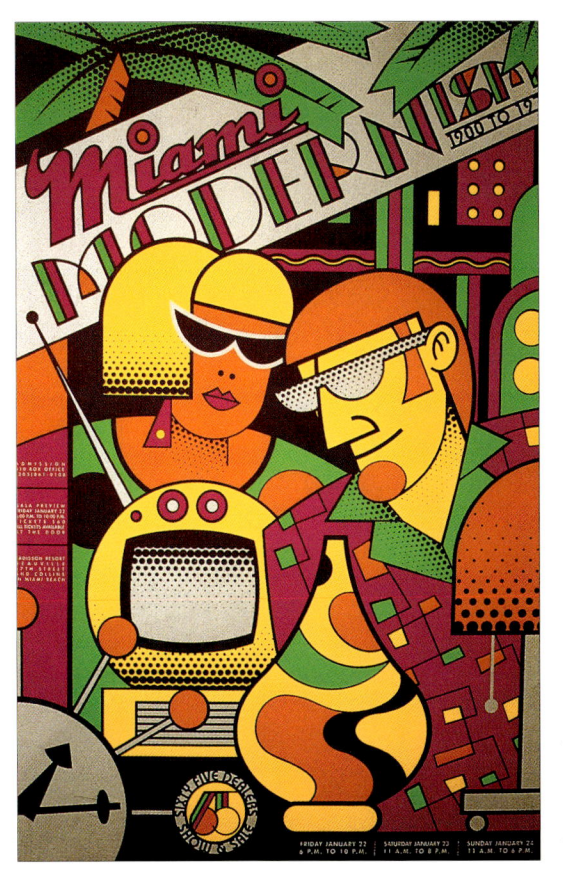

creative firm
  Sayles Graphic
  Design
    Des Moines (Iowa), USA
art director, designer
  John Sayles
client
  Miami Modernism 1999

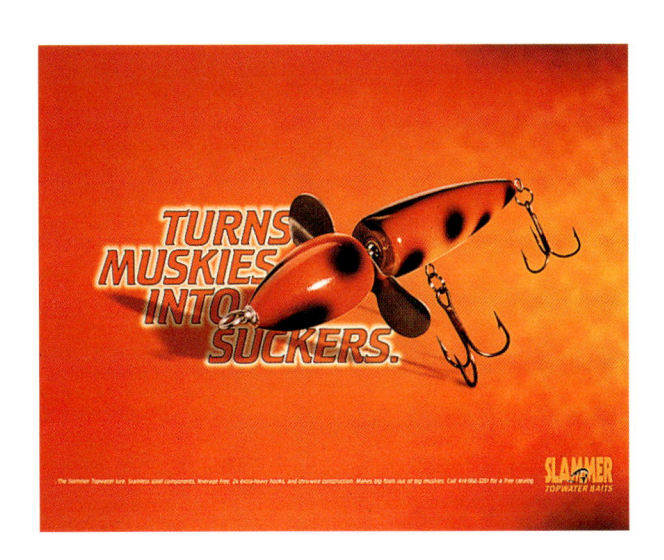

creative firm
  Cramer-Krasselt
    Milwaukee (Wisconsin), USA
creative director
  Neil Casey
art directors
  Matt Hermann
copywriter
  Dan Ames
client
  Slammer

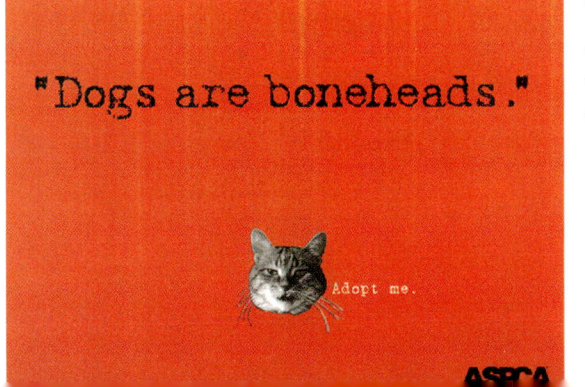

creative firm
  Qualcomm Design Group
    San Diego (California), USA
creative director
  Christopher Lee
designer
  Dave Korinek
client
  Qualcomm

creative firm
  Bleecker & Sullivan
    New York (New York), USA
creative director
  Itzhak Beery
copywriter
  Sela Francis
client
  ASPCA

creative firm
 Cramer-Krasselt
  Milwaukee (Wisconsin), USA
creative director
 Neil Casey
art director
 Matt Hermann
copywriter
 Dan Ames
client
 Slammer

creative firm
 Kinggraphic
  Hong Kong, China
creative director
 Hon Bing-wah
photographer
 Alfred Ko
client
 Hong Kong Graphic Arts Association

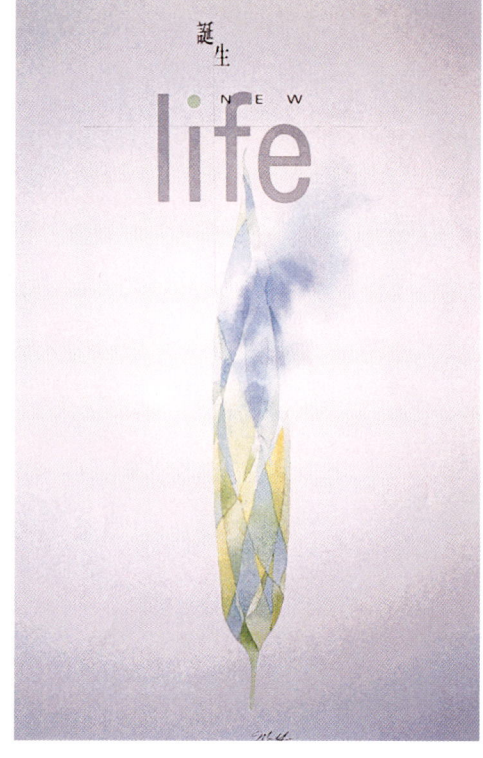

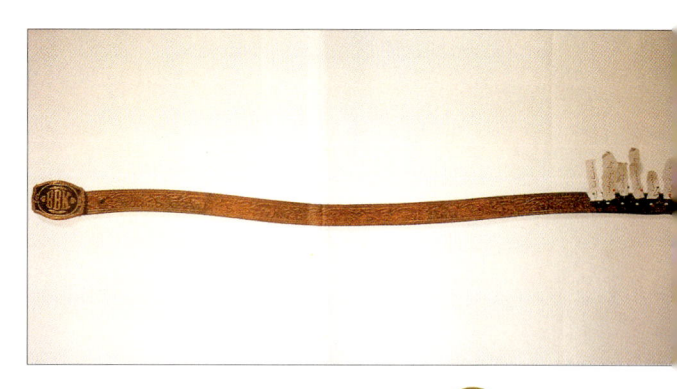

creative firm
 Kinggraphic
  Hong Kong, China
creative director
 So Man-yee
client
 Poster Museum of Beijing

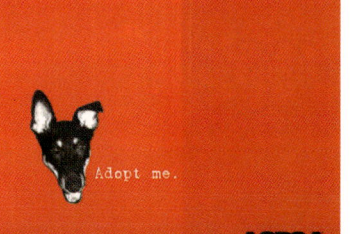

creative firm
 Bleecker & Sullivan
  New York (New York), USA
creative director
 Itzhak Beery
copywriter
 Sela Francis
client
 ASPCA

creative firm
 BBK Studio Inc.
  Grand Rapids (Minnesota), USA
concept
 Kevin Budelmann &
 Yang Kim
creative director
 Kevin Budelmann
designer, typesetter
 Alison Popp
calligrapher
 Matt Ryzenga
copywriters
 Christine MacLean &
 Allison Popp
client
 BBK Studio

creative firm
 Gardner Design
  Wichita (Kansas), USA
art directors, designers
 Bill Gardner & Brian Miller
illustrators
 C.B. Mordan & Brian Miller
client
 Sedgwick County Zoo

creative firm
 Boelts Bros. Associates
  Tuscon (Arizona), USA
creative people
 Eric Boelts, Adanta Arietta,
 Jackson Boelts, & Elicia Taylor
client
 The Institute for Limb Preservation

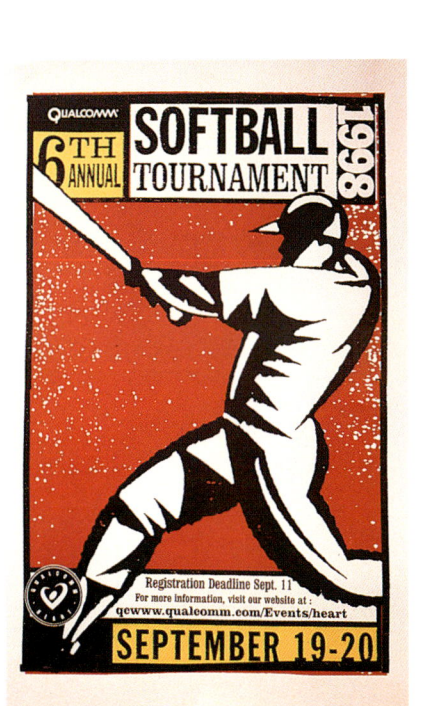

creative firm
 Qualcomm Design Group
  San Diego (California), USA
creative director
 Christopher Lee
designer
 Dean Sipe
client
 Qualcomm

creative firm
 Peter Piper Graphics
  Tokyo, Japan
art director
 Masaki + Fujimoto
photographer
 Mikio Ariga
client
 Neo Vision

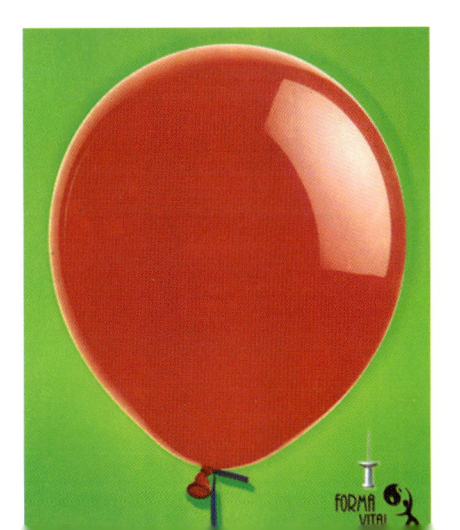

creative firm
 Dieste & Partners Publicidad
  Dallas (Texas), USA
creative director
 Aldo Quevedo
art director
 Chris Sendra
copywriter
 Javier Guemes
client
 Forma Vital

creative firm
  Verba DDB
  Milan, Italy
creative directors
  Enrico Bonomini &
  Francesco Emiliani
illustrator
  Stefano Longoni
copywriter
  Francesco De Luca
client
  Friskies Italia

creative firm
  Peter Piper Graphics
  Tokyo, Japan
art director, design
  Masaki + Fujimoto
designers
  Peter Pan Graphics
photographers
  Masaaki Hiraga & Hideo Shimowasa
client
  Impartmaint

72

creative firm
  August, Lang & Husak, Inc.
  Bethesda (Maryland) USA
creative director
  Chuck Husak
art director
  Brian Burkhart
copywriter
  Trevor Sloan
client
  National Geographic/
  National Public Radio

creative firm
  Popular Mechanics
  New York (New York), USA
art director
  Bryan Canniff
illustrator
  Peter Van Ryzin
client
  Popular Mechanics

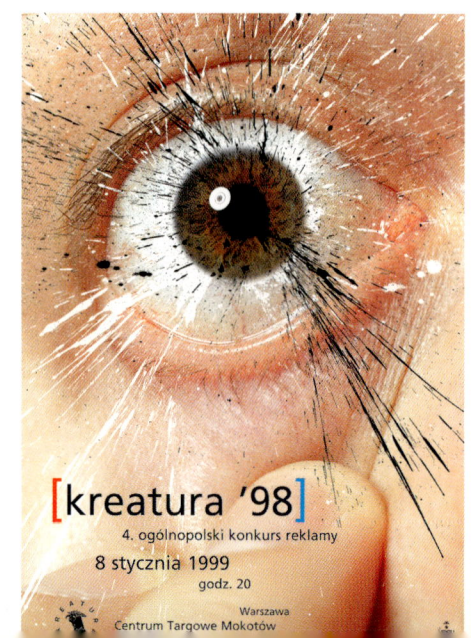

creative firm
  Korek Studio
  Warsaw, Poland
art director, designer, illustrator
  Wojtek Korkuć
photographer
  Włodek Krzemiński
client
  VFP Communications Ltd.

creative firm
 Gardner Design
 Wichita (Kansas), USA
art director, designer
 Brian Miller
photographer
 Rock Island Studios

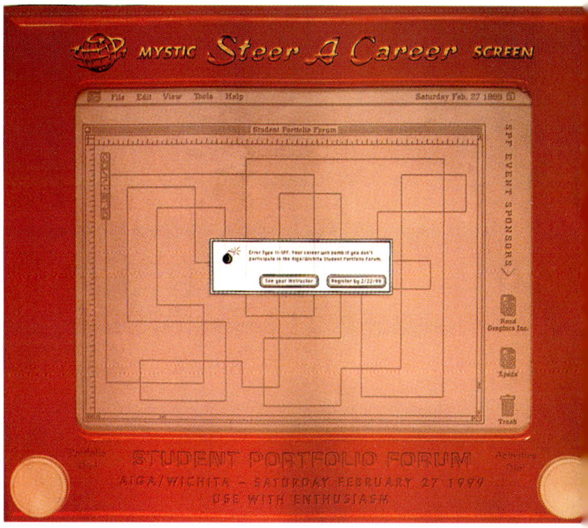

creative firm
 Insight Design Communications
 Wichita (Kansas), USA
art directors
 Sherrie Holdeman & Tracy Holdeman
designer
 Chris Parks
client
 AIGA/Wichita

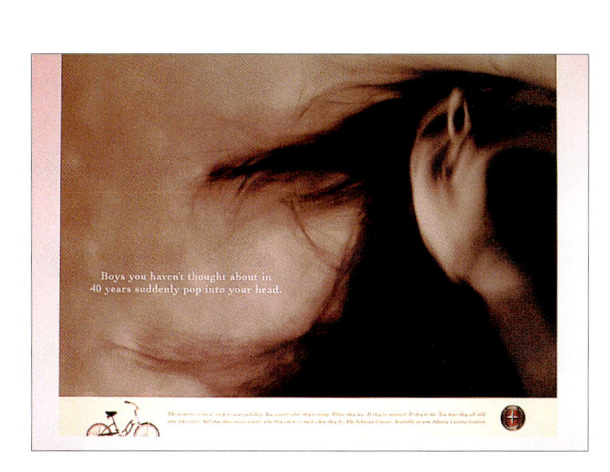

creative firm
 Sawyer Riley Compton
 Atlanta (Georgia), USA
creative director
 Bart Cleveland
art director
 Kevin Thoem
photographer
 David Seijo
copywriter
 Dave Holloway
client
 Atlanta Cycling

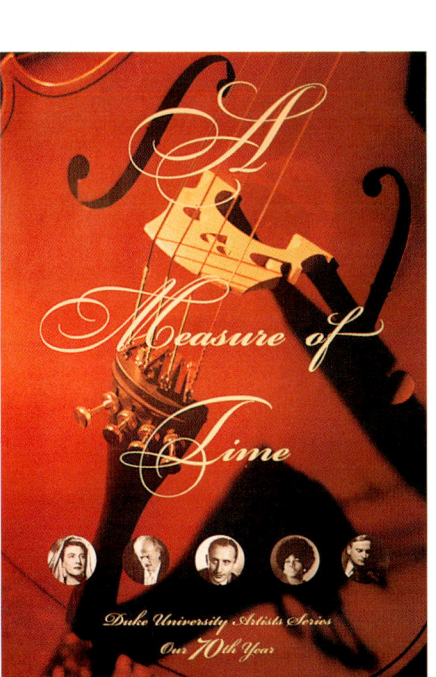

creative firm
 Peter Taflan Marketing
 Communications
 Durham (North Carolina), USA
art director
 Janssen Strother
photographer
 Les Todd
copywriter
 David Terrenoire
client
 Duke University Artists Series

creative firm
 Wet Paper Graphic Design
 Fort Worth (Texas), USA
art director, designer, copywriter
 Lewis Glaser
illustrator
 Don Ivan Punchatz
client
 TCU Art Department

creative firm
 Tiffany & Co.
 New York (New York), USA
creative director
 Stuart De Haan
copywriter
 Ted Pettus
client
 Tiffany & Co.

creative firm
 Cramer-Krasselt
 Milwaukee (Wisconsin), USA
creative director
 Neil Casey
art director
 Matt Hermann
copywriter
 Dan Ames
client
 Slammer

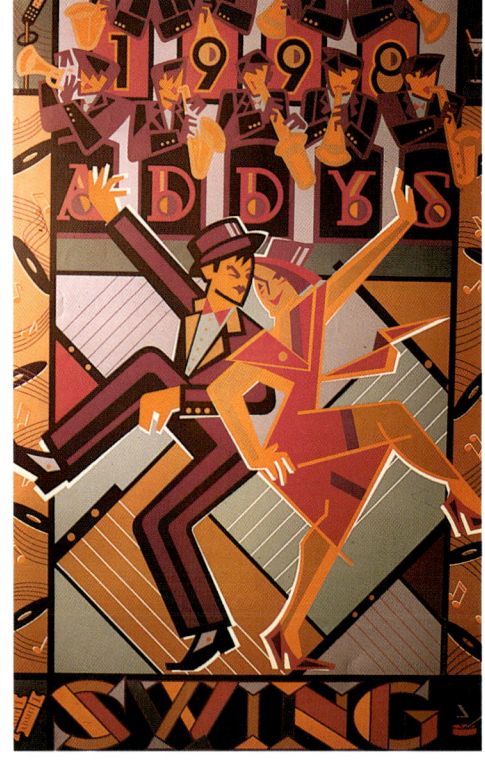

74

creative firm
 The Benchmark Group
 Cincinnati (Ohio), USA
creative people
 John Carpenter, Jen O'Shea,
 Leslie Hall, & Dave Heithaus
client
 Cincinnati Ballet

creative firm
 Sayles Graphic Design
 Des Moines (Iowa), USA
art director, designer
 John Sayles
client
 Advertising Professionals of Des Moines

creative firm
 Faschingbauer & Schaar
 Graz, Austria
creative people
 Siegfried Faschinbauer &
 Dieter Faschinbauer
client
 Jugend Am Werk Steiermark

creative firm
 Tom Fowler, Inc.
  Stanford (Connecticut), USA
creative people
 Thomas G. Fowler
client
 Connecticut Grand Opera & Orchestra

creative firm
 Gardner Design
  Wichita (Kansas), USA
art directors, designers
 Bill Gardner & Brian Miller
client
 March of Dimes

creative firm
 Foley Sackett
  Minneapolis (Minnesota), USA
creative director
 Ron Sackett
art director
 Tim Moran
copywriter
 Johnny Mackin
client
 Art Directors/Copywriters Club

75

creative firm
 Wet Paper Bag Graphic Design
  Fort Worth (Texas), USA
art director, designer, copywriter
 Lewis Glaser
photographer
 Buddy Myers
client
 TCU Dance Department

creative firm
 Wendell Minor Design
  Washington (Connecticut), USA
art director
 Ben Mitchell
designer, illustrator
 Wendell Minor
client
 Muskegon Museum of Art

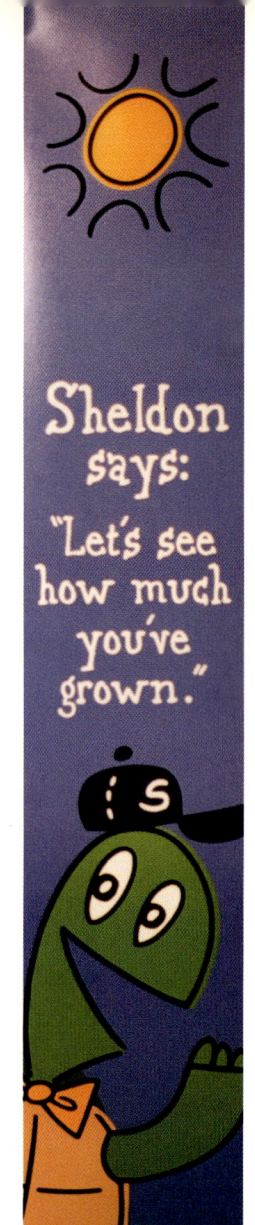

creative firm
 KPR
  New York (New York), USA
creative people
 John Dietz, Paul Weiss, Susana Padron,
 Gerry Borsellino, & Mitch Siegel
client
 Pasteur Mérieux Connaught

creative firm
 Hendlin Visual
  Communications, Inc.
  Minneapolis, (Minnesota), USA
art director
 Larry Skov
photographer
 Ted Wentink
copywriter
 Jon Schumacher
client
 Hendlin Visual Communications, Inc.

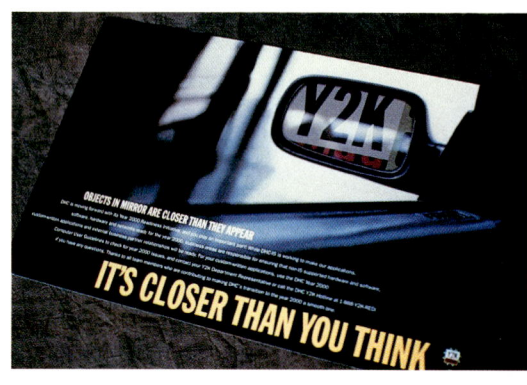

creative firm
 Design Guys
  Minneapolis (Minnesota), USA
creative people
 Steven Sikora & Jay Theige
client
 Target Stores

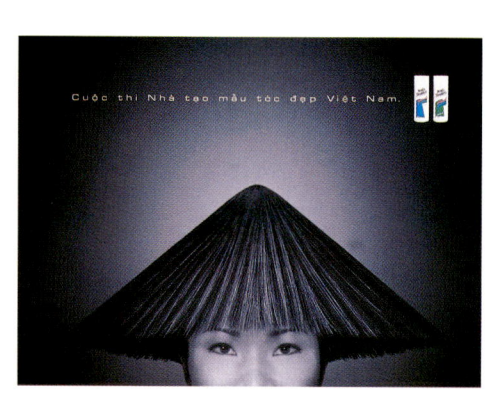

creative firm
 Saatchi + Saatchi Vietnam
  Ho Chi Minh City, Vietnam
creative people
 Paul Ewen, Mike Sands, &
 Le Duc Thang
client
 Procter & Gamble

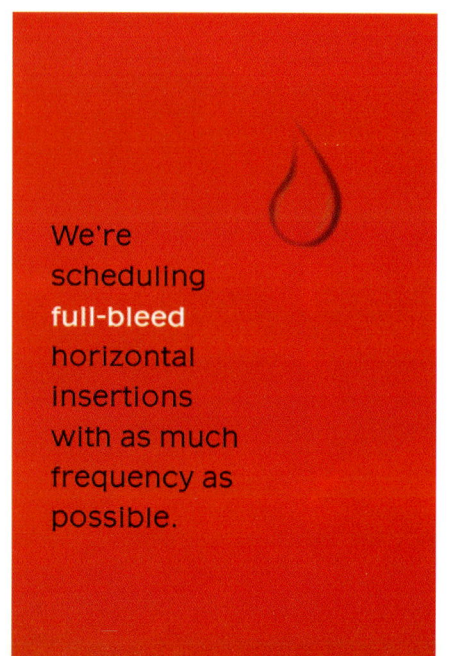

creative firm
 Erwin-Penland Advertising
  Greenville (South Carolina), USA
creative director
 Russ Corvey
studio artist
 Jon Eger
client
 Erwin-Penland

creative firm
  McCann-Erickson Korea Inc.
    Seoul, Korea
creative director
  Jeremy Perrott
art directors
  S.Y. Kim & G.Y. Ahn
copywriter
  W.H. Kim
client
  Levi's Korea

creative firm
  Tom Fowler, Inc.
    Stamford (Connecticut), USA
art director, designer, illustrator
  Thomas G. Fowler
client
  Connecticut Grand Opera & Orchestra

77

creative firm
  Wendell Minor Design
    Washington (Connecticut), USA
designer
  Erik White
illustrator
  Wendell Minor
client
  Harper Collins

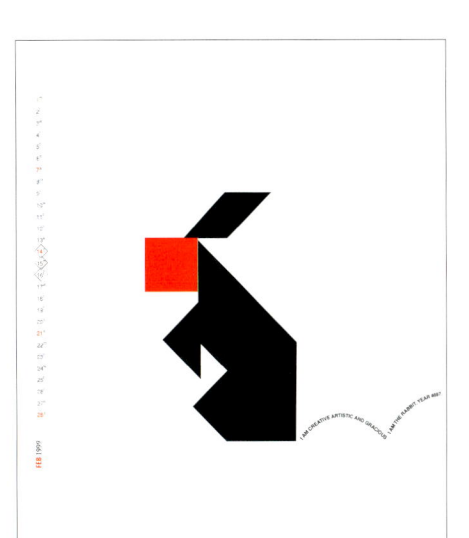

creative firm
  Ellen Bruss Design
    Denver (Colorado), USA
creative people
  G. Carr & Jason C. Otero
client
  Larimer Square

creative firm
  SooHoo Designers
    Torrance (California), USA
creative people
  Patrick SooHoo, Kathy Hirata,
  Daniel Ko, Leo Terrazas, Cindy Hahn,
  Karen Leonard, & Dan Wu
client
  SooHoo Designers

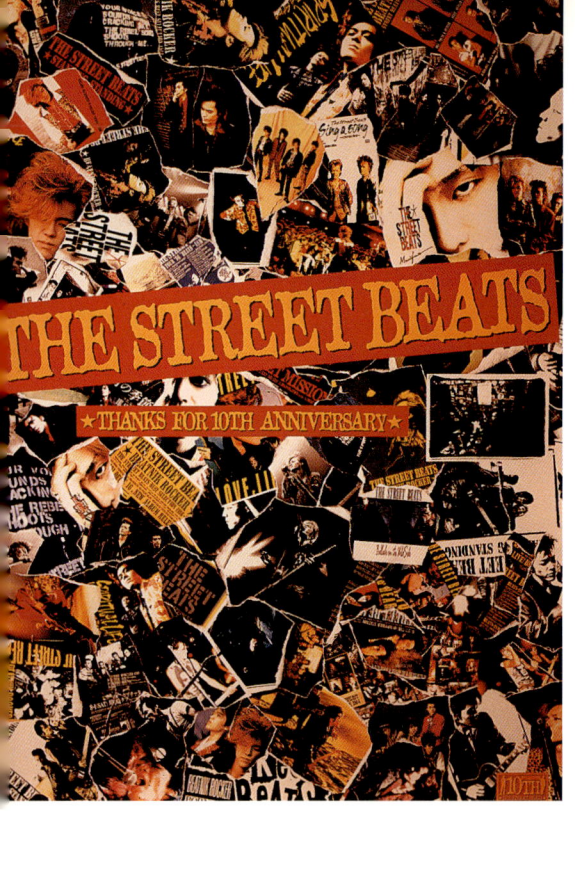

creative firm
  Peter Piper
  Graphics
  Tokyo, Japan
art directors, designers
  Masaki + Fujimoto
client
  Neo Vision

creative firm
  McCann-Erickson
  New York (New York), USA
creative director
  Irwin Warren
art director
  Jeff DiFiore
copywriter
  Stephanie Putter
client
  d-Con

creative firm
  Thompson + Company
  Memphis (Tennessee), USA
creative director
  Trace Hallowell
client
  Memphis Redbirds

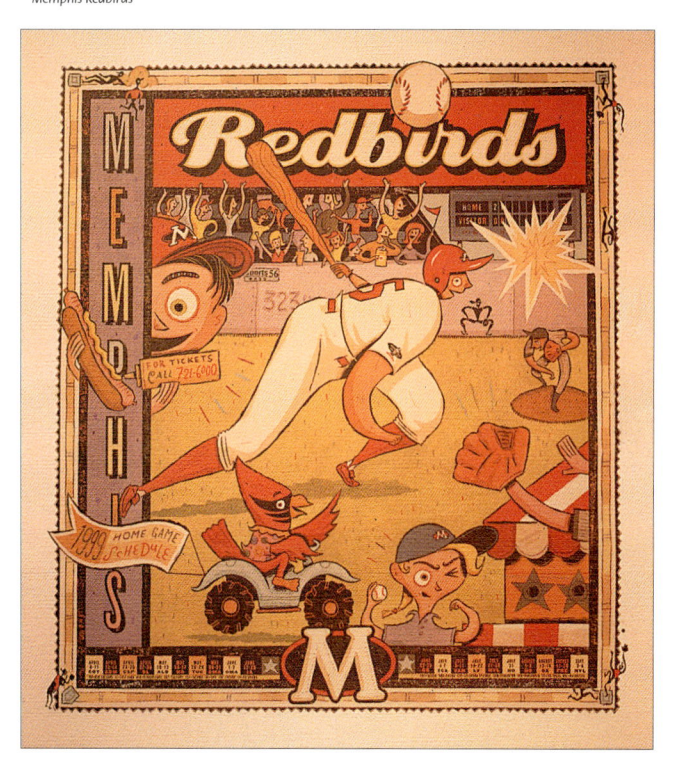

creative firm
  Clarke + Associates LLC
  Somerville (New Jersey), USA
art director
  James DeVito
illustrator
  Judy Reed Silver
copywriter
  Susan Willett
client
  Lucent Technologies

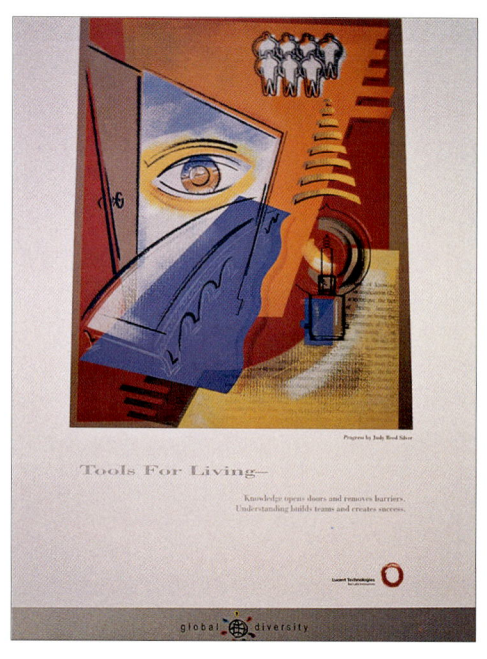

creative firm
  DBD International
  Menomonie (Wisconsin), USA
creative director, artist
  David Brier
photographer
  Photodisc
client
  EarthVision, Inc.

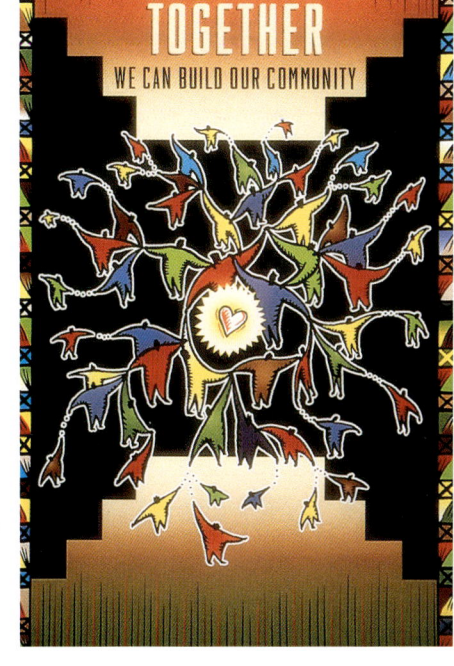

creative firm
  Sharon Sudman/Illustration
  St. Paul (Minnesota), USA
art director
  Terri Kinne
illustrator
  Sharon Sudman
client
  Spaulding & Kinne/Hazelden

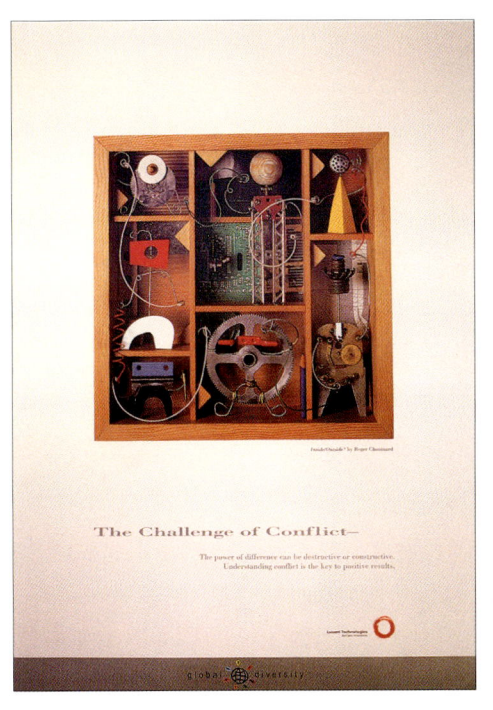

creative firm
  Clarke + Associates LLC
  Somerville (New Jersey), USA
art director
  James DeVito
illustrator
  Roger Chovinard
copywriter
  Susan Willet
client
  Lucent Technologies

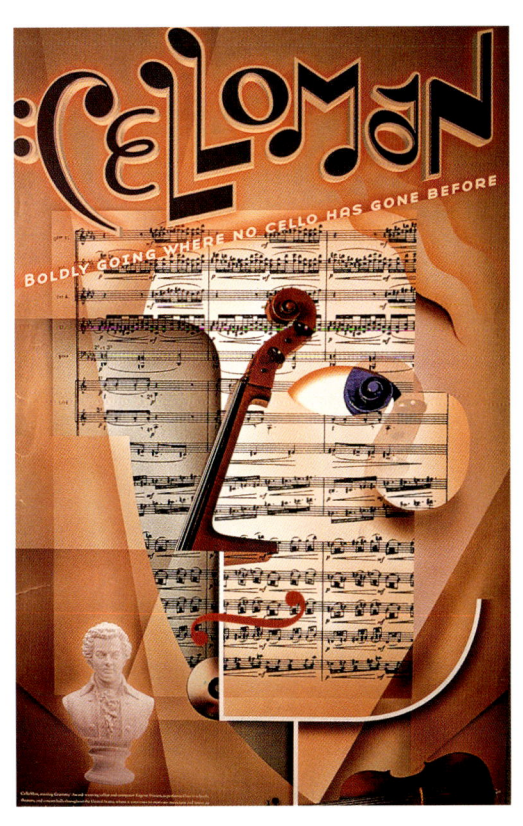

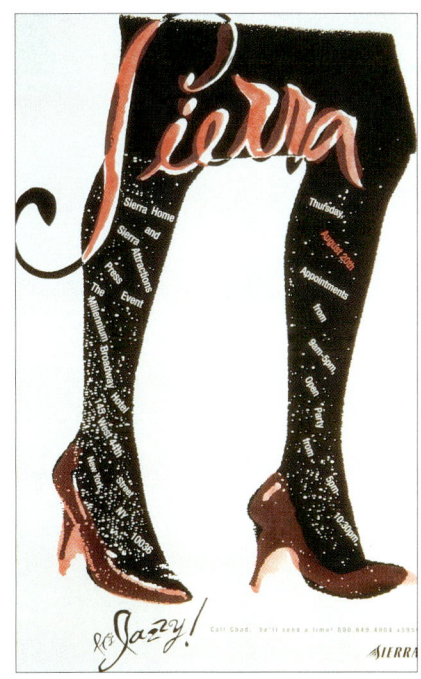

creative firm
  David Lemley Design
  Seattle (Washington), USA
art director
  David Lemley
designers
  Matt Peloza & David Lemley
client
  Sierra On-Line

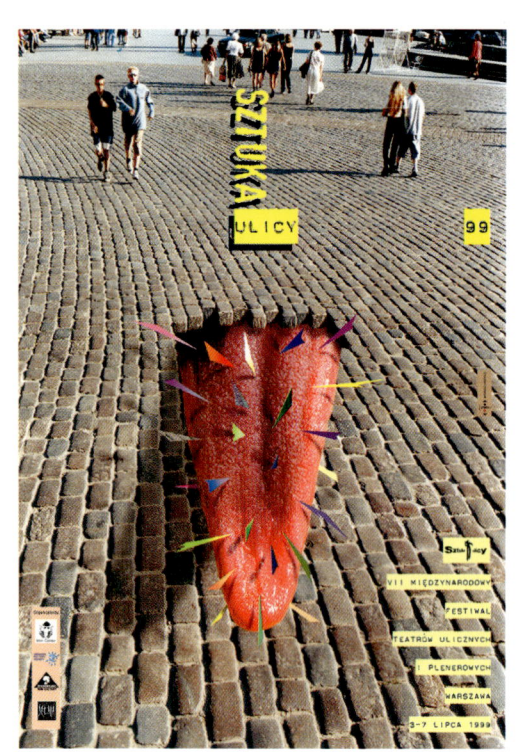

creative firm
  Korek Studio
    Warsaw, Poland
designer, photographer, illustrator
  Wojtek Korkuć
client
  Osrodek Kultury Ochota

creative firm
  Emery Vincent Design Team
    Southbank (Victoria), Australia
creative people
  Emery Vincent Design Team
client
  Workshop 3000

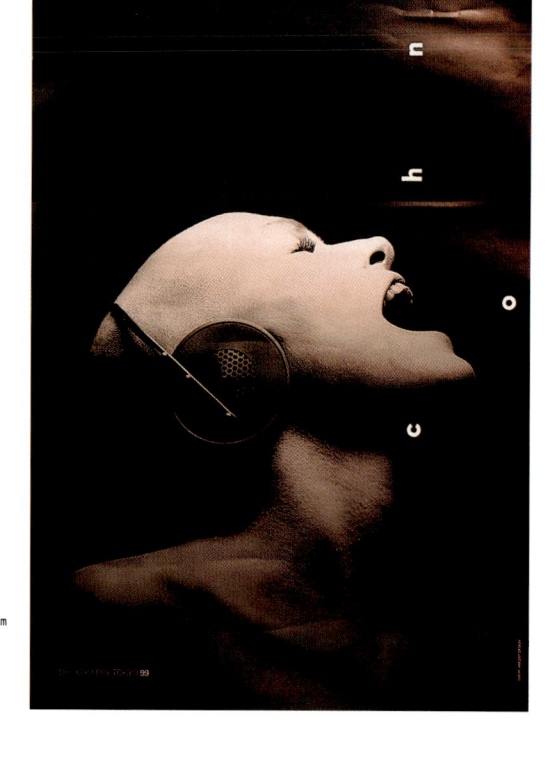

creative firm
  Computer Sciences Corporation
    Falls Church (Virginia), USA
art director
  Mary Jo Ondrejka
designer
  Karen Loehr
copywriter
  Todd Potochnik
client
  Computer Sciences Corporation

creative firm
  30sixty design, inc.
    Los Angeles (California), USA
art director, designer
  Pär Larsson
client
  30sixty design, inc.

creative firm
  Clarke + Associates LLC
    Somerville (New Jersey), USA
art director
  James DeVito
illustrator
  Teresa Cox
copywriter
  Susan Willett
client
  Lucent Technologies

creative firm
  Silver Communications
    New York (New York), USA
creative director
  Gregg Silbert
design director
  Sally Hiesiger
designer
  Chris Weissman
client
  Multex.com

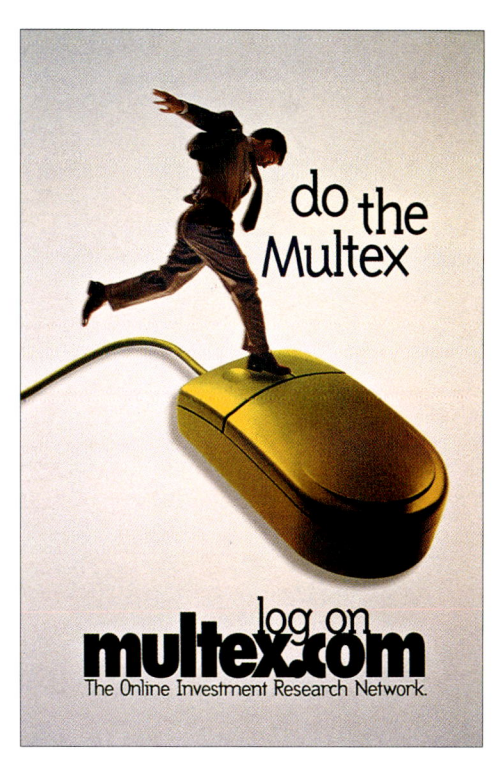

creative firm
  Design Club
    Tokyo, Japan
art director, designer
  Akihiko Tsukamoto
client
  Hershey Japan Ltd.

creative firm
  Fusion Art Institute
    Susono-shi (Shizuoka-ken), Japan
art director
  Hyoman Fumihiko Enokido
designers
  Koshi Ogawa & Hideaki Enokido
photographer
  Toru Kinoshita
client
  JAGDA

creative firm
  Design Club
  Tokyo, Japan
art director, designer
  Akihiko Tsukamoto
client
  Amaguri-Taro Ltd.

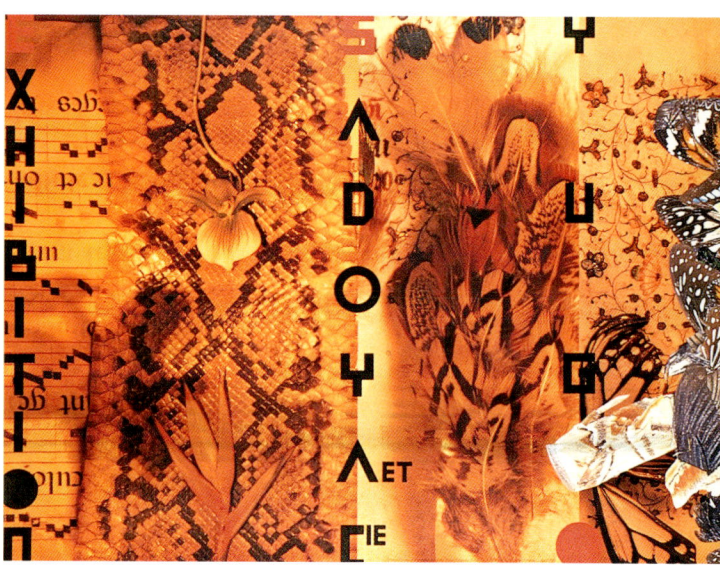

creative firm
  Fusion Art Institute
  Susono-shi (Shizuokako-ken), Japan
art director
  Hyomon Fumihiko Enokido
designers
  Koshi Ogawa & Hideaki Enokido
photographer
  Toru Kinoshita
client
  SADOYAetC<sup>IE</sup>

82

creative firm
  Kan & Lau Design Consultants
  Hong Kong, China
art director, designer
  Freeman Lau Stu Hong
client
  Taipei International Poster
  Invitational Exhibition '99

creative firm
  Design Club
  Tokyo, Japan
art director, designer
  Akihiko Tsukamoto
illustrator
  Radical Suzuki
copywriter
  Masayuki Minoda
client
  Sea Road International
  Corporation

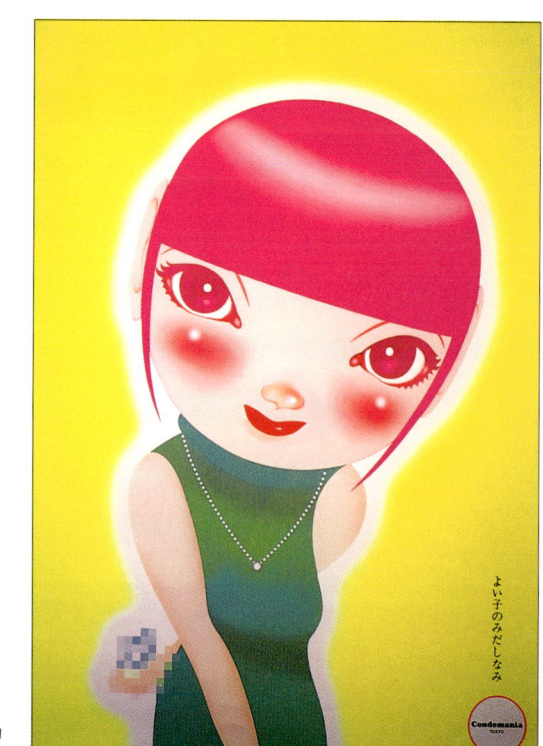

creative firm
  Parham Santana Inc.
  New York (New York), USA
creative director
  William Snyder
art director
  Emily Pak
client
  Bravo Network

creative firm
  Parham Santana Inc.
  New York (New York), USA
creative director
  John Parham
designer
  Annetta Sappenfield
client
  BMG Video

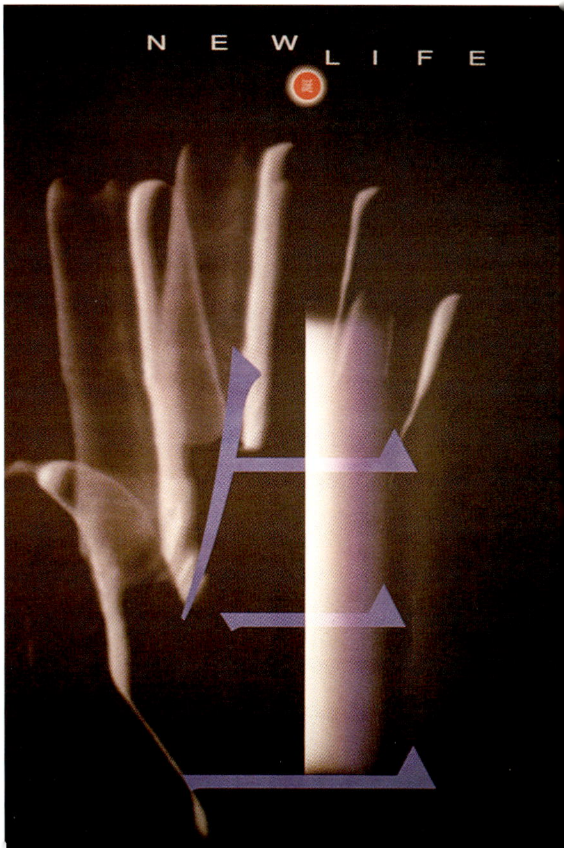

83

creative firm
  Kinggraphic
  Hong Kong, China
creative director
  Hon Bing-wah,
photographer
  Alfred Ko
client
  Poster Museum of Beijing

creative firm
 J. Walter Thompson/N.Y.
  New York (New York), USA
art director
 John Hobbs
copywriter
 Brian Connaughton
client
 National Outdoor Leadership School

creative firm
 Design Machine
  New York (New York), USA
creative people
 Alexander Gelman
client
 The New York Director's Club

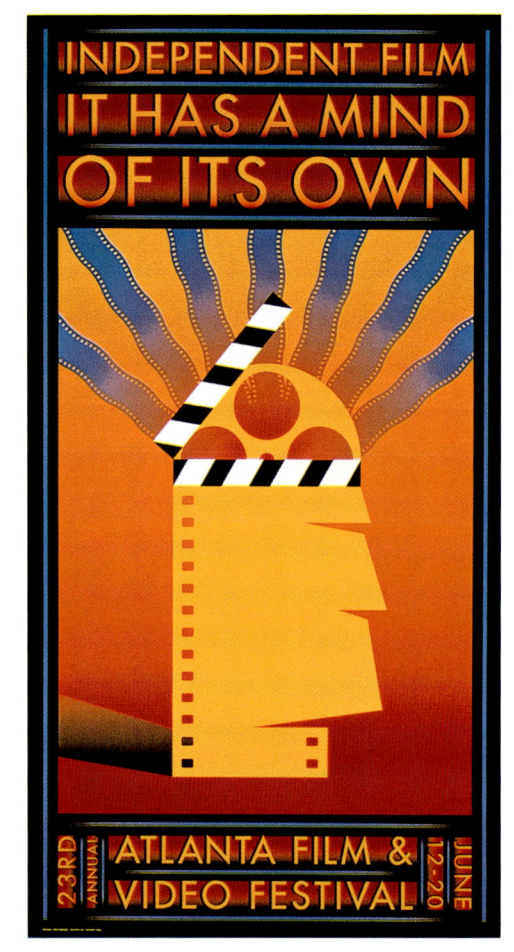

84

creative firm
 Fusion Art Institute
  Sosuni-shi (Shizuoka-ken), Japan
art director
 Hyomon Fumihiko Enokido
designers
 Koshi Agawa & Hideaki Enokido
photographer
 Toru Kinoshita
client
 JAGDA

creative firm
 Deep Design
  Atlanta (Georgia), USA
creative director
 Rick Grimsley
designer, illustrator
 Heath Beeferman
client
 IMAGE Film & Video Center

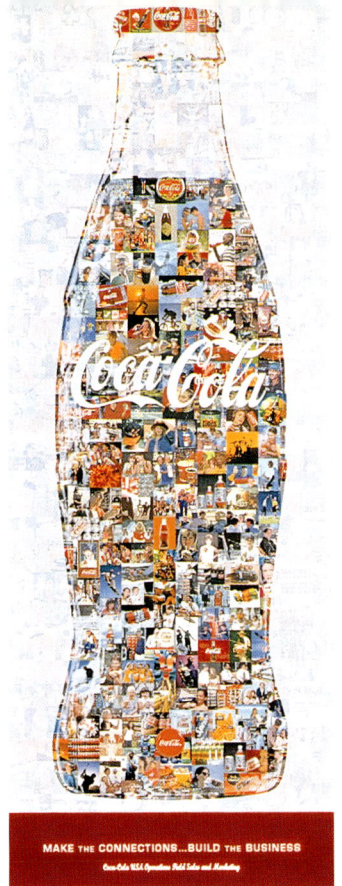

creative firm
 Fine Print, Inc.
  Atlanta (Georgia), USA
creative director
 George Bacso
designer
 Alix Rehbock
client
 The Coca-Cola Company

creative firm
 CommArts, Inc.
  Boulder (Colorado), USA
art directors
 Henry Beer & Janet Martin
designer
 Dave Dute
illustrator
 Phillipe Lardy
client
 Vail Resorts

creative firm
 Clarke + Associates LLC
  Somerville (New Jersey), USA
art director
 James De Vito
illustrator
 Lo Cole
copywriter
 Susan Willett
client
 Lucent Technologies

creative firm
 Augustus Barnett
  Tacoma (Washington), USA
creative director, art director
 Charlie Barnett
designer
 John DiBernardo
illustrator
 Scott Baily
client
 Washington State Fruit Commission/
 Northwest Cherry Growers

creative firm
 Herman Miller Inc.
 Zeeland (Missouri), USA
art director, designer
 Kathy Stanton
client
 Herman Miller Inc.

creative firm
 Leslie Evans
 Design Associates
 Portland (Maine), USA
art directors, designers
 Leslie Evans &
 Tom Hubbard
illustrator
 Patrick Corrigan
client
 Portland Public Market

86

creative firm
 Ogilvy & Mather Frankfurt
 Frankfurt, Germany
creative director
 Ilona Klück & Pit Kho
art director
 Ilona Klück & Birgit Schuster
copywriters
 Pit Kho & Isa Raatz
client
 Miller's Fine Petfood, Munich

creative firm
 Herman Miller Inc. &
 Fairly Painless Advertising
 Zeeland (Michigan), USA
art director
 Steve Frykholm
designer
 Brian Hauch
client
 Herman Miller Inc.

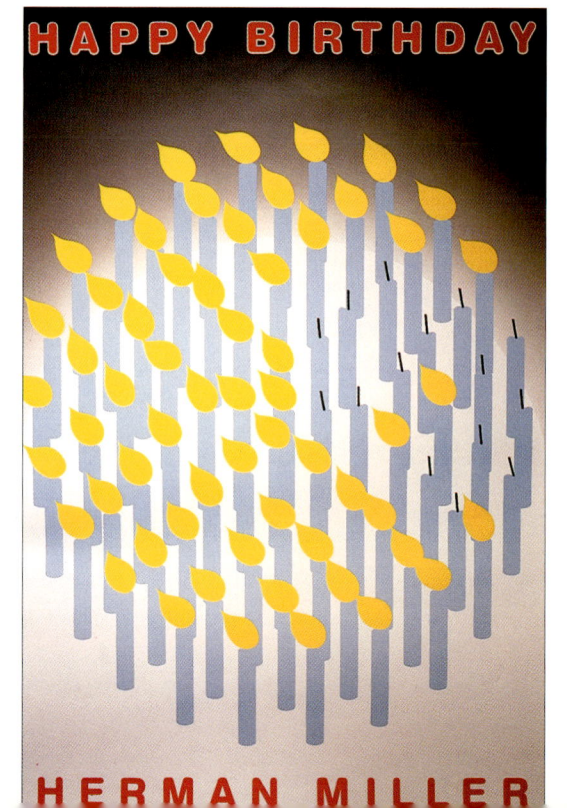

creative firm
 Kinggraphic
  Hong Kong, China
creative director
 Hon Bing-wah
client
 Taiwan Chinese Poster Design Association

creative firm
 Clarke + Associates LLC
  Somerville (New Jersey), USA
art director
 James DeVito
illustrator
 David Diaz
copywriter
 Susan Willett
client
 Lucent Technologies

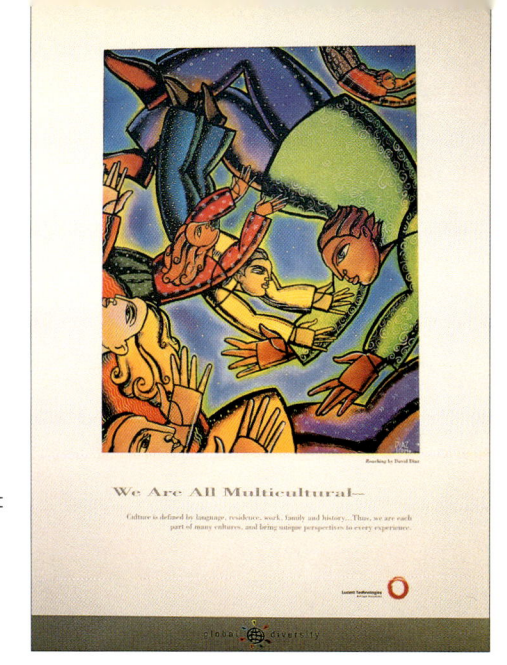

creative firm
 Tiffany & Co.
  New York (New York), USA
creative director
 Stuart De Haan
copywriter
 Ted Pettus
client
 Tiffany & Co.

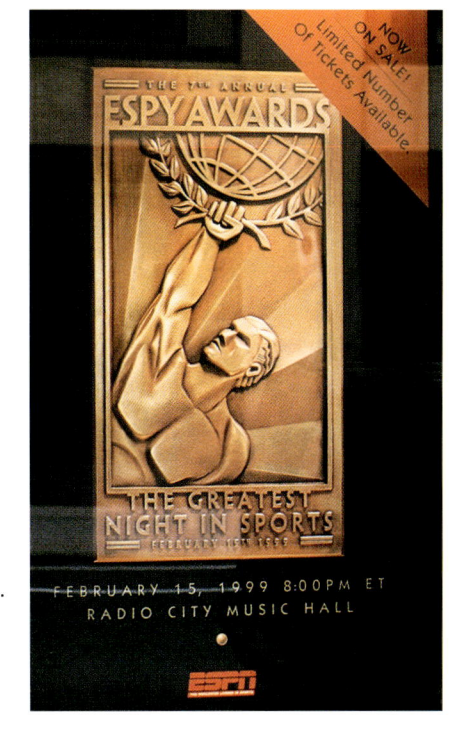

creative firm
 Parham Santana Inc.
  New York (New York), USA
creative director
 Bill Snyder
art director
 Liz Driesbach
client
 ESPN

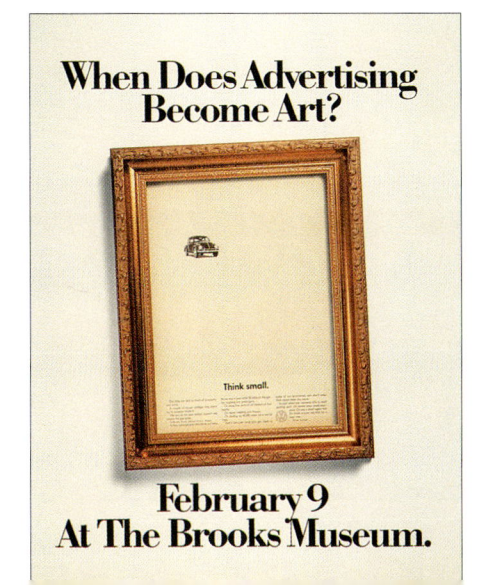

creative firm
 Thompson & Company
  Memphis (Tennessee), USA
client
 Memphis College of Art

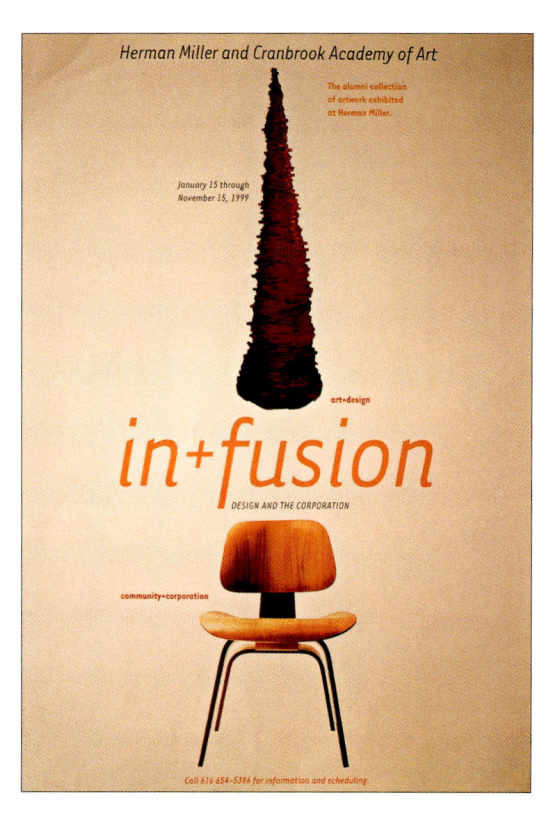

creative firm
 Herman Miller Inc.
  Zeeland (Michigan), USA
art director, designer
 Brian Edlefson
copywriter
 Clark Malcolm
client
 Herman Miller Inc.

creative firm
 Keiler & Company
  Farmington (Connecticut), USA
designer
 Liz Dzilenski
client
 St. Vincents Hospital

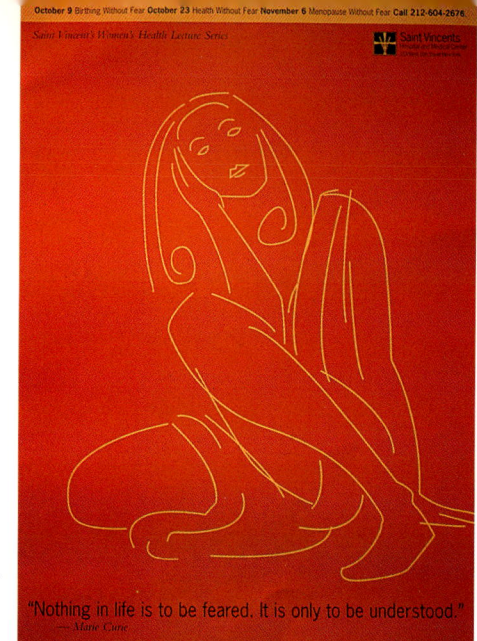

creative firm
 Clarke + Asociates LLC
  Somerville (New Jersey), USA
art director
 James DeVito
illustrator
 William Sloan
copywriter
 Susan Willett
client
 Lucent Technologies

creative firm
 JMC/YR
  Caracas (Miranda), Venezuela
creative people
 Anderes Cruz, Octavio Montiel,
 & Cesar Miliani
client
 Xerox De Venezuela
translation
 Raise your talent to the X Power.

creative firm
 Teamwork Design Ltd.
  Hong Kong, China
creative people
 Gary Tam, Alex Chan, Ivy Wong,
 & Joel Ong
client
 Nuance-Watson (HK) Ltd.

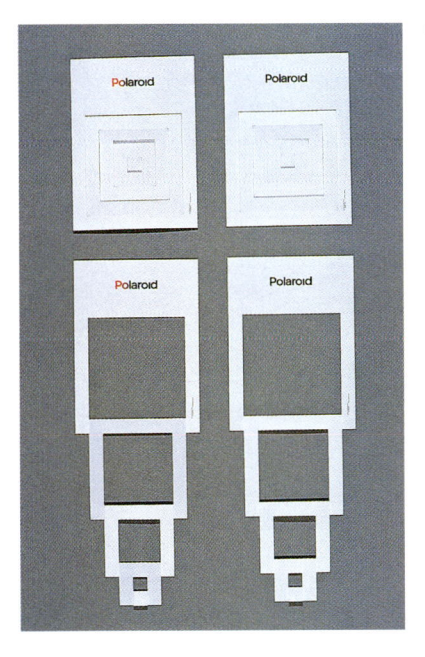

creative firm
 Atelier Tadeusz Piechura
  Lodz, Poland
photographer
 Piotr Tomczyk
client
 Polaroid Polska

creative firm
 Clarke + Associates LLC
  Somerville (New Jersey), USA
art director
 James DeVito
illustrator
 Kelly Stribling Sutherland
copywriter
 Susan Willet
client
 Lucent Technologies

creative firm
 ATW Communications Group
  New York (New York), USA
art director, designer
 Michael Lebron
client
 WinStar Cinema

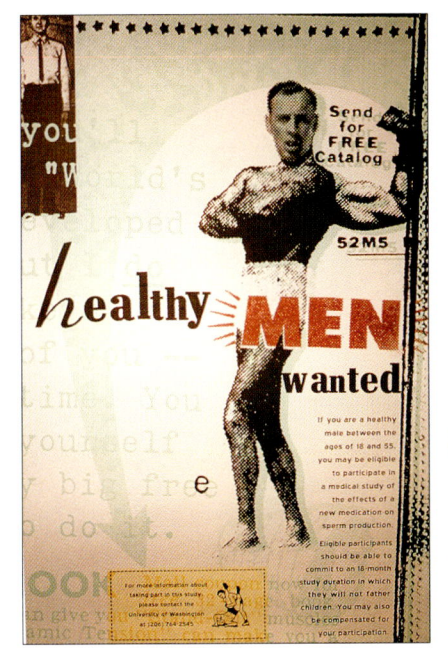

creative firm
 Glaxo Wellcome
 Creative Services
  Research Triangle Park (North Carolina), USA
art directors
 Kevin Dickerson, Todd Coats, & Craig O'Brien
designer, illustrator
 Kevin Dickerson
client
 Glaxo Wellcome Research Services

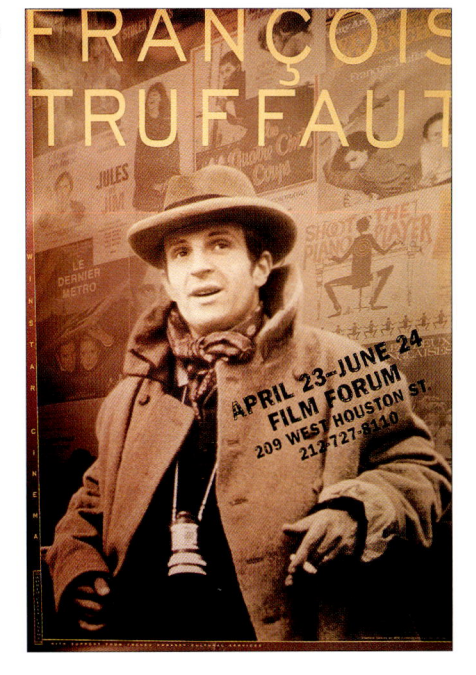

creative firm
 Design Machine
  New York (New York), USA
creative people
 Alexander Gelman
client
 Janou Pakter Inc.

creative firm
 Osoxile S.L.
 Barcelone, Spain
creative people
 Carmelo Henando
client
 Fundacion Caja Rioja

creative firm
 Sommese Design
 State College (Pennsylvania), USA
creative people
 Lanny Sommese
client
 Penn State School of Visual Arts

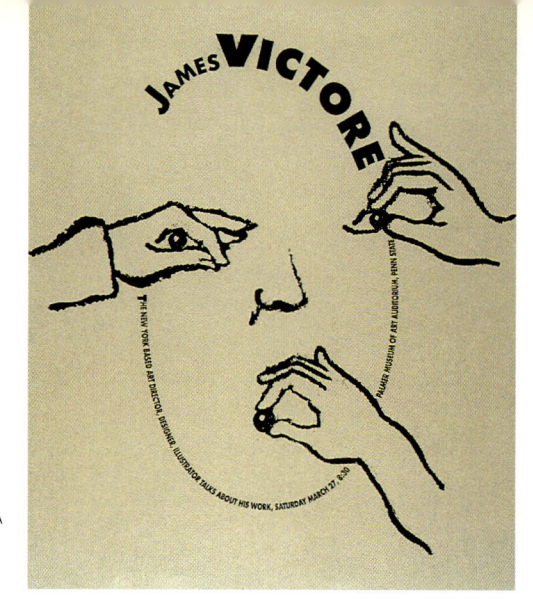

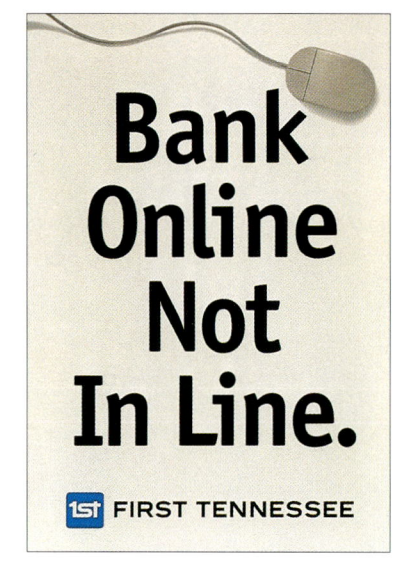

creative firm
 Thompson & Company
 Memphis (Tennessee), USA
art director
 Bill Ainsworth
copywriter
 Jimmy Hamiter
client
 First Tennessee Bank

creative firm
 Thompson & Company
 Memphis (Tennessee), USA
art director, copywriter
 Michael Thompson
 & Sheperd Simmons
client
 Memphis College of Arts

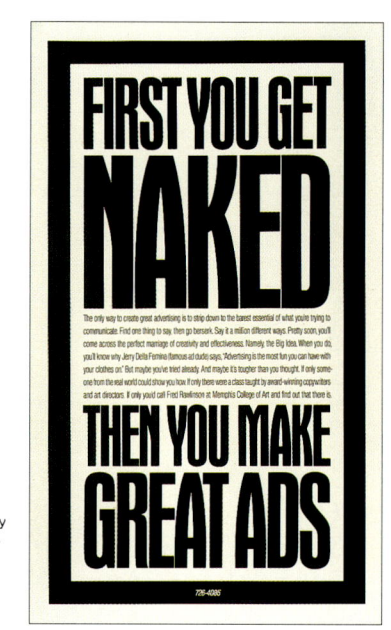

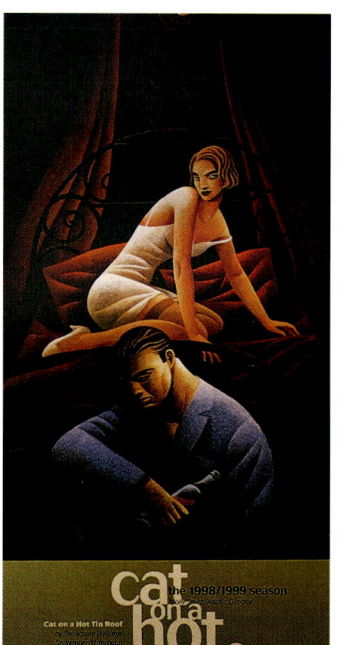

creative firm
 Mires Design, Inc.
 San Diego (California), USA
creative people
 Scott Mires, Neill Archer Roan,
 Miguel Perez, & Laura Connors
illustrator
 Jody Hewgill
client
 Arena Stage

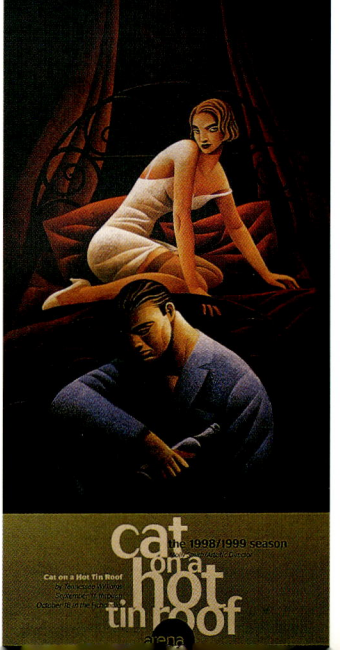

creative firm
 The Widmeyer-Baker Group, Inc.
  Washington (D.C.), USA
creative director
 Tony Frye
designer
 Adam Frew
client
 Iomega

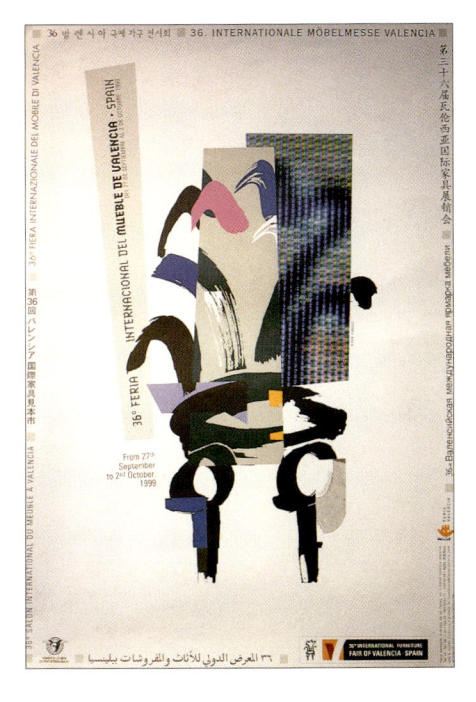

creative firm
 Ford & Earl Associates
  Troy (Michigan), USA
designer
 Barbara Anness
illustrator
 Jon Nason
client
 School-to-Work Oakland Partnership

creative firm
 Pepe Gimeno-Proyecto Grafico
  Godella (Valencia), Spain
creative people
 Pepe Gimeno
client
 Feria International Del Mueble De Valencia

creative firm
 BBK Studio, Inc.
  Grand Rapids (Michigan), USA
designer
 Yang Kim
client
 Herman Miller Inc.

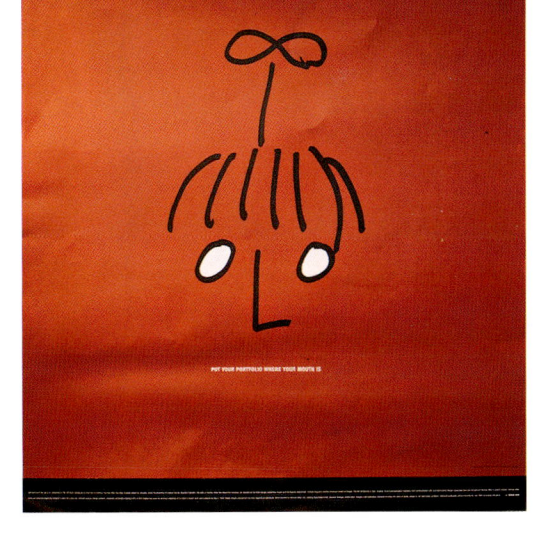

creative firm
 Design Machine
  New York (New York), USA
creative person
 Alexander Gelman
client
 Janou Pakter, Inc.

91

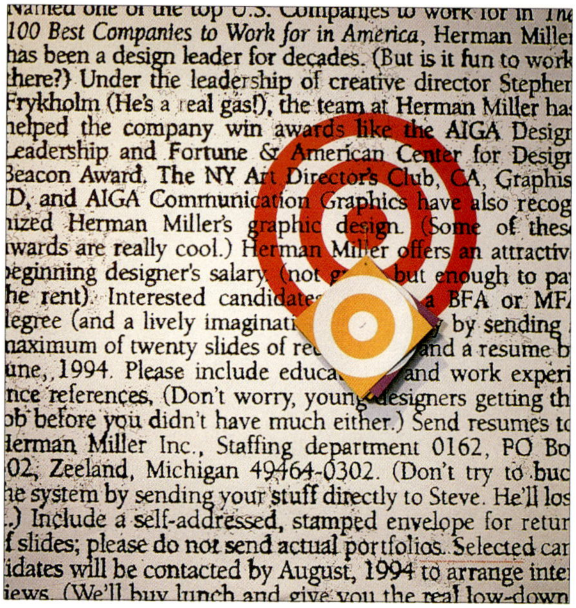

ALCOA FOUNDATION HALL OF AMERICAN INDIANS
CARNEGIE MUSEUM OF NATURAL HISTORY

creative firm
 MARC Advertising
  Pittsburgh (Pennsylvania), USA
creative people
 Ed Fine, Tony Jaffe, Ron Sullivan,
 Kris Knieriem, & Eva Sullivan
client
 Carnegie Museum

creative firm
 BBK Studio, Inc.
  Grand Rapids (Michigan), USA
designer
 Yang Kim
client
 Herman Miller, Inc.

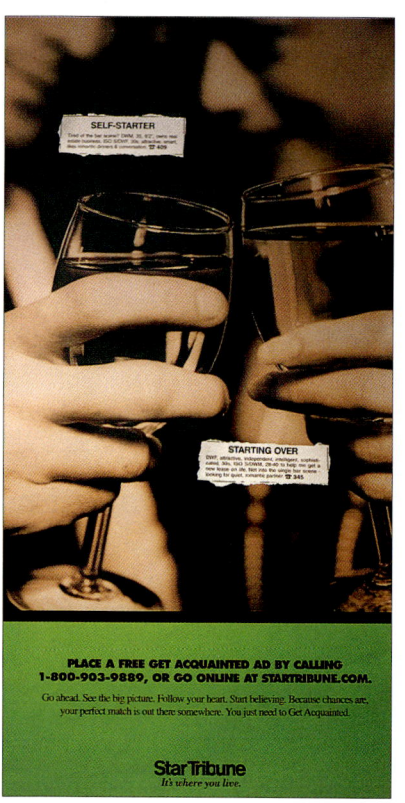

92

creative firm
 Star Tribune
  Minneapolis (Minnesota), USA
designer
 Christopher Weber
client
 Star Tribune

creative firm
 Pepe Gimeno-Proyecto Grafico
  Godella (Valencia), Spain
creative person
 Pepe Gimeno
client
 Feria Internacional
 Del Mueble De Valencia

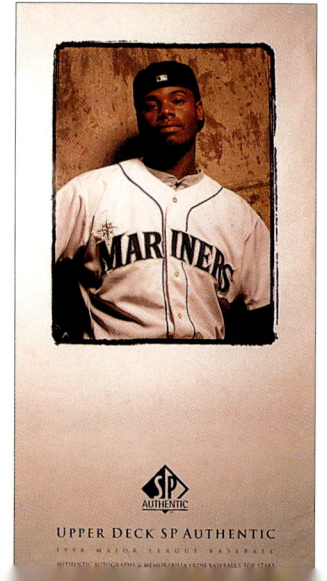

creative firm
 The Upper Deck Company
  Carlsbad (California), USA
designer
 Mary Lou Morreal
client
 The Upper Deck Company

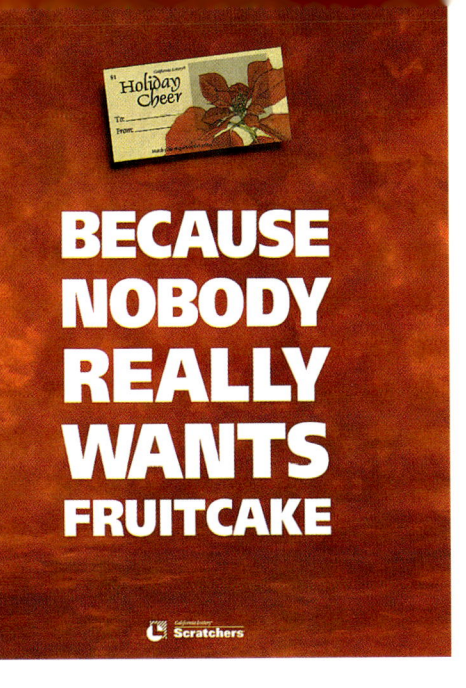

creative firm
 Alcone Marketing Group
  Irvine (California), USA
creative director
 Luis Camano
art director
 Carlos Musquez
photography
 Laura Crosta
copywriter
 Cameron Young
client
 California Lottery

creative firm
 Dieste & Partners Publicidad
  Dallas (Texas), USA
creative director
 Aldo Quevedo
art director
 Chris Sendra
copywriter
 Javier Guemes
client
 Forma Vital

creative firm
 McCann-Erickson Korea Inc.
  Seoul, Korea
creative director
 Jeremy Perrott
art directors
 S.Y. Kim & G.Y. Ahn
copywriter
 W.H. Kim
client
 Levi's Korea

creative firm
 Salisbury State University
  Salisbury (Maryland), USA
designer
 Mike Cooper
client
 Theatre Department

creative firm
 Nelson & Schmidt, Inc.
  Milwaukee (Wisconsin), USA
creative director
 Mark Gale
art director
 Sean Mullen
photographer
 Robert Zimmerman
copywriter
 Bill Stadick
client
 Vision Recumbents

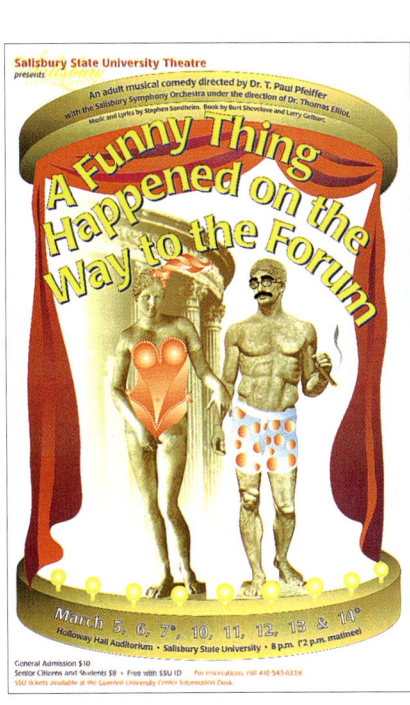

93

# CREATIVITY

## Billboards

creative firm
  Mike Salisbury Communications
  Venice (California), USA
client
  SEAT

creative firm
  J. Walter Thompson/N.Y.
  New York (New York), USA
creative directors
  J. J. Jordan & Michael Hart
art directors, copy writers
  Rick Streed, Anders Carlsson, & Michael Hart
client
  Schieffelin & Somerset Co./J & B Scotch

94

creative firm
  Advico Young & Rubicam
  Zurich-Gockhausen, Switzerland
creative director
  Hansjörg Zürcher
art director
  Dana Wirz
copywriter
  Peter Brönimann
client
  Mountain Marketing

creative firm
  Arnold Ingalls Moranville
  San Francisco (California), USA
art director
  Peter Judd
copywriter
  Jason Siciliano
client
  Infoseek

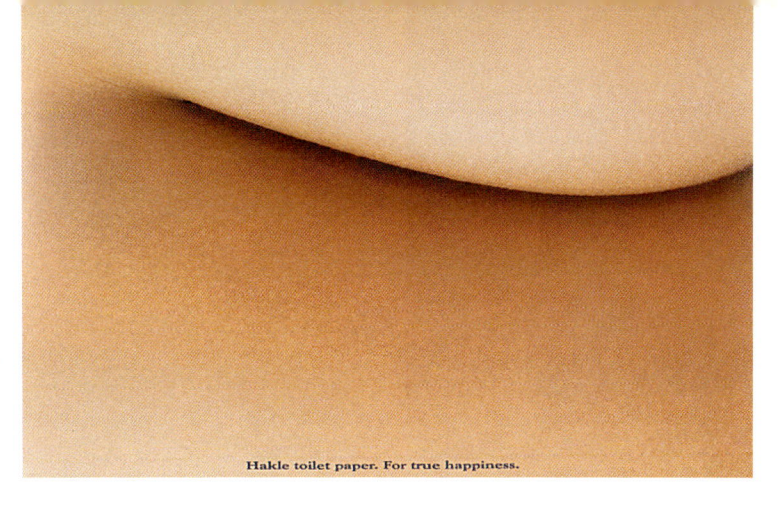

creative firm
  Advico Young & Rubicam
  Zurich-Gockhausen, Switzerland
creative director, copywriter
  Martin Spillman
art directors
  Martin Spillman & Denis Schwarz
client
  Hakle

Hakle toilet paper. For true happiness.

creative firm
  Dynum Nelson & Company
  Pittsburgh (Pennsylvania), USA
creative directors
  John Dynum & Craig Otto
art director
  Anthony Musmanno
client
  Pittsburgh Post-Gazette

Stay Posted.
Pittsburgh Post-Gazette

95

creative firm
  Advico Young & Rubicam
  Zurich-Gockhausen, Switzerland
creative director
  Hansjörg Zürcher
art director
  Mathias Babst
copywriter
  Peter Brönnimann
client
  ZVSM

creative firm
  JMC/Y&R
  Caracas, Venezuela
creative people
  Mary Torres & Jose Navas
client
  Colgate Palmolive

Milk on Tour. Mit den Rolling Stones.

Líder en sonrisas sanas
Colgate

creative firm
  Gauger & Silva Associates
  San Francisco (California), USA
creative people
  Lori Murphy & David Gauger
client
  Commercial Bank

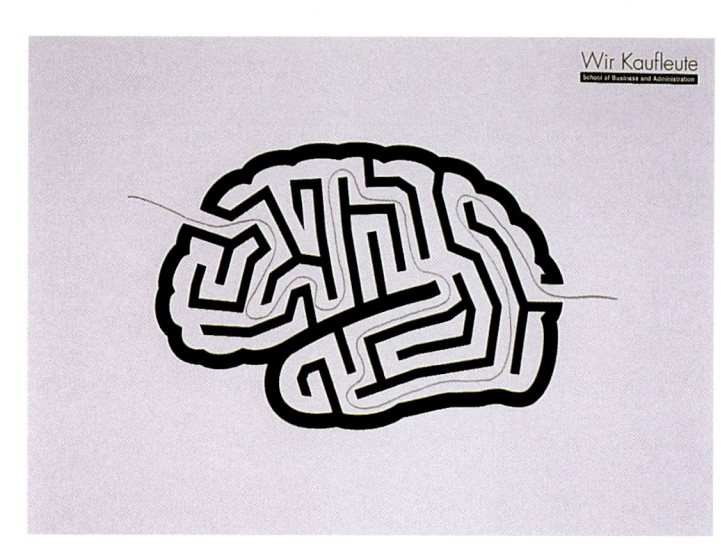

creative firm
  Advico Young & Rubicam
  Zurich-Gockhausen, Switzerland
creative director, copywriter
  Francisco X. Rodon
art directors
  Vanessa Rodriguez & Francisco X. Rodon
client
  School of Business and Administration

96

creative firm
  J. Walter Thompson/N.Y.
  New York (New York), USA
creative directors
  Michael Hart & J.J. Jordan
art directors
  Dennis Soohoo & Andy Green
typographer
  Philip Kelly
photographer
  Mark Weiss
copywriter
  Nick Goodey
client
  Warner-Lambert Co./Trident Gum

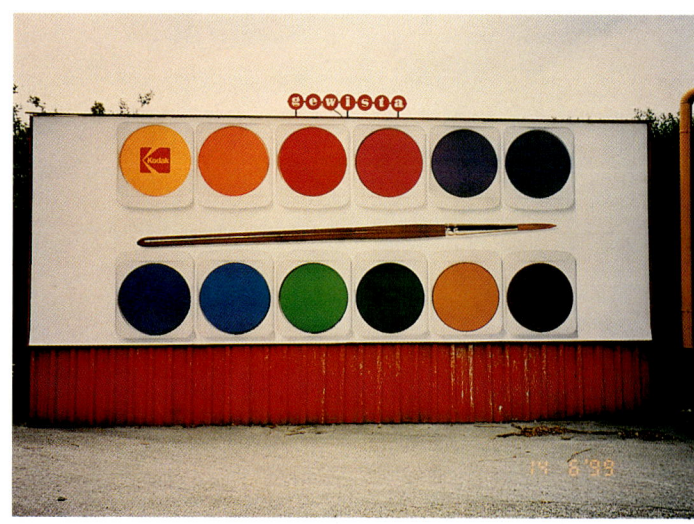

creative firm
  Ogilvy & Mather Frankfurt
  Frankfurt, Germany
creative directors
  Thomas Hofbeck & Dr. Stephan Vogel
art director
  Marco Weber
client
  Kodak Ges.m.b.H, Wien

**Coccolati la pelle.**

Acqua S.Bernardo. Così leggera, così leggeri.

creative firm
  Armando Testa-Turin Italy
  Milan, Italy
creative director
  Roberto Fiore
photographer
  Joe Oppedisano
client
  Aqua.S.Bernardo

DRINKING IN MODERATION BEATS VOMITING IN EXCESS

creative firm
  J. Walter Thompson/N.Y.
  New York (New York), USA
creative directors
  J.J. Jordan & Michael Hart
art directors, copywriters
  Rick Streed, Anders Carlsson, & Michael Hart
client
  Schieffelin & Somerset Co./J & B Scotch

97

**Stay Posted.**
Pittsburgh Post-Gazette

creative firm
  Dymun Nelson & Company
  Pittsburgh (Pennsylvania), USA
creative directors
  John Dymun & Craig Otto
art director
  Tony Shuckhart
client
  Pittsburgh Post-Gazette

"Cash. My favorite four-letter word."
—the Queen
CASINO QUEEN THE LOOSEST SLOTS. PERIOD.

creative firm
  Louis London
  St. Louis (Missouri), USA
art directors
  Joe Ortmeyer & Aaron Segall
copywriters
  Lori Jones & Steve Hunt
client
  The Casino Queen

creative firm
  Alcone Marketing Group
    Irvine (California), USA
creative director, art director
  Luis Camano
designer
  Carlos Musquez
copywriter
  Cameron Young
client
  California Lottery

creative firm
  Advico Young & Rubicam
    Zurich-Gockhausen, Switzerland
creative director, art director, copywriter
  Francisco X. Rodon
client
  Hope and Homes for Children

98

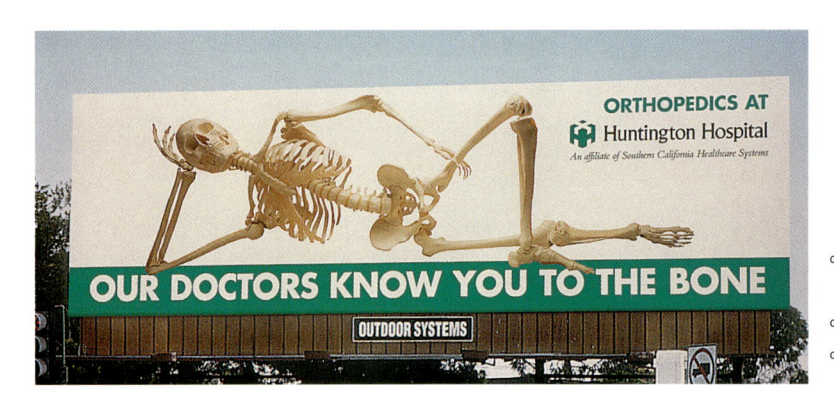

creative firm
  Dennis S. Juett & Associates Inc.
    Pasadena (California), USA
creative people
  Dennis S. Juett & Dennis Scott Juett
client
  Huntington Memorial Hospital

creative firm
  Arnold Ingalls Moranville
    San Francisco (California), USA
art director
  Peter Judd
copywriter
  Jason Siciliano
client
  Infoseek

creative firm
 Design Guys
  Minneapolis (Minnesota), USA
creative people
 Steven Sikora, Gary Patch, & Anne Peterson
client
 Target Stores

creative firm
 J. Walter Thompson/N.Y.
  New York (New York), USA
creative directors
 Ed Evangelista & Chris D'rozario
art director
 Ed Evangelista
designer
 Phil Kelly
copywriters
 Chris D'Rozario & Steve Salinaro
client
 DeBeers

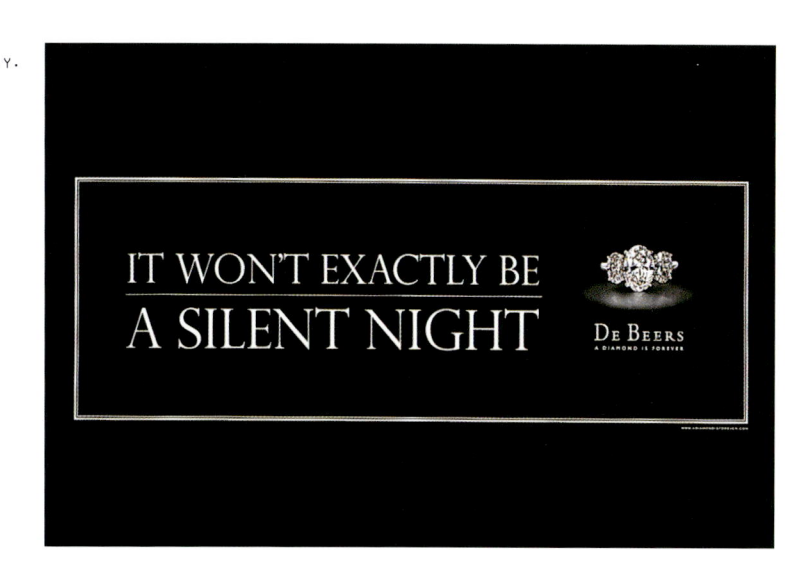

creative firm
 JMC/Y&R
  Caracas, Venezuela
creative people
 Mary Torres, Jose Navas, & Luis Bernardo
client
 FNCS

creative firm
 Spencer Zahn & Associates
  Philadelphia (Pennsylvania), USA
creative director
 Spencer Zahn
art director
 Edward McHugh
client
 Keenan Motors

99

# 29 CREATIVITY

## Annual Reports

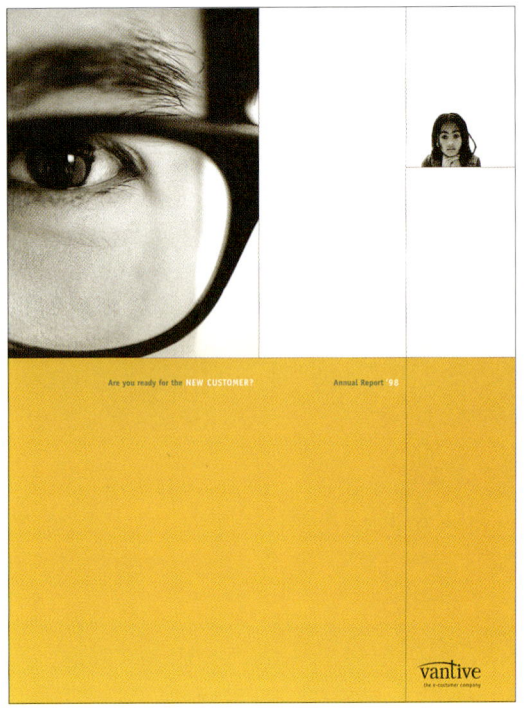

creative firm
 Hornall Anderson
 Design Works
 Seattle (Washington), USA
creative people
 John Hornall, Lisa Cerveny,
 Bruce Branson-Meyer, Jana Nishi,
 Robb Anderson, &
 Michael Brugman
client
 Airborne Express

creative firm
 Addison
 New York (New York), USA
creative director
 David Kohler
art director
 Anna Tan
client
 Eastman Kodak

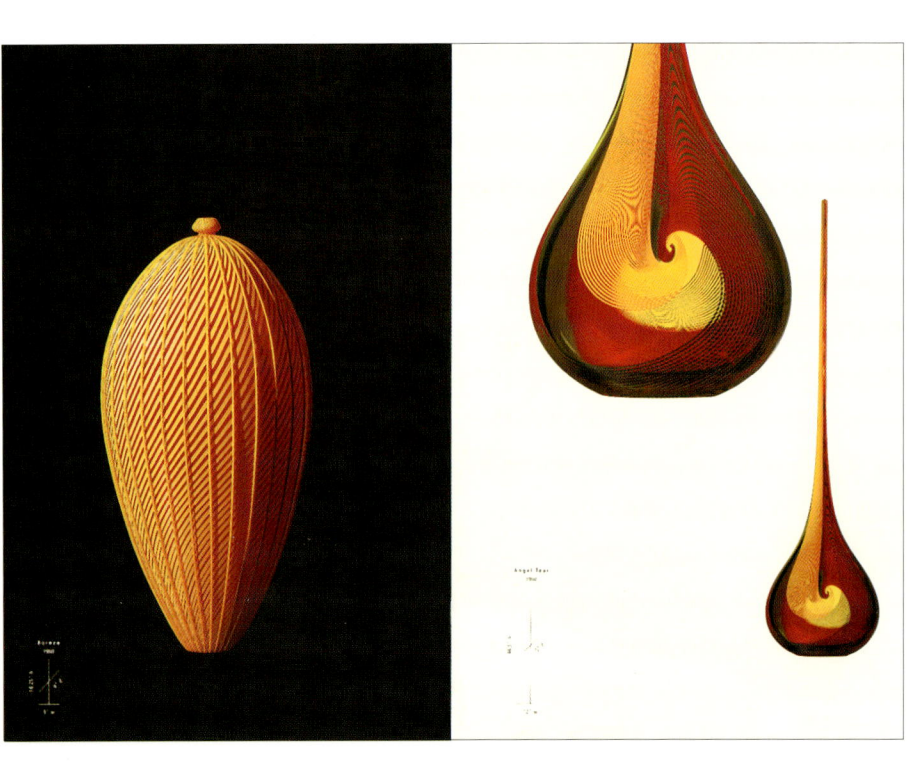

100

creative firm
 Kim Baer Design Associates
 Venice (California), USA
art director
 Kim Baer
photographer
 Mitch Tobias
illustrator
 Jaime Diersing
copywriter
 Michael Lejeune
client
 The Vantive Corpration

creative firm
 Morgan Design Inc.
 New York (New York), USA
creative people
 Clint Morgan
client
 Capital Re

creative firm
 Little & Company
  Minneapolis (Minnesota), USA
client
 Dayton Hudson Corporation

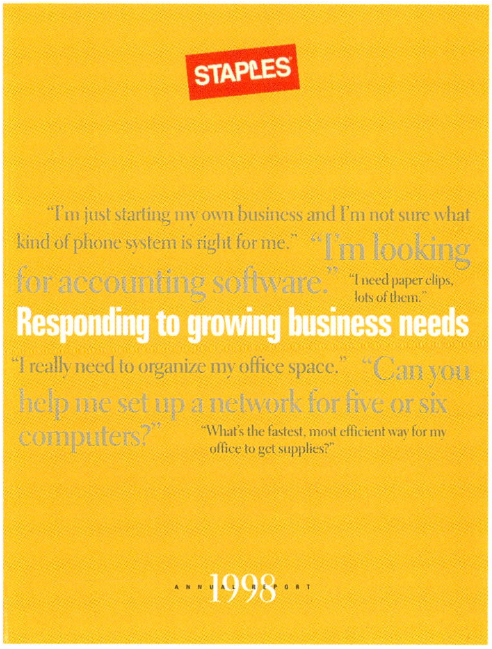

creative firm
 Media Concepts Corp.
  Assonet (Massachusetts), USA
designer
 Chris O'Toole
photographer
 Ron Hagerman
copywriter
 J.D. Siegel
client
 Staples

creative firm
 The Graphic Expression, Inc.
  New York (New York), USA
creative people
 Stephen Ferrari & Sue Balle
client
 Allmerica Financial Corporation

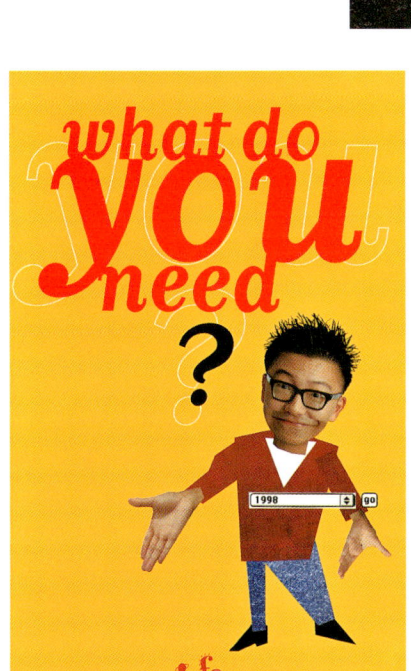

creative firm
 Louey/Rubino
 Design Group Inc.
  Santa Monica (California), USA
art director
 Robert Louey
designer
 Alex Chao
client
 Kaufman and Broad
 Home Corporation

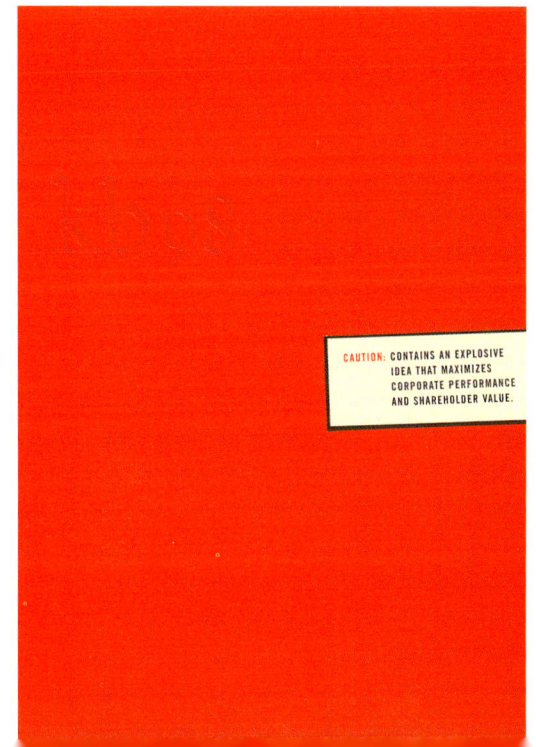

creative firm
 The Leonhardt Group
  Seattle (Washington), USA
art directors
 Tim Young & Jon King
designer
 Tim Young
client
 InfoSpace.com

101

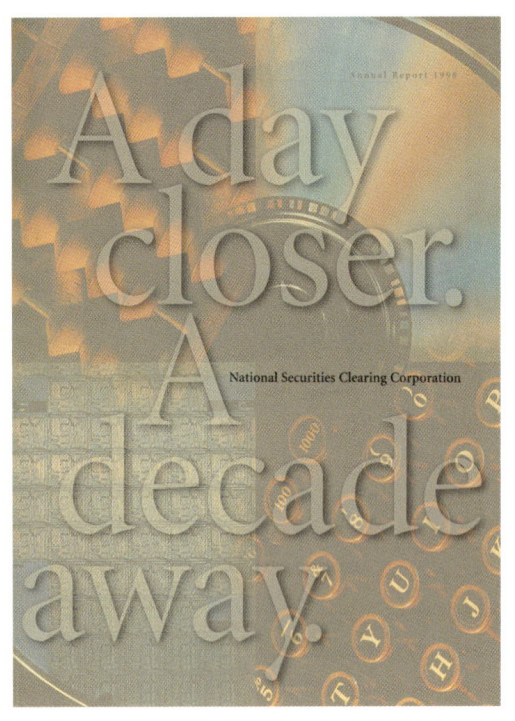

creative firm
 Taylor & Ives Incorporated
 New York (New York), USA
design director
 Ms. Alisa Zamir
senior designer
 Ms. Pamela Brooks
client
 National Securities Clearing Corporation

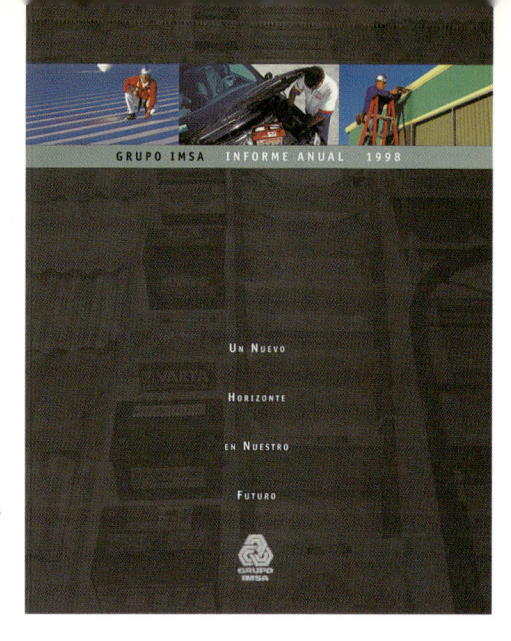

102

creative firm
 Signi
 Mexico City, Mexico
art director
 Daniel Castelao
designer
 Ramon Valdez
client
 IMSA

creative firm
 Besser Design Group
 Santa Monica (California), USA
designer
 Rik Besser
photographer
 Knaver Johnston
client
 Agauron Pharmaceuticals

creative firm
 Broom & Broom
 San Francisco (California), USA
creative director
 David Broom
designer
 Martin McMurray
client
 National Semiconductor Corporation

creative firm
 Cahan & Associates
 San Francisco (California), USA
art director
 Bill Cahan
designer
 Sharrie Brooks
client
 Verilink

Health Care **We can do that.**

creative firm
 Taylor & Ives Incorporated
 New York (New York), USA
design director
 Ms. Alisa Zamir
designer
 Ms. Pamela Brooks
client
 Siemens Corporation

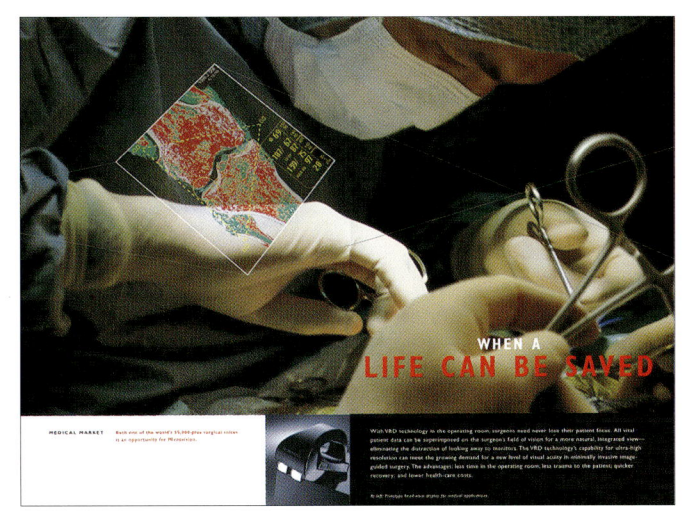

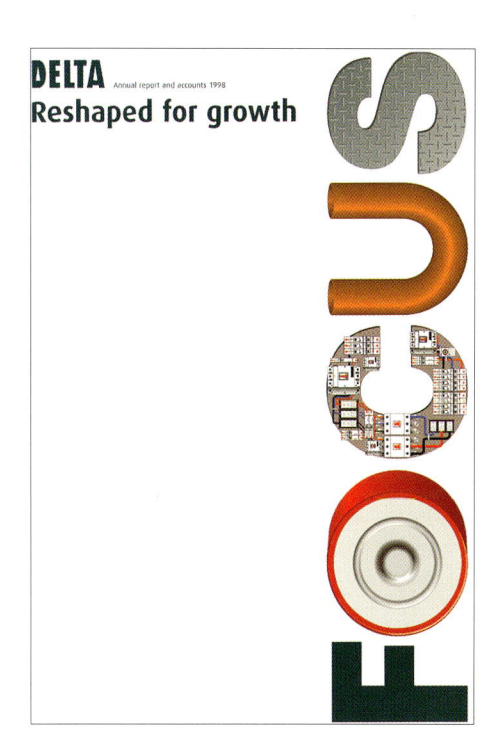

**DELTA** Annual report and accounts 1998
**Reshaped for growth**

FOCUS

creative firm
 The Leonhardt Group
 Seattle (Washington), USA
art directors
 Tim Young & Jon King
designer
 Tim Young
client
 Microvision, Inc.

WHEN A LIFE CAN BE SAVED

MEDICAL MARKET

creative firm
 Tor Pettersen & Partners
 London, England
creative people
 David C. Brown, Chris Birks, & Mike Gill
client
 Delta Group PLC

103

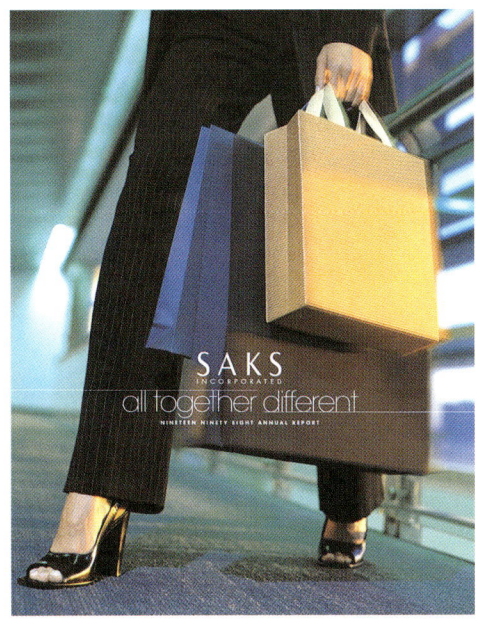

creative firm
 Shar Coulson Design
 Chicago (Illinois), USA
creative director, designer
 Shar Coulson
copywriter
 Cindy Bokhof
client
 Saks Incorporated

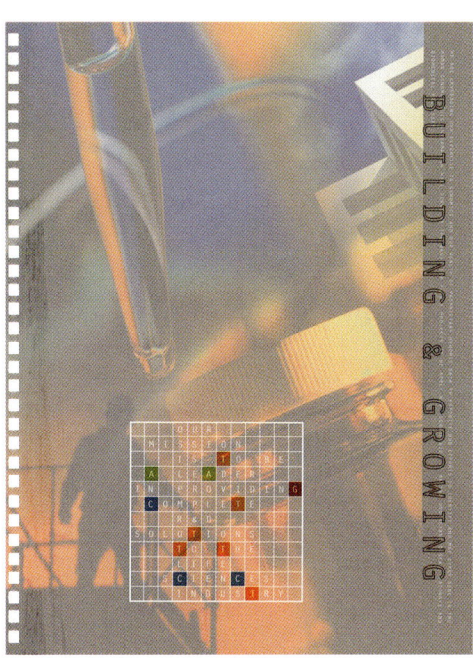

SAKS INCORPORATED
all together different
NINETEEN NINETY EIGHT ANNUAL REPORT

BUILDING & GROWING

creative firm
 1185 Design
 Palo Alto (California), USA
creative people
 Peggy Burke & Nhut Nguyen
client
 Incyte Pharmaceuticals

LEADING

A GROWING

INDUSTRY

1 9 9 8

SOUTHDOWN ANNUAL REPORT

creative firm
 Sessions Group
  Houston (Texas), USA
art director, designer
 Steven Sessions
photographers
 Steve Chen, Otto Nero,
 & Alan Montgomery
client
 Southdown

creative firm
 Leimer Cross Design
  Seattle (Washington), USA
art director, designer
 Kerry Leimer
photographers
 Mark Robert Halper & Tyler Boley
client
 SonoSite, Inc.

104

creative firm
 Addison
  New York (New York), USA
creative director
 David Kohler
art director
 Richard Colbourne
client
 Globalstar

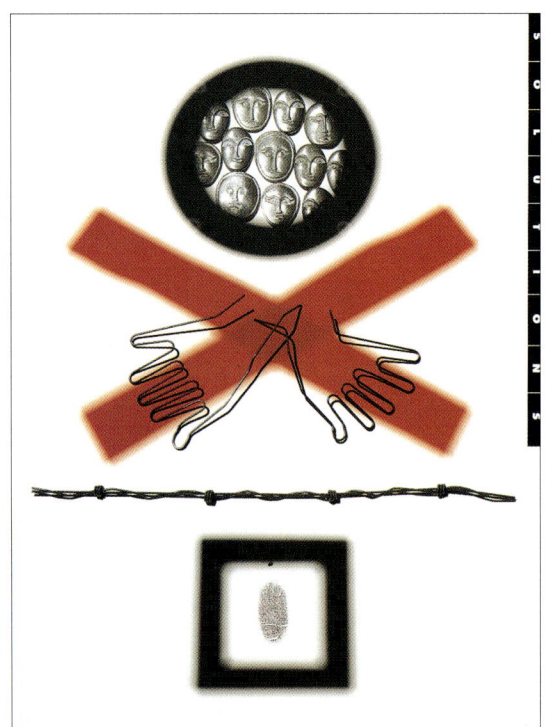

creative firm
 Mortensen Design
  Mountain View (California), USA
creative people
 Gordon Mortensen & PJ Nidecker
client
 Identix, Inc.

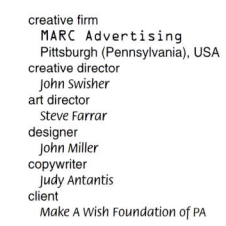

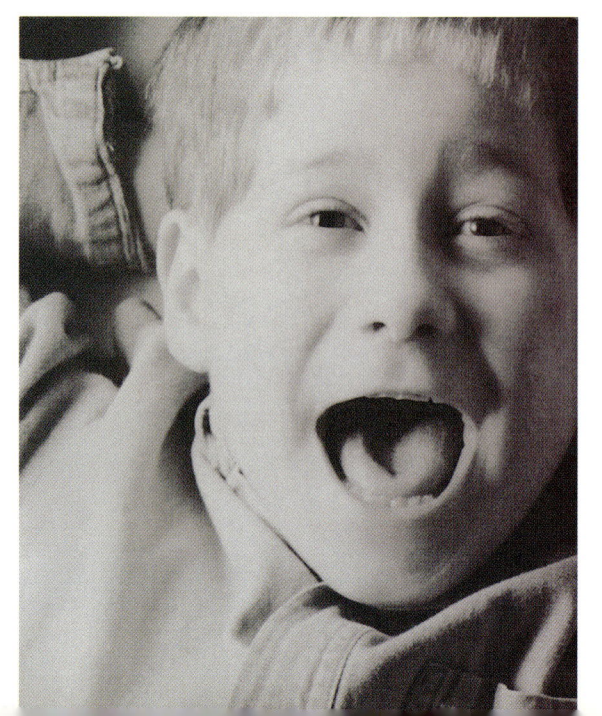

creative firm
 MARC Advertising
  Pittsburgh (Pennsylvania), USA
creative director
 John Swisher
art director
 Steve Farrar
designer
 John Miller
copywriter
 Judy Antantis
client
 Make A Wish Foundation of PA

creative firm
　Savage Design Group, Inc.
　Houston (Texas), USA
creative director
　Paula Savage
art director
　Dahlia Salazar
designer
　Bo Bothe
photographer
　Jack Thompson
copywriter
　Gary Broussard
client
　Strake Jesuit College Preparatory

creative firm
　Emerson, Wajdowicz Studios
　New York (New York), USA
creative director
　Jurek Wajdowicz
designers
　Lisa LaRochelle & Jurek Wajdowicz
photographer
　Antonin Kratochvil
client
　The Rockefeller Foundation

creative firm
　Addison
　New York (New York), USA
creative director
　David Kohler
art director
　Chris Yun
client
　Hershey Foods Corp.

creative firm
　Nolin Larosee Design
　Communications
　Montreal (Québec), Canada
art director
　René Clément
client
　BCE Mobile Communications Inc.

creative firm
　Gottschalk+Ash Int'l
　Zürich, Switzerland
creative people
　Fritz Gottschalk & Barbara Motta
client
　Bank Hofmann AG

creative firm
  The Graphic Expression, Inc.
  New York (New York), USA
creative people
  Stephen Ferrari & Kurt Finkbeiner
client
  Tommy Hilfiger Corporation

creative firm
  Cahan & Associates
  San Francisco (California), USA
art director
  Bill Cahan
designer
  Craig Terrones
client
  Siebel Systems

creative firm
  Cahan & Associates
  San Francisco (California), USA
art director
  Bill Cahan
designer
  Lian Ng
client
  INS

**WYSINSWYG**

1998 annual report

creative firm
  Herman Miller in-house
  design team & BBK
  Zeeland (Michigan), USA
art director
  Steve Frykholm
designer
  Yang Kim (BBK)
copywriters
  Clark Malcolm & Jack Schreur
client
  Herman Miller Inc.

Our reputation keeps expanding.
Most office furniture dealers, interior designers, and facility managers "now perceive Herman Miller as the company to beat." (According to the Wirthlin Worldwide poll of the office furniture industry.)

creative firm
  Addison
  New York (New York), USA
creative director
  David Kohler
art director
  Richard Colbourne
client
  First Pacific Company Limited

board of directors

creative firm
 Carl Thompson Assoc.
 Louisville (Colorado), USA
creative director
 Jonathan Pite
art director
 Tabitha Manresa
designer
 David Morton
client
 Horizon Organic Dairy

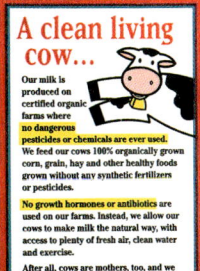

creative firm
 Cahan & Associates
 San Francisco (California), USA
art director
 Bill Cahan
designer
 Sharrie Brooks
client
 Sugen

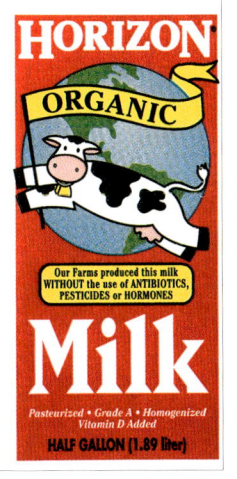

creative firm
 Q Design
 Wiesbaden, Germany
creative people
 Thilo von Debschitz,
 Laurenz Nielbock, &
 Roman Holt
client
 VKE

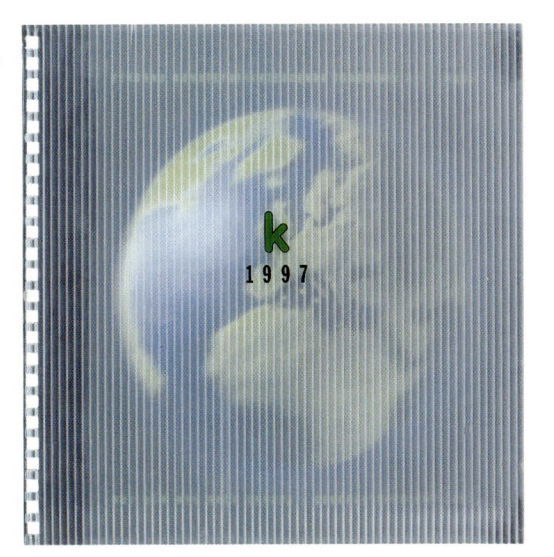

107

creative firm
 Leimer Cross Design
 Seattle (Washington), USA
art director, designer
 Kerry Leimer
photographers
 Jeff Corwin & Tyler Boley
client
 Esterline Technologies

creative firm
 1185 Design
 Palo Alto (California), USA
creative people
 Peggy Burke & Rachel Fitzgibbon
client
 Adobe Systems

creative firm
 Boller Coates & Neu
 Chicago (Illinois), USA
designer
 Robert Mileham
photographer
 Ferguson & Katzman
client
 May Department Stores Co.

creative firm
 Hausman Design, Inc.
 Palo Alto (California), USA
creative people
 Joan L. Hausman & Ellen Hobbs
client
 eBay Inc.

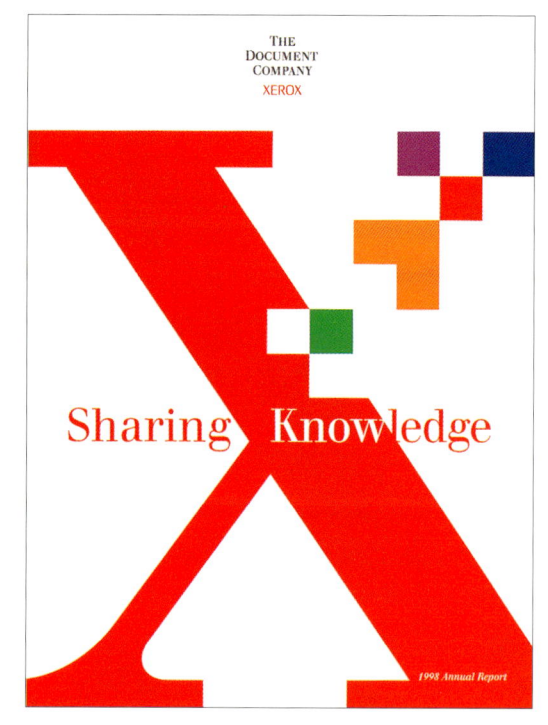

creative firm
 Boller Coates & Neu
 Chicago (Illinois), USA
designer
 Ron Coates
photographer
 Andrew Goodwin
client
 Xerox Corporation

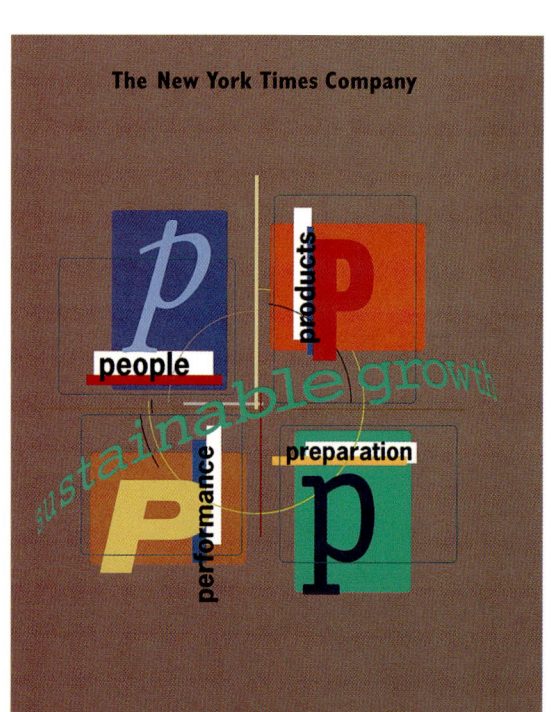

creative firm
 Shari Finger Design
 Rye (New York), USA
designer
 Shari Finger
executive photographer
 William Taufic
illustrator
 Javier Romero
client
 The New York Times Company

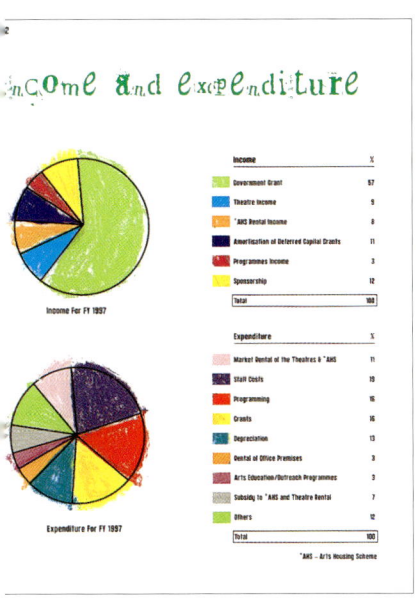

creative firm
 Epigram Pte Ltd
  Singapore
creative director
 Edmund Wee
designer
 Jacke Tan
photographers
 Frank Pinckers & Stephen Koh
client
 National Arts Council

creative firm
 Kan & Lau Design Consultants
  Hong Kong, China
creative director
 Kan Tai-keung
art directors
 Eddy Yu Chi Kong
 & Chau So Hing
designer
 Lerry Ho
photographer
 Bob Davis
computer illustrator
 Ng Cheuk Bong
client
 Kowloon-Canton
 Railway Corporation

creative firm
 Fine Print, Inc.
  Atlanta (Georgia), USA
art directors
 J. Michael Matascik & George Bacso
designer
 J. Michael Matascik
photographer
 Bard Wrisley
client
 Georgia-Pacific

109

creative firm
 Tor Pettersen
 & Partners
  London, England
creative people
 Jeff Davis, Jim Allsopp,
 David Baird, Mike Hingston,
 & Tor Pettersen
client
 Kingfisher PLC

creative firm
 Gottschalk+Ash Int'l
  Zürich, Switzerland
creative people
 Fritz Gottschalk, Erich Gross,
 & Corinne Weibel
client
 Bayerische Hypo- und
 Vereinsbank AG

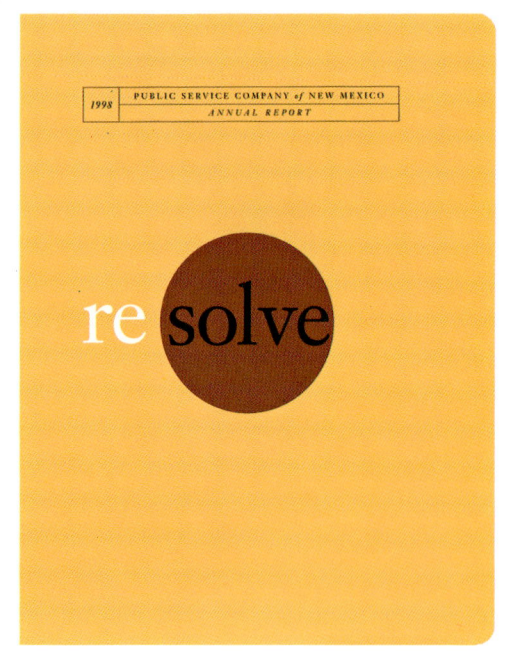

creative firm
  Kilmer & Kilmer
  Design & Advertising
  Albuquerque (New Mexico), USA
creative people
  Richard Kilmer, Brenda Kilmer,
  Randall Marshall, & Gary Kohlman
client
  PNM

creative firm
  Leimer Cross Design
  Seattle (Washington), USA
art director, designer
  Kerry Leimer
photographers
  Jeff Corwin, Charles Blackburn,
  & Tyler Boley
client
  Visio Corporation

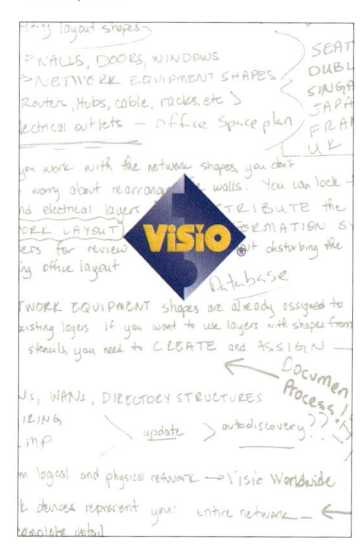

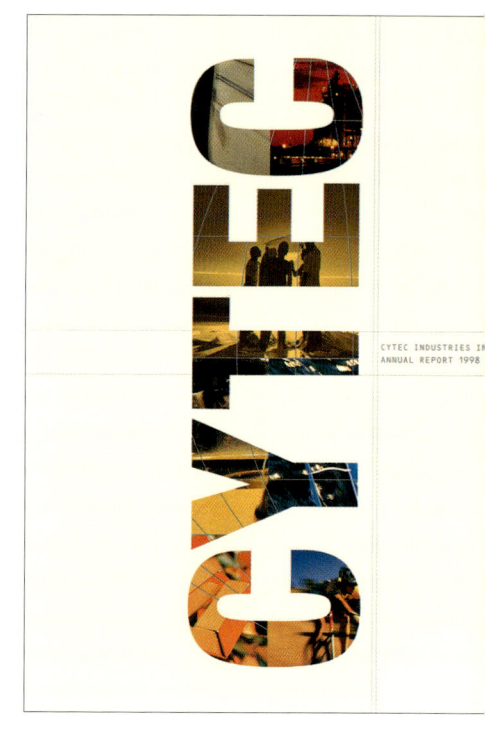

creative firm
  Addison
  New York (New York), USA
creative director
  David Kohler
art director
  Anna Tan
client
  Cytec Industries, Inc.

110

creative firm
  Oh Boy, A Design Company
  San Francisco (California), USA
creative director, art director
  David Salanitro
designer
  Ted Bluey
photographers
  Hunter Wimmer &
  Robertson-Ceco corporate archives
copywriter
  David Salanitro, Ted Bluey,
  Ronald Stephens, & Pat McNulty
client
  Robertson-Ceco

creative firm
  Design Systemat, Inc.
  Makati, Philippines
creative people
  Peachy G. Bunag & Gil Mateo
client
  La Tondena Distillers Inc.

creative firm
 **Baker Designed Communications**
  Santa Monica (California), USA
art director
 *Gary Baker*
designer
 *Louis D'Esposito*
client
 *Minimed Inc.*

creative firm
 **Little & Company**
  Minneapolis (Minnesota), USA
client
 *Wells Fargo & Company*

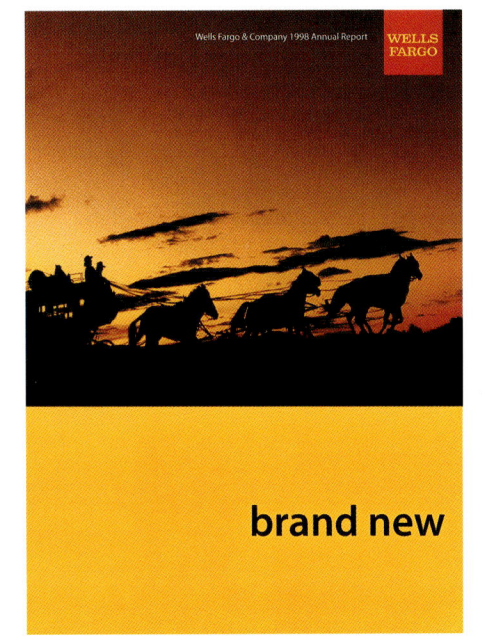

creative firm
 **Nolin Larosee Design Communications**
  Montreal (Québec), Canada
creative director
 *Barbara Jacques*
art directors
 *Barbara Jacques & Michèle Besré*
client
 *Royal Bank of Canada*

111

creative firm
 **Addison**
  New York (New York), USA
creative director
 *David Kohler*
art director
 *Cindy Goldstein*
client
 *General Instrument*

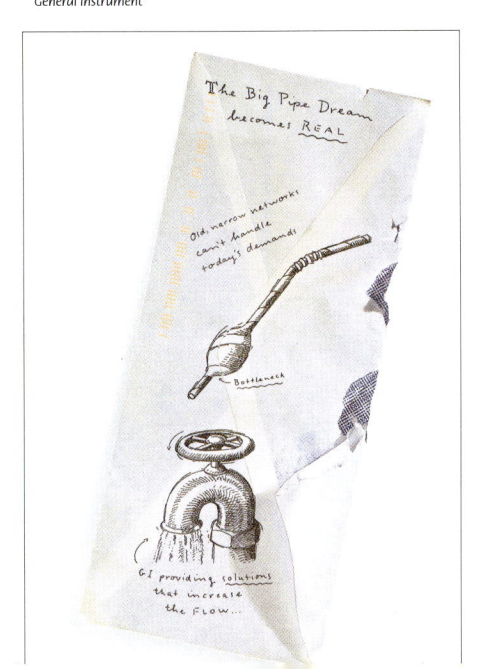

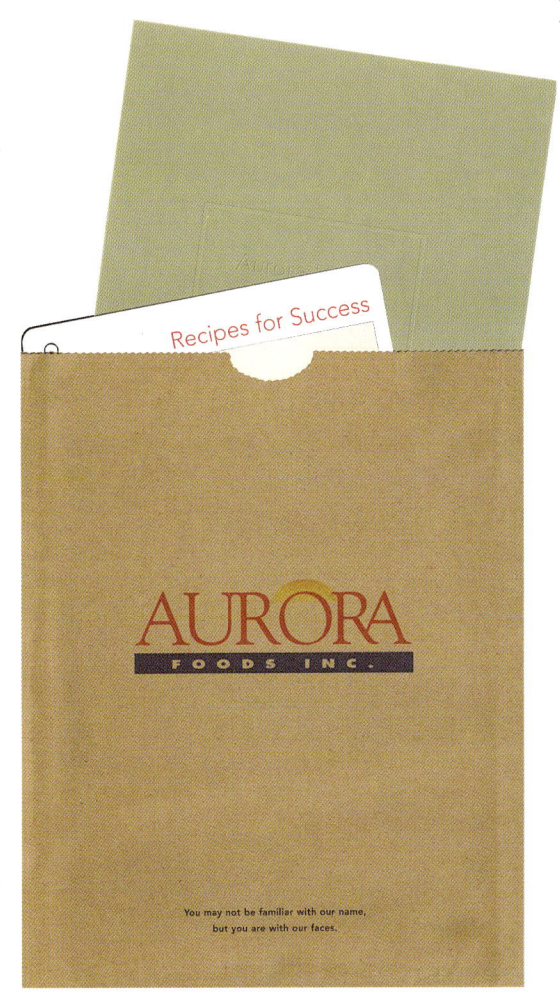

creative firm
 **Cahan & Associates**
  San Francisco (California), USA
art director
 *Bill Cahan*
designer
 *Lian Ng*
client
 *Aurora Foods*

creative firm
  **Casper Design Group**
  Berkeley (California), USA
creative director
  *Bill Ribar*
art director, designer
  *Christopher Buehler*
client
  *PeopleSoft*

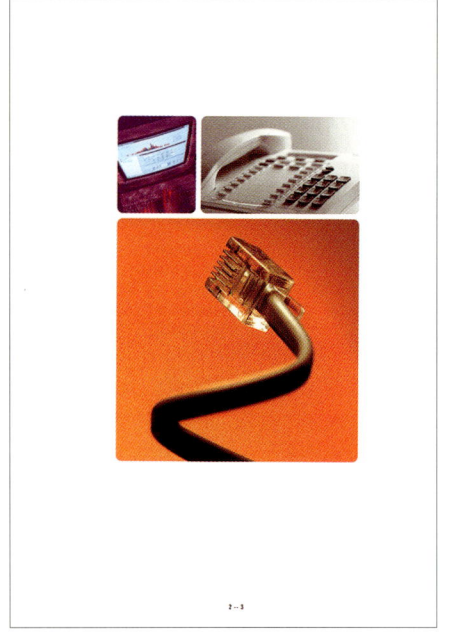

creative firm
  **Iridium Marketing + Design**
  Ottawa (Ontario), Canada
art director
  *Jean-Luc Denat*
production designer
  *Mary Koch*
designer
  *Mario L'Écuyer*
client
  *Mitel Corporation*

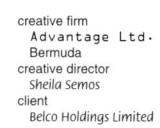

creative firm
  **Advantage Ltd.**
  Bermuda
creative director
  *Sheila Semos*
client
  *Belco Holdings Limited*

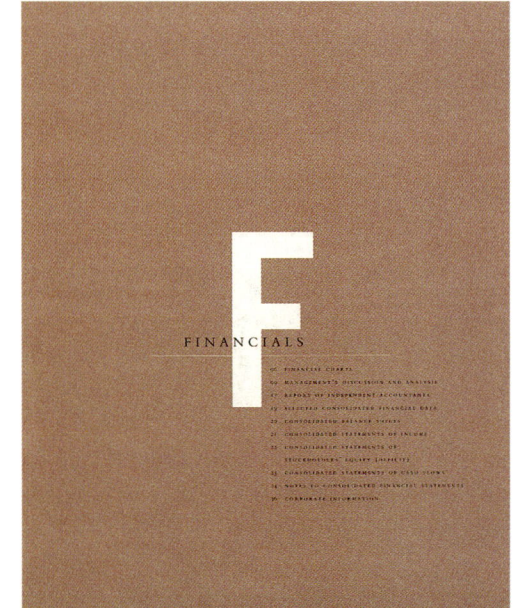

creative firm
  **Cahan & Associates**
  San Francisco (California), USA
art director
  *Bill Cahan*
designer
  *Lian Ng*
client
  *Etec Systems*

creative firm
  **prodialog 2000**
  Munich, Germany
creative people
  *F. Huber, N. Klint,
  K.-H. Langhans, & F. Schwarz*
client
  *TÜV Süddeutschland Holding AG*

creative firm
  The Graphic
  Expression, Inc.
  New York (New York), USA
creative people
  Stephen Ferrari & Monica Gotz
client
  America Online, Inc.

creative firm
  The Leonhardt Group
  Seattle (Washington), USA
art directors
  Greg Morgan & Renee Sullivan
designer
  Lesley Feldman
client
  Media One Group, Inc.

creative firm
  Ted Bertz Design
  Middletown (Connecticut), USA
designers
  Ted Bertz & Mark Terranova
photographer
  Ted Kawalerski
client
  People's Bank

creative firm
  Emerson, Wajdowicz Studios
  New York (New York), USA
art director
  Jurek Wajdowicz
designers
  Lisa LaRochelle & Jurek Wajdowicz
client
  Trickle Up Program

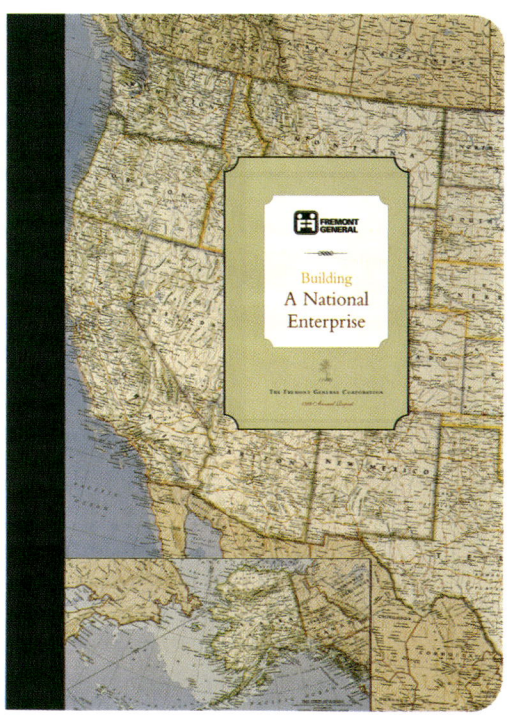

creative firm
  Louey/Rubino
  Design Group Inc.
  Santa Monica (California), USA
art director
  Robert Louey
designer
  Anja Mueller
client
  Fremont General

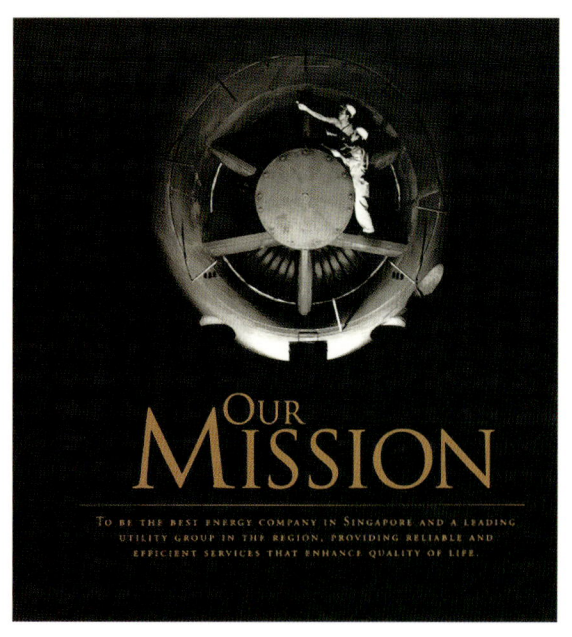

creative firm
 Epigram Pte Ltd
  Singapore
creative director
 Edmund Wee
designer
 Benjy Choo
photographer
 Ken Seet
illustrator
 Jenny Powell (UK)
client
 Singapore Power Ltd

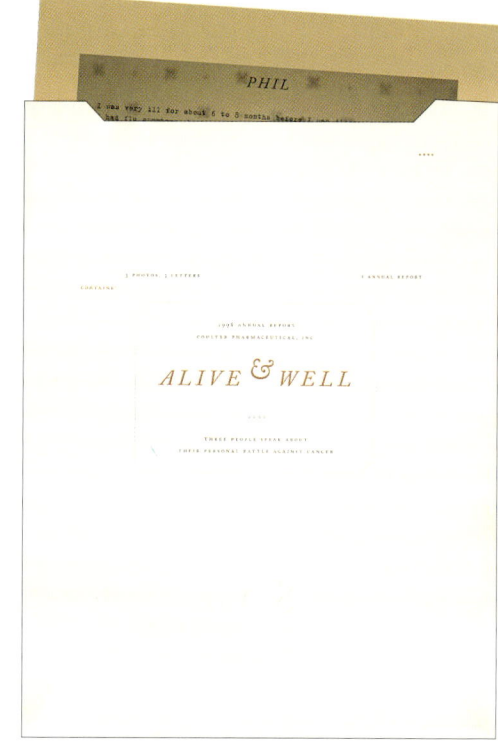

creative firm
 Cahan & Associates
  San Francisco (California), USA
art director
 Bill Cahan
designer
 Kevin Roberson
client
 Coulter Pharmaceutical

creative firm
 Leimer Cross Design
  Seattle (Washington), USA
art director, designer
 Kerry Leimer
photographers
 Tyler Boley & Terry Heffernan
client
 Cutter & Buck

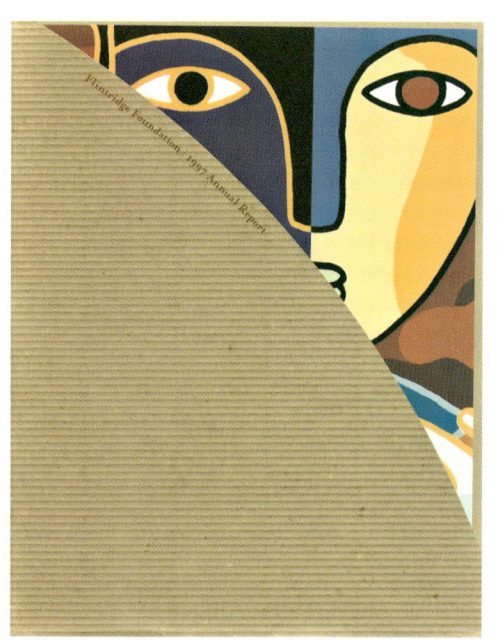

creative firm
 Cliff & Associates
  South Pasadena (California), USA
art director
 Greg Cliff
designer
 Judy Bryan
illustrator
 Jose Ortega
client
 Flintridge Foundation

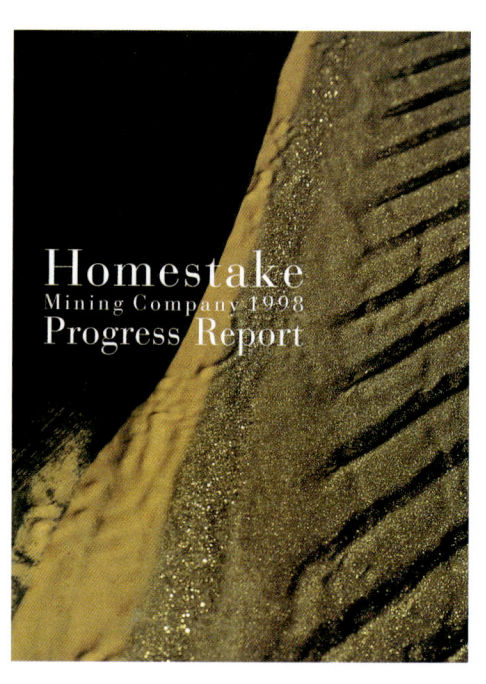

creative firm
 Broom & Broom
  San Francisco (California), USA
creative director
 David Broom
designer
 Deborah Sinclair
client
 Homestake Mining Company

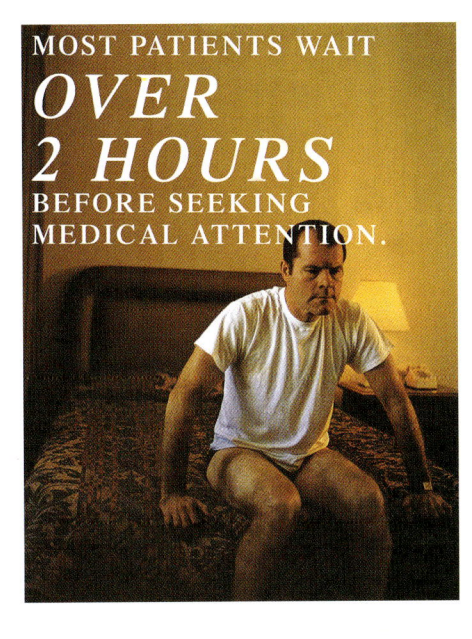

**MOST PATIENTS WAIT OVER 2 HOURS BEFORE SEEKING MEDICAL ATTENTION.**

creative firm
  Cahan & Associates
  San Francisco (California), USA
art director
  Bill Cahan
designer
  Michael Braley
client
  COR Therapeutics

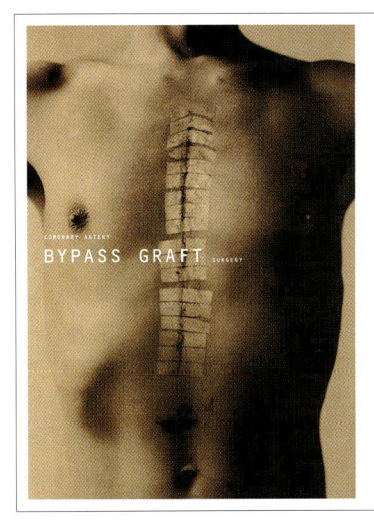

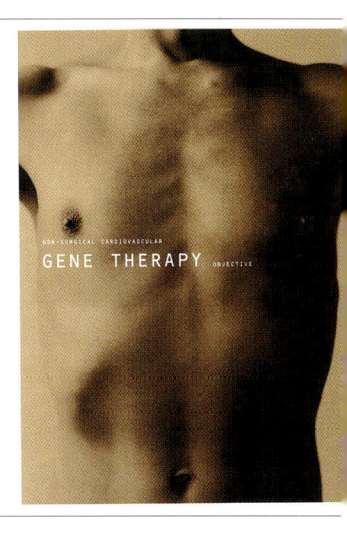

BYPASS GRAFT    GENE THERAPY

creative firm
  Cahan & Associates
  San Francisco (California), USA
art director
  Bill Cahan
designer
  Kevin Roberson
client
  Collateral Therapeutics

creative firm
  What a Concept!
  Coral Gables (Florida), USA
creative people
  Beatrice Muñoz-Reina
client
  Tropical Federal Credit Union

TROPICAL FEDERAL CREDIT UNION
1998 ANNUAL REPORT

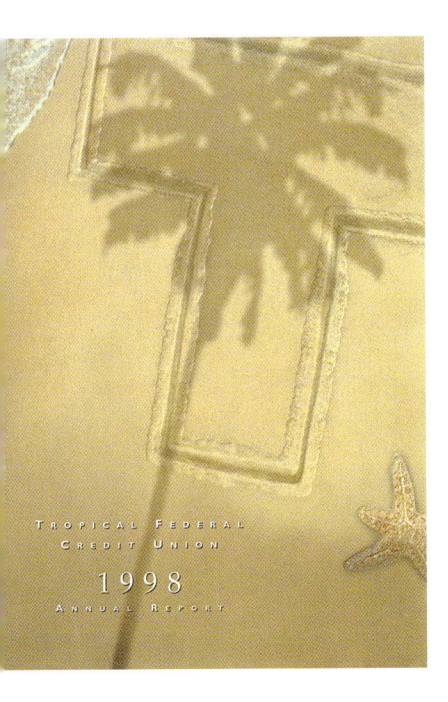

115

creative firm
  Donaldson, Lufkin & Jenrette
  New York (New York), USA
client
  Trump Hotel & Casino Resorts

TRUMP HOTELS & CASINO RESORTS
1998 ANNUAL REPORT

### Založništvo literature

V dejavnosti smo izdali 102 publikaciji v skupni nakladi 206 tisoč izvodov. Od tega je bilo 36 izvirnih del, ostalo pa so bili prevodi. Ponatisov je bilo 11.

creative firm
  KROG
  Ljubljana, Slovenia
art director, designer
  Edi Berk
photographer
  Dragan Arrigler
client
  DZS, Ljubljana

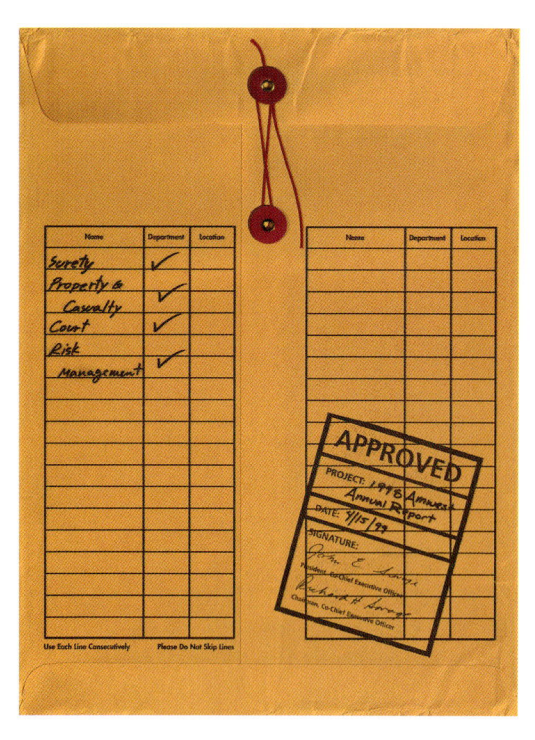

creative firm
  Bloch + Coulter
  Design Group
  Los Angeles (California), USA
creative people
  Heather Gondek, Thomas Bloch,
  & Victoria Coulter
client
  Amwest Insurance Group, Inc.

creative firm
  Baker Designed
  Communications
  Santa Monica (California), USA
creative directors
  Gary Baker & Louis D'Esposito
designer
  Brian Keenan
client
  Dai-Ichi Kangyo Bank of California

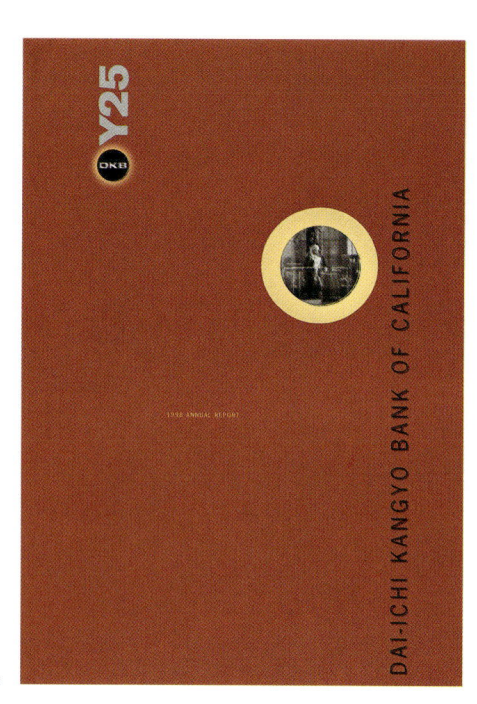

116

creative firm
  Advantage Ltd.
  Bermuda
art director
  Susan Tang Petersen
client
  XL Capital Ltd

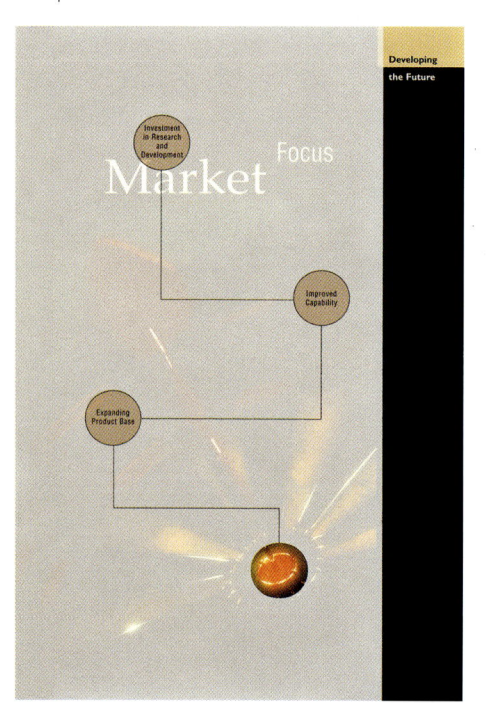

creative firm
  Little & Company
  Minneapolis (Minnesota), USA
client
  E.W. Blanch Holdings Inc.

creative firm
  The Leonhardt Group
  Seattle (Washington), USA
art directors
  Steve Watson & Jon King
designers
  Steve Watson & Ben Graham
client
  Washington Mutual, Inc.

creative firm
  Viadesign
    San Diego (California), USA
creative people
  Eric Schellhorn, Batton Lash,
  Stephan Donche, & Scott Pacheco
client
  Foodmaker

creative firm
  O'Mara & Ryan
    West Vancouver (British Columbia), Canada
creative people
  James O'Mara & Kate Ryan
client
  Vancouver Stock Exchange

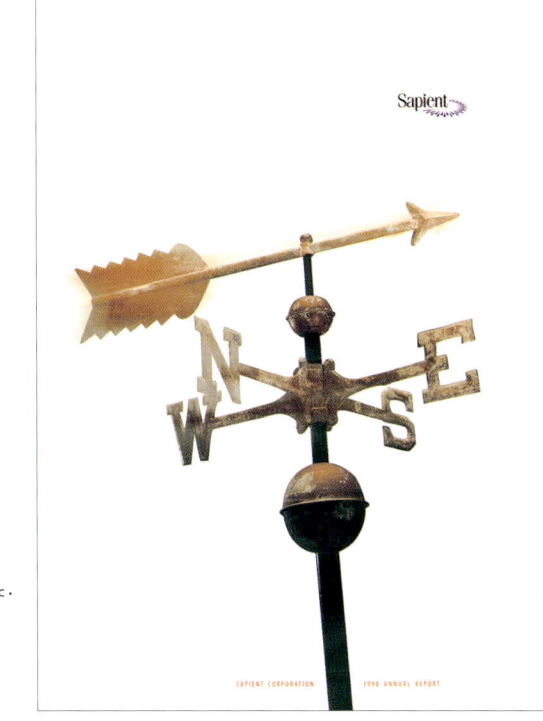

creative firm
  Cahan & Associates
    San Francisco (California), USA
art director
  Bill Cahan
designer
  Bob Dinetz
client
  General Magic

creative firm
  Gill Fishman Associates, Inc.
    Cambridge (Massachusetts), USA
creative director
  Gill Fishman
designer
  Michael Persons
client
  Sapient Corporation

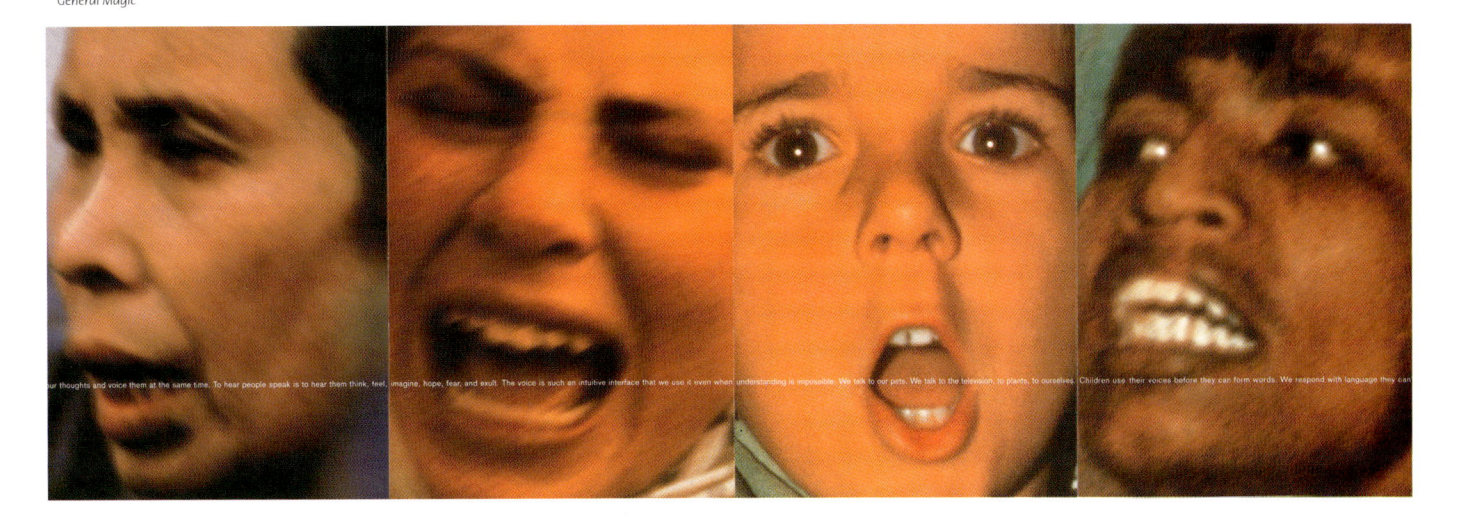

117

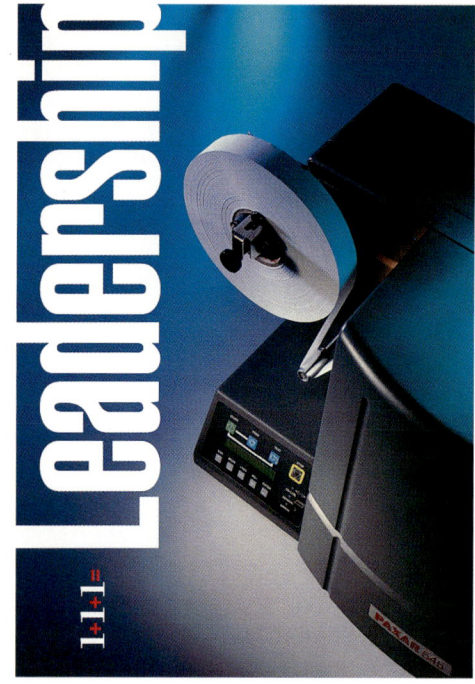

creative firm
 Epigram Pte Ltd
  Singapore
creative director
 Edmund Wee
designer
 Paul Van Der Veer
photographer
 Michael Bradfield
client
 National Computer Board

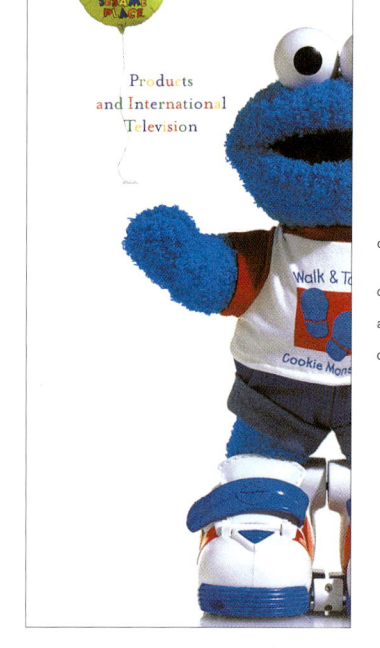

creative firm
 Taylor & Ives Incorporated
  New York (New York), USA
design director
 Ms. Alisa Zamir
designer
 Ms. Heidi Christian
client
 Paxar Corporation

creative firm
 Addison
  New York (New York), USA
creative director
 David Kohler
art director
 Anna Tan
client
 Children's Television Workshop

creative firm
 Emerson, Wajdowicz Studios
  New York (New York), USA
creative director
 Jurek Wajdowicz
designers
 Lisa LaRochelle & Jurek Wajdowicz
photographers
 Victor Mello & others
client
 United Nations Office for Project Services

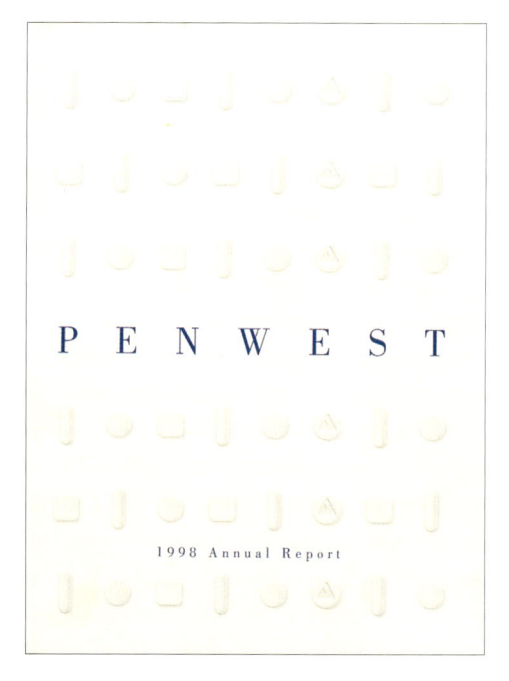

creative firm
 Taylor & Ives
  Incorporated
  New York (New York), USA
design director
 Ms. Alisa Zamir
senior designer
 Mr. Bruce Sugarman
client
 Penwest Pharmaceuticals Co.

118

creative firm
  **Leimer Cross Design**
  Seattle (Washington), USA
art director, designer
  *Kerry Leimer*
photographer
  *Jeff Corwin*
client
  *Microsoft*

creative firm
  **Pinkhaus**
  Miami (Florida), USA
creative director
  *Christopher Vice*
designer
  *Angie Smith*
production
  *Jack Nitowitz*
copywriter
  *Frank Cunningham*
client
  *Sun International Hotels Limited*

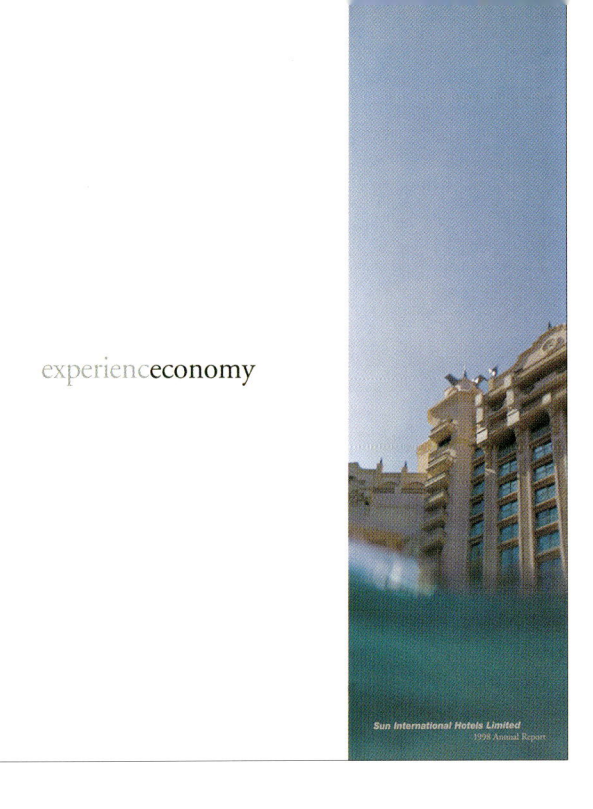

creative firm
  **Kompas Design**
  Ljubljana, Slovenia
designer
  *Matjaz Lazar*
photographer
  *Janet Puksic*
client
  *Iskra Autoelektrika*

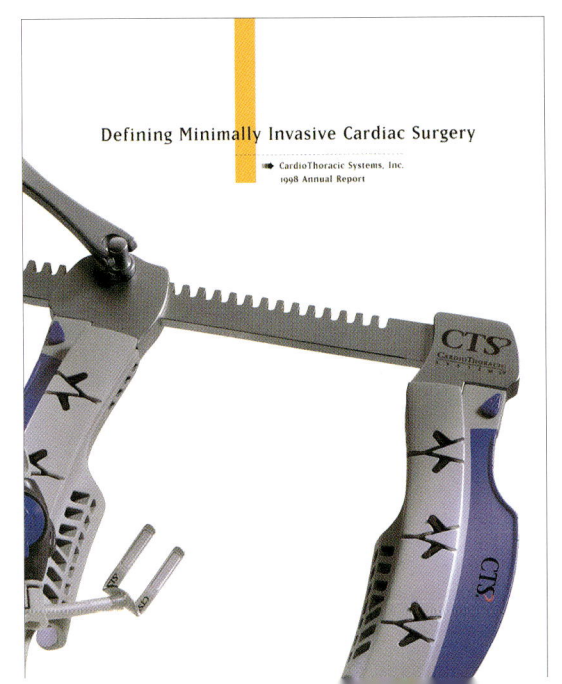

creative firm
  **The Graphic Expression, Inc.**
  New York (New York), USA
creative people
  *Stephen Ferrari & Monica Gotz*
client
  *CardioThoracic Systems, Inc.*

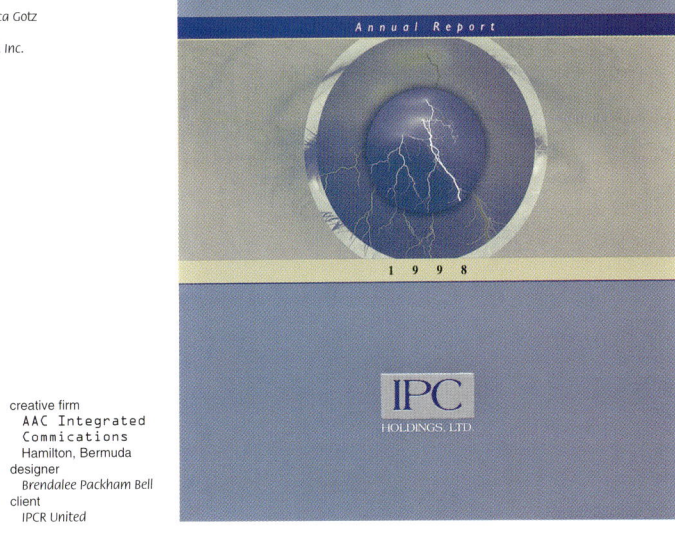

creative firm
  **AAC Integrated Commications**
  Hamilton, Bermuda
designer
  *Brendalee Packham Bell*
client
  *IPCR United*

Bigger. Better. Louder. That was how RadioFest '98 celebrated radio's vibrant role in Singapore. Once again, a month-long extravaganza was held to pay tribute to our listeners for their unstinting support. Launched on 2 Jul 98 at The Ritz Carlton, Radiofest '98 was certainly an event to remember.

creative firm
 Epigram Pte Ltd
  Singapore
creative director
 Edmund Wee
designers
 Beh Kay Yi & Paul Van Der Veer
photographers
 Russel Wong, Frank Pinckers,
 & others
client
 Radio Corporation of Singapore

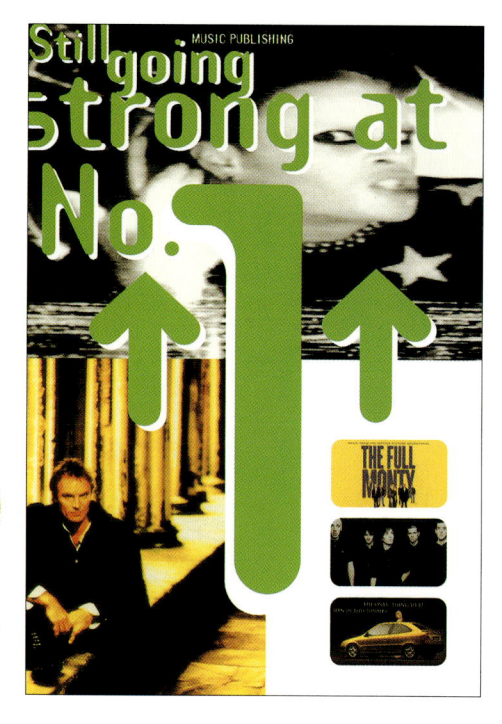

creative firm
 Tor Pettersen
 & Partners
  London, England
creative people
 Jeff Davis, Jim Allsopp,
 Tor Pettersen,
 & Craig Johnson
client
 The EMI Group

120

creative firm
 Addison
  New York (New York), USA
creative director
 David Kohler
art director
 Brian Cunningham
client
 GTECH Holdings Corp.

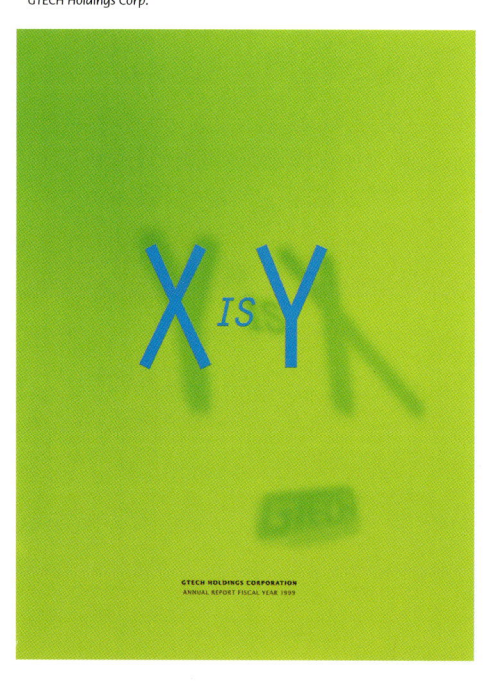

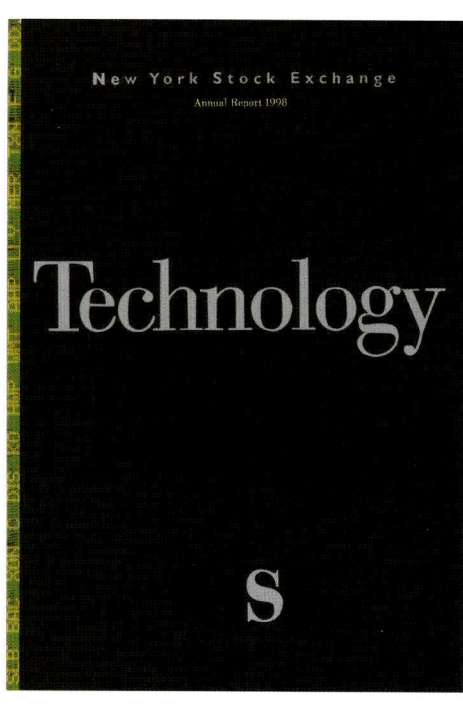

creative firm
 Taylor & Ives Incorporated
  New York (New York), USA
design director
 Ms. Alisa Zamir
senior designer
 Ms. Pamela Brooks
client
 New York Stock Exchange, Inc.

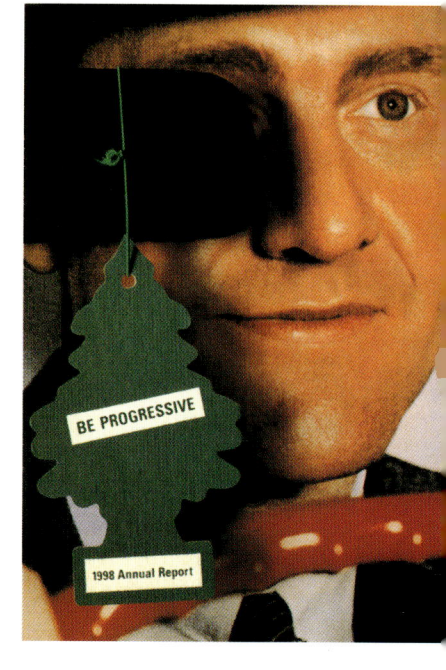

creative firm
 Nesnadny + Schwartz
  Cleveland (Ohio), USA
creative directors
 Mark Schwartz & Joyce Nesnadny
designers
 Joyce Nesnadny & Michelle Moehler
artist
 Stephen Frailey
client
 The Progressive Corporation

creative firm
 Paragraphs Design
  Chicago (Illinois), USA
creative people
 Scott Hickman & Robin Simon
client
 Peapod

creative firm
 Landor Associates
  New York (New York), USA
art director
 Richard Brandt
designers
 Martine Channon
 & Merel Matzinger
client
 Young & Rubicam

creative firm
 Liska + Associates, Inc.
  Chicago (Illinois), USA
art director
 Susanna Barrett
designer
 Aimee Sealfon
client
 Rainforest Alliance

121

creative firm
 Epigram Pte Ltd
  Singapore
creative director
 Edmund Wee
designer
 Jacke Tan
photographer
 Frank Pinckers
client
 Changi General Hospital

creative firm
 Douglas Joseph Partners
  Los Angeles (California), USA
art director
 Doug Joseph
designer
 Scott Lambert
copywriter
 Univision Communications Inc.
client
 Univision Communications Inc.

# 29 CREATIVITY

## Brochures

creative firm
 Emerson, Wajdowicz Studios
  New York (New York), USA
creative director
 Jurek Wajdowicz
designers
 Lisa LaRochelle & Jurek Wajdowicz
photographer
 Antonin Kratochvil
client
 Eddy Specialty Papers

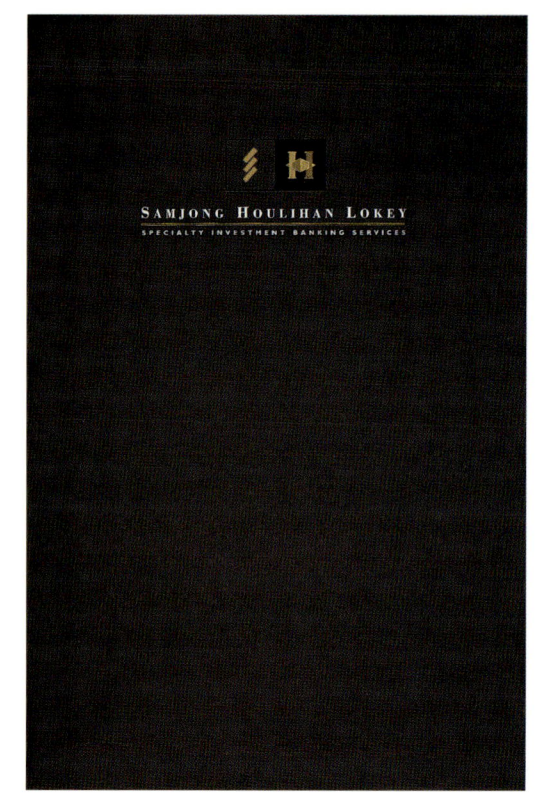

creative firm
 Julia Tam Design
  Palos Verdes (California), USA
art director
 Julia Tam
client
 Samjong Houlihan Lokey

creative firm
 Two Dimensions
  Toronto (Ontario), Canada
creative people
 Queenie Wu, Patrick Dinglesen,
 Yodo Lam & Kam Wai Yu
client
 Two Dimensions

122

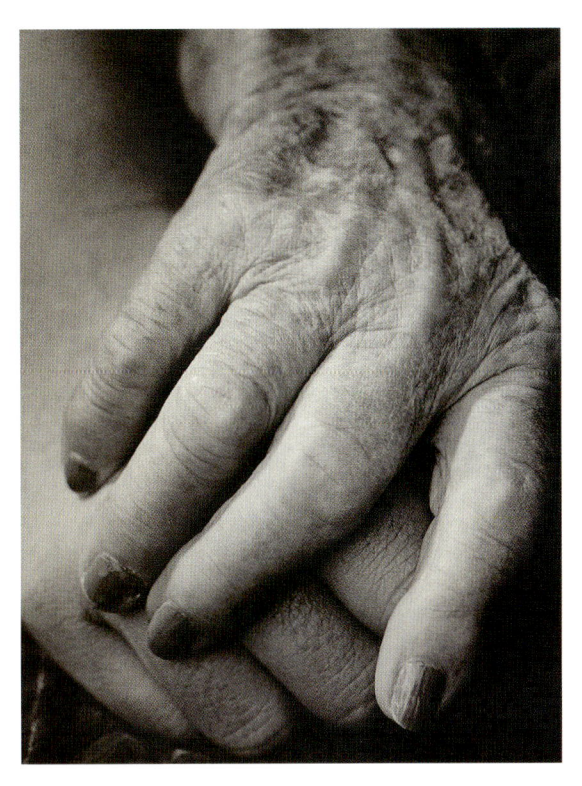

creative firm
 Disneyland Creative Services
  Anaheim (California), USA
creative director
 Scott Starkey
project managers
 Kevi Yoneda & Anthony Giangrande
photographer
 Walter Urie
copywriter
 Tony Serna
client
 Disneyland Community Affairs—Bill Ross

creative firm
 Levine and Associates
  Washington (D.C.), USA
creative people
 Monica Snellings
client
 APCO Worldwide

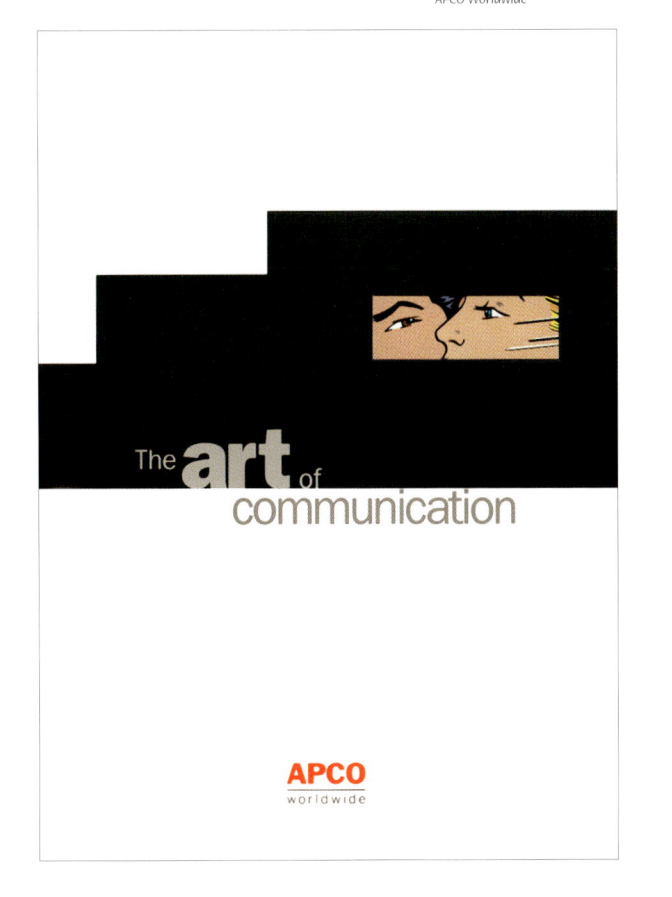

creative firm
 Louis Nelson
 Associates Inc.
  New York (New York), USA
creative people
 Jean Kaim, Louis Nelson,
 Katherine De Paul, & Krisa Briese
client
 Rocky Mountain Productions

creative firm
 Levine And Associates
  Washington (D.C.), USA
creative people
 John Vance, Lena Markley,
 Randi Wright, & Maggie Soldano
client
 Thomas A. Edison Preservation Foundation

123

creative firm
  Gallery Ltd
  Hong Kong, China
creative people
  Benny Cheng, Giles Tse,
  & Kelvin Parker
client
  Gallery Ltd

creative firm
  Fitting Kolbrener, Inc.
  Pittsburgh (Pennsylvania), USA
creative people
  Paul Schifino
client
  Adams Capital Management

124

creative firm
  Dye, Van Mol & Lawrence
  Nashville (Tennessee), USA
creative director
  Chuck Creasy
art director
  Kevin Hinson
client
  Saturn

creative firm
  Greenfield/Belser Ltd.
  Washington (D.C.), USA
creative director
  Burkey Belser
designer
  Tom Cameron
client
  Georgetown Day School

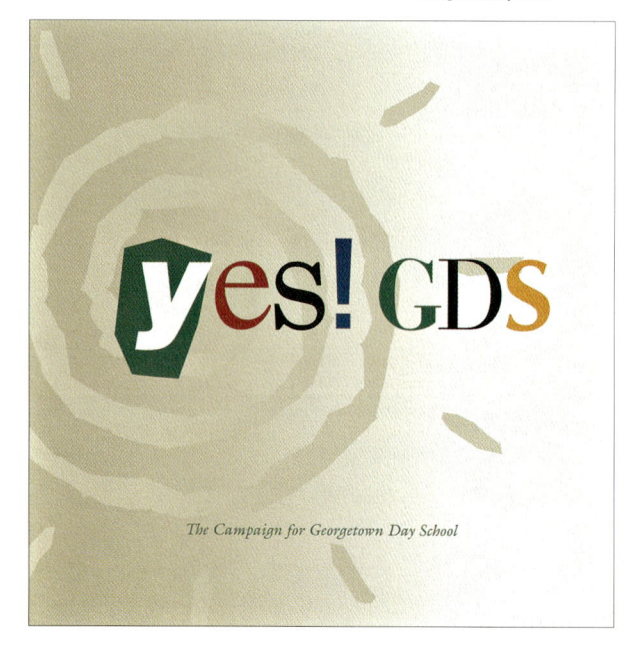

creative firm
  Besser Design Group, Inc.
    Santa Monica (California), USA
designer
  Rik Besser
illustrator
  Nicholas Wilton
client
  Georgia-Pacific Papers

creative firm
  Brad Norr Design
    Minneapolis (Minnesota), USA
art director
  Brad Norr
designers
  Brad Norr, Andrew Bessler, & Daniel Anderson
client
  FastFunds

creative firm
  Talbot Design Group
    Westlake Village (California), USA
creative director
  GayLyn Talbot
art director, designer
  Chris Kosman
client
  Bugle Boy

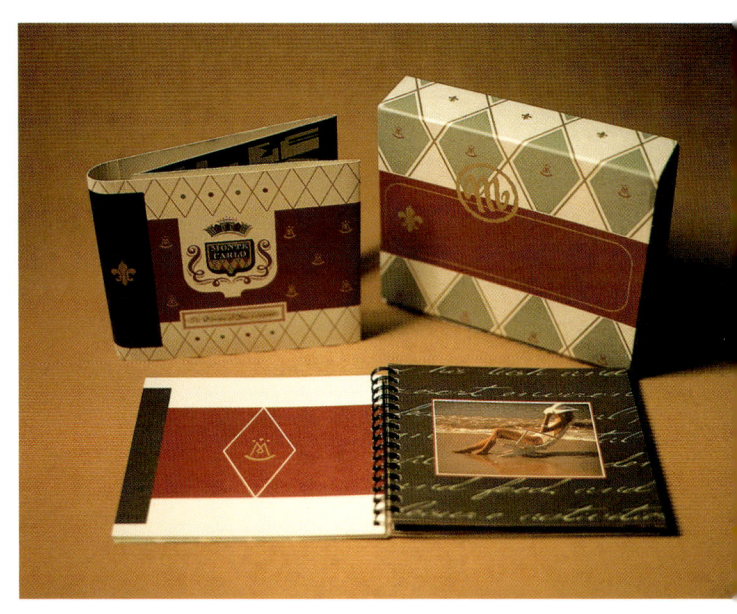

creative firm
  Sayles Graphic Design
    Des Moines (Iowa), USA
art director, designer
  John Sayles
copywriter
  Wendy Lyons
client
  Galileo International

creative firm
 Laura Coe Design Assoc
  San Diego (California), USA
creative director
 Laura Coe Wright
designer
 Leanne Leveillee
client
 Taylor Made Golf Co.

creative firm
 Greenfield/Belser Ltd.
  Washington (D.C.), USA
creative director
 Burkey Belser
designer
 Jeanette Nuzum
client
 Greenfield/Belser Ltd.

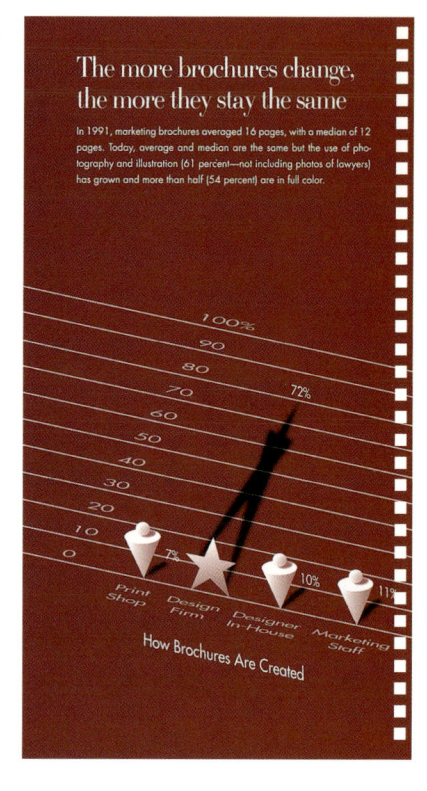

creative firm
 Dugan Valva Contess
  Morristown (New Jersey), USA
creative director
 Stephanie Murrin
art director
 Lisa D'Andrea
copywriter
 Bryan Minogue
client
 AT&T

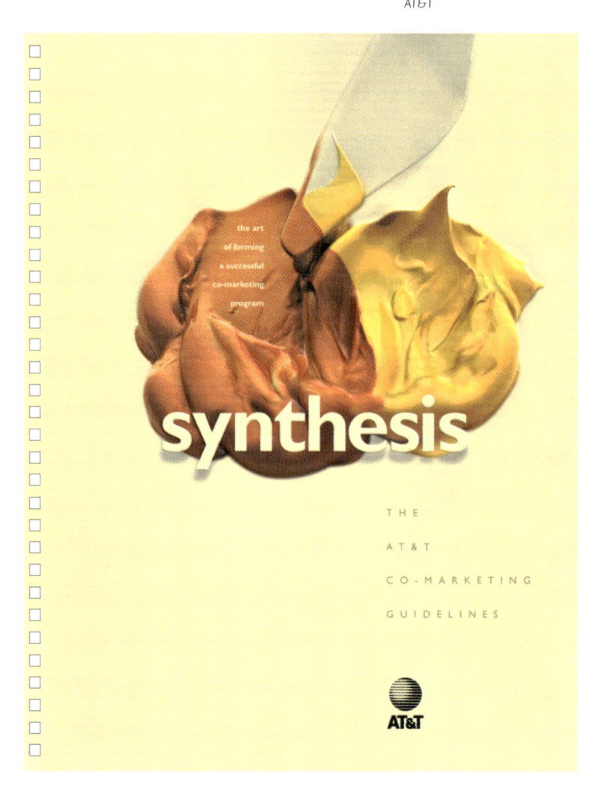

creative firm
 Epigram Pte Ltd
  Singapore
creative director
 Edmund Wee
designer
 Beh Kay Yi
photographer
 Siew Yaw Hoong
client
 Singapore Kerala Association

creative firm
 A to Z communications, inc.
  Pittsburgh (Pennsylvania), USA
graphic designer
 Ed Sutton
client
 Ketchum Pittsburgh

creative firm
 Design Narrative
  London, England
creative people
 Andy Ewan, Alison Beake,
 & Vibe Bangsgaard
client
 Business Lab

127

creative firm
 Mires Design, Inc.
  San Diego (California), USA
art director
 Scott Mires
designer
 Gale Spitzley
photographer
 Chris Wimpey
client
 Taylor Guitars

creative firm
 The Frasier/Bell Group
  Horsham (Pennsylvania), USA
creative director
 Ted Bell
art director, designer
 Bill Healey
copywriter
 Margaret Frasier
client
 Zanders USA

creative firm
  O&J Design, Inc.
  New York (New York), USA
art director
  Barbara Olejniczak
designers
  Christina Mueller & Heishin Ra
client
  Ogilvy & Mather, Inc.

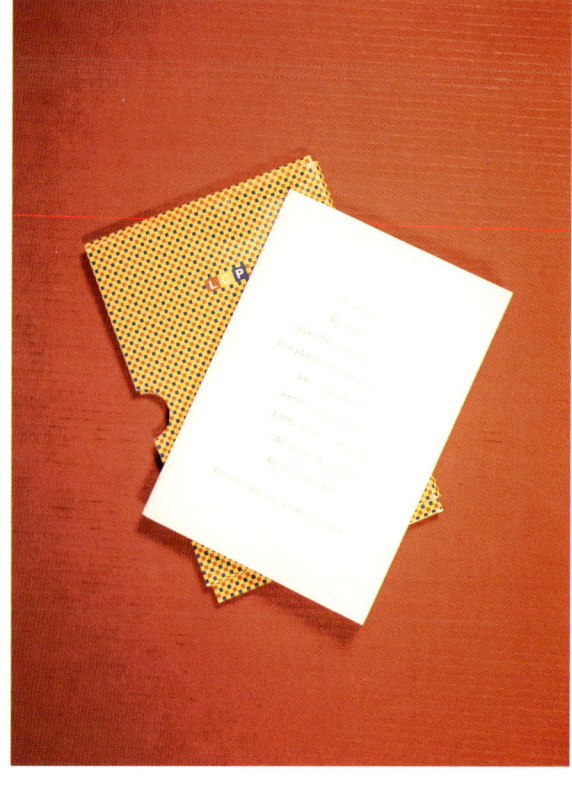

creative firm
  BBK Studio Inc.
  Grand Rapids (Michigan), USA
creative director
  Yang Kim
designers
  Yang Kim & Alison Popp
typesetter
  Alison Popp
client
  Lake County Press

128

creative firm
  Miller & White Advertising
  Terre Haute (Indiana), USA
art director
  Bill White
designers
  Jason Hertenstein & Dannielle Brayer
client
  D&S Investment

creative firm
  Lowe Fox Pavlika
  New York (New York), USA
creative people
  Deb Hiller, Paula Cunyus,
  & Carol Fiorino
client
  RCN

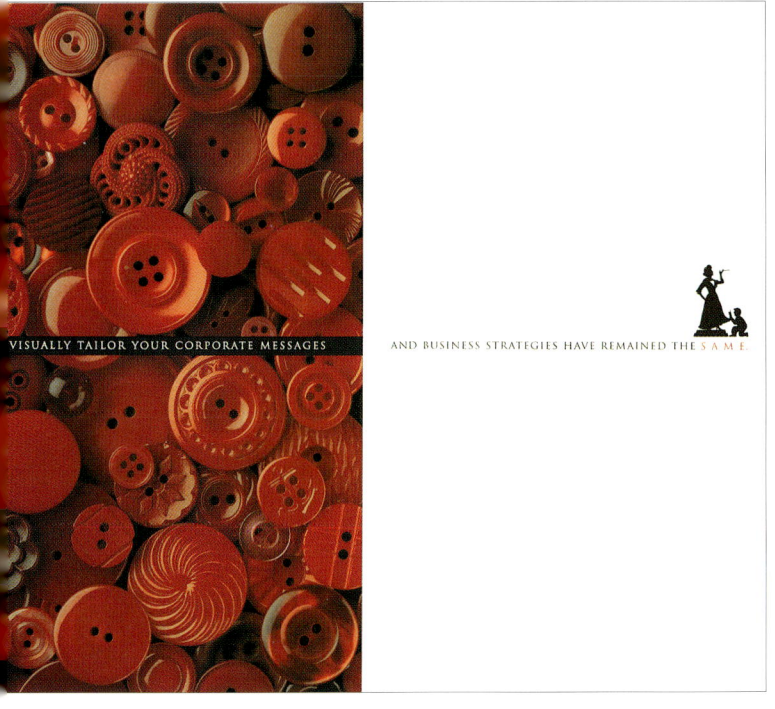

creative firm
  Taylor & Ives Incorporated
  New York (New York), USA
design director
  Ms. Alisa Zamir
designer
  Mr. Takaya Goto

creative firm
  Landor Associates
  New York (New York), USA
art director
  Martine Channon
designer
  Merel Matzinger
client
  Young & Rubicam

129

creative firm
  Louey/Rubino
  Design Group Inc.
  Santa Monica (California), USA
project manager
  Teresa E. Lopez
designer
  Robert Louey
client
  CAST Management Consultants, Inc.

creative firm
  Nolin Larosee
  Design Communications
  Montreal (Québec), Canada
art director
  Barbara Jacques
client
  Nolin Larosée Design Communications

creative firm
  **Lawrence, Mayo & Ponder**
  Newport Beach (California), USA
creative directors
  Lynda Lawrence & Bruce Mayo
art director
  Simone Beaudoin
designer
  Ellen Laning
client
  Lawrence, Mayo & Ponder

130

creative firm
  **Levine And Associates**
  Washington (D.C.), USA
creative people
  John Vance & Laura Latham
client
  National Air and Space Museum

creative firm
  **Kan & Lau Design Consultants**
  Hong Kong, China
creative director, art director, designer
  Kan Tai-keung
photographer
  C.K. Wong
computer illustrator
  Benson Kwun Tin Yau
client
  Kan & Lau Design Consultants

creative firm
  A to Z communications, inc.
  Pittsburgh (Pennsylvania), USA
graphic designer
  Aimee Lazer
client
  A to Z communications, inc.

creative firm
  SHR Perceptual Management
  Scottsdale (Arizona), USA
designer
  Christopher Nagle
client
  Innovative Thinking

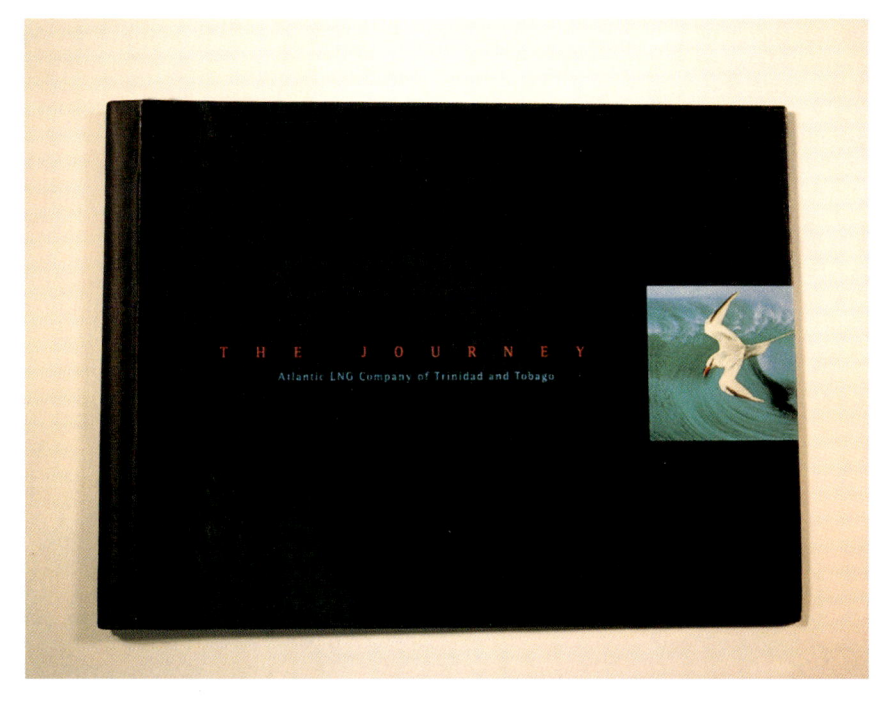

creative firm
  Lonsdale Saatchi & Saatchi Advertising Ltd
  Port of Spain, Trinidad
concept, copywriter
  Anna Walcott
art director
  Garby Woodham
client
  Atlantic LNG Company of Trinidad & Tobago

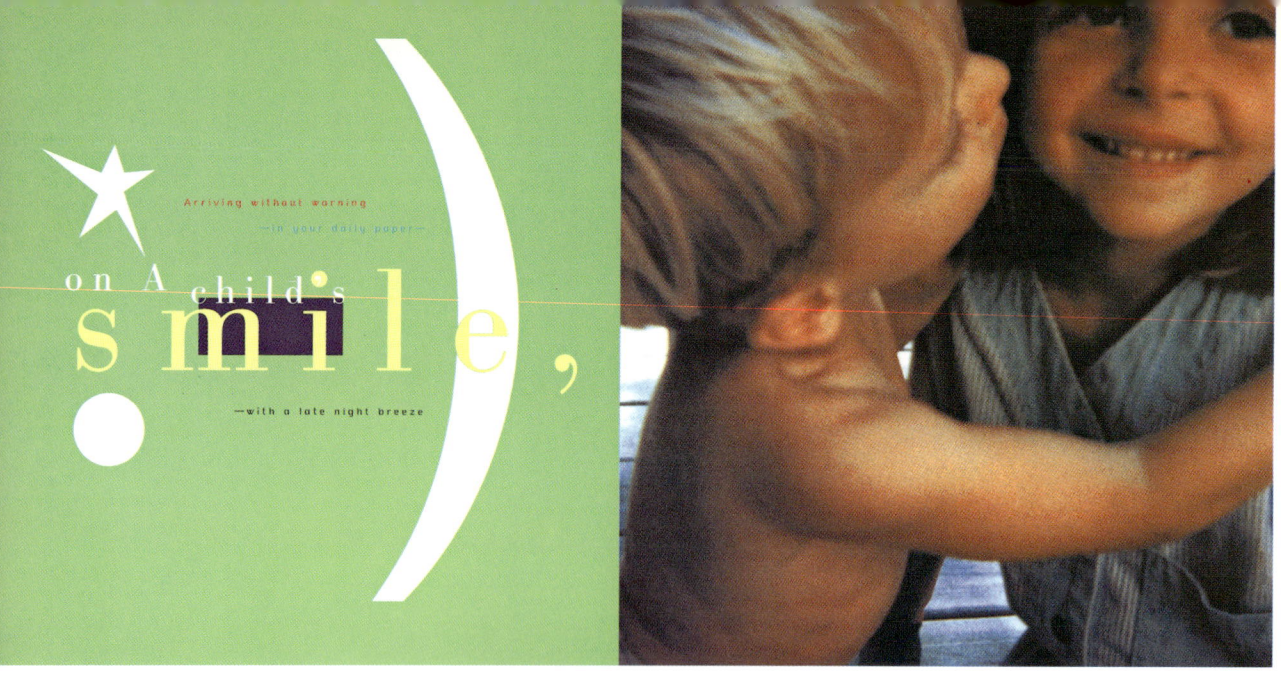

Arriving without warning
—in your daily paper—
on A child's smile,
—with a late night breeze

creative firm
 SrV Unlimited Design
  Darien (Illinois), USA

creative firm
 Watts Graphic Design
  South Melbourne (Victoria), Australia
creative people
 Helen Watts
client
 Specialist Cosmetic Laser Clinic

132

creative firm
 Addison
  New York (New York), USA
creative director
 David Kohler
art director
 Cindy Goldstein
client
 Burlington Industries, Inc.

NANTUCKET BAY
APARTMENTS

Where Dream Living Becomes a Reality

creative firm
 Media Concepts Corp.
  Assonet (Massachusetts), USA
designer
 Kim Noonan
copywriter
 Ed Parr
client
 Gatehouse Companies

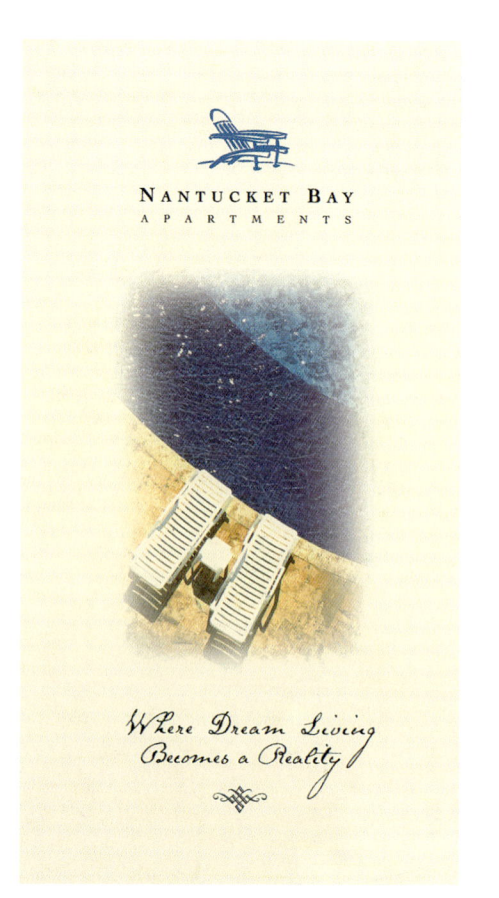

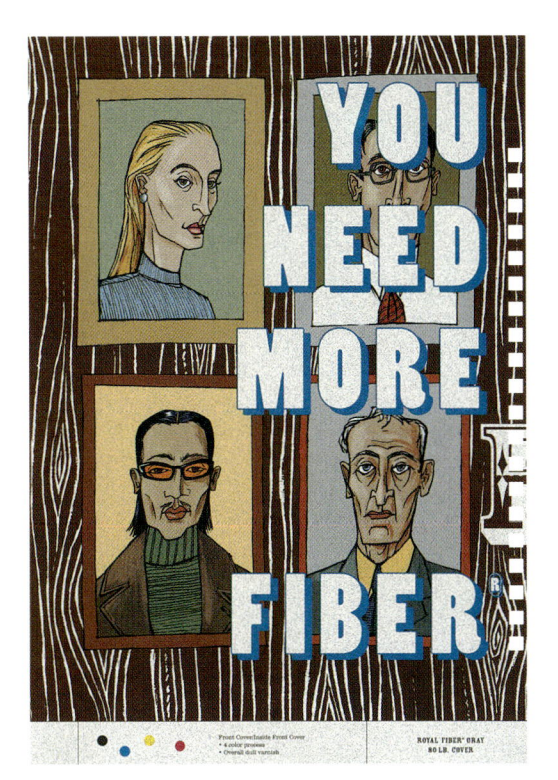

creative firm
  Little & Company
  Minneapolis (Minnesota), USA
client
  Wausau Papers

creative firm
  HDS Marcomm
  Santa Clara (California), USA
art director, designer
  Gayle T. Ono
copywriter
  Seema Khan
client
  Hitachi Data Systems

creative firm
  Besser Design Group
  Santa Monica (California), USA
designer
  Rik Besser
illustrator
  Sudi McCollum
client
  Georgia-Pacific Papers

creative firm
  Jones Studio Limited
  New York (New York), USA
creative people
  Eric Jones & Pui-Pui Li
client
  M2L Inc.

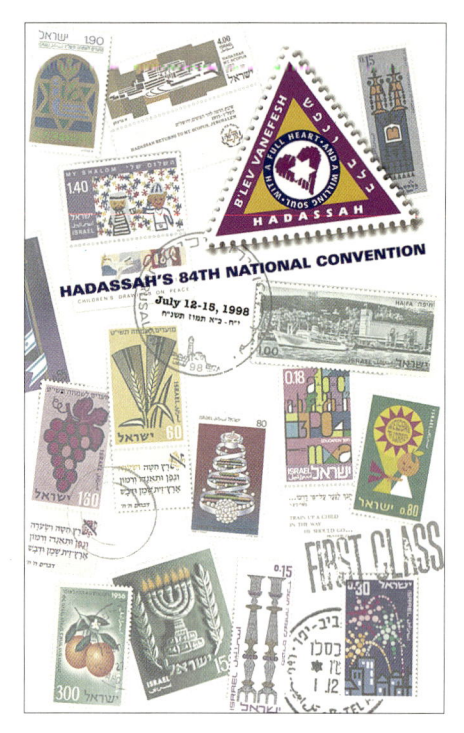

creative firm
  Hadassah Creative
  Services
  New York (New York), USA
creative director
  Michael Cohen
designer
  Irit Hadari
client
  Hadassah Convention
  Department

creative firm
  Malcolm Waddell
  Assoc. Ltd.
  Toronto (Ontario), Canada
creative people
  Bryan Canning, Gary Mansbridge,
  & Malcolm Waddell
client
  Canada Post Corporation

134

creative firm
  Love Packaging Group
  Wichita (Kansas), USA
creative people
  Rick Gimlin, Dustin Commer,
  Lorna McNeill, & Chris West
client
  Love Packaging Group

creative firm
  Leslie Evans Design Associates
  Portland (Maine), USA
art director, designer
  Tom Hubbard
client
  Mariposa

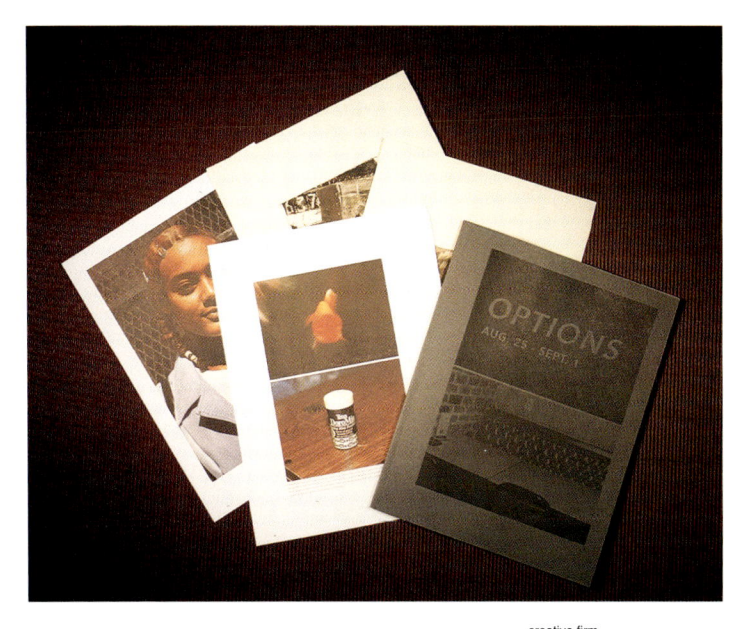

creative firm
 Parham Santana Inc.
  New York (New York), USA
creative director
 William Snyder
art director, designer
 Ann Sappenfield
design services
 Peter Aguanno (Rainbow Programming)
 & Rosie Pisani (Rainbow Programming)
client
 American Movie Classic

creative firm
 Cahan & Associates
  San Francisco (California), USA
art director
 Bill Cahan
designers
 Bob Dinetz & Kevin Roberson
client
 Mohawk Paper Mills

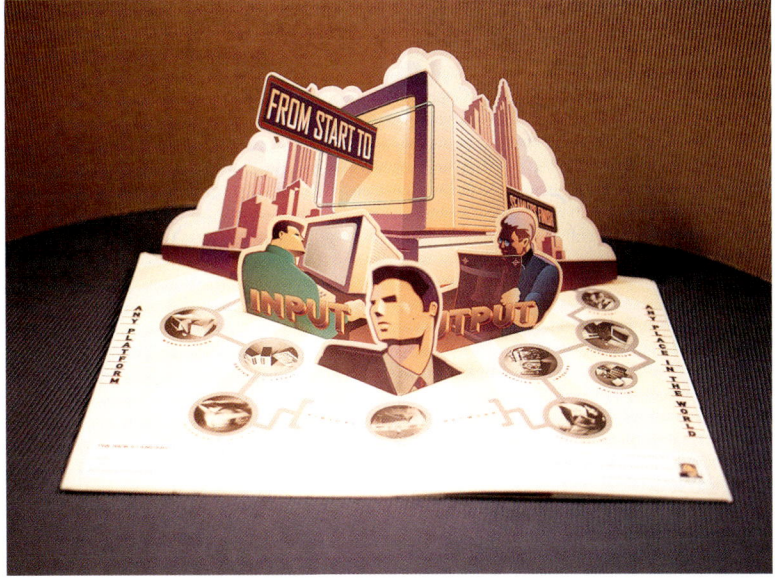

135

creative firm
 DBD International
  Menomonie (Wisconsin), USA
creative director, art director,
designer, copywriter
 David Brier
client
 Digital Minds

creative firm
 CadmusCom
  Richmond (Virginia), USA
designer
 Susan M. Walsh
client
 Mattel/2wo One 2wo

creative firm
 Liska + Associates, Inc.
  Chicago (Illinois), USA
art director
 Marcos Chavez
designer
 Susanna Barrett
client
 modern organic products

136  the most basic organic preparations are often the most effective

creative firm
 BBK Studio Inc.
  Grand Rapids (Michigan), USA
creative director, designer
 Kevin Budelmann
editor
 Dick Holm
photographers
 Nick Merrick & Bob Neumann
illustrator
 Phillipe Weisbecker (Gould Design)
copywriter
 Kate Convissor
client
 Herman Miller

creative firm
 Communication Design Corporation
  Honolulu (Hawaii), USA
creative director, copywriter
 Howard J. Wolff
art director
 Kunio Hayashi
designers
 Kunio Hayashi, Yoko Inui,
 Fred O. Bechlen, & Joy Matsuura
client
 Wimberly Allison Tong & Goo

creative firm
 Little & Company
  Minneapolis (Minnesota), USA
client
 Wausau Papers

creative firm
　The Wyant Simboli Group, Inc.
　　Norwalk (Connecticut), USA
creative people
　Julia Wyant, Karen Olenski, Sheri Cifaldi,
　Paul Neel, & Lance Hertzbach
client
　　GE Capital

creative firm
　　Bellini Design
　　　Oak Brook (Illinois), USA
creative director
　　Eugene Bellini
designer
　　Jeffrey Gallo
client
　　　Consolidated Papers, Inc.

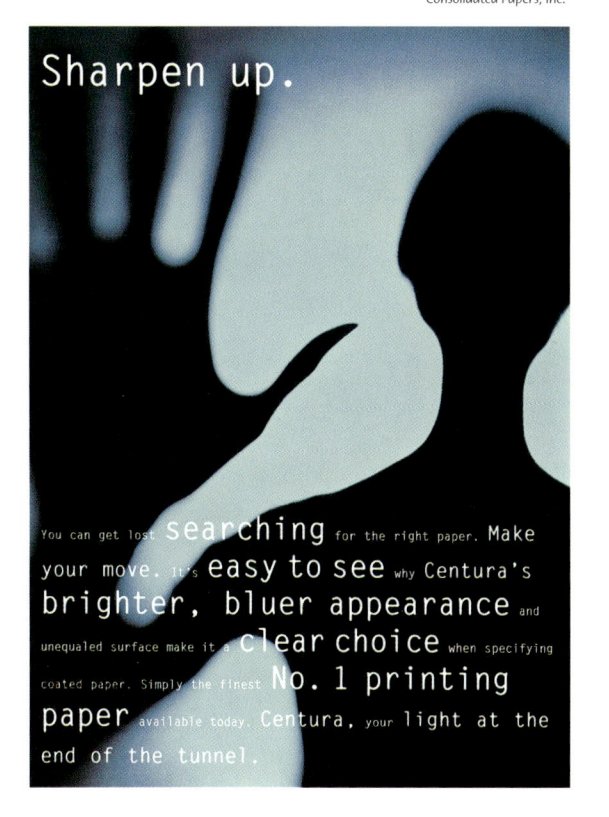

creative firm
　Emerson, Wajdowicz Studios
　　New York (New York), USA
creative director
　Jurek Wajdowicz
designers
　Lisa LaRochelle, Jurek Wajdowicz,
　& Manny Mendez
photographer
　Gueorgui Pinkhassov
client
　Eddy Specialty Papers

creative firm
　　Alan Herman & Associates
　　　Pasadena (California), USA
art director
　　Alan Herman
designer
　　Lee Schamadan
illustrator
　　Chris Gall
client
　　Marwit Capital

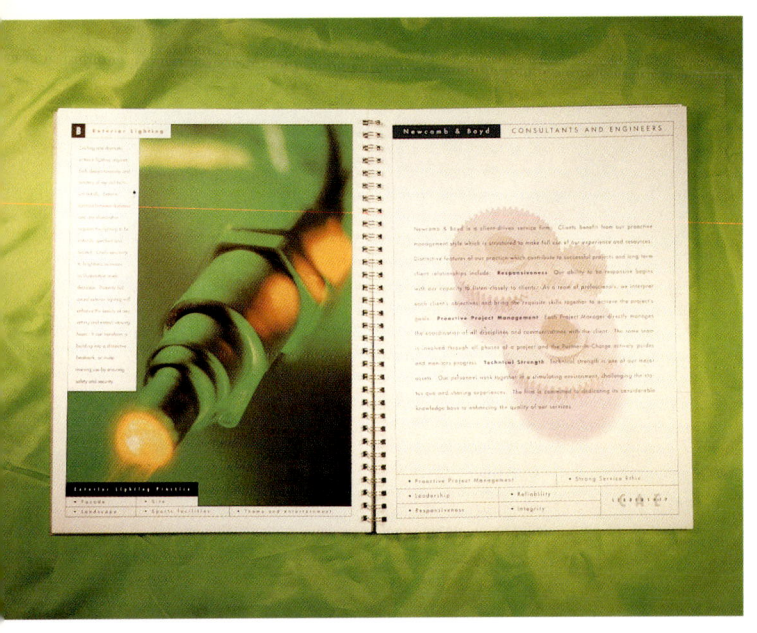

creative firm
 Deep Design
 Atlanta (Georgia), USA
designer
 Rick Grimsley
photographer
 Jerry Burns
client
 Newcomb & Boyd

creative firm
 Braindance
 Atlanta (Georgia), USA
creative people
 Cindy Beebe, Blake Parkman,
 & Tom Wood
client
 Braindance

138

creative firm
 Visual Marketing Associates
 Dayton (Ohio), USA
art directors
 Lynn Sampson & Ken Botts
designer
 Lynn Sampson
photographer
 AGI Photographic Inc.
client
 Visual Marketing Associates

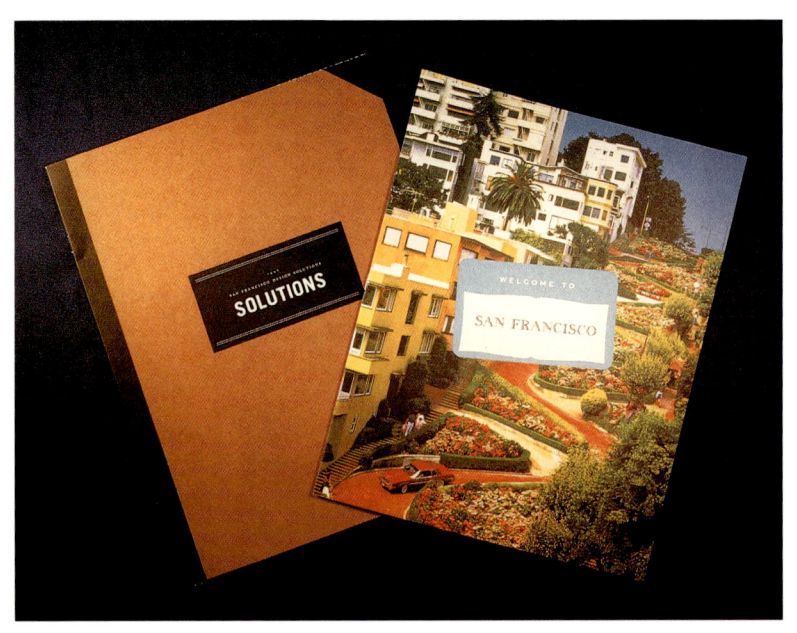

creative firm
 Cahan & Associates
 San Francisco (California), USA
art director
 Bill Cahan
designer
 Kevin Roberson
client
 Bay Area World Trade Center

creative firm
　James Robie Design Associates
　　Los Angeles (California), USA
art directors
　James Robie & Wayne Fujita
designer
　Wayne Fujita
photographer
　Henry Blackham
client
　James Robie Design Associates

creative firm
　Phinney/Bischoff
　Design House
　　Seattle (Washington), USA
art director
　Leslie Phinney
designer
　Cody Rasmussen
copywriter
　Christopher Hughes
client
　Avandel

139

creative firm
　Shari Finger Design
　　Rye (New York), USA
designer
　Shari Finger
illustrator
　Nikolai Punin
copywriter
　Susan Smith
client
　Ortho Biotech

creative firm
　Douglas Joseph Partners
　　Los Angeles (California), USA
art director
　Doug Joseph
designer
　Julie Mellen
client
　3D Systems

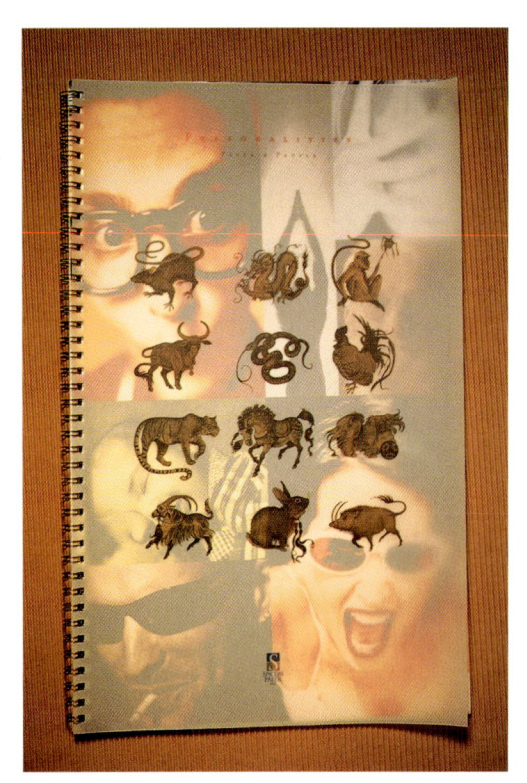

creative firm
  Martin Design Associates
   Los Angeles (California), USA
art director, designer
  Scott Lambert
copywriter
  Ceebs Baily
client
  Spicers Paper

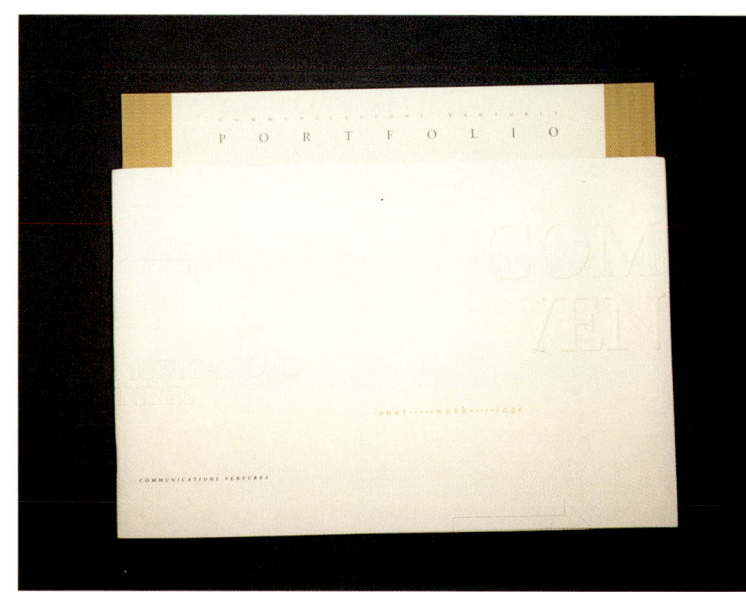

140

creative firm
  Gee + Chung Design
   San Francisco (California), USA
art director
  Earl Gee
designers
  Earl Gee & Fani Chung
photographer
  Scott Peterson
client
  Communications Ventures

creative firm
  Up Design
   Montclair (New Jersey), USA
art director
  Gary Underhill
designer
  Wendy Peters
client
  America's Promise—
  The Alliance for Youth

creative firm
  Sackett Design Associates
   San Francisco (California), USA
creative director
  Mark Sackett
designers
  James Sakamoto, Wendy Wood, & George White
photographers
  Michal Venera & Catherine Buchanan
client
  San Francisco International Airport

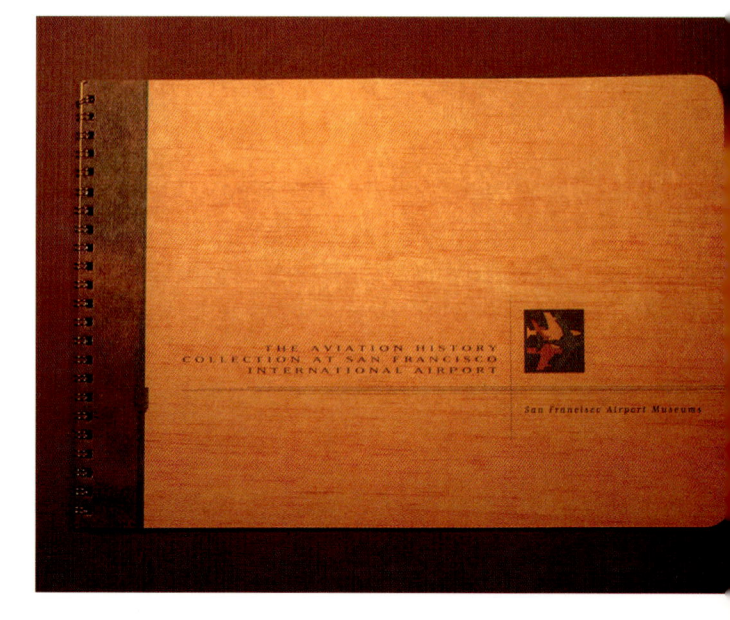

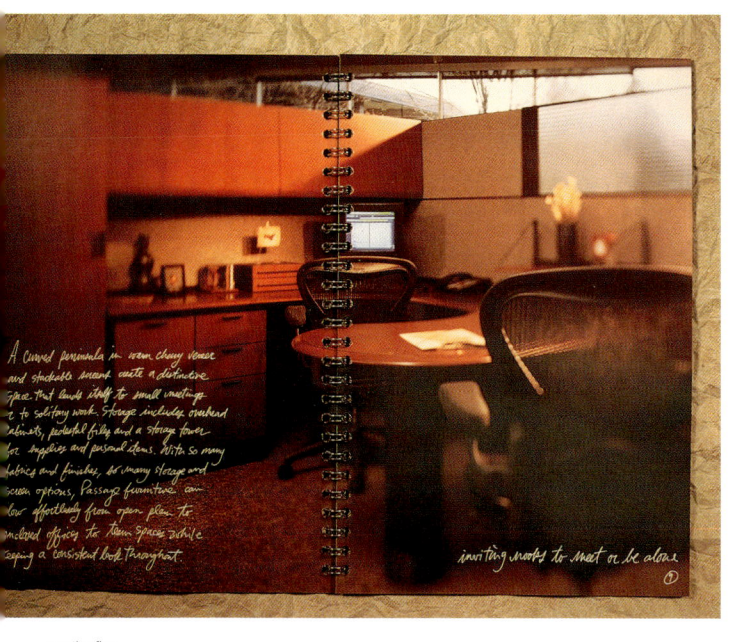

creative firm
 BBK Studio Inc.
  Grand Rapids (Michigan), USA
art director, designer, illustrator
 Kevin Budelmann
editor
 Dick Holm
photographer
 Bob Neumann
copywriter
 Kate Convissor
client
 Herman Miller

creative firm
 Kinggraphic
  Hong Kong, China
creative director
 Hon Bing-wah
designers
 Hon Bing-wah & Sunny Lee
client
 The Hong Kong Printers Association

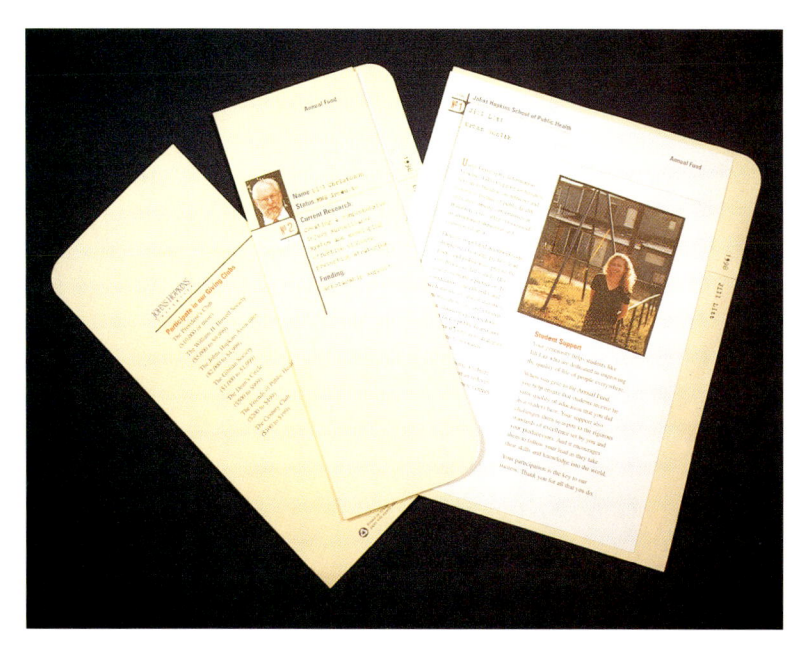

141

creative firm
 Blank—Robert Kent Wilson
  Washington (D.C.), USA
creative people
 Robert Kent Wilson & Adam Cohn
client
 Johns Hopkins University

creative firm
 Hornall Anderson
 Design Works
  Seattle (Washington), USA
creative people
 Jack Anderson, Jana Nishi,
 & Mary Chin Hutchison
client
 Inference Corporation

creative firm
 John Kneapler Design
  New York (New York), USA
creative people
 John Kneapler & Christopher Dietrich
client
 World Financial Properties

creative firm
 Richland Design Associates
  Newton (Massachusetts), USA
art director
 Judith Richland
designers
 Douglas Fortado & Christine Jorge
client
 Investext

creative firm
 Gill Fishman Associates, Inc.
  Cambridge (Massachusetts), USA
creative director
 Gill Fishman
designer
 Michael Persons
photographer
 Bill Truslow
client
 Sapient Corporation

creative firm
  Marion Graphics, L.C.
    Houston (Texas), USA
client
  Baylor College of Medicine

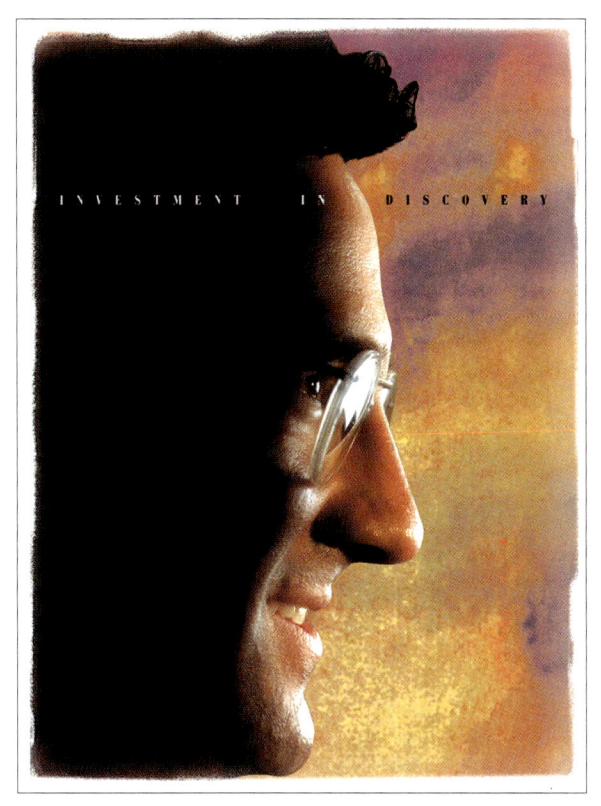

creative firm
  degree inc.
    Osaka, Japan
art director
  Nakanishi Yusaka
designer
  Matsumoto Fumiko
client
  Yoshindo

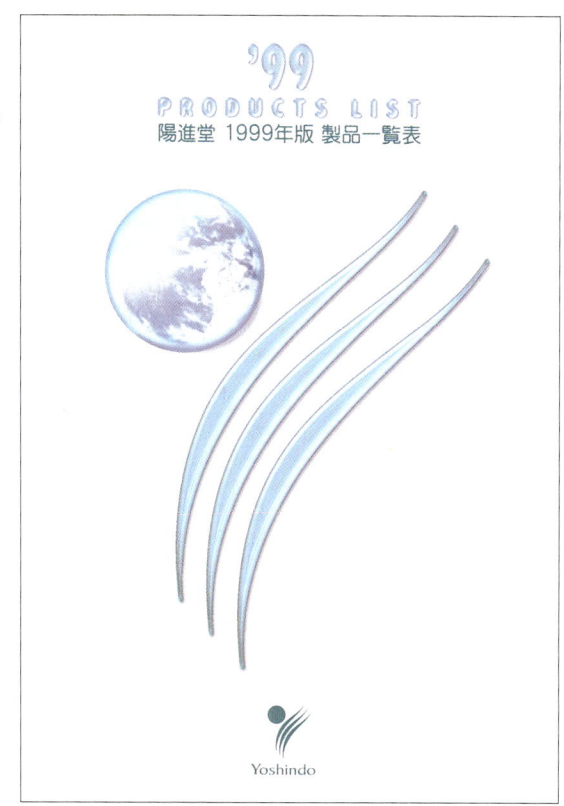

creative firm
  Metzler & Associes
    Paris, France
creative people
  M.A. Herrmann & A. Martiréné
client
  Metzler & Associés

creative firm
  Burrows WCJ
    Shenfield (Essex), England
creative director, copywriter
  Bob Ashwood
art director
  Phil Sutton
client
  Ford Motor Company Ltd.

creative firm
 Interbrand
 Gerstman + Meyers
 New York (New York), USA
creative people
 Juan Concepcion & Melissa Mullin
client
 Interbrand Gerstman + Meyers

creative firm
 Colestudio
 Sebastopol (California), USA
designer
 Michael Cole
photographer
 Bob Stender
painter
 Mark Perlman
client
 Mark Perlman

144

creative firm
 Jones Studio Limited
 New York (New York), USA
creative people
 Pui-Pui Li & Mikio Sekita
client
 Flos USA

creative firm
 WPA Pinfold Ltd
 Leeds, England
creative people
 Andy Probert, Phil Morrison,
 Myles Pinfold, & Richard Hurst
client
 Linpac Group

creative firm
  Michael Orr + Associates, Inc.
  Corning (New York), USA
creative people
  Michael R. Orr, Thomas Freeland, & Gregory Duell
client
  Allsteel

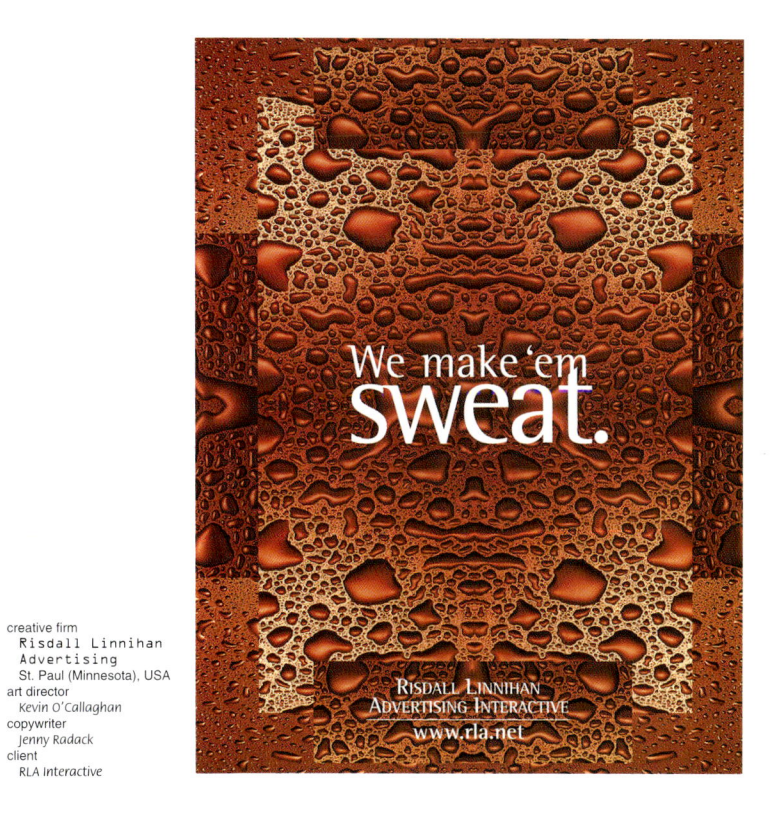

creative firm
  Risdall Linnihan Advertising
  St. Paul (Minnesota), USA
art director
  Kevin O'Callaghan
copywriter
  Jenny Radack
client
  RLA Interactive

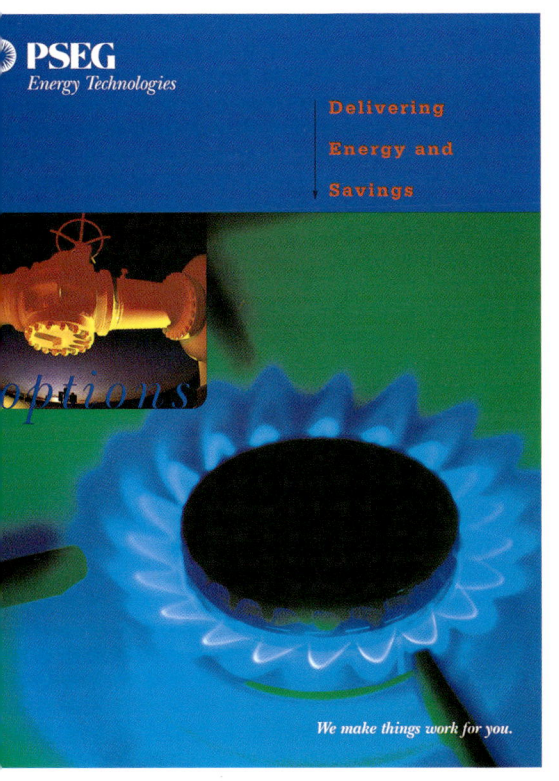

145

creative firm
  Up Design, Inc.
  Montclair (New Jersey), USA
art director
  Gary Underhill
designer
  Carin Manetti
client
  PSE&G

creative firm
  Brian J. Ganton & Associates
  Cedar Grove (New Jersey), USA
art director
  Brian Ganton, Jr.
designer
  Mark Ganton
photographer
  Chris Ganton
copywriter
  Brian Ganton, Sr.
client
  Calico Cottage, Inc.

creative firm
 Besser Design Group
  Santa Monica (California), USA
art director
 Rik Besser
designer
 Kathleen Lamphere
photographer
 Knaver Johnston
copywriter
 Margaret Burger
client
 Windstar Cruises

creative firm
 KPR
  New York (New York), USA
creative people
 John Dietz, Carl Gluck, Paul Weiss,
 Jen Chin, & Ted Whitby
client
 Pastuer Mérieux Connaught

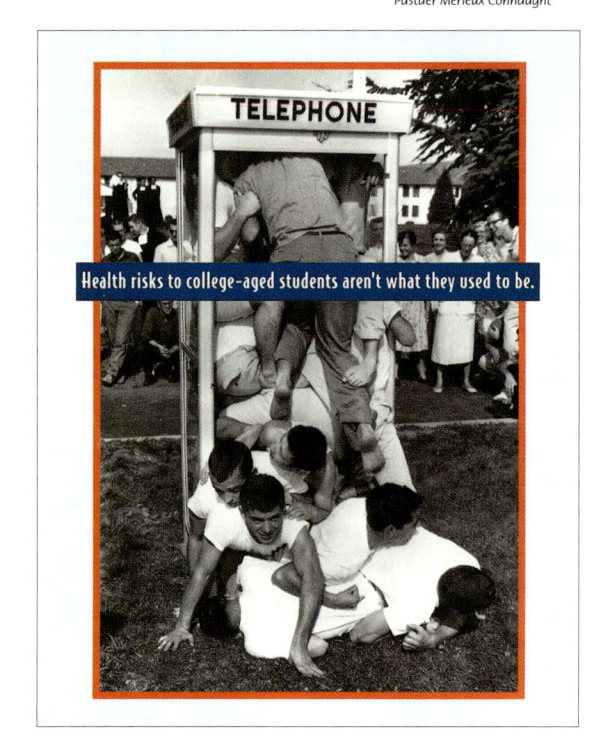

Health risks to college-aged students aren't what they used to be.

146

creative firm
 The Traver Company
  Seattle (Washington), USA
creative people
 Hugh Rodman, Dale Hart,
 & Anne Traver
client
 Iridio

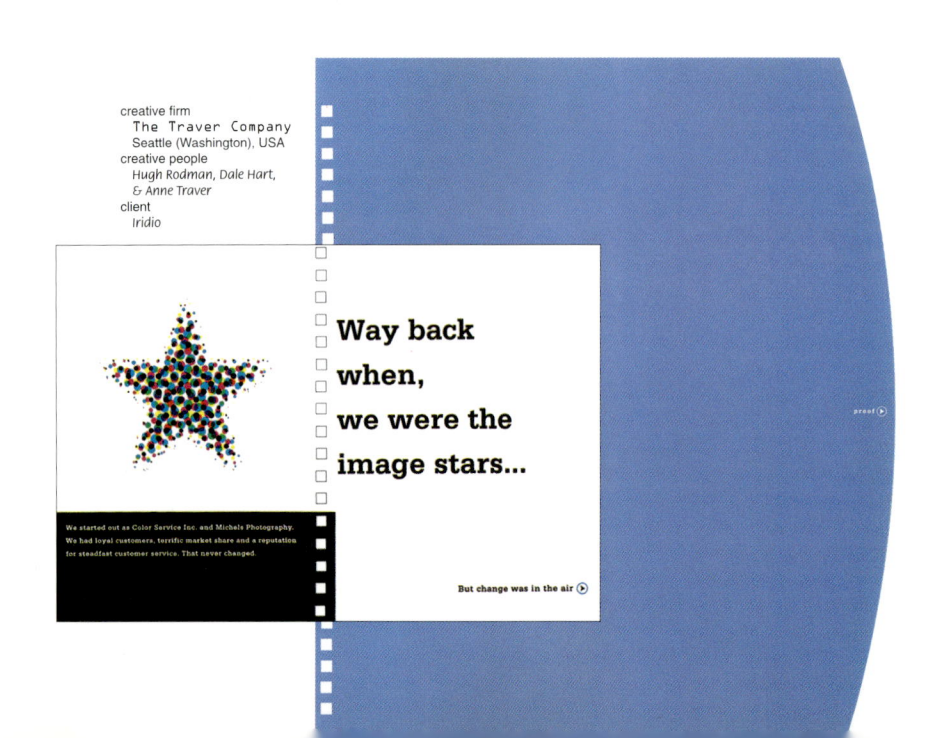

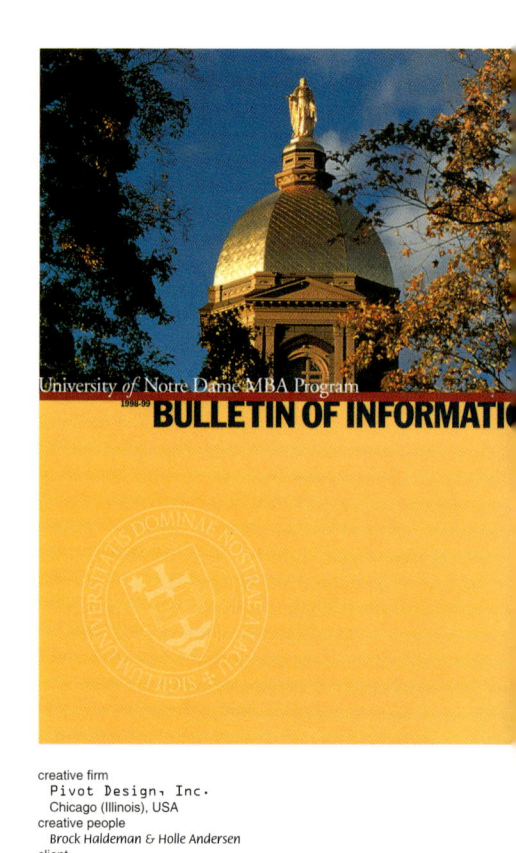

Way back when, we were the image stars...

We started out as Color Service Inc. and Michels Photography. We had loyal customers, terrific market share and a reputation for steadfast customer service. That never changed.

But change was in the air

University of Notre Dame MBA Program
1998-99
BULLETIN OF INFORMATION

creative firm
 Pivot Design, Inc.
  Chicago (Illinois), USA
creative people
 Brock Haldeman & Holle Andersen
client
 University of Notre Dame

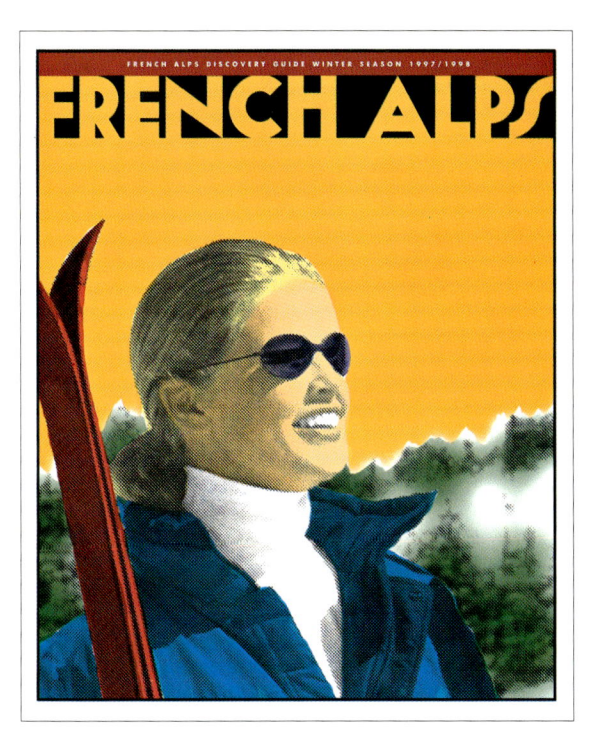

creative firm
 Pivot Design, Inc.
  Chicago (Illinois), USA
creative people
 Brock Haldeman, Tim Hogan,
 & Tracy West
client
 French Government Tourist Office

creative firm
 Faschingbauer & Schaar
  Graz, Austria
creative people
 Siegfred Faschingbauer,
 Dieter Faschingbauer, & Roberto Grill
client
 Jugend Am Werk Steiermark

147

creative firm
 Group C Design
  St. Louis (Missouri), USA
creative people
 Benjamin Franklin
client
 Price Waterhouse Coopers

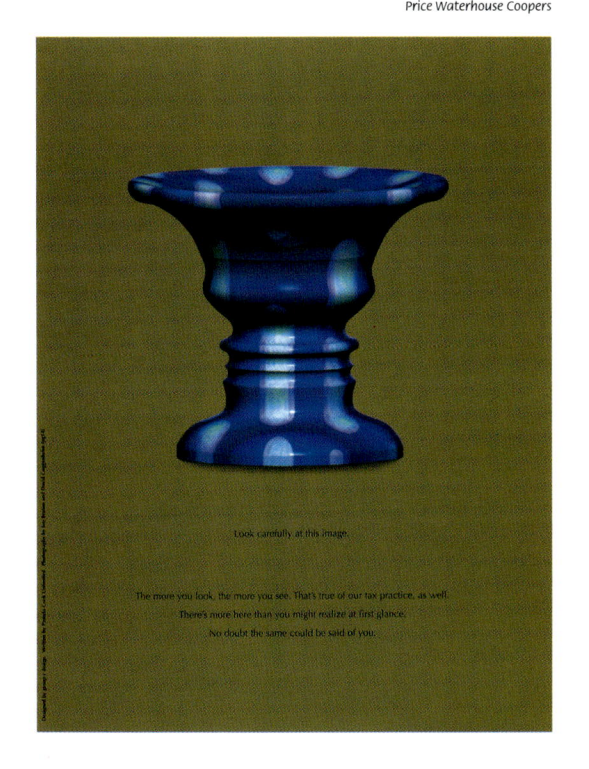

creative firm
 Amy Neiman Design
  Berkeley (California), USA
creative people
 Amy Neiman
client
 INCA (International Nature
 & Cultural Adventures)

creative firm
**Fairly Painless Advertising**
Holland (Michigan), USA
creative director, copywriter
Peter Bell
art director, designer
Brian Hauch
client
Herman Miller

creative firm
**Fader Unda Sohn**
New York (New York), USA
client
Todd Haiman Studio

148

creative firm
**Cahan & Associates**
San Francisco (California), USA
art director
Bill Cahan
designer
Sharrie Brooks
client
Sharpe & Associates

creative firm
**Cahan & Associates**
San Francisco (California), USA
art director
Bill Cahan
designer
Ben Pham
client
Zeum

creative firm
　Cahan & Associates
　　San Francisco (California), USA
art director
　Bill Cahan
designer
　Sharrie Brooks
client
　Sharpe & Associates

creative firm
　Fairly Painless
　Advertising
　　Holland (Michigan), USA
creative director
　Peter Bell
art directors
　Steve Frykholm, Brian Hauch,
　& Tom Crimp
designer
　Brian Hauch
photographer
　Rodney Smith
copywriter
　Clark Malcolm
client
　Herman Miller

creative firm
　McCann-Erickson Korea Inc.
　　Seoul, Korea
creative director
　Jeremy Perrott
art directors
　S.Y. Kim & G.Y. Ahn
designer
　S.W. Choi
copywriter
　W.H. Kim
client
　Levi's Korea

**AT&T, EAT YOUR HEART OUT**

creative firm
　DBD International
　　Menomonie (Wisconsin), USA
creative director,
designer, copywriter
　David Brier
client
　DBD International

creative firm
 DHI
  Vero Beach (Florida), USA
creative people
 Marty Regan
client
 ComEd

creative firm
 Artefact Design
  Palo Alto (California), USA
creative people
 Artefact Design
client
 Geoffrey Nelson

150

creative firm
 Hornall Anderson Design Works
  Seattle (Washington), USA
creative people
 Jack Anderson, Larry Anderson, Mary Hermes,
 Mary Chin Hutchison, & Taro Sakita
client
 TechnoGym, USA Corp

creative firm
 Paragraphs Design
  Chicago (Illinois), USA
creative people
 Scott Hickman & Rachel Radtke
client
 CSC

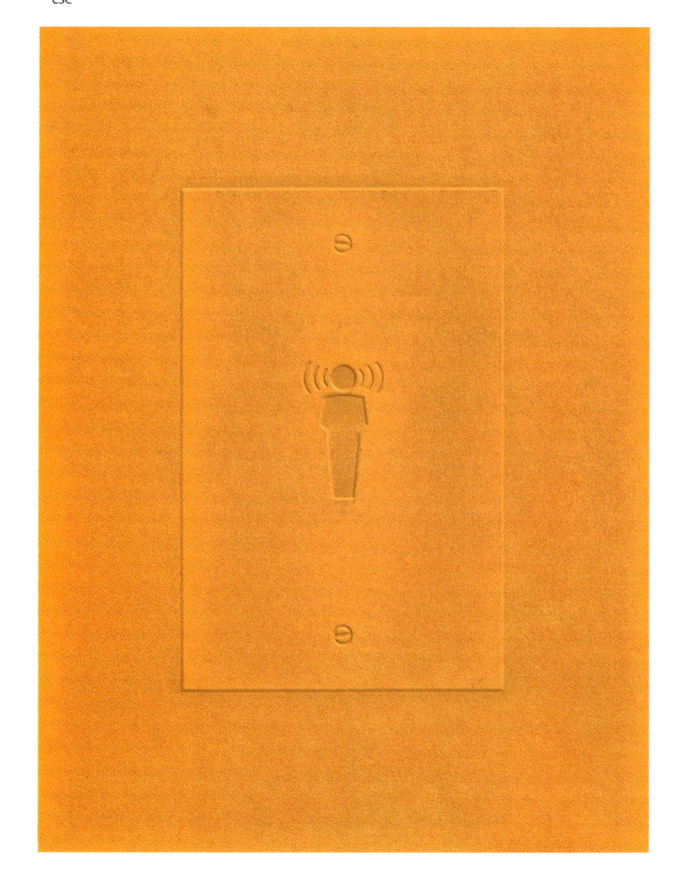

creative firm
 Wages Design
  Atlanta (Georgia), USA
creative people
 Randy Allison
client
 Cadmus

creative firm
 The Benchmark Group
  Cincinnati (Ohio), USA
creative people
 John Forsythe, Jen O'Shea,
 Lesli Hall, & Dave Heithaus
client
 Cincinnati Ballet

creative firm
 Laura Coe Design Assoc
  San Diego (California), USA
creative director
 Laura Coe Wright
designer
 Ryoichi Yotsumoto
client
 Taylor Made Golf Co.

151

creative firm
 Pivot Design, Inc.
  Chicago (Illinois), USA
creative people
 Brock Haldeman & Holle Andersen
client
 Baker & McKenzie

# CREATIVITY

## Catalogs

152

creative firm
  Jowaisas Design
  Cazenovia (New York), USA
designer
  Elizabeth Jowaisas
client
  J.R. Clancy

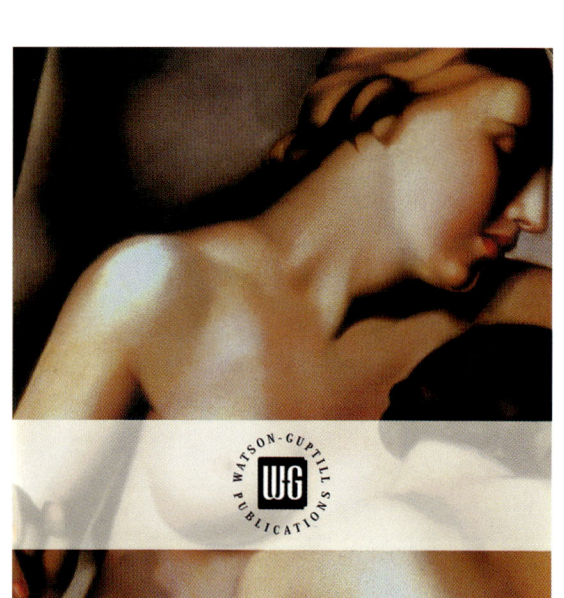

creative firm
  Laura Coe Design Assoc
  San Diego (California), USA
creative director
  Laura Coe Wright
designers
  Leanne Leveillee & Ryoichi Yotsumoto
photographer
  Carl Vandershuit
client
  Taylor Made Golf Co.

creative firm
  Farenga
  Design Group
  New York (New York),
  USA
creative people
  Anthony Farenga
client
  Watson-Guptill Catalog

creative firm
  OXO International's
  in-house art department
  New York (New York), USA
art director, designer
  Jennifer Mariotti Williams
photographer
  John Uher Photograhy
copywriters
  Michelle Sohn &
  Jennifer Mariotti Williams
client
  OXO International

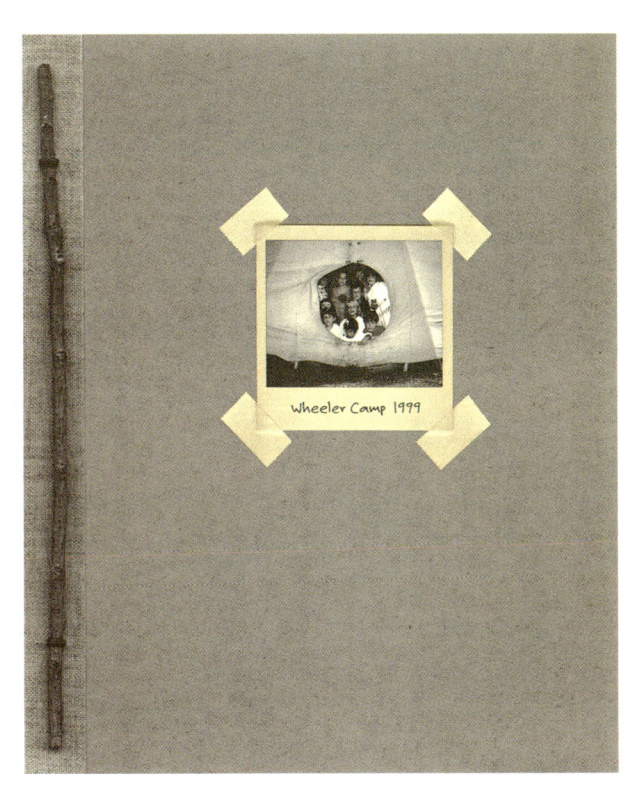

creative firm
  Carpenter Group
  New York (New York), USA
creative director
  John Nishimoto
designer
  Claudia Cataland
client
  Wheeler Summer Day Camp

creative firm
  Hult Fritz Matuszak
  Peoria (Illinois), USA
art director
  Tom Cody
copywriter
  Scott Fishel
client
  Maui Jim, Inc.

creative firm
  Paprika Communications
  Montréal (Québec), Canada
art director
  Louis Gagnon
designers
  Francis Turgeon & Bob Beck
photographer
  Michel Touchette
client
  Baronet

creative firm
  OXO International's in-house art department
  New York (New York), USA
art director
  Jennifer Mariotti Williams
designer
  Stacie Remaly-Wolfe
photographer
  John Uher Photography
client
  OXO International

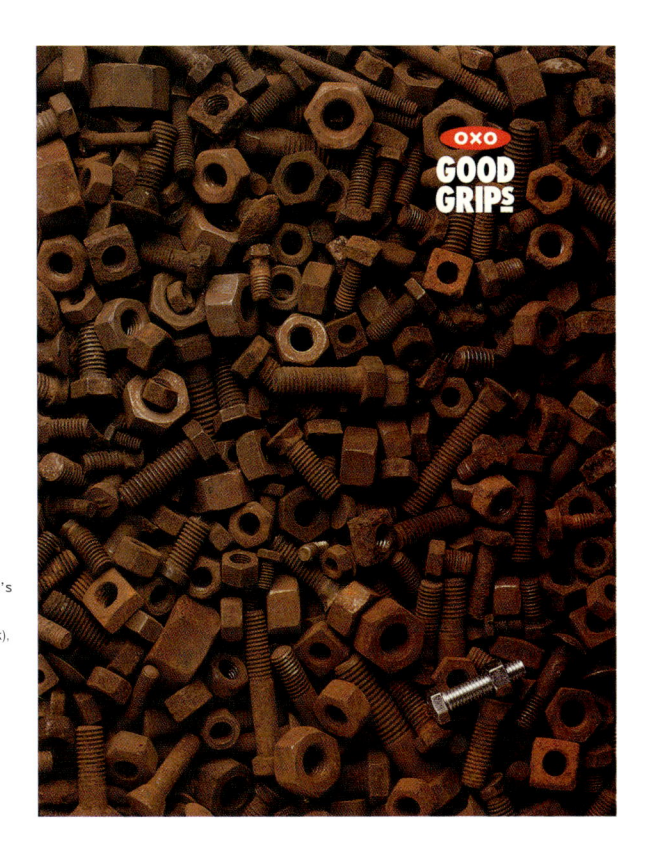

153

creative firm
 Nesnadny + Schwartz
 Cleveland (Ohio), USA
creative directors
 Mark Schwartz &
 Joyce Nesnadny
designers
 Joyce Nesnadny &
 Michelle Moehler
photographers
 Russell Monk & Will Faller
client
 Vassar College

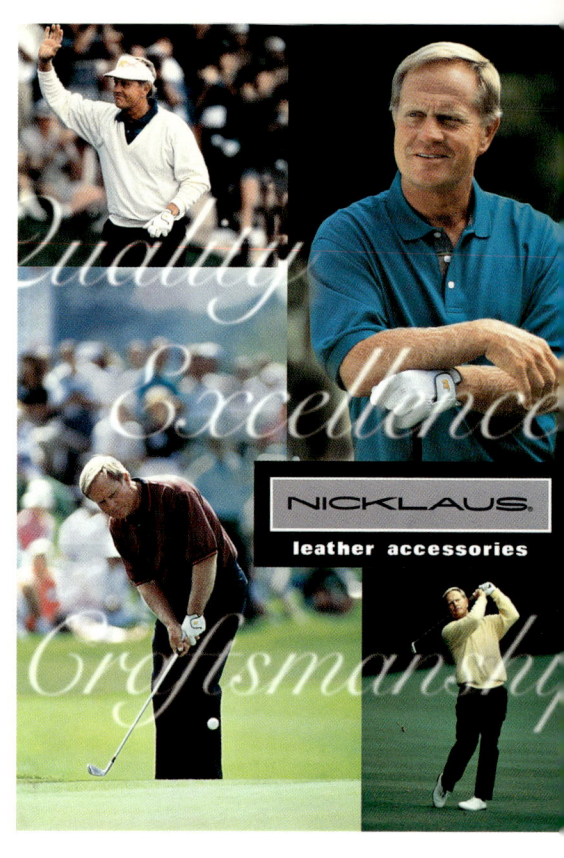

creative firm
 Graphics II
  Wichita Falls (Texas), USA
designer
 Donna Jones-Sudol
photographer
 David Fitzgerald
client
 The Valkyrie Co., Inc.

154

creative firm
 Hershey Communications
 Irvine (California), USA
client
 Esprit

creative firm
 Haase & Knels
  Bremen, Germany
creative directors
 Sibylle Haase & Fritz Haase
art director
 Katja Hirschfelder
photographer
 Hans Hansen
client
 B.T.Dibbern GmbH & Co.KG

creative firm
 Talbot Design Group
  Westlake Village (California), USA
creative director
 Gay Lyn Talbot
art director, designer
 Chris Kosman
photographers
 Doug Hyde & Sydney Cooper
copywriter
 Nina Dillon
client
 Kama Sutra

creative firm
 Gallery Ltd
  Hong Kong, China
creative people
 Benny Cheng, Giles Tse, & Kelvin Parker
client
 Hiap Moh (HK) Ltd

155

creative firm
 winson & terry design
 consultants pte ltd
  Singapore
creative people
 Terry Leu, Evonne Tan, & Joan Low
client
 Pinedale Trading Pte Ltd

creative firm
 Onboard Media
  Miami Beach (Florida), USA
art director
 Dirk Weldon
client
 Onboard Media

creative firm
  Hershey Communications
    Irvine (California), USA
client
  Los Angeles Dodgers

creative firm
  Pinkhaus
    Miami (Florida), USA
creative director
  Christopher Vice
production
  Jack Nitowitz
designer
  John Westmark
copywriter
  Doug Paley
client
  Mercedes Benz

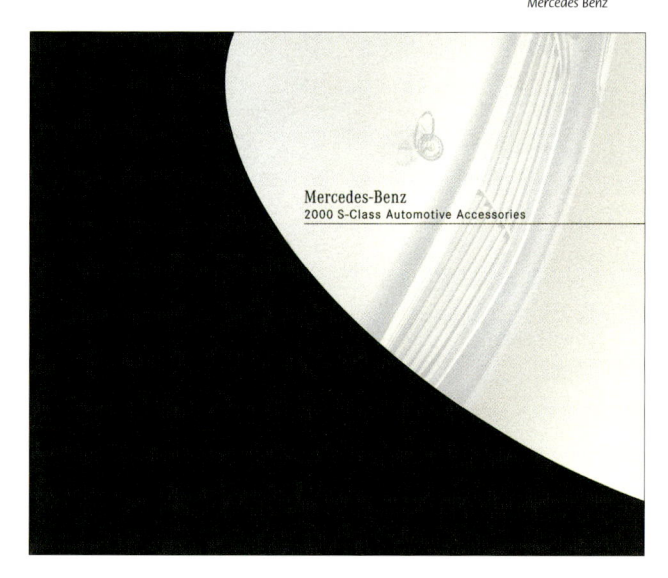

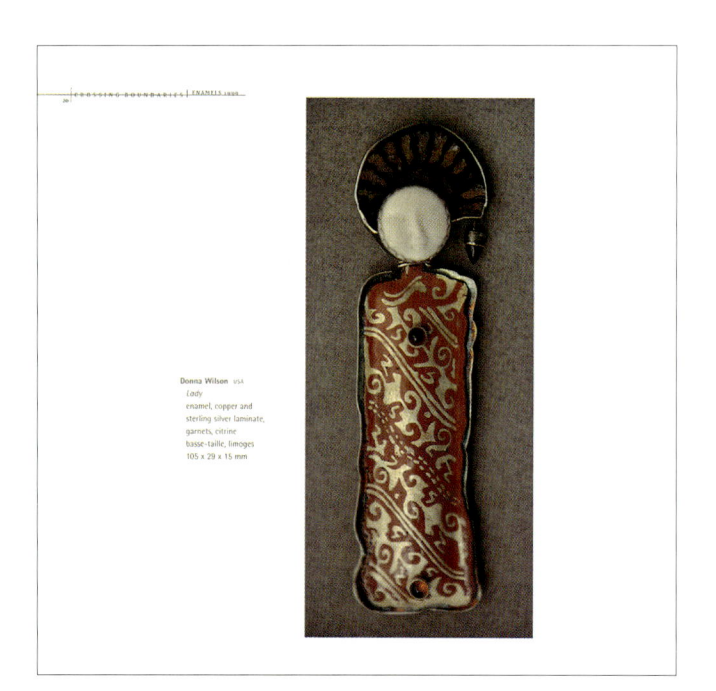

156

creative firm
  Eva Roberts
    Greenville (North Carolina), USA
designers
  Eva Roberts, Julie Spivey,
  & Brandie Knox Kirkman
editorial assistant
  Linda Darty
client
  International Enamelist Society

creative firm
  Design Guys
    Minneapolis (Minnesota), USA
creative people
  Steven Sikora, Lynette Erickson-Sikora,
  Gary Patch, Amy Kirkpatrick,
  & Jay Theige
client
  Target Stores

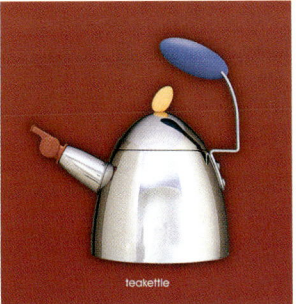

creative firm
 Design Guys
  Minneapolis (Minnesota), USA
creative people
 Steven Sikora & Dawn Selg
client
 Target Stores

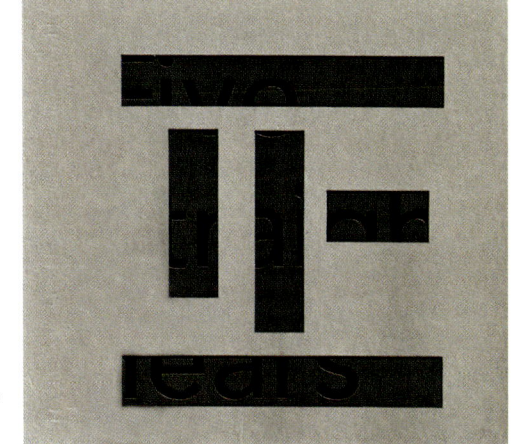

creative firm
 Gallery Ltd
  Hong Kong, China
creative people
 Benny Cheng, Giles Tse,
 & Kelvin Parker
client
 Gallery Ltd

creative firm
 Tiffany & Co.
  New York (New York), USA
creative director
 Stuart DeHaan
art director
 Cynthia Nicolich
copywriter
 Stephanie Van Alyea
client
 Tiffany & Co.

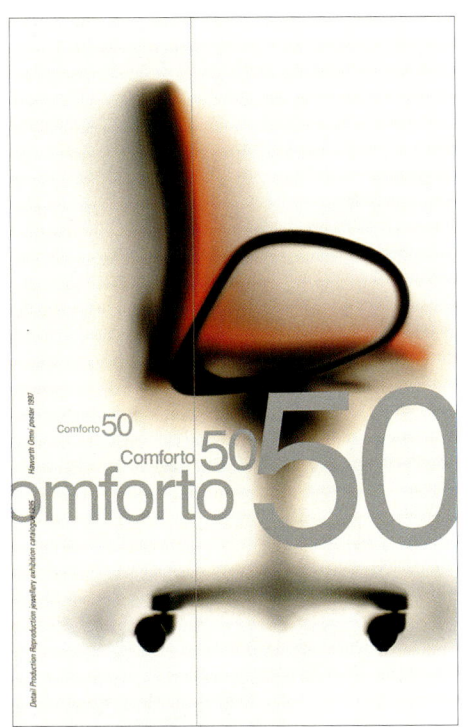

157

creative firm
 Emery Vincent Design
  Southbank (Victoria), Australia
creative people
 Emery Vincent Design
client
 Emery Vincent Design

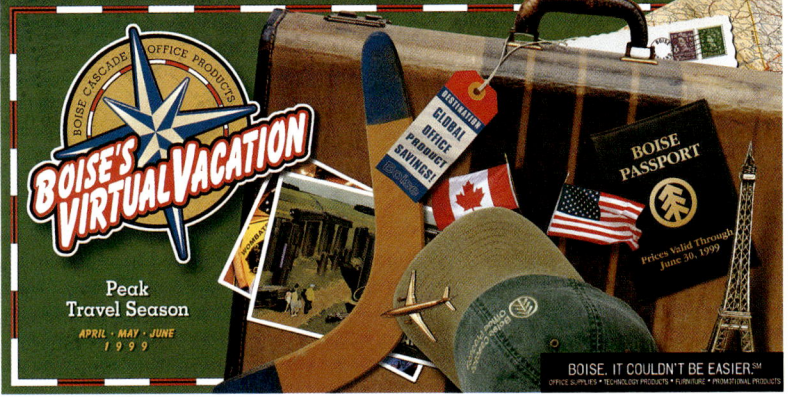

creative firm
 Louis London
  St. Louis (Missouri), USA
art director
 Beth Estes
copywriter
 Staci Yawitz
client
 Boise Cascade Office Products

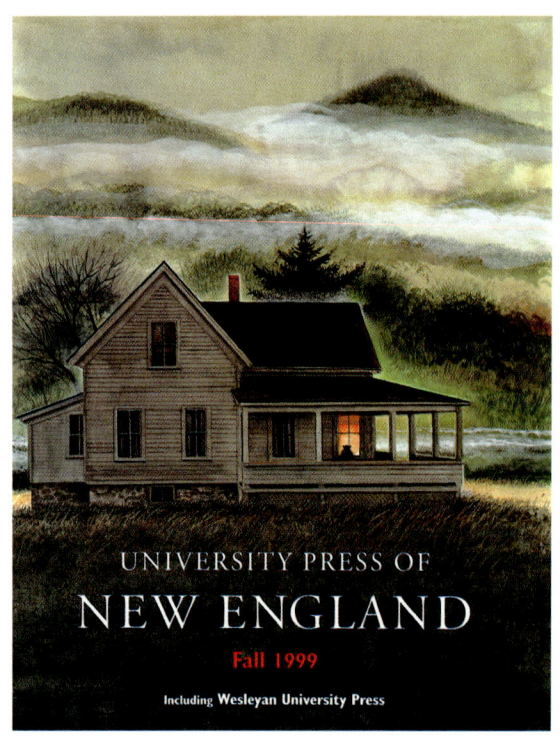

creative firm
  Wendell Minor Design
  Washington (Connecticut), USA
art director
  Mike Burton
illustrator
  Wendell Minor
client
  University Press of New England

158

creative firm
  Paprika Communications
  Montréal (Québec), Canada
art director
  Louis Gagnon
designers
  Francis Turgeon & Bob Beck
photographer
  Michel Touchette
client
  Baronet

creative firm
  Hershey Communications
  Irvine (California), USA
client
  Fao Schwarz

creative firm
  Leslie Evans
  Design Associates
  Portland (Maine), USA
art director
  Leslie Evans
designers
  Leslie Evans, Lori Harley,
  & Shelly Holmquist
copywriter
  Melissa Mirarchi
client
  Stonewall Kitchen

creative firm
  Paprika Communications
    Montréal (Québec), USA
art director
  Louis Gagnon
designers
  Francis Turgeon & Bob Beck
photographer
  Michel Touchette
client
  Baronet

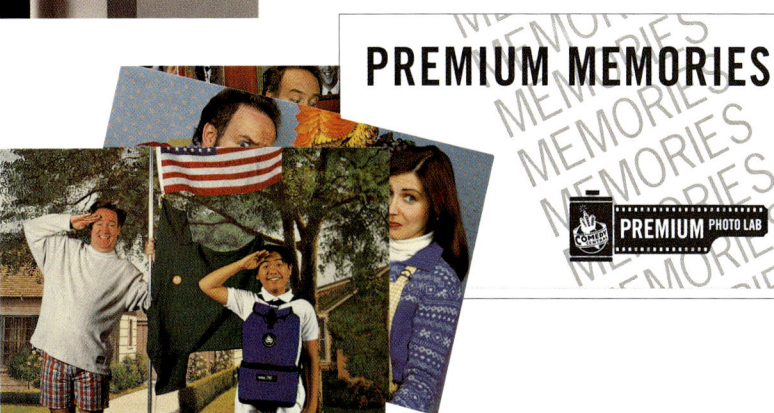

creative firm
  Design Guys
    Minneapolis (Minnesota), USA
creative people
  Steven Sikora & Jay Theige
client
  Target Stores

creative firm
  MTV Networks
  Creative Services
    New York (New York), USA
creative directors
  Scott Wadler & Cheryl Family
designer
  Darren Cox
photographer
  Mark Malabrigo
copywriter
  Ken Saji

159

creative firm
  Nolin Larosee Design
  Communications
    Montréal (Québec), Canada
art director
  Gilles Legault
client
  Bauer Inc.

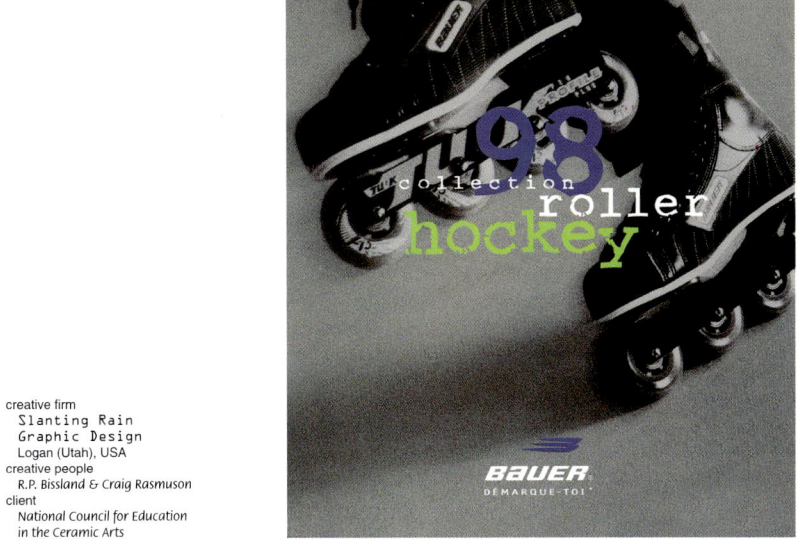

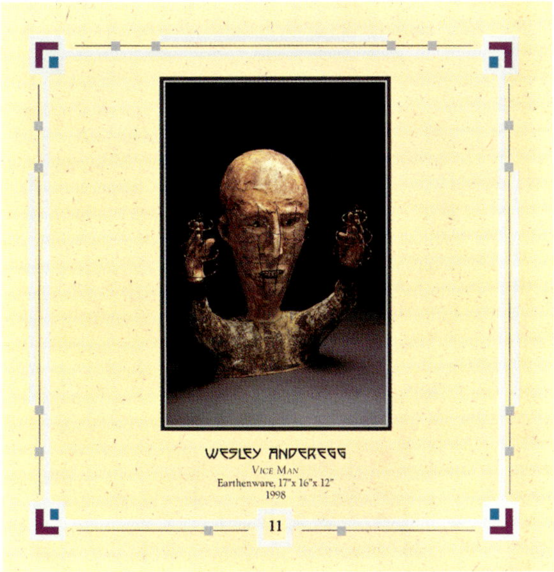

creative firm
  Slanting Rain
  Graphic Design
    Logan (Utah), USA
creative people
  R.P. Bissland & Craig Rasmuson
client
  National Council for Education
  in the Ceramic Arts

creative firm
 Ricardo Mealha Ateger
  Lisbon, Portugal
graphic designer
 Axel Feldmann
illustrator
 Ana Marvarida Lunita
client
 Clube dos Criativos de Portugal

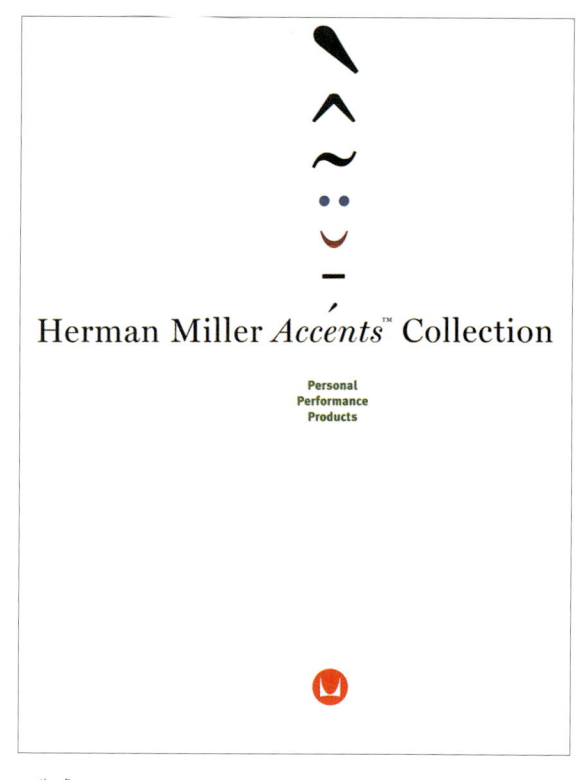

creative firm
 Herman Miller Inc.
  Zeeland (Michigan), USA
art director
 Kathy Stanton
designers
 Brian Edlefson & Sharon Boehm
photographer
 Roger Hill
copywriter
 Dick Holm & Keesha Palmer
client
 Herman Miller Inc.

creative firm
 Jones Studio Limited
  Staten Island (New York), USA
creative people
 Eric Jones, Pui-Pui Li, & Mikio Sekita
client
 ICF

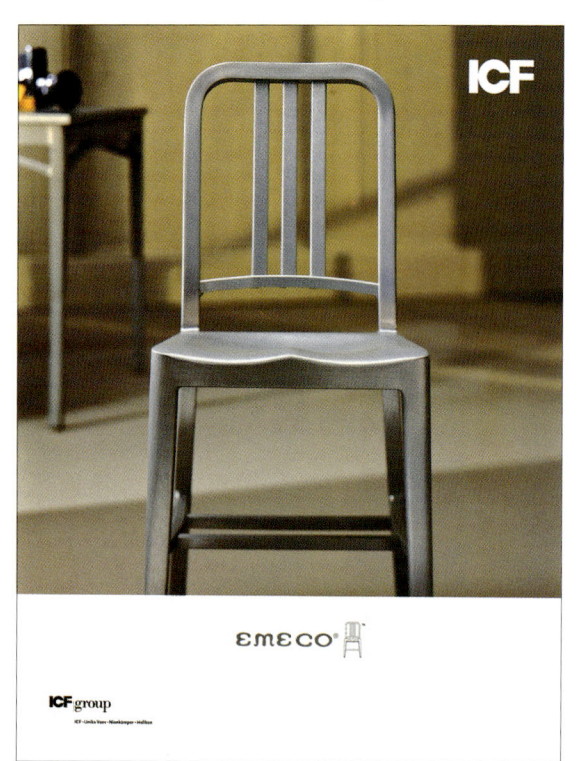

creative firm
 Michael Orr + Associates, Inc.
  Corning (New York), USA
creative people
 Michael R. Orr, Gregory Duell, & Thomas Freeland
client
 Robinson Knife

creative firm
  Seasonal Specialties
  Creative Services
  Eden Prairie (Minnesota), USA
designers
  Barbara J. Roth & Lisa Milan
production
  Deborah Lee, Rene Demel, Michelle Loch,
  Sharon Wilson, & Katrina Snow
client
  Seasonal Specialities LLC

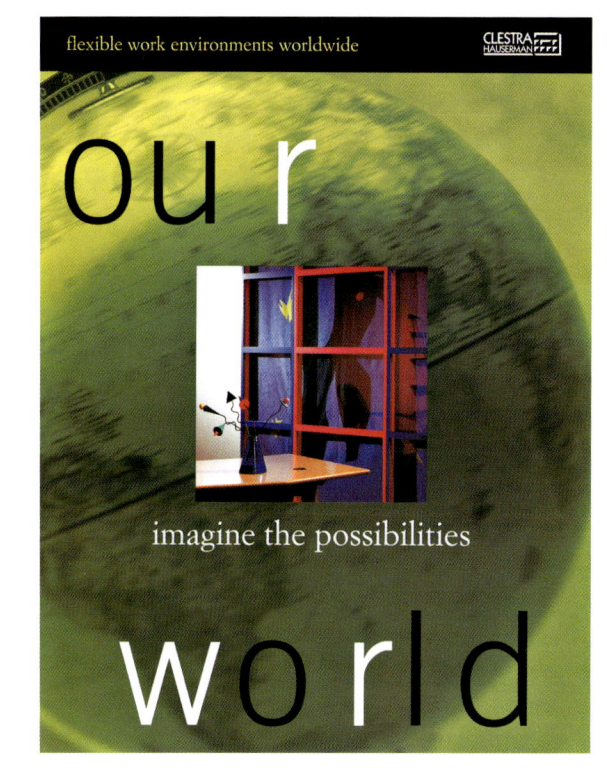

creative firm
  Nesnadny + Schwartz
  Cleveland (Ohio), USA
creative directors
  Mark Schwartz, Joyce Nesnadny,
  & Michelle Moehler
designers
  Joyce Nesnadny, Timothy Lachina,
  Michelle Moehler, & Gregory Oznowich
photographer
  Design Photography, Inc.
client
  Clestra Hauserman

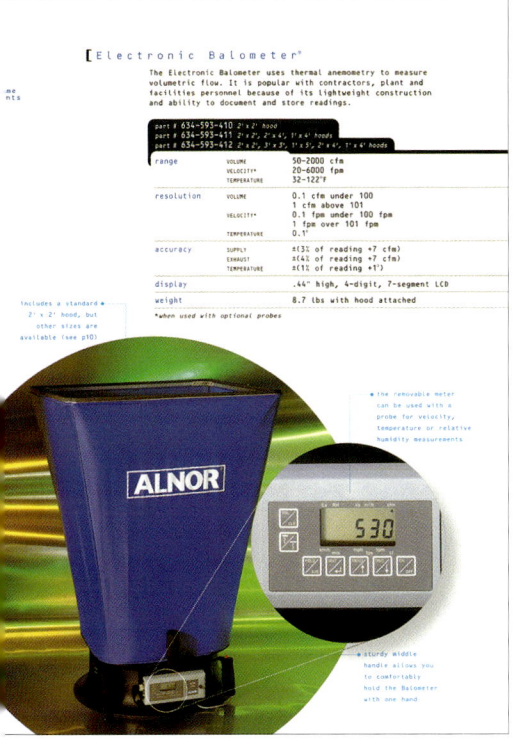

161

creative firm
  Nesnadny + Schwartz
  Cleveland (Ohio), USA
creative directors
  Joyce Nesnadny & Mark Schwartz
designers
  Joyce Nesnadny & Michelle Moehler
photographer
  Robert Muller
client
  Cleveland Institute of Art

creative firm
  Emphasis Seven
  Communications Inc.
  Chicago (Illinois), USA
designer
  Craig Niedermaier
client
  Alnor Instrument Company

creative firm
  Nolin Larosee Design Communications
    Montreal (Québec), Canada
art director
  Louise Filion
client
  Bauer Inc.

162

creative firm
  Hershey Communications
    Irvine (California), USA
client
  Northpark Shopping Center

creative firm
  Hornall Anderson Design Works
    Seattle (Washington), USA
creative people
  Jack Anderson, Lisa Cerveny, & David Bates
client
  Leatherman Tool Group

creative firm
  Nolin Larosee Design Communications
    Montreal (Québec), Canada
art director
  Louise Filion
client
  Bauer Inc.

# CREATIVITY

## Book Jackets

creative firm
  Kan & Lau Design Consultants
  Hong Kong, China
creative director, art director, designer
  Kan Tai-keung
photographer
  C.K. Wong
client
  Kan & Lau Design Consultants

creative firm
  Tangram Strategic Design
  Novara, Italy
creative director, art director, designer
  Enrico Sempi
photographer
  Jill Furmanowsky
client
  Giunti Gruppo Editoriale

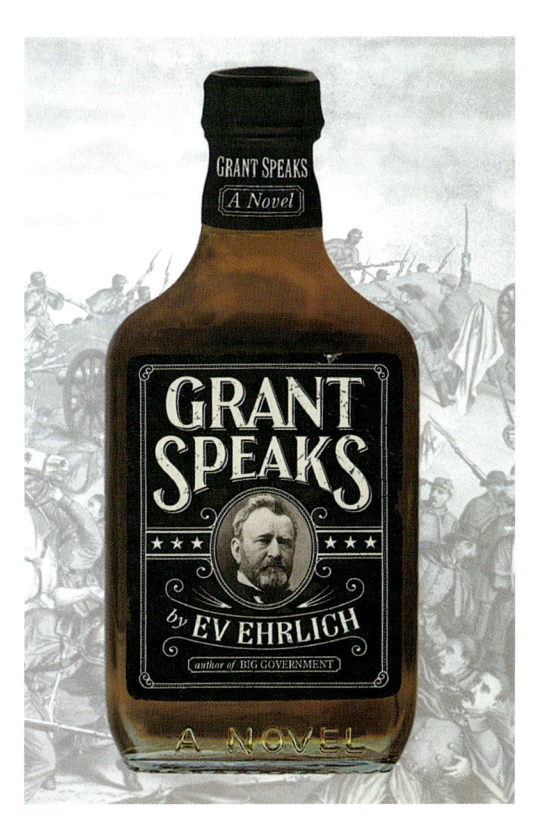

163

creative firm
  Warner Books
  New York (New York), USA
art director
  Jackie Merri Meyer
designer
  John Valk
photographer
  Corbis
client
  Warner Books

creative firm
  Warner Books
  New York (New York), USA
art director, designer
  Flag
photographer
  Joseph Sudek
client
  Warner Books

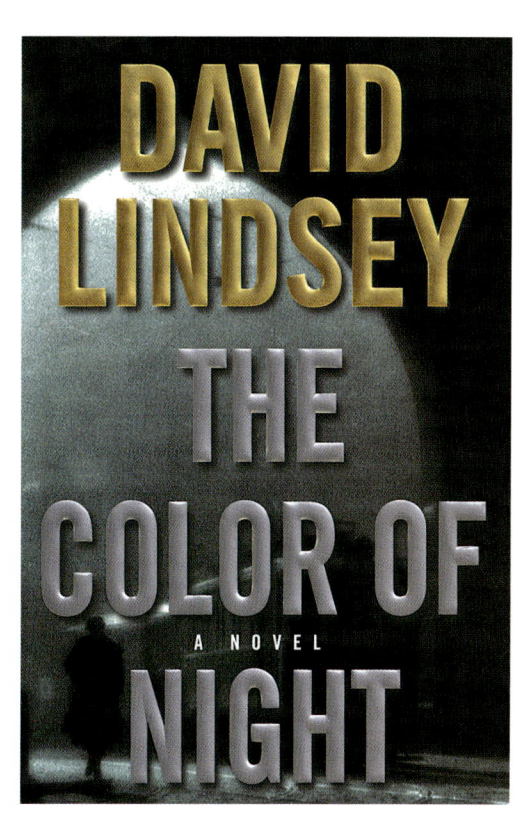

164

creative firm
 Workman Publishing
 New York (New York), USA
designer
 Paul Gamarello
illustrator
 Marc Rosenthal
client
 Workman Publishing

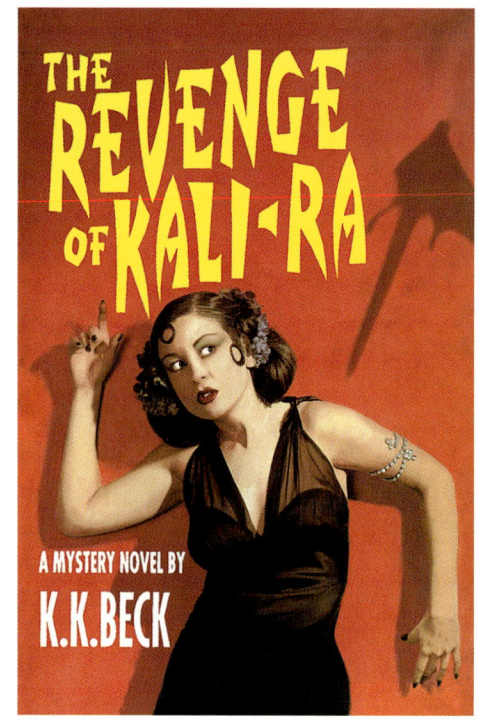

creative firm
 Warner Books
 New York (New York), USA
art director
 Rachel McClain
designer, photographer
 Richard Fahey
client
 Warner Books

creative firm
 Workman Publishing
 New York (New York), USA
creative people
 Paul Hanson
client
 Workman Publishing

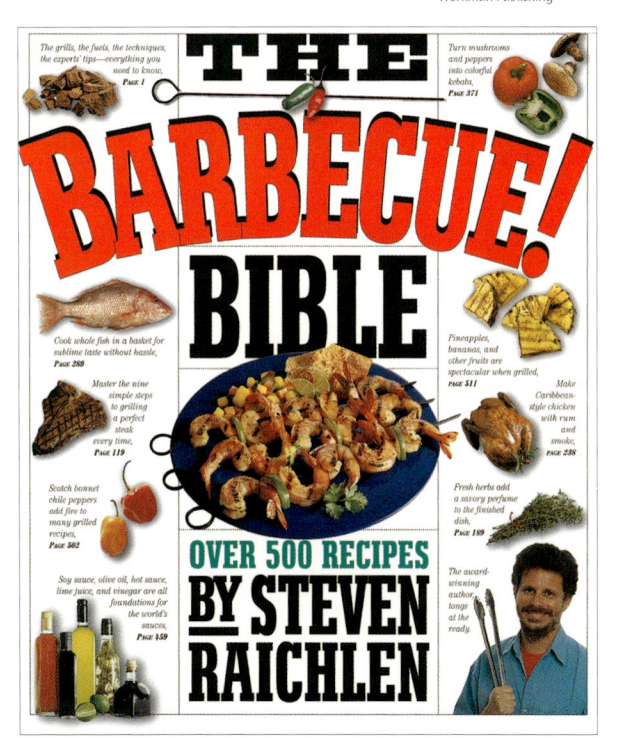

creative firm
 Workman Publishing
 New York (New York), USA
creative people
 Barbara Balch
client
 Workman Publishing

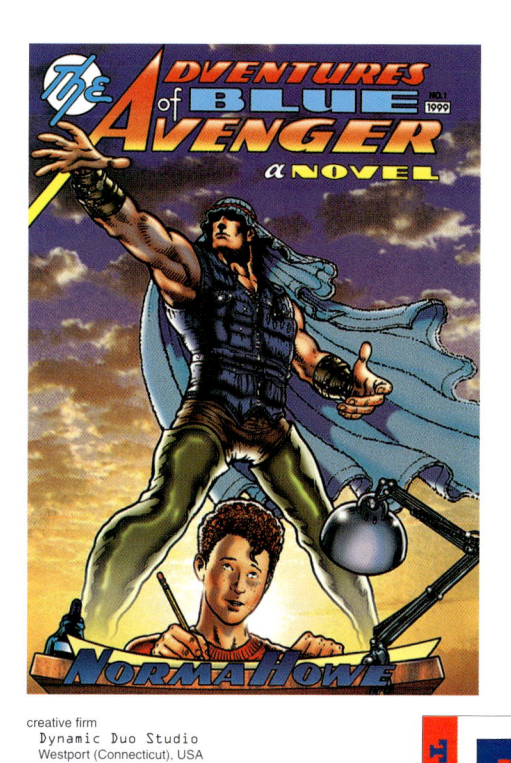

creative firm
 Dynamic Duo Studio
 Westport (Connecticut), USA
art director
 Meredith Baldwin
designer, illustration
 Dynamic Duo Studio
black and white line work,
hand lettering
 Arlen Schumer
computer coloring
 Sherri Wolfgang
client
 Henry Holt Publishing

creative firm
 Workman Publishing
 New York (New York), USA
creative people
 Paul Hanson
client
 Workman Publishing

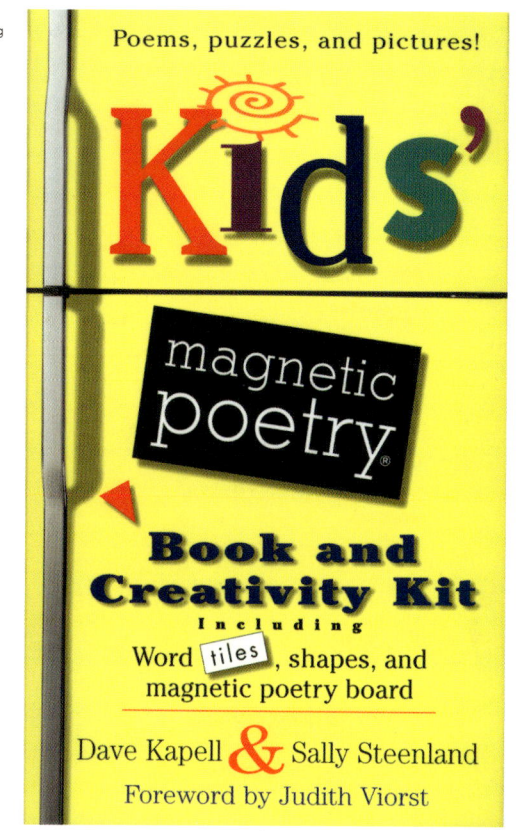

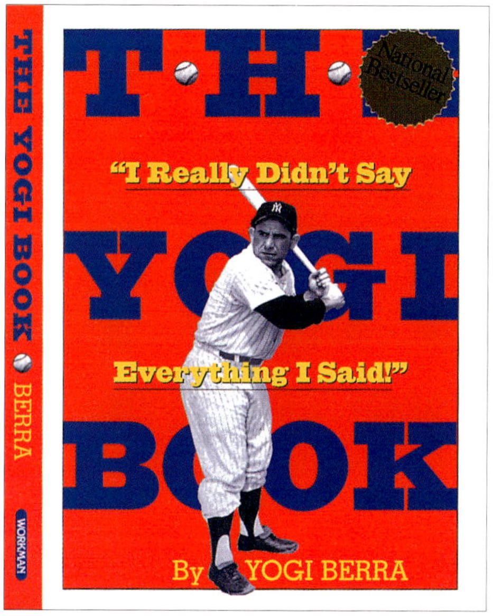

creative firm
 Workman Publishing
 New York (New York), USA
creative people
 Paul Gamarello
client
 Workman Publishing

165

creative firm
 Frank D'Astolfo Design
 New York (New York), USA
client
 University Press of New England

creative firm
 Royce M. Becker Design
 New York (New York), USA
art director
 Laura Hruska
designer
 Royce M. Becker
photographer
 Richard Hamilton Smith
client
 Soho Press

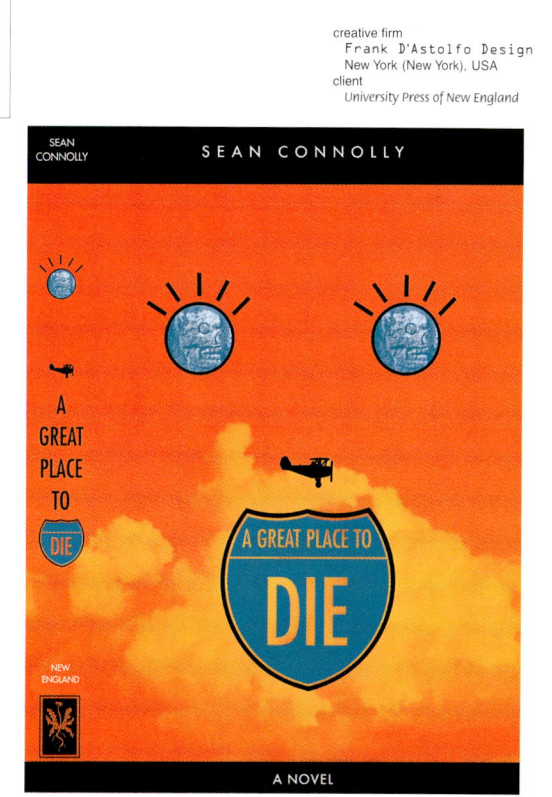

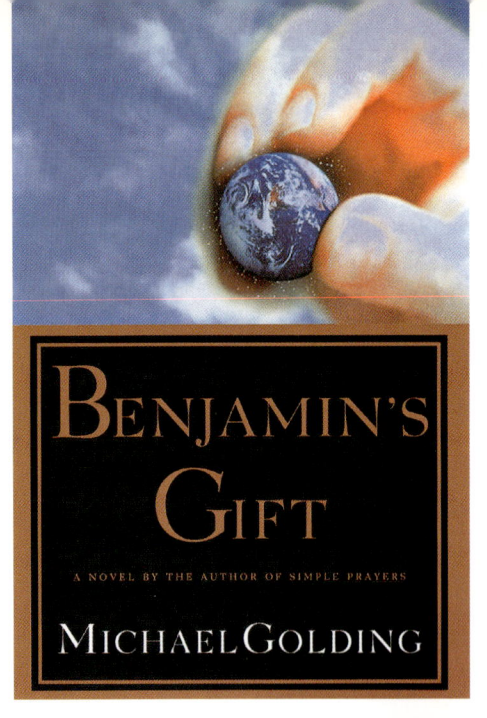

creative firm
　Tangram Strategic Design
　　Novara, Italy
creative director, art director, designer
　Enrico Sempi
client
　Giunti Gruppo Editoriale

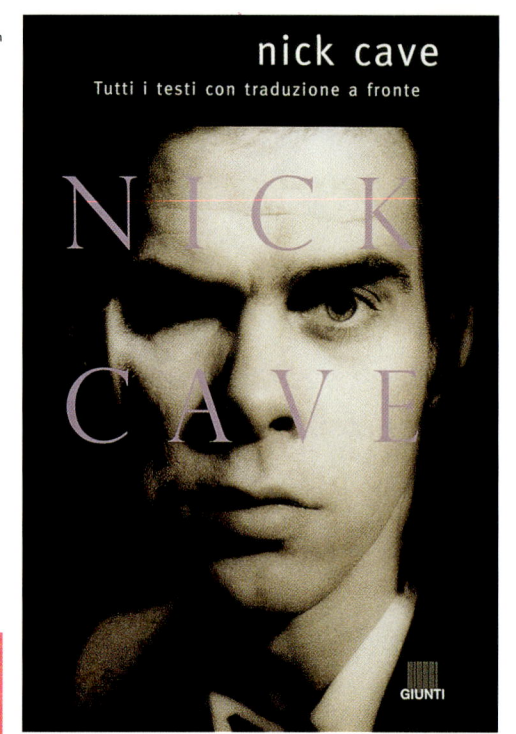

creative firm
　Warner Books
　　New York (New York), USA
art director, designer
　Flag
photographer
　B. Wallach
client
　Warner Books

166

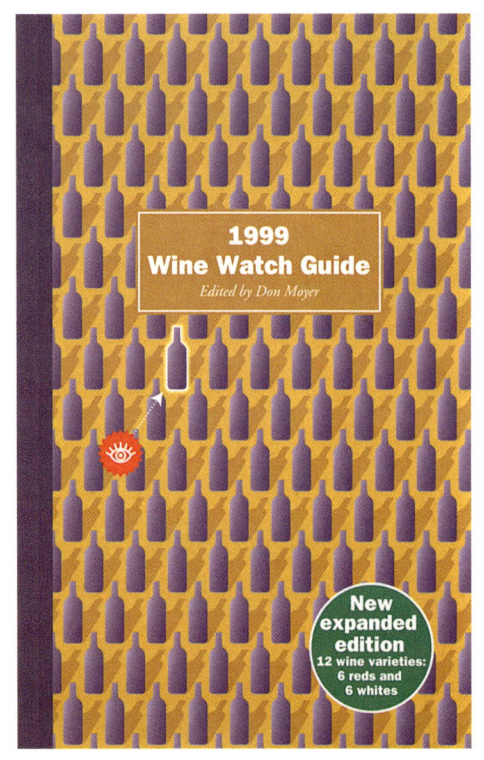

creative firm
　Warner Books
　　New York (New York), USA
art director, designer
　Jacki Merri Meyer
client
　Warner Books

creative firm
　Design Guys
　　Minneapolis (Minnesota), USA
creative people
　Steven Sikora & Jay Theige
client
　Target Stores

creative firm
　Agnew Moyer Smith Inc.
　　Pittsburgh (Pennsylvania), USA
creative people
　Don-Moyer
client
　Agnew Moyer Smith Inc.

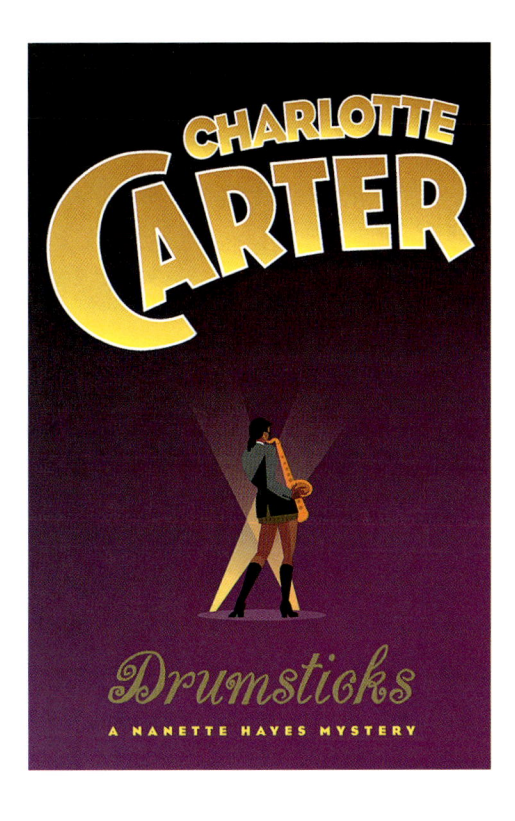

creative firm
  Warner Books
  New York (New York), USA
art director, designer
  Rachel McClain
illustrator
  Paul Rogers
client
  Warner Books

creative firm
  Warner Books
  New York (New York), USA
art director, designer
  Jackie Merri Meyer
photographer
  Jacque Lowe
client
  Warner Books

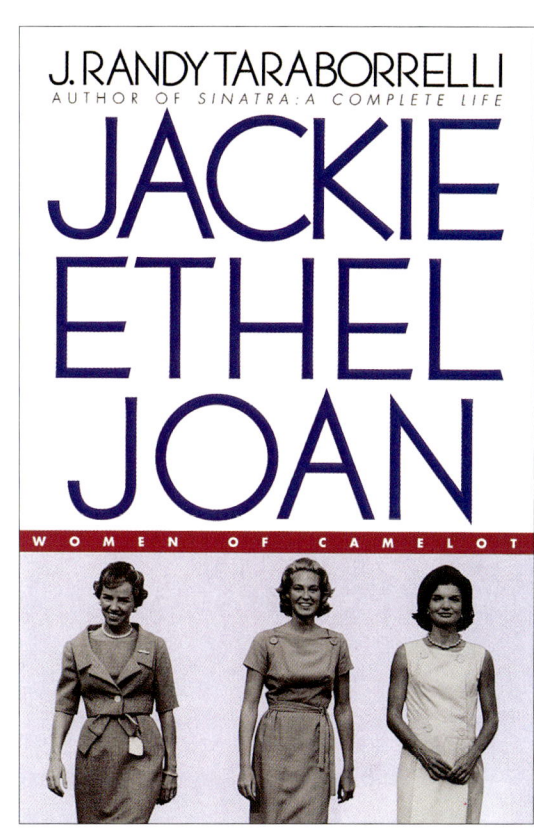

creative firm
  Warner Books
  New York (New York), USA
art director
  Flag
designer
  Jackie Merri Meyer (Flag)
photographers
  Franco Accanero & Michael Neug Bauer
client
  Warner Books

creative firm
  Warner Books
  New York (New York), USA
art director, designer
  Diane Luger
photographer, illustrator
  Herman Estevez
client
  Warner Books

167

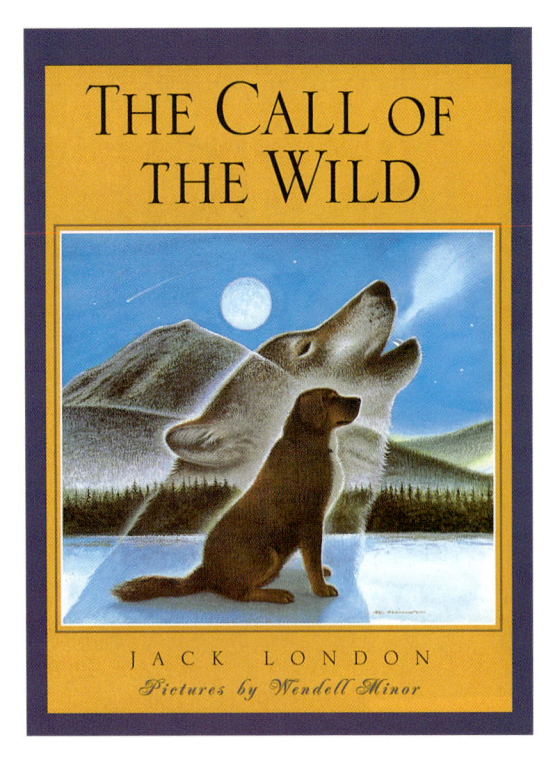

creative firm
 Wendell Minor Design
  Washington (Connecticut), USA
art director
 Nina Barnett
illustrator
 Wendell Minor
client
 Scribners

creative firm
 Warner Books
  New York (New York), USA
art director
 Jackie Merri Meyer
designer
 Paula Scher (Pentagram)
client
 Warner Books

creative firm
 Larsen Design
 + Interactive
  Minneapolis (Minnesota), USA
creative director
 Richelle Huff
design director
 Todd Nesser
client
 The Minneapolis Institute of Arts

creative firm
 Erwin Lefkowitz
 & Associates
  Riverdale (New York), USA
graphic designer
 Ben Gasner
client
 Els Bendheim

creative firm
 Wendell Minor Design
  Washington (Connecticut), USA
art director
 Joseph Montebello
designer, illustrator
 Wendell Minor
client
 Harper Collins

creative firm
 Workman Publishing
  New York (New York), USA
creative people
 Paul Gamarello
client
 Workman Publishing

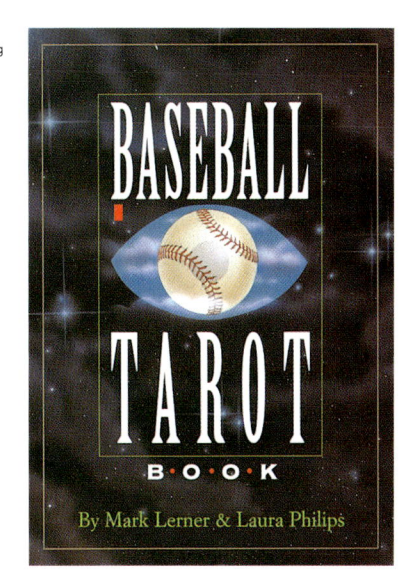

creative firm
 Royce M. Becker Design
  New York (New York), USA
art director
 Marjorie Anderson
designer
 Royce M. Becker
client
 Pantheon Books

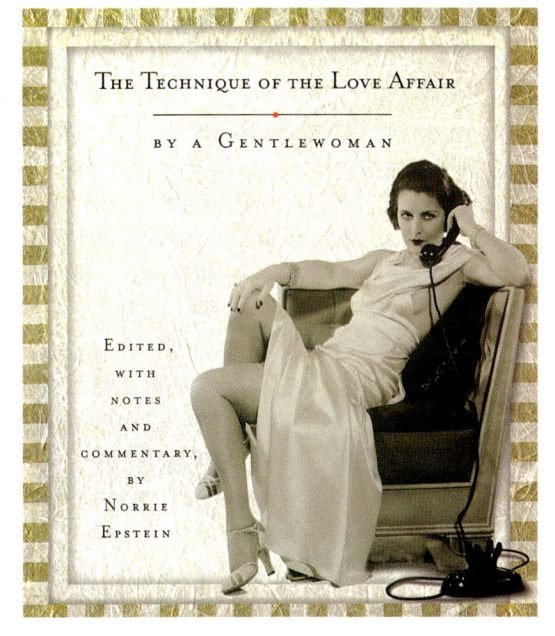

creative firm
 Ukulele Design
  Consultants Pte Ltd
  Singapore
design director
 Kim Chun-wei
designer
 Lynn Lim
client
 The Asia Insurance Co. Ltd

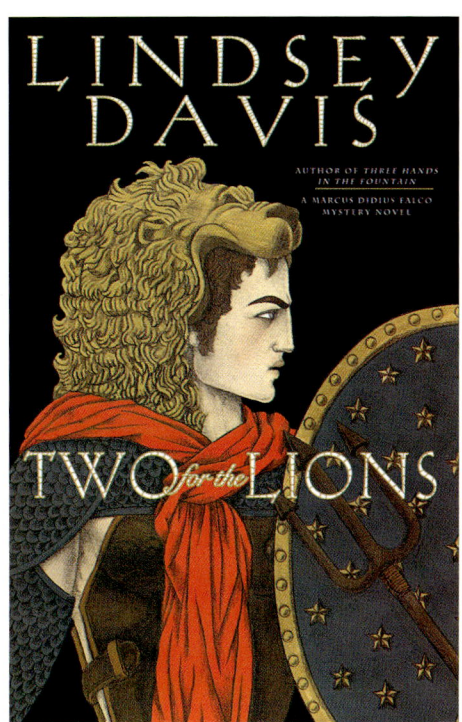

creative firm
 Warner Books
  New York (New York), USA
art director
 Rachel McClain
designer, illustrator
 John Martinez
client
 Warner Books

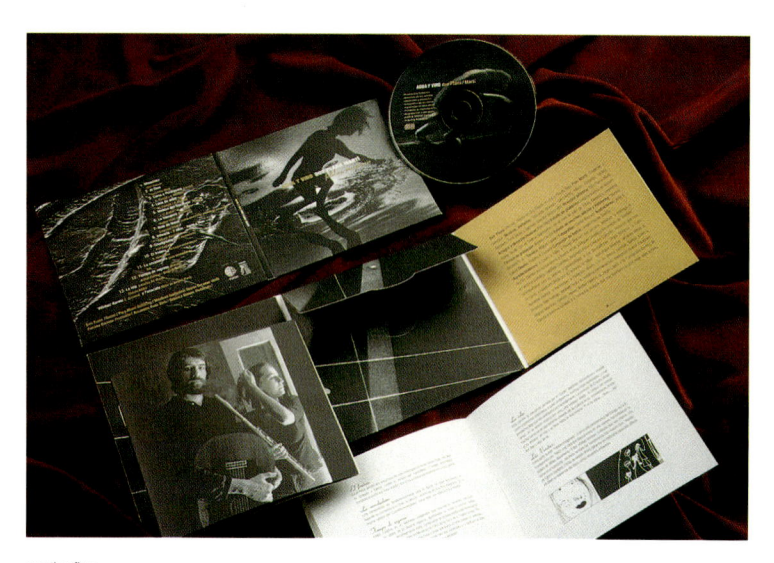

# CREATIVITY

## Records, CDs, Video Packaging

creative firm
 Boldrini & Ficcardi
  Mendoza, Argentina
creative people
 Victor Boldrini, Leonardo Ficcardi, & Pablo Agapito
client
 Instituto Provincial de la Cultura

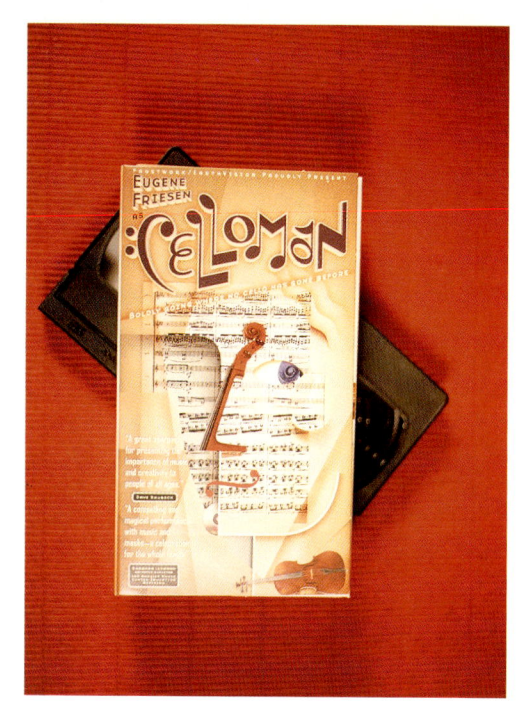

creative firm
 DBD International
  Menomonie (Wisconsin), USA
art director, designer
 David Brier
photographer
 Sean Kernan
client
 DBD International

creative firm
 Infinite Studio
  Savona, Italy
creative people
 Fablo Berruti
art director
 Jenette Williams
designer, photographer, illustrator
 Giorgio Kierkič
client
 BMG Ricordi S.P.A.

creative firm
 HBO
  New York (New York), USA
art director
 Lary Dueno
client
 HBO

170

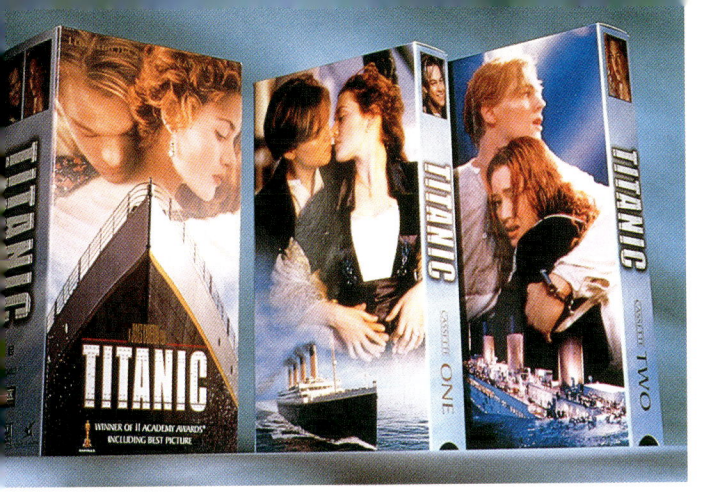

design firm
 30sixty design, inc.
  Los Angeles (California), USA
art director, designer
 Par Larsson
designer
 Russell Koza
client
 Paramount Home Video

creative firm
 Sally Johns Design
  Raleigh (North Carolina), USA
creative people
 Sally Johns & Tito Chazo
client
 Advanced Energy

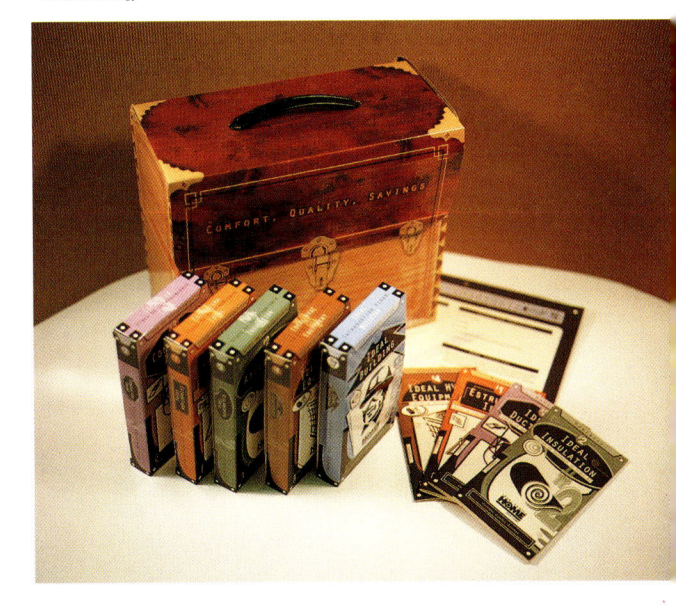

171

creative firm
 Heye & Partner
  Unterhaching, Germany
creative directer
 Alexander Bartel
art director
 Oliver Diehr & Frank Widmann
designer
 Nicole Oberberger
copywriter
 Karin Osenberg
client
 McDonald's

creative firm
 Boldrini & Ficcardi
  Mendoza, Argentina
creative people
 Victor Boldrini & Leonardo Ficcardi
client
 Ediciones Del Uru

creative firm
 Ellen Bruss Design
  Denver (Colorado), USA
creative people
 G. Carr, Charles Carpenter, Matt Coffman,
  & Wendy Keller
client
 chris daniels & the kings

creative firm
 Arista/Nashville
  Nashville (Tennessee), USA
designer
 Missy McKeand
client
 Robert Earl Keen

172

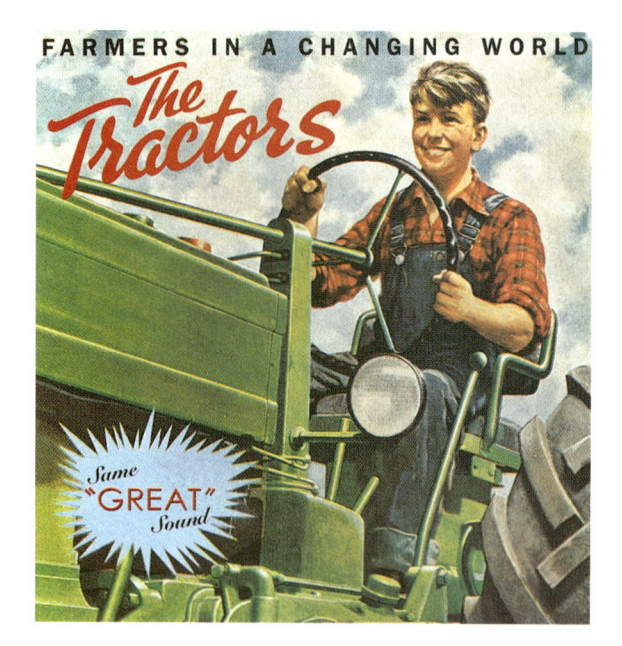

creative firm
 Arista/Nashville
  Nashville (Tennessee), USA
designer
 Maude Gilman-Clapham
client
 The Tractors

creative firm
 O'Mara & Ryan
  Vancouver (British Columbia), Canada
designers
 James O'Mara & Kate Ryan
client
 BMG Classics

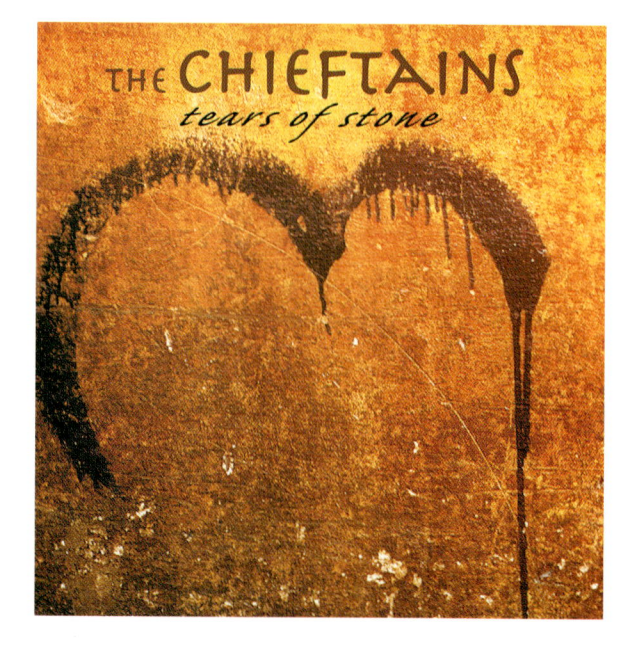

creative firm
 Peter Piper Graphics
  Tokyo (Shibuya-Ku), Japan
art directors, designers
 Masaki & Fujimoto
stylist
 Junko Fujiyama
photographers
 Masaaki Hiraga & Hideo Shimowasa
client
 Inpartmaint

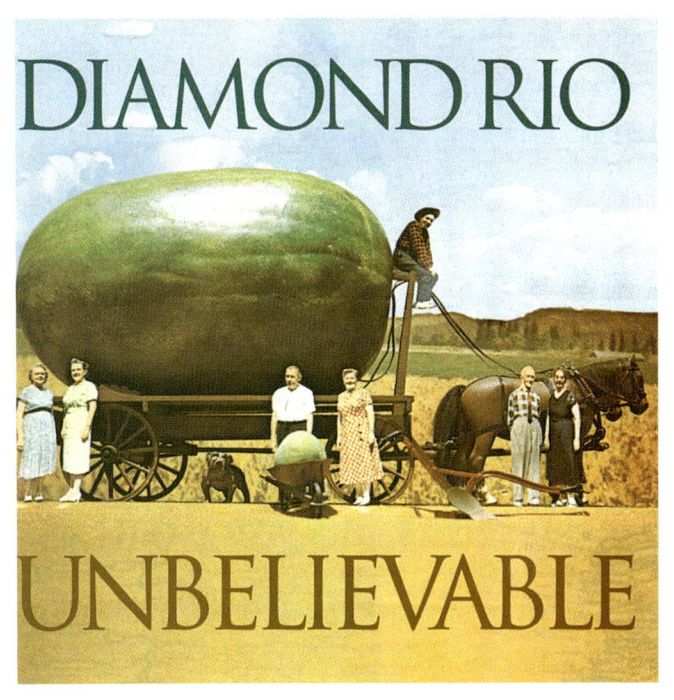

creative firm
 Arista/Nashville
  Nashville (Tennesee), USA
designer
 S. Wade Hunt
client
 Diamond Rio

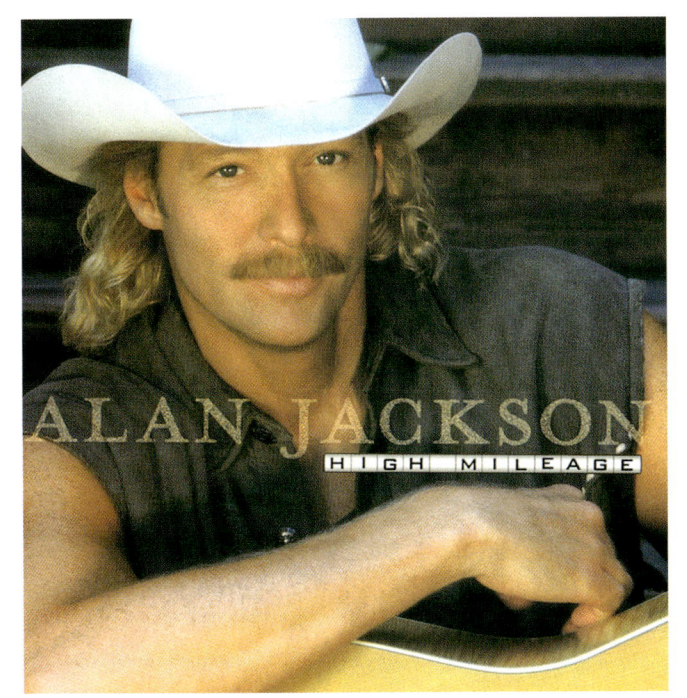

creative firm
 Fitting Kolbrener, Inc.
  Pittsburgh (Pennsylvania), USA
designer
 Kirk Littell
client
 WDUQ.FM

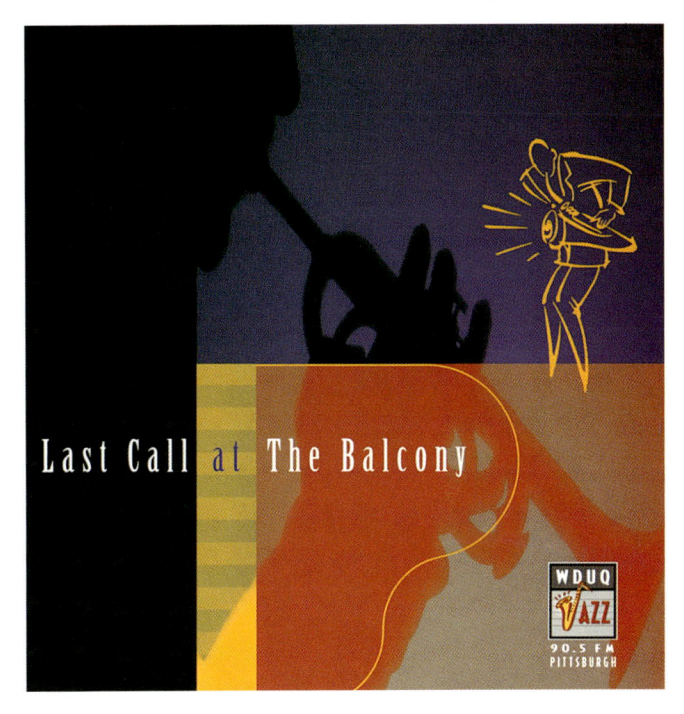

creative firm
 Arista/Nashville
  Nashville (Tennesee), USA
designer
 S. Wade Hunt
client
 Alan Jackson

creative firm
 Infinite Studio
 Albisola (Savona), Italy
creative director
 Fabio Berruti
client
 BMG Ricordi S.P.A.

174

creative firm
 Arista/Nashville
 Nashville (Tennesee), USA
designer
 Missy McKeand
client
 Radney Foster

creative firm
 Blank-Robert Kent Wilson
 Washington (D.C.), USA
creative people
 Robert Kent Wilson & Suzanne Ultman
client
 Red Hat Software/Extreme Linux

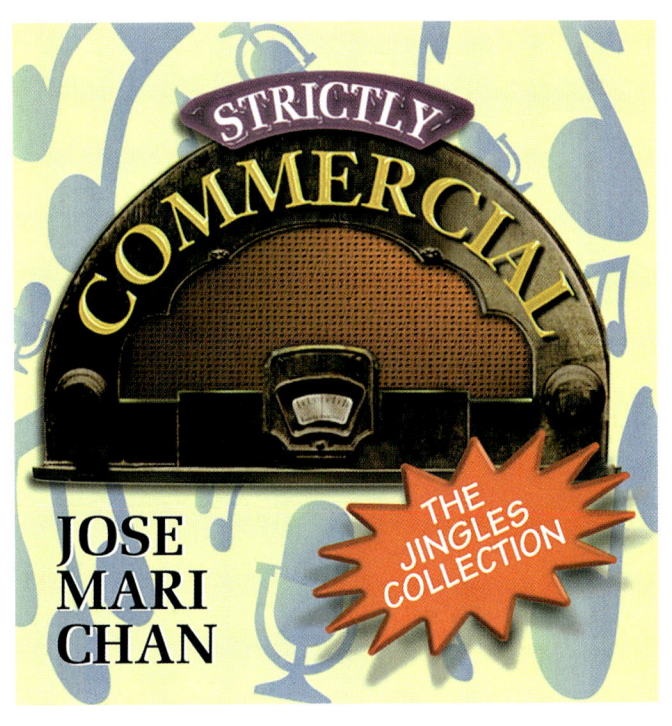

creative firm
  Ad Systems International
    Makati, Philippines
creative people
  Jojo Valerio-Fernandez
client
  Universal Records

creative firm
  Disney Channel Creative Services
    Los Angeles (California), USA
creative people
  Vickie Sum
client
  Disney Channel

175

creative firm
  Rose & Hopp Design
    Oslo, Norway
creative people
  Gina Rose
client
  Norwegian Society of Composers

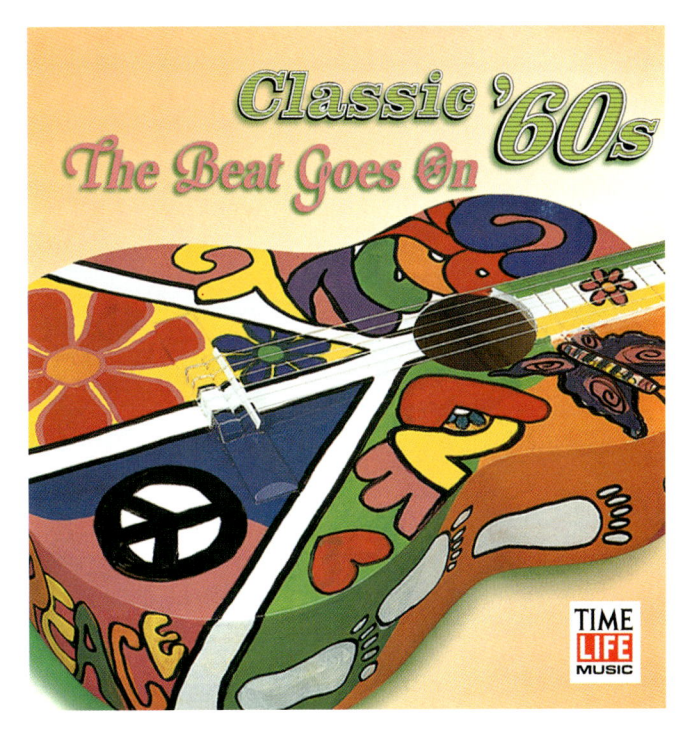

creative firm
  Gold & Associates
    Vedra Beach (Florida), USA
creative people
  Keith Gold & Joseph Vavra
client
  Time Life Music

# CREATIVITY
## Package Designs

creative firm
  BrandEquity International
  Newton (Massachusetts), USA
creative people
  BrandEquity International Design Team
client
  TOZ (Sara Lee)

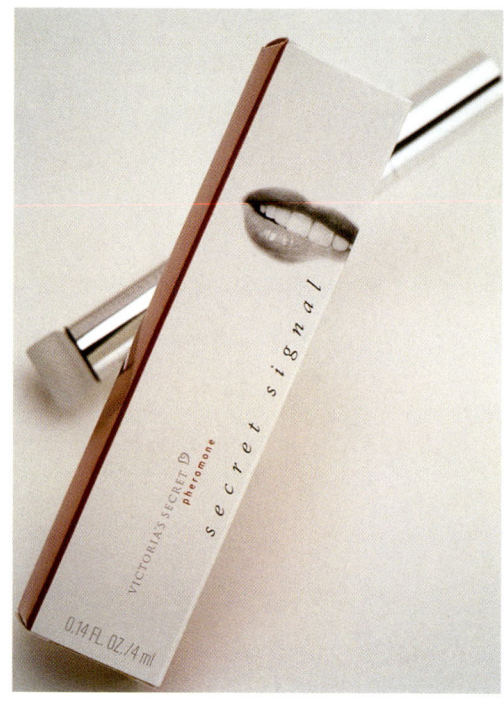

creative firm
  Desgrippes Gobe
  New York (New York), USA
creative director
  Phyllis Aragaki
art director
  Lori Yi
client
  Victoria's Secret

176

creative firm
  Landor Associates
  New York (New York), USA
art director
  Jeremy Dawkins
designer
  Lela Houston
client
  Bath & Body Works

creative firm
  Desgrippes Gobe
  New York (New York), USA
design director
  Susan Berson
designer
  Deirde Tighe
client
  CBI Laboratories

creative firm
  Landor Associates
  New York (New York), USA
art director
  Vicki Arzano
designer
  Lela Houston
client
  Bath & Body Works

creative firm
  The Weber Group, Inc.
  Racine (Wisconsin), USA
creative people
  Anthony Weber & David Sieveking
client
  S.C. Johnson & Son, Inc.

177

creative firm
  Desgrippes Gobe
  New York (New York), USA
design director
  Lori Yi
designer
  Peggy Wong
client
  The Limited, Inc.

creative firm
  Sayles Graphic Design
  Des Moines (Iowa), USA
art director, designer
  John Sayles
client
  Gianna Rose

creative firm
  Fisher Design, Inc.
  Cincinnati (Ohio), USA
creative people
  Eric Hebert & Peter Sexton
client
  Dial Corporation

design firm
  Boldrini & Ficcardi
  Mendoza, Argentina
creative people
  Victor Boldrini & Leonardo Ficcardi
client
  Bodega Viniterra

design firm
  Michael Niblett Design
  Fort Worth (Texas), USA
designer
  Michael Niblett
client
  Michael Niblett Design

178

design firm
  Praxis Disenadores S.C.
  Mexico City, Mexico
art director
  Juan Carlos Rojas
designer
  Nadya Villegas
client
  Valle Redondo S.A.

design firm
  Caldewey Design
  Napa (California), USA
designer
  Jeffrey Caldewey
client
  Inniskillin Vineyards

design firm
  DesignTribe
  San Francisco (California), USA
art director
  Mark Marinozzi
designer
  Dennis Pettigrew
illustrator
  Kelly Burke
client
  DesignTribe

design firm
  Klim Design, Inc.
  Avon (Connecticut), USA
creative people
  Matt Klim
client
  Casa Cuervo, S.A. de C.V.

design firm
  Blackburn's Limited
  London, England
creative, art director
  John Blackburn
designer
  Roberta Oates
illustrator
  Martin Leman
client
  Quinta Do Portal S.A.

creative firm
  Klim Design, Inc.
  Avon (Connecticut), USA
creative people
  Matt Klim
client
  Casa Cuervo, S.A. de C.V.

design firm
  Sterling Group
  New York (New York), USA
creative people
  Simon Lince
client
  Schieffelin & Somerset

creative firm
  M & A Design
    Cape Town, Republic of South Africa
creative people
  Marjoleine Van Der Walt, Jo Pellisier, Stephen Felmore
client
  Woolworths

creative firm
  McElveney & Palozzi Design Group
    Rochester (New York), USA
creative director
  Steve Palozzi
art director, designer
  Ellen Johnson
client
  Upstate Farms

180

creative firm
  Shields Design
    Fresno (California), USA
art director, designer
  Charles Shields
illustrator
  Doug Hansen
client
  G & V Company

creative firm
  Dixon & Parcels Associates
    New York (New York), USA
creative people
  Dixon & Parcels Associates
client
  Florida's Natural Growers

creative firm
  Mark Oliver, Inc.
    Santa Barbara (California), USA
creative people
  Mark Oliver, Brenna Pierce, & Patty Driskel
illustrator
  Grey Newbold
client
  Mountain Sun Juice

creative firm
  The Imagination Company
  Bethel (Vermont), USA
creative director
  Jim Giberti
art director
  Broniven Battaglia
client
  Vermont Pure Spring Water

creative firm
  Hillis Mackey & Company, Inc.
  Minneapolis (Minnesota), USA
creative director
  Terry Mackey
designer
  Terri Gray
client
  The Coca-Cola Company

creative firm
  Interbrand Gerstman & Meyers
  New York (New York), USA
creative people
  Richard Gerstman and staff
client
  Coca-Cola Company

creative firm
  Interbrand Gerstman & Meyers
  New York (New York), USA
creative people
  Chris Sanders & Christian Neidhard
client
  Procter & Gamble

creative firm
  Blackburn's Limited
  London, England
creative director, art director
  John Blackburn
designers
  Belinda Duggan & Roberta Oates
client
  Orchid Drinks

181

creative firm
 Fisher Design, Inc.
  Cincinnati (Ohio), USA
creative people
 Richard W. Deardorff & Sandra Bruce
client
 The Scotts Company

creative firm
 Bailey Design Group, Inc.
  Plymouth Meeting (Pennsylvania), USA
creative director
 David Fiedler
designers
 Lauren Dunoff & Tisha Armour
client
 Johnson & Johnson

182

creative firm
 Nakatsuka Daisuke Inc.
  Tokyo, Japan
creative director
 Shu Uemura
art director
 Daisuke Nakatsuka
designers
 Hiromi Yamada & Kanna Numajiri
client
 Shu Uemura Cosmetics Inc.

creative firm
 Parham Santana Inc.
  New York (New York), USA
creative directors
 Maruchi Santana &
 Lynda Greenblatt (Liz Claiborne)
art directors
 Lori Reinig &
 Barrie Glabman (Liz Claiborne)
designer
 Ann Sappenfield
client
 Liz Claiborne Inc.

creative firm
 Design Resource Center
  Naperville (Illinois), USA
creative people
 John Norman
client
 Ginkgo Intl. Ltd.

creative firm
 Phillips Design Group
  Boston (Massachusetts),USA
art director
 Steve Phillips
designer
 Alison Goudreault
client
 Phillips Design Group

creative firm
 Interbrand Gerstman & Meyers
  New York (New York), USA
creative people
 Rafael Feliciano
client
 Whitehall Robins

183

creative firm
 Laura Coe Design Associates
  San Diego (California), USA
creative director
 Laura Coe Wright
designer
 Leanne Leveillee
client
 Taylor Made Golf Co.

creative firm
 Interbrand Gerstman & Meyers
  New York (New York), USA
creative people
 Jeff Zack & Diana Atkins
client
 Kelloggs

creative firm
 Interbrand Gerstman & Meyers
  New York (New York), USA
creative people
 Rafael Feliciano and staff
client
 Lander

creative firm
 Bailey Design Group, Inc.
  Plymouth Meeting (Pennsylvania), USA
creative director
 David Fiedler
designers
 Lauren Dunoff, Tisha Armour, & Christian Williamson
client
 Cultivations

creative firm
 Design Guys
  Minneapolis (Minnesota), USA
creative people
 Steven Sikora & Jay Theige
client
 Target Stores

184

creative firm
 Tom Fowler, Inc.
  Stamford (Connecticut), USA
creative people
 Elizabeth P. Ball
client
 Chesebrough - Pond's USA Co.

creative firm
 Nakatsuka Daisuke Inc.
  Tokyo, Japan
creative director
 Shu Uemura
art director
 Daisuke Nakatsuka
designer
 Kanna Numajiri
client
 Shu Uemura Cosmetics Inc.

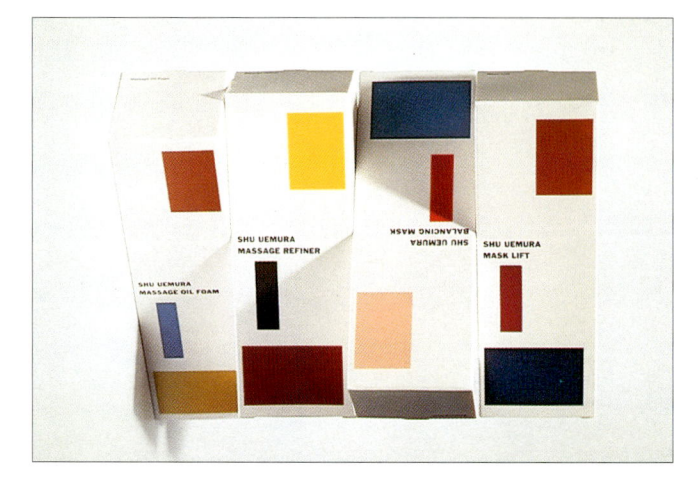

creative firm
 Sterling Group
  New York (New York), USA
creative people
 Janice Pedley
client
 Sara Lee Hosiery

creative firm
 Fisher Design, Inc.
 Cincinnati (Ohio), USA
creative people
 Peter Sexton, Richard W. Deardorff,
 Lynne Chraplivy, & Eric Hebert
client
 Dial Corporation

creative firm
 Sayles Graphic Design
 Des Moines (Iowa), USA
art director, designer
 John Sayles
client
 Gianna Rose

185

creative firm
 Landor Associates
 New York (New York), USA
art director
 Jeremy Dawkins
designer
 Jerry Solon
client
 Hanes Hosiery Inc.

creative firm
 Landor Associates
 New York (New York), USA
art director
 Vicki Arzano
designer
 Lela Houston
client
 Bath & Body Works

creative firm
 LMS Design
 Stamford (Connecticut), USA
creative people
 Richard Shear & Rick Mapes
client
 J. B. Williams

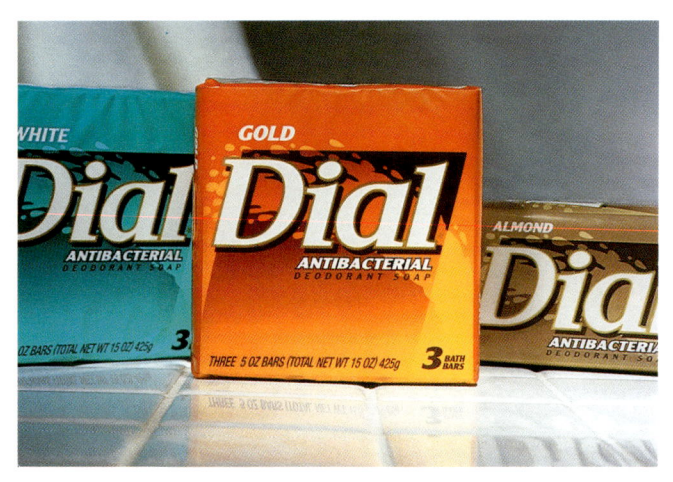

creative firm
  Fisher Design
    Cincinnati (Ohio), USA
creative people
  Peter M. Sexton & Richard W. Deardorff
client
  Dial Corporation

creative firm
  Landor Associates
    New York (New York), USA
art director
  Jeremy Dawkins
designer
  Lela Houston
client
  Bath & Body Works

creative firm
  Fisher Design, Inc.
    Cincinnati (Ohio), USA
creative people
  Angie Martin & Peter Sexton
client
  Colgate - Palmolive

creative firm
  The Weber Group, Inc.
    Racine (Wisconsin), USA
creative people
  Anthony Weber
client
  SC Johnson Wax

creative firm
  The Benchmark Group
    Cincinnati (Ohio), USA
creative people
  Ray Gedean, Chris Forsythe, & Leslie Hall
client
  Soft Sheer Products Inc.

creative firm
  Hillis Mackey & Company, Inc.
    Minneapolis (Minnesota), USA
creative director, designer
  Randy Szarzynski
client
  Target

creative firm
  Springetts
    London, England
client
  Jeyes

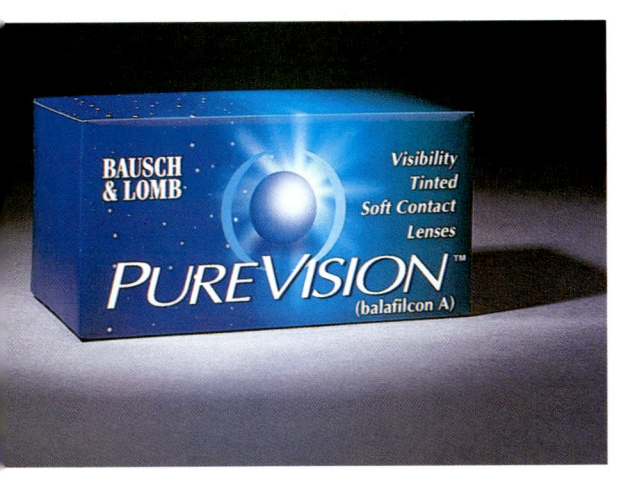

creative firm
  Forward Design, Inc.
    Rochester (New York), USA
creative people
  Daphne Stofer
client
  Bausch & Lomb

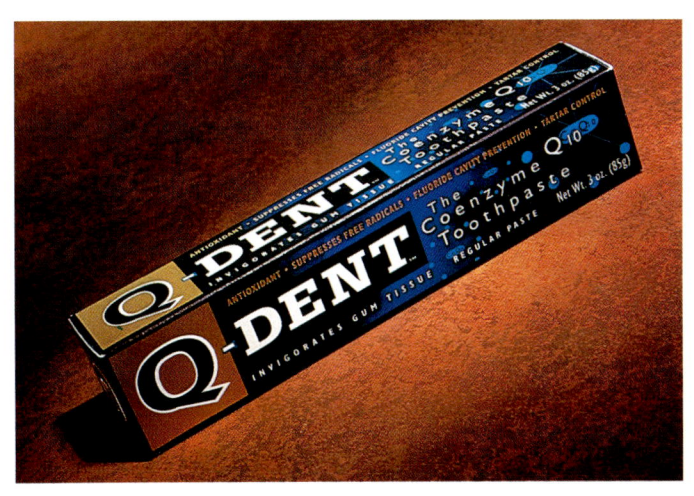

creative firm
  David Lemley Design
    Seattle (Washington), USA
art director
  Alan Lawrence (CD²)
designer
  David Lemley
client
  Q-Pharma

creative firm
  The Weber Group, Inc.
    Racine (Wisconsin), USA
creative people
  Anthony Weber & David Sieveking
client
  S. C. Johnson & Son, Inc.

creative firm
 Haugaard Creative Group, Inc.
 Chicago (Illinois), USA
designer
 José Parado
client
 The Quaker Oats Company

creative firm
 Cornerstone
 New York (New York), USA
art director
 Keith Steimel
designer
 Derek Lou & Martin Yeo
illustrator
 Tom Montini
client
 Desert Glory

188

creative firm
 Dixon & Parcels Associates
 New York (New York), USA
creative people
 Dixon & Parcels Associates
client
 Florida's Natural Growers

creative firm
 Leslie Evans Design Associates
 Portland (Maine), USA
art director
 Leslie Evans & Tom Hubbard
designers
 Leslie Evans, Tom Hubbard & Shoshannah White
client
 Eatzi's

creative firm
 Gaylord Graphics
 Carol Stream (Illinois), USA
creative people
 Jerry Farrell
client
 The Sykes Company

creative firm
  Murrie Lienhart Rysner
  Chicago (Illinois), USA
creative people
  Jim Lienhart
client
  Quaker Oats

creative firm
  Pisarkiewicz Mazur & Co., Inc.
  New York (New York), USA
creative director
  Mary F. Pisarkiewicz
designers
  Nat Estes & Jennifer Harenberg
client
  Kraft Foods, Inc.

creative firm
  Dixon & Parcels Associates
  New York (New York), USA
creative people
  Dixon & Parcels Associates
client
  4C Foods Corp.

creative firm
  Thompson Design Group
  San Francisco (California), USA
art director
  Dennis Thompson
designer
  Kirsten Kandler
illustrator
  Pixar
client
  Nestlé USA

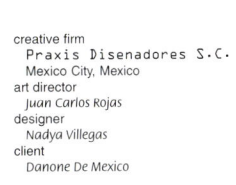

creative firm
  Praxis Disenadores S.C.
  Mexico City, Mexico
art director
  Juan Carlos Rojas
designer
  Nadya Villegas
client
  Danone De Mexico

189

creative firm
 Forward Design, Inc.
  Rochester (New York), USA
creative people
 Daphne Stofer
client
 Canandaigua Wine Company

creative firm
 Klim Design, Inc.
  Avon (Connecticut), USA
creative people
 Matt Klim
client
 Casa Cuervo, S.A. de C.V.

creative firm
 Caldewey Design
  Napa (California), USA
designer
 Jefferey Caldewey
illustrator
 Ronna Nelson
client
 Miner Vineyards

creative firm
 Faltman & Malmen
  Stockholm, Sweden
creative director, art director
 Anders Eliasson
copywriter
 Bo Tidelius
client
 Vin & Sprit

creative firm
 Faltman & Malmen
  Stockholm, Sweden
creative director, art director
 Anders Eliasson
copywriter
 Bo Tidelius
client
 Vin & Sprit

creative firm
 House of Design
  Graz, Austria
art director
 André Stangl
designer
 Thscha Stangl
client
 Domane Muller

creative firm
 Curtis Design LLC
  San Francisco (California), USA
creative people
 David Curtis & Chris Benitez
client
 Vinomex

creative firm
 Caldewey Design
  Napa (California), USA
designer
 Jeffrey Caldewey
client
 Bella Vigna Vineyards

creative firm
 Caldewey Design
  Napa (California), USA
designer
 Jeffrey Caldewey
client
 Allora Vineyards

creative firm
 Caldewey Design
  Napa (California), USA
designer
 Jeffrey Caldewey
client
 Inniskillin Vineyards (Crystal)

creative firm
 Delphine Keim Campbell
 Moscow (Indiana), USA
creative people
 Delphine Keim Campbell
client
 Marilyn Lysohir

creative firm
 Cornerstone
 New York (New York), USA
art director
 Keith Steimel & Sally Clarke
designer, illustrator
 Joe Dimeo
client
 Perrier Group

192

creative firm
 Gauger & Silva Associates
 San Francisco (California), USA
creative people
 Laura Levy & David Gauger
client
 Barbara's Bakery

creative firm
 Thompson Design Group
 San Francisco (California), USA
art director
 Dennis Thompson
designer
 Kirsten Kandler
client
 Nestlé USA

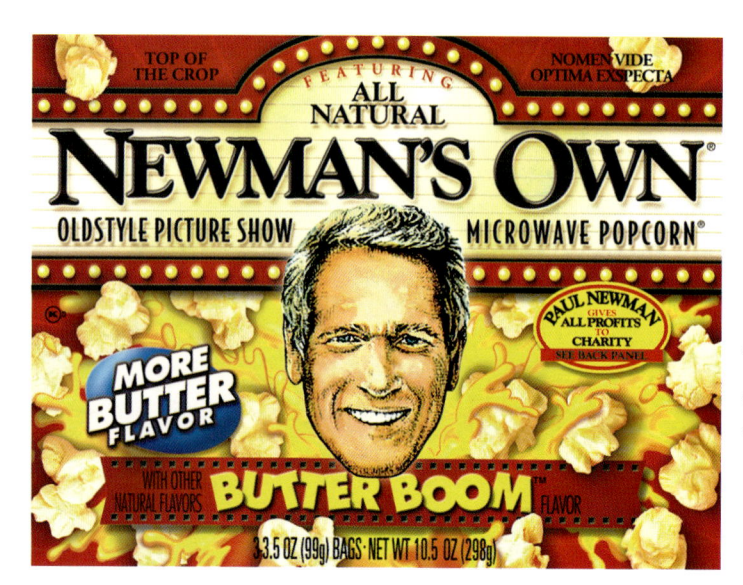

creative firm
 Zunda Design Group
 South Norwalk (Connecticut), USA
creative people
 Charles Zunda, Todd Nickel, Jon Voss, & Frank Navone
client
 Newman's Own

creative firm
 Mark Oliver, Inc.
  Santa Barbara (California), USA
creative people
 Mark Oliver, Brenna Pierce, & Patty Driskel
photographer
 Burke/Triolo
client
 Silverado Food

creative firm
 Tangram Strategic Design
  Novara, Italy
creative director
 Enrico Sempi
art directors
 Enrico Sempi & Antonella Trevisan
designer
 Antonella Trevisan
illustrator
 Guido Rosa
photographer
 Vittorio Zucchelli
client
 Saiwa

193

creative firm
 Thompson Design Group
  San Francisco (California), USA
art director
 Dennis Thompson
designer
 Dave Dzurek
photographer
 Bob Montescleros
client
 Nestlé USA

creative firm
 Springetts
  London, England
client
 Dairy Crest

creative firm
 bonatodesign
  Berwyn (Pennsylvania), USA
creative people
 Donna Bonato Orr & Alvaro Iparraguirre
client
 Schratter Foods Incorporated

creative firm
 KingGraphic
  Hong Kong, China
creative people
 Soman-Yee
client
 Ramada Hotel, China

creative firm
 Artistree Thailand
  Bangkok, Thailand
creative people
 Wichai Limpatiyagorn
client
 Premier Marketing Co., Ltd.

creative firm
 Gauger & Silva Associates
  San Francisco (California), USA
creative people
 Isabelle Laporte & David Gauger
client
 Sunspire

194

creative firm
 RDW Group Inc.
  Providence (Rhode Island), USA
creative people
 Anthony Gill
client
 New England Coffee

creative firm
 McElveney & Palozzi
  Rochester (New York), USA
creative director
 Steve Palozzi
art director, designer
 Ellen Johnson
client
 Upstate Farms

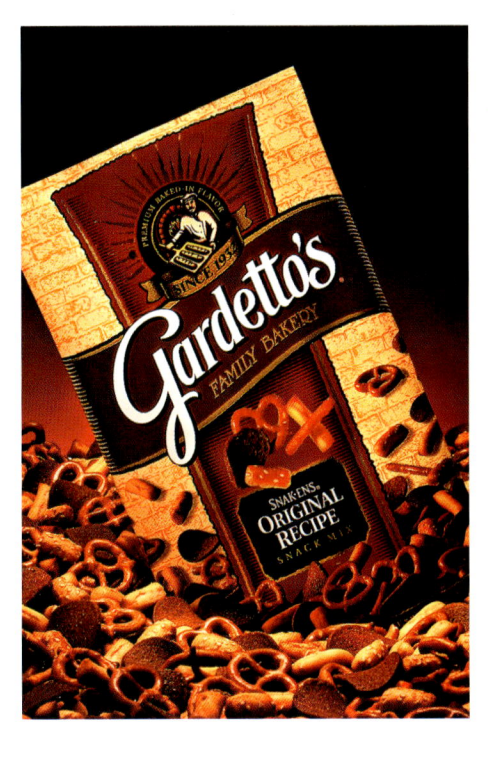

creative firm
 Design North, Inc.
  Racine (Wisconsin), USA
creative people
 Pat Cowan & Jane Marcussen
client
 Gardetto & Co., Inc.

creative firm
 WPA Pinfold
  Leeds, England
creative people
 Hayley Wall
client
 Massarella Catering Group Ltd.

195

creative firm
 Nolin Larosee
 Design Communications
  Montreal, Canada
art director
 Barbara Jacques
client
 Charcuteries Tour Eiffel

creative firm
 McCann-Erickson Korea Inc.
  Seol, Korea
creative director
 Jeremy Perrott
art director
 H. J. Park
designer
 S. H. Yang
client
 Coca-Cola Nestle

creative firm
 Curtis Design LLC
  San Francisco (California), USA
creative people
 David Curtis & Chris Benitez
client
 Fantastic Foods

creative firm
 LMS Design
  Stamford (Connecticut), USA
creative people
 Richard Shear & Alex Williams
client
 General Cigar Company

creative firm
 Gauger & Silva Associates
  San Francisco (California), USA
creative people
 Lori Murphy, John Horvers, & David Gauger
client
 San - J International

creative firm
 Thompson Design Group
  San Francisco (California), USA
art director
 Dennis Thompson
designers
 Veronica Denny & Elizabeth Berta
photographer
 Dennis Mosner
client
 Friskies Petcare, Co., Inc.

creative firm
 The Coleman Group
  Brookline (Massachusetts), USA
creative people
 Selena Bonfilio, Delza Laxamana,
 Ciro Giordano, Mike Wepplo,
 Dave Bied, & Susan Hunter
client
 H. P. Hood, Inc.

196

creative firm
 Gams Chicago
  Chicago (Illinois), USA
creative director
 David Giambrone
art director
 Jason Salas
copywriter
 Faron Greenfield
client
 Blue Haze Cigar Co.

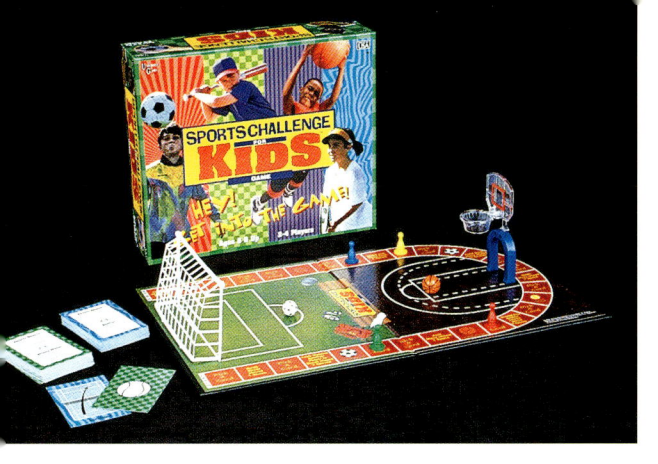

creative firm
  Hunt Weber Clark Associates
   San Francisco (California), USA
creative people
  Nancy Hunt-Weber, Christine Chung, Leigh Krichbaum,
  Jason Bell, & Jim Deeken
client
  University Games

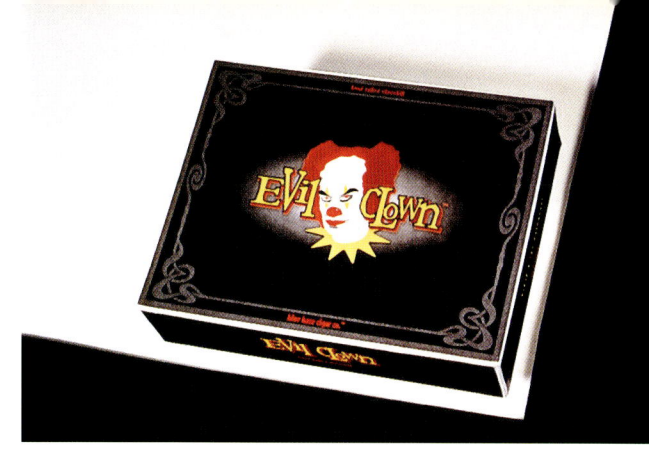

creative firm
  Gams Chicago
   Chicago (Illinois), USA
creative director
  David Giambrone
art director, designer
  Jon Perl
copywriter
  Faron Greenfield
client
  Blue Haze Cigar Co.

creative firm
  Gams Chicago
   Chicago (Illinois), USA
creative director
  David Giambrone
art director, designer
  Betsy Kane
copywriter
  Faron Greenfield
client
  Blue Haze Cigar Co.

197

creative firm
  The Hartz Mountain Corporation
   Secaucus (New Jersey), USA
creative people
  Sheri Mageskerth, Jerry Crum, Ronn Orenstein,
  & Marguerite Chadwick
client
  The Hartz Mountain Corporation

creative firm
  Media Concepts Corp.
   Assonet (Massachusetts), USA
designer
  Rosanne Romiglio
illustrator
  Bill Carroll
client
  Concord Foods, Inc.

creative firm
  Ukulele Design Consultants Pte Ltd.
  Singapore
design director
  Verna Lim
designer
  Lynn Lim
client
  Guan Sang Co Pte Ltd

creative firm
  Axion Design
  San Anselmo (California), USA
project director
  Ronda Hildebrand
client
  Guinness Import Co.

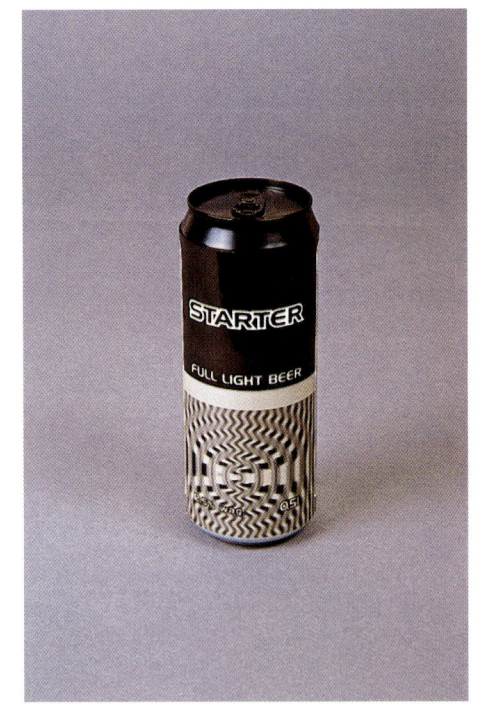

198

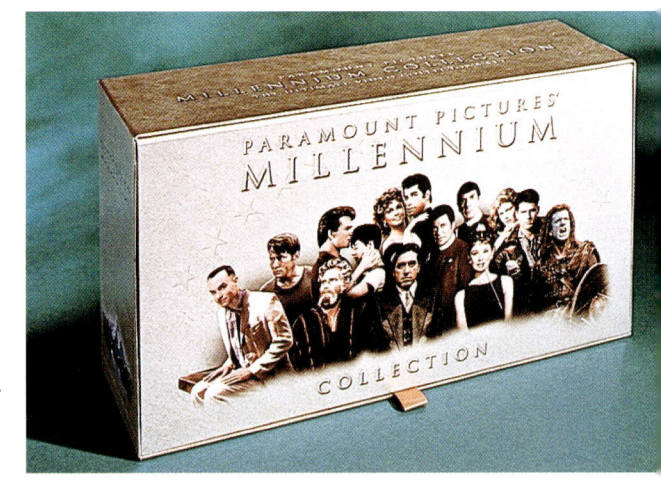

creative firm
  30sixty design, inc.
  Los Angeles (California), USA
art director, designer
  Par Larsson
client
  Paramount Home Video

creative firm
  Moby Dick Group
  Szczecin, Poland
creative people
  Wojciech Mierowski & Tomasz Woody Borawski
client
  Bosman Brewery Co. Ltd

creative firm
  Sally Johns Design
  Raleigh (North Carolina), USA
creative people
  Sally Johns & Tito Chazo
client
  Advanced Energy Corp.

creative firm
  Moby Dick Group
  Szczecin, Poland
creative people
  Wojciech Mierowski, Skawomir Barcz,
  & Tomasz Woody Borawski
client
  Bosman Brewery Co. Ltd.

creative firm
  Parham Santana Inc.
  New York (New York), USA
creative director
  John Parham
designer
  Annetta Sappenfield
creative services
  Jodi Rovin (BMG)
client
  BMG Video

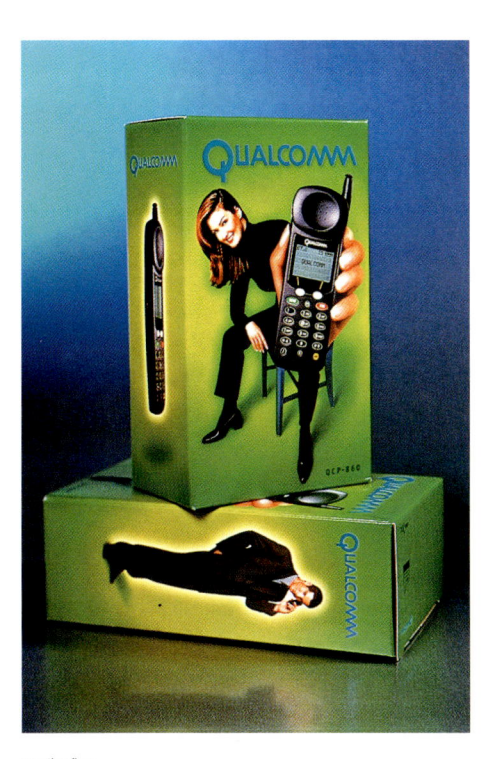

creative firm
  Pearlfisher
  London, England
creative people
  Shaun Bowen & Jonathon Ford
client
  Vin & Sprit

199

creative firm
  Mires Design, Inc.
  San Diego (California), USA
art director
  José A. Serrano
designers
  Deborah Hom & David Adey
photographer
  Carl Vanderschuit
client
  Qualcomm

creative firm
  Sterling Group
  New York (New York), USA
creative people
  Janice Pedley
client
  Austin Nichols

creative firm
  Teamwork Design Ltd.
    Hong Kong, China
creative people
  Gary Tam, Ivy Wong, Alex Chan, & Joel Ong
client
  Nuance-Watson (HK) Ltd.

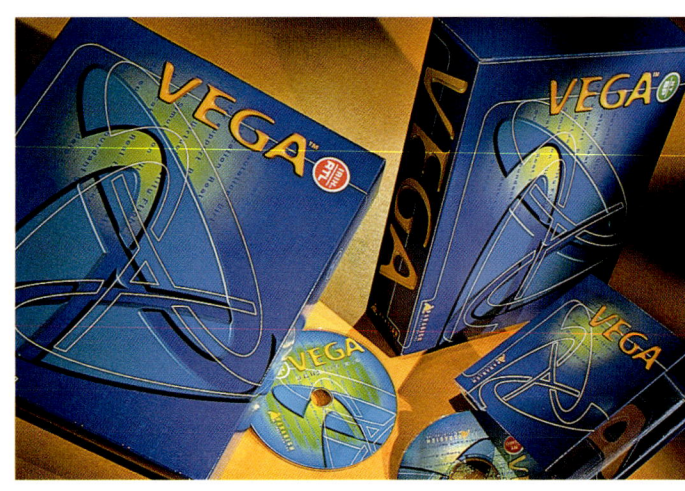

creative firm
  David Carter Design Associates
    Dallas (Texas), USA
creative director
  Lori B. Wilson
designer
  Tien Pham
client
  Paradigm

creative firm
  Moby Dick Group
    Szczecin, Poland
creative people
  Wojciech Mierowski & Tomasz Woody Borawski
client
  Bosman Brewery Co. Ltd.

creative firm
  Seasonal Specialties
  Creative Services
    Eden Prairie (Minnesota), USA
designers
  Jennifer Sheeler, Barbara J. Roth, & Lisa Milan
photo illustrators
  Lisa Milan, Michelle Loch, & Tracy Olson
client
  Seasonal Specialities LLC

creative firm
  Metzler & Associes
    Paris, France
creative director
  M. A. Herrmann
designers
  M. Laporte & Y. Grannec
client
  Canon France

creative firm
  Nakatsuka Daisuke Inc.
  Tokyo, Japan
creative director
  Shu Uemura
art director
  Daisuke Nakatsuka
designer
  Kanna Numajiri
client
  Shu Uemura Cosmetics Inc.

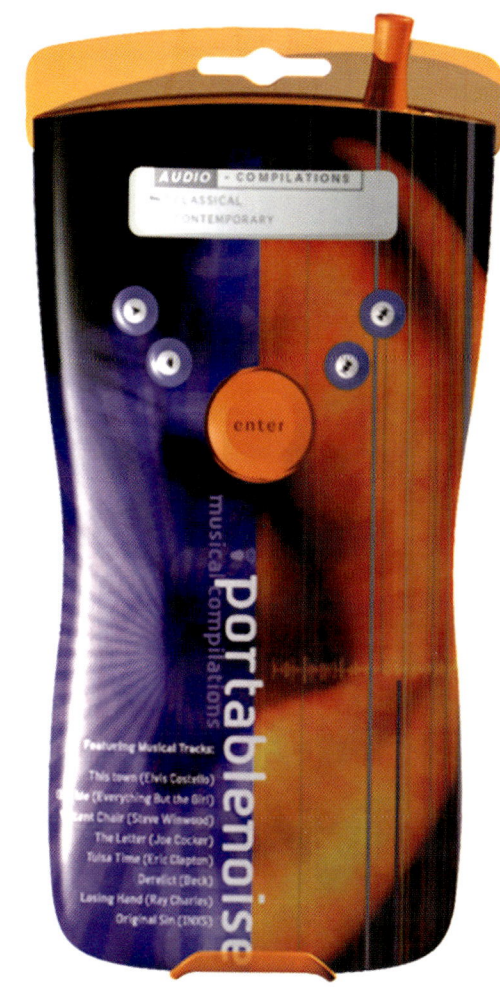

creative firm
  Lunar Design
  Palo Alto (California), USA
creative people
  Tad Toulis, Becky Brown, Tessa Gurney,
  Lea Kobeli, Jeff Hoefer, & Ed Serapio

201

creative firm
  Sterling Group
  New York (New York), USA
creative people
  Stephanie Godkin
client
  Jose Cuervo International

creative firm
  DHI Visual Communication
  Vero Beach (Florida), USA
creative people
  Sean Clinton, Ken Walters, & Carl Miller
client
  The New Piper Aircraft, Inc.

# CREATIVITY
## Calendars

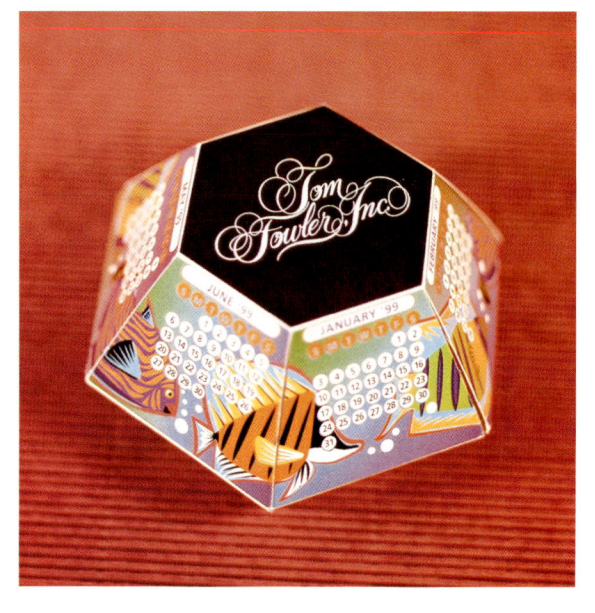

creative firm
  Tom Fowler, Inc.
  Stamford (Connecticut), USA
creative people
  Elizabeth P. Ball
client
  Graphics Three, Inc.

creative firm
  Workman Publishing
  New York (New York), USA
creative people
  Janet Vicaro & Paul Gamarello
client
  Workman Publishing

202

creative firm
  Baker Designed Communications
  Santa Monica (California), USA
creative director
  Gary Baker
designer
  Michelle Wolins
client
  Baker

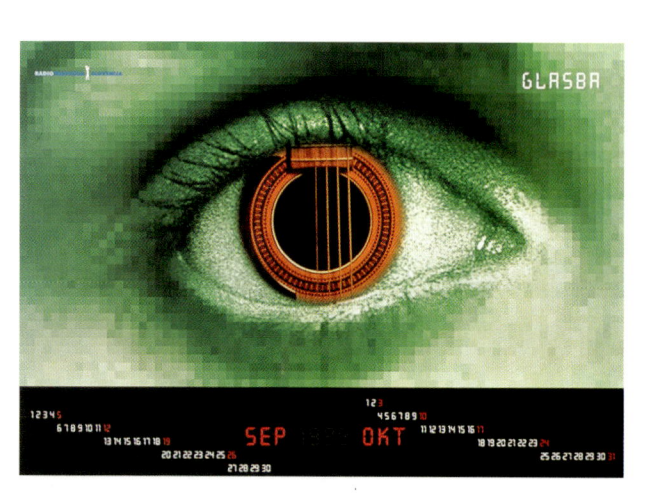

creative firm
  AERIAL
  San Francisco (California), USA
creative people
  Tracy Moon
client
  AERIAL Visual Identity Design

creative firm
  Qualcomm Design Group
  San Diego (California), USA
creative director
  Christopher Lee
client
  Qualcomm

creative firm
  Stan Gellman Graphic Design
  St. Louis (Missouri), USA
creative people
  Teresa Thompson, Mike Donovan,
  Jill Lamden, & Barry Tilson
client
  Bloomington Offset Process Inc.

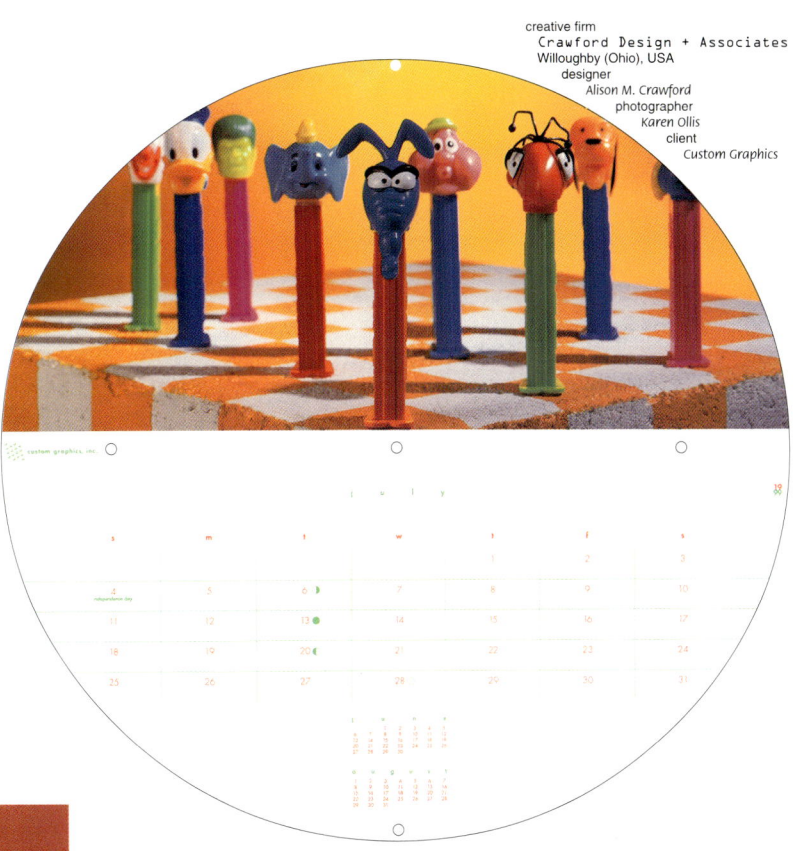

creative firm
  Crawford Design + Associates
  Willoughby (Ohio), USA
designer
  Alison M. Crawford
photographer
  Karen Ollis
client
  Custom Graphics

creative firm
  Computer Sciences Corporation
  Falls Church (Virginia), USA
creative directors
  Karen Loehr & John Farquhar
designer
  Karen Loehr
client
  Compter Sciences Corporation

203

creative firm
  IE Design
  Studio City (California), USA
creative people
  Marcie Carson & David Gilmour
illustrator
  Mirjam Selmi
client
  IE Design

creative firm
  Clarke Thompson
  New York (New York), USA
creative director
  Bud Clarke
designer
  Younie Kim
illustrator
  James Yang
client
  Clarke Thompson

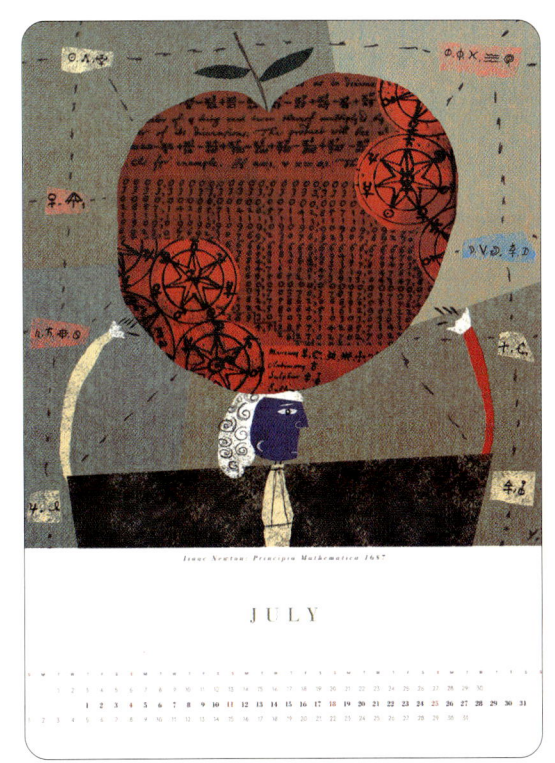

creative firm
 Workman Publishing
  New York (New York), USA
creative people
 Paul Gamarello
client
 Lisa Hollander

creative firm
 AERIAL
  San Francisco
  (California), USA
creative people
 Tracy Moon
client
 AERIAL Visual
 Identity Design

creative firm
 Workman Publishing
  New York (New York), USA
creative people
 Paul Gamarello
client
 Workman Publishing

creative firm
 DBD International
  Menomonie (Wisconsin), USA
art director, designer, illustrator
 David Brier
client
 DBD International

creative firm
 Paprika Communications
  Montréal (Québec), Canada
art director
 Louis Gagnon
designer
 Francis Turgeon
illustrator
 Bruce Roberts
client
 Baronet

creative firm
  Belyea
    Seattle (Washington), USA
art director
  Patricia Belyea
designer
  Ron Lars Hansen
photographer
  Rosanne Olson
client
  Belyea

creative firm
  All Media Projects Ltd (Ample)
    St. Clair, Trinidad & Tobago
art director
  Desmond Jutla
graphic designer
  Illya Furlonge-Walker
client
  Colonial Life Insuranc Company (Trinidad) Ltd

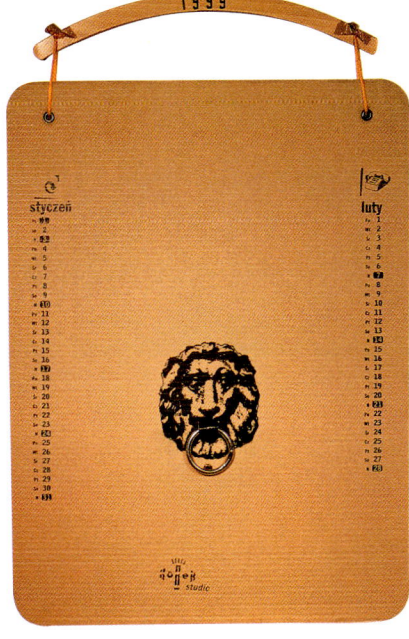

creative firm
  Korek Studio
    Warsaw, Poland
art director
  Wojtek Korkuć
client
  Korek Studio

205

creative firm
  AAC Integrated Commications
    Hamilton, Bermuda
art director, illustrator
  Rhona Emmerson
digital artists
  Ceral Undo & Janine Advice
client
  BF&W Insurance Group

creative firm
  Workman Publishing
    New York (New York), USA
creative people
  Paul Hanson & Jeanne Hogel

206

creative firm
  Workman Publishing
  New York (New York), USA
creative people
  Janet Vicaro & Paul Gamarello
client
  Workman Publishing

creative firm
  Kompas Design
  Ljubljana, Slovenia
art director
  Zare Kerin
designer
  Anka Bernik
photographer
  Bogdan Kladnik
client
  Imos Ljubljana

creative firm
  Catalyst Direct, Inc.
  Rochester (New York), USA
creative directors
  Meghan Labonge & Kevin Schroer
senior art director
  Jennifer Wagner
copywriter
  Frank Brady
client
  Catalyst Direct, Inc.

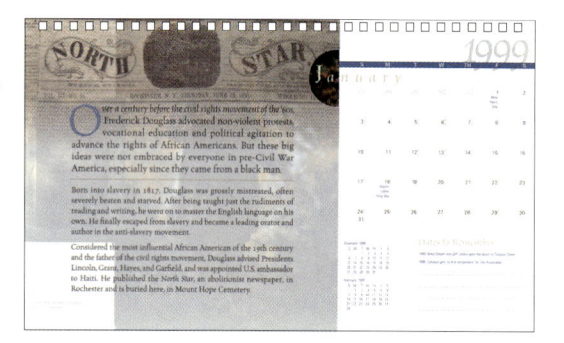

creative firm
  Workman Publishing
  New York (New York), USA
creative people
  Paul Gamarello
client
  Workman Publishing

creative firm
  Vogue Magazine
  New York (New York), USA
designer
  Pamela Gelbert
client
  Vogue Magazine

# CREATIVITY

## Direct Mail Pieces

creative firm
**The Benchmark Group**
Cincinnati (Ohio), USA
creative people
John Carpenter, Chris Forsythe,
Ken Neade, & Leslie Hall
client
Centerline Software, Inc.

creative firm
**Fairly Painless Advertising**
Holland (Michigan), USA
creative director
Chris Cook
art director, designer
Brian Hauch
client
Drawform

creative firm
**Gallery Ltd**
Hong Kong, China
creative people
Benny Cheng, Rayond Fu,
& Kelvin Parker
client
Gallery Ltd

creative firm
**Everest Integrated Communications Pvt. Ltd.**
Mumbai (Maharashtra), India
creative people
Mr. Uday Parkar &
Mr. Vijay Subramaniam
client
Matheran Bachao Samiti

creative firm
**Dana Buckley, Inc.**
New York (New York), USA
art director
Jim Streacker

207

creative firm
 winson & terry
 design consultants
 pte ltd
 Singapore
creative people
 Ong Kah Yong & Winson Sit
client
 Symantec Singapore Pte Ltd.

creative firm
 The Benchmark
 Group
 Cincinnati (Ohio), USA
creative people
 John Carpenter,
 Chris Forsythe, & Leslie Hall
client
 Millennia III, Inc.

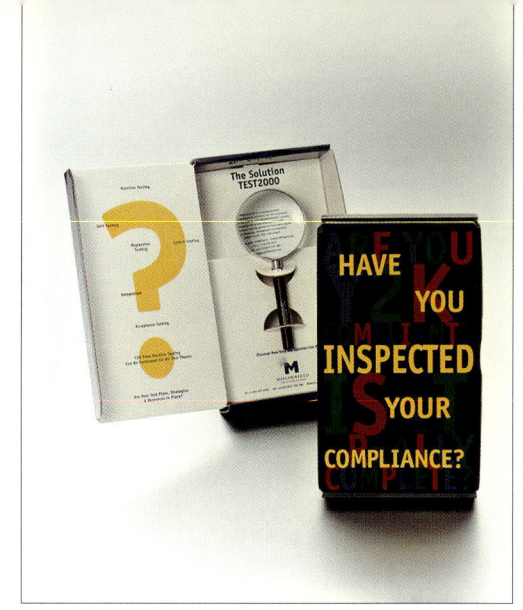

208

creative firm
 Braindance
 Atlanta (Georgia), USA
creative people
 Blake Parkman, Tom Wood,
 Cindy Beebee, David Schulz,
 & Mark Synder
client
 Braindance

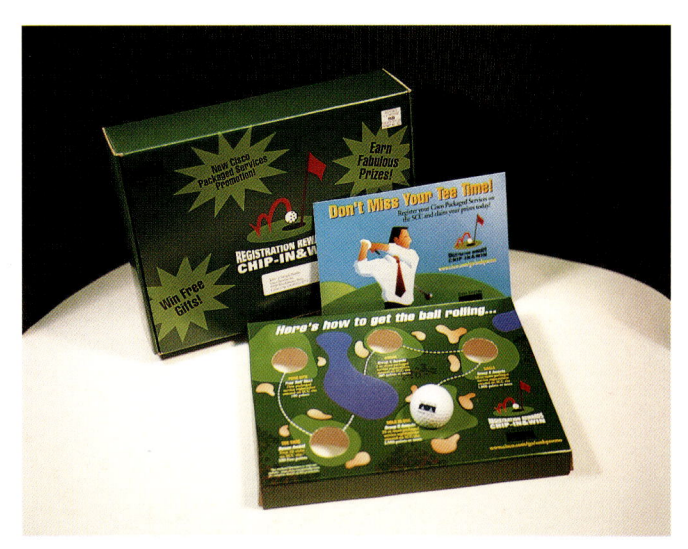

creative firm
 Jack Nadel, Inc.
 Los Angeles (California), USA
creative director, illustrator
 Scott Brown
copywriter
 Robert Buckingham
client
 Cisco Systems, Inc.

creative firm
 Flowers
 & Fedele
 Dallas (Texas), USA
creative director
 Anthony Fedele
art director
 Aaron Steele
copywriter
 J. Frederick
client
 Cinema Tech

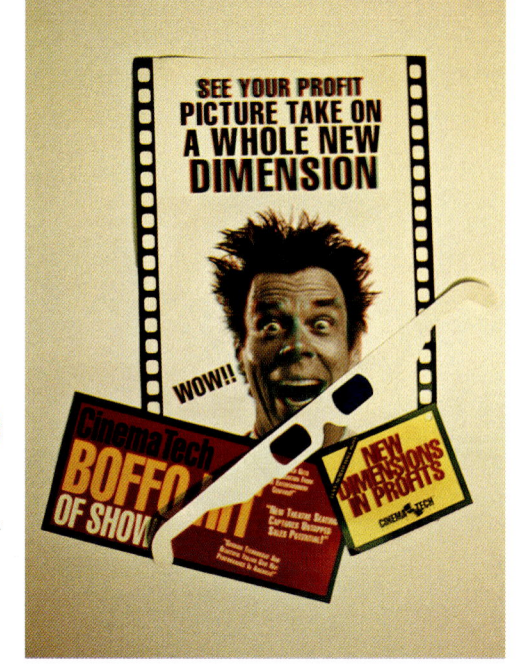

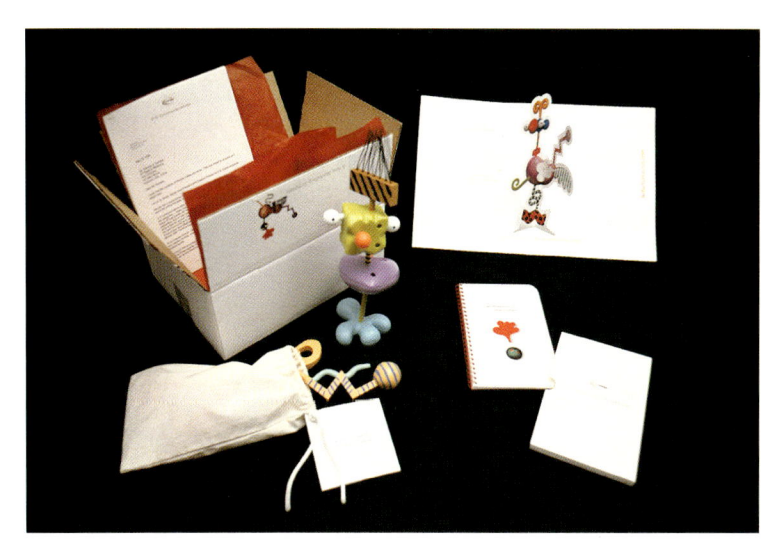

creative firm
 Dugan Valva Contess
  Morristown (New Jersey), USA
creative director
 Stephanie Murrin
art director
 Karen Zinn
copywriter
 Nina Sloan
client
 Dugan Valva Contess

creative firm
 C-E Communications
  Warren (Michigan), USA
creative directors
 Susan Logar, Raymond Allston,
 & Jim Krechnyak
art directors
 Jim Krechnyak & Terry Sharbach
copywriter
 Jennifer Thomas & Molly Schechter
client
 C-E Communications

creative firm
 DHI Visual Communciation
  Vero Beach (Florida), USA
creative people
 Sandra Vogt & Carl Miller
client
 DHI Visual Communication

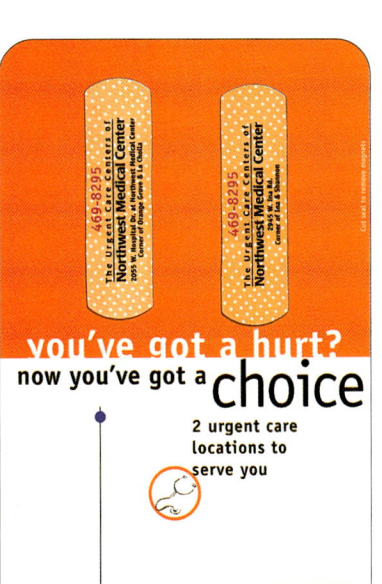

209

creative firm
 Boelts Bros. Associates
  Tucson (Arizona), USA
creative people
 Kerry Stratford
client
 Northwest Medical Center

creative firm
 Louis London
  St. Louis (Missouri), USA
art director
 David Penn
digital retouching
 Beth Estes
copywriter
 Staci Yawitz
client
 Boise Cascade Office Products

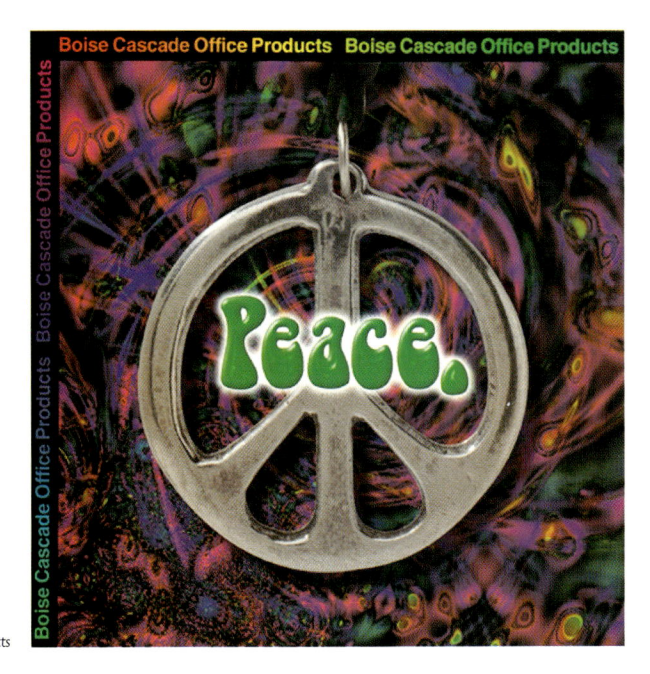

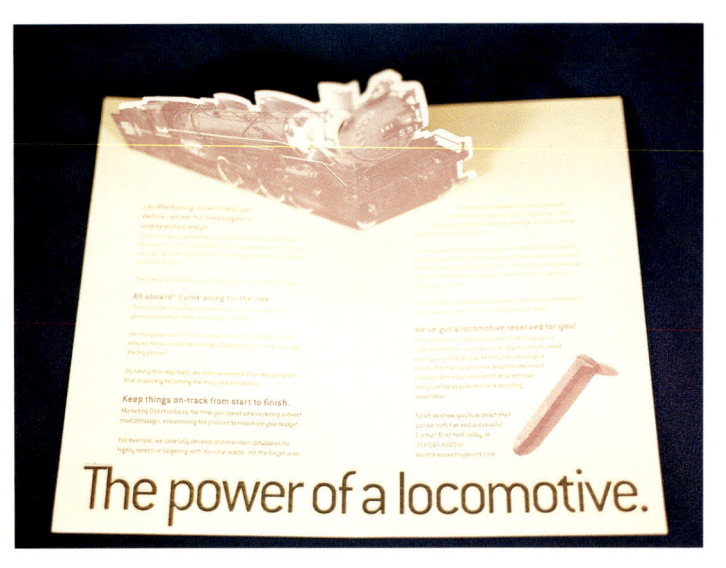

creative firm
  Metropolis Design
    St. Louis (Missouri), USA
creative people
  Andy Quevreaux
client
  Marketing Direct

creative firm
  Sackett Design Associates
    San Francisco (California), USA
designers
  James Sakamoto & Mark Sackett
copywriter
  Diane Olberg
client
  Charles Schwab & Co., Inc.

creative firm
  Ukulele Design
  Consultants Pte Ltd.
    Singapore
design director
  Kim Chun-wei
designer
  Lee Shin Kee
copywriter
  Roger Hiew
client
  Lucent Technologies (S) Pte Ltd.

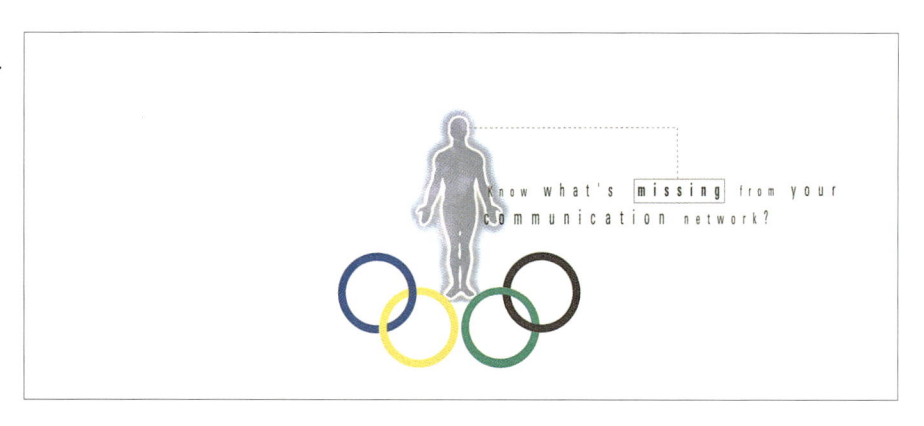

210

creative firm
  AJF Marketing
    Piscataway (New Jersey), USA
creative people
  Justin Brindisi & Paul Borkowski
client
  AJF Marketing

creative firm
 degree inc.
  Osaka, Japan
art director
 Nabawishi Yasaka
designer
 Matsumoto Fumiko
client
 degree inc.

creative firm
 Lowe Fox Pavlika
  New York (New York), USA
creative people
 Bob Buzas & Jeremy Feldman
client
 MONY

211

creative firm
 Kopf Zimmermann Schultheis
  Hauppauge (New York), USA
art director
 Art Zimmermann
photographer
 Richard Shepard
copywriter
 Michael Schiano
client
 GN Netcom, Inc.

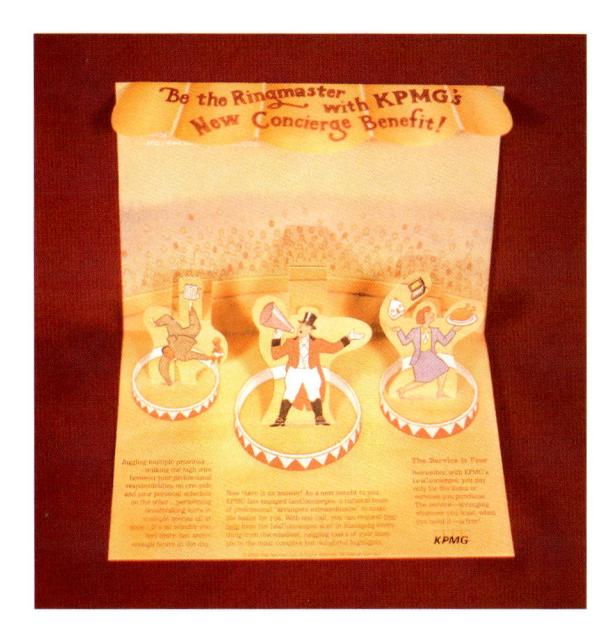

creative firm
 Clarke & Associates LLC
  Somerville (New Jersey), USA
art director
 Ken Thorlton
illustrator
 Robert Saunders
client
 KPMG

212

creative firm
 Fader Unda Sohn
 New York (New York), USA
client
 Todd Haiman Studio

creative firm
 Callahan and Company
 Baltimore (Maryland), USA
creative people
 Paula Sloane, Kate Cogswell, Geoff Graham,
 Bruce Weller, Andrea Cipriani, Patrick Walkinshaw,
 Charles Freeman, & Deborah Mazzoleni
client
 Callahan and Company

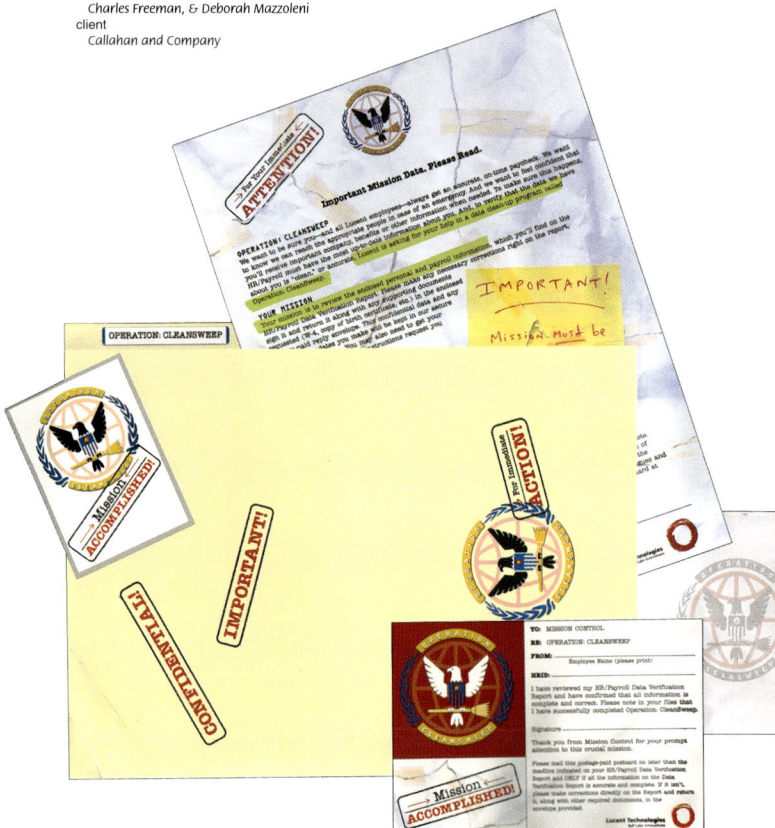

creative firm
 DHI Visual Communication
 Vero Beach (Florida), USA
creative people
 Marty Regan & Carl Miller
client
 DHI Visual Communication

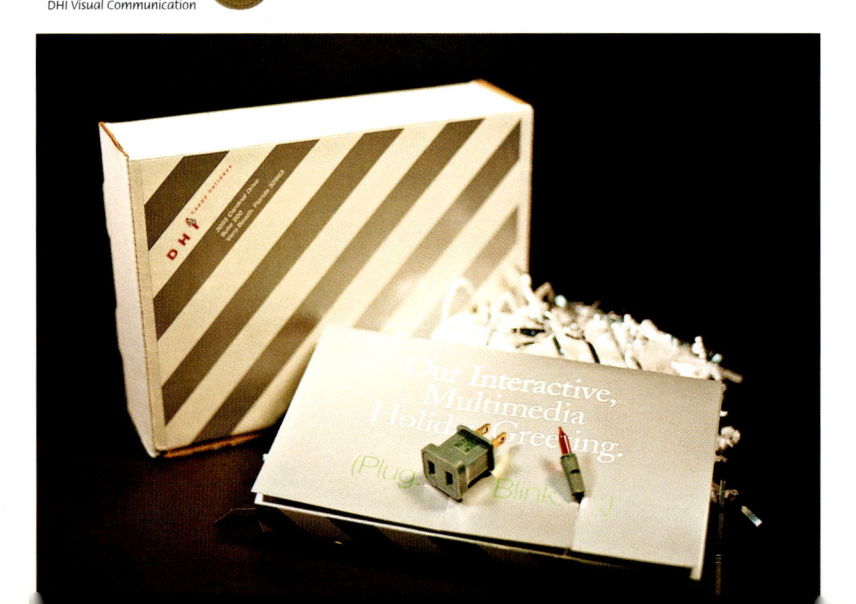

creative firm
 Clarke & Associates LLC
 Somerville (New Jersey), USA
creative director
 Susan Willett
art director
 Ken Thorlton
copywriter
 Nancy Cavallo
client
 Lucent Technologies

creative firm
  Hult Fritz Matuszak
  Peoria (Illinois), USA
art director
  Dave Wiggins
copywriter
  Scott Fishel
client
  Maui Jim, Inc.

creative firm
  Wong•Wong•Boack, Inc.
  San Francisco (California), USA
creative people
  Ben Wong, Penelope Wong, Homan Lee,
  Pagely Tucker, Yolanda Petriz-Morris, &
  Phuong-Mai Bui-Quang
client
  Cisco Systems, Inc.

creative firm
  Spencer Zahn & Associates
  Philadelphia (Pennsylvania), USA
creative director
  Spencer Zahn
art director
  Joseph McCarthy
client
  DC 2

creative firm
  HDS Marcomm
  Santa Clara (California), USA
art director, designer
  Michael McCann
copywriter
  Taya Graham
client
  Hitachi Data Systems

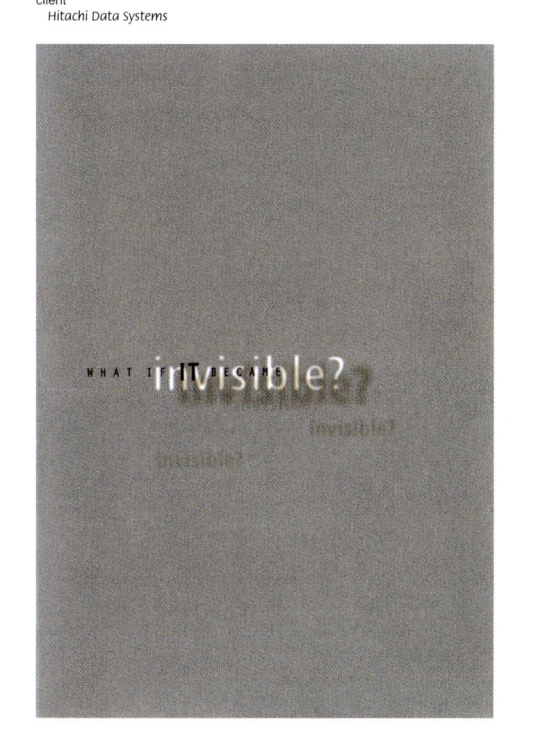

creative firm
  Artefact Design
  Palo Alto (California), USA
creative people
  Artefact Design
client
  Network Appliance

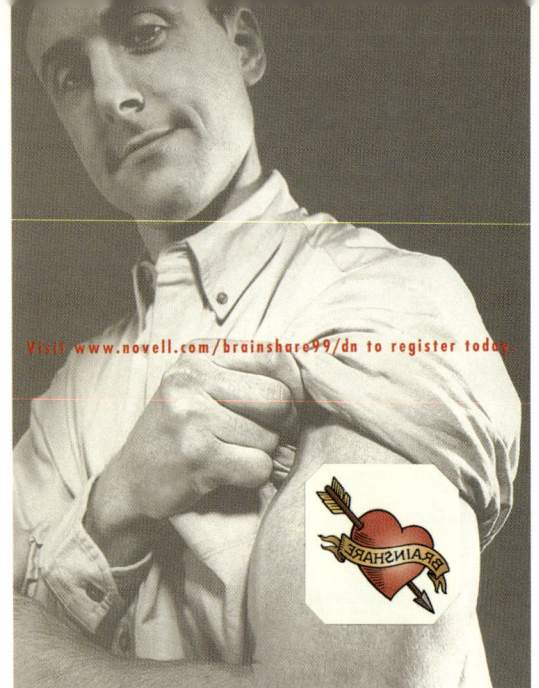

creative firm
  **Wunderman Cato Johnson**
  San Francisco (California), USA
creative directors
  John Meyer & Steve Alfano
art director
  Shannon Brown
copywriter
  Ida Gamban
client
  Novell

creative firm
  **Morgan & Partners**
  Jacksonville (Florida), USA
art director
  Bryan Cox
production
  Brian Thompson
copywriter
  Kathy Bronson
client
  Jacksonville Chamber of Commerce

creative firm
  **Whitney Stinger**
  Clayton (Missouri), USA
creative director
  Michael Whitney
production
  Karl Stinger
client
  Whitney Stinger

creative firm
  **Lawrence, Mayo & Ponder**
  Newport Beach (California), USA
creative directors
  Lynda Lawrence & Bruce Mayo
art director
  Simone Beavdoin
designer
  Brenda Tradii
copywriters
  Lynda Lawrence & Rick Underwood
client
  Lawrence, Mayo & Ponder

creative firm
  **Ambush Communication**
  New York (New York), USA
art director
  Keith Mastandrea
client
  Crain Communication Inc.

creative firm
  Sides & Associates, Inc.
    Lafayette (Louisiana), USA
creative director
  Larry Sides
art director
  Will Bailey
client
  SECON

We're taking your whiz, we're checking it twice, we're gonna find out who's naughty or nice.

creative firm
  H2D, Inc.
    Milwaukee (Wisconsin), USA
creative people
  Joseph Hausch & Allan Haas
client
  H2D, Inc.

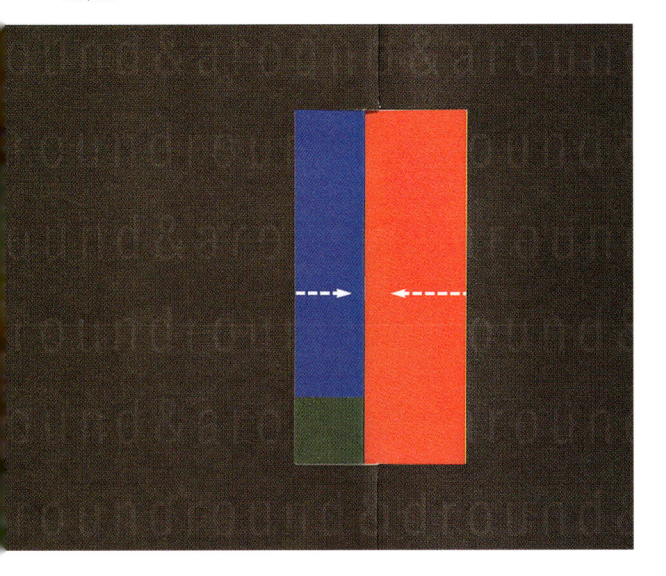

creative firm
  Redbook Promotion Dept.
    New York (New York), USA
creative director
  Denise Benay
art director
  Joel Benay
client
  Redbook Magazine

Do your **network** choices lead you to a **BIG PUZZLE?** Let us put your choice clearly into perspective you. Novell.

creative firm
  Burrows WCJ
    Shenfield (Essex), England
creative director
  Roydon Hearne
art director
  Robin Lowry
copywriters
  Graham Woods & Joan Dance
client
  Silverstone Race Circuit (UK)

creative firm
  winson & terry design consultants pte ltd
    Singapore
creative people
  Karine Low
client
  Novell Singapore Pte Ltd.

creative firm
 M & A Design
 Cape Town,
 Republic of South Africa
creative people
 Marjoleine Van Der Walt
 & Louise Kelly
copywriter
 Dena Benatan
client
 Woolworths

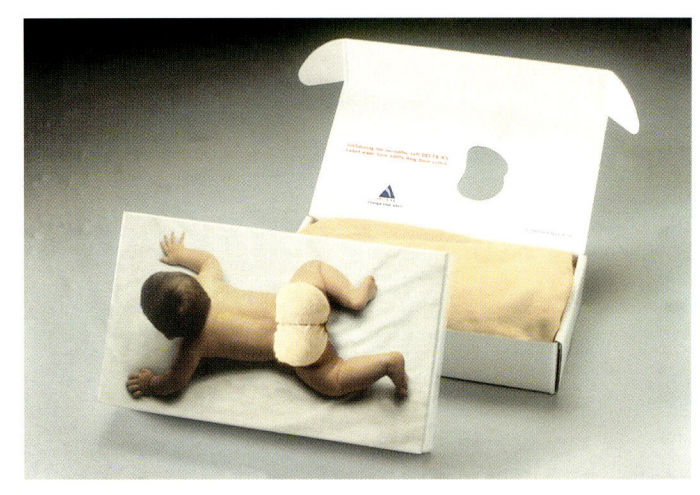

creative firm
 Sawyer
 Riley Compton
 Atlanta (Georgia), USA
creative director
 Bart Cleveland
art director
 Kevin Thoem
photographer
 Greg Slater
copywriter
 Brett Compton
client
 Delta Apparel

{ WE'RE RELOCATING OUR NEST... }

... BUT THAT DOESN'T MEAN WE
HAVE CHANGED OUR FEATHERS.

YOU CAN EXPECT THE SAME LEVEL OF
COMMITMENT FROM
THE TEAM AT UKULELE.
IN FACT, WITH A BIGGER PREMISE
AND FRESHER AIR UP THERE,
WE'RE ALL GEARED UP TO BRING YOU
THE WHOLE NEW OUTLOOK IN
COMMUNICATIONS AND DESIGN.

HERE'S WISHING YOU AN
EARLY BIRD'S SEASON'S GREETINGS.

OUR NEW ADDRESS EFFECTIVE
TUESDAY, 12 NOV 96
8 NEW INDUSTRIAL RD
#02-03 LHK 3 BUILDING
SINGAPORE 536200
TEL: (65) 281 8482
FAX: (65) 281 1418

UKULELE ADVERTISING & DESIGN

216

I was on cloud nine

creative firm
 Ukulele Design
 Consultants
 Pte Ltd.
 Sinapore
design director
 Kim Chun-wei
designer
 Lee Shin Kee
copywriter
 Evelyn Teng
client
 Paper Dimension(s)
 Pte Ltd.

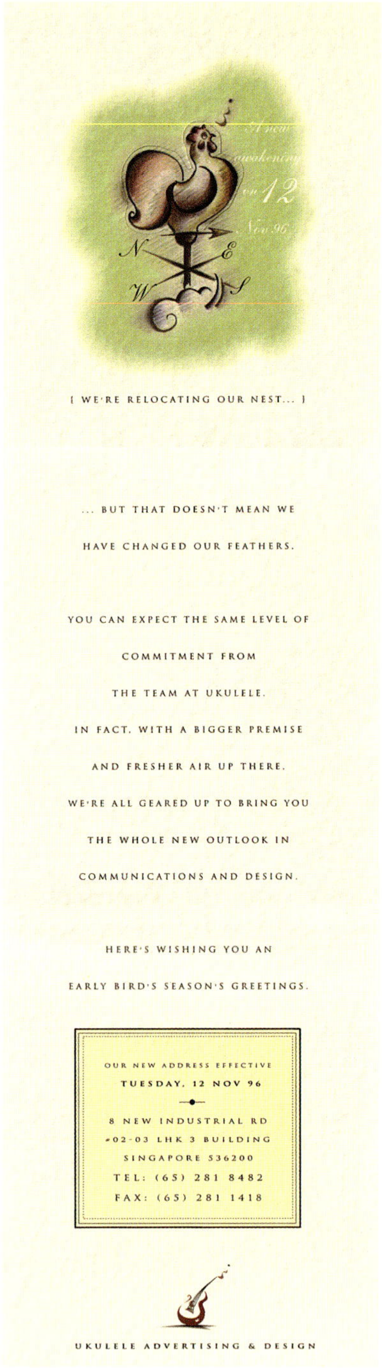

creative firm
 Ukulele Design Consultants Pte Ltd.
 Singapore
design director
 Verna Lim
client
 Ukulele Design Consultants Pte Ltd.

We've taken

Simplicity

and given it a voice.

creative firm
 Dymun Nelson & Company
 Pittsburgh (Pennsylvania), USA
creative directors
 John Dymun & Craig Otto
art director
 Anthony Musmanno
copywriter
 Terrence MClusky
client
 Pittsburgh Paints

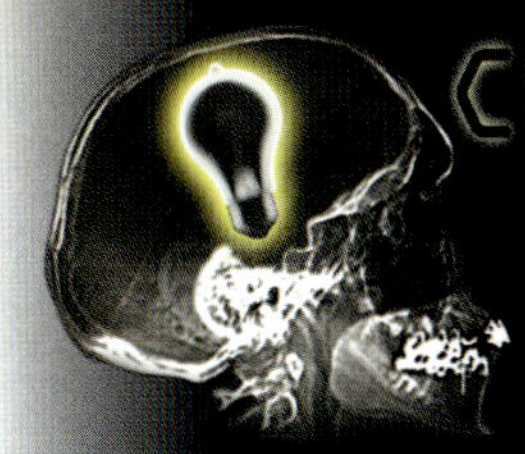

# CREATIVITY

## T-shirts

creative firm
  **Whitney Stinger**
  Clayton (Missouri), USA
creative director
  Michael Whitney
production
  Karl Stinger
client
  Littlefield Unlimited

creative firm
  **Jack Nadel, Inc.**
  Los Angeles (California), USA
creative director, illustrator
  Scott Brown
client
  D.A.R.E. America

creative firm
  **Hausman Design, Inc.**
  Palo Alto (California), USA
creative people
  Joan L. Hausman & Linda Aryani
client
  Hausman Design, Inc.

creative firm
  **Human•I•Tees**
  Fairlawn (New Jersey), USA
art director
  Donna Martines

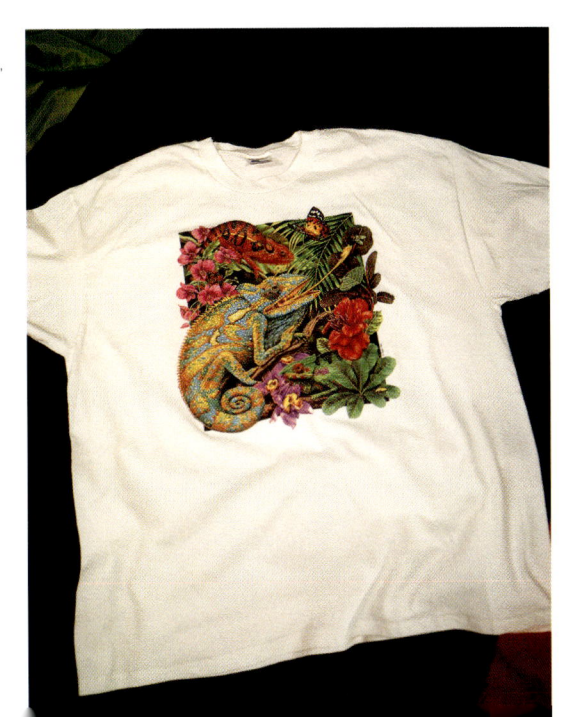

217

creative firm
Stan Gellman Graphic Design
St. Louis (Missouri), USA
creative people
Barry Tilson & Mike Donovan
client
Peernet Group, Inc.

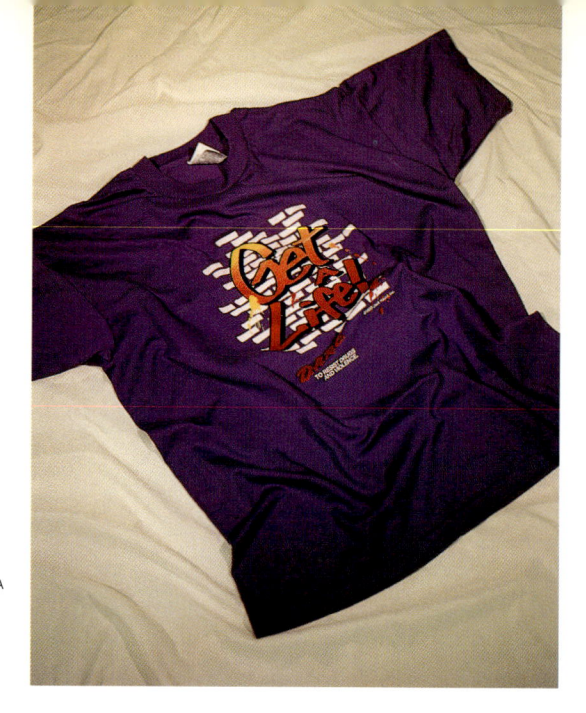

creative firm
JWT Specialized Communications
St. Louis
Los Angeles (California), USA
creative director, copywriter
Tim Kidwell
art director
Gene Kuehnle
client
Federal Express

creative firm
Ukulele Design Consultants Pte Ltd
Singapore
design director
Kim Chun-wei
designer
Lee Shin Kee
client
The Jeunes Shop

218

creative firm
Jack Nadel, Inc.
Los Angeles (California), USA
creative director, illustrator
Scott Brown
client
D.A.R.E. America

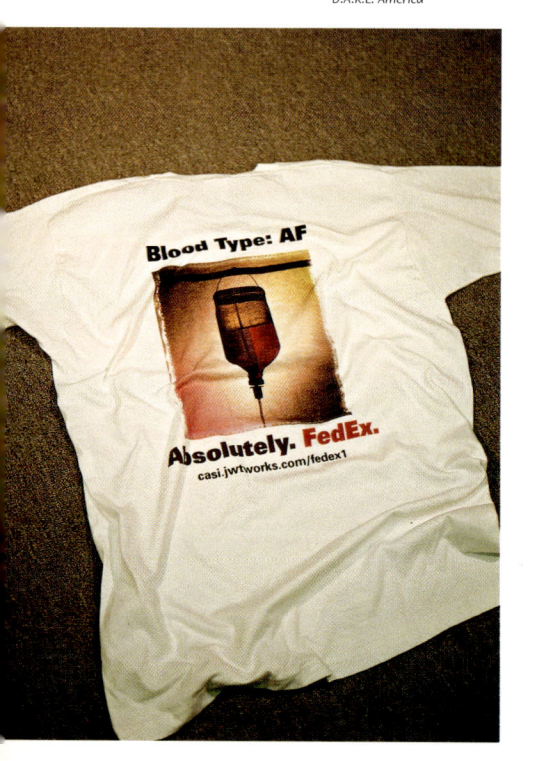

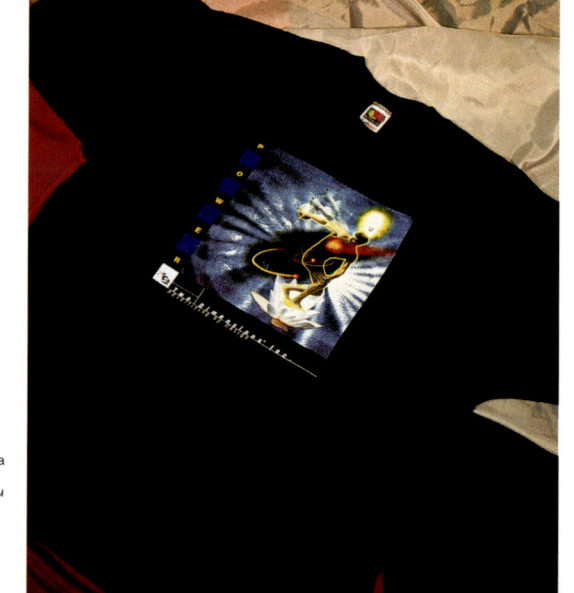

creative firm
Two Dimensions
Toronto (Ontairo), Canada
creative people
Queenie Wu & Kam Wai Yu
client
Two Dimensions

# CREATIVITY 29
## Promotional Pieces

creative firm
  **Savage Design Group, Inc.**
  Houston (Texas), USA
creative people
  Paula Savage, Dahlia Salazar,
  Robin Tooms, Barbara Weeke, Bo Bothe,
  Molly Glasgow, Doug Hebert, Tracy Price,
  Kenny Ragland, Yi May Yang, & Jay Stevens
client
  Savage Design Group

creative firm
  **Dookim Inc.**
  Seoul, Korea
creative people
  Doo Kim & Yeon J. Hong
client
  Dookim Inc.

creative firm
  **The Ungar Group**
  Chicago (Illinois), USA
creative people
  Tom Ungar & Mark Ingraham
client
  Newell Rubbermaid

creative firm
  **Robert Meyers**
  Cuyahoga Falls (Ohio), USA
creative director, designer
  Robert Meyers
client
  Mark & Myrna Mason

creative firm
 Jack Nadel, Inc.
  Los Angeles (California), USA
creative director, illustrator
 Scott Brown
client
 Scott Brown

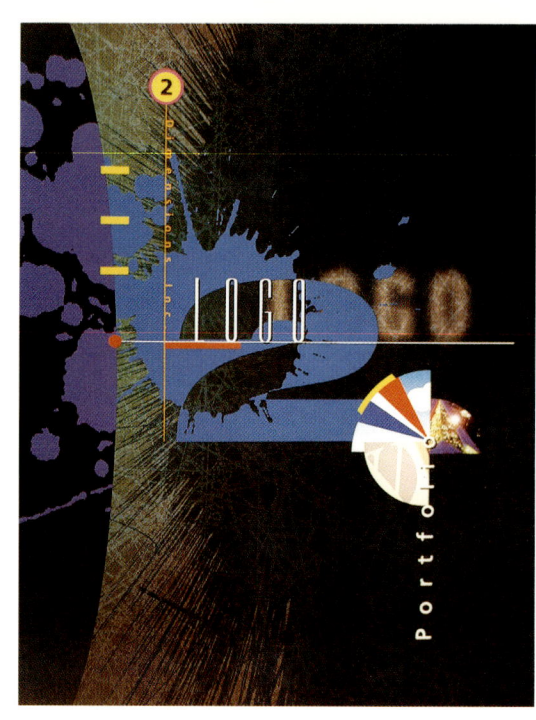

creative firm
 Two Dimensions
  Toronto (Ontario), Canada
creative people
 Queeni Wu, Patrick Dinglesen,
 Vodo Lam, & Kam Wai Yu
client
 Two Dimensions

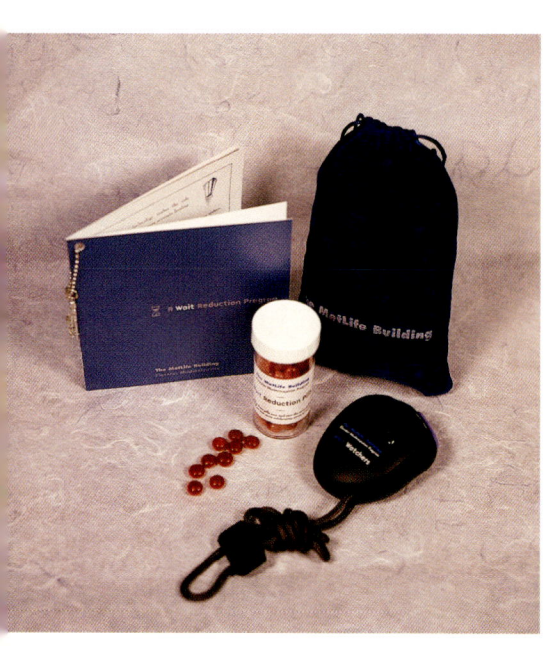

220

creative firm
 Wages Design
  Atlanta (Georgia), USA
creative people
 Randy Allison
client
 Cadmus

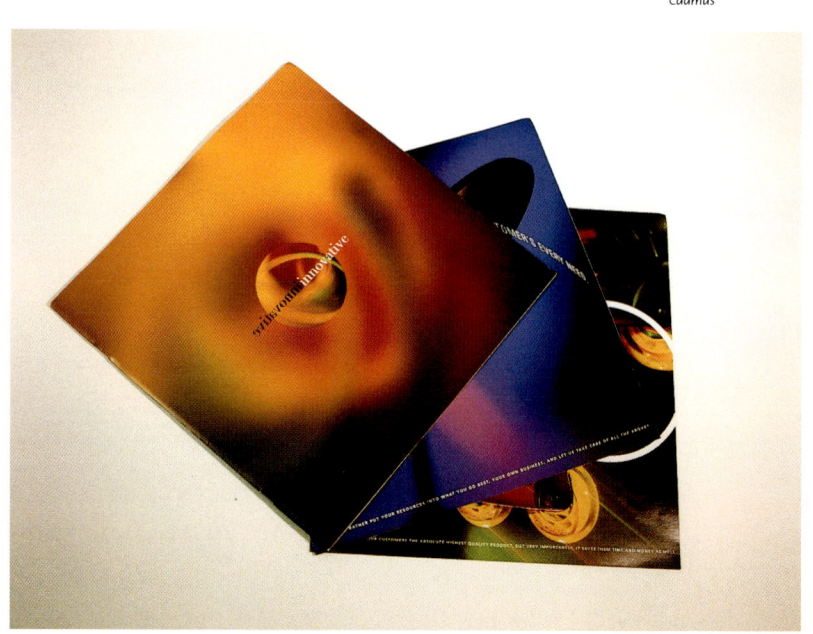

creative firm
 NPM Advertising
  New York (New York), USA
art director, designer
 Brian Wong
copywriters
 Arthur Lohman & Paul Summer
client
 Metlife

creative firm
  Studio Gallo
    San Antonio (Texas), USA
creative people
  Clare Rihn-Smith
client
  Rosario's Mexican Cafe

creative firm
  Richland Design Associates
    Newton (Massachusetts), USA
art director
  Judith Richland
designers
  Douglas Fortad & Christine Jorge
client
  Investext

221

creative firm
  Estudio Ray
    Phoenix (Arizona), USA
creative people
  Joe Ray, Christine Ray, & Leslie Link
client
  Estudio Ray

creative firm
  Disneyland Creative Services
    Anaheim (California), USA
creative director
  Scott Starkey
project manager
  Beth Campbell
coordinator
  Marilyn Carter
production designers
  Dathan Shore & Michael Firman
illustrator
  Korobkin & Associates
client
  Disneyland Food Operations: Michael Berry,
  Disneyland Marketing Services: Paula Freeman

creative firm
  McGaughy Design
    Falls Church (Virginia), USA
designer
  Malcolm McGaughy
client
  National Adult Baseball Assoc.

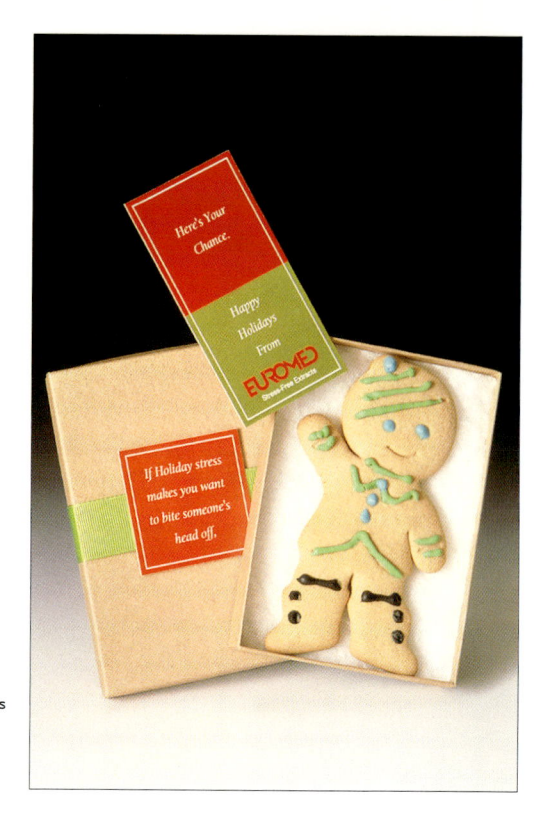

creative firm
  Gauger & Silva Associates
    San Francisco (California), USA
creative people
  Isabelle Laporte & David Gauger
client
  Euromed

creative firm
  HBO
    New York (New York), USA
art director
  Venus R. Dennsion
designers
  Venus Dennison & Frances Richer
client
  HBO

creative firm
  Agnew Moyer Smith Inc.
    Pittsburgh (Pennsylvania), USA
creative people
  Norm Goldberg, Kurt Hess, &
  George Heidekat
client
  Agnew Moyer Smith Inc.

creative firm
  Kim Baer Design Associates
    Venice (California), USA
art director
  Kim Baer
designer
  Barbara Cooper
client
  The Getty Conservation Institute

creative firm
  David Carter Design Associates
    Dallas (Texas), USA
creative director
  Lori B. Wilson
designer
  Katherine Baronet
client
  David Carter

223

creative firm
  BBK Studio Inc.
    Grand Rapids (Michigan), USA
creative director, designer, typesetter
  Yang Kim
illustrator
  Rebecca Gibson
copywriters
  Yang Kim & Betty Harag
client
  The Etheridge Company

creative firm
  Fairly Painless Advertising
    Holland (Michigan), USA
creative director, art director
  Cheryl Bell
designer
  Eunhee Hoffman
client
  Herman Miller

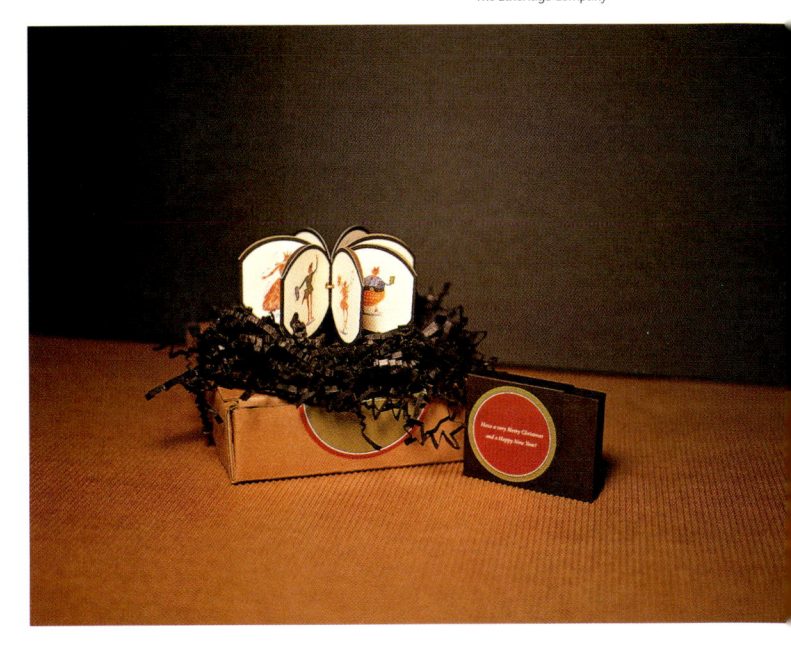

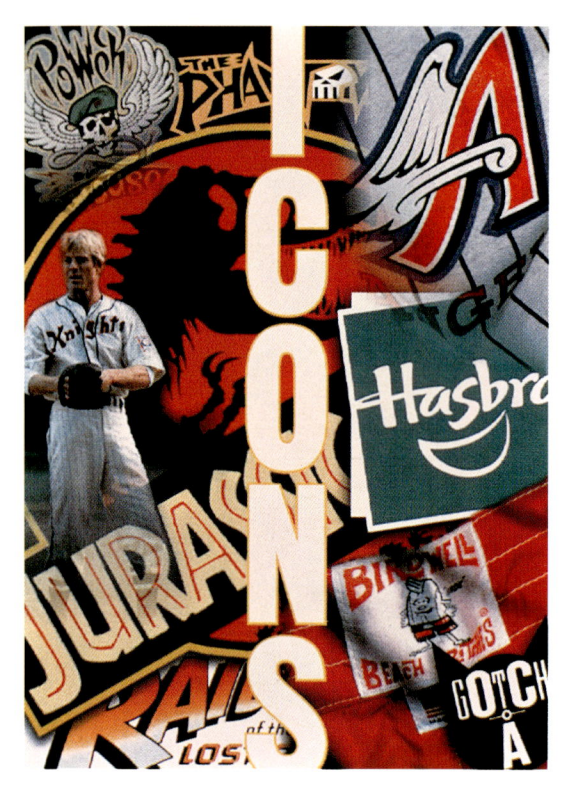

creative firm
  Salisbury LLC
    Venice (California), USA
creative people
  Mike Salisbury & Tor Naerheim
client
  Salisbury LLC

creative firm
  David Lemley Design
    Seattle (Washington), USA
designers
  David Lemley & Matt Peloza
preacher
  David Lemley
client
  One Reel (Bumbershoot)

224

creative firm
  iridium Marketing + Design
    Ottawa (Ontario), USA
creative people
  Étienne Bessette, Jean-Luc Denat,
  Stephen J. Hards, & Lucero Sánchez
client
  iridium

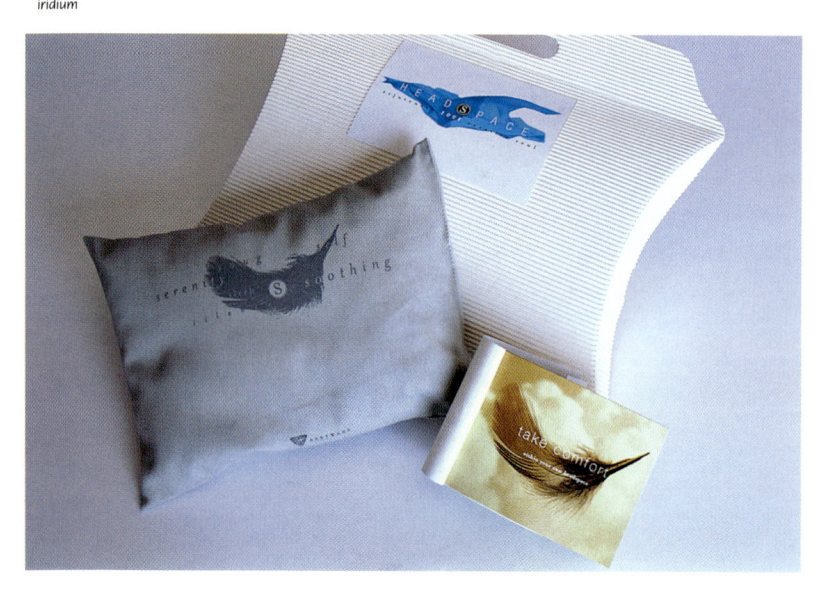

creative firm
  Love Packaging Group
    Wichita (Kansas), USA
creative people
  Rick Gimlin & Mitch McCollough
client
  Love Packaging Group

creative firm
  David Lemley Design
    Seattle (Washington), USA
creative director
  Robert Raible (The Bon Marché)
designer, illustrator
  David Lemley
production
  Matt Peloza
copywriters
  The Bon Marché staff
client
  Seattle Public Schools/The Bon Marché

creative firm
  Design Guys
    Minneapolis (Minnesota), USA
creative people
  Steven Sikora & Dawn Selg
client
  Target Stores

225

creative firm
  Buck Consultants
    St. Louis (Missouri), USA
creative people
  Communications Division of Buck Consultants
client
  Buck Consultants

creative firm
  Jensen Design Assoc. Inc.
    Long Beach (California), USA
creative people
  David Jensen & Robert Rayburn
client
  Jensen Design Assoc. Inc.

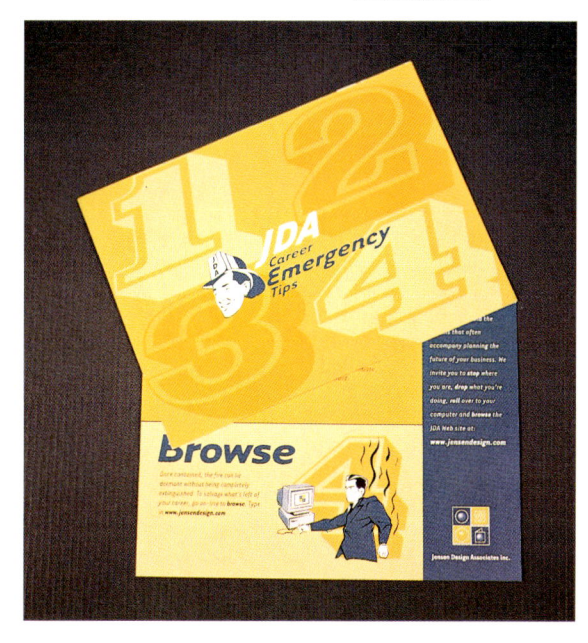

creative firm
  Evenson Design Group
    Culver City (California), USA
creative people
  Stan Evenson, Tricia Rauen, & Bob Dombroski
client
  Evenson Design Group

creative firm
  Disney Design Group
    Lake Buena Vista (Florida), USA
art director, designer
  Mike Wood
photographers
  Joe Brooks, Walt Disney World Photography
calligrapher
  Rita Tyrell
client
  Walt Disney World Attractions Merch.

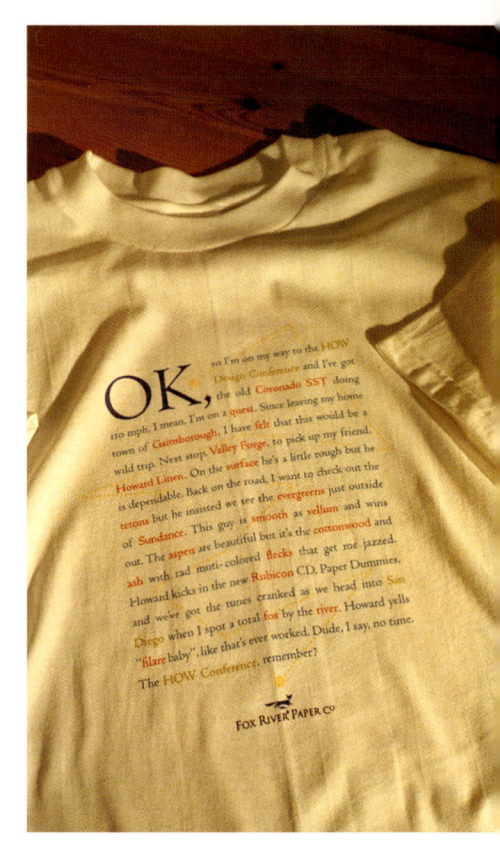

226

creative firm
  Lambert Design
    Los Angeles (California), USA
designer, copywriter
  Scott Lambert
client
  Fox River Paper

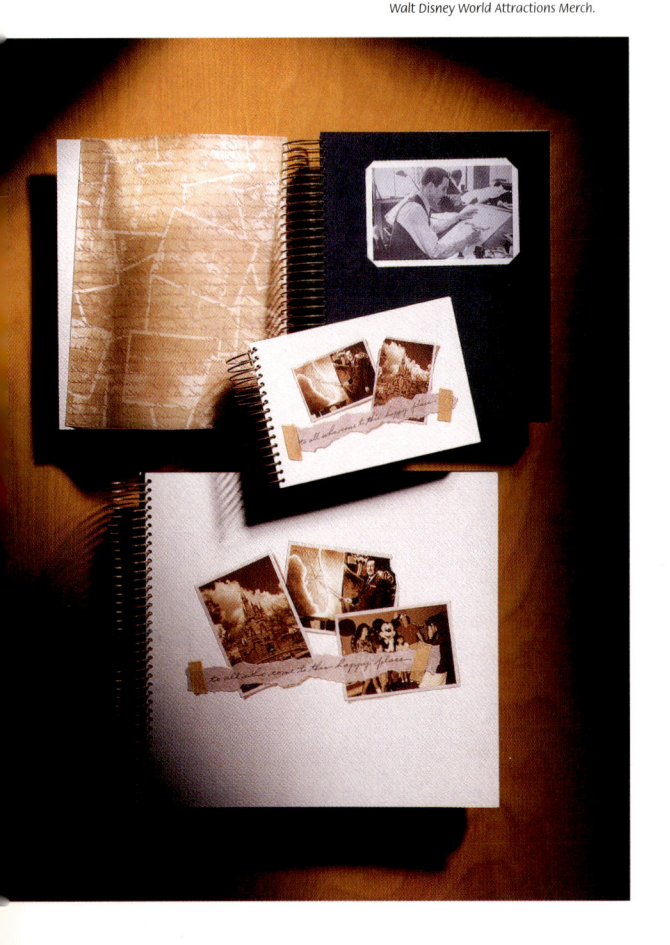

creative firm
  Adkins/Balchunas
    Providence (Rhode Island), USA
creative people
  Jerry Balchunas & Michelle Phaneuf
client
  The Groceria

creative firm
 Warkulwiz Design Associates
  Philadelphia (Pennsylvania), USA
creative people
 Robert J. Warkulwiz & Kirsten Engstrom
client
 DAK Associates Inc..

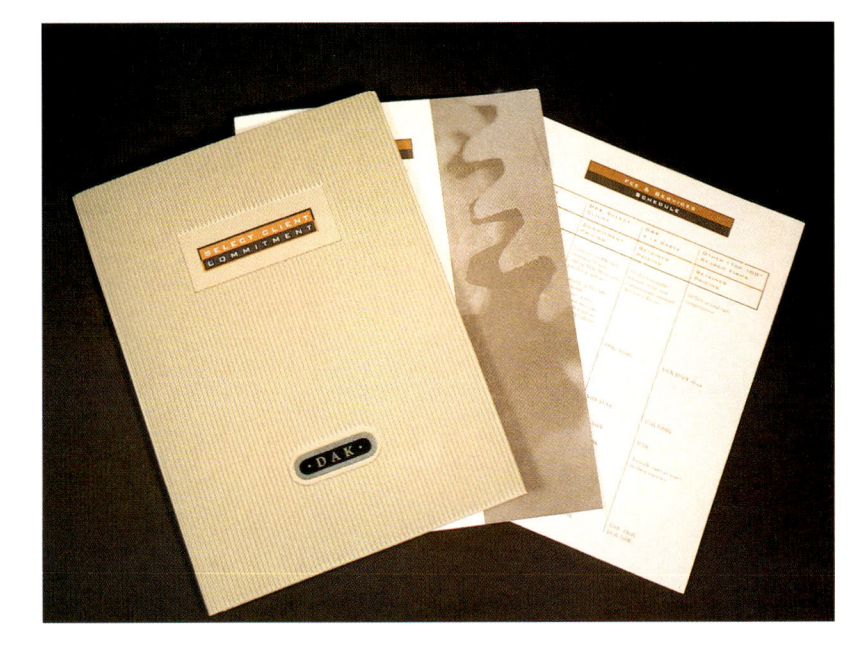

designer
 Andrea Brown
  Denver (Colorado), USA
client
 Aaron & Sabina Brown

227

creative firm
 Teikna Graphic Design Inc.
  Toronto (Ontario), Canada
art director
 Claudia Neri
production
 Garry Campbell
client
 Butterfield + Robinson

creative firm
 Buck Consultants
  St. Louis (Missouri), USA
creative people
 Communications Division of Buck Consultants
client
 Buck Consultants

228

creative firm
  Dye, Van Mol & Lawrence
  Nashville (Tennessee), USA
creative director
  Chuck Creasy
art director
  Kevin Hinson
client
  Middle Tennessee Council Boy Scouts of America

creative firm
  The Marketing Continuum
  Dallas (Texas), USA
art director
  G.M. Crimm
copywriter
  John Hill
client
  Labatt Visa

creative firm
  Primary Design, Inc.
  Haverhill (Massachusetts), USA
designer
  Jules Epstein
client
  Primary Design, Inc.

creative firm
  HBO
  New York (New York), USA
art director
  Don Crawford
client
  HBO

creative firm
 De Goede + Others Inc
  Chicago (Illinois), USA
creative people
 Jan de Goede & Nancy Nord de Goede
client
 De Goede + Others Inc

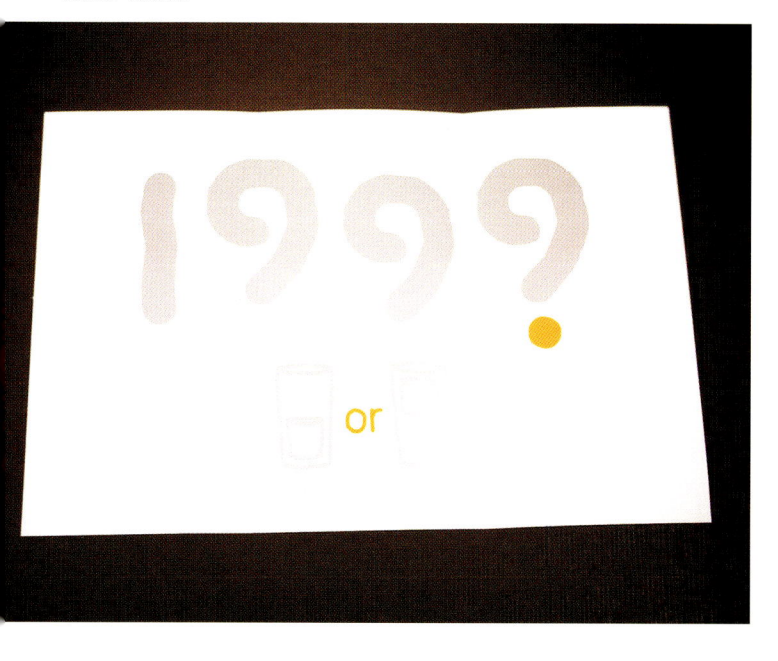

creative firm
 Ellen Bruss Design
  Denver (Colorado), USA
creative people
 Ellen Bruss & Charles Carpenter
client
 Pacific Star Supper Club

creative firm
 Kim Baer Design Associates
  Venice (California), USA
designers
 Kim Baer, Barbara Cooper,
 Maggie van Oppen, Liz Roberts,
 Helen Duval, & Michael Lejeune

creative firm
 The Traver Company
  Seattle (Washington), USA
art directors
 Anne Traver & Dale Hart
designer
 Christopher Downs
photographer
 Iridio
client
 Iridio

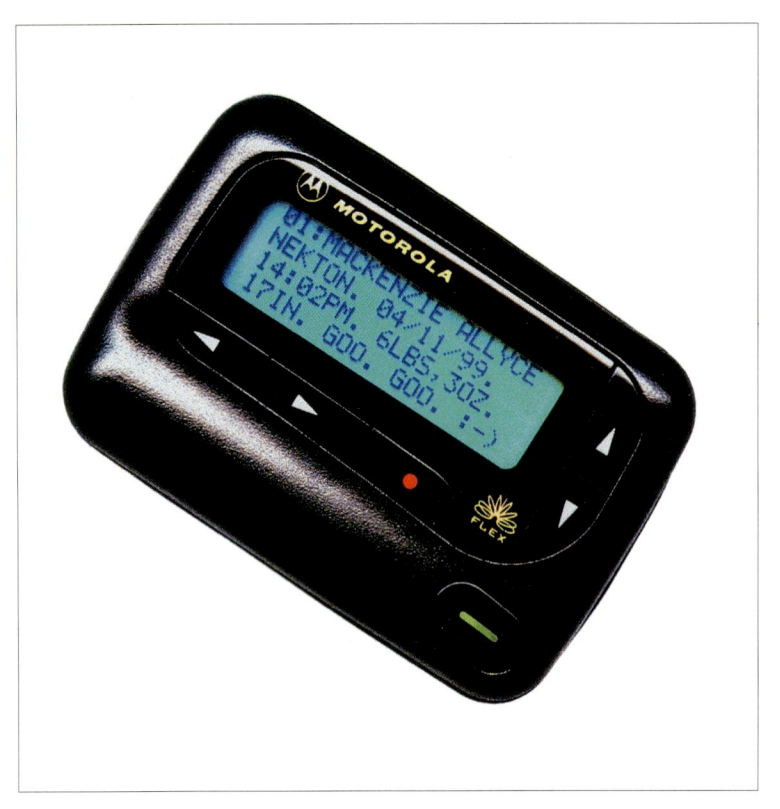

creative firm
  Saatchi & Saatchi NY
  New York (New York), USA
art director, copywriter
  Dabni Harvey
client
  Mr. & Mrs. James Nekton

creative firm
  Planets Ads & Design Pte Ltd
  Singapore
creative director
  Harukazu Suzuki
client
  Edo Sushi (Singapore)

230

creative firm
  Disneyland Creative Services
  Anaheim (California), USA
creative director
  Scott Starkey
coordinator
  Marilyn Carter
designers
  Mike Puchalski, Dathan Shore,
  David Riley & Associates, &
  Barton/Komai/Dunnahoe
client
  Disneyland Merchandise

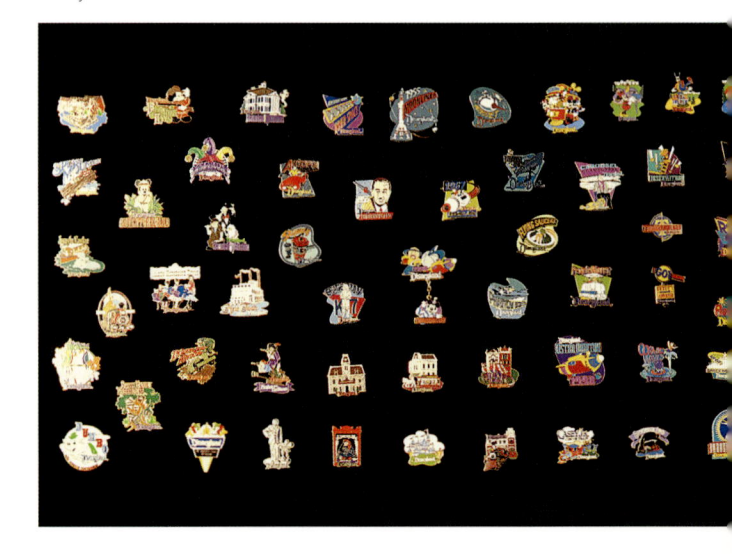

creative firm
  John Brady Design Consultants
  Pittsburgh (Pennsylvania), USA
creative people
  Kathy Grubb, Jim Bolander,
  Rick Madison, & Carl Chiocca
client
  General Nutrition Corporation

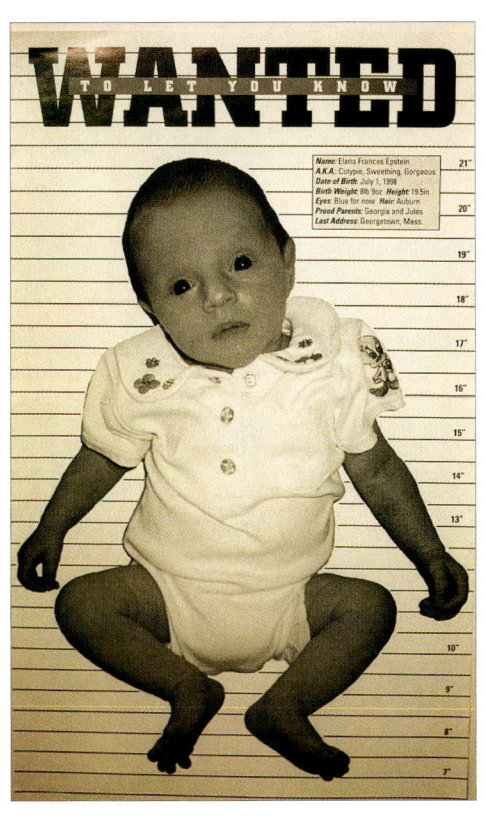

creative firm
  Primary Design, Inc.
    Haverhill (Massachusetts), USA
designer
  Jules Epstein
client
  Elana Frances Epstein

creative firm
  Streamline Communication Ltd.
    Hong Kong, China
creative director, art director, copywriter
  Lawrence Yu
client
  Streamline Communication Ltd.

231

creative firm
  Interbrand Gerstman + Meyers
    New York (New York), USA
creative people
  Juan Concepcion
client
  Interbrand Gerstman + Meyers

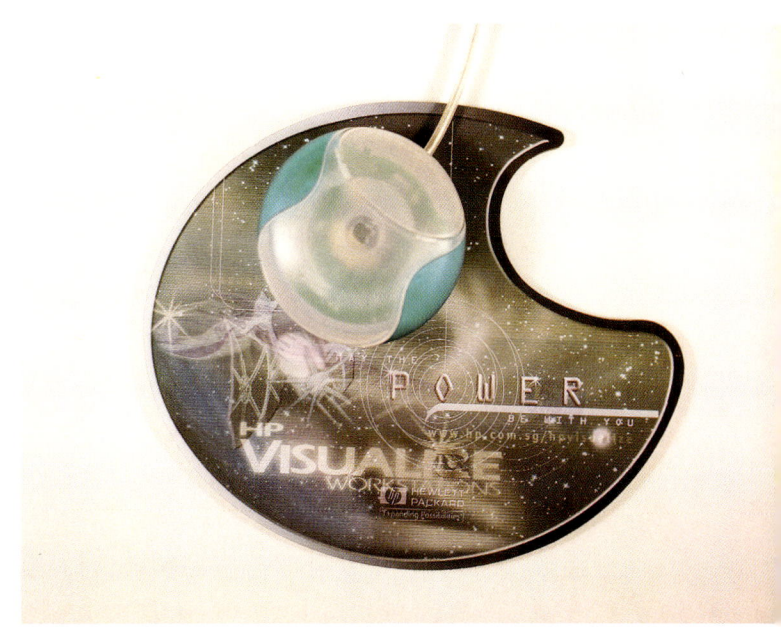

creative firm
  Ukulele Design Consultants Pte Ltd.
    Singapore
design director
  Kim Chun-wei
designer
  Lynn Lim
client
  Hewlett-Packard Singapore

creative firm
  Kompas Design
  Ljubljana, (Slovenia)
designer
  Zare Kerin
photographer
  Janel Puksic
copywriter
  Rok Kvaternik
client
  Zalozba Rokus, D.O.O.

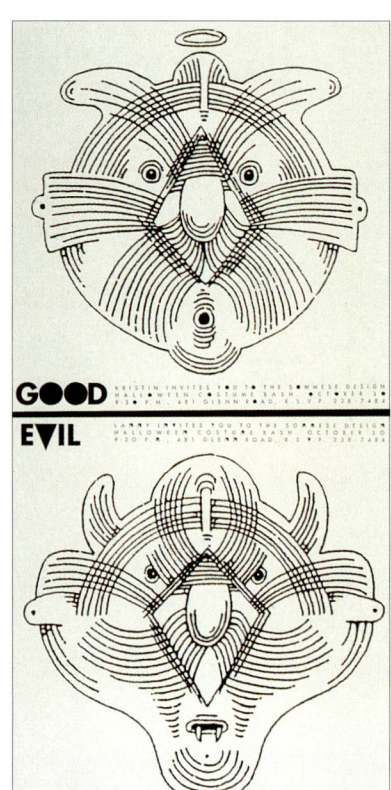

creative firm
  Sommese Design
  State College (Pennsylvania), USA
creative people
  Lanny Sommese & Kristin Sommese
client
  Sommese Design

232

creative firm
  Adkins/Balchunas
  Providence (Rhode Island), USA
creative people
  Jerry Balchunas & Michelle Phaneuf
client
  Autocrat, Inc.

creative firm
  Tangram Strategic Design
  Novara, Italy
creative director, art director, designer
  Enrico Sempi
client
  Tangram Strategic Design

creative firm
  **Gregory group**
    Dallas (Texas), USA
creative director
  Jon Gregory
art director
  Craig Lloyd
illustrator
  Craig Frazier
client
  Gregory group

creative firm
  **Wendell Minor Design**
    Washington (Connecticut), USA
art director
  Rebecca Petrie
designer, illustrator
  Wendell Minor
client
  Hancock Shaker Village

233

creative firm
  **Pirman Communications Inc.**
    De Pere (Wisconsin), USA
creative people
  Brian Pirman
client
  Abbott Pennings High School

creative firm
  **Sayles Graphic Design**
    Des Moines (Iowa), USA
art director, designer
  John Sayles
copywriter
  Wendy Lyons
client
  Muscular Dystrophy Association

creative firm
  Wong•Wong•Boyack, Inc.
  San Francisco (California), USA
creative people
  Ben Wong, Penelope Wong,
  HoMan Lee, Pagely Tucker,
  Yolanda Petriz-Morris, &
  Phuong-Mai Bui-Quang
client
  Cisco Systems, Inc.

creative firm
  Windigo-Graphics Division
  Morristown (New Jersey), USA
production
  CDM Sound Studios, N.Y.
jacket design
  Windigo, Janet Ralli
client
  Marjorie Gubelmann

234

creative firm
  Greenfield/Belser Ltd.
  Washington (D.C.), USA
creative director, designer
  Burkey Belser
client
  Fine Arts Engraving

creative firm
  Alain M. Flores/Controles Graficos
  San Cristobal, Mexico
creative director, designer
  Alain Mauricio Flores Monterrubio
client
  World Boxing Council

creative firm
  A+B (In Exile)
  Ljubljana, Slovenia
creative people
  Eduard Cehovin
client
  A Atalanta

creative firm
  Redbook Promotion Dept.
  New York (New York), USA
creative director
  Denise Benay
art director
  Joel Benay
client
  Redbook Magazine

creative firm
  SooHoo Designers
  Torrance (California), USA
creative people
  Patrick Soohoo, Kathy Hirata,
  Daniel Ko, Cindy Hahn, Karen Leonard,
  Dan Wu, & Leo Terrazas
client
  SooHoo Designers

235

creative firm
  Design Objectives Pte Ltd
  Singapore
creative people
  Ronnie S C Tan
client
  Singapore Post Pte Ltd

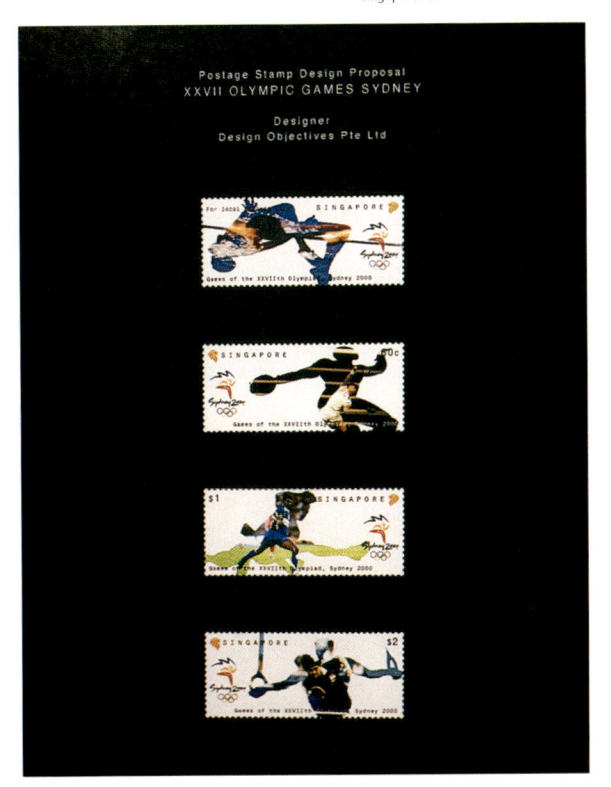

236

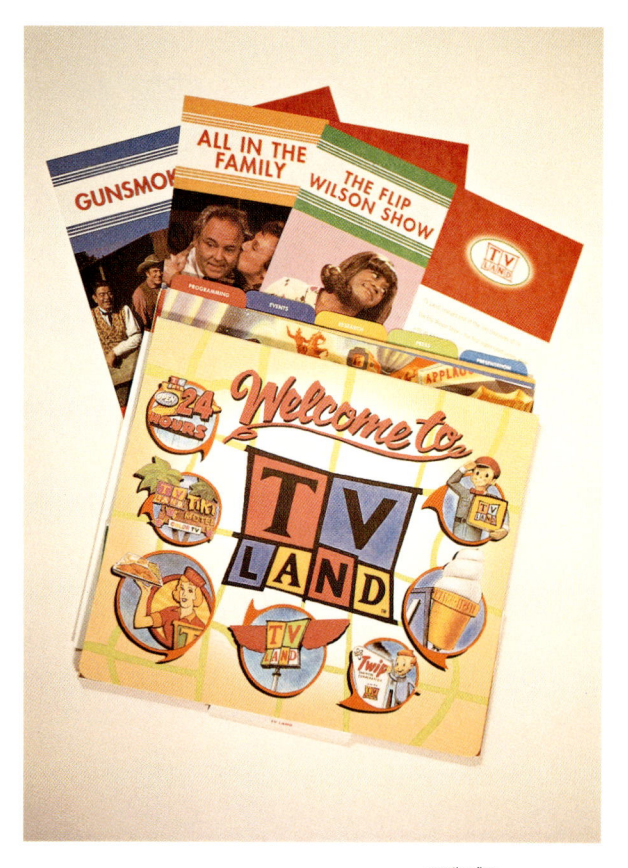

creative firm
 TV Land
  New York (New York), USA
agency
 Spot Design/Kristina DeCorpo
creative director
 Kim Rosenblum
art director
 Matt Duntemann
producer
 Karen Levy
designer
 Claudia Brandenburg
illustrator
 Ross MacDonald
copywriter
 David Rieth
client
 Ad Sales

creative firm
 Metzler & Associes
  Paris, France
creative people
 M.A. Herrmann & I. Tonnel
client
 Metzler & Associés

creative firm
 A+B (In Exile)
  Ljubljana, Slovenia
creative people
 Cehovin E.
client
 Author—Cehovin E.

creative firm
 Pisarkiewicz Mazur & Co., Inc.
  New York (New York), USA
creative people
 Linda Farber, Beth Lieberman, & Christie Shin
client
 Pisarkiewicz Mazur & Co., Inc.

creative firm
 Stephanie Knopp Designs
  Philadelphia (Pennsylvania), USA
creative people
 Stephanie Knopp
client
 Stephanie Knopp

creative firm
 The Traver Company
  Seattle (Washington), USA
creative people
 Margo Sepanski & Christopher Downs
client
 Vulcan Northwest

creative firm
 The Traver Company
  Seattle (Washington), USA
creative people
 Anne Traver, Dale Hart,
 Christopher Downs, John Koval,
 & Yvette Tinsley
client
 ESM Consulting Engineers

creative firm
 Mike Salisbury Communications
  Venice (California), USA

creative firm
  Mires Design, Inc.
    San Diego (California), USA
art director
  John Ball
designers
  Gale Spitzley & Jeff Samaripa
photographers
  John Ball, Jeff Samaripa,
  David Adey, Scott Mires, & Bob Shaddox
illustrators
  Jeff Samaripa & David Adey
client
  Mires Design, Inc.

creative firm
  Tom Fowler, Inc.
    Stamford (Connecticut), USA
creative people
  Thomas G. Fowler & Elizabeth P. Ball
client
  Tom Fowler, Inc.

238

creative firm
  Gallery Ltd
    Hong Kong, China
creative people
  Benny Cheng, Raymond Fu,
  & Kelvin Parker
client
  Sylvia & Cheuk Hung

creative firm
  The Sloan Group
    New York (New York), USA
creative directors
  Cliff Sloan & Wyndy Wilder
designer
  Alison Oliver
client
  China Grill

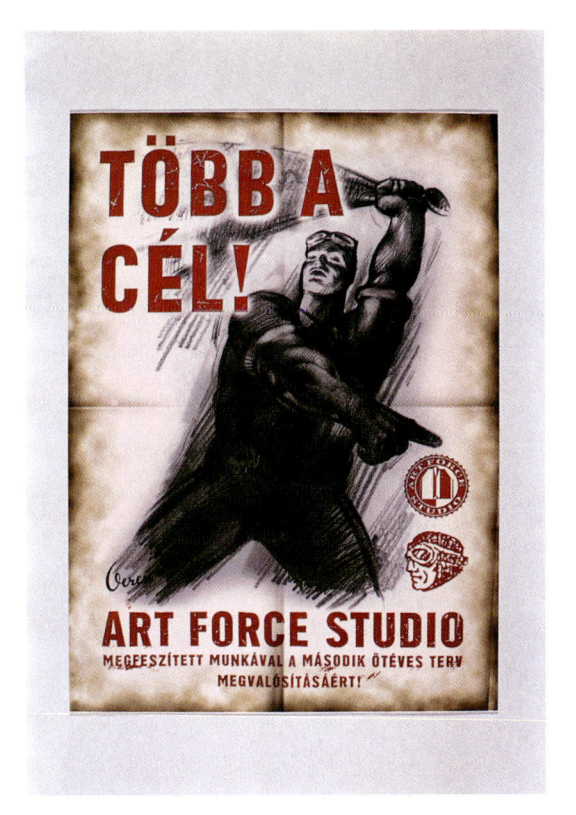

creative firm
  Art Force Studio
    Budapest, Hungary
creative people
  Veress Tama's
client
  Art Force Studio

creative firm
  FRANTZ/Corporate Imaging
    Rye (New Hampshire), USA
creative people
  Richard C. Frantz & Susan Frantz
client
  FRANTZ/Corporate Imaging

239

creative firm
  Nolin Larosee Design
  Communications
    Montréal (Québec), Canada
art director
  Louise Filion
client
  Montréal International

creative firm
  Lissac
    Paris, France
creative people
  Pierre Lissac
client
  Pierre Lissac

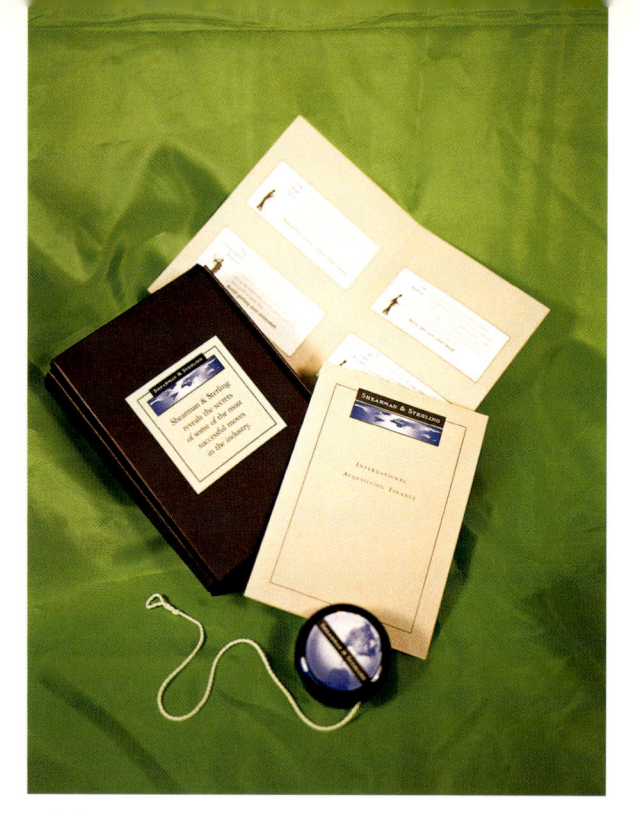

creative firm
  Ross Culbert & Lavery
  New York (New York), USA
creative people
  Peter Ross, Kathy Sobb, & Lucy White
client
  Shearman & Sterling

creative firm
  Oswaldo Mendes
  Belém, Brazil
creative people
  Oswaldo Mendes & Eduardo Reis
client
  Mendes Publicidade Ltda.

240

creative firm
  Evenson Design Group
  Culver City (California), USA
creative people
  Stan Evenson, Tricia Rauen,
  John Krause, & Emma Whipple
client
  Evenson Design Group

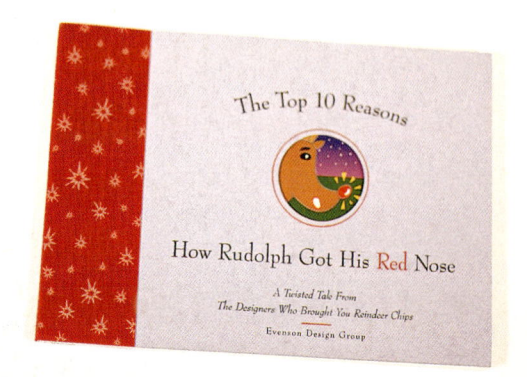

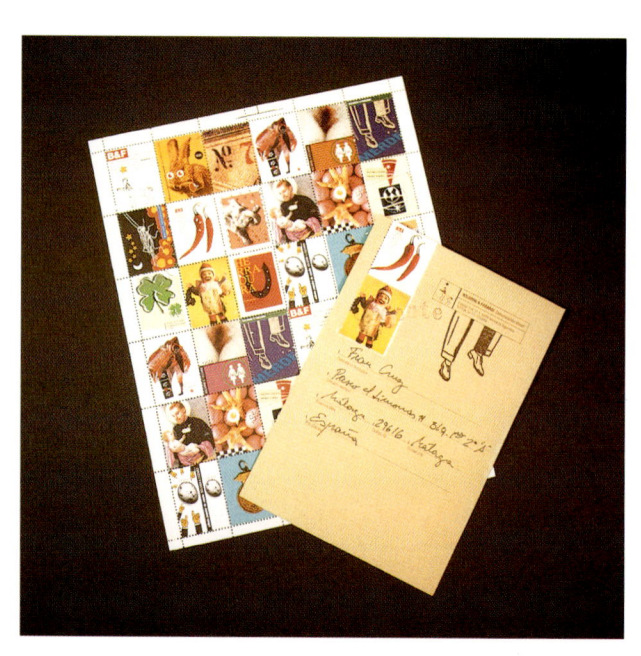

creative firm
  Boldrini & Ficcardi
  Mendoza, Argentina
creative people
  Victor Boldrini & Leonardo Ficcardi
client
  Boldrini & Ficcardi

creative firm
 Pirman Communications Inc.
 De Pere (Wisconsin), USA
creative people
 Brian Pirman
client
 Brian Pirman

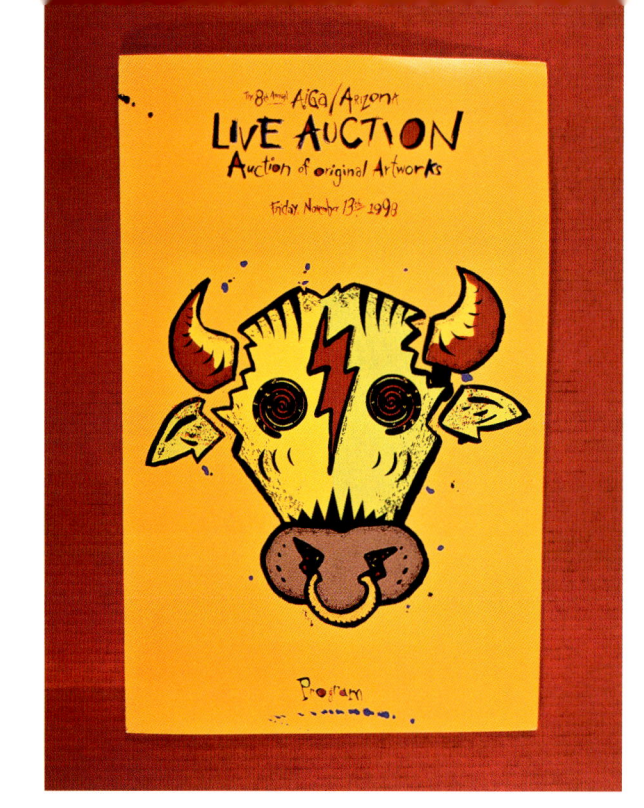

creative firm
 Estudio Ray
 Phoenix (Arizona), USA
creative people
 Joe Ray, Christine Ray, & Leslie Link
client
 AIGA

creative firm
 Burkhardt & Hillman
 New York (New York), USA
creative people
 Rena Wong & Dimitrios Petsas
client
 Ron Burkhardt's 40th Birthday Party

creative firm
 Evenson Design Group
 Culver City (California), USA
creative people
 Stan Evenson, Peggy Woo, &
 Dan Cosgrove
client
 Universal Studios Florida

creative firm
 Watts Graphic Design
  South Melbourne (Victoria), Australia
art director
 Helen Watts
designer
 Sally Varne
client
 Brivis Climate Systems

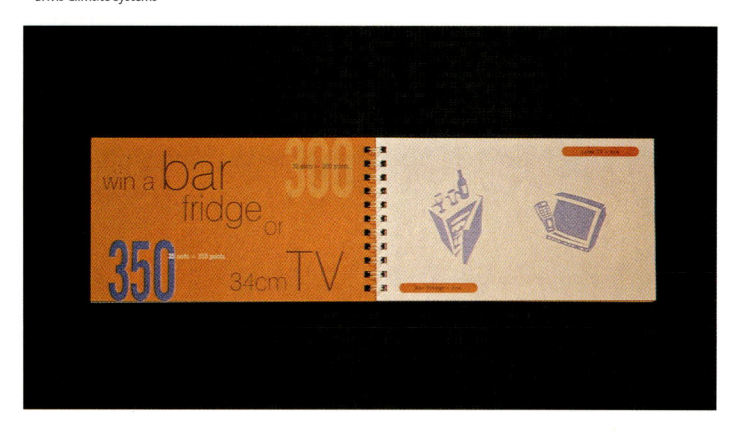

creative firm
 Nickelodeon
  New York (New York), USA
art director
 Laurie Hinzman
project manager
 Betsy Flounders
designer
 Lisa Cohen
illustrator, copywriter
 Laurie Keller
client
 Nickelodeon Talent Department

242

creative firm
 Disney Design Group
  Lake Buena Vista (Florida), USA
art directors, designers
 Mike Wood & Darren Wilson
illustrators
 Brian Blackmore & Alex Maher
client
 Walt Disney World Attractions
 Merchandise Special Events

creative firm
 Hunt Weber Clark Associates
  San Francisco (California), USA
creative people
 Leigh Krichbaum, Jim Deeken,
 Christine Chung, & Nancy Hunt-Weber
client
 Hunt Weber Clark Associates

creative firm
 Hornall Anderson Design Works
  Seattle (Washington), USA
creative people
 Jack Anderson, Lisa Cerveny,
 David Bates, & Alan Florsheim
client
 Leatherman Tool Group

creative firm
 Nickelodeon
  New York (New York), USA
art director
 Laurie Hinzman
designer
 Jennifer Juliano
illustrator
 Sara Fanelli
client
 Nickelodeon

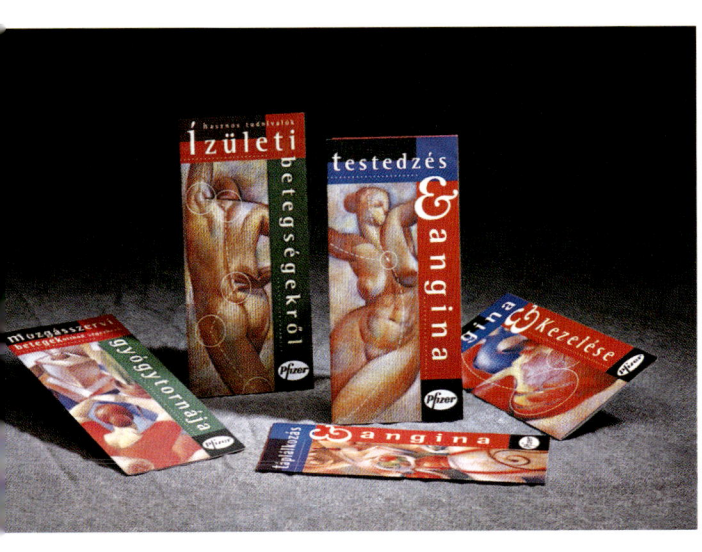

243

creative firm
 Greenfield/Belser Ltd.
  Washington (D.C.), USA
creative director
 Burkey Belser
designer
 Tom Cameron
client
 Tonkon Torp

creative firm
 Art Force Studio
  Budapest, Hungary
creative people
 Zoltàn Halasi
client
 Fotop Studio

creative firm
  Cornerstone
    New York (New York), USA
creative people
  Buster Waslar
art directors
  Keith Steimel, Sally Clarke
designers
  Mo Pizzi, Keith Steimel, & Sally Clarke
client
  Pfizer, Inc.

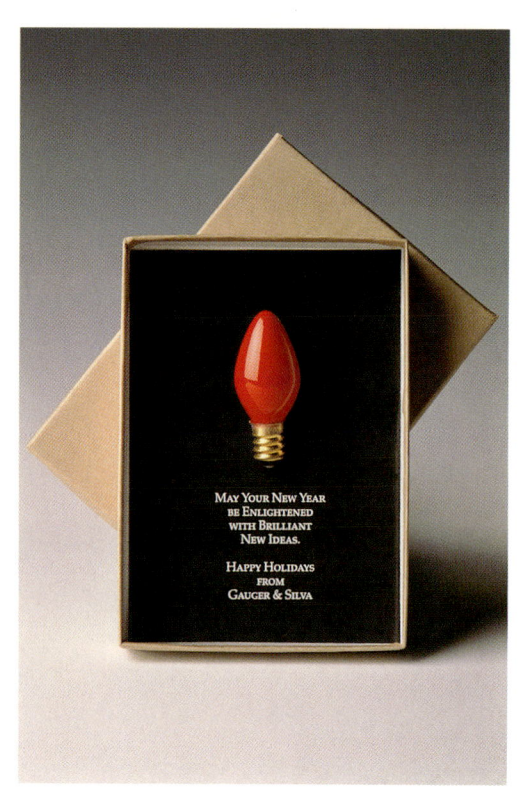

creative firm
  Gauger & Silva Associates
    San Francisco (California), USA
creative people
  Bob Ankers & David Gauger
client
  Gauger & Silva Associates

creative firm
  Sayles Graphic Design
    Des Moines (Iowa), USA
art director, designer
  John Sayles
copywriter
  Wendy Lyons
client
  CDW Comdex

creative firm
  Love Packaging Group
    Wichita (Kansas), USA
creative people
  Rick Gimlin & Mitch McCullough
client
  Love Packaging Group

creative firm
  Cahan & Associates
  San Francisco (California), USA
art director
  Bill Cahan
designer
  Ben Pham
client
  Zeum

creative firm
  FRCH Design Worldwide
  (Cincinnati)
  New York (New York), USA
creative people
  Meredith Belafsky &
  Michael Beeghly
client
  AIGA Cincinnati

245

creative firm
  30sixty design, inc.
  Los Angeles (California), USA
art director, designer
  Pär Larsson
client
  30sixty design, inc.

creative firm
  Young & Roeher Group
  Portland (Oregon), USA
creative director
  David Galluzzo
art director
  Barbara Baugnon
copywriter
  Jo Ann Lunt
client
  Young & Roehr

creative firm
  Terry O Communications Inc.
    Scarborough (Ontario), Canada
art directors
  Terry O'Connor & Helen Fong O'Connor
package designer
  Terry O'Connor
client
  George Bond Sports

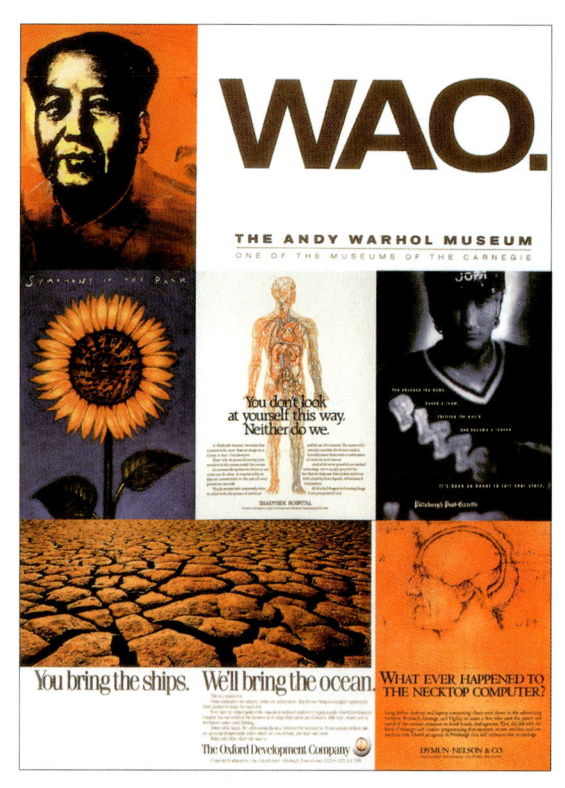

creative firm
  Dymun Nelson & Company
    Pittsburgh (Pennsylvania), USA
creative director, copywriter
  John Dymun
art director
  Anthony Musmanno
electronic designer
  Robyn Riel
client
  Dymun Nelson & Company

246

creative firm
  Gee + Chung Design
    San Francisco (California), USA
art director
  Earl Gee
designers
  Earl Gee & Fani Chung
photographer
  Kevin Irby
client
  Applied Materials

creative firm
  1185 Design
    Palo Alto (California), USA
creative people
  Peggy Burke & Joan Takenaka
client
  when.com

creative firm
**Hendlin Visual Communications, Inc.**
Minneapolis (Minnesota), USA
art director
Larry Skov
photographer
Ted Wentink
audio
Toby's Tunes
copywriter
Jon Schumacher
client
Hendlin Visual Communications, Inc.

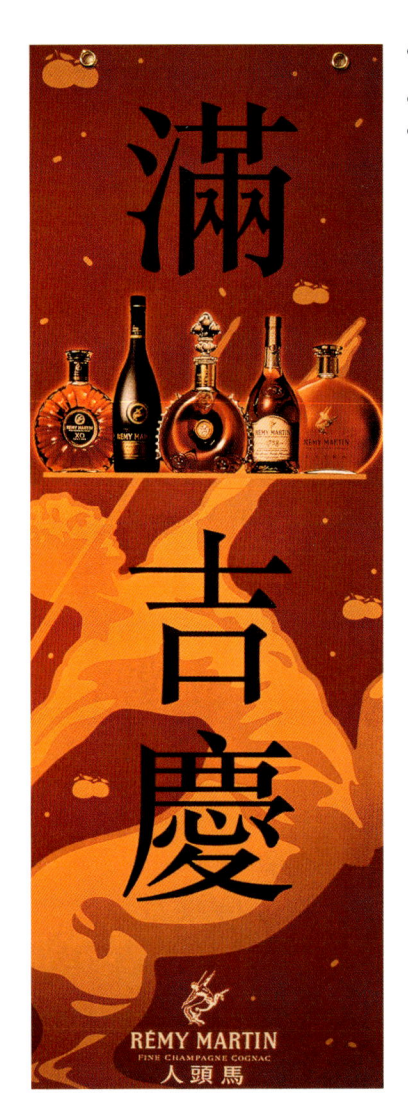

creative firm
**L3 Advertising Inc.**
New York (New York), USA
creative people
Nicholas Tsang & Charles Lui
client
Remy Amerique, Inc.

creative firm
**Disney Design Group**
Lake Buena Vista (Florida), USA
art director
Mark Seppala
designer
Thomas Scott
illustrators
Larry Moore & Christian Milch
copywriter
Troy Schmidt
client
Walt Disney Attractions Product Development

creative firm
**IE Design**
Studio City (California), USA
creative people
Marcie Carson
client
Good Gracious Events

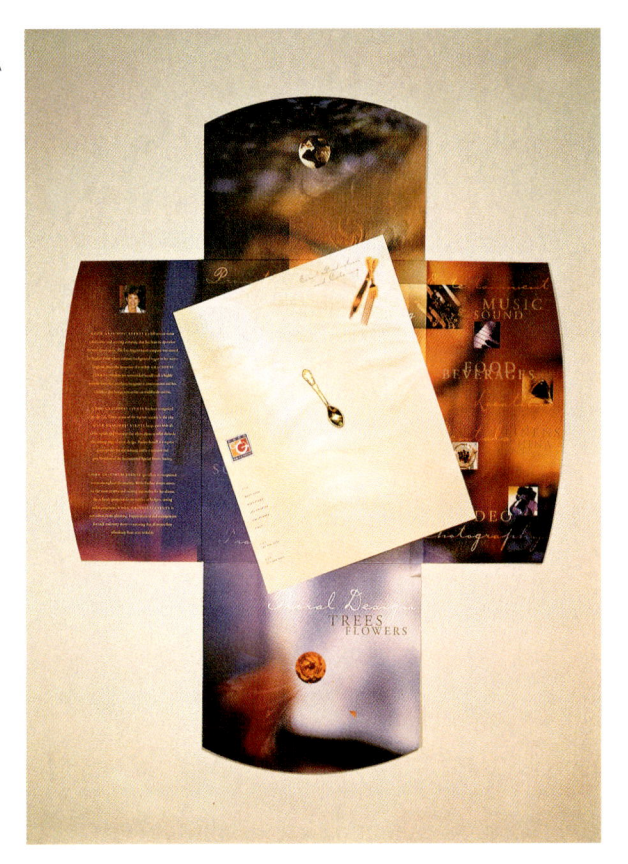

creative firm
    McGaughy Design
    Falls Church (Virginia), USA
designers
    Malcolm McGaughy
client
    McGaughy Design

creative firm
    Larsen Design + Interactive
    Minneapolis (Minnesota), USA
creative director
    Tim Larsen
designer
    Sascha Boecker
client
    Larsen Design + Interactive

248

creative firm
    Larsen Design + Interactive
    Minneapolis (Minnesota), USA
art directors
    Gayle Jorgens & Paul Wharton
client
    Novellus Systems, Inc.

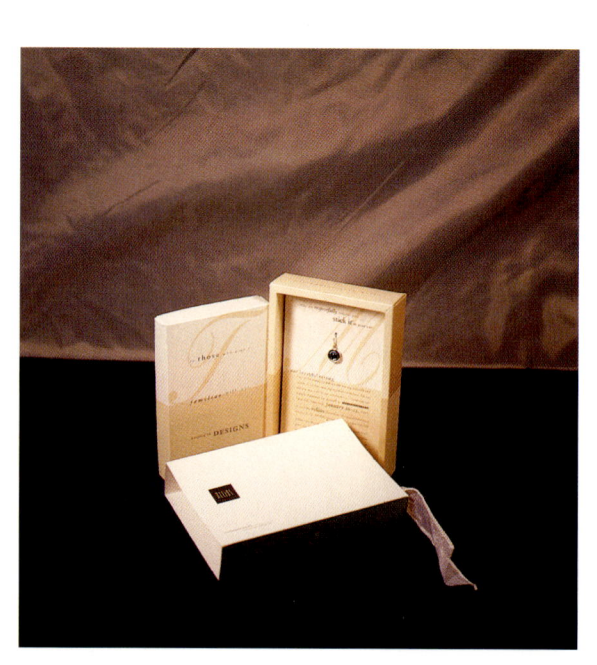

creative firm
    Kilmer & Kilmer
    Design & Advertising
    Albuquerque (New Mexico), USA
creative people
    Richard Kilmer, Randall Marshall,
    & Paul Brandenburger
client
    Relios

creative firm
  Design Club
    Tokyo, Japan
art director, designer
  Akihiko Tsukamoto
illustrator
  Yenpitsu Nemoto
copywriter
  Haruki Nagumo
client
  Yamato Inc.
  Arjo Wiggins Fine Paper Ltd.

creative firm
  Paprika Communications
    Montréal (Québec), Canada
art director
  Louis Gagnon
designer
  Francis Turgeon
client
  Paprika

249

creative firm
  David Carter
  Design Associates
    Dallas (Texas), USA
creative director
  Lori B. Wilson
designer
  Tabitha Bogard
client
  Atlantis Resort

creative firm
  Greenfield/Belser Ltd.
    Washington (D.C.), USA
creative director
  Burkey Belser
designer
  Tom Cameron
client
  D'Ancona

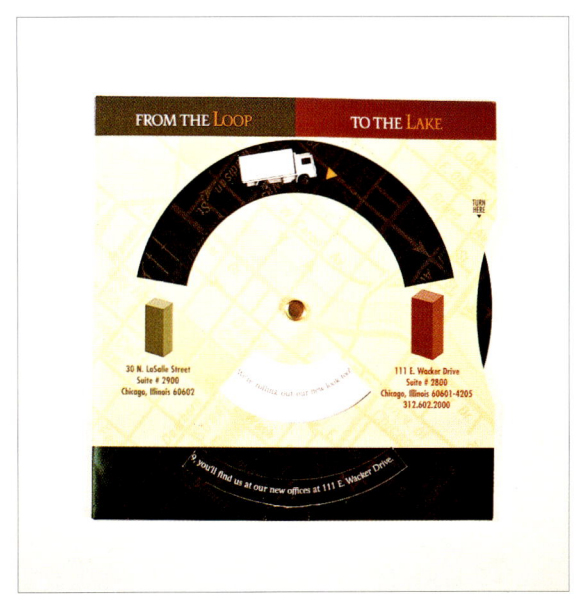

creative firm
  Mires Design, Inc.
  San Diego (California), USA
art director
  John Ball
designer
  Gale Spitzley
illustrators
  Miguel Perez & Jeff Samaripa
client
  Mires Design, Inc.

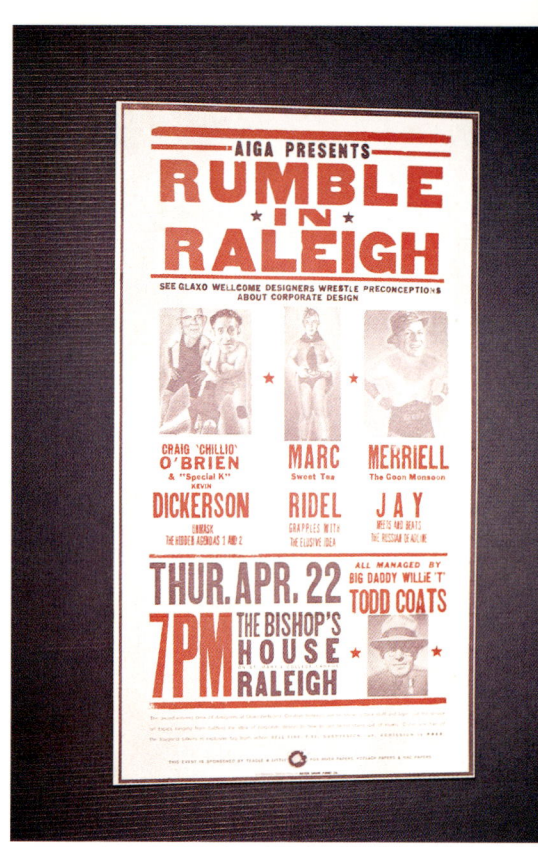

250

creative firm
  Glaxo Wellcome Creative Services
  Research Triangle Park (North Carolina), USA
art directors, designers
  Todd Coats, Kevin Dickerson, & Craig O Brien
client
  AIGA Raleigh

creative firm
  Ross Culbert & Lavery
  New York (New York), USA
creative people
  Ross Culbert & Lavery
client
  Ross Culbert & Lavery

creative firm
  Pearlfisher
  London, England
creative people
  Kim Hardy & Jonathon Ford
client
  Pearlfisher

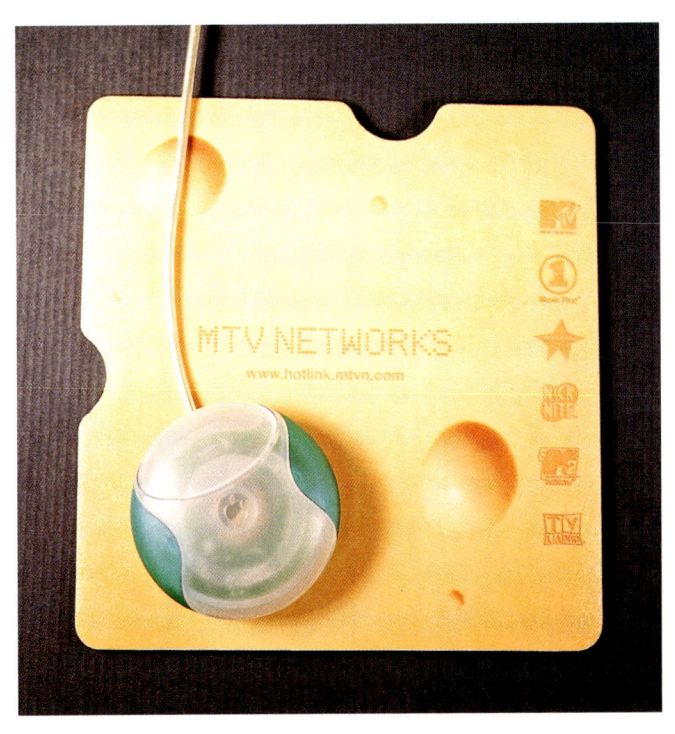

creative firm
   MTV Networks Creative Services
      New York (New York), USA
creative directors
   Scott Wadler & Cheryl Family
designer
   Nok Acharee

creative firm
   Alcone Marketing Group
      Irvine (California), USA
creative director
   Luis Camano
art director
   Carlso Musquez
copywriter
   Cameron Young
client
   Airtouch

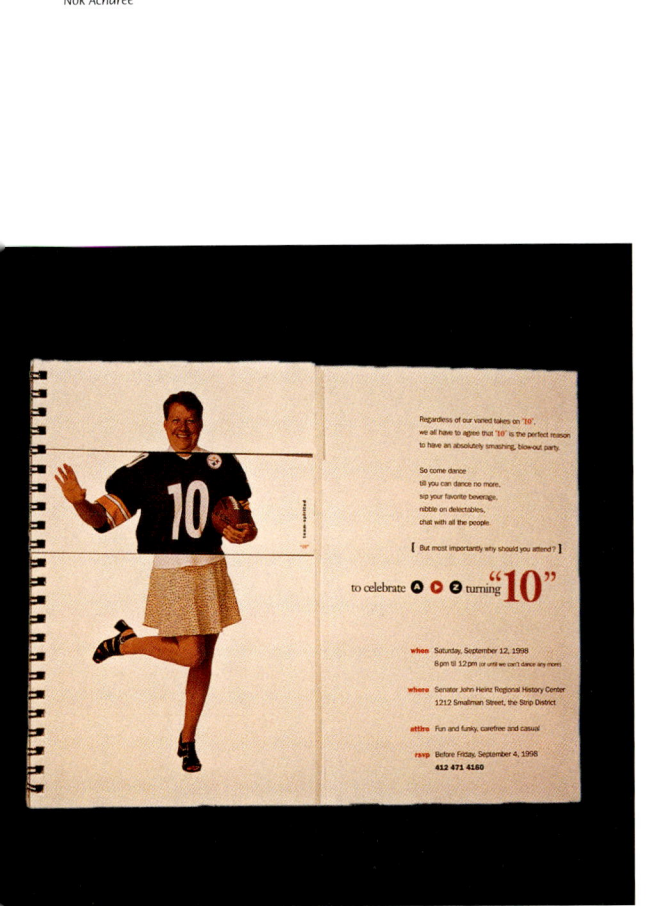

251

creative firm
   Kinggraphic
      Hong Kong, China
creative directors
   Hon Bing-wah & So Man-yee
client
   Kinggraphic

creative firm
   A to Z communications, inc.
      Pittsburgh (Pennsylvania), USA
creative director
   Goldie Z. Ostrow
graphic designers
   Vonnie Hornburg & Cheryl Roder-Quill
copywriter
   Ann Hornak
client
   A to Z communications, inc.

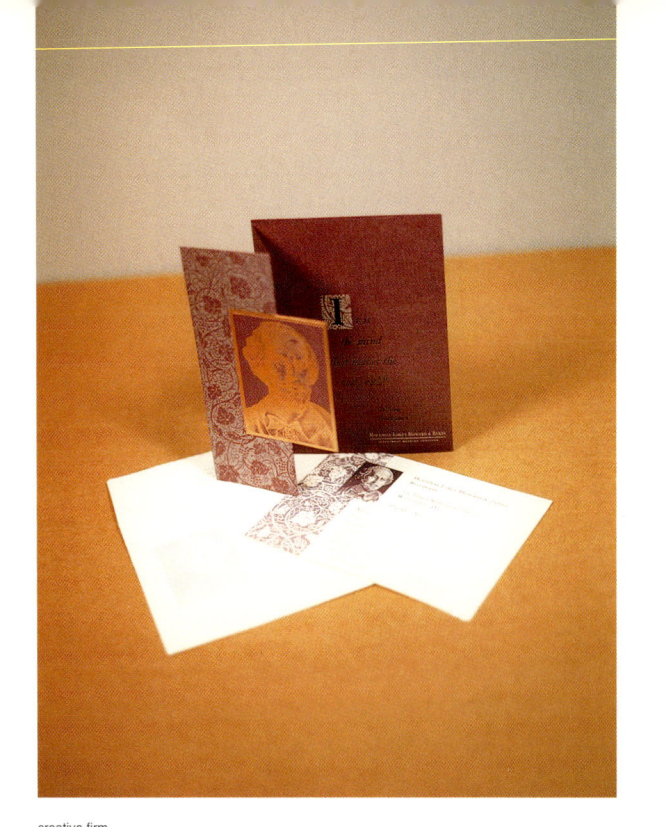

creative firm
  Julia Tam Design
    Palos Verdes (California), USA
art director
  Julia Tam
illustrator
  Ken Barton
client
  Houlihan Lokey Howard & Zukin

252

creative firm
  SGI
    New York (New York), USA
creative people
  Scott Greenlee & Frank White
client
  SGI

creative firm
  Rose + Hopp Design
    Oslo, Norway
creative people
  Gina Rose
client
  Rose + Hopp Design

creative firm
  Dynamic Duo Studio
    Westport (Connecticut), USA
designer, illustration
  Dynamic Duo Studio
black and white line work,
hand lettering, copywriter
  Arlen Schumer
computer coloring
  Sherri Wolfgang
client
  Dynamic Duo Studio

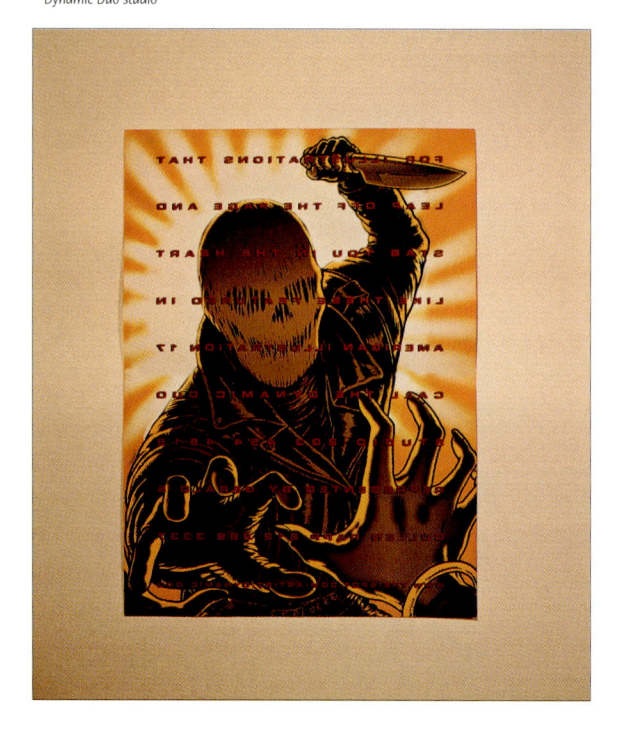

creative firm
  Lazywood Press
  Houston (Texas), USA
concept
  Paula Murphy
designer
  Trinh Pham
client
  My Table

creative firm
  Gallery Ltd
  Hong Kong, China
creative people
  Benny Cheng, Giles Tse,
  & Kelvin Parker
client
  Hiap Moh (HK) Ltd

creative firm
  James Robie Design Associates
  Los Angeles (California), USA
art director
  James Robie
designer
  Karen Nakatani
client
  The Hump Sushi Bar & Restaurant

253

creative firm
  Alcone Marketing Group
  Irvine (California), USA
creative director
  Kevin Favell
art director
  Carlos Musquez
copywriter
  Cameron Young
client
  Alcone Marketing Group

creative firm
  dk design
  NoHo Arts District (California), USA
art director, designer
  Dianne Krausse
computer illustrator
  Tony Copolillo
client
  Six Flags Over Texas

creative firm
  Gauger & Silva Associates
  San Francisco (California), USA
creative people
  Isabelle Laporte & David Gauger
client
  Euromed

254

creative firm
  Gauger & Silva Associates
  San Francisco (California), USA
creative people
  Isabelle Laporte & David Gauger
client
  Euromed

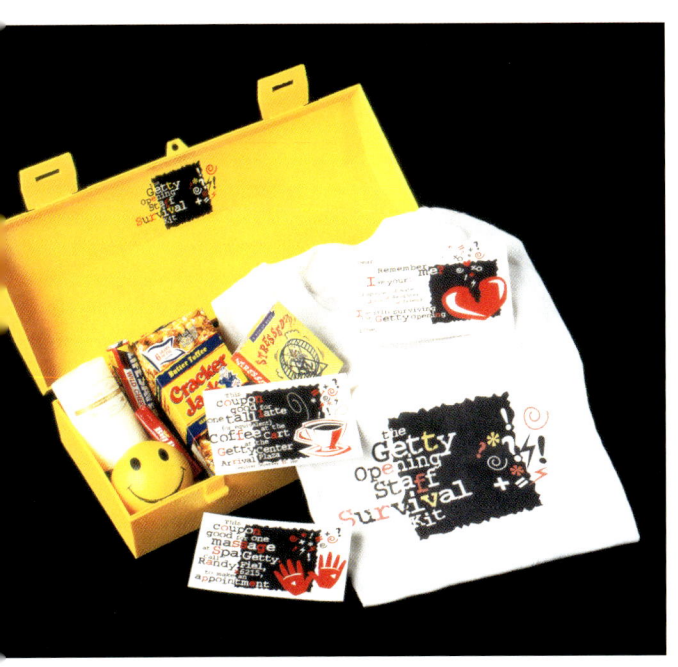

creative firm
  James Robie Design Associates
   Los Angeles (California), USA
art directors
  James Robie & Wayne Fujita
designer
  Karen Nakatani
client
  J. Paul Getty Trust

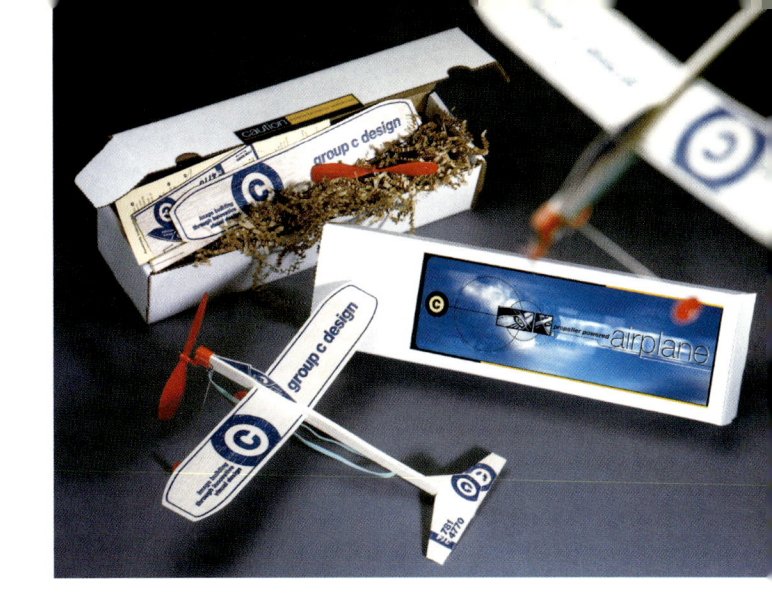

creative firm
  Group C Design
   St. Louis (Missouri), USA
creative people
  Benjamin Franklin
client
  Group C Design

creative firm
  Gauger & Silva Associates
   San Francisco (California), USA
creative people
  Isabelle Laporte & David Gauger
client
  Euromed

255

creative firm
  Deep Design
   Atlanta (Georgia), USA
designer
  Mark Steingruber
client
  Porsche Cars North America

creative firm
 Oxygen Inc.
  Chicago (Illinois), USA
creative people
 Penina Goodman & Michelle Goldish
client
 Oxygen Inc.

creative firm
 kor group
  Boston (Massachusetts), USA
creative people
 Anne Callahan, Karen Dendy,
 MB Sawyer, Jim Gibson, & Brian Acevedo
client
 kor group

creative firm
 Love Packaging Group
  Wichita (Kansas), USA
creative people
 Chris West & Mitch McCollough
client
 Love Packaging Group

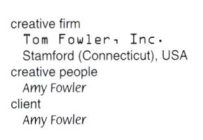

creative firm
  Tom Fowler, Inc.
    Stamford (Connecticut), USA
creative people
  Amy Fowler
client
  Amy Fowler

creative firm
  Gaylord Graphics
    Carol Stream (Illinois), USA
creative people
  Jerry Farrell
client
  Gaylord Container Corp.

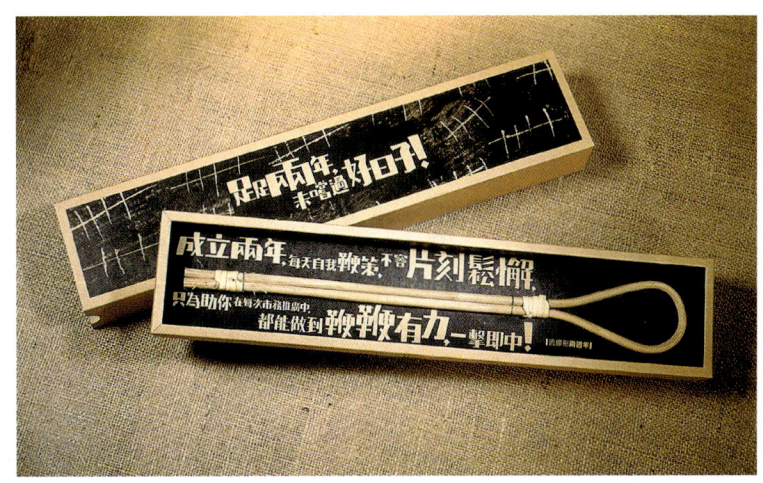

creative firm
  Streamline Communication Ltd.
    Hong Kong, China
creative director, art director
  Lawrence Yu
designers
  Lawrence Yu & Doris Lee
illustrator, typographer
  Doris Lee
copywriter
  Grace Ip
client
  Streamline Communication Ltd.

creative firm
  Love Packaging Group
    Wichita (Kansas), USA
creative people
  Rick Gimlin
client
  Love Packaging Group

257

# CREATIVITY

**Trademarks/ Logos**

creative firm
 NDW Communications
  Horsham (Pennsylvannia), USA
 art director, designer, illustrator
  Tom Brill
 client
  American Cyanamid

**PHANTOM**
INSECTICIDE/TERMITICIDE

creative firm
 Hornall Anderson Design Works
  Seattle (Washington), USA
 creative people
  Jack Anderson, Debra McCloskey,
  & Holly Finlayson
 client
  Personify

creative firm
 Sessions Group
  Houston (Texas), USA
 art director, designer
  Steven Sessions
 client
  Phantom Lighting

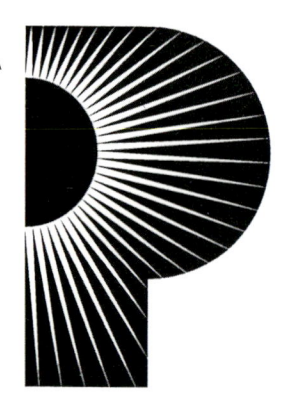

258

creative firm
 Arte-Final,
 Design E Publicidade, LDA
  Lisboa, Portugal
 designer
  António Antunes
 client
  Cinel

**CINEL**

creative firm
 Neil Motts & Associates, Inc.
  Canal Winchester (Ohio), USA
 creative people
  Neil Motts & Steve Gunder
 client
  Eclipse Interactive Publishing, Inc.

**ECLIPSE**
INTERACTIVE PUBLISHING, INC.

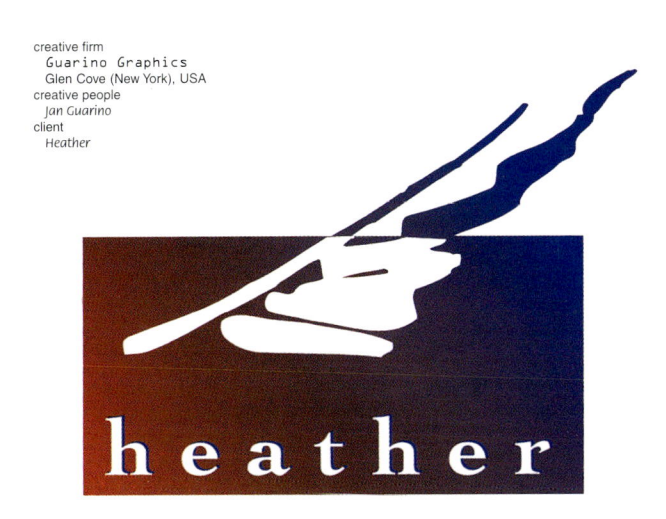

creative firm
 Guarino Graphics
 Glen Cove (New York), USA
creative people
 Jan Guarino
client
 Heather

creative firm
 Pisarkiewicz Mazur & Co., Inc.
 New York (New York), USA
designers
 Linda Farber, Beth Lieberman, & Luca Gasperi
client
 Cybersmith, Inc.

creative firm
 Ambush Communication
 New York (New York), USA
art directors
 Yuk-Chun Yu & Keith Mastandrea
client
 Crain Communication Inc.

259

creative firm
 Mortensen Design
 Mountain View (California), USA
art director
 Gordon Mortensen
designer
 PJ Nidecker
client
 Mirapoint, Inc.

creative firm
 J.R. Navarro & Associates Inc.
 Los Angeles (California), USA
client
 Petersen Automotive Museum

creative firm
 Metzler & Associes
 Paris, France
designer
 M.A. Herrmann
client
 Charles Neuville

creative firm
 Beggs Design
  Palo Alto (California), USA
creative director, art director,
designer, illustrator
 Lee Beggs
client
 Aveo, Inc.

creative firm
 A+B (In Exile)
  Ljubljana, Slovenia
creative people
 Eduard Cehovin
client
 A Atalanta

creative firm
 HBO
  New York (New York), USA
art director, designer
 Gary Dueno
client
 HBO

creative firm
 The Parker Group
  Park Ridge (Illinois), USA
designer
 Rex Parker
client
 Heavenly Pet Center

260

creative firm
 Murrie Lienhart Rysner
  Chicago (Illinois), USA
creative people
 Michael Kelly & Horst Mickler
client
 Drs. Keyes & Toraason

DRS. KEYES & TORAASON
DENTAL ASSOCIATES, LTD.

creative firm
 Forward Design, Inc.
  Rochester (New York), USA
creative people
 Daphne Stofer
client
 Bausch & Lomb

creative firm
 Braindance
  Atlanta (Georgia), USA
creative people
 Blake Parkman & Cindy Beebe
client
 Braindance

creative firm
 Insight Design Communications
  Wichita (Kansas), USA
art directors, designers
 Sherrie Holdeman & Tracy Holdeman
client
 With-A-Twist

creative firm
 Love Packaging Group
  Wichita (Kansas), USA
creative people
 Chris West & Rick Gimlin
client
 Interex

creative firm
 Landor Associates
  New York (New York), USA
art director
 Robert Matza
designers
 Bob Schroeder & Godfried Konnings
client
 Hyperion

261

creative firm
 Landor Associates
  New York (New York), USA
art director, designer
 Robert Matza
client
 GeoCities

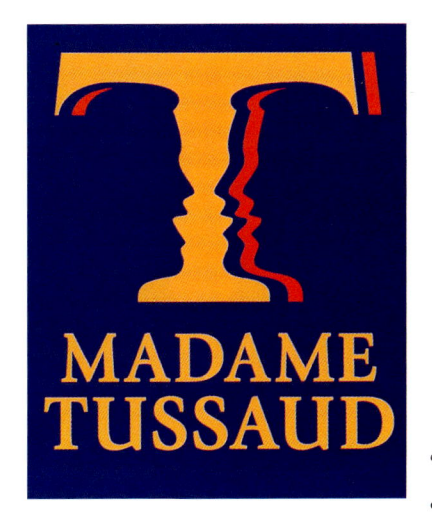

creative firm
 Pearlfisher
  London, England
creative people
 Sarah Butler & Jonathon Ford
client
 The Tussauds Group

creative firm
 Miller & White Advertising
  Terre Haute (Indiana), USA
art director
 Bill White
designer
 Robert Burch
client
 Thompson Thrift Development

creative firm
 Robert Meyers
  Cuyahoga Falls (Ohio), USA
designer
 Robert Meyers
client
 Shadyside Chamber of Commerce

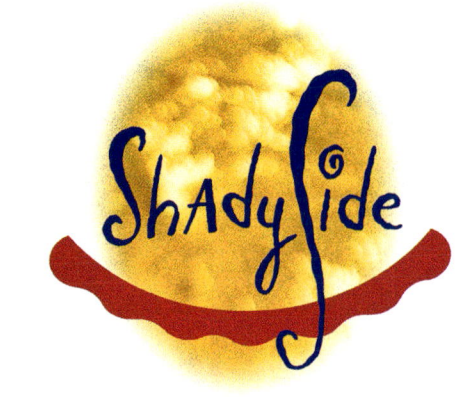

creative firm
 Artefact Design
  Palo Alto (California), USA
creative people
 Artefact Design
client
 The Stanford Fund

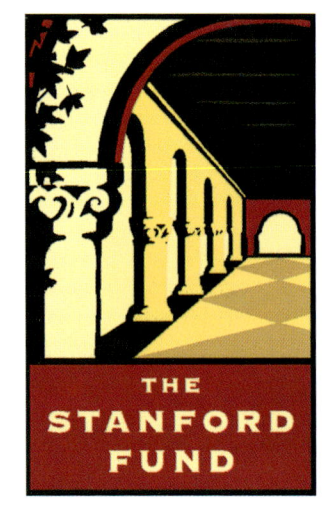

creative firm
 Tangram Strategic Design
  Novara, Italy
creative director
 Enrico Sempi
art director, designer
 Antonella Trevisan
illustrator
 Guido Rosa
client
 Camera di Commercio di Vicenza

262

creative firm
 Peter Taflan Marketing Communications
  Durham (North Carolina), USA
art director
 Janssen Strother
illustrator
 Jim Brown
client
 The Renaissance Handyman

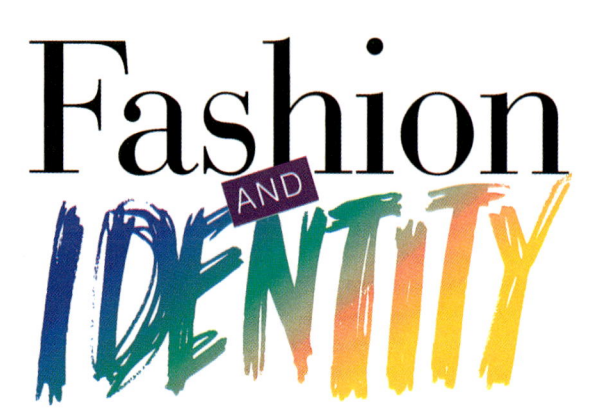

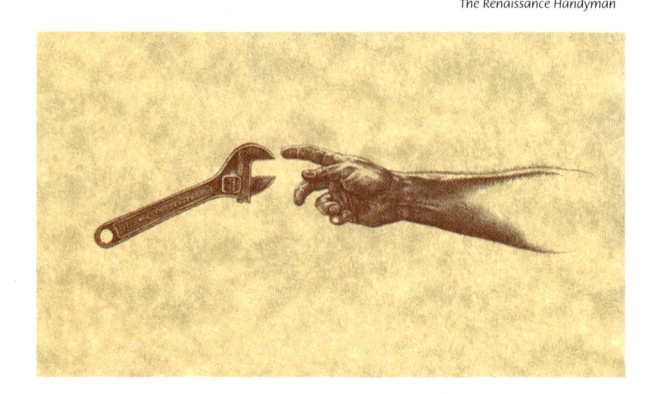

creative firm
 Murrie Lienhart Rysner
  Chicago (Illinois), USA
creative people
 Jim Lienhart
client
 Fashion Institute

creative firm
　Landor New York
　　New York (New York), USA
creative director
　Carlos Sanchez
art director
　Martine Channon
designer
　Soo Jin Yum
client
　Traverse City
　Convention &
　Visitor's Bureau

creative firm
　Design Guys
　　Minneapolis (Minnesota), USA
creative people
　Steven Sikora, Amy Kirkpatrick,
　& Anne Peterson
lettering
　Todd ap Jones
client
　Target Stores

TRAVERSE CITY
*A World Apart*

THE SAINT JOHN'S BIBLE

creative firm
　Addison Whitney
　　Charlotte (North Carolina), USA
art director
　Lori Earnhardt
graphic designer
　Michael Sells
client
　Epicor Software Corporation

creative firm
　Landkamer Partners
　　San Francisco (California), USA
creative people
　Mark Landkamer & Gene Clark
client
　ILOG

epicor
Software Corporation

ILOG

263

creative firm
　Gauger & Silva Associates
　　San Francisco (California), USA
creative people
　Bob Ankers, Matt Vanselow,
　David Gauger, & Dividend Homes, Inc.
client
　Dividend Homes, Inc.

multex.com℠

COYOTE ESTATES

creative firm
　Silver Communications, Inc.
　　New York (New York), USA
creative director
　Gregg Sibert
design director
　Sally Hiesiger
senior designer
　Chris Weissman
client
　multex.com

creative firm
  Nolin Larosee Design Communications
    Montreal (Québec), Canada
  art director
    Loise Filion
  client
    Allegro Films

creative firm
  L-Square Design
    Strategy
    Hong Kong, China
  creative people
    Ben Lai
  client
    Interactive Media

creative firm
  Mires Design, Inc.
    San Diego (California), USA
  art directors
    José A. Serrano & Brian Fandetti
  designers
    José A. Serrano & Miguel Perez
  illustrator
    Miguel Perez
  client
    Yellow Pages

creative firm
  Nolin Larosee
    Design Communications
    Montreal (Québec), Canada
  art director
    Gilles Legault
  client
    Bauer Nike Hockey Inc.

264

creative firm
  Art 270, Inc.
    Jenkintown (Pennsylvania), USA
  art director
    Carl Mill
  designer
    Holly Kempf
  client
    Priority Call Management

creative firm
  Mike Salisbury Communications
    Venice (California), USA

creative firm
 Jowaisas Design
 Cazenovia (New York), USA
designer
 Elizabeth Jowaisas
client
 Cazenovia Public
 Library

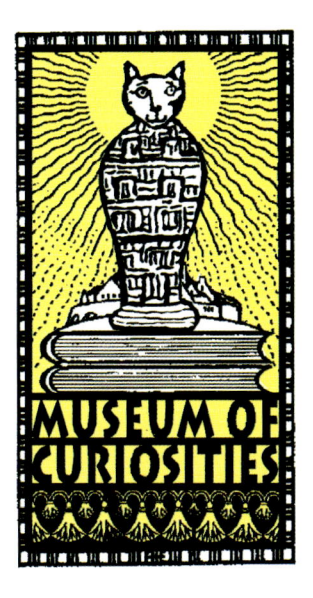

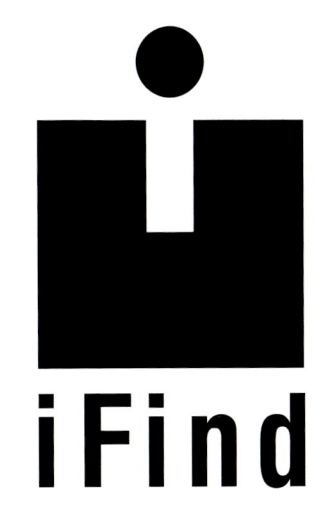

creative firm
 Laura Kay Design
 Ashland (Oregon), USA
creative people
 Laura Kay & Donald Kay
client
 Fareed & Co. for Motorola

creative firm
 Diane Foug Design
 San Francisco (California), USA
creative people
 Diane Foug
client
 La Salle Properties

creative firm
 Armstrong Graphics
 Minneapolis (Minnesota), USA
art director, designer, illustrator
 Bruce Armstrong
client
 Familink

265

creative firm
 Parham Santana Inc.
 New York (New York), USA
creative director
 William Snyder (Parham Santana)
art director
 Emily Pak (Parham Santana)
design director
 Peter Aguanno (Rainbow Programming)
print production manager
 Janet Nicosia (Rainbow Programming)
client
 Bravo Networks

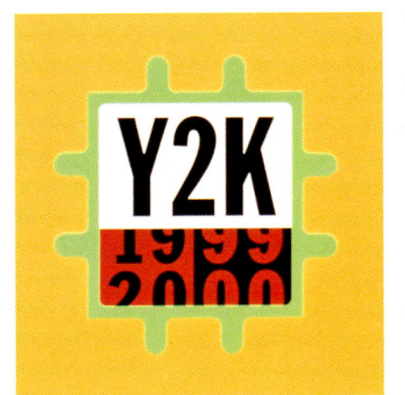

creative firm
 Design Guys
 Minneapolis
 (Minnesota), USA
creative people
 Steven Sikora &
 Jay Theige
client
 Target Stores

creative firm
 Curtis Design LLC
  San Francisco (California), USA
creative people
 David Curtis & Chris Benitez
client
 La Fabrica

creative firm
 Primary Design
  Haverhill (Massachusetts), USA
creative director
 Jules Epstein
designer
 Allison Davis
client
 Beacon/Corcoran Jennison Partners

creative firm
 Primary Design, Inc.
  Haverhill (Massachusetts), USA
designer
 Jules Epstein
client
 Corcoran Jennison Company

creative firm
 JGA, Inc.
  Southfield (Michigan), USA
creative people
 Tony Camilletti,
 Brian Eastman,
 & Mike Farris
client
 Pennsylvania Fashions

creative firm
 A+B (In Exile)
  Ljubljana, Slovenia
creative people
 Eduard Cehovin
client
 National Examination Center
 "25th Conference East Meet West"

creative firm
 Arte-Final, Design E Pub, LDA
  Lisboa, Portugal
designer
 António Antunes
client
 Cocise

266

creative firm
 Nakatsuka Daisuke Inc.
  Tokyo, Japan
creative director
 Daisuke Nakatsuka
art directors
 Daisuke Nakatsuka & Yoshifumi Nakasima
copywriters
 Daisuke Nakatsuka & Junko Nakatsuka
typographer
 Tadanori Yokoo
client
 Nakatsuka Daisuke Inc.

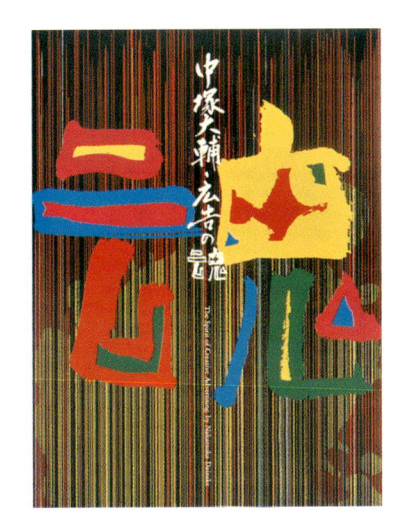

creative firm
 Gardner Design
  Wichita (Kansas), USA
creative director
 Bill Gardner
art directors
 Bill Gardner &
 Chris Parks
designer
 Chris Parks
client
 Piranha

creative firm
 30sixty design, inc.
  Los Angeles (California), USA
art director
 Chris Jaszkowiak
designers
 Gary Pelzman & Marilyn Pelzman
client
 King's Seafood
 Company

creative firm
 Obata Design, Inc.
  St. Louis (Missouri), USA
creative people
 Beth Gellman
client
 Maryville Data Systems

267

creative firm
 Gill Fishman Associates, Inc.
  Cambridge (Massachusetts), USA
creative director
 Gill Fishman
designer
 Michael Persons
client
 Yes Strategies, Inc.

creative firm
 Congdon & Company
  Greenwich (Connecticut), USA
creative people
 Arthur Congdon
client
 BMG

creative firm
  'Tudes, Graphic Design
    Friendswood (Texas), USA
creative people
  Sandy Newcomb
client
  Suntrac Radiation Services, Inc.

creative firm
  Zenn Graphic Design
    Los Angeles (California), USA
creative people
  Zengo Yoshida
client
  WellCare Solutions, Inc.

creative firm
  Gauger & Silva Associates
    San Francisco (California), USA
creative people
  Bob Ankers & David Gauger
client
  Dividend Homes, Inc.

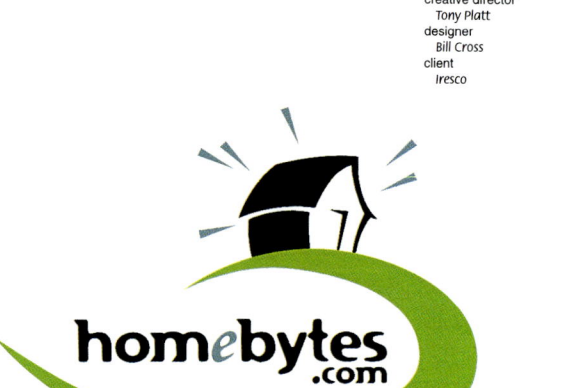

creative firm
  Cadmus Com
    Richmond (Virginia), USA
creative director
  Tony Platt
designer
  Bill Cross
client
  Iresco

268

creative firm
  Nolin Larosee Design Communications
    Montreal (Québec), Canada
art director
  Louise Filion
client
  Provigo

creative firm
  Curtis Design LLC
    San Francisco (California), USA
creative people
  David Curtis & Wendy Rogell
client
  A Xerox new enterprise co.

creative firm
  Plant Ads & Design Pte Ltd
  Singapore
creative director
  Harukazu Suzuki
client
  Profex International
  Limited (Singapore)

**ProfEx**
INTERNATIONAL LIMITED

creative firm
  Iridium Marketing + Design
  Ottawa (Ontario), Canada
art director
  Jean-Luc Denat
designer
  Mario L'Écyer
illustrator
  David Plunkert
client
  Iridium

**IRIDIUM**

creative firm
  David Lemley Design
  Seattle (Washington), USA
designer
  David Lemley
client
  David Lemley Design

creative firm
  Mortensen Design
  Mountain View (California), USA
art director
  Gordon Mortensen
designers
  Wendy Chon & Gordon Mortensen
client
  Tamalpais Bank

**TamalpaisBank**

269

creative firm
  Fisher Design, Inc.
  Cincinnati (Ohio), USA
creative people
  Richard W. Deardorff
client
  Cypress Prepress, Inc.

**Chobe**
CHILWERO

creative firm
  DHI Visual Communication
  Vero Beach (Florida), USA
creative people
  Marjorie Shropshire & Carl Miller
client
  Abercrombie & Kent

creative firm
 Rutgers University
 New Brunswick (New Jersey), USA
art director, designer, illustrator
 John Van Cleaf
client
 RUnet 2000

creative firm
 Gill Fishman Associates, Inc.
 Cambridge (Massachusetts), USA
creative director
 Gill Fishman
designer
 Michael Persons
client
 Sapient Corporation

creative firm
 Beggs Design
 Palo Alto (California), USA
creative director, art director,
designer, illustrator
 Lee Beggs
client
 dpiX, Inc.

creative firm
 Sapient (Studio Archetype)
 San Francisco (California), USA
creative people
 Jennifer Anderson, Mathew Carlson,
 & Grant Peterson
client
 ShareWave

270

creative firm
 David Morris Creative Inc.
 Jersey City (New Jersey), USA
art director
 Gregory Roll
designer
 Denise Spirito
client
 OpenCon Systems Inc.

creative firm
 Tom Fowler, Inc.
 Stamford (Connecticut), USA
creative people
 Karl S. Maruyama
client
 Eventra

creative firm
  Oxygen Inc.
    Chicago (Illinois), USA
creative people
  Penina Goodman
client
  Moondoggie

creative firm
  Next Year's News, Inc.
    Toledo (Ohio), USA
creative people
  Andrea Colon & Chris Hoffman
client
  American Assoc. for the Study of Liver Diseases

creative firm
  Ambush Communication
    New York (New York), USA
art directors
  Yuk-Chun Yu & Keith Mastandrea
client
  Advanstar Communications

creative firm
  Gill Fishman Associates, Inc.
    Cambridge (Massachusetts), USA
creative director
  Gill Fishman
designer, illustrator
  Alicia Ozyjowski
client
  Logal Software

creative firm
  Focus Design
    San Rafael (California), USA
creative people
  Brian Jacobson
client
  Spectrum Photographic & Imaging

creative firm
  Kim Baer Design Associates
    Venice (California), USA
art director
  Kim Baer
designer
  Barbara Cooper
client
  Net Zero

creative firm
  Obata Design, Inc.
  St. Louis (Missouri), USA
creative people
  Wade Howell & Chris Haller
client
  Affiniti

**AFFINITI**

creative firm
  AERIAL
  San Francisco (California), USA
creative people
  Tracy Moon, Stephanie West, & Kimberly Cross
client
  Tribe Pictures

TRiBE
[moving]
Pictures

creative firm
  L-Square Design Strategy
  Hong Kong, China
creative people
  Ben Lai
client
  Im Fine Porcelain

"I'm china"
I.M.fine porcelain

272

creative firm
  Kuo Design
  New York (New York), USA
creative people
  Bongchan Kim
client
  Kentucky Horse Park

creative firm
  James Robie Design Associates
  Los Angeles (California), USA
art directors
  James Robie & Wayne Fujita
designer
  Karen Nakatani
client
  The Hump Sushi Bar & Restaurant

the Hump
SUSHI BAR & RESTAURANT

H₂OTEL

creative firm
  Paprika Communications
  Montréal (Québec), Canada
art director
  Louis Gagnon
designer
  Francis Turgeon
client
  Hotel Le Germain

creative firm
  Wunderman Cato Johnson
  San Francisco (California), USA
creative director
  John Meyer
art director
  Silvia Grossmann
client
  Xerox

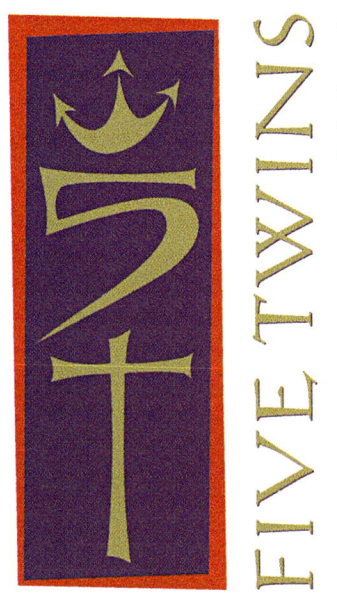

**MOBILEDOC**™

creative firm
  David Carter Design Associates
  Dallas (Texas), USA
creative director
  Lori B. Wilson
designer
  Sharon Lejeune
client
  Atlantis Resort

FIVE TWINS

creative firm
  Congdon & Company
  Greenwich (Connecticut), USA
creative people
  Arthur Congdon
client
  Corp Air

[i]e design

273

creative firm
  IE Design
  Studio City (California), USA
creative people
  Marcie Carson
illustrator
  Mirjam Selmi
client
  IE Design

creative firm
  Pat Taylor Inc.
  Washington (D.C.), USA
art director, designer
  Pat Taylor
client
  Patricia M. Sitar Center
  for the Arts

**COVANTA**™
solutions

creative firm
  Addison Whitney
  Charlotte (North Carolina), USA
art director
  Lori Earnhardt
client
  Covanta

creative firm
  Congdon & Company
  Greenwich (Connecticut), USA
creative people
  Arthur Congdon
client
  Hypernex

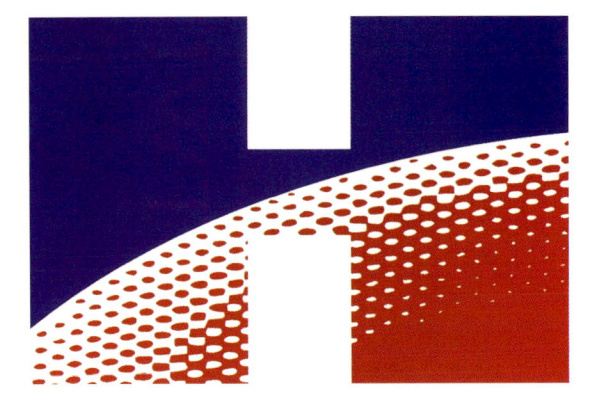

creative firm
  Cahan & Associates
  San Francisco (California), USA
art director
  Bill Cahan
designer
  Michael Braley
client
  InQuizit

creative firm
  Frank D'Astolfo Design
  New York (New York), USA
client
  International Arts Movement

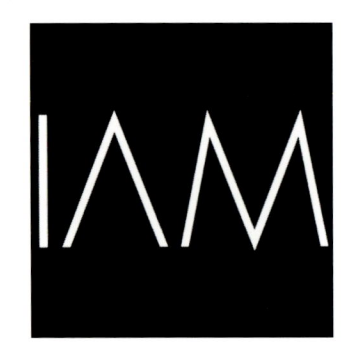

creative firm
  Rick Johnson & Company, Inc.
  Albuquerque (New Mexico), USA
designer
  Tim McGrath
client
  New Mexico Economic Development

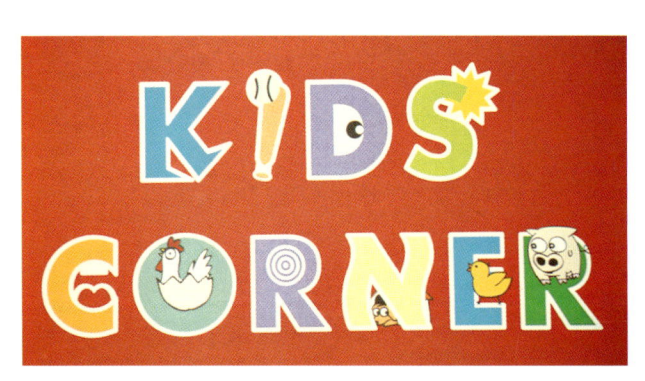

274

creative firm
  Teamwork Design Ltd.
  Hong Kong, China
creative people
  Gary Tam, Ivy Wong, Alex Chan, & Joel Ong
client
  Nuance-Watson (HK) Ltd.

creative firm
  Gardner Design
  Wichita (Kansas), USA
designer
  Brian Miller
client
  Artistree

creative firm
  Congdon & Company
  Greenwich (Connecticut), USA
creative people
  Arthur Congdon
client
  Novasource

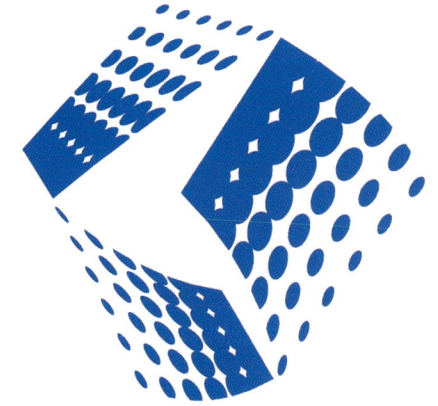

creative firm
  Hornall Anderson Design Works
  Seattle (Washington), USA
creative people
  Jack Anderson & Mike Calkins
client
  Hammerquist & Halverson

creative firm
  Metzler & Associes
  Paris, France
designer
  M.A. Herrmann
client
  Meccano

creative firm
  Artefact Design
  Palo Alto (California), USA
creative people
  Artefact Design
client
  Webcor Builders

275

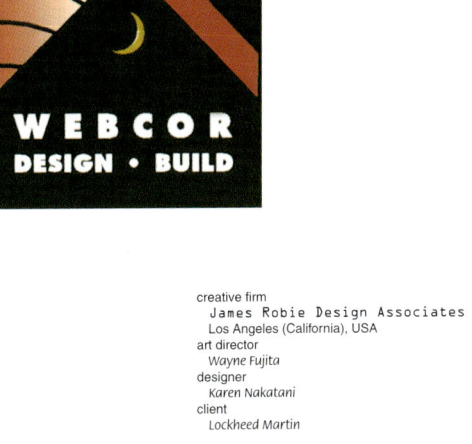

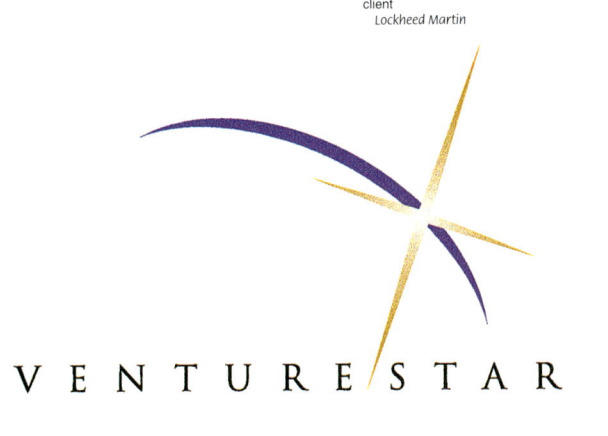

creative firm
  James Robie Design Associates
  Los Angeles (California), USA
art director
  Wayne Fujita
designer
  Karen Nakatani
client
  Lockheed Martin

creative firm
  Gardner Design
  Wichita (Kansas), USA
art directors
  Travis Brown, Brian Miller, & Bill Gardner
designer
  Travis Brown
client
  Roosevelt's American Eatery

creative firm
 The Imagination Company
  Bethel (Vermont), USA
creative director
 Jim Giberti
art directors
 Mark Connolly
 & Steve Frigard
client
 The Imagination
 Studios

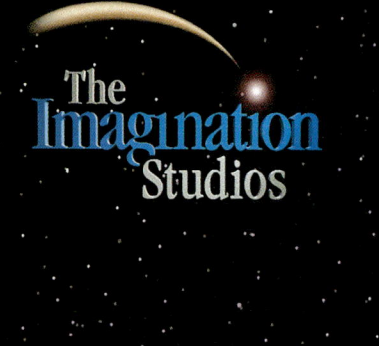

creative firm
 Hornall Anderson Design Works
  Seattle (Washington), USA
creative people
 Jack Anderson & David Bates
client
 Anderson Pellet

creative firm
 Fisher Design, Inc.
  Cincinnati (Ohio), USA
creative people
 Fisher Design
client
 Hasbro, Inc.

creative firm
 Landor Associates
  New York (New York), USA
art director
 Robert Matza
designers
 Jeremy Dawkins, Brett Traylor,
 & Merel Matzinger
client
 Iridium

276

creative firm
 Landor Associates
  New York (New York), USA
art director, designer
 Richard Brandt
client
 Florida USA

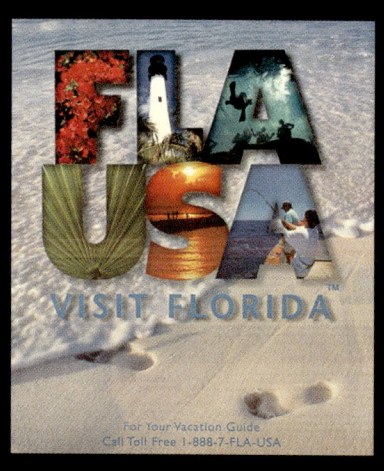

creative firm
 Landor Associates
  New York (New York), USA
designer
 Alan Dye
client
 Youth Power/Just Say No

creative firm
 Planet Ads & Design Pte Ltd
  Singapore
creative director
 Harukazu Suzuki
client
 Comm Pte Ltd (Singapore)

creative firm
 Gardner Design
  Wichita (Kansas), USA
art director, designer
 Bill Gardner
client
 Buzz Cuts Maximum Lawncare

creative firm
 MTV Networks Creative Services
  New York (New York), USA
creative directors
 Scott Wadler & Cheryl Family
designer
 Andrew Lopez

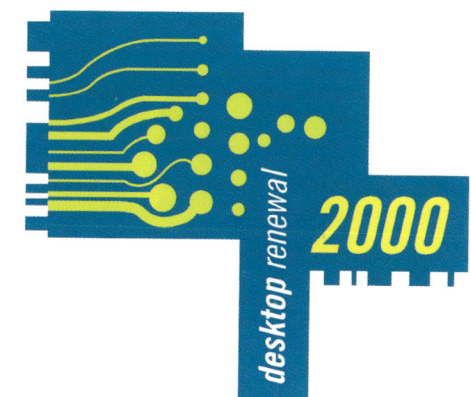

creative firm
 Sabingrafik, Inc.
  Carlsbad (California), USA
creative director
 Dene Oliver
art director
 Marilee Bankers
designer, illustrator
 Tracy Sabin
client
 Oliver McMillan

277

creative firm
 Addison Whitney
  Charlotte (North Carolina), USA
art director
 Lori Earnhardt
client
 Olive Garden

creative firm
 Conflux Design
  Rockford (Illinois), USA
designer
 Greg Fedorev
client
 Mission Studios

# CREATIVITY
## Letterheads/ Stationery

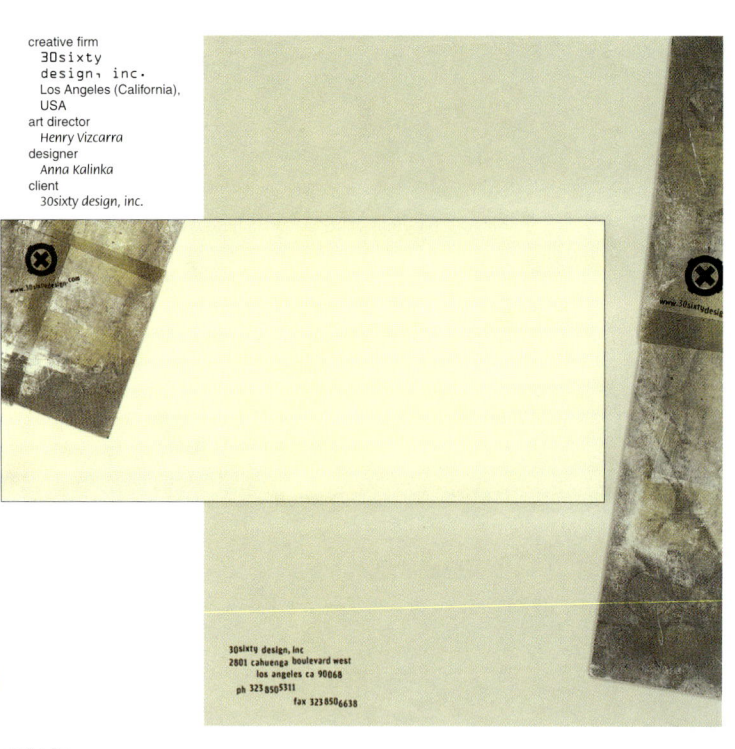

creative firm
**30sixty design, inc.**
Los Angeles (California), USA
art director
Henry Vizcarra
designer
Anna Kalinka
client
30sixty design, inc.

278

creative firm
**Heye + Partner**
Unterhaching, Germany
creative director
Norbert Herold
art directors
Detlev Schmidt & Frank Widmann
designer
Frank Widmann
client
Reinhold Laugallies Plane Rental

creative firm
**O&J Design, Inc.**
New York (New York), USA
art director
Barbara Olejniczak
designer
Heishin Ra
client
The Acme Idea Company

creative firm
**Deep Design**
Atlanta (Georgia), USA
art director
Edward Jett
designer, illustrator
Philip Shore
client
Dr. Smith's Veterinary Collectibles

creative firm
 RDW Group Inc
  Providence
  (Rhode Island), USA
creative people
 Anthony Gill
client
 New England Coffee

creative firm
 Miller & White Advertising
  Terre Haute (Indiana), USA
art director
 Bill White
designer
 Jason Hertenstein
client
 D&S Investment

279

creative firm
 The Zimmerman Agency
  Tallahassee (Florida), USA
creative director
 Doug Engel
art director
 John Towler
production
 Emily Barron
client
 Premier Roasters

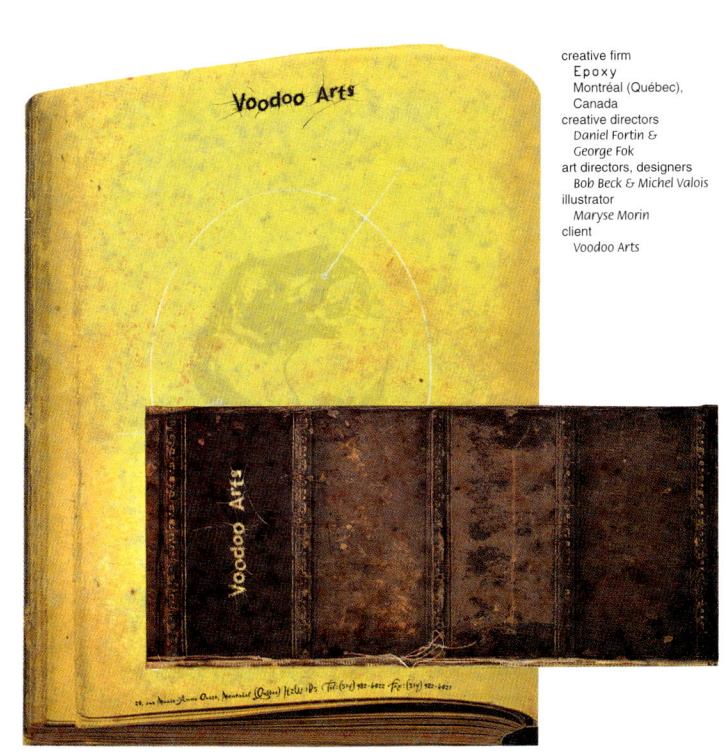

creative firm
 Epoxy
  Montréal (Québec),
  Canada
creative directors
 Daniel Fortin &
 George Fok
art directors, designers
 Bob Beck & Michel Valois
illustrator
 Maryse Morin
client
 Voodoo Arts

creative firm
  Iridium Marketing + Design
  Ottawa (Ontario), Canada
art director
  Jean-Luc Denat
designer
  Etienne Bessette
photographer
  Headlight
client
  Headlight Innovative Imagery

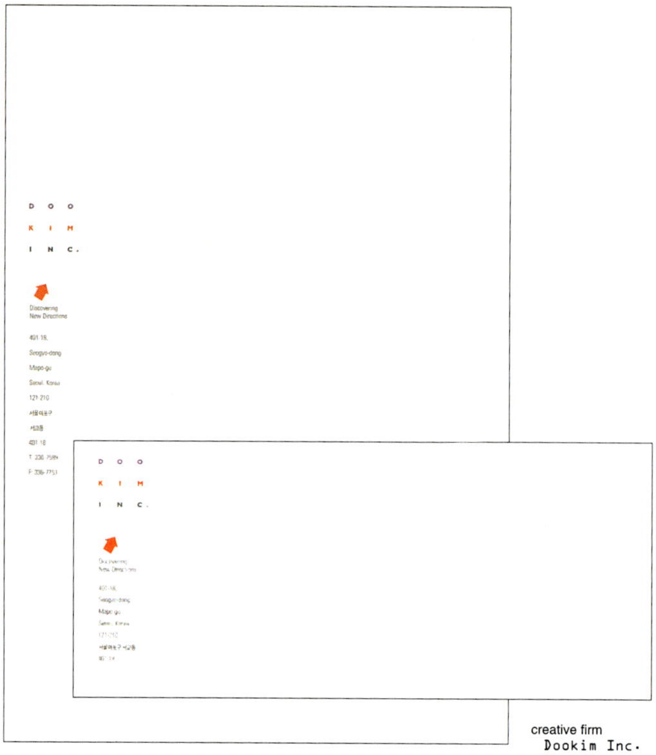

creative firm
  Dookim Inc.
  Seoul, Korea
creative people
  Doo Kim
client
  Dookim Inc.

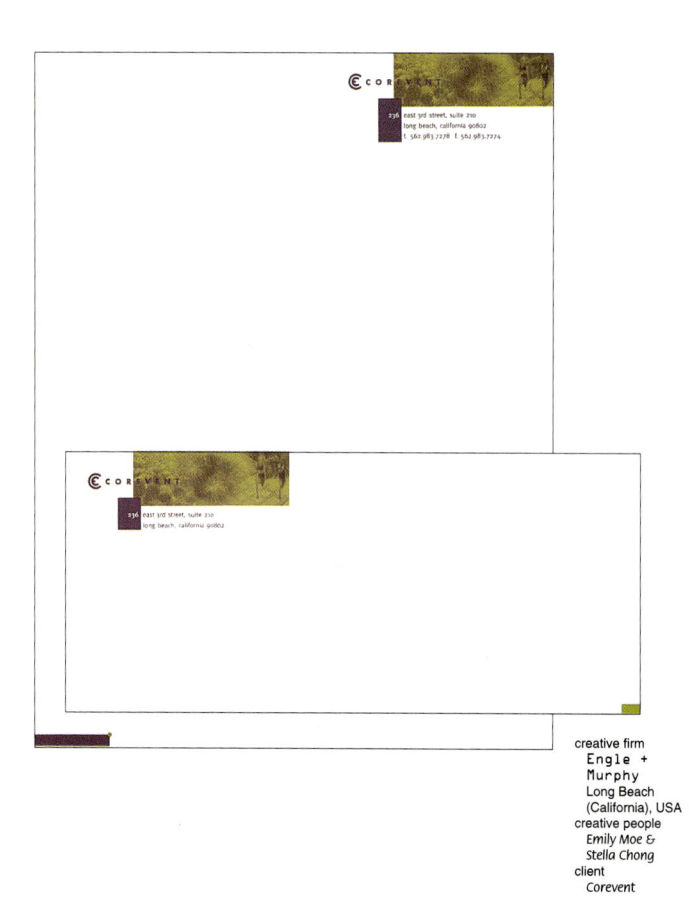

280

creative firm
  Engle +
  Murphy
  Long Beach
  (California), USA
creative people
  Emily Moe &
  Stella Chong
client
  Corevent

creative firm
  Metropolis Design
  St. Louis (Missouri), USA
creative people
  Andy Quevreaux
client
  FP Mobile Television

creative firm
  DBD International
  Menomonie (Wisconsin), USA
art director, designer, illustrator
  David Brier
client
  Digital Minds

creative firm
  Hornall Anderson Design Works
  Seattle (Washington), USA
creative people
  John Hornall, Julie Lock, & Mary Chin Hutchison
client
  NextRx Corporation

281

creative firm
  Hull Creative Group
  Boston (Massachusetts), USA
art director
  Caryl Hull
designer
  Michelle Perreault
client
  TranSysoft

creative firm
  Sayles Graphic Design
  Des Moines (Iowa), USA
art director, designer
  John Sayles
client
  Casa Bonita

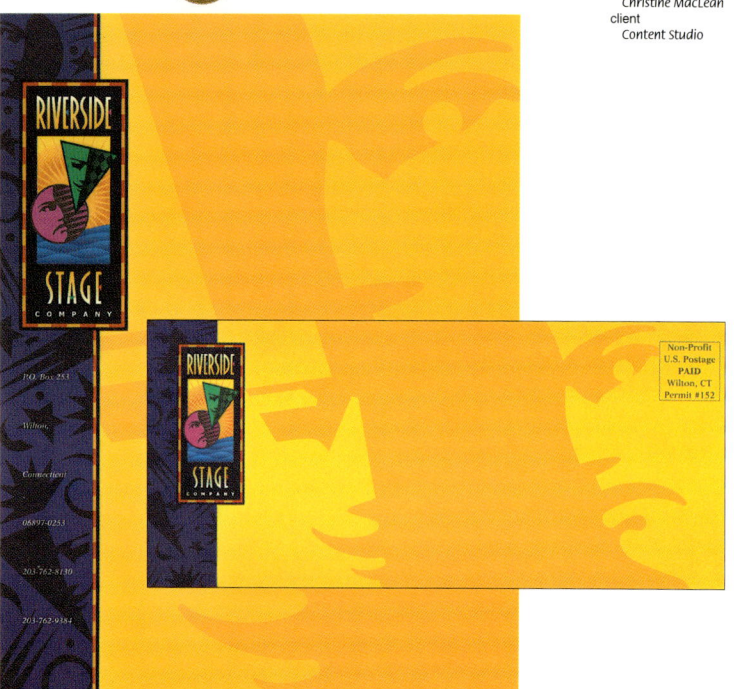

creative firm
　Zunda Design Group
　　South Norwalk (Connecticut), USA
creative people
　　Charles Zunda
client
　　Riverside Stage Company

creative firm
　　BBK Studio Inc.
　　　Grand Rapids (Michigan),
　　　USA
creative director, designer
　　　Yang Kim
copywriter
　　　Christine MacLean
client
　　　Content Studio

282

creative firm
　Goldforest Advertising
　　Miami (Florida), USA
client
　　Stern & Company LLP

creative firm
　Design Objectives Pte Ltd
　　Singapore
creative people
　　Ronnie S C Tan
client
　　Failsafe Corporation (Singapore)

creative firm
 A+B (In Exile)
  Ljubljana, Slovenia
creative people
 E. Čehovin
client
 A Atalanta

creative firm
 Gensler
 Studio 585
  San Francisco
  (California), USA
creative people
 Jane Brady,
 Chris Seager, &
 Cathy Terashita
client
 Kenmark

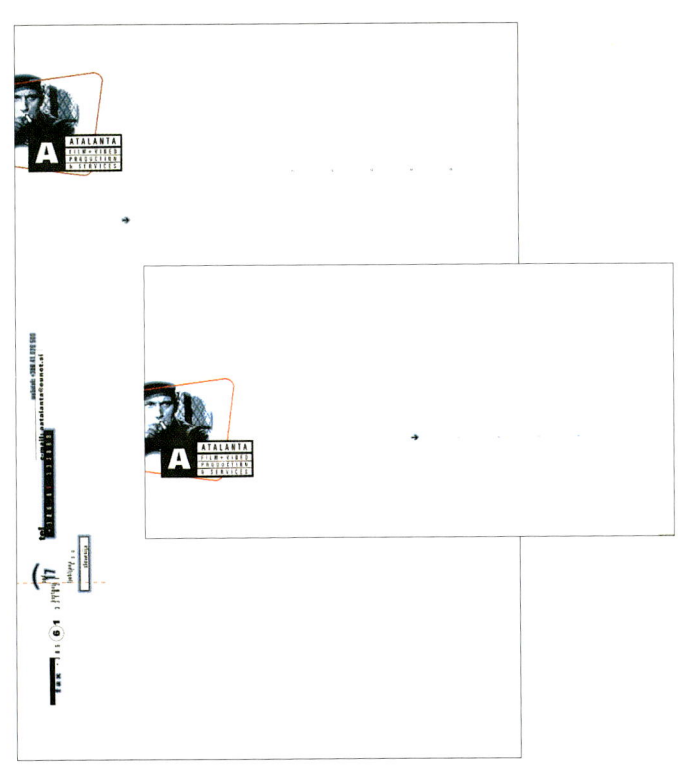

283

creative firm
 Louey/Rubino Design Group Inc.
  Santa Monica (California), USA
art director
 Robert Louey
project manager
 Teresa E. Lopez
designer
 Anja Mueller
client
 Platinum Advisors

creative firm
 Gardner Design
  Wichita (Kansas), USA
art director
 Bill Gardner
designer
 Brian Miller
client
 Paul Chauncey
 Photography

creative firm
　Haan and Associates
　　Advertising, Inc.
　　West Lafayette (Indiana), USA
creative people
　Li Zhang
client
　Purdue University

creative firm
　1185 Design
　　Palo Alto (California), USA
creative people
　Peggy Burke & Dave Prescott
client
　when.com

284

creative firm
　The Traver Company
　　Seattle (Washington), USA
creative people
　Dale Hart & Christopher Downs
client
　ESM Consulting Engineers

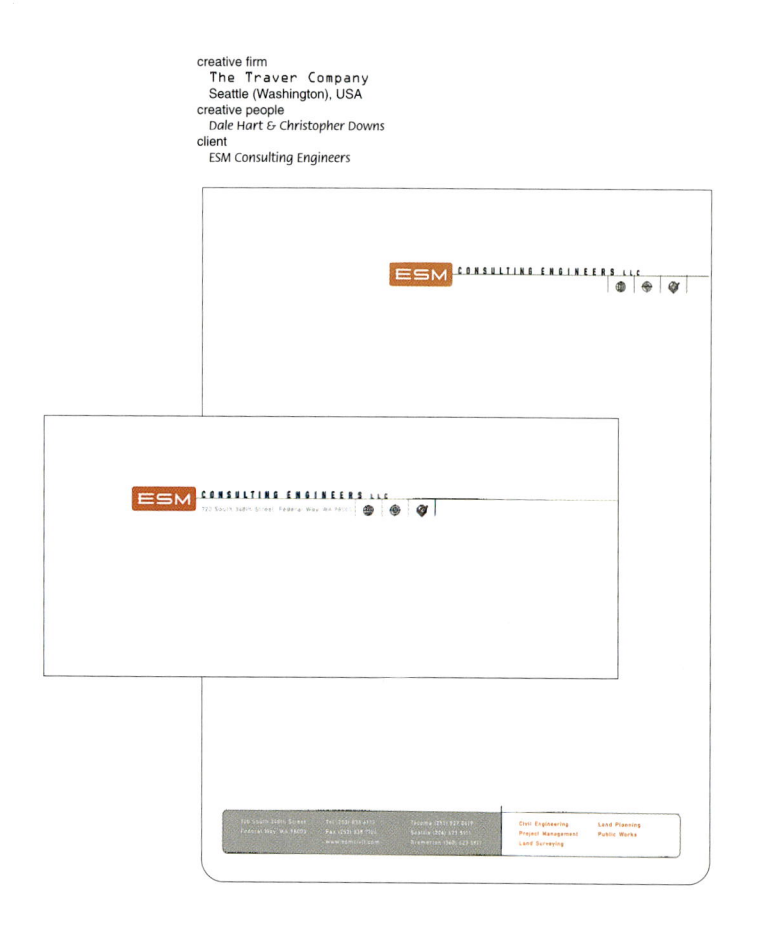

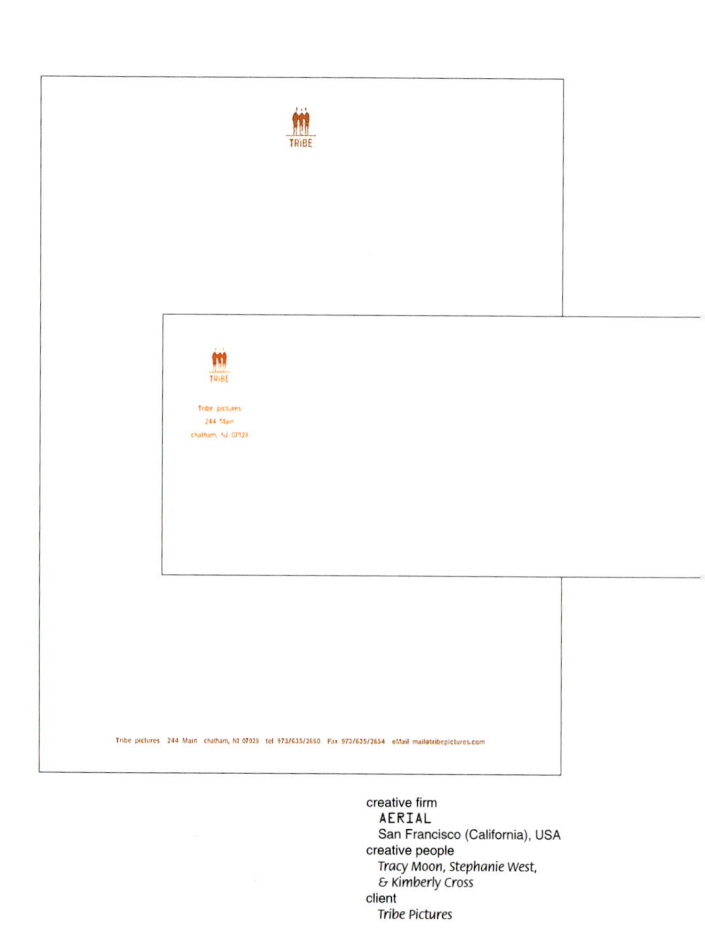

creative firm
　AERIAL
　　San Francisco (California), USA
creative people
　Tracy Moon, Stephanie West,
　& Kimberly Cross
client
　Tribe Pictures

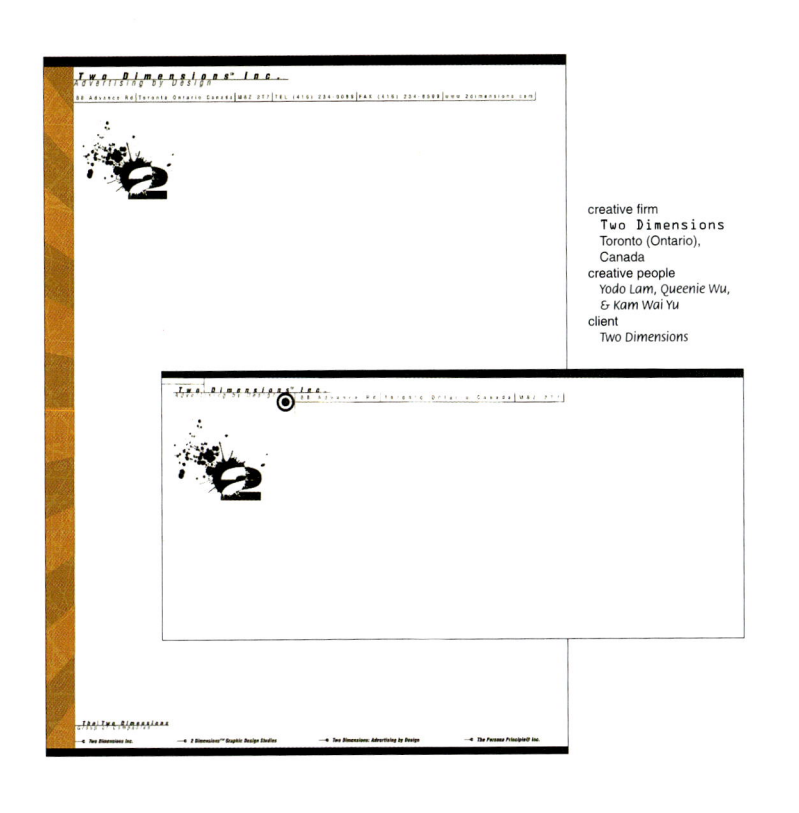

creative firm
  Two Dimensions
  Toronto (Ontario),
  Canada
creative people
  Yodo Lam, Queenie Wu,
  & Kam Wai Yu
client
  Two Dimensions

creative firm
  A to Z communications, inc.
  Pittsburgh (Pennsylvania), USA
designer
  Vonnie Hornburg
client
  Ketchum Pittsburgh

285

creative firm
  Visual Marketing Associates
  Dayton (Ohio), USA
art directors
  Tracy Meiners, Jason Selke, & Ken Botts
designer
  Jason Selke
client
  CYND Snowboarding Apparel

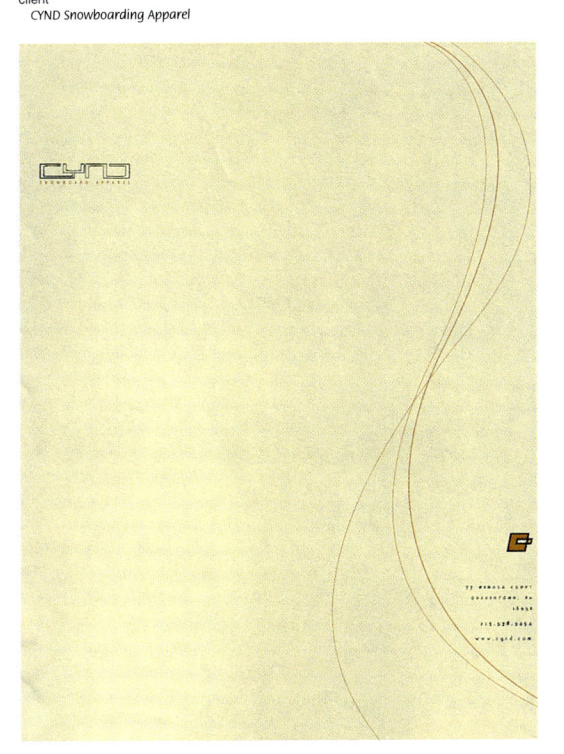

creative firm
  Pink Coyote
  Design, Inc.
  New York
  (New York), USA
creative director
  Amber Reshen
art director
  Joel Ponzan
client
  Crews N Production
  Services

creative firm
  Watts Graphic Design
    South Melbourne (Victoria), Australia
creative people
  Peter Watts
client
  Blackwood Studios

creative firm
  Kim Baer Design Associates
    Venice (California), USA
art director
  Kim Baer
designer
  Liz Roberts
client
  The Ant Farm

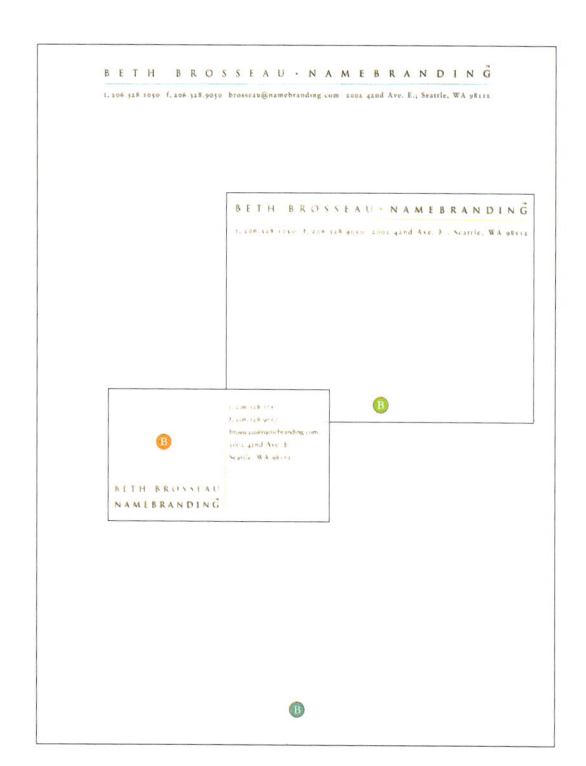

creative firm
  The Traver Company
    Seattle (Washington), USA
creative people
  Hugh Rodman & Anne Traver
client
  Beth Brosseau Namebranding

creative firm
  Sapient
  (Studio
  Archetype)
    San Francisco
    (California), USA
creative people
  Henrik Olsen,
  Jessie Thacker, &
  Michael Bebe
client
  Spring Street

creative firm
 Werkhaus Design
  Seattle (Washington), USA
creative people
 Christina Stein
client
 Clear Blue Sky Productions

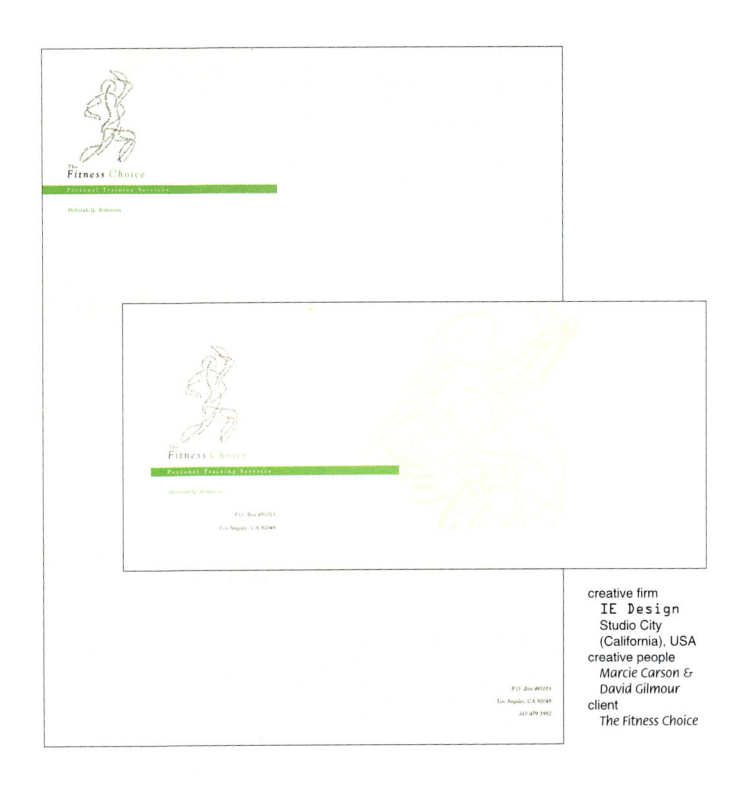

creative firm
 IE Design
  Studio City
  (California), USA
creative people
 Marcie Carson &
 David Gilmour
client
 The Fitness Choice

287

creative firm
 Oakley Design Studios
  Portland (Oregon), USA
designer
 Tim Oakley
client
 Oakley Design Studios

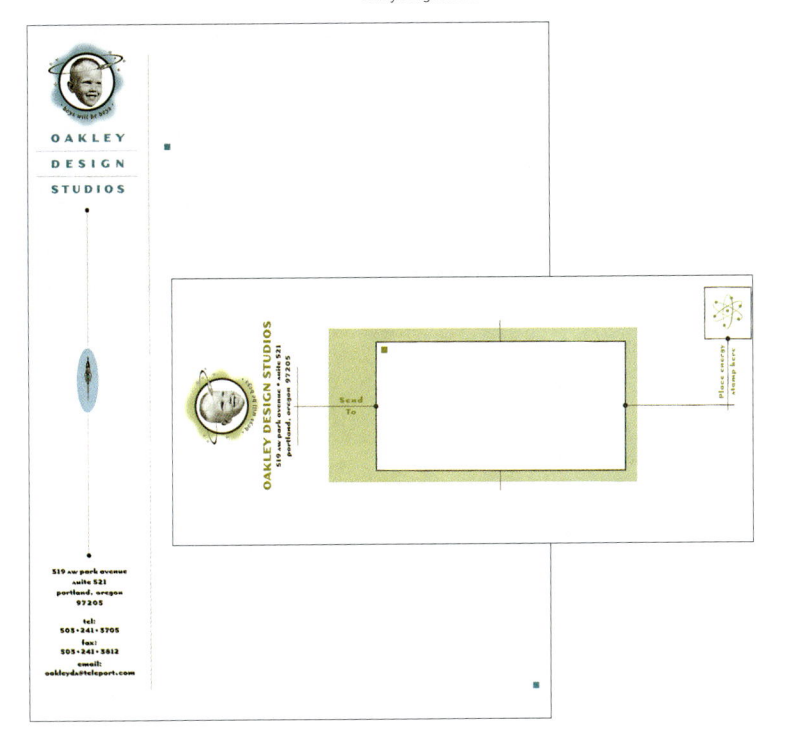

creative firm
 Zeewy Design
  Paoli (Pennsylvania), USA
designer
 Orly Zeewy
illustrator
 Kathryn Adams
copywriter
 Linda Angew
client
 Dr. McSurdy & Staff

creative firm
  AERIAL
  San Francisco (California), USA
creative people
  Tracy Moon & Stephanie West
client
  Collage Salon

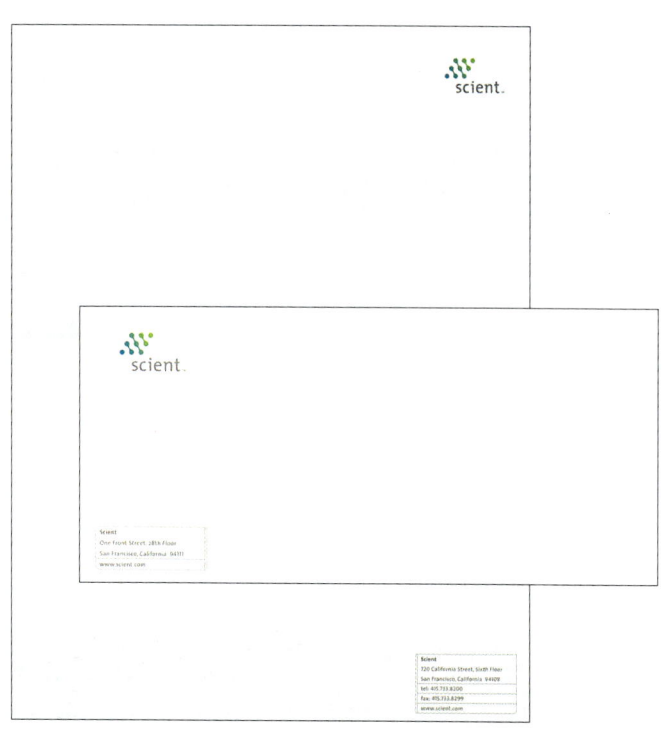

creative firm
  Spencer Zahn
  & Associates
  Philadelphhia
  (Pennsylvania), USA
creative director
  Spencer Zahn
art director
  Joseph McCarthy
client
  World OM Day

creative firm
  Sapient (Studio Archetype)
  San Francisco (California), USA
creative people
  Jack Herr & Matt Carlson
client
  Scient

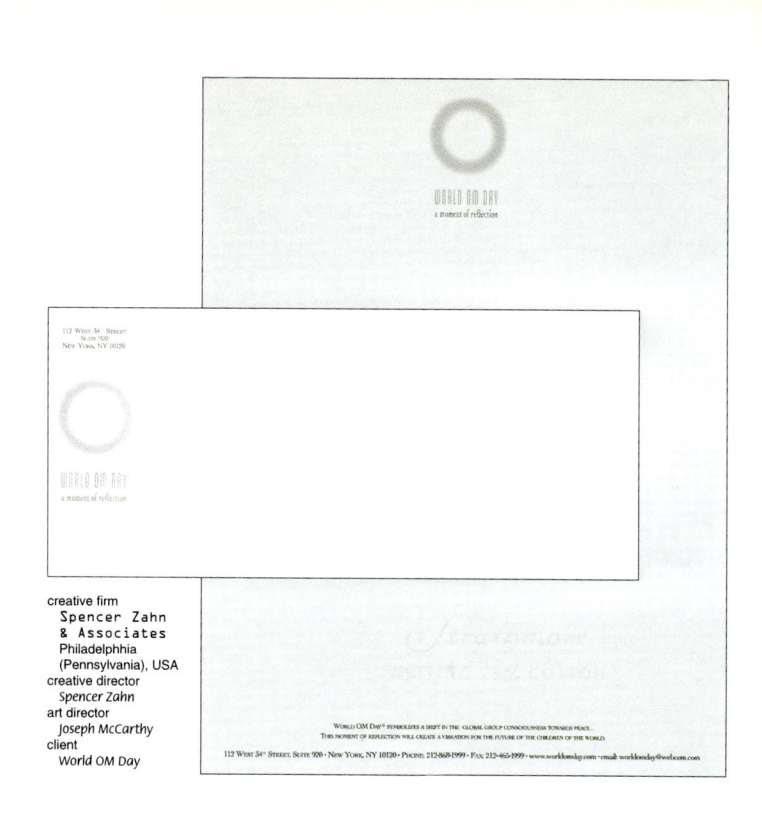

creative firm
  Brad Norr Design
  Minneapolis (Minnesota), USA
art director
  Brad Norr
designer
  Andrew Bessler
client
  Cybernet Systems Inc.

creative firm
 David Lemley Design
  Seattle (Washington), USA
designers
 David Lemley & Matt Peloza
client
 Appliant, Inc.

creative firm
 Insight Design Communications
  Wichita (Kansas), USA
creative people
 Sherrie Holdeman & Tracy Holdeman
client
 CLOTIA

289

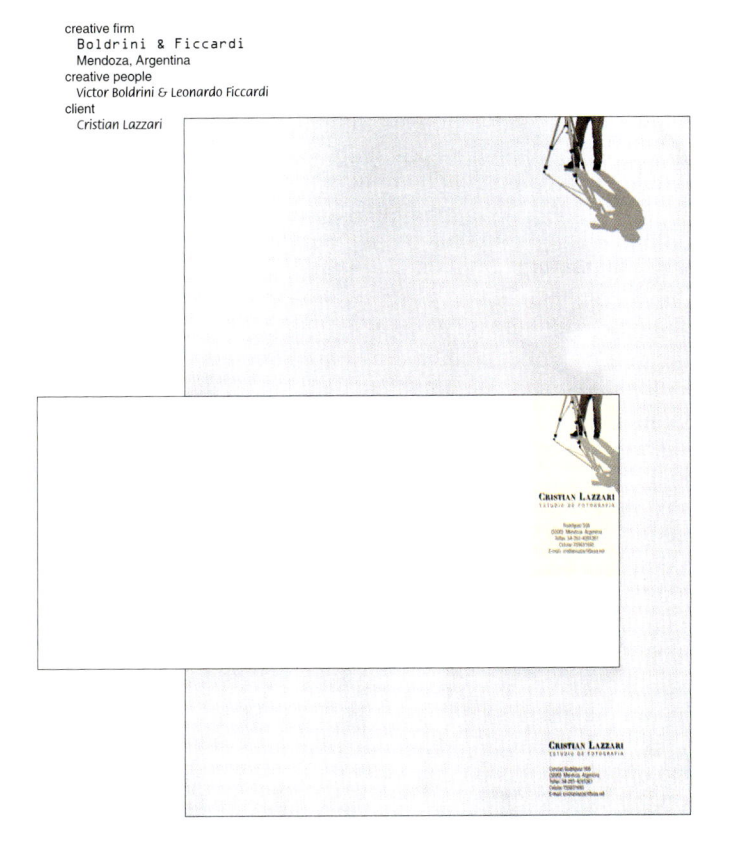

creative firm
 Boldrini & Ficcardi
  Mendoza, Argentina
creative people
 Victor Boldrini & Leonardo Ficcardi
client
 Cristian Lazzari

creative firm
 NPM Advertising
  New York (New York), USA
art director
 Yuk-Chun Yu
designer
 Rob Silverman
client
 Brown Harris Stevens/Mosbacher

creative firm
 Cahan & Associates
  San Francisco (California), USA
art director
 Bill Cahan
designer
 Ben Pham
client
 Zeum

creative firm
 DHI Visual Communication
  Vero Beach (Florida), USA
creative people
 Marty Regan & Carl Miller
client
 DHI Visual Communication

creative firm
 House of Design
  Ciraz, Austria
art directors, designers
 André Stangl & Mischa Stangl
client
 Strobl Baugestibh

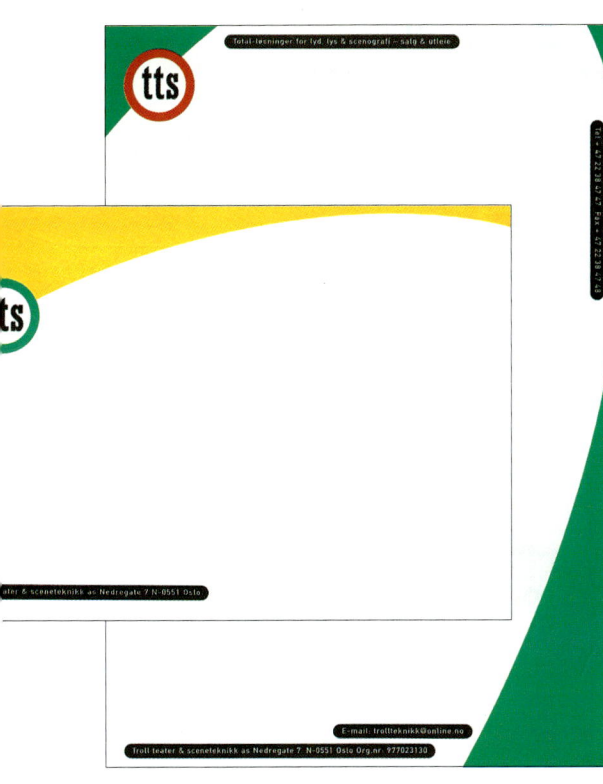

creative firm
 Rose + Hopp Design
  Oslo, Norway
creative people
 Gina Rose
client
 TTS

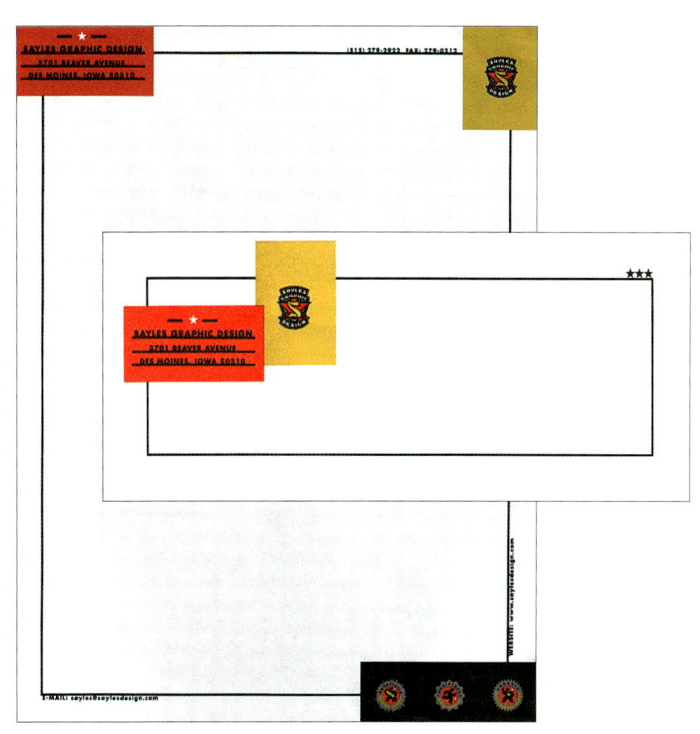

creative firm
 Sayles Graphic Design
  Des Moines (Iowa), USA
art director, designer
 John Sayles
client
 Sayles Graphic Design

291

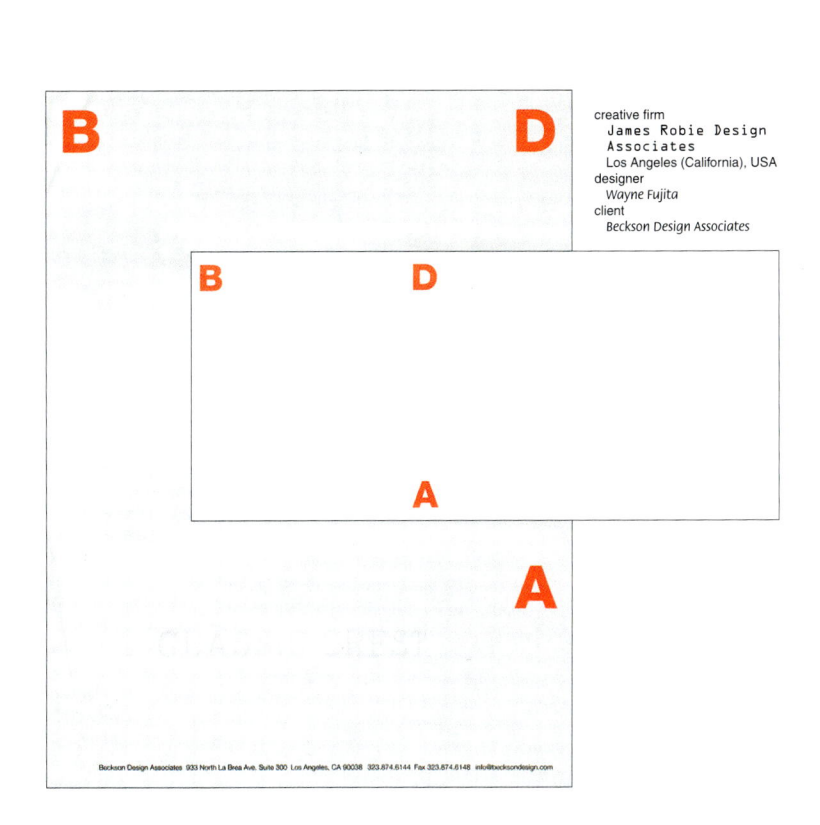

creative firm
 James Robie Design Associates
  Los Angeles (California), USA
designer
 Wayne Fujita
client
 Beckson Design Associates

creative firm
 Belyea
  Seattle (Washington), USA
art director
 Patricia Belyea
designer
 Ron Lars Hansen
client
 Belyea

# CREATIVITY
## Corporate Identity Manuals

creative firm
 Handler Design Group, Inc.
  White Plains (New York), USA
creative people
 Bruce Handler, John Ryan,
 & Dennis Weinberg
client
 Empire Blue Cross/Blue Shield

creative firm
 Michael Orr +
 Associates, Inc.
  Corning (New York), USA
creative people
 Michael R. Orr,
 Gregory Duell,
 & Thomas Freeland
client
 United Health Services

292

creative firm
 BrandEquity International
  Newton (Massachusetts), USA
creative people
 BrandEquity team
client
 Staples

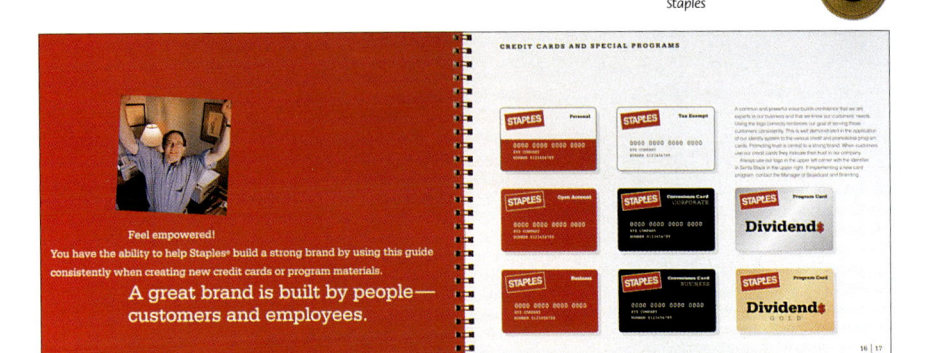

creative firm
 World Studio
  New York (New York), USA
creative people
 David Sterling & Noreen Leahey
client
 The Metropolitan Opera

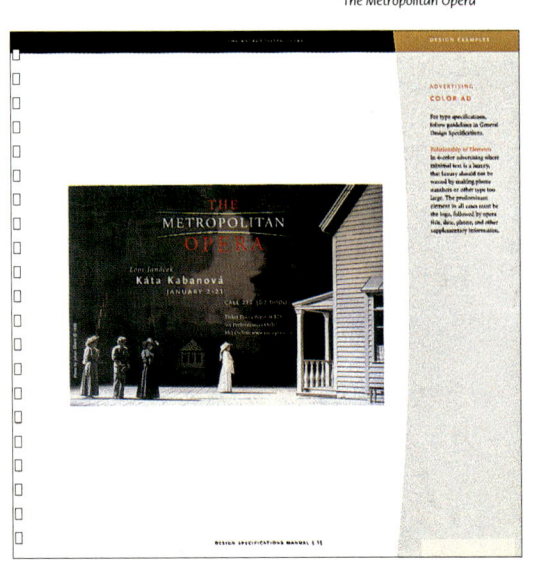

creative firm
 DCG Chicago
  Chicago (Illinois), USA
creative people
 Hugh Lambert,
 Jeri Dimalanta, & Anne Siegel
client
 National Association of Realtors

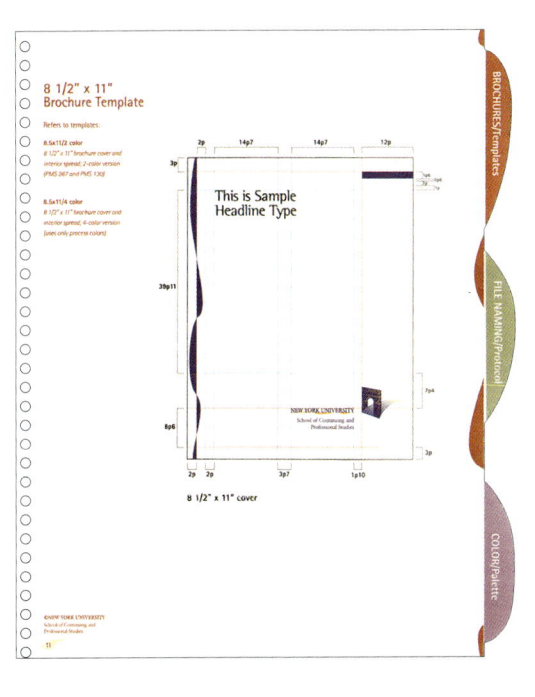

creative firm
O&J Design, Inc.
New York (New York),
USA
art director
Andrzej Olejniczak
designers
Leslie Nayman &
Andrzej Olejniczak
client
New York University School
of Continuing Education
and Professional Studies

creative firm
Hornall Anderson Design Works
Seattle (Washington), USA
creative people
John Hornall, Katha Dalton, & Holly Finlayson
client
Washington Mutual Bank

creative firm
Nickelodeon
New York (New York), USA
creative director
Kim Rosenblum
art director
Kenna Kay
producer
Tammy Brown
designer
Noel Claro
photographer
Steffany Rubin
illustrator
Chip Wass
copywriter
Sharon Lesser

293

creative firm
Nolin Larosee Design
Communications
Montreal (Québec), Canada
art director
Barbara Jacques
client
Rôtisseries St-Hubert Ltée

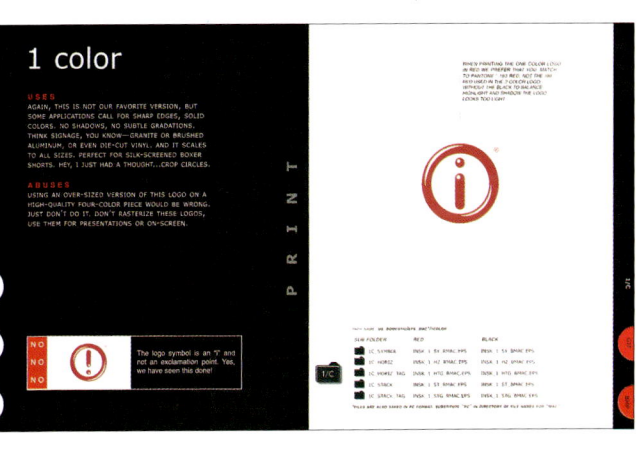

creative firm
Sapient (Studio Archetype)
San Francisco (California), USA
creative people
Bob Skubic, Thomas Gehring,
Chuck Adsit, Steven Cavalieri,
& Grant Peterson
client
Infoseek

# CREATIVITY

## Signage, Environmental Graphics

294

creative firm
 Nicholson Design
  Encinitas (California), USA
creative people
 Joe C. Nicholson
client
 Centre City Development Corporation

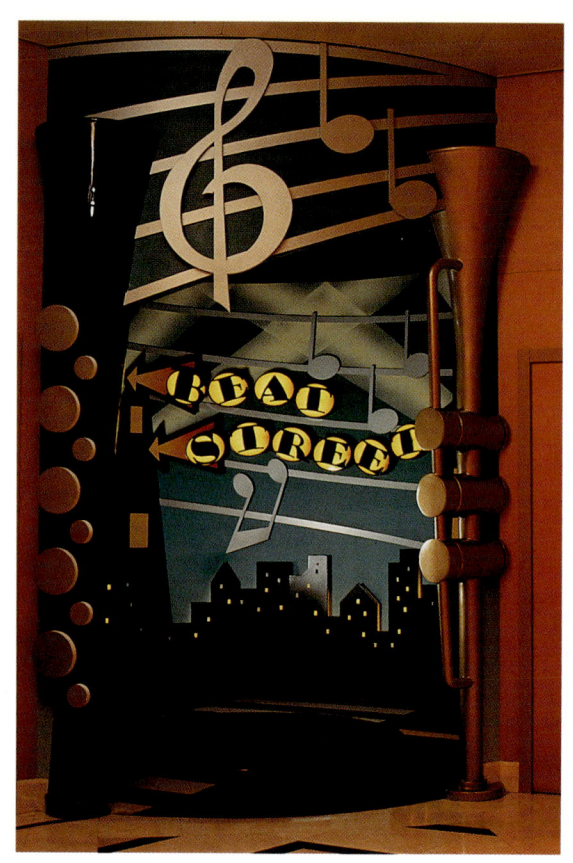

creative firm
 David Carter
 Design Associates
  Dallas (Texas), USA
creative director
 Lori B. Wilson
client
 Disney Cruise Line

creative firm
 BrandEquity International
  Newton (Massachusetts), USA
creative people
 BrandEquity Design team
client
 TŌZ (Sara Lee)

creative firm
 Schafer
  Oak Park (Illinois), USA
creative people
 Dale Wennlund, Steve Prosser,
 Jube Manderico, Jeri Bademian-Elsie,
 Corbin Pulliam, & Jennifer Sweas
client
 Fedco Incorporated

creative firm
　FRCH Design Worldwide
　　(Cincinnati)
　　New York (New York), USA
creative people
　Tessa Westermeyer, Jeff Waggoner,
　Denise Labus, & Paul Lechleiter
client
　FootAction,
　　division of Footstar Corporation

creative firm
　Emery Vincent Design
　　Southbank (Victoria), Australia
creative people
　Emery Vincent Design team
client
　Peter Elliott Architects

295

creative firm
　Gensler Studio 585
　　San Francisco (California), USA
creative people
　Michael Bodziner, Jeff Henry,
　Beth Novitsky, Cathy Terashita,
　Chris Seager, Julie Lochowski-Haney,
　& Jodi Chen
client
　Briggs & Riley

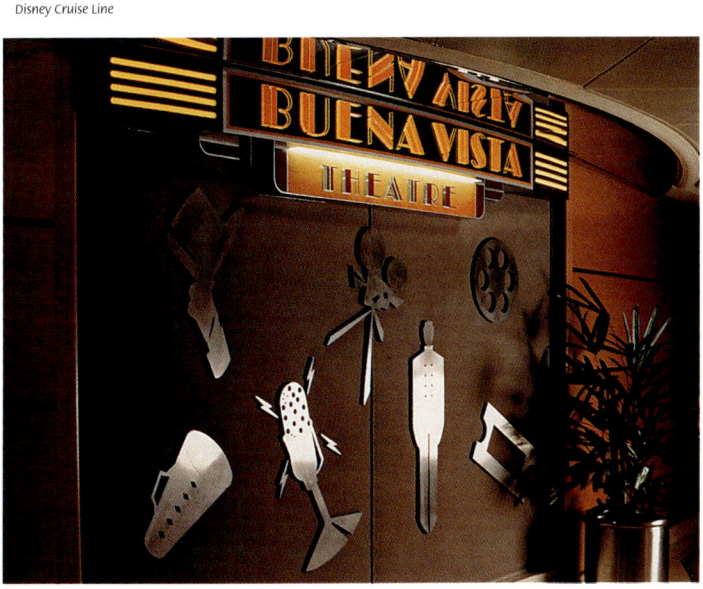

creative firm
　David Carter Design Associates
　　Dallas (Texas), USA
creative director
　Lori B. Wilson
designers
　Gary Loboue & Cynthia Carter
client
　Disney Cruise Line

creative firm
　Jensen Design Assoc. Inc.
　Long Beach (California), USA
creative people
　David Jensen
client
　Philharmonic Society of Orange County

creative firm
　Hornall Anderson
　Design Works
　Seattle (Washington), USA
creative people
　Jack Anderson & Cliff Chung
client
　Bollé

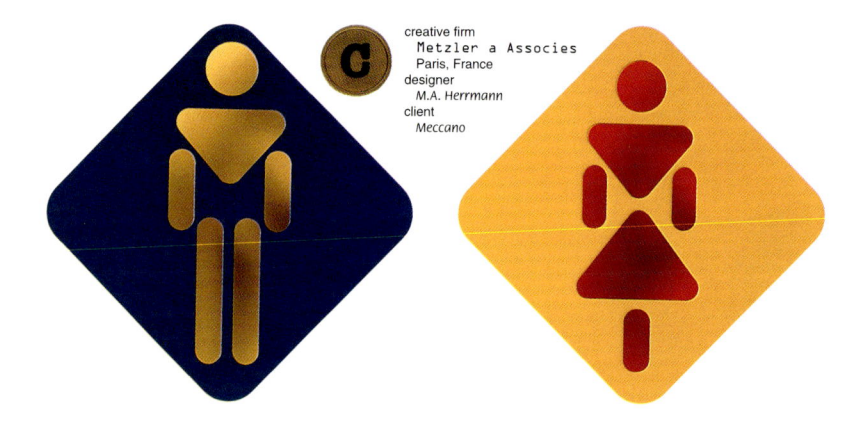

creative firm
　Metzler a Associes
　Paris, France
designer
　M.A. Herrmann
client
　Meccano

296

creative firm
　Design Systemat, Inc.
　Makati, Philippines
creative people
　Angel L. Bunag & Jessie Aquino
client
　Red Ribbon Bakeshop

creative firm
　CommArts, Inc.
　Boulder (Colorado), USA
creative people
　Henry Beer, John Ward, Paul Mack,
　Dave Dute, Jim Babinchak,
　Mike Demmings, Chuck Desmoineaux,
　Amie Echols, Eric Fowles,
　Aaron Howell, Dale Hubbard,
　Grady Huff, Kristian Kluver,
　Jim Redington, & Kurt Sinclair
client
　The Mills Corporation

creative firm
  FRCH Design
  Worldwide
  (Cincinnati)
  New York (New York),
  USA
creative people
  Ray Berberich,
  Michael Beeghly,
  & Jenny Bollin
client
  The Keeneland
  Association

creative firm
  Nicholson Design
  Encinitas (California), USA
creative people
  Joe C. Nicholson

creative firm
  David Carter
  Design Associates
  Dallas (Texas), USA
creative director
  Lori B. Wilson
designer
  Cynthia Carter
client
  Disney Cruise Line

297

creative firm
  Emery Vincent Design
  Southbank (Victoria), Australia
creative people
  Emery Vincent Design team
client
  The Ian Potter Museum of Art

creative firm
  Michael Courtney Design
  Seattle (Washington), USA
designers
  Mike Courtney & Michelle Riek
client
  Rosche Services

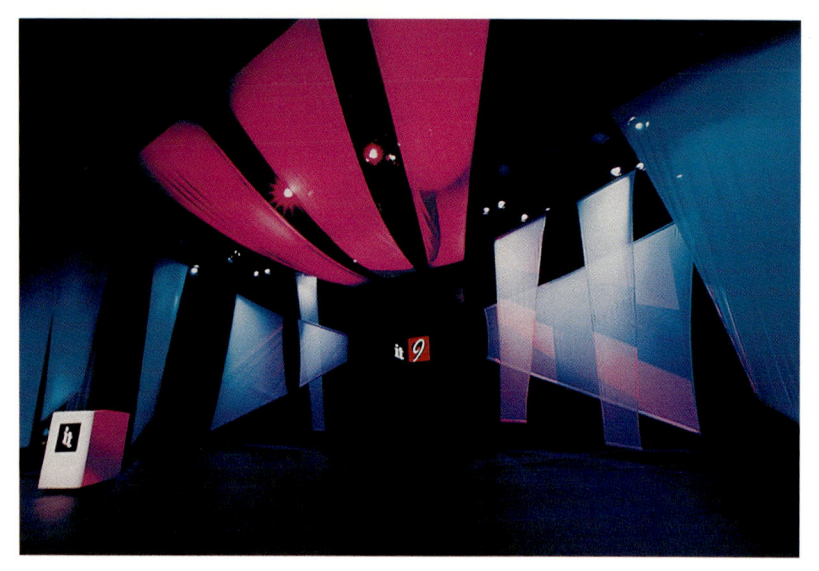

creative firm
 SHR Perceptual Management
  Scottsdale (Arizona), USA
designer
 Christopher Nagle
client
 Innovative Thinking

creative firm
 Hornall Anderson Design Works
  Seattle (Washington), USA
creative people
 John Hornall, Cliff Chung, & Alan Florsheim
client
 NextRx Corporation

298

creative firm
 FRCH Design Worldwide
  (Cincinnati)
  New York (New York), USA
creative people
 Ray Berberich, Michael Beeghly,
 Sandra Pancoe, & Trish Baum
client
 Paramount Group, Inc.

creative firm
 Hornall Anderson Design Works
  Seattle (Washington), USA
creative people
 Jack Anderson, Cliff Chung, David Bates,
 Mike Calkins, & Alan Florsheim
client
 Novell, Inc.

creative firm
  Laura Coe Design Assoc
  San Diego (California), USA
creative director
  Laura Coe Wright
designers
  Leanne Leveillee & Denise Heisey
client
  Taylor Made Golf Co.

creative firm
  Gensler Studio 585
  San Francisco (California), USA
creative people
  Jeff Henry, Beth Novitsky, Katie Price,
  Mark Sanders, & Dian Duvall
client
  Pacific Union Real Estate

299

creative firm
  Virginia Museum
  of Fine Arts
  Richmond (Virginia), USA
designer
  Kennah Harcum
fabricator
  Holiday Signs,
  Richmond, VA
client
  Virginia Museum of Fine Arts

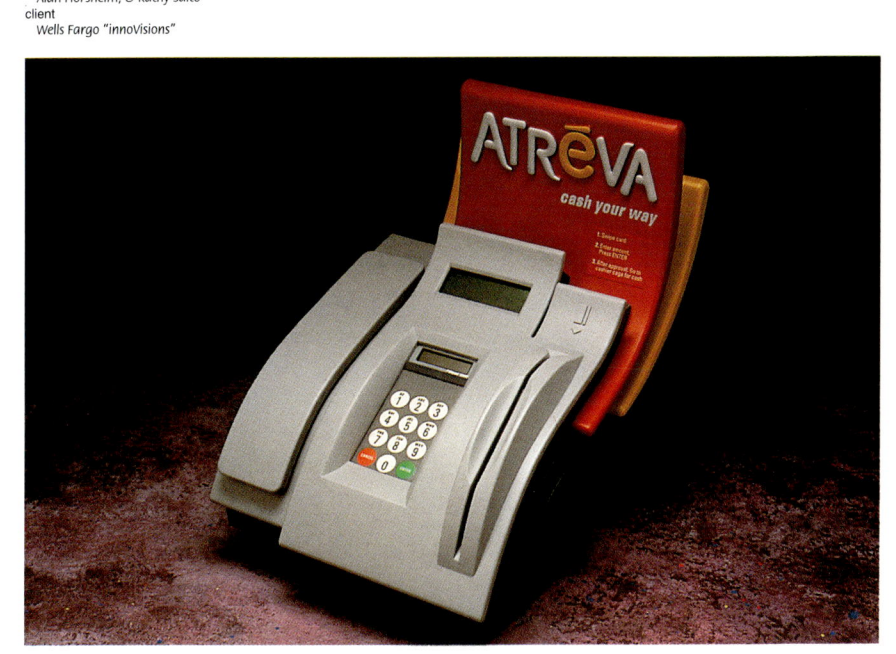

creative firm
  Hornall Anderson Design Works
  Seattle (Washington), USA
creative people
  Jack Anderson, Chris Sallquist, Cliff Chung,
  Alan Florsheim, & Kathy Saito
client
  Wells Fargo "innoVisions"

# CREATIVITY
## Editorial Designs

300

creative firm
  SHR Perceptual Management
  Scottsdale (Arizona), USA
designer
  Mike Barton
photographer
  Bob Carey
client
  Innovative Thinking

creative firm
  Mires Design
  San Diego (California), USA
art director
  John Ball
designer
  Deborah Hom
illustrator
  Dave Adey
client
  Anacomp

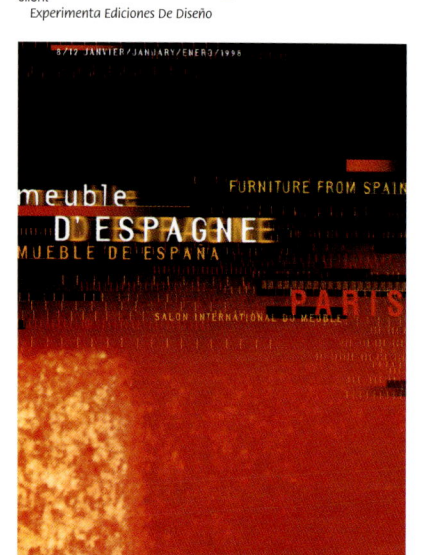

creative firm
  Akron Beacon Journal
  Akron (Ohio), USA
designer, illustrator
  John Backderf
client
  Akron Beacon Journal

creative firm
  Pepe Gimeno-
  Proyecto Grafico
  Godella (Valencia), Spain
creative people
  Pepe Gimeno
client
  Experimenta Ediciones De Diseño

creative firm
American Lawyer Media
New York (New York), USA
art director, designer
Morris Stubbs
photo editor
T.L. Litt
client
The American Lawyer

creative firm
American Lawyer Media
New York (New York), USA
art director, designer
Joan Ferrell
photo editor
T.L. Litt
client
The American Lawyer

creative firm
Akron Beacon Journal
Akron (Ohio), USA
client
Akron Beacon Journal

creative firm
GSO Magazine
Trumbull (Connecticut), USA
art director, designer
Gloria Melfi
fashion editor
Eileen Rafferty Broderick
photographer
Tom Hopkins

creative firm
Ce Disena
Santiago, Chile
creative director
Paula Celedón
photographer
Miguel Etchepare
food stylist
Paula Murtado
client
Banco A. Edwards

301

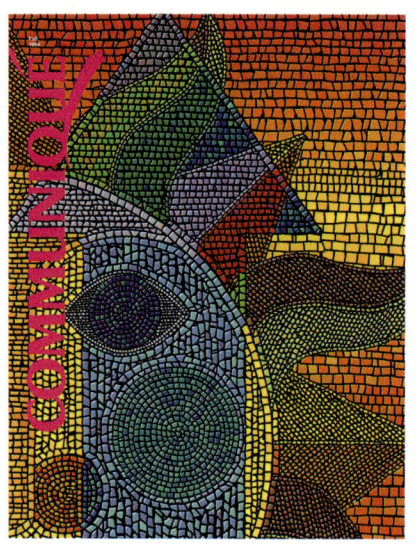

creative firm
 Mueller & Wister, Inc.
  Norristown (Pennsylvania), USA
creative people
 Denise Cotter, Ilene Hass, & Wolfgang Mueller
client
 Wyeth-Ayerst Laboratories

creative firm
 CMP Media/
 VARBusiness
  Jericho (New York),
  USA
art director
 David Loewy
illustrator
 Chriss Gall

creative firm
 Birmingham Studios
  Putnam Valley (New York), USA
creative people
 Pauline Cianciolo &
 Lloyd P. Birmingham
client
 Republic of Palau

creative firm
 Onboard Media
  Miami Beach (Florida), USA
art director
 Dirk Weldon
editor
 Pamela Jaccarino
illustrator
 Glenn Hilario
client
 Sandals

creative firm
 People Specials
  New York (New York), USA
art director
 Gregory Monfries
client
 People Specials,
 The 50 Most Beautiful People 1999

creative firm
  Paprika Communications
    Montréal (Québec), Canada
art director
  Louis Gagnon
designer
  François Leclerc
client
  Unisource

creative firm
  Communication Design Corporation
    Honolulu (Hawaii), USA
art director, designer
  Kunio Hayashi
photographer, copywriter
  Allan Seiden
client
  Network Media

creative firm
  Tieken Design & Creative Services
    Phoenix (Arizona), USA
creative director
  Fred E. Tieken
designers
  Colleen Hale & Fred E. Tieken
illustrator
  Sandy Appleoff
client
  Ritz-Carlton Magazine/SCG Publishing

creative firm
  People Magazine
    New York (New York), USA
creative people
  Hillie Pitzer
client
  People Magazine

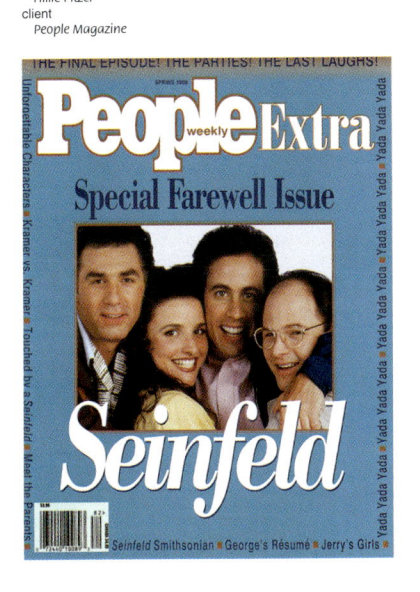

creative firm
  Tieken Design & Creative Services
    Phoenix (Arizona), USA
creative director
  Fred E. Tieken
designer
  Colleen Hale
illustrator
  Garrian Manning
client
  Tycoon Magazine/SCG Publishing

303

creative firm
 Communication Design Corporation
 Honolulu (Hawaii), USA
art director
 Kunio Hayashi
designer
 Yoko Inui
photographer
 Linda Ching
copywriter
 Reiko Ibano
client
 Network Media

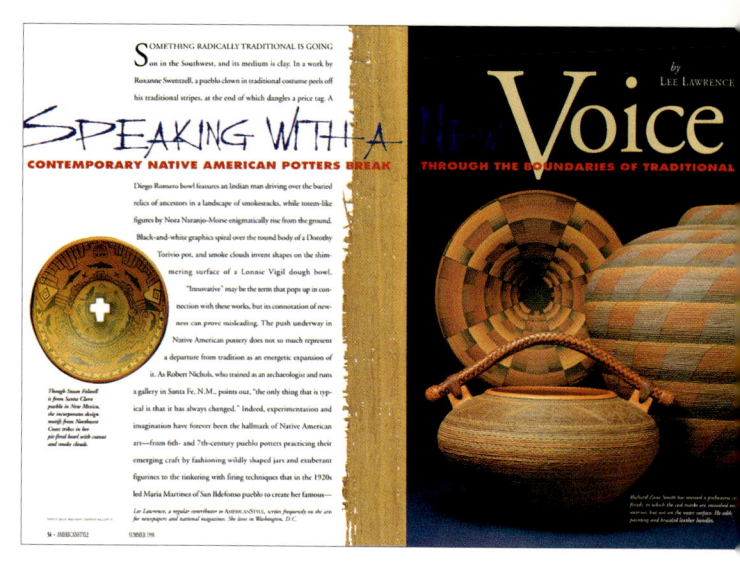

creative firm
 Dever Designs
 Laurel (Maryland), USA
art director, designer
 Jeffrey L. Dever
client
 American Style Magazine

creative firm
 Dever Designs
 Laurel (Maryland), USA
art directors
 Jeffrey L. Dever & Emily Martin Kendall
designer
 Emily Martin Kendall
illustrator
 Sean Kelly
client
 Government Windows Nt Magazine

creative firm
 People Specials
 New York (New York), USA
art directors
 Gregory Monfries & Janice Hogan
client
 People Specials,
 The 25 Most Intriguing People

creative firm
 People Specials
 New York (New York), USA
art director
 Gregory Monfries
designer
 Stephen Wilder
client
 People Specials,
 The 25 Most Intriguing People

creative firm
**Communication Design Corporation**
Honolulu (Hawaii), USA
art director
Kunio Hayashi
editor
Susumu Michizoe
designer
Yoko Inui
photographer
Linny Morris Cunningham
copywriter
Mark Cunningham
translation
Yasuko Tashiro
client
Pacifica

creative firm
**Communication Design Corporation**
Honolulu (Hawaii), USA
art director
Kunio Hayashi
designer
Yoko Inui
photographer
Linda Ching
copywriter
Reiko Ibano
client
Network Media

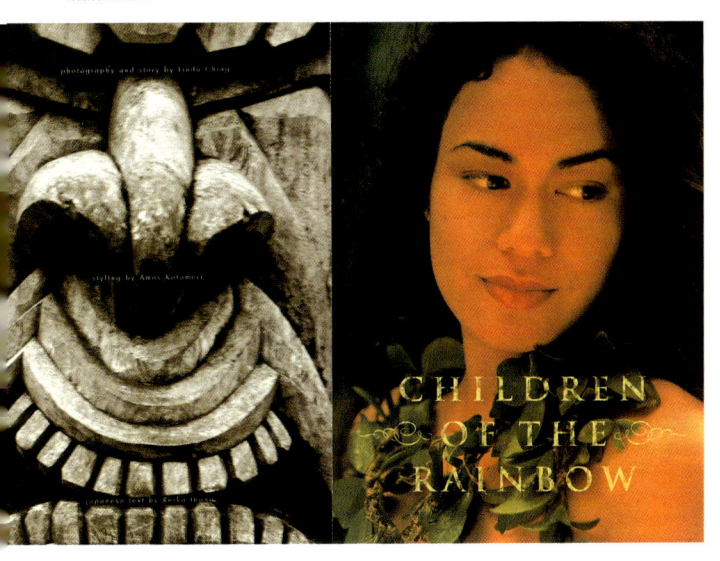

creative firm
**Bard Communications**
New York (New York), USA
design director, photographer
Rick Bard
client
Manhattan Magazine

creative firm
**Communication Design Corporation**
Honolulu (Hawaii), USA
art director
Kunio Hayashi
designer
Yoko Inui
photographer
Linda Ching
copywriter
Reiko Ibano
client
Network Media

creative firm
**People Specials**
New York (New York), USA
art director
Gregory Monfries
client
People Specials,
The 25 Most Intriguing People

creative firm
 Popular Mechanics
 New York (New York), USA
art director
 Bryan Canniff
illustrator
 Tom Freeman
client
 Popular Mechanics

creative firm
 People Magazine
 New York (New York), USA
creative people
 Hillie Pitzer
client
 People Magazine

creative firm
 People Specials
 New York (New York), USA
art director
 Gregory Monfries
client
 People Specials,
 Hollywood's Happy Couples

creative firm
 Jowaisas Design
 Cazenovia (New York), USA
editor
 Eric Johnson
designer
 Elizabeth Jowaisas
client
 Carrier Corporation

creative firm
 JA Design Solutions
 Coppell (Texas), USA
designer
 Jean Ashenfelter
composition
 Jon Mosier
client
 GTE Supply

creative firm
 Dever Designs
  Laurel (Maryland), USA
art directors
 Jeffrey L. Dever & Emily Martin Kendall
designer, illustrator
 Jeffrey L. Dever
client
 Liberty Magazine

creative firm
 Popular Mechanics
  New York (New York), USA
art director
 Bryan Canniff
illustrators
 Richard Chasemore & Hans Jenssen
client
 Popular Mechanics

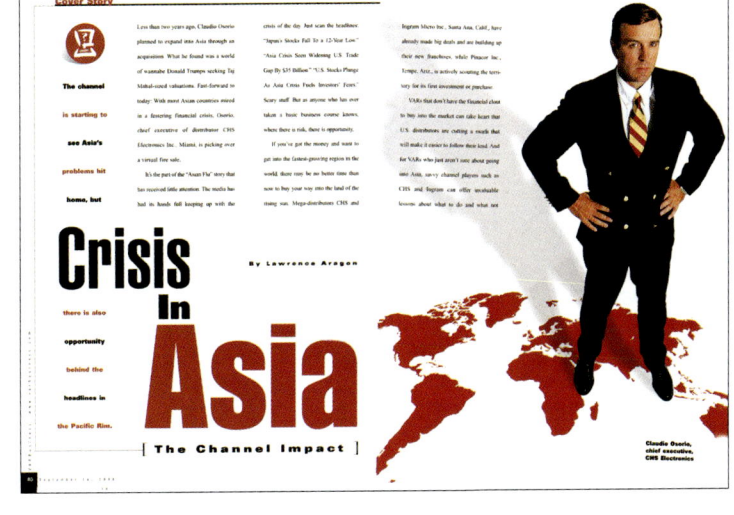

307

creative firm
 CMP Media/VARBusiness
  Jericho (New York), USA
art director
 David Loewy

creative firm
 Communication
 Design Corporation
  Honolulu (Hawaii), USA
art director
 Kunio Hayashi
editor
 Susumu Michizoe
designer
 Yoko Inui
photographer
 Linny Morris Cunningham
copywriter
 Mark Cunningham
translation
 Yasuko Tashiro
client
 Pacifica

creative firm
 360 Degrees, Inc.
  New York (New York), USA
creative people
 Janine Weitenauer & Suzanne Jennerich
client
 Lewit & Lewinter

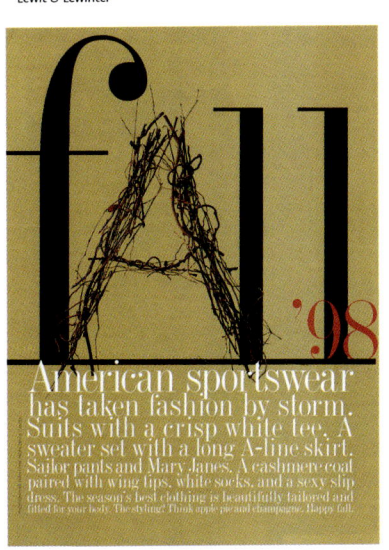

creative firm
    Communication Design Corporation
    Honolulu (Hawaii), USA
art director, designer
    Kunio Hayashi
editor
    Susumu Michizoe
photographer
    David B. Fleetham
copywriter
    Akiko Yoshitomi
client
    Pacifica

308

creative firm
    People Magazine
    New York (New York), USA
creative people
    Tom Allison
client
    People Magazine

creative firm
    People Specials
    New York (New York), USA
art directors
    Gregory Monfries & Janice Hogan
client
    People Specials, The 50 Most Beautiful People 1999

creative firm
    People Specials
    New York (New York), USA
art director
    Gregory Monfries
client
    People Specials,
    The 50 Most Beautiful People 1999

creative firm
  Bard Communications
  New York (New York), USA
design director, photographer
  Rick Bard
client
  Manhattan Magazine

creative firm
  People Specials
  New York (New York), USA
art directors
  Gregory Monfries &
  Ronnie Brandwein-Keats
client
  People Specials,
  The 50 Most Beautiful People 1999

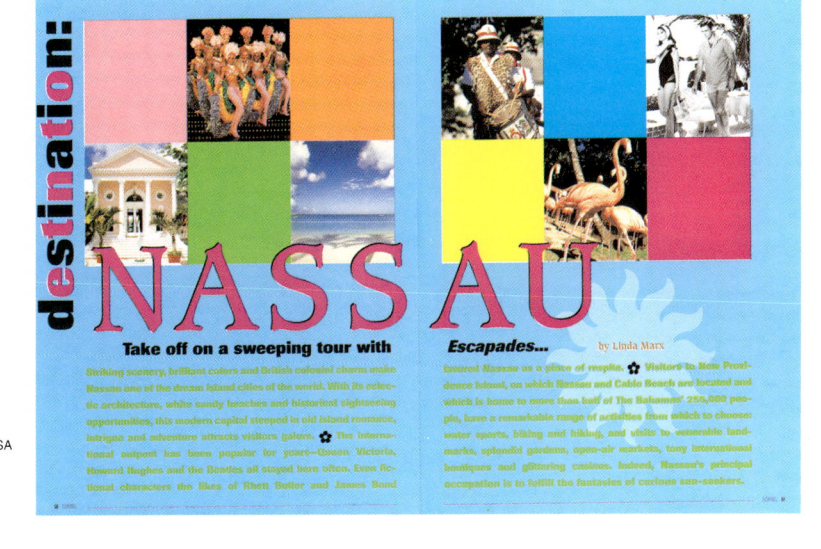

309

creative firm
  Onboard Media
  Miami Beach (Florida), USA
art director
  Dirk Weldon
client
  Sandals/Beaches Resorts

creative firm
  People Magazine
  New York (New York), USA
creative people
  Hillie Pitzer
client
  People Magazine

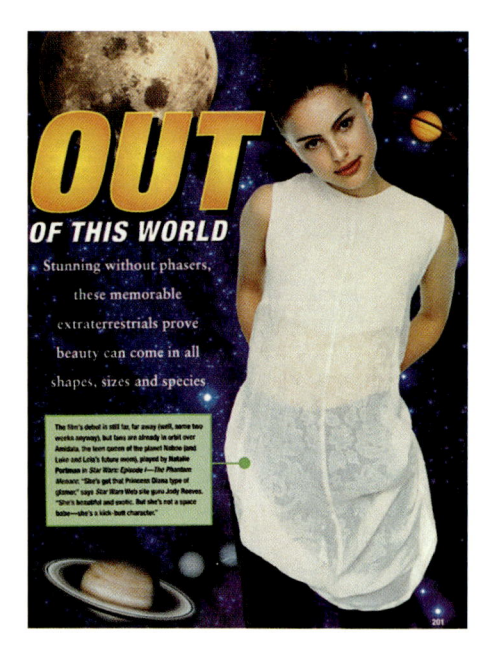

310

creative firm
 People Specials
 New York (New York), USA
art directors
 Gregory Monfries & Ronnie Brandwein-Keats
client
 People Specials, The 50 Most Beautiful People 1999

creative firm
 People Specials
 New York (New York), USA
art director
 Gregory Monfries
designer
 Stephen Wilder
client
 People Specials,
 The 25 Most Intriguing People

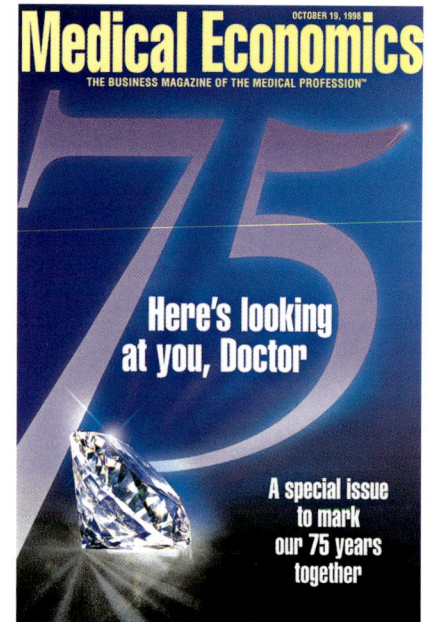

creative firm
 Medical Economics
 Montvale (New Jersey), USA
art director
 Roger Dowd
editor
 Anne Finger
designer
 Ann Weber
client
 Medical Economics

creative firm
 Philadelphia 76ers
 Philadelphia (Pennsylvania), USA
creative people
 Charles Bennett, Peggy Moroz, Leslie Syrden,
 Dave Coskey, Lara White, & Mark Elmore

creative firm
 Erwin Zinger
 Graphic Design
 Groningen, Netherlands
creative people
 Erwin Zinger &
 Coen Springelkamp
client
 Scapino

creative firm
**Popular Mechanics**
New York (New York), USA
art director, illustrator
Bryan Canniff
client
*Popular Mechanics*

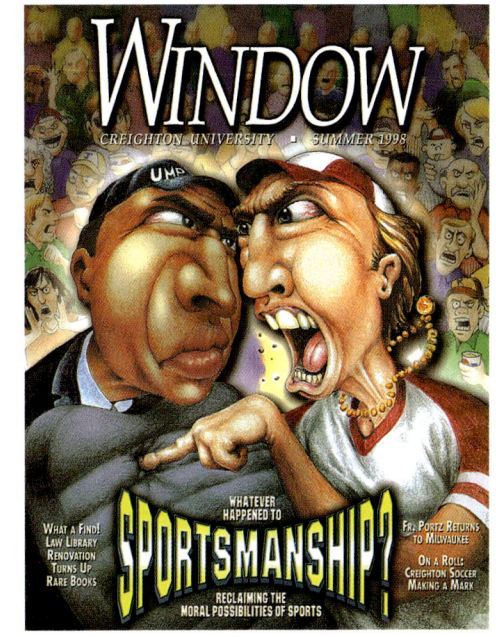

creative firm
**Dever Designs**
Laurel (Maryland), USA
art directors
Jeffrey L. Dever & Emily Martin Kendall
designer
Emily Martin Kendall
illustrator
Kim Barnes
client
*Liberty Magazine*

creative firm
**Dotzler Creative Arts**
Omaha (Nebraska), USA
client
*Creighton University*

creative firm
**People Magazine**
New York (New York), USA
creative people
Hillie Pitzer
client
*People Magazine*

creative firm
**People Magazine**
New York (New York), USA
creative people
Phil Simone
client
*People Magazine*

311

# CREATIVITY
## Magazine Covers

creative firm
  Onboard Media
  Miami Beach (Florida), USA
art director
  Karen Sorota
client
  Airtours

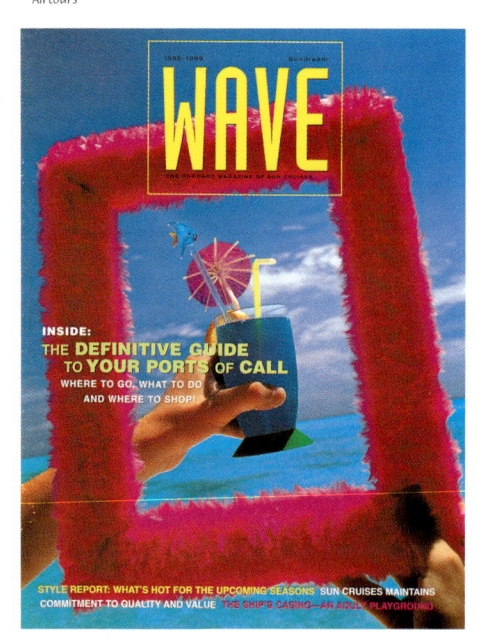

creative firm
  Dynamic Duo Studio
  Westport (Connecticut), USA
designers, illustrators
  Dynamic Duo Studio
computer colorist
  Sherri Wolfgang
black & white line work, hand lettering
  Arlen Schumer
client
  New York Magazine

creative firm
  People Magazine
  New York (New York), USA
creative people
  Hillie Pitzer
client
  People Magazine

312

creative firm
  People Magazine
  New York (New York), USA
creative people
  Phil Simone
client
  People Magazine

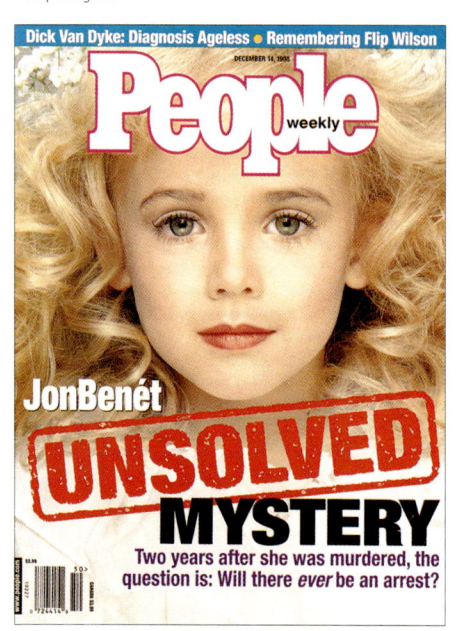

creative firm
  People Magazine
  New York (New York), USA
creative people
  Hillie Pitzer
client
  People Magazine

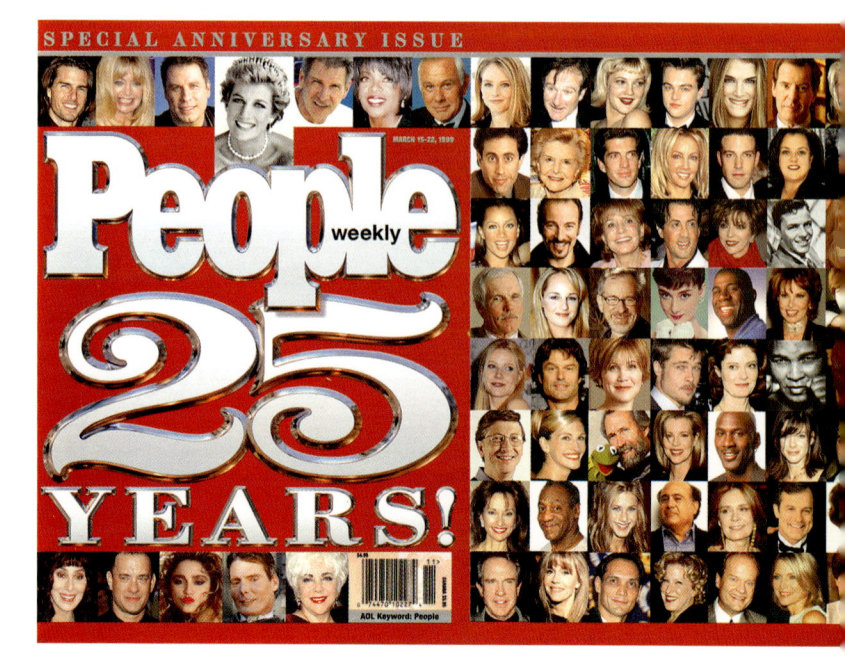

creative firm
  Heye + Partner
  Unterhaching, Germany
creative director, photographer
  Norbert Herold
art director
  Karlheinz Müller
client
  Markenartikel

creative firm
  John Brady Design Consultants
  Pittsburgh (Pennsylvania), USA
creative people
  Jim Bolander, Kevin Kennedy, Rick Madison,
  Bill Ochsenhirt, Dave Roos, & Carl Chiocca
client
  Carnegie Magazine

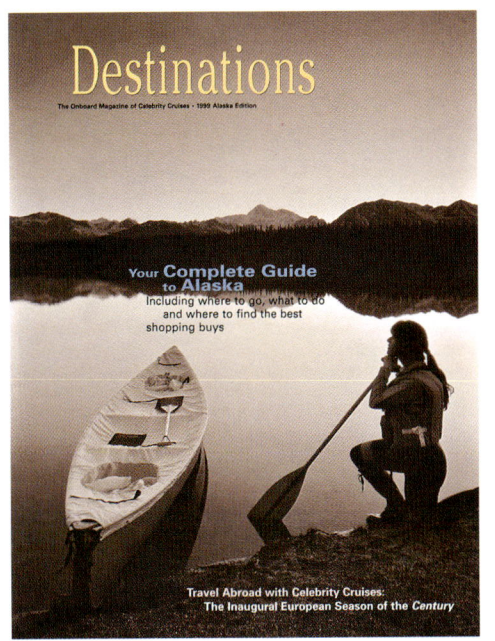

creative firm
  Onboard Media
  Miami Beach (Florida), USA
art director
  Karen Sorota
client
  Celebrity Cruises

313

designer
  Rick Sealock
  Milo (Alberta), Canada
creative people
  Rick Sealock
editor
  Kris Vester
client
  Home Home Publications

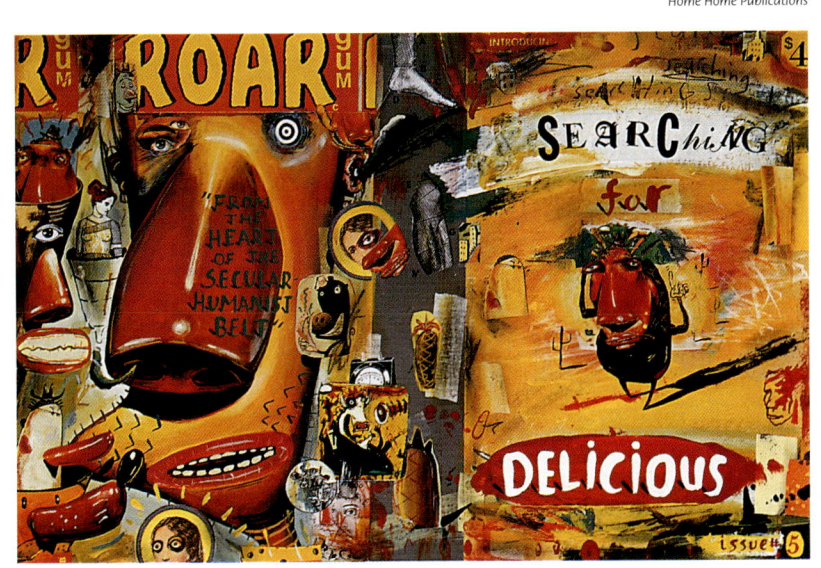

creative firm
  Onboard Media
  Miami Beach (Florida), USA
art director
  Karen Sorota
client
  Royal Caribbean International Cruiseline

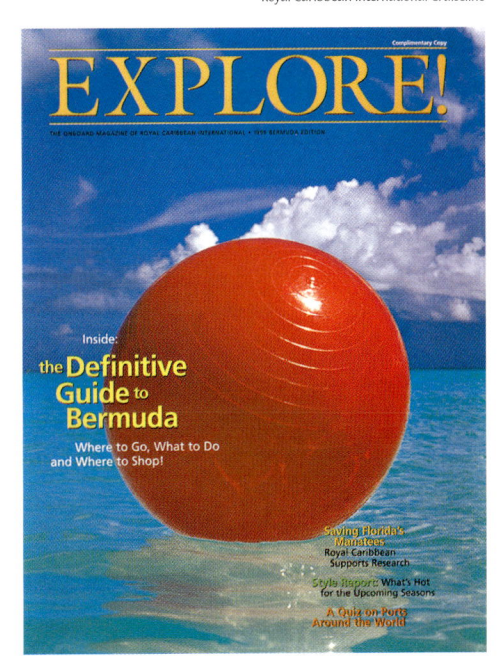

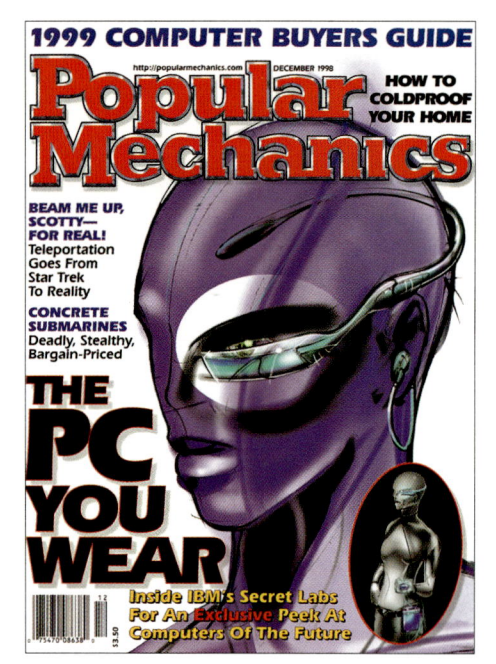

creative firm
  Popular Mechanics
  New York (New York), USA
art director
  Bryan Canniff
illustrator
  Karl Zeeso

314

creative firm
  SIGN Kommunikation GmbH
  Frankfurt, Germany
creative people
  Dieter Waider
client
  Beltz-Verlag GmbH

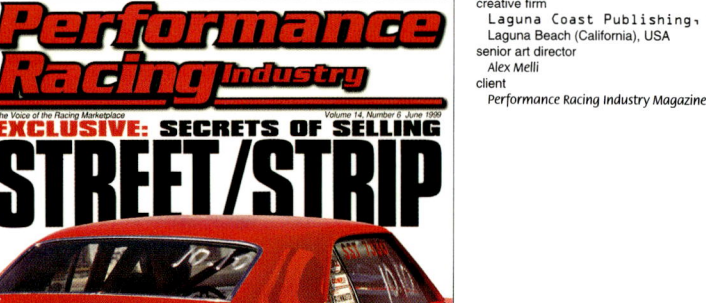

creative firm
  Richland Design Associates
  Newton (Massachusetts), USA
art director
  Judith Richland
designer
  Douglas Fortadd
illustrator
  Amy Vansguard
client
  Thomson Financial

creative firm
  Laguna Coast Publishing, Inc.
  Laguna Beach (California), USA
senior art director
  Alex Melli
client
  Performance Racing Industry Magazine

creative firm
  American Lawyer Media
  New York (New York), USA
art director, designer
  Joan Ferrell
illustrator
  Will Crocker
client
  The American Lawyer

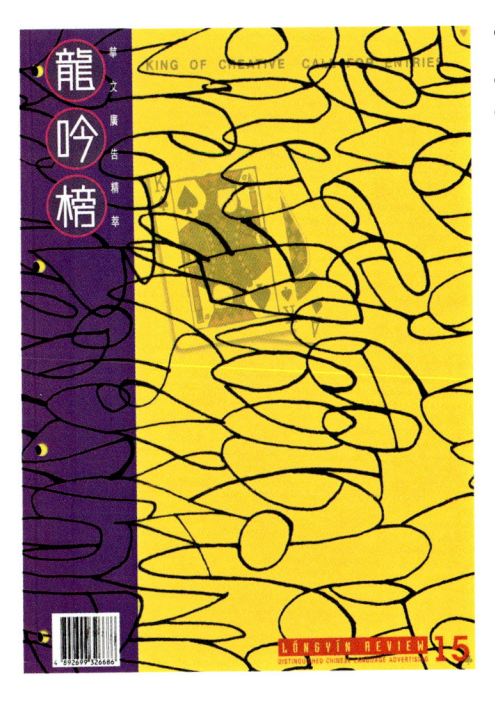

creative firm
  Gallery Ltd
  Hong Kong, China
creative people
  Benny Cheng & Raymond Fu
client
  Longyin Review Ltd

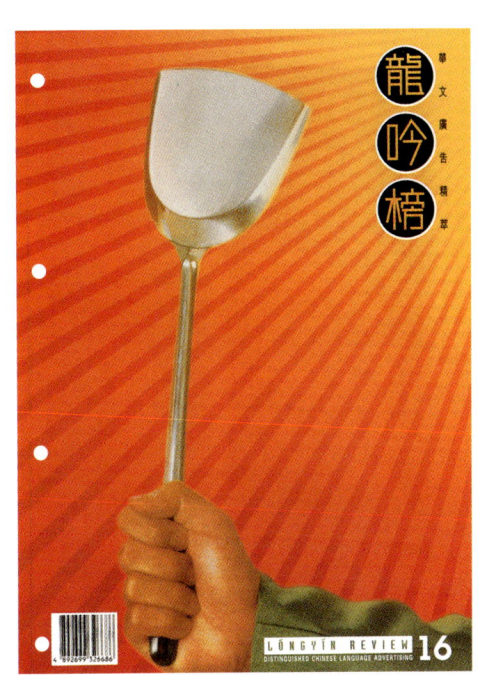

creative firm
  Gallery Ltd
  Hong Kong, China
creative people
  Benny Cheng & Raymond Fu
client
  Longyin Review Ltd

creative firm
  Bard Communications
  New York (New York), USA
design director, photographer
  Rick Bard
client
  Manhattan Magazine

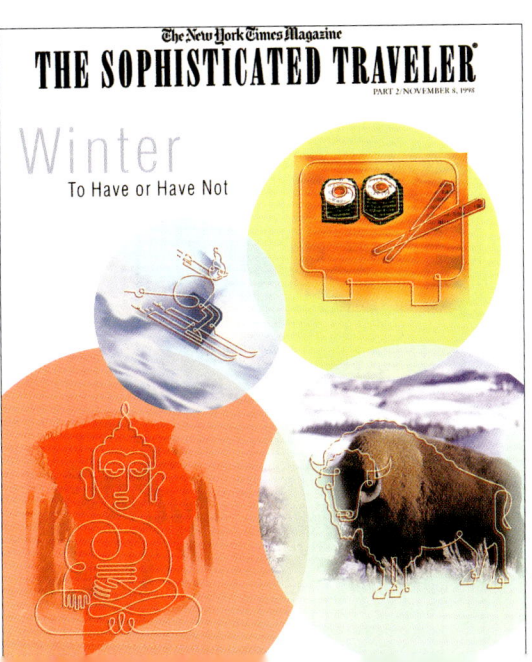

creative firm
  NYT Magazine
  New York (New York), USA
art director
  Ken McFarlin
illustrator
  Otto Steininger
client
  The New York Times Magazine

creative firm
  Arts Image Creative Group
  Oklahoma City (Oklahoma), USA
creative people
  Fred Welch & Mark Holly
client
  Backstage Pass Magazine

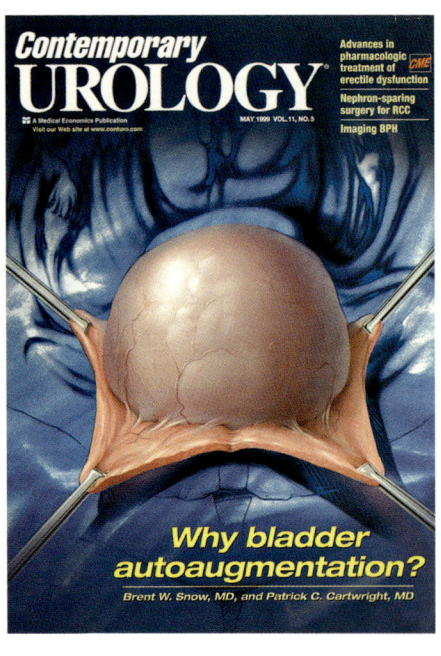

creative firm
  Medical Economics Company
  Montvale (New Jersey), USA
art director
  Irene Brady
illustrator
  Craig Kiefer
client
  Contemporary Urology

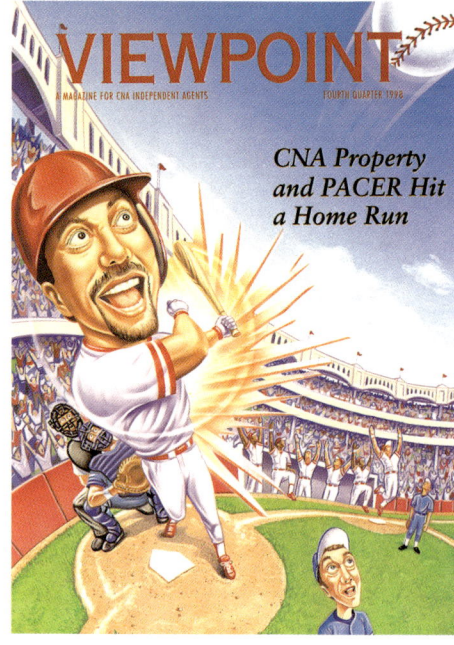

creative firm
  Alain M. Flores
  San Cristobal, Mexico
designer, illustrator
  Alain Mauricio Flores Monterrubio
client
  World Boxing Council

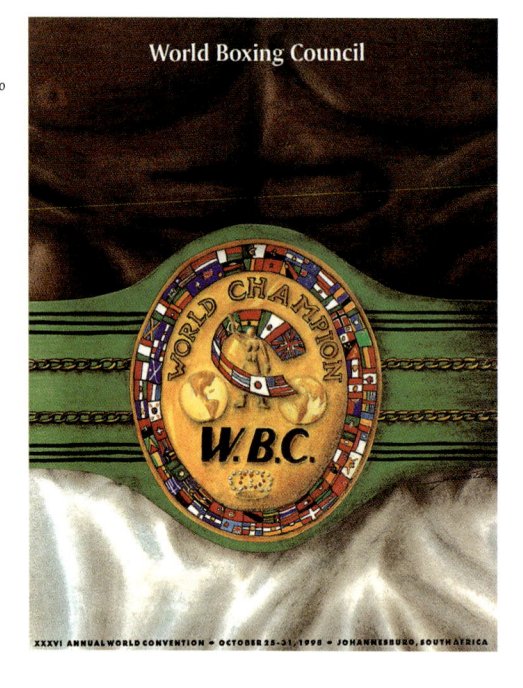

creative firm
  CNA Insurance
  Chicago (Illinois), USA
designer
  Kevin Meyers
illustrator
  Joe McDermott
client
  CNA Insurance

316

creative firm
  Popular Mechanics
  New York (New York), USA
art director
  Bryan Canniff
illustrator
  Tom Freeman
client
  Popular Mechanics

creative firm
  Glimpses Advertising
  Agana (Guam), USA
creative people
  Manuel C. Lujan & Amy V. Preuss
client
  Hard Rock Cafe Guam

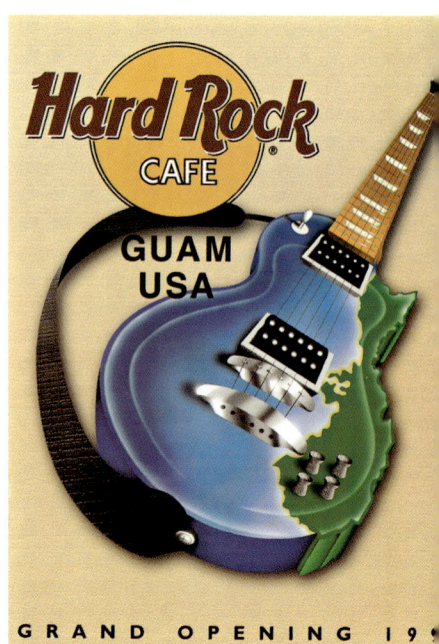

creative firm
 Laguna Coast Publishing, Inc.
 Laguna Beach (California), USA
senior art director
 Alex Melli
client
 Performance Racing Industry Magazine

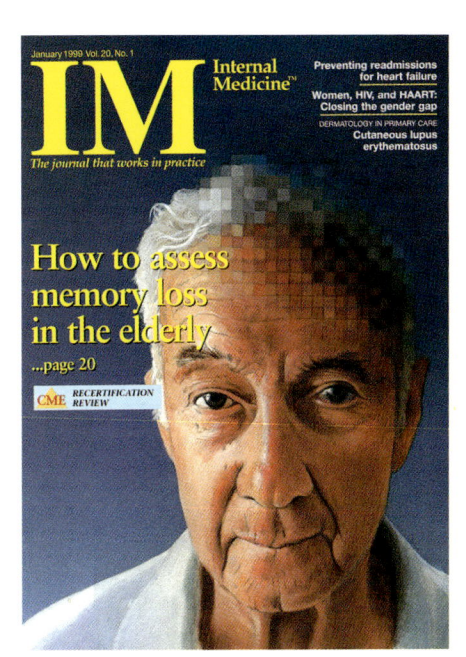

creative firm
 Medical Economics Company
 Montvale (New Jersey), USA
art director
 Irene Brady
illustrator
 Sharon Ellis
client
 IM Internal Medicine

creative firm
 SIGN Kommunikation GmbH
 Frankfurt, Germany
creative people
 Dieter Waider
client
 Beltz-Verlag GmbH

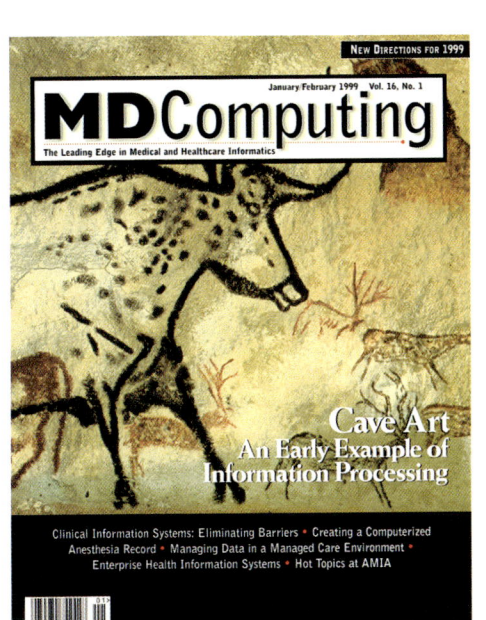

creative firm
 CMP Media/VARBusiness
 Jericho (New York), USA
art director
 David Loewy
illustrator
 Chris Gall

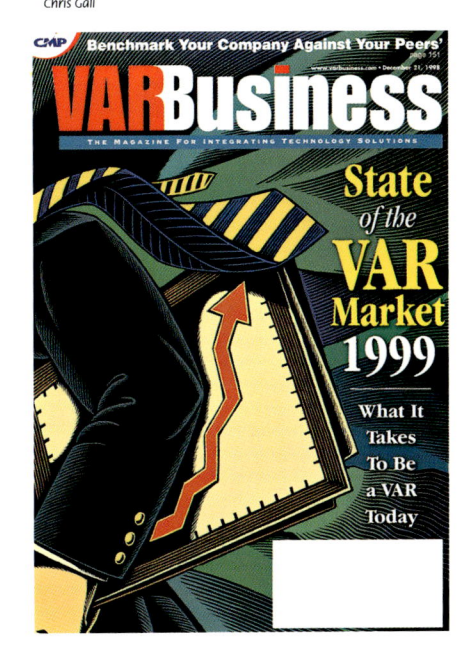

creative firm
 Heaven & Earth Designs
 New York (New York), USA
creative people
 Karliese Greiner-Laurie & Madeline R. Kraner
client
 Springer-Verlag New York Inc.

creative firm
 Boelts Bros. Associates
  Tucson (Arizona), USA
creative people
 Kerry Stratford, Jackson Boelts, & Eric Boelts
client
 The Tucson Arts District Partnership

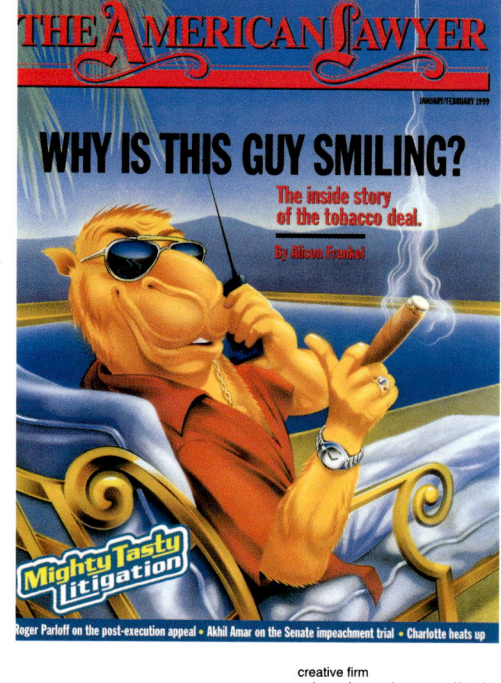

creative firm
 American Lawyer Media
  New York (New York), USA
art director
 Joan Ferrell
designer
 Sue Llewellyn
illustrator
 Dave Miller
client
 The American Lawyer

318

creative firm
 CMP Media
  Jericho (New York), USA
creative people
 Anne Cooney, Marc Burckhardt, & Gene Fedele
client
 Computer Reseller News

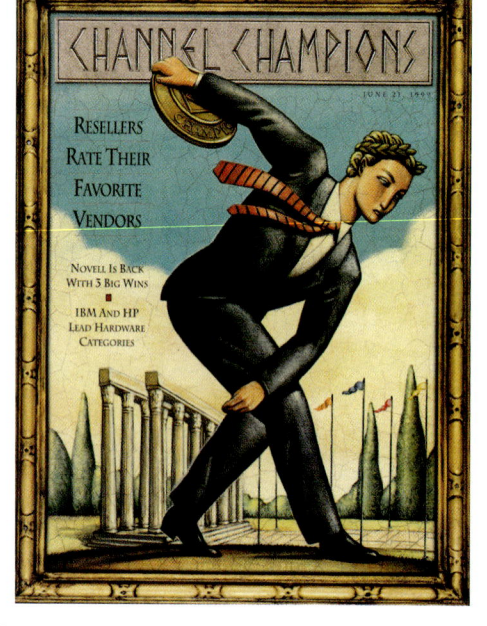

creative firm
 Circus
  Nagoya, Japan
art director, illustrator
 Shigeharu "Smiley" Kato
designer
 Masayuki Azuma
client
 Kento's Co., Ltd

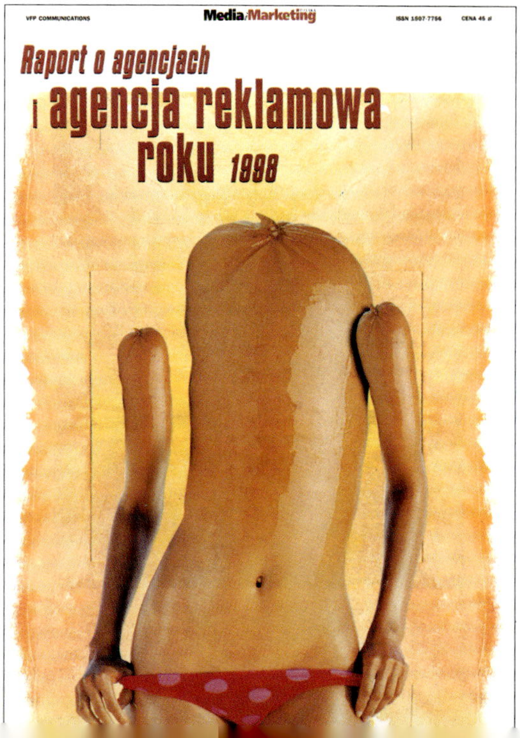

creative firm
 Korek Studio
  Warsaw, Poland
art director, designer, illustrator
 Wojtek Korkuć
client
 VFP Communications Ltd.

creative firm
  American Lawyer Media
  New York (New York), USA
art director, designer
  Joan Ferrell
photo editor
  T.L. Litt
photographer
  Karen Kuehn
client
  The American Lawyer

creative firm
  The Beacon Journal
  Akron (Ohio), USA
art director, designer
  Kathy Hagedorn
photographer
  Ed Suba, Jr.

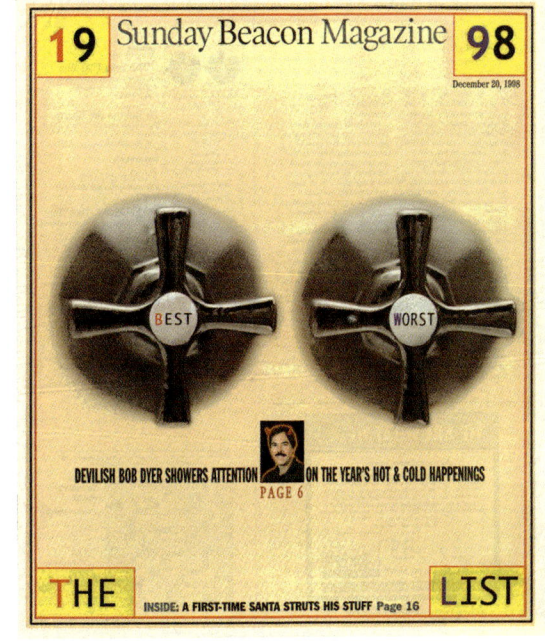

creative firm
  GSO Magazine
  Trumbull (Connecticut), USA
art director, designer
  Gloria Melfi
photographer
  Jim Herity

creative firm
  GSO Magazine
  Trumbull (Connecticut), USA
art director, designer
  Gloria Melfi
illustrator
  Steven Keller

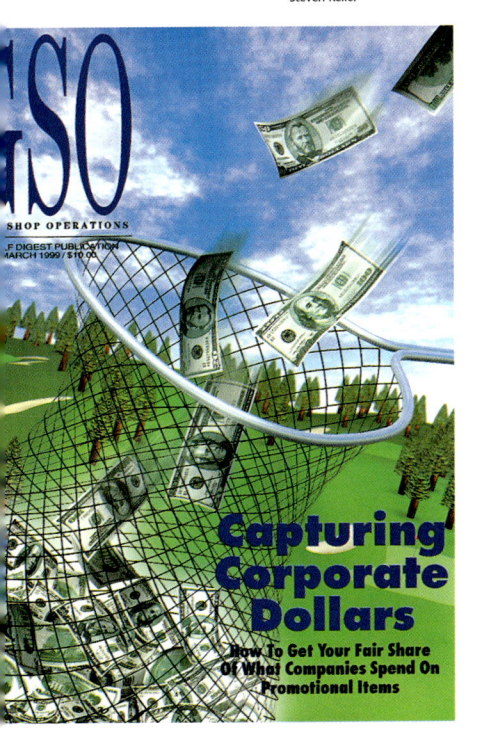

creative firm
  Gallery Ltd
  Hong Kong, China
creative people
  Benny Cheng & Raymond Fu
client
  Longyin Review Ltd

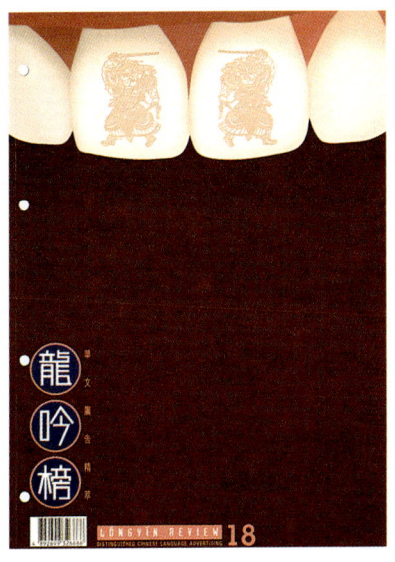

319

# CREATIVITY

## Public Service Ads Campaign

---

**SELECT A CAUSE TO SUPPORT**

**JWT CHARITY DRIVE**
BE A PART OF IT. VISIT JWTCARES.CHI.JWT.COM

320

creative firm
 J. Walter Thompson
 Chicago (Illinois), USA
art director
 Mark Westman
copywriter
 Pam Anderson
client
 JWT Charity Drive

---

**WHEN SOME YOUNG MAMMALS ARE DRIVEN TO SUICIDE WE RUSH TO SAVE THEM.**

**NOW WE'RE ASKING YOU TO RUSH TO SAVE OUR KIDS.**

creative firm
 Illidge Thorp & Partners
 Advertising
 McMahons Point, Australia
creative director
 Bruce Illidge
art director
 Barry Moss
client
 Sydney City Mission

---

creative firm
 J. Walter Thompson
 Chicago (Illinois), USA
art director
 Mark Westman
copywriter
 Pam Anderson
client
 JWT Charity Drive

---

creative firm
 Cramer-Krasselt
 Milwaukee (Wisconsin), USA
creative directors
 Neil Casey & Paul Counsel
art directors
 Dave Hofmann & Vince DeMarinis
copywriter
 Pat Pritchard
client
 Sojourner Truth House

---

**YOU DON'T NEED BRUISES TO HAVE SCARS.**

SOJOURNER TRUTH HOUSE
Call For Help (414) 933-2722

---

**ANY QUESTIONS ABOUT YOUR CHARITY?**

**JWT Charity Drive. Be a Part of It.**
Starts December 10th!

THE UNITED WAY   AMERICAN CANCER SOCIETY   OFF THE STREET CLUB
VISIT THE JWT CHARITY WEB-SITE AT JWTCARES.CHI.JWT.COM

creative firm
 Young & Rubicam Mexico
  Mexico City, Mexico
 creative director, copywriter
  Yuri Alvarado
 art directors
  Mauricio Castillo & Gumersindo Inglemo
 director creative services
  Enrique Laguardia
 client
  Departamento Del Distrito Federal

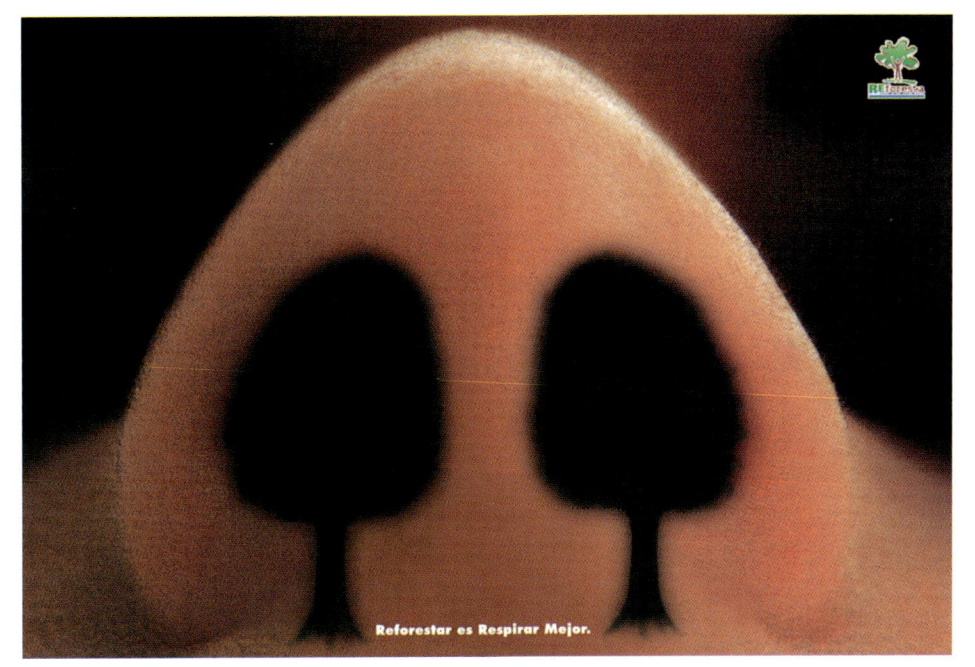

Reforestar es Respirar Mejor.

creative firm
 Mudra Communications Limited
  Ahmedabad (Gujarat), India
 creative people
  Sabu Paul & Yogesh Bhavsar
 client
  The Indian Express

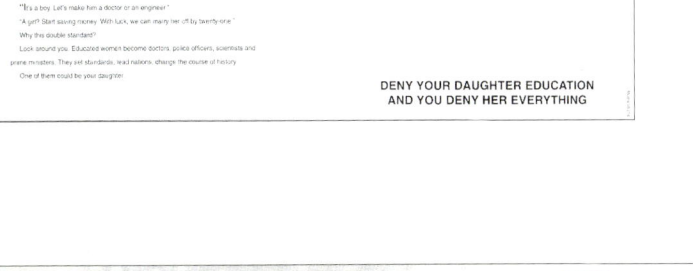

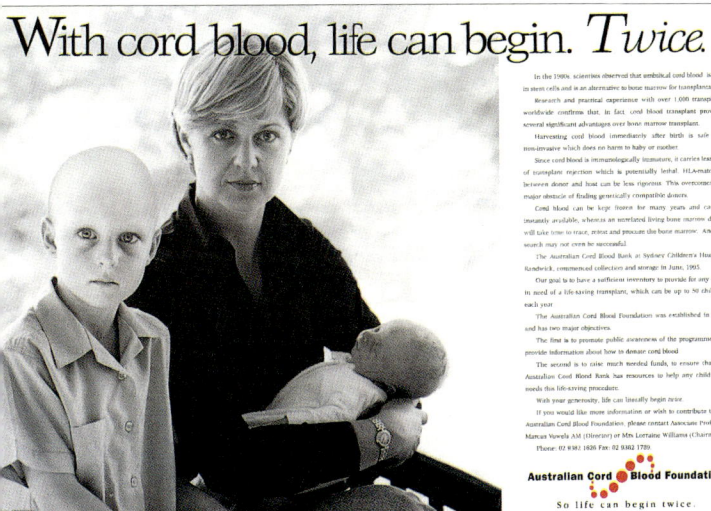

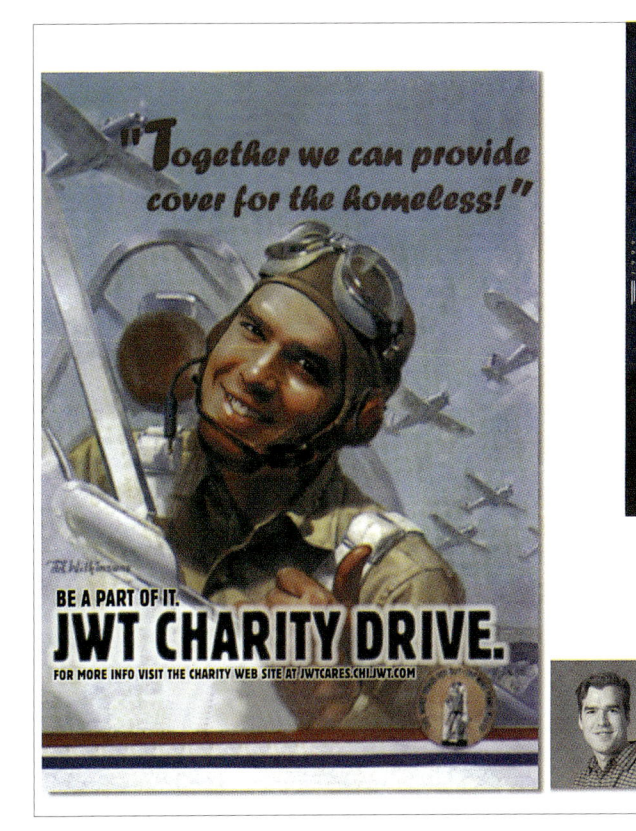

A reminder that nobody is born this way.

"It's a boy. Let's make him a doctor or an engineer."
"A girl? Start saving money. With luck, we can marry her off by twenty-one."
Why this double standard?
Look around you. Educated women become doctors, police officers, scientists and prime ministers. They set standards, lead nations, change the course of history.
One of them could be your daughter.

DENY YOUR DAUGHTER EDUCATION
AND YOU DENY HER EVERYTHING

"Together we can provide cover for the homeless!"

BE A PART OF IT.
JWT CHARITY DRIVE.
FOR MORE INFO VISIT THE CHARITY WEB SITE AT JWTCARES.CHI.JWT.COM

creative firm
 J. Walter Thompson
  Chicago (Illinois), USA
 art director
  Mark Westman
 copywriter
  Pam Anderson
 client
  JWT Charity Drive

# With cord blood, life can begin. *Twice.*

Australian Cord Blood Foundation
So life can begin twice.

creative firm
 Sudler & Hennessey
  North Sydney, Australia
 creative people
  Robert Lallamant & Chris Bull
 client
  Australian Cord Blood Foundation

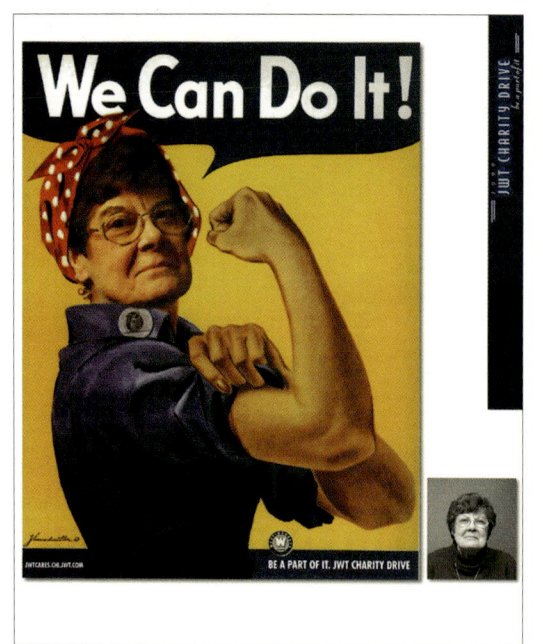

creative firm
  J. Walter Thompson
    Chicago (Illinois), USA
art director
  Mark Westman
copywriter
  Pam Anderson
client
  JWT Charity Drive

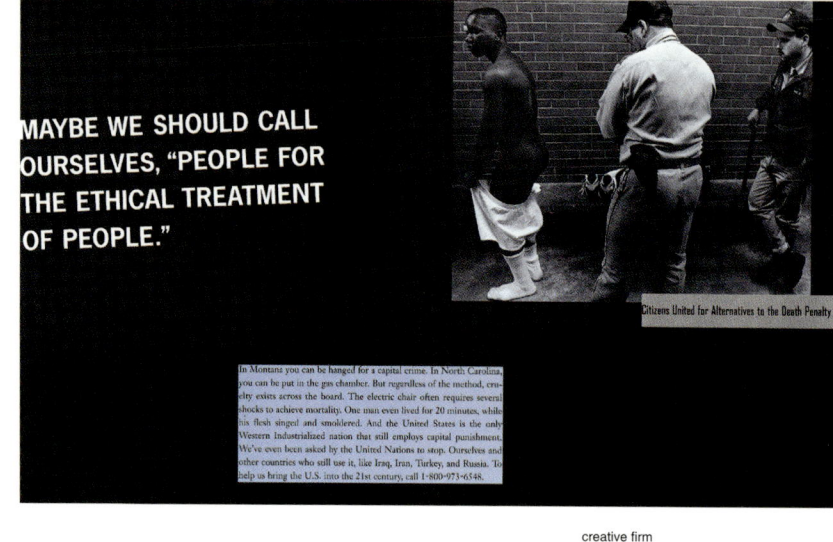

creative firm
  Sawyer Riley Compton
    Atlanta (Georgia), USA
creative director, art director
  Bart Cleveland
photographer
  Ken Light
copywriter
  Cathy Carlisi
client
  Citizens for Alternatives to the Death Penalty

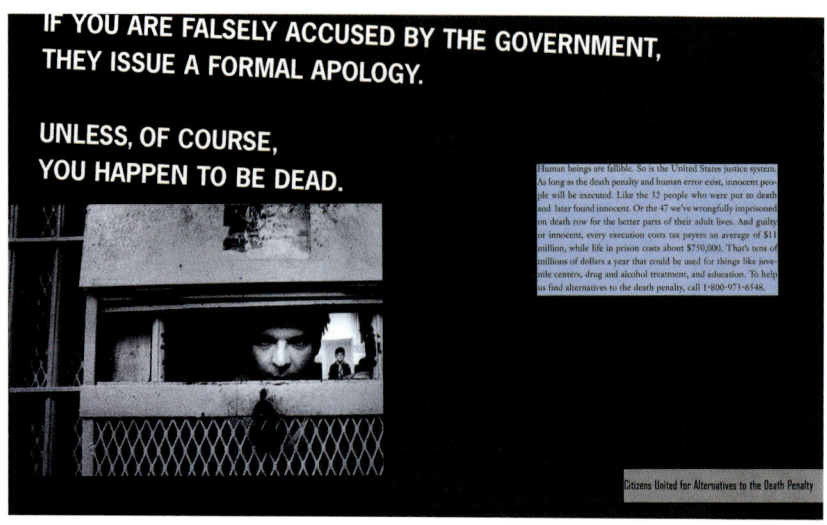

322

creative firm
  Sawyer Riley Compton
    Atlanta (Georgia), USA
creative director, art director
  Bart Cleveland
photographer
  Ken Light
copywriter
  Cathy Carlisi
client
  Citizens for Alternatives to the Death Penalty

creative firm
  Nelson & Schmidt, Inc.
    Milwaukee (Wisconsin), USA
creative director
  Mark Gale
art director
  Sean Mullen
photographer
  Ricco Photo.
illustrator
  Bob Zimmerman
copywriters
  Maggie Kenny & Sean Mullen
client
  Illinois Attorney General

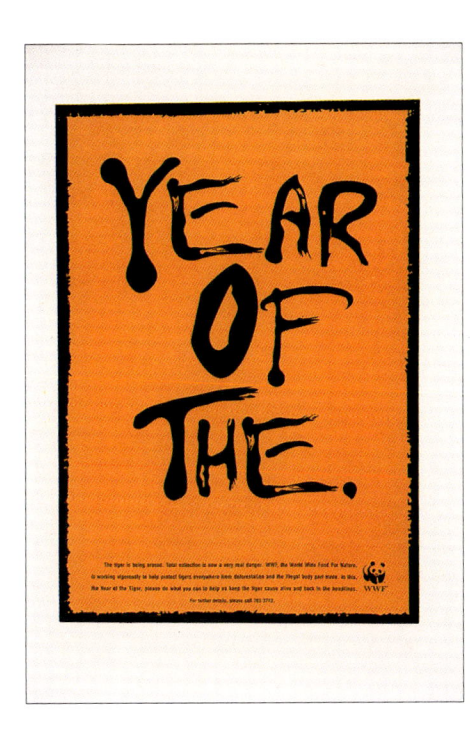

creative firm
  Saatchi & Saatchi Vietnam
  Ho Chi Minh City, Vietnam
creative people
  Paul Ewen, Le Duc Thang, & Mike Sands
client
  World Wide Fund For Nature (WWF)

translation
  The year of the .

The tiger is being erased. Total extinction is now a very real danger. WWF, the World Wide Fund For Nature, is working vigorously to help protect tigers from deforestation and the illegal body part trade. In this, the Year of the Tiger, please do what you can to help us keep the tiger cause alive and back in the headlines.

creative firm
  Publicis Union 45 SDN BHD
  Petaling Jaya (Selangor), Malaysia
art director
  Bobby Chan
copywriter
  Victor Ng
client
  Concerned for Sungai Selangor

creative firm
  Young & Rubicam Mexico
  Mexico City, Mexico
creative directors
  Enrique Laguardia,
  Fernando Torres, &
  Hermann Blackaller
art director
  Hermann Blackaller
copywriter
  Fernando Torres
client
  Casa Cuervo

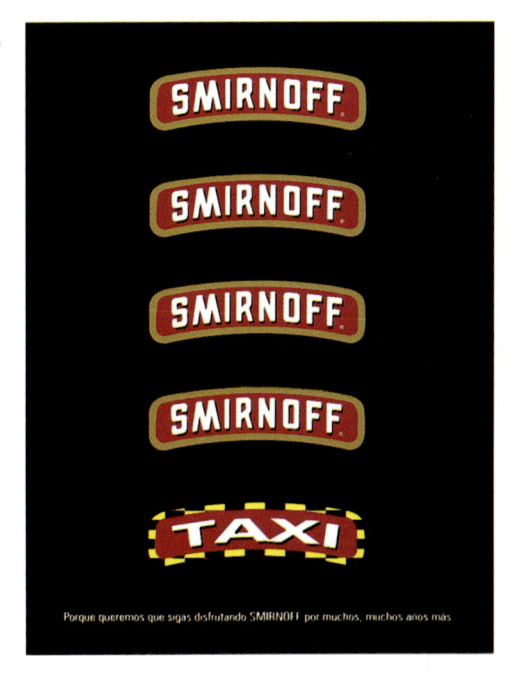

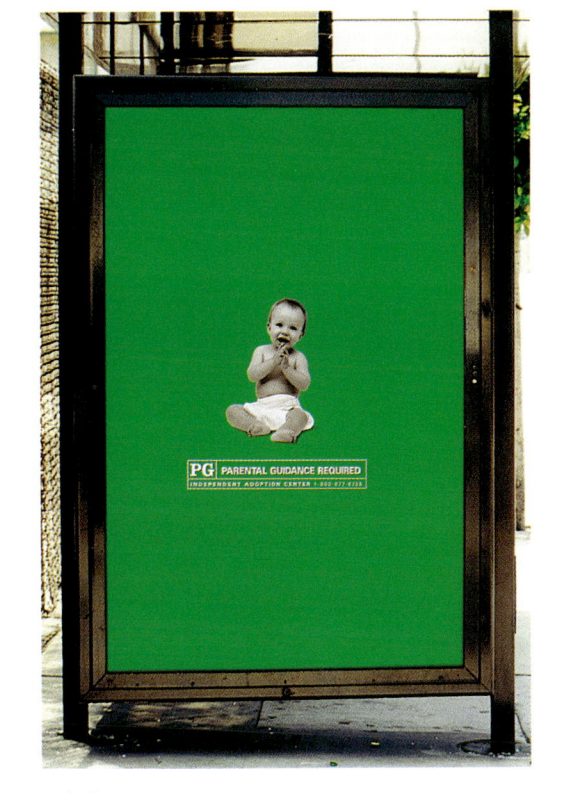

323

creative firm
  Bald & Beautiful
  Venice (California), USA
creative director
  Luis Camano
art director
  Carlos Musquez
copywriter
  Cameron Young
client
  Independent Adoption Center

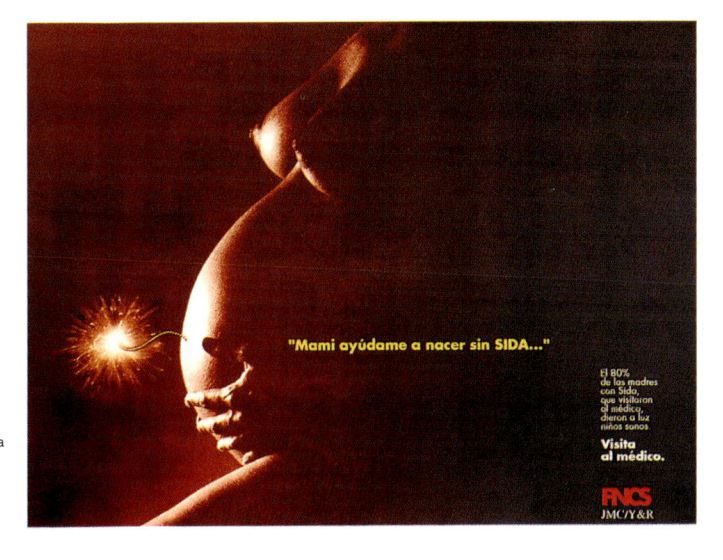

creative firm
  JMC/Y&R
  Caracas (Miranda), Venezuela
creative people
  Mary Torres, Jose Navas,
  & Luis Bernardo
client
  FNCS

creative firm
  Ogilvy & Mather Frankfurt
  Frankfurt, Germany
creative director, copywriter
  Johannes Krempl
art director
  Patrick They
client
  WWF Germany, Frankfurt

"The significant black shape of the German island 'Sylt' is very famous. The shape of this island is used as a sticker on cars, bags, etc. to say, 'I've been there.'"

"Sylt is also known as a nature reserve. When a crashed freighter spilled oil onto the coast of Sylt, it could have dramatically affected the wildlife. We made this ad showing just the famous shape of Sylt as an oil stain. The stickers never use words, so we didn't use a headline."

translation
  The mud flats:
  If an oil tanker crashed, this would be it.
  This time only 10,000 seabirds died.
  WWF goes to court.
  Protection must be improved.
  Help us: (bank account).

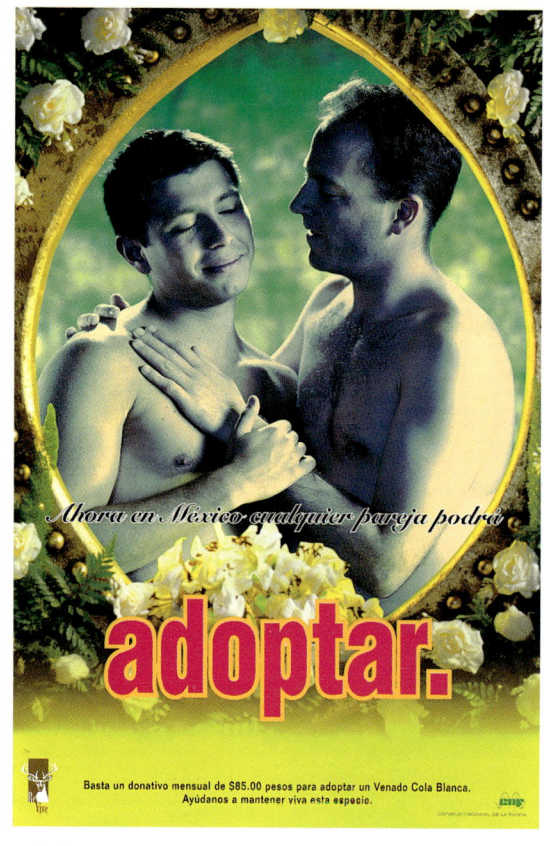

324

creative firm
  Young & Rubicam Mexico
  Mexico City, Mexico
creative director
  Mauricio Castillo
art directors
  Emiliano Vega, Mauricio Castillo,
  & Gumersindo Ingelmo
photographer
  Miguel Icaza
copywriter
  Enrique Laguardia L.
client
  Consejo Nacional De La Fauna

creative firm
  Nelson & Schmidt, Inc.
  Milwaukee (Wisconsin), USA
creative director
  Mark Gale
art director
  Sean Mullen
photographer
  Ricco Photo.
illustrator
  Bob Zimmerman
copywriters
  Maggie Kenny & Sean Mullen
client
  Illinois Attorney General

creative firm
  Sawyer Riley Compton
  Atlanta (Georgia), USA
creative director, art director
  Bart Cleveland
photographer
  Ken Light
copywriter
  Cathy Carlisi
client
  Citizens for Alternatives to
  the Death Penalty

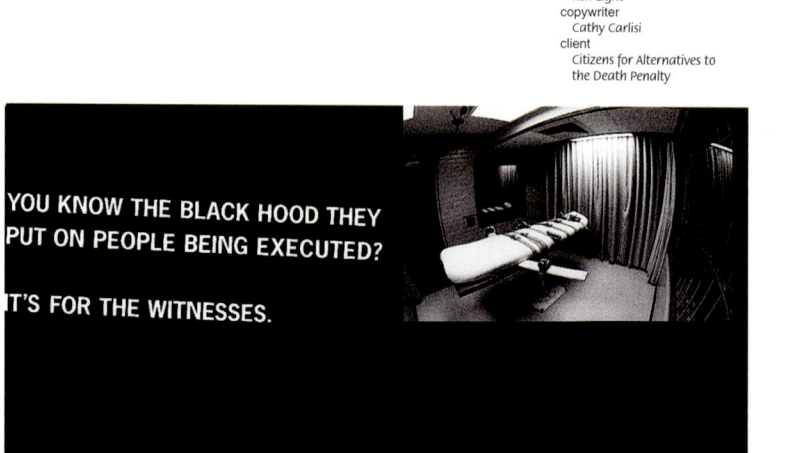

CREATIVITY 29
Public Service Ads
Campaign

creative firm
  J. Walter Thompson
  Chicago (Illinois), USA
art director
  Mark Westman
copywriter
  Pam Anderson
client
  JWT Charity Drive

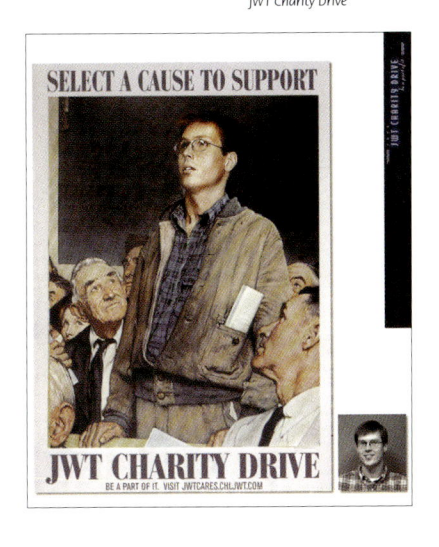

creative firm
  Nelson & Schmidt, Inc.
  Milwaukee (Wisconsin), USA
creative director
  Mark Gale
art director
  Sean Mullen
photographer
  Ricco Photo.
illustrator
  Bob Zimmerman
copywriters
  Maggie Kenny & Sean Mullen
client
  Illinois Attorney General

creative firm
  Dye, Van Mol & Lawrence
  Nashville (Tennessee), USA
creative director
  Chuck Creasy
art director
  Dale Addy
client
  Goodwill

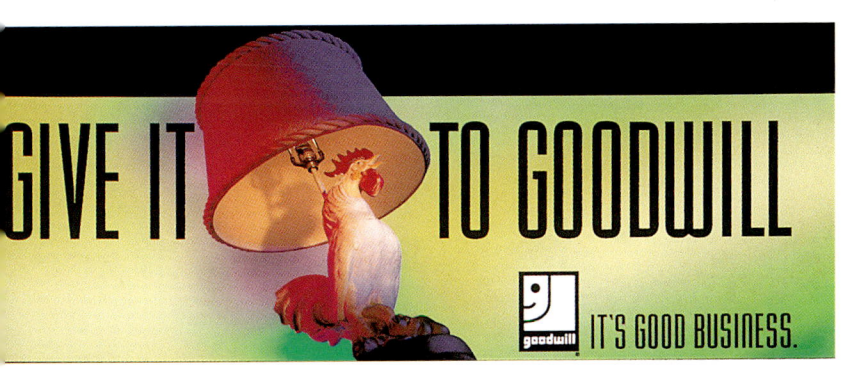

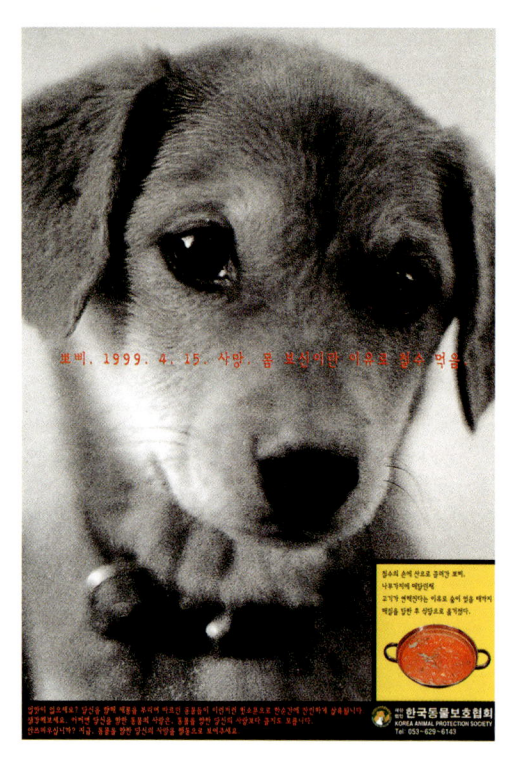

326

creative firm
McCann-Erickson Korea Inc.
Seoul, Korea
creative director
Jeremy Perrott
art directors
S.Y. Kim & G.Y. Ahn
copywriter
W.H. Kim
client
Korea Animal Protection Association

translation
Puppy. Died 1999.4.15.
Eaten by Chulsoo.

Tied to a tree and beaten to death for tenderer meat. Baked and eaten by Chulsoo to increase his vigor.

It's the dog you live with.
Because of groundless rumors, thousands of animals are dying everyday. Tasteless? Do something about it.

Show your love for animals through action.
Call 053-629-6143.

translation
Kitty. Died 1999.5.13.
Drunk by Doosik.

Stabbed in the heart with a dagger, chopped to pieces, and boiled in hot water until the bones were completely melted. Drunk by Doosik to cure his neuralgia.

It's the cat you sleep with.
Because of groundless rumors, thousands of animals are dying everyday. Painful? Do something about it.

Show your love for animals through action.
Call 053-629-6143.

creative firm
Mudra Communications Limited
Ahmedabad (Gujarat), India
creative people
Sabu Paul & Falguni Mathur
client
Sun Pharmaceutical Industries Ltd.

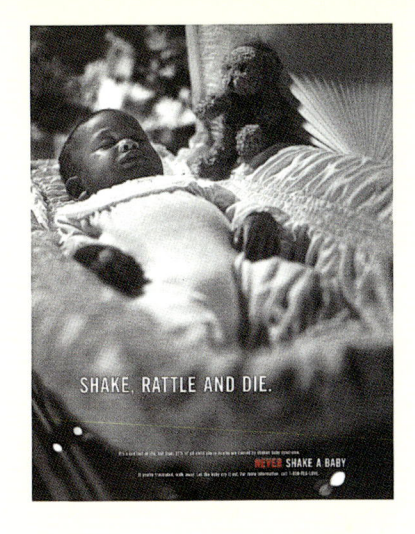

creative firm
  The Zimmerman Agency
    Tallahassee (Florida), USA
creative director
  Doug Engel
art director
  Mark Limbach
production
  Gwendy Vea
photographer
  Sandro
copywriters
  Jason Piroth & Doug Engel
client
  Family Preservation & Support Services

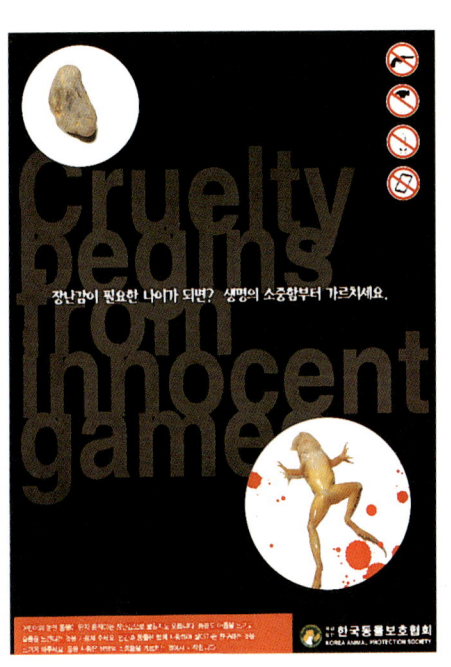

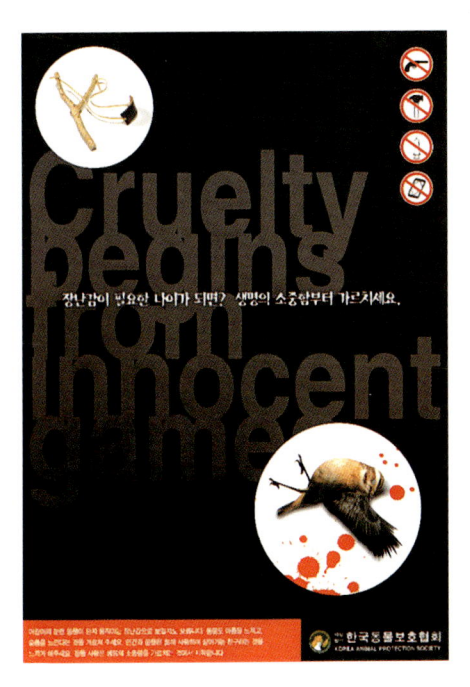

creative firm
  McCann-Erickson Korea Inc.
    Seoul, Korea
creative director
  Jeremy Perrott
art directors
  S.Y. Kim & G.Y. Ahn
copywriter
  W.H. Kim
client
  Korea Animal Protection Association

translation
  Cruelty begins with innocent games. When your kids reach the age when they need toys, teach them the value of life first.

  Children may not notice that animals have a life. Teach them that animals feel pain just like humans. Teach them that animals also have life. Animals are not toys. Teach them that animals are the human being's closest friends.

  Loving animals starts with teaching the importance of life.

creative firm
  JMC/Y&R
    Caracas (Miranda), Venezuela
creative people
  Mary Torres, J. Navas, & Luis Bernardo
client
  FNCS

translation
(top)
  "Mommy, help me to be born without AIDS."

  The 80% of mothers with AIDS who visited a doctor, gave birth to absolutely healthy babies.

  Visit a doctor.

(bottom)
  "Mommy, help me to be born without AIDS."

  Visit a doctor.

327

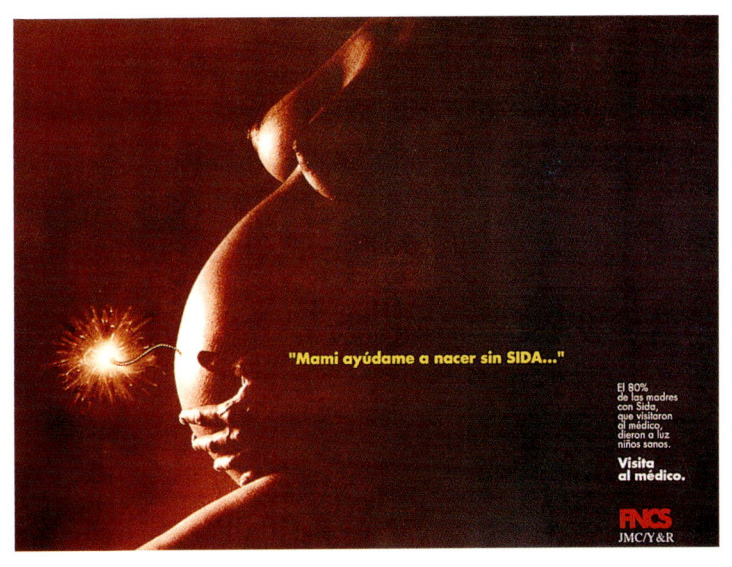

# CREATIVITY
## Creative Achievement for Art, Illustration

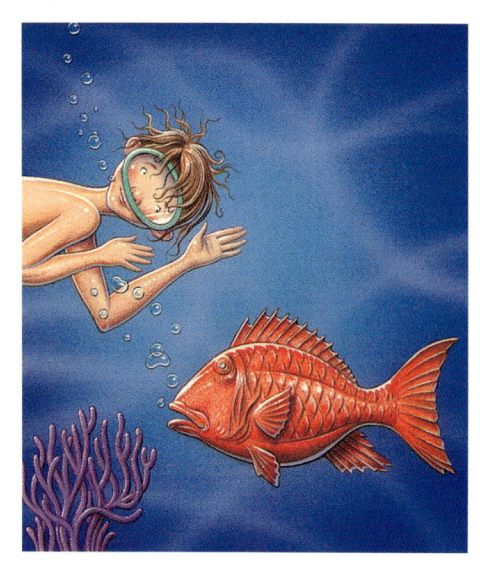

creative firm
  Mires Design
  Carlsbad (California), USA
art director
  John Ball
illustrator
  Tracy Sabin
client
  Harcourt Brace & Co.

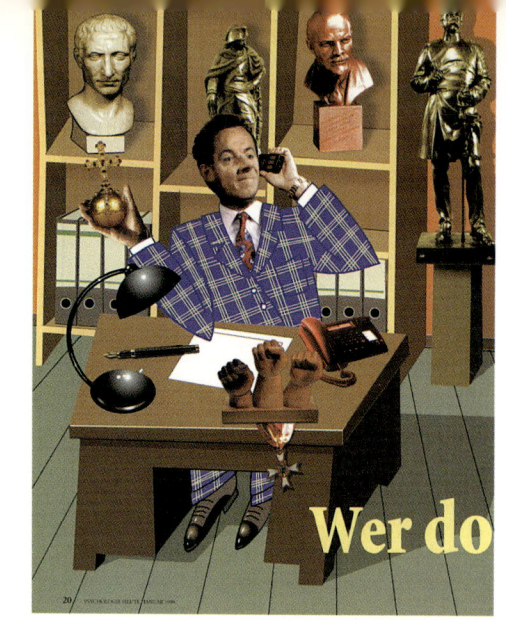

creative firm
  Playboy Enterprises, Inc.
  Chicago (Illinois), USA
art director, designer
  Tom Staebler
client
  Playboy

creative firm
  SIGN Kommunikation GmbH
  Frankfurt, Germany
creative people
  Erich Maas
client
  Beltz-Verlag GmbH

328

creative firm
  Wet Paper Bag Graphic Design
  Fort Worth (Texas), USA
designer
  Lewis Glaser
illustrator
  Don Ivan Punchatz
client
  TCU Art Department

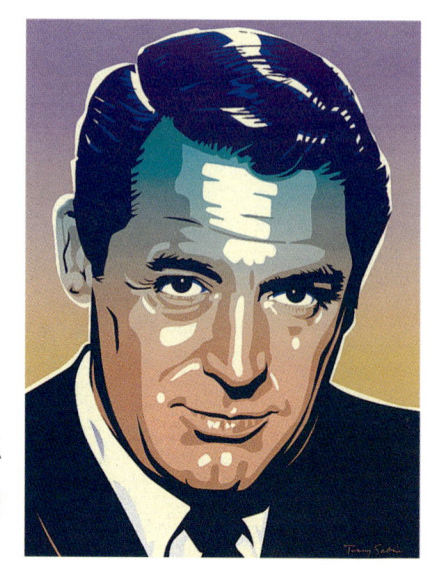

creative firm
  Sabingrafik, Inc.
  Carlsbad (California), USA
art director
  Jim Gordon
illustrator
  Tracy Sabin
client
  Gordon Screen Printing

creative firm
 Wendell Minor Design
  Washington (Connecticut), USA
art director
 Al Cetta
designer, illustrator
 Wendell Minor
client
 HarperCollins

creative firm
 Sabingrafik, Inc.
  Carlsbad (California), USA
art directors
 Tom Burke & Tom Morrison
illustrator
 Tracy Sabin
client
 Morrison & Burke Screen Printers

creative firm
 People Specials
  New York (New York), USA
art director
 Gregory Monfries
illustrator
 Michael Elins
client
 People Specials,
 The 25 Most Intriguing People

329

creative firm
 Wendell Minor Design
  Washington (Connecticut), USA
art director
 Michael Farmer
illustrator
 Wendell Minor
client
 Browndeer Press/Harcourt Brace

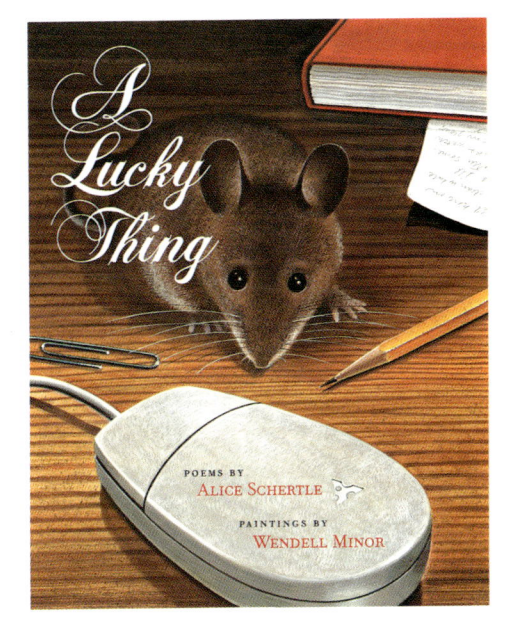

creative firm
 TV Land
  New York (New York), USA
agency
 Spot Design/Kristina DeCorpo
creative director
 Kim Rosenblum
art director
 Matt Duntemann
producer
 Karen Levy
designer
 Claudia Brandenburg
illustrator
 Ross MacDonald
copywriter
 David Rieth
client
 Ad Sales

creative firm
 U.S. Postal Service
  Washington (D.C.), USA
art director
 Phil Jordan
illustrator
 Nicholas Gaetano
client
 U.S. Postal Service

creative firm
 Wendell Minor Design
  Washington (Connecticut), USA
designer, illustrator
 Wendell Minor
client
 Delacorte Press

330

illustrator
 W.B. Park
  Altamonte Springs (Florida), USA
client
 American Bar Association

creative firm
 McNulty Design
  Carlsbad (California), USA
art director
 MAry McNulty
illustrator
 Tracy Sabin
client
 Star One

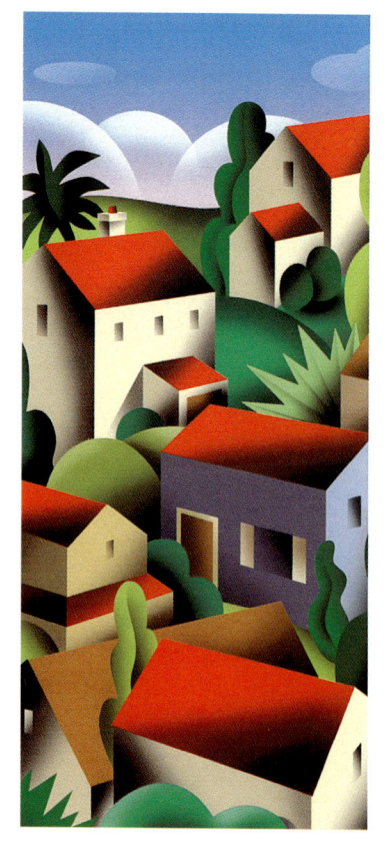

creative firm
 U.S. Postal Service
  Washington (D.C.), USA
art director
 Phil Jordan
illustrator
 Attila Hejja
client
 U.S. Postal Service

creative firm
　RDW Group Inc
　　Providence (Rhode Island), USA
creative people
　Anthony Gill
client
　New England Coffee Co.

creative firm
　Wendell Minor Design
　　Washington (Connecticut), USA
art director
　Nina Barnett
illustrator
　Wendell Minor
client
　Scribners

creative firm
　BBK Studio Inc.
　　Grand Rapids
　　(Michigan), USA
creative director, designer
　Michael Barile
illustrators
　Michael Barile &
　Allen McKinney
prepress
　Graphic Impressions
client
　BBK Studio

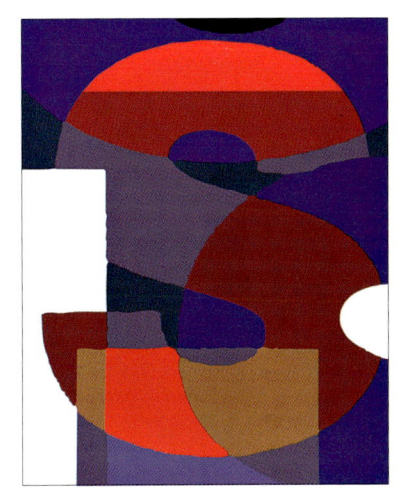

331

creative firm
　U.S. Postal Service
　　Washington (D.C.), USA
art director
　Ethel Kessler
illustrator
　Whitney Sherman
client
　U.S. Postal Service

creative firm
　American Medical News
　　Chicago (Illinois), USA
art director, designer
　Meredith Hogan
illustrator
　Jonathan Barkat

creative firm
    Playboy Enterprises, Inc.
    Chicago (Illinois), USA
art director, designer
    Tom Staebler
client
    Playboy

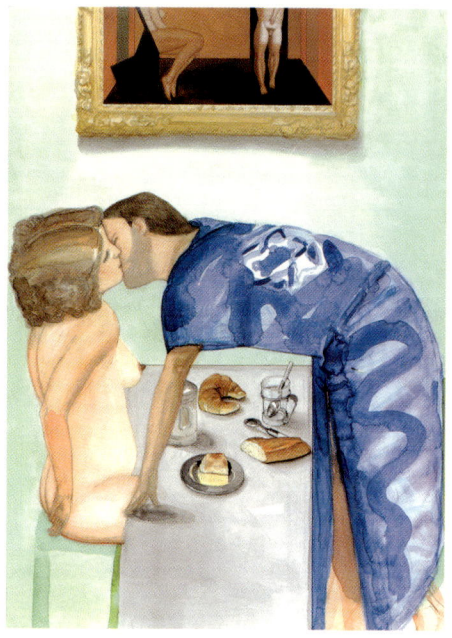

creative firm
    Playboy Enterprises, Inc.
    Chicago (Illinois), USA
art director
    Tom Staebler
designer
    Kerig Pope
artist
    Pat Andrea
client
    Playboy

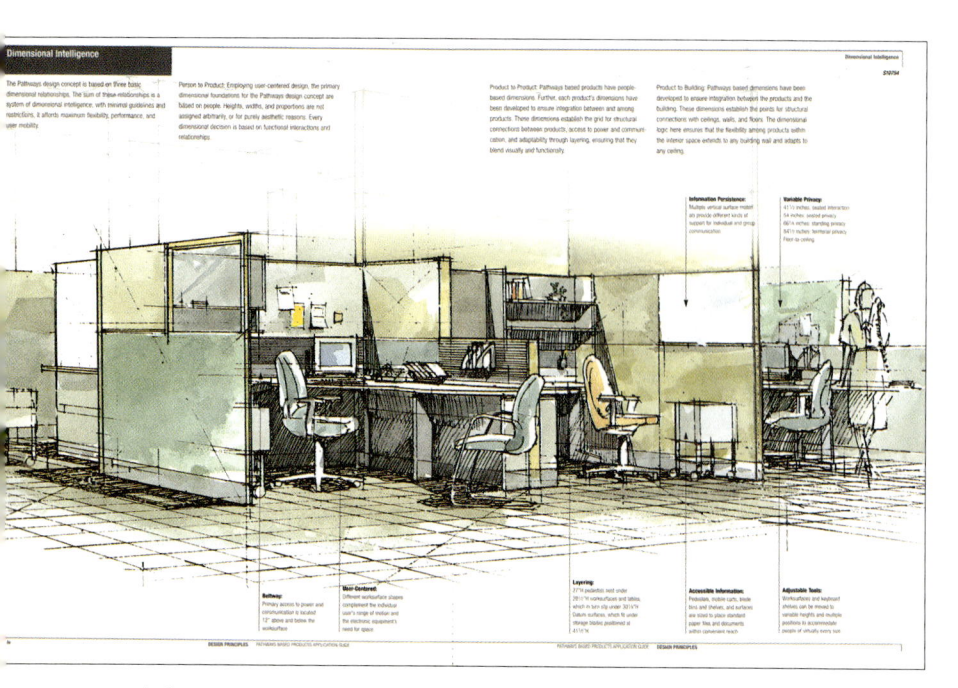

332

creative firm
    Agnew Moyer Smith Inc.
    Pittsburgh (Pennsylvania), USA
creative people
    Rita Lee, Molly Bigelow, Gina Datres,
    Rick Henkel, Clarence Bartley,
    Jonathan Hill, Giovanni Bacigalupi,
    Carlos Peterson
client
    Steelcase Inc.

creative firm
    People Specials
    New York (New York), USA
art director
    Gregory Monfries
illustrator
    Thomas Fluharty
client
    People Specials, The 25 Most Intriguing People

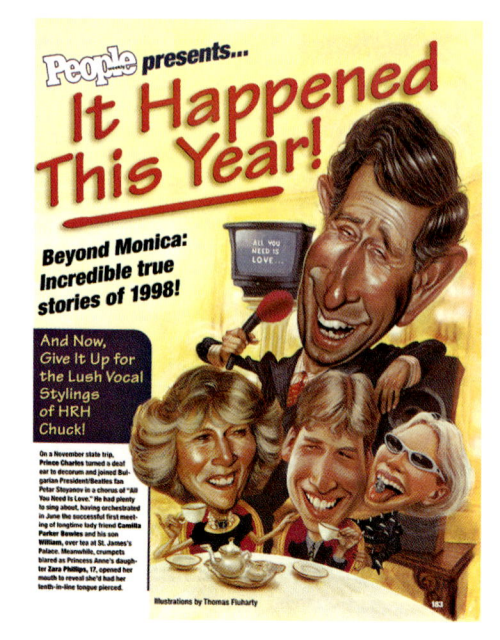

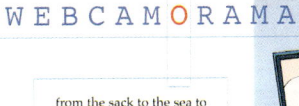

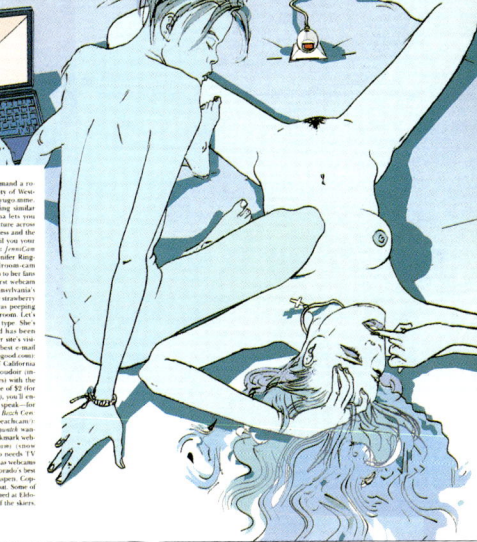

creative firm
 Playboy Enterprises, Inc.
  Chicago (Illinois), USA
art director
 Tom Staebler
designer
 Kerig Pope
artist
 Phil Hale
client
 Playboy

creative firm
 Popluar Mechanics
  New York (New York), USA
art director
 Bryan Canniff
illustrator
 Paul Blumstein
client
 Popular Mechanics

creative firm
 Playboy Enterprises, Inc.
  Chicago (Illinois), USA
art director
 Tom Staebler
designer
 Kerig Pope
artist
 Istvan Banyai
client
 Playboy

creative firm
 Medical Economics
  Montvale (New Jersey), USA
art director
 Roger Dowd
designer
 Elyse Carter
illustrator
 J.T. Morrow
client
 Medical Economics

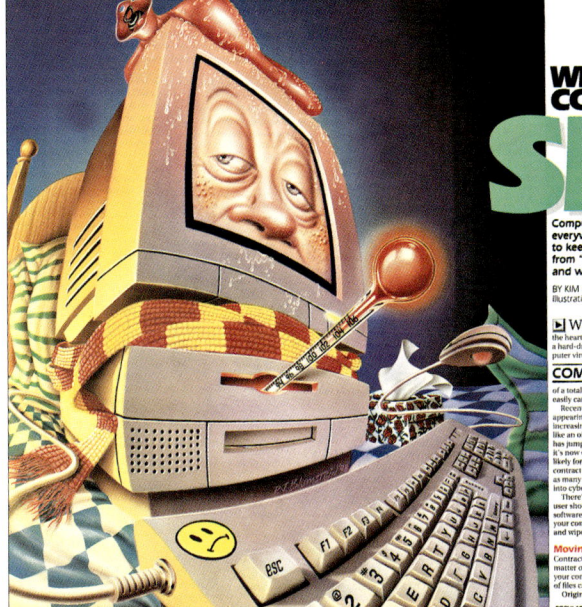

333

creative firm
 Hadassah Creative Services
 New York (New York), USA
creative director
 Michael Cohen
designer
 Jennifer Norton
illustrator
 José Ortega
client
 Hadassah Exhibit and Display Department

creative firm
 The Wyant Simboli Group, Inc.
 Norwalk (Connecticut), USA
creative people
 Julia Wyant, Karen Olenski, Sheri Cifaldi,
 Paul Neel, & Lance Hertzback
client
 GE Capital

creative firm
 Julia Tam Design
 Palos Verdes (California), USA
art director
 Julia Tam
illustrator
 Tim Webb
client
 MetaChem, Inc.

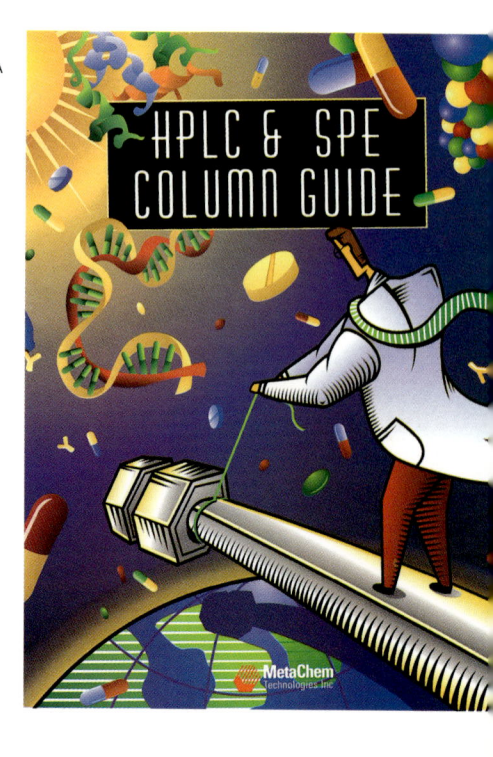

creative firm
 Lensa Film SDN BHD
 Kaula Lumpur, Malaysia
creative people
 Mr. Ak Don Cham Pi

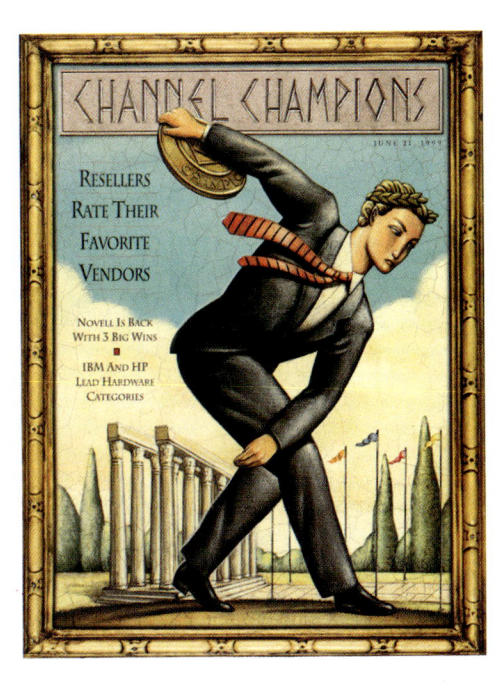

creative firm
 CMP Media
  Jericho (New York), USA
creative people
 Anne Cooney, Marc Burckhardt, & Gene Fedele
client
 Computer Reseller News

creative firm
 Dynamic Duo Studio
  Westport (Connecticut), USA
magazine art director
 Brandon Kavulla
designers, illustrators
 The Dynamic Duo Studio:
  Arlen Schumer (black and white linework)
  Sherri Wolfgang (computer coloring)
client
 VIBE Magazine

creative firm
 Playboy Enterprises, Inc.
  Chicago (Illinois), USA
art director
 Tom Staebler
designer
 Len Willis
artist
 Rafal Olbinski
client
 Playboy

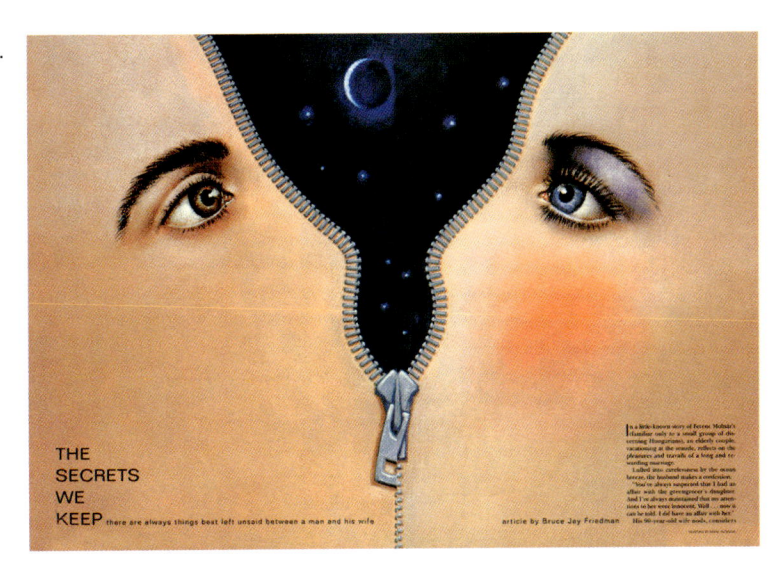

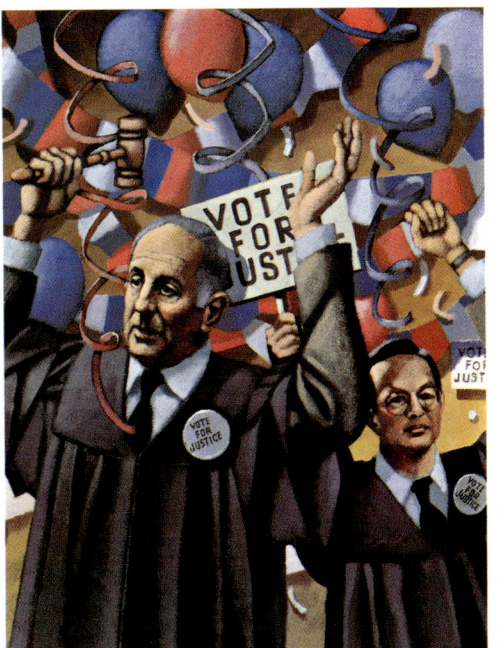

creative firm
 American Lawyer Media
  New York (New York), USA
art director
 Joan Ferrell
designer
 Sue Llewellyn
illustrator
 John Howard
client
 The American Lawyer

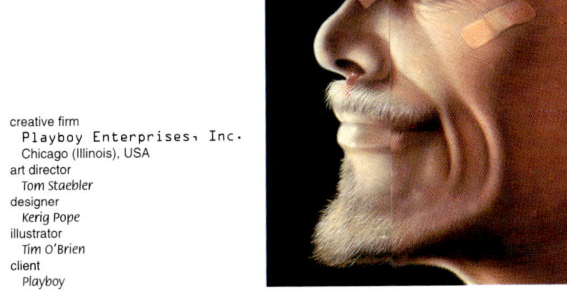

creative firm
 Playboy Enterprises, Inc.
  Chicago (Illinois), USA
art director
 Tom Staebler
designer
 Kerig Pope
illustrator
 Tim O'Brien
client
 Playboy

creative firm
 Eni Oken-3D Artist
  Los Angeles (California), USA
creative people
 Eni Oken
client
 Eni Oken

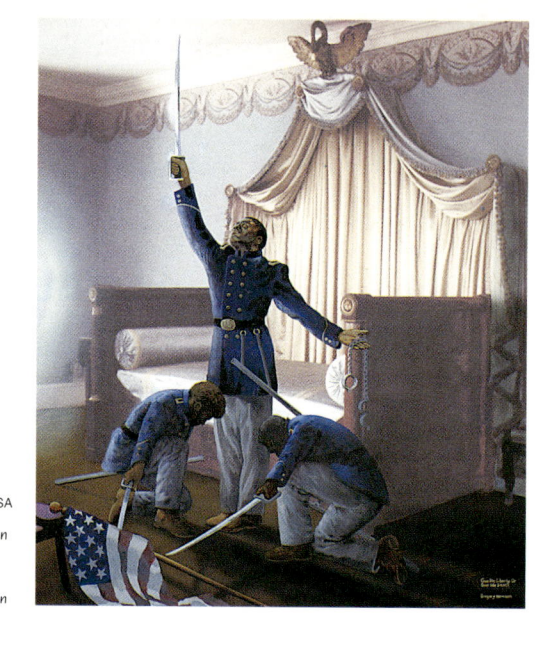

creative firm
 Gregory
 Newson
 Design
  New York
  (New York), USA
creative people
 Gregory Newson
canvas trafer
 Pixation
client
 Gregory Newson

creative firm
 Sorensen Illustrates
  San Francisco (California), USA
art director
 Liz Scoggins (Flair Communications)
illustrator
 Marcos Sorensen
client
 Lucky Strike

336

creative firm
 Medical Economics
  Montvale (New Jersey), USA
art director
 Jeffrey T. Beavers
illustrator
 Quade Paul
client
 Patient Care Magazine

creative firm
 Hadassah Creative Services
  New York (New York), USA
designers
 Irit Hadar & Michael Cohen
illustrator
 Joel Nakamura
client
 Hadassah Fund Raising Division

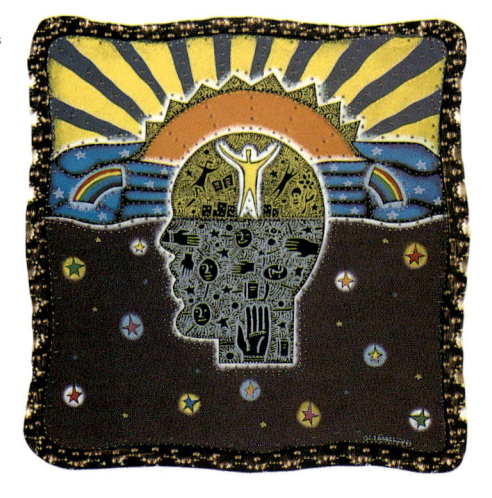

creative firm
 Sorensen Illustrates
 San Francisco (California), USA
art director
 Jandos Rothstein
illustrator
 Marcos Sorensen
client
 Washington Film Festival

creative firm
 Communication Design, Inc.
 Richmond (Virginia), USA
art director
 Ron Saikowski
illustrator
 Robert Meganck
client
 The Washington Times

creative firm
 Murphy Design Inc.
 Milo (Alberta), Canada
creative people
 Rick Sealock & Murphy Design Inc.
client
 Fortran Printing

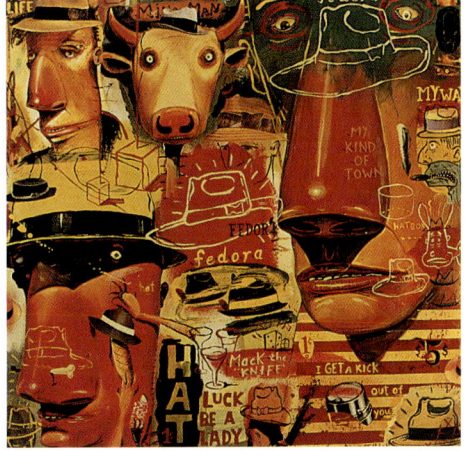

creative firm
 Communication Design, Inc.
 Richmond (Virginia), USA
art director
 Jandos Rothstein
illustrator
 Robert Meganck
client
 Washington City Paper

creative firm
 Sorensen Illustrates
 San Francisco (California), USA
art director
 Bob Maharry
illustrator
 Marcos Sorensen
client
 Epilepsy Foundation

337

# CREATIVITY
## Creative Achievement for Photography

**10 BILLION VOLTS**
PHOTOGRAPHY BY NICK DJORDJEVIC

creative firm
  Chris Collins Studio
  New York (New York), USA
creative people
  Chris Collins
client
  Chris Collins

creative firm
  Genesis Fine Art Photography
  Perth, Australia
designer, photographer
  Nick Djordjevic
client
  Genesis Fine Art Photography

creative firm
  Concept CA-Studio JMV
  Miami (Florida), USA
creative people
  Armando Cardenas, Jose M. Vidaurre,
  Alberto Hernandez, & Humberto D'Ascoli
client
  Cedesa

creative firm
  Fader Unda Sohn
  New York (New York), USA
creative people
  Fader Unda Sohn
client
  Todd Haiman Studio

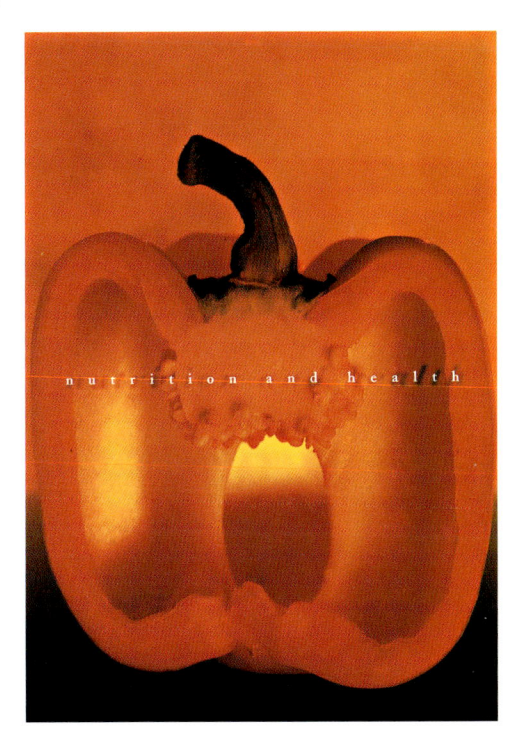

creative firm
  Emerson,
  Wajdowicz Studios
    New York (New York), USA
creative director
  Jurek Wajdowicz
designers
  Lisa LaRochelle, Jurek Wajdowicz,
  & Manuel Mendez
photographer
  Gueorgui Pinkhassov
client
  Eddy Specialty Papers

creative firm
  Signi
    Naucalpan (Edo de Mexico), Mexico
designer
  Nora Schwasky
photographer
  Gabriel Covian
client
  Savia

creative firm
  Lawrence, Mayo & Ponder
    Newport Beach (California), USA
creative directors
  Lynda Lawrence & Bruce Mayo
art director
  Simone Beaudoin
designer
  Ellen Laning
photographer
  Leonard Myszynski
client
  Lawrence, Mayo & Ponder

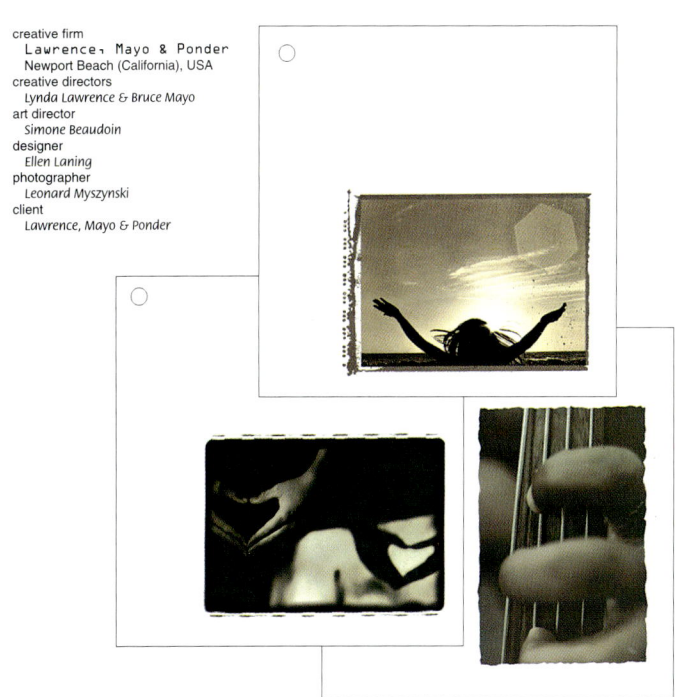

creative firm
  Chris Collins Studio
    New York (New York), USA
creative people
  Chris Collins
client
  Chris Collins

creative firm
  Prisma Photography
    Southport (Connecticut), USA
designer, photographer
  Peter J. Pezzella
client
  Prisma Photography

creative firm
  People Magazine Special Issues
  New York (New York), USA
picture editor
  Maddy Miller
photographer
  Richard Corman

creative firm
  Bard Communications
  New York (New York), USA
design director, photographer
  Rick Bard
client
  Manhattan Magazine

340

creative firm
  People Magazine
  Special Issues
  New York (New York), USA
picture editor
  Maddy Miller
photographer
  Norman Jean Roy

creative firm
  Nesnadny +
  Schwartz
  Cleveland (Ohio), USA
creative director
  Mark Schwartz
designer
  Michelle Moehler
photographer
  Larry Fink
client
  The George Gund
  Foundation

creative firm
  People Magazine
  Special Issues
  New York
  (New York), USA
picture editor
  Maddy Miller
photographer
  George Holz

creative firm
 People Magazine
 Special Issues
 New York
 (New York), USA
photo editor
 Maddy Miller
photographer
 George Lange

creative firm
 Nesnadny +
 Schwartz
 Cleveland
 (Ohio), USA
creative directors
 Mark Schwartz &
 Joyce Nesnadny
designers
 Joyce Nesnadny &
 Michelle Moehler
artist
 Stephen Frailey
client
 The Progressive
 Corporation

creative firm
 People Magazine Special Issues
 New York (New York), USA
picture editor
 Ann Tortorelli
photographer
 Bob Frame

creative firm
 American Lawyer Media
 New York (New York), USA
art director, designer
 Joan Ferrell
photo editor
 T.L. Litt
photographer
 Michael Bowles
client
 The American Lawyer

creative firm
 Emerson, Wajdowicz Studios
 New York (New York), USA
creative director
 Jurek Wajdowicz
designers
 Lisa LaRochelle & Jurek Wajdowicz
photographer
 Antonin Kratochvil
client
 The Rockefeller Foundation

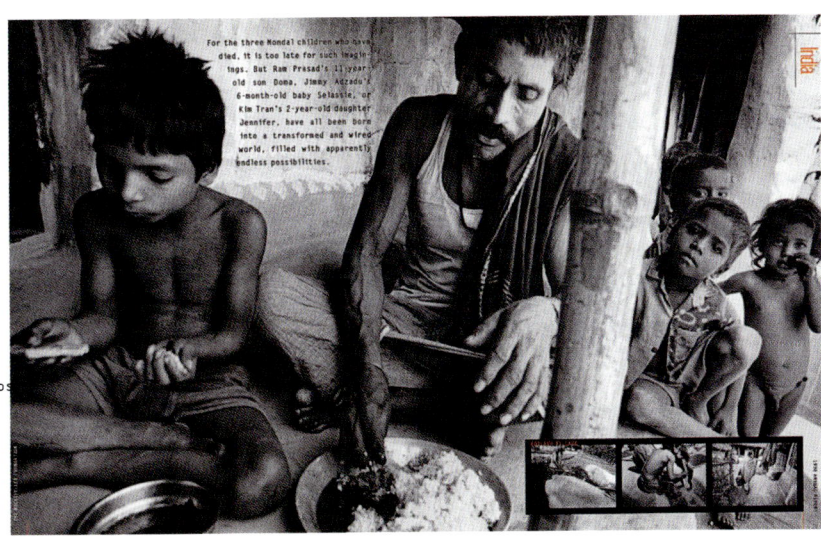

creative firm
**Greg Pease Photography**
Baltimore (Maryland), USA
creative people
*Greg Pease*

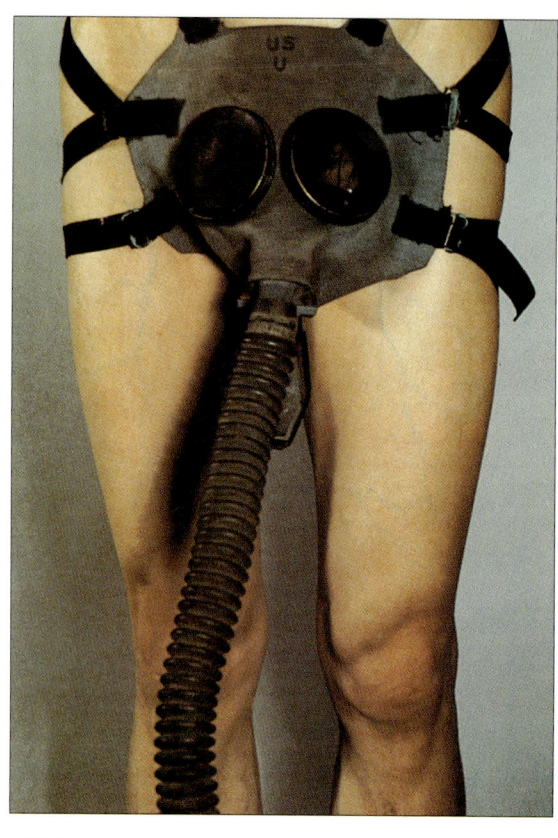

creative firm
**66 communication inc.**
New York (New York), USA
creative people
*Chin-Chih Yang*

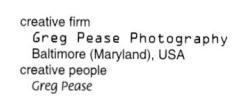

342

creative firm
**Garry Kan Photography**
Calgary (Alberta), Canada
art director, photographer
*Garry Kan*

creative firm
**Greg Pease Photography**
Baltimore (Maryland), USA
creative people
*Greg Pease*

creative firm
**Greg Pease Photography**
Baltimore (Maryland), USA
creative people
*Greg Pease*

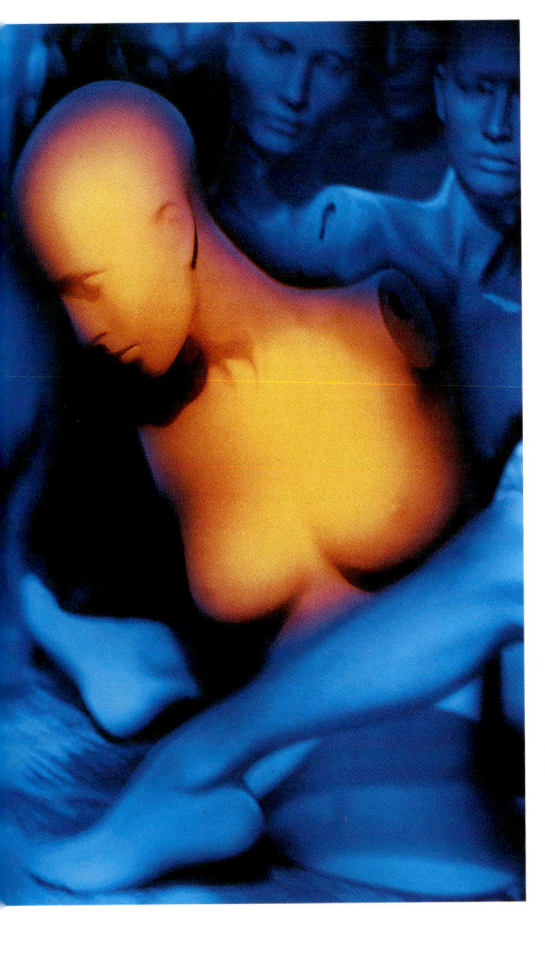

creative firm
  VanderSchuit Studio
  San Diego
  (California), USA
creative people
  Carl VanderSchuit

creative firm
  Blu Bird Productions S.R.L. (internal)
  Milan, Italy
c.a.d., photographer
  Joe Oppedisano
client
  Mares

creative firm
  Mires Design
  San Diego (California), USA
creative people
  Jose Serrano
client
  Qualcomm

creative firm
  VanderSchuit Studio
  San Diego (California), USA
creative people
  Carl VanderSchuit
client
  Single Image

343

# CREATIVITY 29
## Creative Achievement for Typography

creative firm
  Nesnadny + Schwartz
  Cleveland (Ohio), USA
creative directors
  Mark Schwartz & Joyce Nesnadny
designers
  Joyce Nesnadny & Michelle Moehler
artist
  Stephen Frailey
client
  The Progressive Corporation

creative firm
  Popular Mechanics
  New York (New York), USA
art director
  Bryan Canniff
photographer
  David Dewhurst
client
  Popular Mechanics

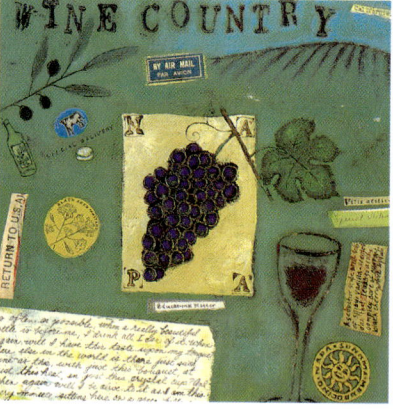

344

creative firm
  Artefact Design
  Palo Alto (California), USA
creative people
  Artefact Design
client
  Artefact Design

creative firm
  Gallery Ltd
  Hong Kong, China
creative people
  Benny Cheng, Raymond Fu, & Kelvin Parker
client
  Gallery Ltd

creative firm
  Artefact Design
  Palo Alto (California), USA
creative people
  Artefact Design
client
  Artefact Design

# CREATIVITY
## Consumer TVc
## Singles

creative firm
  Advico Young & Rubicam
  Zurich-Gockhausen, Switzerland
creative directors
  Francisco X. Rodon & Martin Spillmann
client
  Swissair

creative firm
  Advico Young & Rubicam
  Zurich-Gockhausen, Switzerland
creative director
  Hansjörg Zürcher
art director
  Mathias Bapst
client
  ZVSM

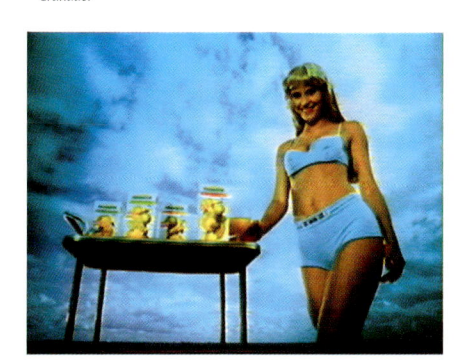

creative firm
  Advico Young & Rubicam
  Zurich-Gockhausen, Switzerland
creative director, copywriter
  Peter Brönnimann
art director
  Héléne Forster
client
  Egger Tyres

345

creative firm
  Advico Young & Rubicam
  Zurich-Gockhausen, Switzerland
creative director
  Martin Spillmann
art directors
  Martin Spillmann & Alain Picard
copywriters
  Martin Spillmann & Denis Schwarz
client
  Granador

creative firm
  Advico Young & Rubicam
  Zurich-Gockhausen, Switzerland
creative director, copywriter
  Martin Spillmann
art director
  Denis Schwarz
client
  Giuseppe Citterio

creative firm
  Advico Young & Rubicam
  Zurich-Gockhausen, Switzerland
creative director, art director, copywriter
  Martin Spillmann
client
  Hakle

creative firm
  Advico Young & Rubicam
  Zurich-Gockhausen, Switzerland
creative director
  Martin Spillmann
art director
  Roland Scotoni
copywriter
  Iwan Weidmann
client
  Museum of Creation, Zurich

creative firm
  Bleecker & Sullivan
  New York (New York), USA
creative director
  Itzhak Beery
copywriter
  Sela Francis
client
  ASPCA

creative firm
  Burkhardt & Hillman/WestWayne
  New York (New York), USA
creative people
  Rebecca Mirkin & Ron Burkhardt
client
  BellSouth Yellow Pages

creative firm
  Campbell-Ewald
  Advertising
  Warren (Michigan), USA
creative directors
  Jim Gorman & Joe Putty
art director
  John Clarey
copywriter
  Jon Stewart
client
  Chevrolet Truck

creative firm
  Campbell-Ewald
  Advertising
  Warren (Michigan), USA
creative people
  Bill Ludwig, Lance Mald,
  Vince Murray, Steve Williams,
  & Betty Meadows
client
  DirecTV

creative firm
  Campbell-Ewald
  Advertising
  Warren (Michigan), USA
creative people
  Bill Ludwig, Arthur Mitchell,
  David Johns, Patrick O'Leary, Robin Todd,
  Mary Ellen Krawczyk, & Denise Sidlow
client
  Chevrolet Motor Division

creative firm
  Campbell-Ewald
  Advertising
  Warren (Michigan), USA
creative directors
  Jim Gorman & Joe Putty
art director
  John Clarey
copywriter
  Jon Stewart
client
  Chevrolet Truck

creative firm
  Cramer-Krasselt
  Milwaukee (Wisconsin), USA
creative director
  Neil Casey
art director
  David Hofmann
copywriter
  Michael Bednar
client
  Birds Eye

creative firm
  Cramer-Krasselt
  Milwaukee (Wisconsin), USA
creative director
  Neil Casey
art director
  David Hofmann
copywriter
  Pat Pritchard
client
  Master Lock

346

creative firm
  Design Guys
  Minneapolis (Minnesota), USA
creative director, art director, copywriter
  Steven Sikora
producer
  John Lick
director
  Rich Michel
editor
  Tony Fischer
flame art
  Mark Youngren
client
  Target Stores

creative firm
  Dieste & Partners Publicidad
  Dallas (Texas), USA
executive creative director
  Aldo Quevedo
art director
  Paty Martinez
senior copywriter
  Iañki Escudero
client
  Pizza Hut

creative firm
  Dieste & Partners Publicidad
  Dallas (Texas), USA
executive creative director
  Aldo Quevedo
art director
  Paty Martinez
senior copywriter
  Iañki Escudero
client
  Pizza Hut

creative firm
  Dymun Nelson & Company
  Pittsburgh (Pennsylvania), USA
creative directors
  John Dymun & Craig Otto
art director
  Craig Otto
producer
  Sandy Stewart
copywriter
  John Dymun
client
  Dollar Bank

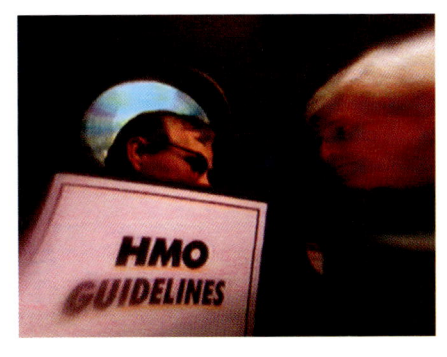

creative firm
  Erwin-Penland Advertising
  Greenville (South Carolina), USA
creative director
  Russ Corvey
broadcast producer
  Randall Owens
senior art director
  Jerold Murry
client
  HealthFirst

creative firm
  Faltman & Malmn
  Stockholm, Sweden
art director
  Björn Nordfors
copywriter
  Patrik Moks
client
  Svenska Spel

347

creative firm
  Flynn, Sabatino & Day
  Cincinnati (Ohio), USA
creative director
  James Browning
producer
  Bethann Thompson
client
  Avomark Auto Insurance

creative firm
  Grey Daiko Advertising Inc.
  Tokyo (Minato-ku), Japan
creative director
  Miyagawa Kanji
tv planners
  Kamiutsuri Akira & Namiki Hideki
copywriter
  Tomiyama Yukika
production company
  River Run, Inc.
client
  Calpis Ajinomoto Danone Japan Co., LTD.

creative firm
  GREY GmbH & Co. KG
  Düsseldorf, Germany
creative director
  Renate Günther-Greene
producer
  Michael Maschke
director
  Johnny Cohen
dop
  Eric Dumage
client
  Groupe Moulinex/Krups

creative firm
 J. Walter Thompson
  Chicago (Illinois), USA
art director
 Colleen Smith
copywriter
 Liz Taylor
client
 Partnership for a Drug Free America

creative firm
 J. Walter Thompson
  Chicago (Illinois), USA
gcd
 Dennis Ryan
art director
 Kevin Seavitt
copywriter
 Derek Sherman
client
 NABISCO/Air Crisps

creative firm
 J. Walter Thompson/N.Y.
  New York (New York), USA
creative directors
 Stuart Mickle, John Morrison,
 & Bill Hamilton
art director
 Alain Briere
copywriter
 Peter Seterdahl
producer
 Mark Sitley
client
 Merrill Lynch

creative firm
 J. Walter Thompson/N.Y.
  New York (New York), USA
creative directors
 Stuart Mickle, John Morrison,
 & Bill Hamilton
art director
 Alain Briere
copywriter
 Peter Seterdahl
producer
 Mark Sitley
client
 Merrill Lynch

creative firm
 J. Walter Thompson/N.Y.
  New York (New York), USA
creative directors
 David Smith & Mickey Paxton
art directors
 John Hobbs & Mickey Paxton
copywriters
 Brian Connaughton & David Smith
producer
 Paul Roy
client
 Lipton Brisk

creative firm
 J. Walter Thompson/N.Y.
  New York (New York), USA
creative director
 Brian Sitts
art director
 Randy Freeman
copywriter
 Kevin Doyle
producer
 Paul Roy
client
 Warner Lambert - Rolaids

creative firm
 J. Walter Thompson/N.Y.
  New York (New York), USA
creative director
 Brian Sitts
art director
 Randy Freeman
copywriter
 Kevin Doyle
producer
 Paul Roy
client
 Warner Lambert - Rolaids

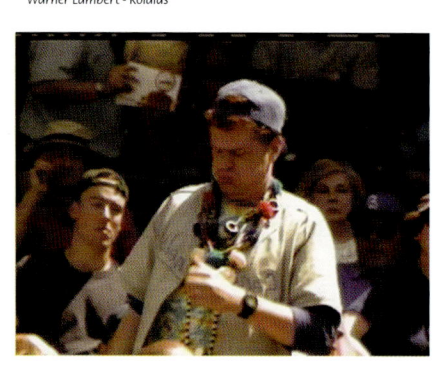

creative firm
 J. Walter Thompson/N.Y.
  New York (New York), USA
art director
 DJ Pierce
copywriter
 Scott Duchon
producer
 Lauren Bayer
director
 Frank Samuel
production company
 Vamp Film
client
 Blades, Board & Skate

creative firm
 J. Walter Thompson/N.Y.
  New York (New York), USA
art director
 Joe Massaro
copywriter
 George Parker
producer
 Susan Smitman
client
 Qwest

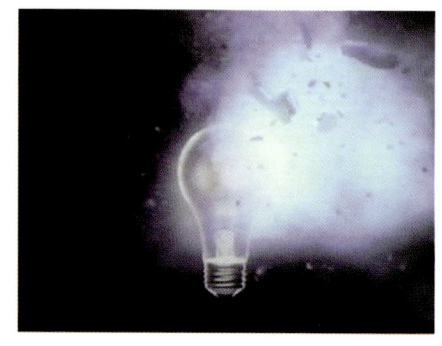

348

creative firm
 J. Walter Thompson/N.Y.
 New York (New York), USA
creative director
 Alan Platt
art director
 Thomas Hayo
copywriter
 Ronald Wohlman
producer
 Jill Rothman
client
 Kellogg's Raisin Bran Crunch

creative firm
 J. Walter Thompson/N.Y.
 New York (New York), USA
art director
 Joe Massaro
copywriter
 George Parker
producer
 Susan Smitman
client
 Qwest

creative firm
 J. Walter Thompson/N.Y.
 New York (New York), USA
art director
 DJ Pierce
copywriter
 Scott Duchon
director
 Chris Plum
producer
 Cathern Colbert
client
 Blades, Board & Skate

creative firm
 J. Walter Thompson
 Chicago (Illinois), USA
gcd
 Dennis Ryan
art director
 Kevin Seavitt
copywriter
 Derek Sherman
client
 NABISCO/Air Crisps

creative firm
 J. Walter Thompson
 Chicago (Illinois), USA
gcd
 Mark Silviera
art director
 Craig Schwartz
copywriter
 Jeff Martin
client
 KRAFT/Miracle Whip Flavors

creative firm
 J. Walter Thompson
 Chicago (Illinois), USA
creative director
 Peter Griffth
client
 Partnership for a Drug Free America

creative firm
 J. Walter Thompson
 Chicago (Illinois), USA
gcd
 Mark Silviera
art director
 Craig Schwartz
copywriter
 Jeff Martin
client
 KRAFT/Miracle Whip Flavors

creative firm
 J. Walter Thompson
 Chicago (Illinois), USA
gcd
 Jeff York
creative director
 Doug Kamp
art director
 Pam Anderson
copywriter
 Greg Oreskovich
client
 DELL

creative firm
 J. Walter Thompson
 Chicago (Illinois), USA
gcd
 Jeff York
art director
 Mark Westman
copywriter
 Miguel Barron
client
 Blockbuster/Video Game Rentals

349

creative firm
  J. Walter Thompson
  Chicago (Illinois), USA
gcd
  Mark Silviera
art director
  Craig Schwartz
copywriter
  Jeff Martin
client
  KRAFT/Miracle Whip Flavors

creative firm
  J. Walter Thompson
  Chicago (Illinois), USA
gcd
  Mark Silviera
art director
  Craig Schwartz
copywriter
  Jeff Martin
client
  KRAFT/Miracle Whip Flavors

creative firm
  JMC/Y&R
  Caracas (Miranda), Venezuela
creative people
  Orlando Monteleone & Elida Montilla
client
  PDV

350

creative firm
  JMC/Y&R
  Caracas (Miranda), Venezuela
creative people
  Orlando Monteleone & A. Hontoria
client
  Catana

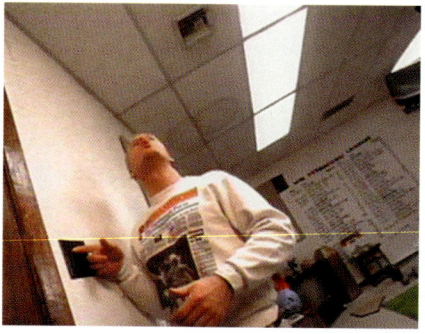

creative firm
  egan/st. james
  Pittsburgh (Pennsylvania), USA
creative directors
  Lee St. James, Bill Garrison, & Jay Giesen
art director
  Jay Giesen
agency producer
  Nan Quatchak
copywriter
  Bill Garrison
client
  Pittsburgh Pirates

creative firm
  egan/st. james
  Pittsburgh (Pennsylvania), USA
creative directors
  Lee St. James, Bill Garrison, & Jay Giesen
art director
  Jay Giesen
agency producer
  Nan Quatchak
copywriter
  Bill Garrison
client
  Pittsburgh Pirates

creative firm
  egan/st. james
  Pittsburgh (Pennsylvania), USA
creative directors
  Lee St. James, Jim Anderson, & David Wachter
art director
  David Wachter
agency producer
  Marilyn Salley
copywriter
  Jim Anderson
client
  Zippo Manufacturing Company

creative firm
  Louis London
  St. Louis (Missouri), USA
art directors
  Joe Ortmeyer & Aaron Segall
copywriters
  Lori Jones & Steve Hunt
client
  The Casino Queen

creative firm
  MARC Advertising
  Pittsburgh (Pennsylvania), USA
creative people
  Ed Fine, Tony Jaffe, Cathy Bowen,
  & John Hapach
client
  Tru Serv Corporation/Taylor Rental Division

creative firm
 MARC Advertising
 Pittsburgh (Pennsylvania), USA
creative people
 Ed Fine, Tony Jaffe, Holly Humphrey,
 & John Swisher
client
 Rite Aid Corporation

creative firm
 MARC Advertising
 Pittsburgh (Pennsylvania), USA
creative people
 Ed Fine, Tony Jaffe, John Swisher,
 & Holly Humphrey
client
 Rite Aid Corporation

creative firm
 MARC Advertising
 Pittsburgh (Pennsylvania), USA
creative people
 Ed Fine, Tony Jaffe, Holly Humphrey,
 & John Swisher
client
 Rite Aid Corporation

creative firm
 McCann-Erickson Korea Inc.
 Seoul, Korea
creative director
 Jeremy Perrott
art directors
 H.J. Park & Y.C. Kim
client
 Coca-Cola Nestle

creative firm
 McCann-Erickson Korea Inc.
 Seoul, Korea
creative director
 Jeremy Perrott
art directors
 G.Y. Ahn & S.Y. Kim
client
 Coca-Cola Korea

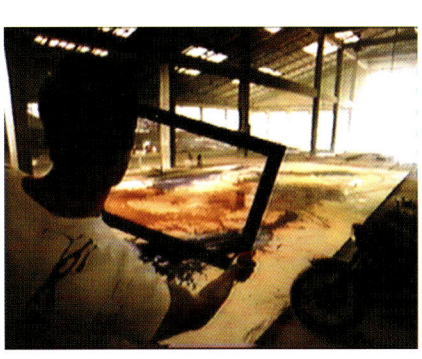

creative firm
 McCann-Erickson Korea Inc.
 Seoul, Korea
creative director
 Jeremy Perrott
art directors
 G.Y. Ahn & S.Y. Kim
client
 Levi's Korea

creative firm
 McCann-Erickson Korea Inc.
 Seoul, Korea
creative director
 Jeremy Perrott
art directors
 H.J. Park & Y.C. Kim
client
 Nestle Korea

creative firm
 McCann-Erickson NZ
 Auckland, New Zealand
national creative director
 Carolyn Reid
agency producer
 Hannah Godwin
client
 New Zealand Insurance

creative firm
 McCann-Erickson Sydney
 North Sydney, Australia
creative people
 Paul Kamzelas & Jamie Kwong
client
 Rebel Sport Limited

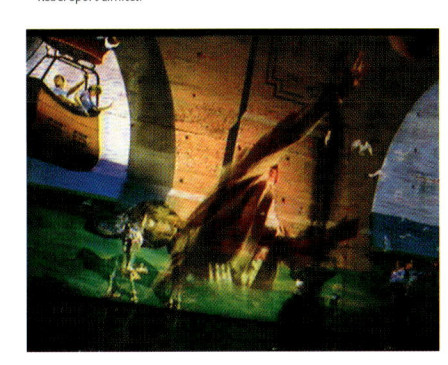

creative firm
  McCann-Erickson Sydney
  North Sydney, Australia
creative people
  Paul Kamzelas & Jamie Kwong
client
  Rebel Sport Limited

creative firm
  McCann-Erickson Sydney
  North Sydney, Australia
creative people
  Angeline Ebejer & Michael Lee
client
  Nescafe

creative firm
  McCann-Erickson Sydney
  North Sydney, Australia
creative people
  Paul Kamzelas & Jamie Kwong
client
  Rebel Sport Limited

352

creative firm
  McCann-Erickson
  New York (New York), USA
creative directors
  Jonathan Cranin & Joyce King Thomas
art director
  Chris Cereda
copywriter
  Eric Goldstein
producer
  Greg Lotus
client
  MasterCard

creative firm
  McCann-Erickson
  New York (New York), USA
creative directors
  Jonathan Cranin & Joyce King Thomas
art director
  Chris Cereda
producer
  Greg Lotus
copywriter
  Eric Goldstein
client
  MasterCard

creative firm
  McCann-Erickson
  New York (New York), USA
creative directors
  Joyce King Thomas
art director
  Jacques Borris
producer
  Corsa USA
copywriter
  Lisa Brandriff
client
  MasterCard

creative firm
  McCann-Erickson
  New York (New York), USA
creative director, copywriter
  Joyce King Thomas
art director
  Louisa Wilson
producer
  Kelley Long
client
  MasterCard

creative firm
  McCann-Erickson
  New York (New York), USA
creative director
  Douglas Toews
art director
  Diane Stratton-Crooke
producers
  Judi Nierman & Claire Anderson
copywriter
  Caitlin Ewing
client
  L'Oreal

creative firm
  Mountain View Productions, Ltd.
  New York (New York), USA
client
  Marsahll/Yezzi Inc.

creative firm
  Nickelodeon (Nick Jr.)
  New York (New York), USA
art director
  George Guzman
producer
  Sharon Ngoi
copywriter
  Karen Kuflik
director of animation
  Chris Gilligan
production manager
  Donna Watts

creative firm
  Nickelodeon
  New York (New York), USA
executive producer
  Agi Fodor
director
  Anastasia Kedroe
art director
  George Guzman
designer
  Andrew Ulanoff
animator
  Joe Silver
copywriter
  Joe Boyd
production
  Donna Watts & Adrienne Torrisi

creative firm
  Ogilvy & Mather Frankfurt
  Frankfurt, Germany
creative director
  Thomas Hofbeck & Dr. Stephan Vogel
art director
  Thomas Hofbeck
copywriter
  Dr. Stephan Vogel
client
  Osram GmbH, München

creative firm
  Ogilvy & Mather Frankfurt
  Frankfurt, Germany
creative director
  Johannes Krempl
art director
  Traudel Linder
copywriter
  Anna Kohlhaupt
client
  Nestlé Dairy Chilled Products, Frankfurt

creative firm
  Ogilvy & Mather Frankfurt
  Frankfurt, Germany
creative directors
  Pit Kho & Ilona Klück
art director
  Ilona Klück
copywriter
  Pit Kho
client
  Advance Bank Munich

creative firm
  Ogilvy & Mather Frankfurt
  Frankfurt, Germany
creative director, copywriter
  Dr. Stephan Vogel
art directors
  Dr. Stephan Vogel & Christian Mommertz
client
  Ogilvy & Mather Frankfurt

353

creative firm
  RDW Group Inc.
  Providence (Rhode Island), USA
creative people
  Anthony Gill & Dan Madole
client
  Roger William Park Zoo

creative firm
  Bozell Worldwide
  Providence (Rhode Island), USA
creative people
  Anthony Gill
client
  DBS Bank

creative firm
  RDW Group Inc.
  Providence (Rhode Island), USA
creative people
  Anthony Gill & Dan Madole
client
  City of Providence

354

creative firm
  Tamir Cohen J.W.T.
  Tel-Aviv, Israel
creative people
  Orit Ringel & Anita Rave
director
  Haim Buzaglo
client
  Tempo

creative firm
  Tamir Cohen J.W.T.
  Tel-Aviv, Israel
creative people
  Tali Cohen & Pnina Ofir
director
  Yariv Gaver
client
  Pele-Phone Communications

creative firm
  Tamir Cohen J.W.T.
  Tel-Aviv, Israel
creative people
  Orit Ringel
director
  Yariv Gaver
client
  Tempo

creative firm
  Tamir Cohen J.W.T.
  Tel-Aviv, Israel
creative people
  Tali Cohen & Pnina Ofir
director
  Oded Davidoff
client
  Pele-Phone Communications

creative firm
  TBWA/BDDP SPA
  Milan, Italy
copywriter
  Bruno Cataldo
art
  Nieo Marchesi
client
  McDonald's

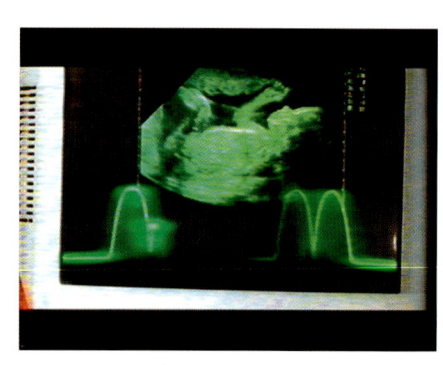

creative firm
  TBWA/BDDP SPA
  Milan, Italy
copywriter
  Bruno Cataldo
art
  Nieo Marchesi
client
  McDonald's

creative firm
  TBWA/BDDP SPA
  Milan, Italy
copywriter
  Antonio De Santis
art
  Giorgio Cignoni
client
  Honda Automobili Italia SPA

creative firm
  TBWA/BDDP SPA
  Milan, Italy
copywriter
  Emilio Haimann
art
  Marco Ravanetti
client
  Aprilia

creative firm
  Temerlin McClain
  Irving (Texas), USA
creative directors
  Matt Manroe & Vinny Minchillo
acd/art director
  Barbara Stampley
copywriter
  Vinny Minchillo
client
  American Airlines

creative firm
  Temerlin McClain
  Irving (Texas), USA
creative directors
  Bill Oakley, David Wilgus, & Diane Seimetz
art director
  David Wilgus
copywriter
  Diane Seimetz
client
  American Airlines

creative firm
  Temerlin McClain
  Irving (Texas), USA
creative director
  Glenn Ashley
art director
  Karen Selkey
copywriter
  Michael Tuggle
client
  JCPenney

creative firm
  Temerlin McClain
  Irving (Texas), USA
creative director, art director, copywriter
  Artie Megibben
client
  Nationwide

creative firm
  Temerlin McClain
  Irving (Texas), USA
creative director
  Glenn Ashley
art director
  Karen Selkey
copywriter
  Priscilla Siegel
client
  JCPenney

creative firm
  Temerlin McClain
  Irving (Texas), USA
creative director
  Glenn Ashley
art director
  Craig Anderson
copywriter
  Steve Taylor
client
  JCPenney

creative firm
  Temerlin McClain
  Irving (Texas), USA
creative director
  Artie Megibben
art director
  Gary Smith
copywriters
  Jim Weber & Melvin Strobbe
client
  Subaru

355

creative firm
  Temerlin McClain
  Irving (Texas), USA
creative director
  Glenn Ashley
art directors
  Karen Selkey & Craig Anderson
copywriters
  Michael Tuggle & Steve Taylor
client
  JCPenney

creative firm
  Temerlin McClain
  Irving (Texas), USA
creative directors
  Glenn Ashley & Janet Ferguson
art director
  Janet Ferguson
copywriter
  Priscilla Siegel
client
  JCPenney

creative firm
  Temerlin McClain
  Irving (Texas), USA
creative director
  Artie Megibben
art director
  Donna Lempert
copywriters
  Steve Spencer
client
  Subaru

creative firm
  Temerlin McClain
  Irving (Texas), USA
creative director
  Artie Megibben
art director
  Virgil Adams
copywriter
  Jim Weber
client
  Subaru

creative firm
  Temerlin McClain
  Irving (Texas), USA
creative director
  Artie Megibben
art director
  Virgil Adams
copywriter
  Jim Weber
client
  Nationwide

creative firm
  The Benchmark Group
  Cincinnati (Ohio), USA
creative people
  John Carpenter, Leslie Hall,
  & Jen O'Shea
client
  Cincinnati Ballet

356

creative firm
  The Ungar Group
  Chicago (Illinois), USA
creative people
  Tom Ungar, Mark Ingraham,
  & Janet Tomaskovic
client
  Sanford

creative firm
  Verba DDB
  Milan, Italy
director
  Gianfranco Marabelli
art
  Laura Trovalusci
copywriter
  Luca Gelmuzzi
client
  Henkel

creative firm
  Verba DDB
  Milan, Italy
directors
  Stefano Longoni & Francesco Emiliani
art
  Stefano Longoni
copywriter
  Francesco Emiliani
client
  Spontex Italia

creative firm
  Verba DDB
  Milan, Italy
director
  Enrico Bonomini
art
  Mariangela Storti
copywriters
  Enrico Bonomini
  & Frediano Tavano
client
  Autogerma

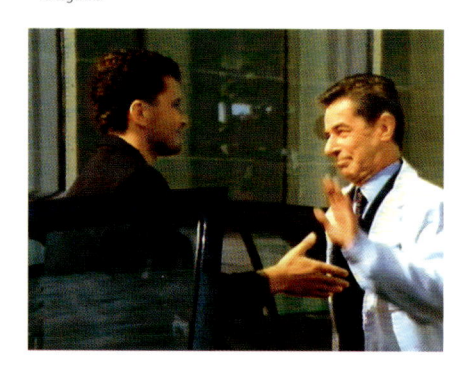

creative firm
  VH1 On Air Promos
  New York (New York), USA
copywriter, director, producer
  Briton McAdams
executive producers
  Geoffrey Whelan & Linda Danner

creative firm
  Wray Ward Laseter
  Advertising
  Charlotte (North Carolina), USA
creative director
  Jennifer Appleby
copywriter
  Tom Cocke
producer
  Sheila B. Dulin
client
  Carolina Beverage Corp.

creative firm
　Young & Rubicam Mexico
　　Mexico City, Mexico
creative directors
　Yuri Alvarado & Ignacio Zeleny
art director
　Walter Sendra
producer
　Bernardo Salum
director of creative serv.
　Enrique Laguardia Longega
copywriter
　Ignacio Zeleny
client
　Whitehall Robins

creative firm
　Young & Rubicam Mexico
　　Mexico City, Mexico
creative directors
　Enrique Laguardia, Yuri Alvarado,
　& Hector San Roman
art directors
　Alberto Najera & Avril Olachea
producer
　Bernardo Salum
copywriter
　Hector San Roman
client
　Grupo Modelo

creative firm
　Advico Young & Rubicam
　　Zurich-Gockhausen, Switzerland
creative director, art director, copywriter
　Dieter Hofmann
client
　Migros

# CREATIVITY 29
## Consumer TVc Campaign

creative firm
　BBDO Minneapolis
　　Minneapolis (Minnesota), USA
creative director
　Denny Haley
art director
　Steve Michels-Boyce
producers
　Amy Jo Schulteis, Payy Lum-Hughes,
　& Jackie Vidor
copywriter
　Karen Lokensgard
client
　Jennie-O Foods Corp.

creative firm
　BGS DMB&B
　　Milan, Italy
producer
　Ego Maniac
director
　Boss U. Around
copywriter
　Pen Sword
client
　Sara Lee/Champion

creative firm
　CadmusCom
　　Richmond (Virginia), USA
creative directors
　Kelly O'Keefe & Robin Konieczny
art director
　J. B. Hopkins
producers
　Sheila Fox & Karen Smith
director
　Ali Selim
copywriter
　Brian Fox
client
　Office Furniture USA

creative firm
  Campbell-Ewald
  Advertising
    Warren (Michigan), USA
creative directors
  Jim Gorman & Joe Putty
art director
  John Clarey
copywriter
  Jon Stewart
client
  Chevrolet Truck

creative firm
  Campbell-Ewald
  Advertising
    Warren (Michigan), USA
creative directors
  Jim Gorman & Joe Putty
art director
  John Clarey
copywriter
  Jon Stewart
client
  Chevrolet Truck

creative firm
  Cramer-Krasselt
    Milwaukee (Wisconsin), USA
creative director
  Michael Bednar
art director
  Jon Grider
copywriter
  Mark Henderson
client
  Allen Edmonds

creative firm
  Dymun Nelson & Company
    Pittsburgh (Pennsylvania), USA
creative directors
  John Dymun & Craig Otto
copywriter
  John Dymun
art director
  Craig Otto
producer
  Sandy Stewart
client
  Dollar Bank

creative firm
  Grey Advertising Inc.
    New York (New York), USA
creative people
  Rob Batocco, Eric Finkelstein, Richie Solomon,
  Ugo Pergolotti, & Sallie Moore
client
  Six Flags

creative firm
  Grey Daiko Advertising Inc.
    Tokyo, (Minato-ku), Japan
creative directors
  Soeda Masayoshi & Matsushima Chikako
art director
  Nakajima Tatsuhisa
copywriter
  Matsushima Chikako
tv planner
  Serizawa Yoichiro
production company
  River Run, Inc.
client
  Proctor & Gamble Far East, Inc.

creative firm
  GREY GmbH & Co. KG
    Düsseldorf, Germany
creative directors
  Barbara Dibué & Adam Owett
producer
  Siglinde Kubicek
director
  David Ondricek
dop
  Jan Velicky
client
  Effem - Kitekat

creative firm
  GREY GmbH & Co. KG
    Düsseldorf, Germany
creative directors
  Barbara Dibué & Adam Owett
producer
  Robert Leisewitz
director
  Wayne Gibson
dop
  Wance Burberry
client
  Effem - Kitekat

creative firm
  Heye + Partner
    Unterhaching, Germany
creative directors
  Martin Kiebling & Alexander Bartel
producer
  Sascha Driesang
art director
  Frank Widmann
copywriter
  Jan Okusluk
client
  McDonald's Austria

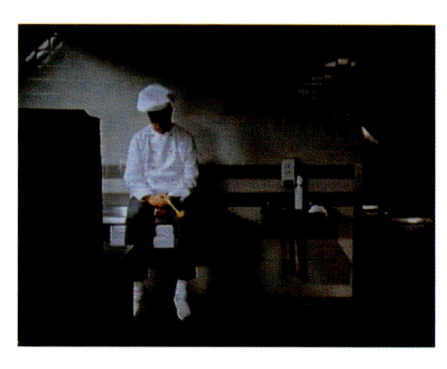

358

creative firm
  J. Walter Thompson
  Chicago (Illinois), USA
gcd
  Mark Silviera
art director
  Craig Schwartz
copywriter
  Jeff Martin
client
  KRAFT/Miracle Whip Flavors

creative firm
  J. Walter Thompson
  Chicago (Illinois), USA
gcd
  Mark Silviera
art director
  Craig Schwartz
copywriter
  Jeff Martin
client
  KRAFT/Miracle Whip Squeeze

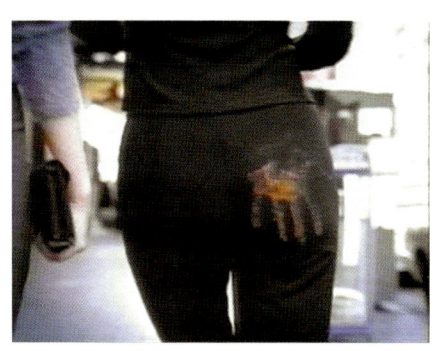

creative firm
  J. Walter Thompson
  Chicago (Illinois), USA
gcd
  Dennis Ryan
art director
  Kevin Seavitt
copywriter
  Derek Sherman
client
  NABISCO/Air Crisps

creative firm
  J. Walter Thompson/N.Y.
  New York (New York), USA
creative director
  Stuart Mickle, John Morrison, & Bill Hamilton
art director
  Alain Briere
copywriter
  Peter Seterdahl
producer
  Mark Sitley
client
  Merrill Lynch

creative firm
  J. Walter Thompson/N.Y.
  New York (New York), USA
creative director
  Brian Sitts
art director
  Randy Freeman
copywriter
  Kevin Doyle
producer
  Paul Roy
client
  KRAFT/Miracle Whip Squeeze

creative firm
  J. Walter Thompson/N.Y.
  New York (New York), USA
creative director
  Alan Platt
art director
  Thomas Hayo
copywriter
  Ronald Wohlman
producer
  Jill Rothman
client
  Kelloggs Raisin Bran Crunch

creative firm
  J.J. Sedelmaier Prod., Inc.
  New York (New York), USA
agency producer, art director, copywriter
  Ken Giddon
director
  J.J. Sedelmaier
designer
  Douglas Fraser
head animator
  David Wachtenheim
client
  Rothman's

creative firm
  J.J. Sedelmaier Prod., Inc.
  New York (New York), USA
agency producer, art director, copywriter
  Ken Giddon
director
  J.J. Sedelmaier
designer
  Douglas Fraser
head animator
  Brian Gaidry
client
  Rothman's

creative firm
  JMC/YR
  Caracas (Miranda), Venezuela
creative people
  Mabel Ruiz & Ruben Perez
client
  EL Universal

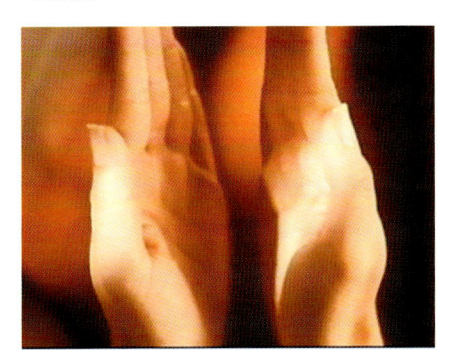

creative firm
  Louis London
    St. Louis (Missouri), USA
art directors
  Joe Ortmeyer & Aaron Segall
copywriters
  Lori Jones & Steve Hunt
client
  The Casino Queen

creative firm
  Louis London
    St. Louis (Missouri), USA
art director
  Aaron Segall
copywriter
  Lori Jones
client
  Postnet.com

creative firm
  MARC Advertising
    Pittsburgh (Pennsylvania), USA
creative people
  Ed Fine, Tony Jaffe, Holly Humphrey,
  & John Swisher
client
  Rite Aid Corporation

360

creative firm
  McCann-Erickson Sydney
    North Sydney, Australia
creative people
  Paul Kamzelas & Jamie Kwong
client
  Rebel Sport Limited

creative firm
  McCann-Erickson
    New York (New York), USA
creative directors
  Joyce King Thomas & Jonathan Cranin
art director
  Chris Cereda
copywriter
  Eric Goldstein
producer
  Kelley Long
client
  MasterCard

creative firm
  Nick-at-Nite
    New York (New York), USA
producer, copywriter
  Mark Sullivan

creative firm
  Nick-at-Nite
    New York (New York), USA
creative director
  Matthew Duntemann
art directors
  Jim Spegman, Scott Stowell, & Chip Wass
executive producer
  Gwen Powell
producer
  Michelle Band
designer
  Scott Stowell
illustrator
  Chip Wass

creative firm
  Nickelodeon
    New York (New York), USA
creative director
  Agi Fodor
art director
  Marie Hyon
producers
  Rich Williams, Victoria Stewart,
  & Rich Barry
copywriters
  Victoria Stewart, Rich Barry, & Rick Groel

creative firm
  Nickelodeon
    New York (New York), USA
executive producer
  Agi Fodor
art director
  Konk Productions
director
  Chris Koch

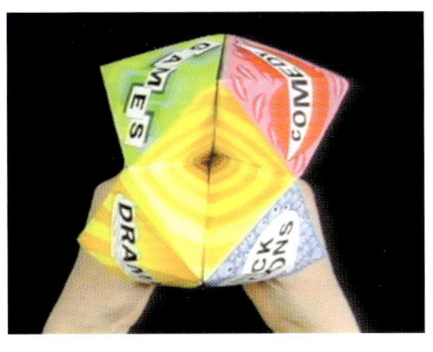

creative firm
  Nickelodeon
    New York (New York), USA
creative director
  Kim Rosenblum
art directors
  Kenna Kay & Jim Spegman
producer
  Gwenevere Powell
directors
  Jim Matison & Lucy Blackwell
production company
  Colossal Pictures

creative firm
  Tamir Cohen J.W.T.
    Chicago (Illinois), USA
creative people
  Tal Raviv, Itay Galon, & Gilad Rozen
director
  Moshe Yom Tov
client
  Strauss

creative firm
  Tamir Cohen J.W.T.
    Chicago (Illinois), USA
director
  Yigal Shilon
client
  Amir Marketing

creative firm
  Temerlin McClain
    Irving (Texas), USA
creative director
  Grant Swain
art director
  Karen Selkey
copywriter
  Priscilla Siegel
client
  JCPenney

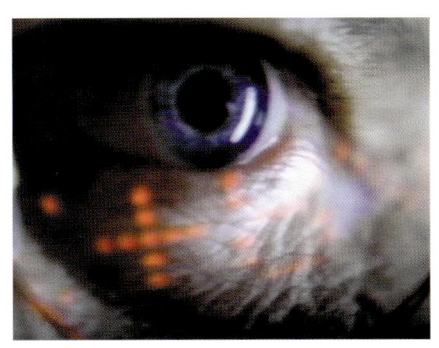

creative firm
  Temerlin McClain
    Irving (Texas), USA
creative director
  Grant Swain
art director
  Scott Morris
copywriter
  Shep Kellam
client
  NationsBank

creative firm
  Temerlin McClain
    Irving (Texas), USA
creative director
  Glenn Ashley
art directors
  Randee Paur & James Hughes
copywriters
  Sandra Luciano, Lisa Johnson, & Glenn Ashley
client
  JCPenney

361

creative firm
  Temerlin McClain
    Irving (Texas), USA
creative director
  Grant Swain
art directors
  John McEown & Scott Morris
copywriters
  Shep Kellam & Grant Swain
client
  NationsBank

creative firm
  The Imagination Company
    Bethel (Vermont), USA
creative director, producer
  Jim Giberti
cameraman, editor
  Steve Frigard
client
  Tri-State Lottery

creative firm
  Verba DDB
    Milan, Italy
creative director
  Francesco Emiliani
art director
  Andrea Maggioni
copywriter
  Frediano Tavano
client
  Garda Bibite

creative firm
 VH1 On Air Promos
 New York (New York), USA
director
 Rob Grobengieser
producers
 Geoffrey Whelan, Linda Danner,
 & Rob Grobengieser
copywriter
 Gary T. Carlin

# CREATIVITY
## Corporate, TVc Single

362

creative firm
 Dye, Van Mol & Lawrence
 Nashville (Tennessee), USA
creative director
 Chuck Creasy
client
 CCA

creative firm
 Erwin-Penland Advertising
 Greenville (South Carolina), USA
creative director
 Russ Corvey
broadcast producer
 Randall Owens
art director
 Jerry O'Malley
copywriters
 Tom Leach & Brandon Walters
client
 Bell Atlantic Mobile

creative firm
 Dieste & Partners Publicidad
 Dallas (Texas), USA
creative director
 Aldo Quevedo
art director
 Roberto Saucedo
copywriter
 Javier Guemes
client
 Major League Soccer

creative firm
 J. Walter Thompson/N.Y.
 New York (New York), USA
creative directors
 Stuart Mickle, John Morrison, & Bill Hamilton
art director
 Alan Brier
producer
 Mark Sitley
copywriter
 Michael Eilperin
client
 Merrill Lynch

creative firm
 JMC/YR
 Caracas (Miranda), Venezuela
creative people
 Cesar Milianai, A. Hontoria
 & Andres Cruz
client
 PDVSA

creative firm
 McCann-Erickson Sydney
 North Sydney, Australia
creative people
 Paul Kamzelas & Jamie Kwong
client
 Levi Strauss

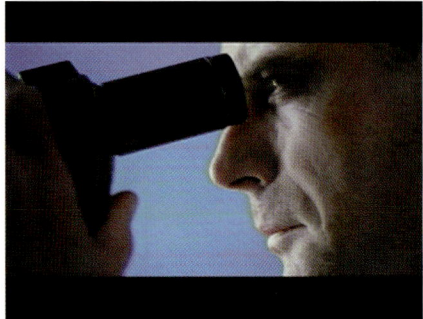

creative firm
  McCann-Erickson
  New York (New York), USA
creative director
  Jonathan Cranin
art director
  Dan Miyahara
producer
  Sally Hotchkiss
copywriter
  Pete Jones
client
  Salomon Smith Barney

creative firm
  Primal Screen
  Atlanta (Georgia), USA
art director
  Douglass Grimmett
designer
  Noeve Warren
animation
  Joe Peery & Primal Screen
copywriter
  Chris Kelly
sound
  Stephen Mank
client
  Cartoon Network

creative firm
  Temerlin McClain
  Irving (Texas), USA
creative director
  Bill Oakley
art director
  Brad White
copywriters
  Leigh Sander, John Lennon, &
  Paul McCartney
client
  Nortel Networks

creative firm
  Dye, Van Mol & Lawrence
  Nashville (Tennessee), USA
creative director
  Chuck Creasy
client
  CCA

# CREATIVITY 29
## Corporate TVc Campaign

creative firm
  JMC/Y&R
  Caracas (Miranda), Venezuela
creative people
  Juan M. Mendez, Matias Padron, &
  M. Barnola
client
  Banco Mercantil

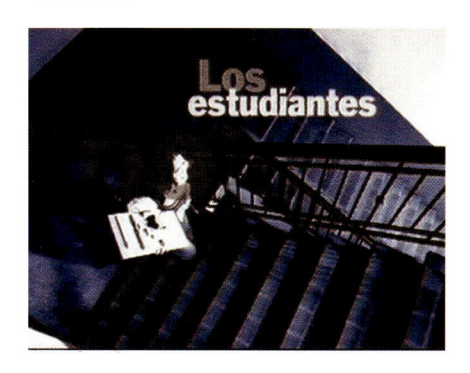

creative firm
  McCann-Erickson
  New York (New York), USA
creative directors
  Gib Marquardt & Paul Behnen
art director
  Paul Behnen
producer
  Linda Kramer
copywriter
  Gib Marquardt
client
  Lucent

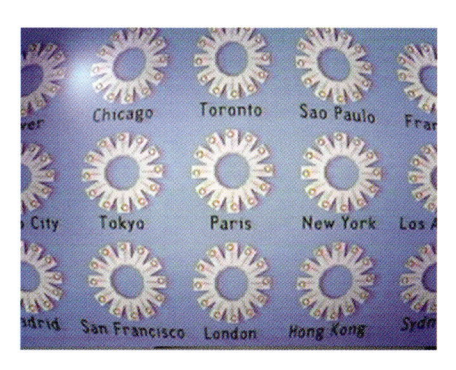

creative firm
  McCann-Erickson
  New York (New York), USA
creative director
  Jonathan Cranin
art director
  K.J. Bowen
producer
  Sally Hotchkiss
copywriter
  Pete Jones
client
  AON

# CREATIVITY
## Public Service, TV
## Single

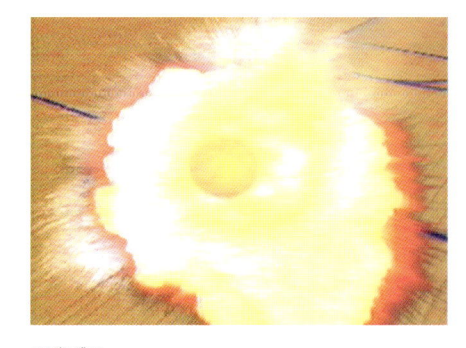

creative firm
 Conflux Design
  Rockford (Illinois), USA
director
 Greg Fedorev
sound
 Rick Nielsen
producer
 Scott Fustin
client
 Rock Valley College

creative firm
 Dieste & Partners
  Publicidad
  Dallas (Texas), USA
creative director
 Aldo Quevedo
art director
 Patty Martinez
copywriter
 Iñaki Escudero
client
 Nelson-Tebedo

creative firm
 J.J. Sedelmaier Prod., Inc.
  White Plains (New York), USA
producer, director
 J.J. Sedelmaier
copywriters
 J.J. Sedelmaier & Adrian Tomine
music
 Pomposello Productions
client
 Art Directors Club

creative firm
 J.J. Sedelmaier Prod., Inc.
  White Plains (New York), USA
directors
 J.J. Sedelmaier & David Wachtenheim
copywriter
 Robert Smigel
producer
 J.J. Sedelmaier
animation, design
 David Wachtenheim
client
 NBC/Saturday Night Live

creative firm
 J.J. Sedelmaier Prod., Inc.
  White Plains (New York), USA
art directors
 J.J. Sedelmaier & Jeff Hopfer
copywriter
 Ron Henderson & J.J. Sedelmaier
producer
 J.J. Sedelmaier
animator, designer
 Brian Gaidry
client
 Episcopal New Church Center

creative firm
 J.J. Sedelmaier Prod., Inc.
  White Plains (New York), USA
copywriter
 Robert Smigel
producer, director
 J.J. Sedelmaier
animators
 Don McGrath & Mike Wetterhahn
client
 NBC/Saturday Night Live

creative firm
 J.J. Sedelmaier Prod., Inc.
  White Plains (New York), USA
copywriters
 Robert Smigel, Michelle Saks Smigel, & Adam McKay
producer, director
 J.J. Sedelmaier
designers
 J.J. Sedelmaier & Dave Lovelace
animator
 Dave Lovelace
client
 NBC/Saturday Night Live

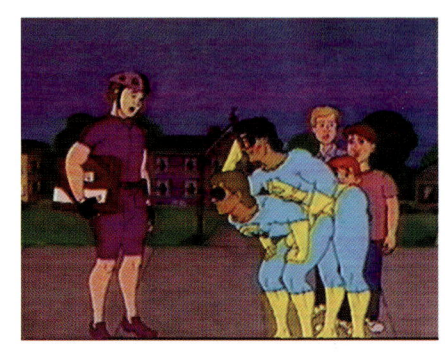

creative firm
 J.J. Sedelmaier Prod., Inc.
 White Plains (New York), USA
copywriters
 Robert Smigel & Stephen Colbert
directors
 Dave Lovelace & J.J. Sedelmaier
designers
 J.J. Sedelmaier & Dave Lovelace
producer
 J.J. Sedelmaier
client
 NBC/Saturday Night Live

creative firm
 J.J. Sedelmaier Prod., Inc.
 White Plains (New York), USA
copywriters
 Robert Smigel, Adam McKay, & Louis C.K.
director, designer
 Dave Lovelace
producer
 J.J. Sedelmaier
client
 NBC/Saturday Night Live

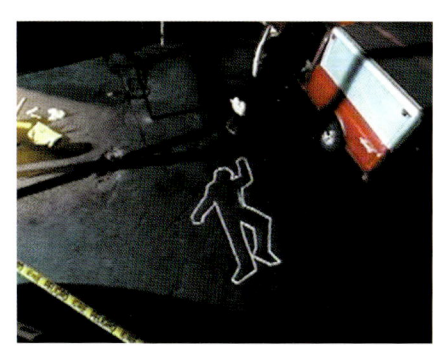

creative firm
 JMC/Y&R
 Caracas (Miranda), Venezuela
creative people
 Ruben Perez, Mabel Ruiz, R. Amiel,
 & Enelio Farina
client
 AVSD

creative firm
 Ogilvy & Mather Frankfurt
 Frankfurt, Germany
creative director
 Delle Krause
art director
 Christian Mommertz
copywriter
 Christian Seifert
client
 SWR Television Station Baden-Baden

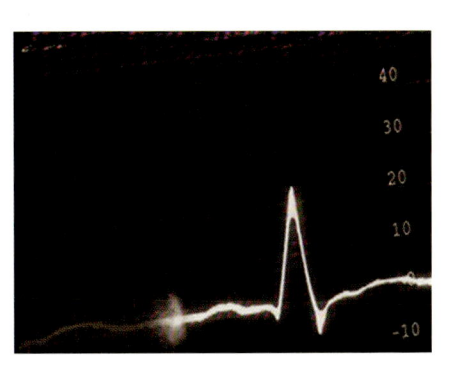

creative firm
 Ogilvy & Mather Frankfurt
 Frankfurt, Germany
creative director
 Bernd Lange & Gregor Seitz
art director
 Gregor Seitz
copywriter
 Bernd Lange
client
 German Heart Foundation, Frankfurt

creative firm
 Ogilvy & Mather Frankfurt
 Frankfurt, Germany
creative director
 Johannes Krempl
art director
 Patrick They
copywriters
 Johannes Krempl & Patrick They
client
 WWF Germany Frankfurt

365

creative firm
 Ogilvy & Mather Frankfurt
 Frankfurt, Germany
creative director
 Johannes Krempl
art director
 Patrick They
copywriter
 Johannes Krempl & Patrick They
client
 SWR Television Station Baden Baden

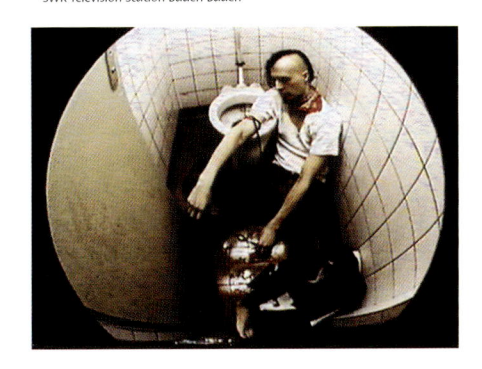

creative firm
 Pontes/Buckley Advertising Inc.
 Boston (Massachusetts), USA
creative people
 Ed Pontes & Michael Kizilbash
client
 Massachusetts Council on Compulsive Gambling

design firm
 Prospect Associates
 Silver Springs (Maryland), USA
creative director, copywriter
 Lynda Bardfield
client
 State of Georgia

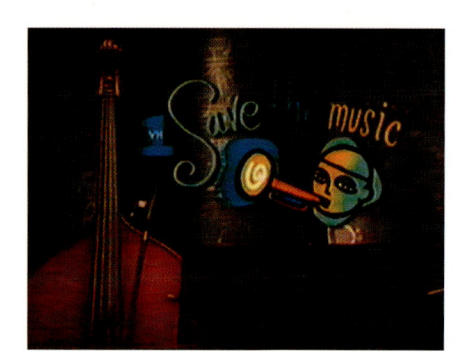

creative firm
 VH1 On Air Promos
 New York (New York), USA
directors
 Rob Grobengieser & Briton McAdams
producers
 Geoffrey Whelan, Linda Danner, & David Chustz
copywriter
 Briton McAdams

creative firm
 Young & Rubicam Mexico
 Mexico City, Mexico
creative directors
 Yuri Alvarado & Ignacio Zeleny
art director
 Walter Sendra
producer
 Bernardo Salum
director of creative services
 Enrique Laguardia Longega
copywriter
 Ignacio Zeleny
client
 Derechos Humanos

creative firm
 Young & Rubicam Mexico
 Mexico City, Mexico
creative director, copywriter
 Yuri Alvarado
art director
 Mauricio Castillo
producer
 Bernardo Salum
director of creative services
 Enrique Laguardia Longega
client
 Donacion De Corneas

# CREATIVITY 29
## Public Service TVc Campaign

creative firm
 Dye, Van Mol & Lawrence
 Nashville (Tennessee), USA
creative director
 Chuck Creasy
art director
 Dale Addy
client
 Goodwill

creative firm
 GREY GmbH & Co. KG
 Düsseldorf, Germany
creative director
 Renate Günther-Greene
producer, dop
 Claude Mougin
director
 Wilfried Seegers
client
 RVA-Alpha Telefon Voluntary Agency

creative firm
 VH1 On Air Promos
 New York (New York), USA
copywriters
 Adam Dolgins, Brit McAdams,
 & Geoffrey Whelan
directors
 Joe Kanellitsas, Linda Danner, Rob Grobengieser,
 & Brit McAdams
producers
 Mike Benson, Linda Danner, Geoffrey Whelan,
 David Chustz, & Joe Kanellitsas

# CREATIVITY 29
## Show Openings, IDs, Titles

creative firm
 Amgen Inc. Marketing
Communications Dept.
 Thousand Oaks (California), USA
creative director
 Lesa Barnes
producers
 Lesa Barnes & Marc Lion
art director
 Brent Sizemore
animation design & production
 Radical 3D
client
 Amgen Inc.

creative firm
 E! On Air Design
 Los Angeles (California), USA
creative director
 Amy Nagasawa
art director
 Reuben Lee
producer
 Samira Sahebi
director of photography
 Stephen Von Bjorn
production coordinator
 Heather Hope
compositor
 Marco Bacich
client
 E. Entertainment Television

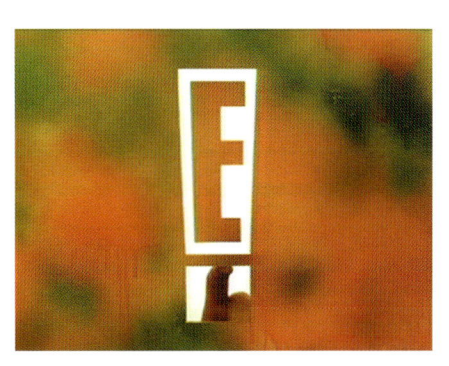

creative firm
 E! On Air Design
 Los Angeles (California), USA
creative director
 Amy Nagasawa
art director
 Reuben Lee
producer
 Samira Sahebi
director of photography
 Stephen Von Bjorn
production coordinator
 Heather Hope
compositor
 Marco Bacich
client
 E. Entertainment Television

creative firm
 E! On Air Design
 Los Angeles (California), USA
creative director
 Amy Nagasawa
art director
 Reuben Lee
producer
 Samira Sahebi
director of photography
 Stephen Von Bjorn
production coordinator
 Heather Hope
compositor
 Marco Bacich
client
 E. Entertainment Television

367

creative firm
 Eyeidea
 Thousand Oaks (California), USA
creative director
 Chad Anderson
client
 Big Little Films

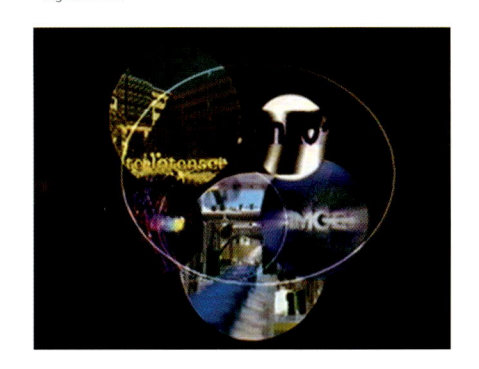

creative firm
 MTV Design
 New York (New York), USA
creative people
 Catherine Chesters & Jenny Rask
client
 MTV Networks

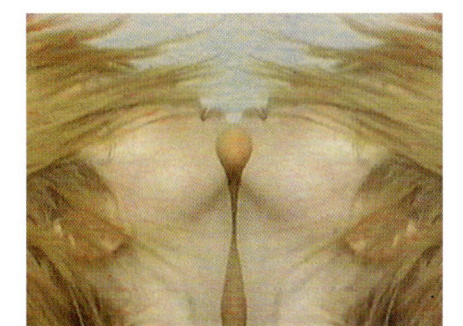

creative firm
 MTV Design
 New York (New York), USA
creative people
 Jenny Rask
client
 MTV Networks

creative firm
  MTV Design
  New York (New York), USA
creative people
  Paul Villacis & Pakorn Bupphavesa
client
  MTV Networks

creative firm
  MTV Design
  New York (New York), USA
creative people
  Greg Hahn, Todd St. John,
  & Pakorn Bupphavesa
client
  MTV Networks

creative firm
  MTV Design
  New York (New York), USA
creative people
  Pual Villacis, Rodger Belknap,
  & Olivier Spencer
client
  MTV Networks

368

creative firm
  Nickelodeon
  New York (New York), USA
creative director
  Agi Fodor
producers
  Niels Schuurmans & Jeremy Lipkin
art director
  Matthew Duntemann
directors, designers
  Todd Mueller & Ken Largent
compositor
  Eben Mears

creative firm
  Nickelodeon
  New York (New York), USA
executive producer
  Agi Fodor
animator
  Steve Erdman
audio
  Tom Clack

creative firm
  Nickelodeon
  New York (New York), USA
creative director
  Kim Rosenblum
art director
  Kenna Kay
director
  Chris Gilligan
producers
  Victoria Stewart
designer
  Laurie Keller
production company
  Pitch Productions

creative firm
  Nickelodeon
  New York (New York), USA
producer
  Adam Idelson
art director
  George Guzman
animators
  Klasky Csupo
music
  Mark Mothersbaugh
production manager
  Hilary Wolk
vp creative
  Niels Schuurmans

creative firm
  Noggin
  New York (New York), USA
art director
  Steve Thomas
animator
  Head Gear
project manager
  Jocelyn Hassenfeld

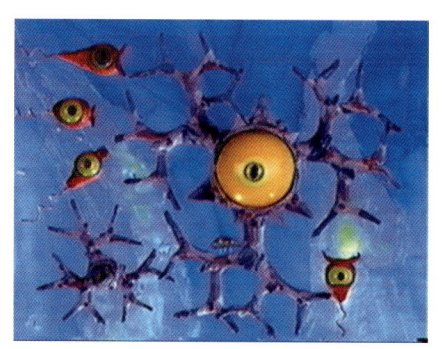

creative firm
  Noggin
  New York (New York), USA
animator
  Head Gear
project manager
  Jocelyn Hassenfeld

creative firm
 Noggin
 New York (New York), USA
art director
 Steve Thomas
animator
 Protozoa
project manager
 Jocelyn Hassenfeld

creative firm
 Primal Screen
 Atlanta (Georgia), USA
creative director
 Michael Ouweleen
sound
 Stehphen Mank
composer
 Raymond Scott

animator
 Primal Screen
project director
 Douglass Grimmett
orchestra
 Seattle Philharmonic
client
 Cartoon Network

creative firm
 Primal Screen
 Atlanta (Georgia), USA
art director
 Douglass Grimmett
animator
 Joe Peery & Primal Screen
music & sound
 Stephen Mank
copywriter
 Chris Kelly
client
 Primal Screen

creative firm
 VH-1 On-Air Graphics
 New York (New York), USA
art director
 DeDe Sullivan
designers
 Phil Han & Neil DuFine

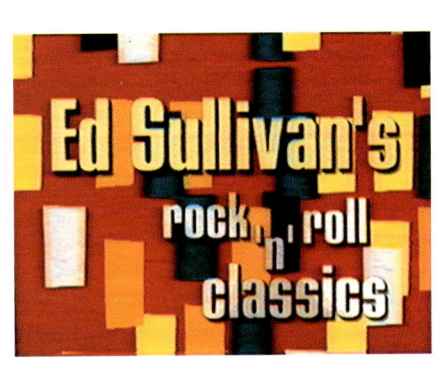

creative firm
 VH-1 On-Air Graphics
 New York (New York), USA
art director
 DeDe Sullivan
designer
 Neil DuFine

creative firm
 VH-1 On-Air Graphics
 New York (New York), USA
art director
 DeDe Sullivan
designer
 Neil DuFine

369

creative firm
 VH-1 On-Air Graphics
 New York (New York), USA
art director
 DeDe Sullivan
designer
 Phil Han

creative firm
 VH-1 On-Air Graphics
 New York (New York), USA
art director
 DeDe Sullivan
designer
 Phil Han

creative firm
 VH-1 On-Air Graphics
 New York (New York), USA
art director
 DeDe Sullivan
designer
 Phil Han

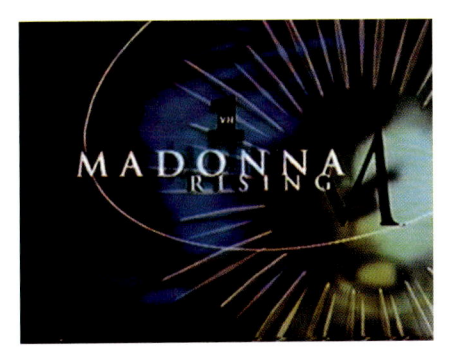

creative firm
  VH-1 On-Air Graphics
  New York (New York), USA
art director
  DeDe Sullivan
designer
  Phil Han

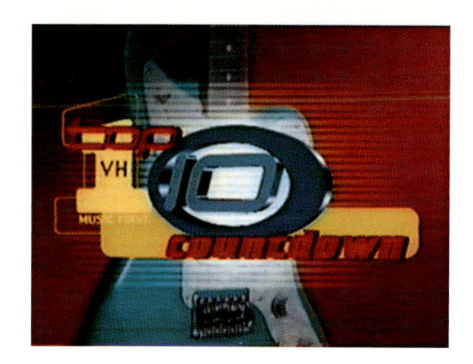

creative firm
  VH-1 On-Air Graphics
  New York (New York), USA
art director
  DeDe Sullivan
designer
  Julie Hirschfeld

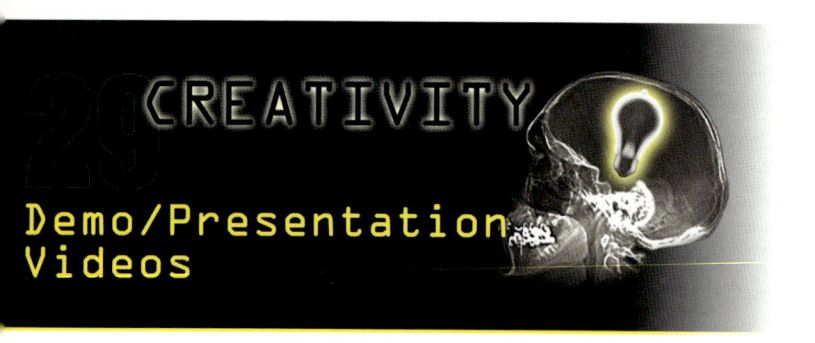

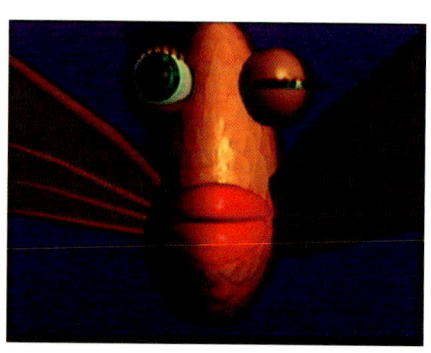

# 29 CREATIVITY
## Demo/Presentation Videos

creative firm
  Conflux Design
  Rockford (Illinois), USA
creative directors
  Greg Fedorev & Scott Fustin
client
  Conflux Design

creative firm
  Dixon Productions Ltd.
  Lower Hutt (Wellington), New Zealand
diirector, copywriter
  Grant Dixon
camera
  Sean O'Donnell
sound
  Grant Lawley
editor
  David Stubbs
client
  The New Zealand Mountain Safety Council

creative firm
  EyeIdea
  Thousand Oaks (California), USA
creative people
  Chad Anderson
client
  EyeIdea

creative firm
  Film Magic Limited
  Hong Kong, China
director
  Fung Tze Cheong, Percy
creative director
  Stephen Siu
art director
  Au Hing Cheong
agency producer
  Kiwi Chan
post production
  Benny Yip
photographer
  David Ng
music
  Philip Tang
animator
  Wong Kan Chuen
client
  GMCC/China Telecom

creative firm
  Interbrand Gerstman + Meyers
  New York (New York), USA
creative people
  Lynne Stewart, Richard Slechta,
  & Donnalynn Civello
client
  Unicef

creative firm
  Louis London
  St. Louis (Missouri), USA
art directors
  Daved Bannecke & Anne Oller
copywriter
  Laura Tomlinson
client
  Trizec • Hahn

creative firm
  Nick-at-Nite/TV Land
  New York (New York), USA
creative director
  Kim Rosenblum
producers
  Dave Herman & David Kerwin
  (Konk Productions)
copywriter
  Dave Goldenberg
director
  Chris Koch (Konk Productions)

creative firm
  Nickelodeon
  New York (New York), USA
producers
  Gwen Powell & Neil Krupnick
director
  Chris Koch

creative firm
  Noggin
  New York (New York), USA
creative people
  Jocelyn Hassenfeld, Karen Kuflik, Andrew Yernoff,
  Big Blue Dot, & Dave Buron

371

creative firm
  Cramer-Krasselt
  Milwaukee (Wisconsin), USA
creative director, copywriter
  Michael Bednar
art director
  John Grider
client
  Fiserv

CREATIVITY 29
Corporate Videos

creative firm
 Innovision, Inc.
  Concord (Massachusetts), USA
producer
 Marilyn H. Knight
director
 Peter Cutler
copywriters
 Marilyn H. Knight & Peter Cutler
client
 GTE Corporation

creative firm
 Louis London
  St. Louis (Missouri), USA
copywriter
 Doug Outman
art director
 Mark Masterson
client
 Southwestern Bell Telephone

creative firm
 Prospera
  Minneapolis (Minnesota), USA
producer, director
 Susan Wagner
client
 Lutheran Brotherhood

372

creative firm
 SHR Perceptual
 Management
  Scottsdale (Arizona), USA
art director
 Mike Barton
client
 Sensory Science

creative firm
 The Chelmar Group
  Monrovia (California), USA
creative people
 Michelle Palmer, Marc Griffith,
 & Mark Leach
client
 The Salvation Army Adult
 Rehabilitation Center

creative firm
 The Sloan Group
  New York (New York), USA
creative directors
 Cliff Sloan & Wyndy Wilder
designer
 Curt Neuman
client
 Miss Universe

creative firm
 The Sloan Group
  New York (New York), USA
creative directors
 Cliff Sloan & Wyndy Wilder
designer
 Curt Neuman
client
 ESPN

creative firm
 Nick-at-Nite
  New York (New York), USA
producer
 Mark Sullivan (Konk Productions)
project manager
 Karen Dragotto
copywriter
 David Rieth

# CREATIVITY
## Web Site Designs

creative firm
 Think New Ideas, Inc.
 Boston (Massachusetts), USA
creative people
 Think New Ideas, Inc.
client
 Avon

creative firm
 Oh Boy, A Design Company
 San Francisco (California), USA
creative director
 David Salanitro
designer
 Alice Chang
photographer
 Hunter Wimmer
illustrator
 Kathryn Otoshi
copywriter
 David Salanitro
web coding
 IOsphere
client
 Oh Boy, A Design Company

373

creative firm
 AJF Marketing
 Piscataway (New Jersey), USA
creative people
 Justin Brindisi
client
 SM Electric

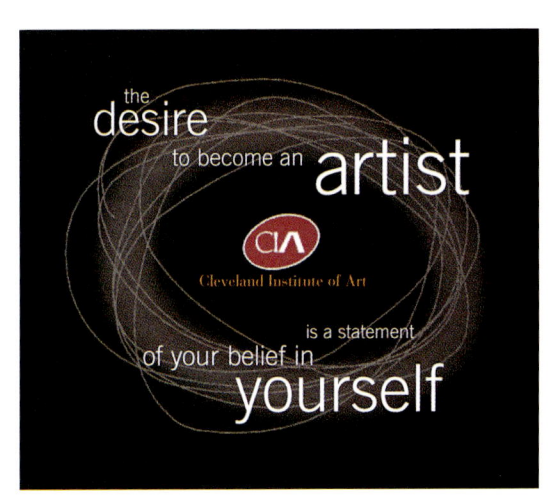

creative firm
 Nesnadny + Schwartz
 Cleveland (Ohio), USA
creative director
 Mark Schwartz
designers
 Timothy Lachina, Michelle Moehler,
 Brian Lavy, & Cynthia Lowry
photographer
 Robert Muller
client
 Cleveland Institute of Art

creative firm
 Digital Navigation
 Cleveland (Ohio), USA
creative director
 Leo Zimmerman
interactive design director
 Susan Lesko
copywriter
 Erin Johnson
client
 Today's Office

creative firm
  Jensen Design Assoc. Inc.
    Long Beach (California), USA
creative people
  David Jensen
client
  Jensen Design Assoc. Inc.

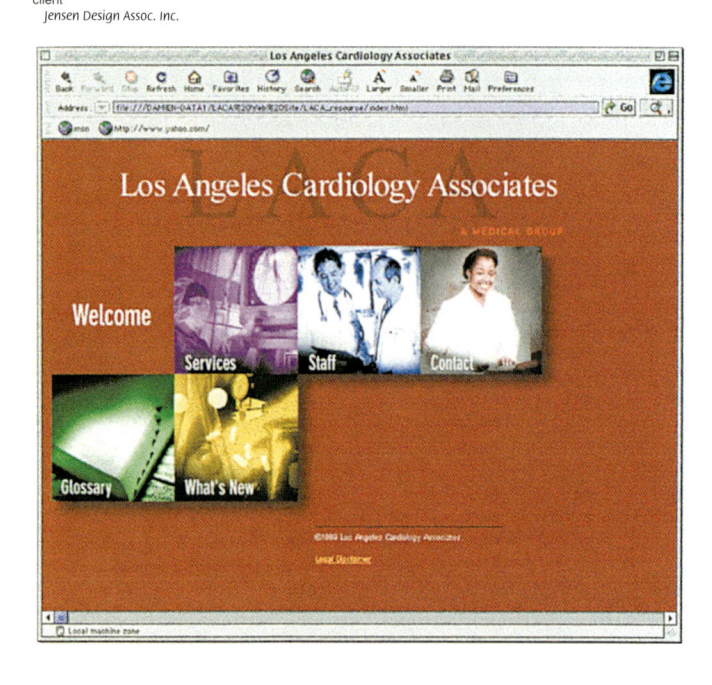

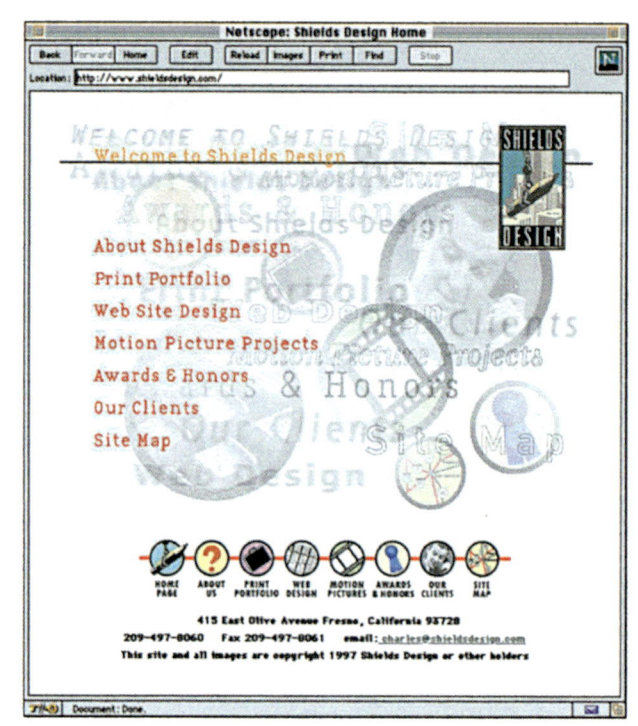

creative firm
  Shields Design
    Fresno (California), USA
art director, structural designer
  Stephanie Wong
designer
  Charles Shields
client
  Shields Design

374

creative firm
  The Wyant Simboli Group, Inc.
    Norwalk (Connecticut), USA
creative people
  Julia Wyat & Sheri Cifaldi
client
  Tod Bryant Photography

creative firm
  IBM Corporate Internet
    New York (New York), USA
creative director
  Jennifer Kilian
web art director
  Victor H. Chan
corporate design strategist
  Patricia Pallisco
designer
  Alex Wright
client
  IBM Corporate Internet

creative firm
  Savage Design Group, Inc.
  Houston (Texas), USA
creative director
  Paula Savage
art director
  Doug Hebert
designer, programmer
  Molly Glasgow
client
  FKP, Inc.

creative firm
  BBK Studio Inc.
  Grand Rapids (Michigan), USA
creative director
  Kevin Budelmann
designers
  Kevin Budelmann, Alison Popp,
  & Jeff Sikkema
coding
  Jeff Sikkema
editors
  Christine MacLean &
  Deb Wieringa
client
  Herman Miller

creative firm
  BBK Studio Inc.
  Grand Rapids (Michigan), USA
creative director
  Kevin Budelmann
designers
  Kevin Budelmann, Alison Popp,
  & Steven Joswick
coding
  Jeff Sikkema
editors
  Julie Ridl, various
client
  Herman Miller

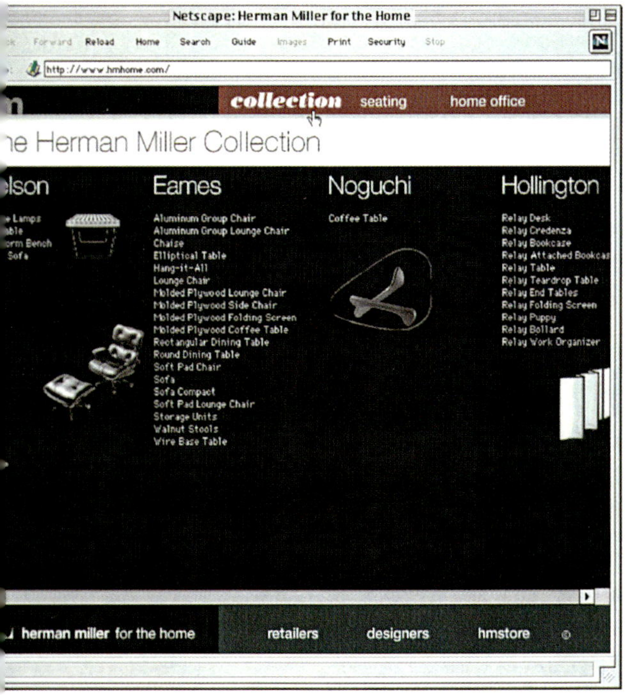

375

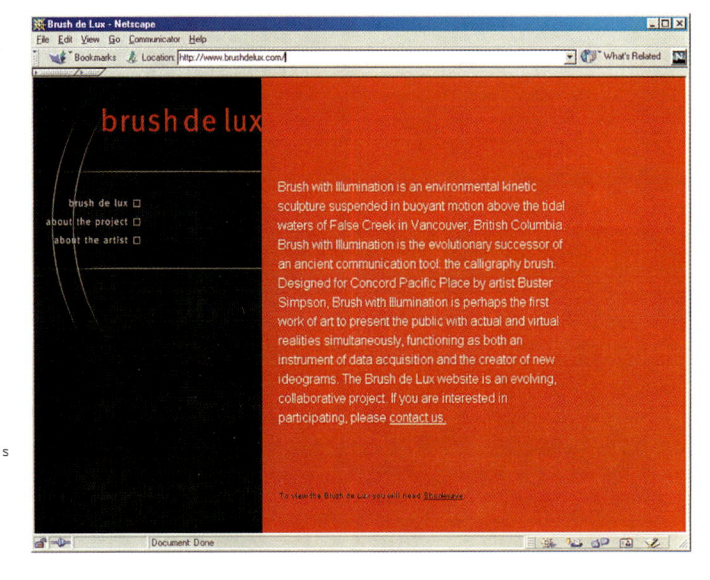

creative firm
  Hornall Anderson Design Works
  Seattle (Washington), USA
creative people
  Eulah Sheffield, Danny Campbell, &
  Robb Anderson
client
  Buster Simpson

creative firm
    Penguin Design.Com
    Newburgh (Indiana), USA
creative director
    Jim Hough
art director, designer
    Sue Hall
client
    Penguin Design.Com

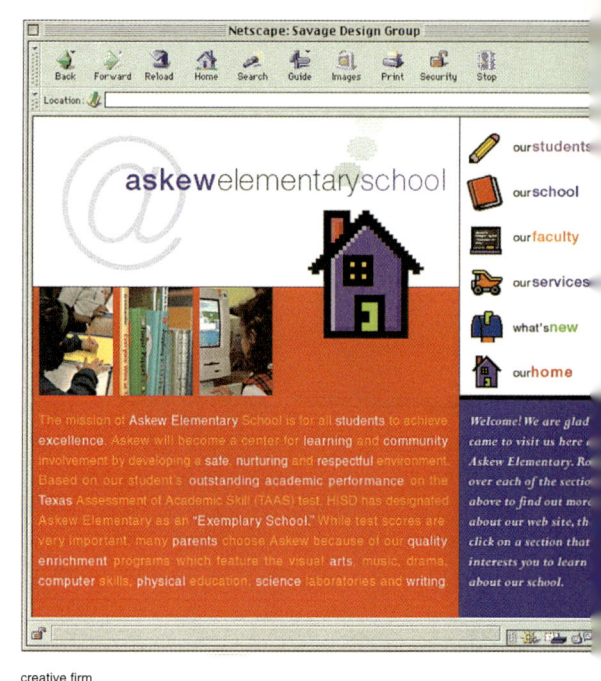

376

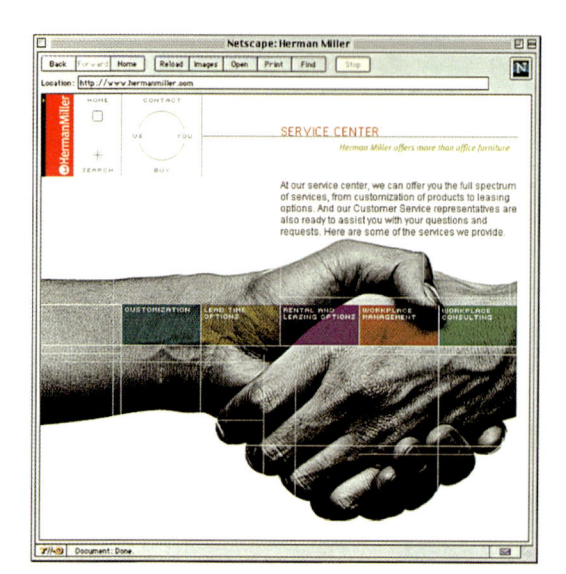

creative firm
    BBK Studio Inc.
    Grand Rapids (Michigan), USA
creative director
    Kevin Budelmann
editor
    Julie Ridl
client
    Herman Miller Inc.

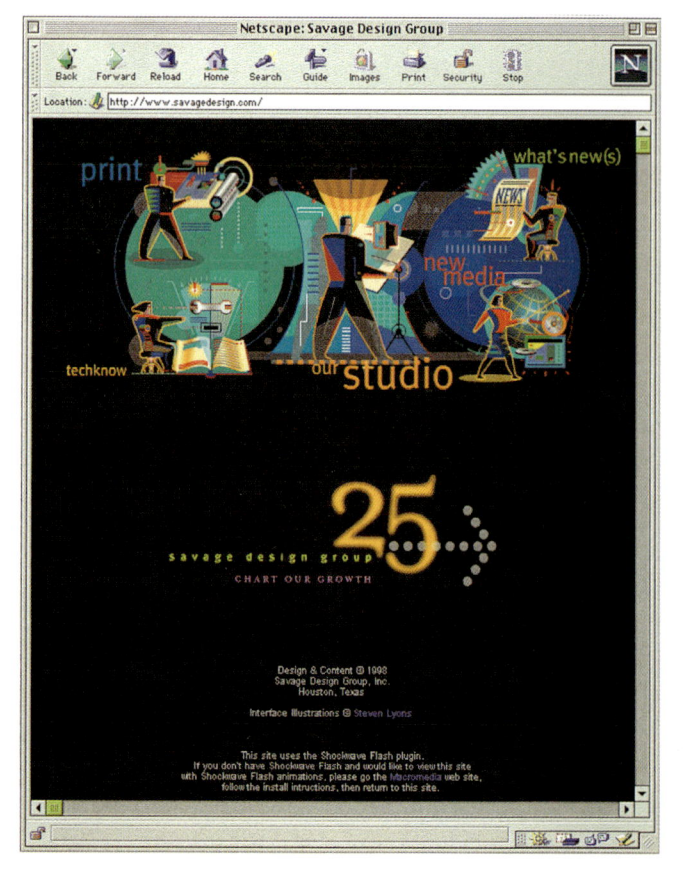

creative firm
    Savage Design Group, Inc.
    Houston (Texas), USA
creative director
    Paula Savage
art director
    Bo Bothe
designers
    Bo Bothe, Molly Glasgow,
    Alicia Noack, & Yi May Yang
programming
    Yi May Yang
animation
    Pat Duffy
client
    Askew Elementary School

creative firm
    Savage Design Group, Inc.
    Houston (Texas), USA
creative director
    Paula Savage
art director
    Doug Hebert
illustrator
    Steven Lyons
programming
    Tony Adams
animation
    Robin Tooms
client
    Savage Design Group

creative firm
 Penguin Design.Com
  Newburgh (Indiana), USA
creative director
 Jim Hough
art director, designer
 Sue Hall
client
 Injury Law Advice. Com

creative firm
 Stackig/TMP
  McLean (Virginia), USA
creative people
 David Gorodetski &
 Lindsay Hall
client
 Tellium

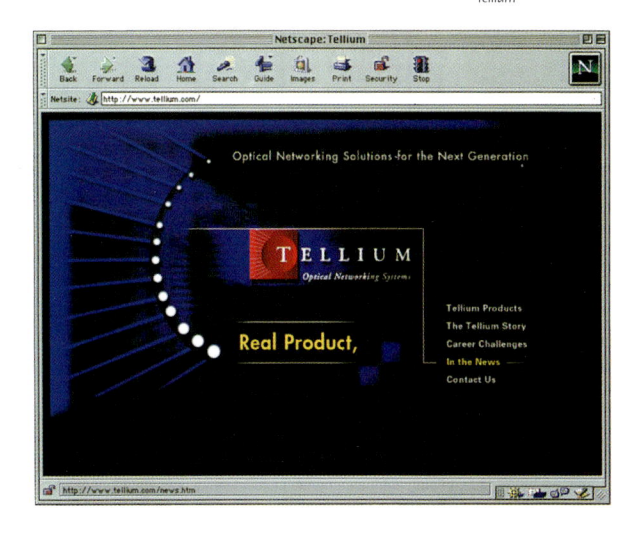

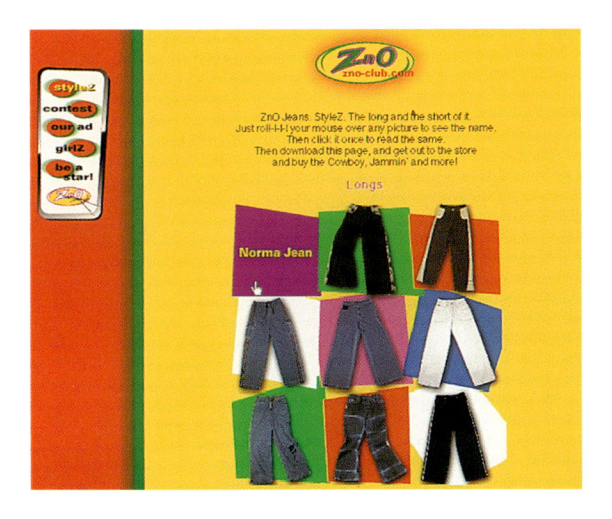

creative firm
 DLS Design
  New York (New York), USA
designers
 David Schiffer &
 Eve Gonsenhauser
client
 CHIC By H.I.S.

creative firm
 MTV Networks Creative Services
  New York (New York), USA
creative director, editor
 Cheryl Family
multimedia director
 Alan Perler
multimedia manager
 Mark Malabrigo
copywriters
 Mia Quagliarello & Rachel Roswal
client
 MTV Networks Creative Services

# CREATIVITY

## CD-ROMs

creative firm
   30sixty design, Inc.
     Los Angeles (California) USA
art director
   Pär Larsson
designers
   Rickard Olsson, Pär Larsson,
   Suppasak Viboonlarp, &
   Peggy Martin
client
   Viacom Consumer Products

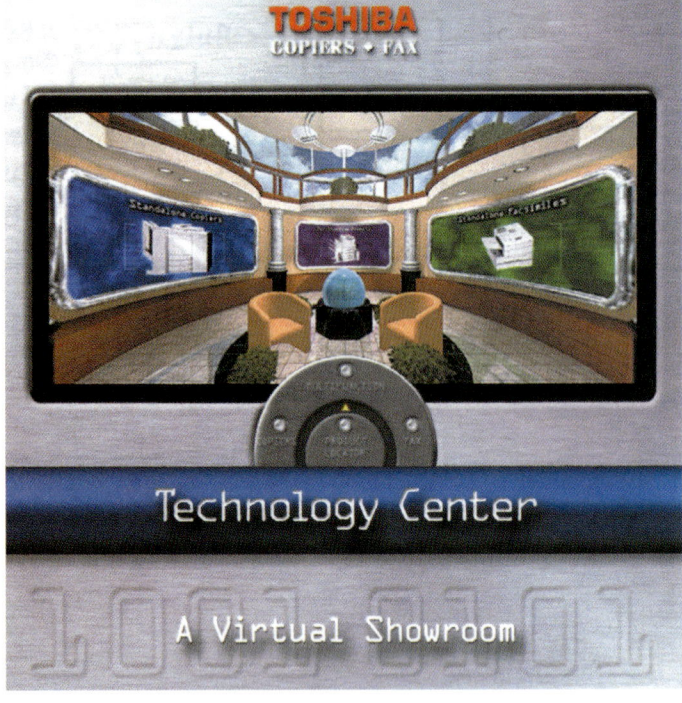

378

creative firm
   Impact Communications Group
     Fountain Valley (California), USA
creative people
   Brad Vinikow
client
   Toshiba EID

creative firm
   Metaforce Interactive
     Norristown (Pennsylvania), USA
creative people
   Eric Mueller & Kurt Mueller
client
   Metaforce Interactive

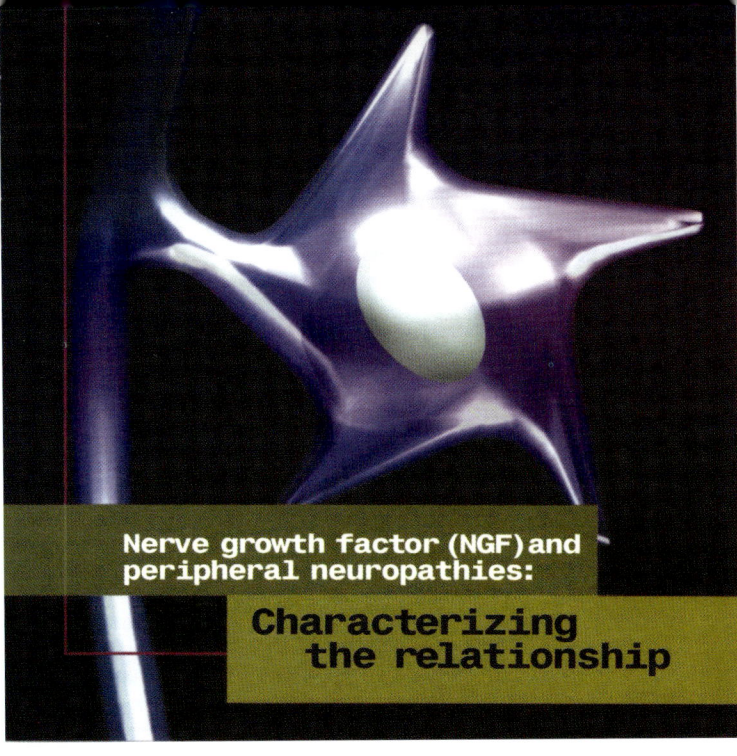

creative firm
  Lewis Gale Bozell
    Ft. Lee (New Jersey), USA
art director
  Kevin Thompson
copywriter
  Elyn Ramon
client
  Genentech, Inc.

creative firm
  Estudio Ray
    Phoenix (Arizona), USA
creative people
  Joe Ray, Christine Ray, & Leslie Link
interactive sites
  Frank Ybarra
client
  Estudio Ray

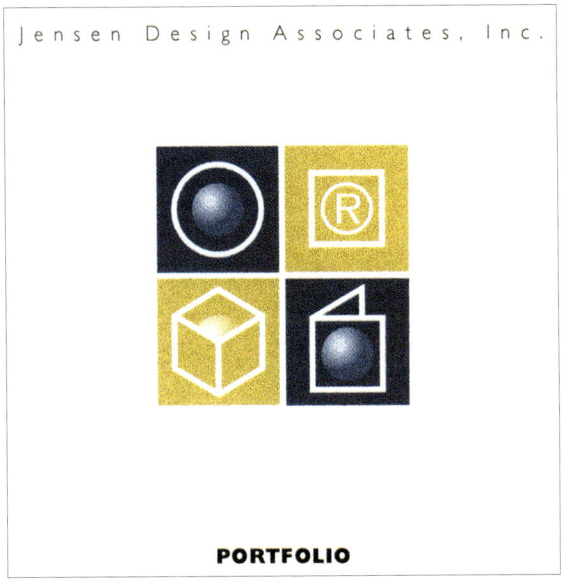

379

creative firm
  Jensen Design Assoc, Inc.
    Long Beach (California), USA
creative people
  David Jensen & Robert Rayburn
client
  Jensen Design Assoc, Inc.

# CREATIVITY

# Index

## CREATIVE FIRMS

### symbols
1185 Design 103, 107, 246, 284
30sixty design, inc. 80, 171, 198, 245, 267, 278, 378
360 Degrees, Inc. 56, 307
66 communication inc. 6, 342

### A
A to Z communications, inc. 127, 131, 251, 285
A+B (In Exile) 235, 236, 260, 266, 283
AAC Integrated Commications 119, 205
Ad Systems International 175
Addison 100, 104, 105, 106, 110, 111, 118, 120, 132
Addison Whitney 263, 273, 277
Adkins/Balchunas 226, 232
Advantage Ltd. 112, 116
Advico Young & Rubicam 38, 94, 95, 96, 98, 345, 346, 357
AERIAL 202, 204, 272, 284, 288
Agnew Moyer Smith Inc. 166, 222, 332
AJF Marketing 210, 373
Akron Beacon Journal 300, 301
Alain M. Flores 234, 316
Alan Herman & Associates 137
Alcone Marketing Group 11, 37, 93, 98, 251, 253
All Media Projects Ltd (Ample) 205
Ambush Communication 51, 214, 259, 271
American Lawyer Media 301, 314, 318, 319, 335, 341
American Medical News 331
Amgen Inc.Marketing Communicati 367
Ammirati Puris Lintas/Column 10, 11
Amy Neiman Design 147
Andrea Brown 227
Arista/Nashville 172, 173, 174
Armando Testa-Rome Italy 24
Armando Testa-Turin Italy 97
Armstrong Graphics 29, 265
Arnold Ingalls Moranville 94, 98
Art 270, Inc. 264
Art Force Studio 239, 243
Arte-Final, Design E Publicidade 258, 266
Artefact Design 150, 213, 262, 275, 344
Artistree Thailand 194
Arts Image Creative Group 315
Atelier Tadeusz Piechura 89
ATW Communications Group 89
August, Lang & Husak, Inc. 72
Augustus Barnett 85
Axion Design 198
Aydlotte & Cartwright 17, 45

### B
Bailey Design Group, Inc. 182, 184
Baker Designed Communications 111, 116, 202
Bald & Beautiful 63, 323
Bard Communications 305, 309, 315, 340
Batey Ads (Pte) Ltd 66, 67, 68
BBDO Minneapolis 357
BBK Studio Inc. 70, 91, 92, 128, 136, 141, 223, 282, 331, 375, 376
Beggs Design 260, 270
Bellini Design 137
Belyea 57, 205, 291
Besser Design Group 102, 125, 133, 146
BGS DMB&B 38, 357
Birmingham Studios 302
Blackburn's Limited 179, 181
Blank-Robert Kent Wilson 68, 141, 174
Bleecker & Sullivan 11, 55, 69, 70, 346
Bloch + Coulter Design Group 116
Blu Bird Productions S.R.L. 343
Boelts Bros. Associates 71, 209, 318
Boldrini & Ficcardi 170, 171, 178, 240, 289
Boller Coates & Neu 108
bonatodesign 193
Botfeld, Kevin 33
Bozell Kamstra 43
Bozell Worldwide 353
Brad Norr Design 125, 288
Braindance 138, 208, 261
BrandEquity International 176, 292, 294
Brian J. Ganton & Associates 145
Broom & Broom 102, 114
Brown, Andrea 227
Bryan Nimeth 22
Buck Consultants 225, 227
Burkhardt & Hillman 42, 54, 63, 241, 346
Burrows WCJ 143, 215

### C
C-E Communications 209
Cadmus Com 10, 23, 32, 135, 268, 357
Cahan & Associates 102, 106, 107, 111, 112, 114, 115, 117, 135, 138, 148, 149, 245, 274, 290
Caldewey Design 178, 190, 191
Callahan and Company 67, 212
Campbell-Ewald Advertising 33, 346, 358
Carl Thompson Assoc. 107
Carpenter Group 153
Casper Design Group 112
Catalyst Direct, Inc. 50, 206
Ce Disena 301
Chris Collins Studio 12, 338, 339
Circus 318
Clarke & Associates LLC 78, 79, 81, 85, 87, 88, 89, 211, 212
Clarke Thompson 203
Cliff & Associates 114
CMP Media 302, 307, 317, 318, 335
CNA Insurance 316
Colestudio 144
CommArts, Inc. 85, 296
Communication Design Corporation 136, 303, 304, 305, 307, 308
Communication Design, Inc. 337
Computer Sciences Corporation 80, 203
Concept CA-Studio JMV 68, 338
Conflux Design 277, 364, 370
Congdon & Company 267, 273, 274, 275
Controles Graficos 234
Cornerstone 188, 192, 244
Cramer-Krasselt 35, 47, 61, 62, 64, 69, 70, 74, 320, 346, 358, 371
Crawford Design + Associates 203
Curtis Design LLC 191, 195, 266, 268

### D
Dana Buckley, Inc. 207
David Carter Design Associates 200, 223, 249, 273, 294, 295, 297
David Lemley Design 79, 187, 224, 225, 269, 289
David Morris Creative Inc. 270
DBD International 79, 135, 149, 170, 204, 281
DCG Chicago 292
De Goede + Others Inc 229
Deep Design 84, 138, 255, 278
degree inc. 143, 211
Delphine Keim Campbell 192
Dennis S. Juett & Associates Inc 24, 98
Dente & Cristina, Inc. 41
Desgrippes Gobe 176, 177
Design Club 66, 81, 82, 249
Design Guys 13, 76, 99, 156, 157, 159, 166, 184, 225, 263, 265, 347
Design Machine 38, 84, 89, 91
Design Narrative 127
Design North, Inc. 195
Design Objectives Pte Ltd 235, 282
Design Resource Center 182
Design Systemat, Inc. 110, 296
DesignTribe 179
Dever Designs 304, 307, 311
DHI 150
DHI Visual Communication 201, 209, 212, 269, 290
Diane Foug Design 265
Dieste & Partners Publicidad 34, 71, 93, 347, 362, 364
Digital Navigation 373
Disney Channel Creative Services 175
Disney Design Group 226, 242, 247
Disneyland Creative Services 123, 221, 230
Dixon & Parcels Associates 180, 188, 189
Dixon Productions Ltd. 370
dk design 254
DLS Design 377
Donaldson, Lufkin & Jenrette 115
Dookim Inc. 219, 280
Dotzler Creative Arts 311
Douglas Joseph Partners 121, 139
Dugan Valva Contess 126, 209
Dye, Van Mol & Lawrence 42, 124, 228, 325, 362, 363, 366
Dymun Nelson & Company 14, 22, 23, 44, 95, 97, 216, 246, 347, 358
Dynamic Duo Studio 165, 252, 312, 335

### E
E! On Air Design 367
egan/st. james 30, 350
Ellen Bruss Design 77, 172, 229
Emerson, Wajdowicz Studios 105, 113, 118, 122, 137, 339, 341
Emery Vincent Design 80, 157, 295, 297
Emphasis Seven Communications Inc 55, 161
Engle + Murphy 280
Eni Oken-3D Artist 336
Epigram Pte Ltd 109, 114, 118, 120, 121, 126
Epoxy 279
Erwin Lefkowitz & Associates 168
Erwin Zinger Graphic Design 310
Erwin-Penland Advertising 76, 347, 362
Estudio Ray 221, 241, 379
Eva Roberts 156
Evenson Design Group 226, 240, 241
Everest Integrated Communications 207
Eyeidea 367, 370

### F
Fader Unda Sohn 148, 212, 338
Fairly Painless Advertising 26, 48, 58, 86, 148, 149, 207, 223
Faltman & Malmen 190, 347
Farenga Design Group 152
Faschingbauer & Schaar 74, 147
FCB Singapore 18
Film Magic Limited 370
Fine Print, Inc. 85, 109
Fisher Design, Inc. 177, 182, 185, 186, 269, 276
Fitting Kolbrener, Inc. 124, 173
Flowers & Fedele 208
Flynn, Sabatino & Day 347
Focus Design 271
Foley Sackett 16, 17, 68, 75
Ford & Earl Associates 91
Forward Design, Inc. 187, 190, 260
Frank D'Astolfo Design 165, 274
FRANTZ/Corporate Imaging 239
FRCH Design Worldwide (Cincinnati) 245, 295, 297, 298
Fry Hammond Barr 8, 16, 24, 36, 66
Funk & Associates 37
Fusion Art Institute 81, 82, 84

### G
Gallery Ltd 48, 52, 60, 62, 124, 155, 157, 207, 238, 253, 315, 319, 344
Gams Chicago 196, 197
Gardner Design 71, 73, 75, 267, 274, 275, 277, 283
Garry Kan Photography 342
Gauger & Silva Associates 13, 26, 53, 96, 192, 194, 196, 222, 244, 254, 255, 263, 268
Gaylord Graphics 188, 257
Gee + Chung Design 140, 246
Genesis Fine Art Photography 338
Gensler Studio 585 283, 295, 299
Gill Fishman Associates, Inc. 117, 142, 267, 270, 271
Glaxo Wellcome Creative Services 89, 250
Glimpses Advertising 316
Gold & Associates 175
Goldforest Advertising 282
Gottschalk+Ash Int'l 105, 109
Graphics II 154
Greenfield/Belser Ltd. 124, 126, 234, 243, 249
Greg Pease Photography 342
Gregory Newson 336
Gregory group 233
Grey Advertising 40, 358
Grey Daiko Advertising Inc. 13, 347, 358
GREY GmbH & Co. KG 347, 358, 366
Group C Design 147, 255
GSO Magazine 301, 319
Guarino Graphics 259

### H
H2D, Inc. 215
Haan and Associates Advertising, 284
Haase & Knels 154
Hadassah Creative Services 134, 334, 336
Handler Design Group, Inc. 292
Haugaard Creative Group, Inc. 188
Hausman Design, Inc. 108, 217
HBO 58, 170, 222, 228, 260
HDS Marcomm 133, 213
Heaven & Earth Designs 317
Hendlin Visual Communications, Inc 76, 247
Herman Miller Inc. 86, 88, 106, 160
Hershey Communications 154, 156, 158, 162
Heye + Partner 53, 171, 278, 313, 358
Hillis Mackey & Company, Inc. 181, 187
Hindustan Thompson Associates 25
Hornall Anderson Design Works 100, 142, 150, 162, 243, 258, 275, 276, 281, 293, 296, 298, 299, 375
House of Design 191, 290
Hull Creative Group 281
Hult Fritz Matuszak 153, 213
Human•l•Tees 217
Hunt Weber Clark Associates 197, 242

### I
IBM Corporate Internet 374
IE Design 203, 247, 273, 287
Illidge Thorp & Partners Advertis 320
Impact Communications Group 378
Infinite Studio 170, 174
Innovision, Inc. 372
Insight Design Communications 73, 261, 289
Interbrand Gerstman + Meyers 144, 181, 183, 231, 371
Iridium Marketing + Design 112, 224, 269, 280
iridium Marketing + Design 224

### J
J. Sposato 66
J. Walter Thompson 12, 15, 20, 26, 37, 40, 320, 321, 322, 325, 348, 349, 350, 359
J. Walter Thompson/N.Y. 6, 30, 35, 39, 40, 84, 94, 96, 97, 99, 348, 349, 359, 362
J.J. Sedelmaier Prod., Inc. 359, 364, 365
J.R. Navarro & Associates Inc. 259
JA Design Solutions 306
Jack Nadel, Inc. 208, 217, 218, 220
James Robie Design Associates 139, 253, 255, 272, 275, 291
Jensen Design Assoc. Inc. 225, 296, 374, 379
JGA, Inc. 50, 266
JMC/Y&R 5, 18, 19, 21, 27, 28, 53, 88, 95, 99, 323, 327, 350, 359, 362, 363, 365
John Brady Design Consultants 230, 313
John Kneapler Design 142
Jones Studio Limited 31, 133, 144, 160
Jowaisas Design 152, 265, 306
Julia Tam Design 122, 252, 334
JWT Specialized Communications 10, 50, 54, 218
JWT Specialized Communications 50

### K
Kan & Lau Design Consultants 82, 109, 130, 163
Keiler & Company 88
Ketchum Advertising 14, 15, 17
Kevin Botfeld 33
Kilmer & Kilmer Design & Advertis 110, 248
Kim Baer Design Associates 100, 223, 229, 271, 286
Kinggraphic 70, 83, 87, 141, 194, 251
Klim Design, Inc. 179, 190
Kompas Design 119, 206, 232
Kopf Zimmermann Schultheis 211
kor group 256
Korek Studio 72, 80, 205, 318
KPR 5, 18, 48, 76, 146
KROG 115
Kuo Design 272

### L
L-Square Design Strategy 264, 272
L3 Advertising Inc. 14, 23, 247
Laguna Coast Publishing, Inc. 314, 317
Lambert Design 226
Landkamer Partners 263
Landor Associates 121, 129, 176, 177, 185, 186, 261, 276
Landor New York 263
LaRowe Advertising 49
Larsen Design + Interactive 168, 248
Laura Coe Design Associates 126, 151, 152, 183, 299
Laura Kay Design 265
Lawrence, Mayo & Ponder 130, 214, 339
Lazywood Press 253
Leimer Cross Design 104, 107, 110, 114, 119
Lensa Film SDN BHD 334
Leslie Evans Design Associates 41, 86, 134, 158, 188
Levine And Associates 123, 130
Lewis Gale Bozell 379
Liska + Associates, Inc. 121, 136
Lissac 239
Little & Company 101, 111, 116, 133, 136
LMS Design 185, 196
Lonsdale Saatchi & Saatchi Advertis 131
Louey/Rubino Design Group Inc. 101, 113, 129, 283
Louis London 36, 46, 49, 51, 56, 97, 157, 209, 350, 360, 371, 372
Louis Nelson Associates Inc. 123
Love Packaging Group 134, 224, 244, 256, 257, 261
Lowe Fox Pavlika 44, 128, 211

380

Lunar Design 201

**M**

M & A Design 180, 216
Malcolm Waddell Assoc. Ltd. 134
MARC Advertising 22, 28, 92, 104, 350, 351, 360
Marion Graphics, L.C. 143
Mark Oliver, Inc. 180, 193
Martin Design Associates 140
McCann-Erickson 25, 31, 78, 352, 360, 363
McCann-Erickson Korea Inc. 5, 77, 93, 149, 195, 326, 327, 351
McCann-Erickson NZ 351
McCann-Erickson Sydney 351, 352, 360, 362
McElveney & Palozzi Design Group 180,194
McGaughy Design 222, 248
McNulty Design 330
Media Concepts Corp. 101, 132, 197
Medical Economics Company 310, 316, 317, 333, 336
Metaforce Interactive 378
Metropolis Design 210, 280
Metzler & Associes 143, 200, 236, 259, 275, 296
Michael Courtney Design 297
Michael Niblett Design 178
Michael Orr + Associates, Inc. 145, 160, 292
Mike Salisbury Communications 52, 65, 94, 237, 264
Miller & White Advertising 128, 262, 279
Mires Design, Inc. 43, 54, 90, 127, 199, 238, 250, 264, 300, 328, 343
Moby Dick Group 198, 199, 200
Morgan & Partners 6, 24, 61, 214
Morgan Design Inc. 100
Mortensen Design 104, 259, 269
Mountain View Productions, Ltd. 352
MTV Design 367, 368
MTV Networks Creative Services 159, 251, 277, 377
Mudra Communications Limited 321, 326
Mueller & Wister, Inc. 302
Murphy Design Inc. 337
Murrie Lienhart Rysner 189, 260, 262

**N**

Nakatsuka Daisuke Inc. 34, 182, 184, 201, 267
NDW Communications 258
Neil Motts & Associates, Inc. 258
Nelson & Schmidt, Inc. 16, 93, 322, 324, 325
Nesnadny + Schwartz 120, 154, 161, 340, 341, 344, 373
Next Year's News, Inc. 271
Nicholson Design 294, 297
Nick-at-Nite 360, 372
Nick-at-Nite/TV Land 371
Nickelodeon 242, 243, 293, 353, 360, 361, 368, 371
Nickelodeon (Nick Jr.) 353
Noggin 368, 369, 371
Nolin Larosee Design Communications 105, 111, 129, 159, 162, 195, 239, 264, 268, 293
NPM Advertising 220, 289
NYT Magazine 315

**O**

O&J Design, Inc. 128, 278, 293
Oakley Design Studios 287
Obata Design, Inc. 267, 272
Ogilvy & Mather Frankfurt 14, 15, 51, 86, 96, 324, 353, 365
Oh Boy, A Design Company 110, 373
O'Mara & Ryan 117, 172
Onboard Media 155, 302, 309, 312, 313
Ososxile S.L. 90
Oswaldo Mendes 54, 55, 240
OXO International's in-house art 152, 153
Oxygen Inc. 256, 271

**P**

Paprika Communications 153, 158, 159, 204, 249, 272, 303
Paragraphs Design 121, 150
Parham Santana Inc. 17, 83, 87, 135, 182, 199, 265
Pat Taylor Inc. 273
Paul Kaza Assoc. 16, 28
Pearlfisher 199, 250, 261
Penguin Design.Com 376, 377
People Magazine 303, 306, 308, 309, 311, 312
People Magazine Special Issues 302, 304, 305, 306, 308, 309, 310, 329, 332, 340, 341
Pepe Gimeno-Proyecto Grafico 91, 92, 300
Peter Piper Graphics 71, 72, 78, 173
Peter Taflan Marketing Communicat 73, 262
Philadelphia 76ers 22, 51, 310
Phillips Design Group 183
Phinney/Bischoff Design House 139
Pink Coyote Design, Inc. 285
Pinkhaus 119, 156
Pirman Communications Inc. 233, 241
Pisarkiewicz Mazur & Co., Inc. 36, 189, 236, 259
Pivot Design, Inc. 146, 147, 151
Planet Ads & Design Pte Ltd 277, 230, 269
Playboy Enterprises, Inc. 328, 332, 333, 335
Pontes/Buckley Advertising Inc. 365
Popular Mechanics 72, 306, 307, 311, 314, 316, 333, 344
Praxis Disenadores S.C. 178, 189
Primal Screen 363, 369
Primary Design, Inc. 228, 231, 266
Prisma Photography 339
prodialog 2000 112
Propeller Communication AB 62
Prospect Associates 365
Prospera 372
Publicis Union 45 SDN BHD 323

**Q**

Q Design 107
Qualcomm Design Group 69, 71, 202

**R**

RDW Group Inc. 25, 194, 279, 331, 353
Redbook Promotion Dept. 215, 235
Ricardo Mealha Ateger 160
Richland Design Associates 142, 221, 314
Rick Johnson & Company, Inc. 274
Rick Sealock 313
Risdall Linihan Advertising 55, 145
Robert Meyers 219, 262
Rose + Hopp Design 175, 252, 291
Ross Culbert & Lavery 240, 250
Royce M. Becker Design 165, 169
Rutgers University 270

**S**

Saatchi & Saatchi NY 230
Saatchi & Saatchi Vietnam 19, 76, 323
Sabingrafik, Inc. 277, 328, 329
Sackett Design Associates 140, 210
Salisbury LLC 224
Salisbury State University 93
Sally Johns Design 171, 198
Sapient (Studio Archeptype) 270, 286, 288, 293
Savage Design Group, Inc. 105, 219, 375, 376
Sawyer Riley Compton 7, 9, 11, 15, 29, 31, 45, 46, 47, 49, 52, 64, 65, 73, 216, 322, 324
Sayles Graphic Design 69, 74, 125, 177, 185, 233, 244, 281, 291
Schafer 294
Sealock, Rick 313
Seasonal Specialties Creative Services 161, 200
Sessions Group 104, 258
SGI 252
Shar Coulson Design 103
Shari Finger Design 108, 139
Sharon Sudman/Illustration 79
Shields Design 180, 374
SHR Perceptual Management 131, 298, 300, 372
Sides & Associates, Inc. 215
SIGN Kommunikation GmbH 314, 317, 328
Signi 102, 339
Silver Communications, Inc. 81, 263
Slanting Rain Graphic Design 159
Sommese Design 90, 232
SooHoo Designers 77, 235
Sorensen Illustrates 336, 337
Spencer Zahn & Associates 99, 288
Springetts 187, 193
SrV Unlimited Design 132
Stackig/TMP 48, 377
Stan Gellman Graphic Design 203, 218
Star Tribune 92
Stephanie Knopp Designs 237
Sterling Group 179, 184, 199, 201
Streamline Communication Ltd. 231, 257
Studio Gallo 221
Sudler & Hennessey 52, 321

**T**

Talbot Design Group 125, 155
Tamir Cohen J.W.T. 354, 361
Tangram Strategic Design 163, 166, 193, 232, 262
Taylor & Ives Incorporated 102, 103, 118, 120, 129
TBWA/BDDP SPA 354
Teamwork Design Ltd. 88, 200, 274
Ted Bertz Design 67, 113
Teikna Graphic Design Inc. 227
Temerlin McClain 8, 42, 45, 48, 50, 354, 355, 356, 361, 363
Terry O Communications Inc. 246
The Beacon Journal 319
The Benchmark Group 68, 74, 151, 186, 207, 208, 356
The Chelmar Group 372
The Coleman Group 196
The Frasier/Bell Group 46, 49, 127
The Graphic Expression, Inc. 101, 106, 113, 119
The Hartz Mountain Corporation 197
The Imagination Company 20, 181, 276, 361
The Leonhardt Group 101, 103, 113, 116
The Marketing Continuum 228
The Miller Group 35
The Parker Group 260
The Signature Agency 60
The Sloan Group 17, 238, 372
The Traver Company 146, 229, 237, 284, 286
The Ungar Group 10, 45, 46, 47, 49, 50, 56, 57, 59, 219, 356
The Upper Deck Company 92
The Weber Group, Inc. 177, 186, 187
The Widmeyer-Baker Group, Inc. 91
The Wyant Simboli Group, Inc. 137, 334, 374
The Zimmerman Agency 7, 23, 41, 279, 327
Think New Ideas, Inc. 373
Thompson & Company 78, 87, 90
Thompson Design Group 189, 192, 193, 196
Tieken Design & Creative Services 57, 303
Tiffany & Co. 74, 87, 157
Tom Fowler, Inc. 75, 77, 184, 202, 238, 257, 270
Tor Pettersen & Partners 103, 109, 120
Trikaya Grey Advertising India Ltd. 29
'Tudes, Graphic Design 268
TV Land 236, 329
Two Dimensions 122, 218, 220, 285

**U**

U.S. Postal Service 330, 331
Ukulele Design Consultants Pte Ltd. 34, 169, 198, 210, 216, 218, 231
Up Design, Inc. 140, 145

**V**

VanderSchuit Studio 343
VARBusiness 302, 307, 317
Verba 9, 16, 30, 67
Verba DDB 7, 33, 39, 72, 356, 361
VH-1 On-Air Graphics 369, 370
VH1 On Air Promos 356, 362, 366
Viadesign 117
Virginia Museum of Fine Arts 299

Visual Marketing Associates 138, 285
Vogue Magazine 13, 206

**W**

Wages Design 151, 220
Warkulwiz Design Associates 227
Warner Books 163, 164, 166, 167, 168, 169
Watts Graphic Design 132, 242, 286
Wendell Minor Design 67, 75, 77, 158, 168, 169, 233, 329, 330, 331
Werkhaus Design 287
Wet Paper Bag Graphic Design 69, 75, 328
Wet Paper Graphic Design 73
What a Concept! 115
Whitney Stinger 214, 217
Windigo-Graphics Division 234
winson & terry design consultants 155, 208, 215
Wong•Wong•Boyack, Inc. 213, 234
Workman Publishing 164, 165, 169, 202, 204, 205, 206
World Studio 292
WPA Pinfold Ltd 144, 195
Wray Ward Laseter Advertising 24, 25, 27, 32, 43, 44, 356
Wright Ideas, Inc. 54, 63
Wunderman Cato Johnson 61, 214, 273

**Y**

Young & Roehr Group 51, 59, 60, 245
Young & Rubicam Mexico 5, 12, 19, 321, 323, 324, 357, 366

**Z**

Zebra Design 66
Zeewy Design 287
Zenn Graphic Design 268
Zunda Design Group 59, 192, 282

# CLIENTS

## symbols

30sixty design, inc. 80, 245, 278
3D Systems 139
3M Pharmaceuticals 18
4C Foods Corp. 189

**A**

A Atalanta 235, 260, 283
A to Z communications, inc. 131, 251
Aaron & Sabina Brown 227
Abbott Pennings High School 233
Abercrombie & Kent 269
Acme Idea Company, The 278
ACSYS Professional Staffing 61
Ad Sales 236, 329
Adams Capital Management 124
Adidas Singapore 18
Adobe Systems 107
Advance Bank Munich 353
Advanced Energy Corp. 171, 198
Advanstar Communications 271
Advertising Professionals of Des Moines 74
AERIAL Visual Identity Design 202, 204
Affiniti 272
Agauron Pharmaceuticals 102
Agnew Moyer Smith Inc. 166, 222
AIGA 241
AIGA Cincinnati 245
AIGA Raleigh 250
AIGA/Wichita 73
Airborne Express 100
AIRTOUCH 37
Airtouch 11, 251
Airtours 312
Akron Beacon Journal 300, 301
Alan Jackson 173
Alcone Marketing Group 253
Allegro Films 264
Allen Edmonds 358
Allmerica Financial Corporation 101
Allora Vineyards 191
Allsteel 145
Alnor Instrument Company 161
Amaguri-Taro Ltd. 82
America Online, Inc. 113
American Airlines 354, 355
American Assoc. for the Study of Liver Diseases 271

American Bar Association 330
American Cyanamid 258
American Express Int. Inc. Frankfurt 14, 15
American Hardware Maunfacturers Assn. 57
American Lawyer, The 301, 314, 318, 319, 335, 341
American Movie Classic 135
American Style Magazine 304
America's Promise—The Alliance for Youth 140
Amgen Inc. 367
Amir Marketing 361
Amwest Insurance Group, Inc. 116
Amy Fowler 257
Anacomp 300
Anderson Pellet 276
Andy Warhol Museum,The 22, 44
Ant Farm, The 286
AON 363
APCO Worldwide 123
Appliant, Inc. 289
Applied Materials 246
Aprilia 354
APWM, Inc. 6
Aqua.S.Bernardo 97
Arena Stage 43, 90
Art Directors Club 364
Art Directors/Copywriters Club 75
Art Force Studio 239
Artefact Design 344
Artistree 274
Asia Insurance Co. Ltd,The 169
Askew Elementary School 376
ASPCA 11, 69, 70, 346
AT&T 126
Atlanta Cycling 73
Atlantic LNG Company of Trinidad & Tobago 131
Atlantis Resort 249, 273
Aurora Foods 111
Austin Nichols 199
Australian Cord Blood Foundation 321
Autocrat, Inc. 232
Autogerma 7, 9, 33, 67, 356
Avandel 139
Aveo, Inc. 260
Avomark Auto Insurance 347
Avon 373
AVSD 365

**B**

B.T.Dibbern GmbH & Co.KG 154
Bacardi 13
Backstage Pass Magazine 315
Baker 202
Baker & McKenzie 151
Banco A. Edwards 75
Banco Mercantil 27, 363
Bank Hofmann AG 105
Barbara's Bakery 192
Barilla Japan 13
Baronet 153, 158, 159, 204
Bath & Body Works 176, 177, 185, 186
Bauer Inc. 159, 162
Bauer Nike Hockey Inc. 264
Bausch & Lomb 187, 260
Bay Area World Trade Center 138
Bayerische Hypo-und Vereinsbank AG 109
Baylor College of Medicine 143
BBK Studio 70, 331
BCE Mobile Communications Inc. 105
Beacon/Corcoran Jennison Partners 266
Beckson Design Associates 291
Belco Holdings Limited 112
Bell Atlantic Mobile 362
Bell Atlantic Yellow Pages 23
Bella Vigne Vineyards 191
BellSouth Yellow Pages 346
Beltz-Verlag GmbH 314, 317, 328
Belyea 205, 291
Beth Brosseau Namebranding 286
BF&W Insurance Group 205
Big Little Films 367
Birds Eye 346
Blackwood Studios 286

381

Blades, Board & Skate  20, 39, 348, 349
Blockbuster/Video Game Rentals  349
Bloomington Offset Process Inc.  203
Blue Haze Cigar Co.  196, 197
BMG  267
BMG Classics  172
BMG Ricordi S.P.A.  170, 174
BMG Video  83, 199
Bodega Viniterra  178
Boise Cascade Office Products  157, 209
Boldrini & Ficcardi  240
Bollé  296
Bosman Brewery Co. Ltd.  198, 199, 200
Braindance  138, 208, 261
Bravo Network  83, 265
Brian Pirman  241
Briggs & Riley  295
Brivis Climate Systems  242
Brooks Rehabilitation Hospital  24
Brown, Scott  220
Brown Harris Stevens/Mosbacher  289
Browndeer Press/Harcourt Brace  329
BSI, Inc  48
Buck Consultants  225, 227
Bugle Boy  125
Burlington Industries, Inc.  132
Business Lab  127
Buster Simpson  375
Butterfield + Robinson  227
Buzz Cuts Maximum Lawncare  277

**C**

C-E Communications  209
Cadmus  151, 220
Calico Cottage, Inc.  145
California Lottery  93, 98
Callahan and Company  212
Calpis Ajinomoto Danone Japan Co., LTD.  347
Camera di Commercio di Vicenza  262
Campari  30
Canada Post Corporation  134
Canandaigua Wine Company  190
Canon France  200
Capital Re  100
CardioThoracic Systems, Inc.  119
Carnegie Magazine  313
Carnegie Museum  22, 92
Carnegie Science Center  43
Carolina Beverage Corp.  356
Carrier Corporation  306
Cartoon Network  363, 369
Casa Bonita  281
Casa Cuervo, S.A. de C.V.  179, 190, 323
CASE AG  47, 61
Casino Queen, The  97, 350, 360
Cassina USA  31
CAST Management Consultants, Inc.  129
Catalyst Direct, Inc.  206
Catana  350
Cazenovia Public Library  265
CBI Laboratories  176
CCA  42, 362, 363
CDW Comdex  244
Cedesa  68, 338
Cehovin E.  236
Celebrity Cruises  313
Centerline Software, Inc.  207
Centre City Development Corporation  294
CFI  60
Changi General Hospital  121
Charcuteries Tour Eiffel  195
Charles Neuville  259
Charles Schwab & Co., Inc.  210
Charles Village Community Benifits District  67
Chase  14
Cheesebrough-Pond's USA Co.  184
CheezWhiz  12, 40
Chevrolet  33
Chevrolet Motor Division  346

Chevrolet Truck  346, 358
CHIC By H.I.S.  377
Children's Television Workshop  118
China Grill  238
Chris Collins  338, 339
chris daniels & the kings  172
Cincinnati Ballet  68, 74, 151, 356
Cinel  258
Cinema Tech  208
Cinemax  58
Cisco Systems, Inc.  208, 213, 234
Citizens for Alternatives to the Death Penalty  322, 324
City of Providence  353
Clarke Thompson  203
Clear Blue Sky Productions  287
Clestra Hauserman  161
Cleveland Baseball  22
Cleveland Institute of Art  161, 373
CLOTIA  289
Clown Hall of Fame  16
Clube dos Criativos de Portugal  160
CNA Insurance  316
CNN Newsource  64
Coca-Cola Company, The  85, 181
Coca-Cola Nestle  195, 351
Cocise  266
Colgate Palmolive  18, 95, 186
Collage Salon  288
Collateral Therapeutics  115
Colombo Design  16
Colonial Life Insurance Company (Trinidad) Ltd  205
ComEd  150
Comm Pte Ltd (Singapore)  277
Commercial Bank  96
Communications Ventures  140
Compter Sciences Corporation  203
Computer Reseller News  318, 335
Computer Sciences Corporation  80
Concerned for Sungai Selangor  323
Concord Foods, Inc.  197
Conflux Design  370
Connecticut Grand Opera & Orchestra  75, 77
Consejo Nacional De La Fauna  324
Consolidated Papers, Inc.  137
Contemporary Urology  316
Content Studio  282
COR Therapeutics  115
Corcoran Jennison Company  266
Corevent  280
Corp Air  273
Corporcion C. Carabobo  53
Coulter Pharmaceutical  114
Covanta  273
CPDN  54, 63
Crain Communication Inc.  51, 214, 259
Creative Circus  45, 47
Creighton University  311
Crews N Production Services  285
Cristian Lazzari  289
CSC  150
Cultivations  184
Custom Graphics  203
Cutter & Buck  114
Cybernet Systems Inc.  288
Cybersmith, Inc.  36, 259
CYND Snowboarding Apparel  285
Cypress Prepress, Inc.  269
Cytec Industries, Inc.  110

**D**

D&S Investment  128, 279
d-Con  78
D.A.R.E. America  217, 218
Dai-Ichi Kangyo Bank of California  116
Dairy Crest  193
DAK Associates Inc..  227
D'Ancona  249
Danone de Mexico  12, 189
David Carter  223
David Lemley Design  269
Dayton Hudson Corporation  101
DBD International  149, 170, 204
DBS Bank  353
DC 2  213
De Goede + Others Inc  229
DeBeers  40, 99
degree inc.  211
Delacorte Press  330
DELL  37, 349
DELL Computers  10, 11, 38
Delta Apparel  47, 49, 216
Delta Group PLC  103
Dennis & Company  27

Departamento Del Distrito Federal  321
Derechos Humanos  366
Desert Glory  188
DesignTribe  179
DHI Visual Communication  209, 212, 290
Dial Corporation  177, 185, 186
Diamond Rio  173
Digital Minds  135, 281
DirecTV  346
Disney Channel  175
Disney Cruise Line  294, 295, 297
Disneyland Community Affairs—Bill Ross  123
Disneyland Food Operations  221
Disneyland Merchandise  230
Dividend Homes, Inc.  263, 268
Dollar Bank  347, 358
Domane Muller  191
Donacion De Corneas  366
Donna Martines  217
Dookim Inc.  219, 280
dpiX, Inc.  270
Dr. McSurdy & Staff  287
Dr. Smith's Veterinary Collectibles  278
Drawform  207
Drs. Keyes & Toraason  260
Dublin Ranch  26
Dugan Valva Contess  209
Duke University Artists Series  73
Durham Fair Association  67
DX Photography  51
Dymun Nelson & Company  246
Dynamic Duo Studio  252
DZS, Ljubljana  115

**E**

E.Entertainment Television  367
E.W. Blanch Holdings Inc.  116
EarthVision, Inc.  79
Eastman Kodak  100
Eaton Corporation  47, 65
Eaton Feature  46
Eatzi's  188
eBay Inc.  108
Eclipse Interactive Publishing, Inc.  258
Eddy Specialty Papers  122, 137, 339
Ediciones Del Uru  171
Edo Sushi (Singapore)  230
Edward Don & Company  46
Effem-Kitekat  358
Egger Tyres  345
El Universal  5, 27, 359
Elana Frances Epstein  231
Elisabeth Arden  5
Els Bendheim  168
Emery Vincent Design  157
EMI Group, The  120
Empire Blue Cross/Blue Shield  292
Eni Oken  336
Epicor Software Corporation  263
Epilepsy Foundation  337
Episcopal New Church Center  364
Erwin-Penland  76
ESM Consulting Engineers  237, 284
ESPN  87, 372
Esprit  154
Esterline Technologies  107
Estudio Ray  221, 379
Etc Systems  112
Etheridge Company, The  223
Euromed  222, 254, 255
Evenson Design Group  226, 240
Eventra  270
Experimenta Ediciones De Diseño  300
Eyeldea  370

**F**

Failsafe Corporation (Singapore)  282
Familink  265
Family Preservation & Support Services  327
Fantastic Foods  195
Fao Schwarz  158
Fareed & Co. for Motorola  265
Fashion Institute  262
FastFunds  125
Fedco Incorporated  294
Federal Express  10, 218
Feria Internacional Del Mueble De Valencia  91, 92

Fine Arts Engraving  234
First Chicago NBD Bank  49
First Pacific Company Limited  106
First Tennessee Bank  90
FischerSkis U.S.  20
Fiserv  371
Fitness Choice, The  287
FKP, Inc.  375
Flintridge Foundation  114
Florida USA  276
Florida's Natural Growers  180, 188
Flos USA  144
FNCS  99, 323, 327
Focus Properties  26
Foodmaker  117
FootAction, division of Footstar Corporation  295
Ford Motor Company Ltd.  143
Forma Vital  71, 93
Fortran Printing  337
Fotop Studio  243
Fox Family Channel  17
Fox River Paper  226
FP Mobile Television  280
FRANTZ/Corporate Imaging  239
Freightliner  59
Fremont General  113
French Government Tourist Office  147
Friskies Italia  72
Friskies Petcare, Co., Inc.  196
Fundacion Caja Rioja  90

**G**

G & V Company  180
Galileo International  125
Gallery Ltd  124, 157, 207, 344
Garda Bibite  361
Gardetto & Co., Inc.  195
Gaston Health Care  24, 32
Gatehouse Companies  132
Gauger & Silva Associates  244
Gaylord Container Corp.  257
GE Capital  137, 334
Genentech, Inc.  379
General Cigar Company  196
General Instrument  111
General Magic  117
General Nutrition Corporation  230
Genesis Fine Art Photography  338
GeoCities  261
Geoffrey Nelson  150
George Bond Sports  246
George Gund Foundation, The  340
Georgetown Day School  124
Georgia-Pacific  109
Georgia-Pacific Papers  125, 133
German Heart Foundation, Frankfurt  365
Getty Conservation Institute, The  223
Gianna Rose  177, 185
Ginkgo Intl. Ltd.  182
Giunti Gruppo Editoriale  163, 166
Giuseppe Citterio  345
Glaxo Wellcome Research Services  89
Globalstar  104
GMCC/China Telecom  370
GN Netcom, Inc.  211
Go Card  54
Goetze's Candy Co.  35
Good Gracious Events  247
Goodwill  325, 366
Gordon Screen Printing  328
Goto, Mr. Takaya  129
Government Windows Nt Magazine  304
Governo do Pará  55
Granador  345
Graphics Three, Inc.  202
Great American Audio  59
Greenfield/Belser Ltd.  126
Gregory group  233
Gregory Newson  336
Groceria, The  226
Group C Design  255
Groupe Moulinex/Krups  347
Grupo Modelo  357
GTE  45
GTE Corporation  372
GTE Supply  306
GTECH Holdings Corp.  120
Guan Sang Co Pte Ltd  198
Guinness Import Co.  198

**H**

H+B Lifescience Co., Ltd.  34

H. P. Hood, Inc.  196
H2D, Inc.  215
Hadassah Convention Department  134
Hadassah Exhibit and Display Department  334
Hadassah Fund Raising Division  336
Hakle  95, 345
Hammerquist & Halverson  275
Hancock Shaker Village  233
Hanes Hosiery Inc.  185
Hanson, Paul & Jeanne Hogel  205
Harcourt Brace & Co.  328
Hard Rock Cafe Guam  316
HarperCollins  77, 169, 329
Hartz Mountain Corporation, The  197
Hasbro, Inc.  276
Hathaway  41
Hausman Design, Inc.  217
HBO  170, 222, 228, 260
Headlight Innovative Imagery  280
HealthFirst  347
Heather  259
Heavenly Pet Center  260
Henderson House B&B  29
Hendlin Visual Communications, Inc.  76, 247
Henkel  356
Henry Holt Publishing  165
Herman Miller, Inc.  48, 58, 86, 88, 91, 92, 106, 136, 141, 148, 149, 160, 223, 375, 376
Hershey Foods Corp.  105
Hershey Japan Ltd.  81
Hewlett-Packard Singapore  231
Hiap Moh (HK) Ltd  48, 52, 60, 155, 253
Hindustan Lever Ltd  25
Hitachi Data Systems  133, 213
Hogel, Jeanne & Paul Hanson  205
Home Home Publications  313
Homestake Mining Company  114
Honda Automobili Italia SPA  354
Hong Kong Graphic Arts Association  70
Hong Kong Printers Association, The  141
Hope and Homes for Children  98
Horizon Organic Dairy  107
Hotel Le Germain  272
Hotel Tverskaya  7
Houlihan Lokey Howard & Zukin  252
Hump Sushi Bar & Restaurant, The  253, 272
Hunt Weber Clark Associates  242
Huntington Memorial Hospital  24, 98
Hyperion  261
Hypernex  274

**I**

I.N.A. National Insurance  24
Ian Potter Museum of Art, The  297
IBM Corporate Internet  374
ICF  160
Identix, Inc.  104
IE Design  203, 273
IFS Industrial + Financial Systems  57
Illinois Attorney General  322, 324, 325
ILOG  263
Im Fine Porcelain  272
IM Internal Medicine  317
IMAGE Film & Video Center  84
Imagination Studios, The  276
Imagine Foods  13
Imos Ljubljana  206
Impartmaint  72
IMSA  102
INCA (International Nature & Cultural Adventures)  147
Incyte Pharmaceuticals  103
Independent Adoption Center  323
Independent Film Channel, The  17
Indian Express, The  321
Inference Corporation  142
Infoseek  94, 98, 293
InfoSpace.com  101
Injury Law Advice. Com  377
Inniskillin Vineyards  178, 191
Innovative Thinking  131, 298, 300
Inpartmaint  173
InQuizit  274

INS 106
Institute for Limb Preservation, The 71
Instituto Provincial de la Cultura 170
Interactive Media 264
Interbrand Gerstman + Meyers 144, 231
Interex 261
International Arts Movement 274
International Enamelist Society 156
Investext 142, 221
Iomega 91
IPCR United 119
Iresco 268
Iridio 146, 229
Iridium 224, 269, 276
Iskra Autoelektrika 119

**J**
J. B. Williams 185
J. Paul Getty Trust 255
J.R. Clancy 152
Jacksonville Chamber of Commerce 214
JAGDA 81, 84
James Hardie Building Products 9, 31
James Robie Design Associates 139
Janou Pakter, Inc. 89, 91
Janssen Pharmaceutica 5
JCPenney 355, 361
Jennie-O Foods Corp. 357
Jensen Design Assoc. Inc. 225, 374, 379
Jeunes Shop, The 218
Jewelers on Fifth 55
Jeyes 187
JGA, Inc. 50
JMC-Web Page 18
JMC/Y&R 18, 19
Jockey 40
Johns Hopkins University 141
Johnson & Johnson 182
Johnson Controls 62, 64
Jose Cuervo International 201
Jugend Am Werk Steiermark 74, 147
Junior Achievement 44
Junior League of Charlotte 25
Just My Size 42
JWT Charity Drive 320, 321, 322, 325

**K**
Kama Sutra 155
Kan & Lau Design Consultants 130, 163
Kaufman and Broad Home Corporation 101
Keenan Motors 99
Keeneland Association, The 297
Kellogg's 35
Kelloggs Raisin Bran Crunch 349, 359
Kenmark 283
Kennedy Space Center Visitor Complex 16
Kento's Co., Ltd 318
Kentucky Horse Park 272
Ketchum Pittsburgh 127, 285
Kingfisher PLC 109
Kinggraphic 251
King's Seafood Company 267
KMC Telecom Inc. 55
Kodak Ges.m.b.H, Wien 96
kor group 256
Korea Animal Protection Association 326, 327
Korek Studio 205
Kowloon-Canton Railway Corporation 109
KPMG 211
Kraft Foods, Inc. 189
KRAFT/Miracle Whip Flavors 349, 350, 359
KRAFT/Miracle Whip Squeeze 359

**L**
La Fabrica 266
La Salle Properties 265
La Tondena Distillers Inc. 110
Labatt Visa 228
Lake County Press 128
Lander 183
Larimer Square 77
Larsen Design + Interactive 248
Lawrence, Mayo & Ponder 130, 214, 339

Leatherman Tool Group 162, 243
Levi Strauss 362
Levis 65
Levi's Korea 77, 93, 149, 351
Lewit & Lewinter 307
Liberty Magazine 307, 311
Limited, Inc., The 177
Linpac Group 144
Lipton Brisk 348
Lisa Hollander 204
Littlefield Unlimited 217
Liz Claiborne Inc. 182
Lockheed Martin 275
Logal Software 271
Longyin Review Ltd 315, 319
L'Oreal 352
Los Angeles Dodgers 156
Love Packaging Group 134, 224, 244, 256, 257
Lucent Technologies 78, 79, 81, 85, 87, 88, 89, 212, 363
Lucent Technologies (S) Pte Ltd. 210
Lucky Strike 336
Lutheran Brotherhood 372

**M**
M2L Inc. 133
Make A Wish Foundation 28
Make A Wish Foundation of PA 104
Manhattan Magazine 305, 309, 315, 340
Mann House, The 54
March of Dimes 75
Mares 343
Marilyn Lysohir 192
Mariposa 134
Marjorie Gubelmann 234
Mark & Myrna Mason 219
Mark Perlman 144
Markenartikel 313
Marketing Direct 210
Marsahll/Yezzi Inc. 352
Marwit Capital 137
Maryville Data Systems 267
Massachusetts Council on Compulsive Gambling 365
Massarella Catering Group Ltd. 195
Master Lock 346
MasterCard 25, 352, 360
Matheran Bachao Samiti 207
Mattel/2wo One 2wo 135
Maui Jim, Inc. 153, 213
Mauritius Tourism Information Service 29
MaxMara 41
May Department Stores Co. 50, 108
Mayfair House 23
McDonald's 171, 354
McDonald's Austria 358
McGaughy Design 248
McIlhenny Company 34
Meccano 275, 296
Media One Group, Inc. 113
Medical Economics 310, 333
Memphis College of Arts 87, 90
Memphis Redbirds 78
Mendes Publicidade Ltda. 55, 240
Mercedes Benz 156
Merrill Lynch 15, 26, 348, 359, 362
MetaChem, Inc. 334
Metaforce Interactive 378
Metlife 220
Metropolitan Opera, The 292
Metzler & Associés 143, 236
Miami Modernism 1999 69
Michael Niblett Design 178
Microsoft 119
Microvision, Inc. 103
Middle Tennessee Council Boy Scouts of America 228
Migros 357
Millennia III, Inc. 208
Miller Brewing Company 46
Miller's Fine Petfood, Munich 86
Mills Corporation, The 296
Miner Vineyards 190
Minimed Inc. 111
Ministry of Health 67, 68
Minneapolis Institute of Arts, The 168
Mint Museum of Craft & Design 32, 43
Miracle Printing Co. Ltd. 62
Mirapoint, Inc. 259
Mires Design, Inc. 238, 250
Miss Universe 372

Mission Studios 277
Mitel Corporation 112
Mitsubishi Wireless Digital Cellular Phones 11
modern organic products 136
Mohawk Paper Mills 135
Montréal International 239
MONY 211
Moondoggie 271
Morrison & Burke Screen Printers 329
Mountain Marketing 38, 94
Mountain Sun Juice 180
Mr. & Mrs. James Nekton 230
Mr. Ak Don Cham Pi 334
Mr. Takaya Goto 129
Mrs. Bairds 34
MTV Networks 367, 368, 377
multex.com 81, 263
Muscular Dystrophy Association 233
Museum of Creation, Zurich 346
Muskegon Museum of Art 75
My Table 253

**N**
NABISCO/Air Crisps 348, 349, 359
Nakatsuka Daisuke Inc. 267
Narcissus 41
National Adult Baseball Assoc. 222
National Air and Space Museum 130
National Arts Council 109
National Association of Realtors 292
National Computer Board 118
National Council for Education in the Ceramic Ar 159
National Examination Center "25th Conference East 266
National Geographic/National Public Radio 72
National Outdoor Leadership School 84
National Securities Clearing Corporation 102
National Semiconductor Corporation 102
NationsBank 361
Nationwide 355, 356
NBC/Saturday Night Live 364, 365
Nekton, Mr. & Mrs. James 230
Nelson-Tebedo 364
Neo Vision 71, 78
Nescafe 352
Nestlé Dairy Chilled Products, Frankfurt 353
Nestle Korea 351
Nestlé USA 189, 192, 193
Net Zero 271
Network Appliance 213
Network Media 303, 304, 305
New England Coffee Co. 194, 279, 331
New Mexico Economic Development 274
New Piper Aircraft, Inc., The 201
New York Director's Club, The 84
New York Magazine 312
New York Stock Exchange, Inc. 120
New York Times Company, The 108
New York Times Magazine, The 315
New York University School of Continuing Education 293
New Zealand Insurance 351
New Zealand Mountain Safety Council, The 370
Newcomb & Boyd 138
Newell Rubbermaid 45, 47, 50, 59, 219
Newman's Own 192
NextRx Corporation 281, 298
Nickelodeon 243
Nickelodeon Talent Department 242
Piranha 267
Nok Acharee 251
Nolin Larosée Design Communications 129
Nortel Networks 48, 50, 363
Northpark Shopping Center 162
Northwest Medical Center 209
Norwegian Society of Composers 175
Novartis 19
Novasource 275
Novell 61, 214, 298
Novell Singapore Pte Ltd. 215
Novellus Systems, Inc. 248
Nuance-Watson (HK) Ltd. 88, 200, 274

**O**
O Liberal 54
Oakley Design Studios 287
Office Furniture USA 10, 32, 357
Ogilvy & Mather Frankfurt 51, 353
Ogilvy & Mather, Inc. 128
Oh Boy, A Design Company 373
Olive Garden 277
Oliver McMillan 277
Onboard Media 155
One Reel (Bumbershoot) 224
Oneida 12
Onstar 33
OpenCon Systems Inc. 270
Orchid Drinks 181
Orlando Sentinel Interactive 36
Ortho Biotech 139
Osram GmbH, München 353
Osrodek Kultury Ochota 80
Outdoor Life Network 63
OXO International 152, 153
Oxygen Inc. 256

**P**
Pacific Star Supper Club 229
Pacific Union Real Estate 299
Pacifica 305, 307, 308
Pantheon Books 169
Paper Dimension(s) Pte Ltd. 216
Paprika 249
Paradigm 200
Paramount Group, Inc. 298
Paramount Home Video 171, 198
Partnership for a Drug Free America 348, 349
Pasteur Mérieux Connaught 48, 76, 146
Patient Care Magazine 336
Patricia M. Sitar Center for the Arts 273
Paul Chauncey Photography 283
Paul Hanson & Jeanne Hogel 205
Paxar Corporation 118
PDV 350
PDVSA 362
Peapod 121
Pearlfisher 250
Peernet Group, Inc. 218
Pele-Phone Communications 354
Penguin Design.Com 376
Penn State School of Visual Arts 90
Pennsylvania Fashions 266
Penwest Pharmaceuticals Co. 118
People Magazine 303, 306, 308, 309, 311, 312
People Specials, Hollywood's Happy Couples 306
People Specials, The 25 Most Intriguing People 304, 305, 310, 329, 332
People Specials, The 50 Most Beautiful People 1999 302, 308, 309, 310
People's Bank 113
PeopleSoft 112
Performance Racing Industry Magazine 314, 317
Perrier Group 192
Personify 258
Peter Elliott Architects 295
Petersen Automotive Museum 259
Pfizer, Inc. 244
Pfizer Pty Ltd 52
Phantom Lighting 258
Philadelphia 76ers 22, 51
Philharmonic Society of Orange County 296
Phillips Design Group 183
Pi, Mr. Ak Don Cham 334
Pierre Lissac 239
Pinedale Trading Pte Ltd 155
Pisarkiewicz Mazur & Co., Inc. 236
Pittsburgh Paints 216
Pittsburgh Pirates 17, 350
Pittsburgh Post-Gazette 14, 23, 95, 97
Pizza Hut 347
Platinum Advisors 283
Playboy 328, 332, 333, 335
PNM 110
Poetry-in-Motion 68
Polaroid Polska 89
Pony Express Delivery Service 46, 52, 65
Popular Mechanics 72, 306, 307, 311, 316, 333, 344
Porsche Cars North America 255

Portland Public Market 86
Poster Museum of Beijing 70, 83
Postnet.com 36, 360
Premier Marketing Co., Ltd. 194
Premier Roasters 279
Price Waterhouse Coopers 147
Primal Screen 369
Primary Design, Inc. 228
Priority Call Management 264
Prisma Photography 339
Procter & Gamble 19, 76, 181
Proctor & Gamble Far East, Inc. 358
Profex International Limited (Singapore) 269
Progressive Corporation, The 120, 341, 344
Provigo 268
PSE&G 145
Purdue University 284

**Q**
Q-Pharma 187
Quaker Oats 188, 189
Qualcomm 69, 71, 199, 202, 343
Quinta Do Portal S.A. 179
Qwest 348, 349

**R**
Radio Corporation of Singapore 120
Radney Foster 174
Rainforest Alliance 121
Ramada Hotel, China 194
RCN 128
Rebel Sport Limited 351, 352, 360
Red Hat Software/Extreme Linux 174
Red Ribbon Bakeshop 296
Redbook Magazine 215, 235
Reddi-Wip 35
Reinhold Laugallies Plane Rental 278
Relios 248
Remy Amerique, Inc. 247
Renaissance Handyman, The 262
Republic of Palau 302
Richmond Symphony 23
Rite Aid Corporation 351, 360
Ritz-Carlton 7, 15, 29
Ritz-Carlton Magazine/SCG Publishing 303
Riverside Stage Company 282
RLA Interactive 145
Robert Earl Keen 172
Robertson-Ceco 110
Robinson Knife 160
Rock Island Studios 73
Rock Valley College 364
Rockefeller Foundation, The 105, 341
Rocky Mountain Productions 123
Roger William Park Zoo 353
Rollerblade 52
Ron Burkhardt's 40th Birthday Party 217
Roosevelt's American Eatery 275
Rosario's Mexican Cafe 221
Rosche Services 297
Rose + Hopp Design 252
Ross Culbert & Lavery 250
Ross Simonds 25
Rothman's 359
Rôtisseries St-Hubert Ltée 293
Royal Bank of Canada 111
Royal Caribbean International Cruiseline 313
RUnet 2000 270
RVA-Alpha Telefon Voluntary Agency 366

**S**
S.C. Johnson & Son, Inc. 177, 187
SADOYAetCie 82
Saiwa 193
Saks Incorporated 103
Salisbury LLC 224
Salomon Smith Barney 363
Salvation Army Adult Rehabilitation Center, The 372
Samjong Houlihan Lokey 122
San-J International 196
San Francisco International Airport 140

Sandals 302
Sandals/Beaches Resorts 309
Sanford 10, 49, 56, 356
Sapient Corporation 117, 142, 270
Sara Lee Hosiery 184
Sara Lee/Champion 38, 357
Saturn 124
Savage Design Group 219, 376
Savia 339
Sayles Graphic Design 291
SC Johnson Wax 186
Scanner 57
Scapino 310
Schieffelin & Somerset 179
Schieffelin & Somerset Co./J&B Scotch 6, 30, 94, 97
School of Business and Administration 96
School-to-Work Oakland Partnership 91
Schratter Foods Incorporated 193
Scient 288
Scott Brown 220
Scotts Company, The 182
Scribners 168, 331
Sea Road International Corporation 82
Seasonal Specialities LLC 161, 200
SEAT 94
Seattle Public Schools/The Bon Marché 225
SECON 215
Sedgwick County Zoo 71
Sensory Science 372
SGI 252
Shadyside Chamber of Commerce 262
ShareWave 270
Sharpe & Associates 148, 149
Shearman & Sterling 240
Shields Design 374
Shu Uemura Cosmetics Inc. 182, 184, 201
Siebel Systems 106
Siemens Corporation 103
Sierra On-Line 79
Sigma-Aldrich 54
Silverado Food 193
Silverstone Race Circuit (UK) 215
Singapore Anti-Narcotics Association 66
Singapore Kerala Association 126
Singapore Post Pte Ltd 235
Singapore Power Ltd 114
Single Image 343
Six Flags 358
Six Flags Over Texas 254
Slammer 69, 70, 74
SM Electric 373
Soft Sheer Products Inc. 186
Soho Press 165
Sojourner Truth House 320
Sommese Design 232
SonoSite, Inc. 104
SooHoo Designers 77, 235
Southdown 104
Southern Oregon University 37
Southwestern Bell Telephone 372
Spaulding & Kinne/Hazelden 79
Specialist Cosmetic Laser Clinic 132
Spectrum Photographic & Imaging 271
Spicers Paper 140
Spontex Italia 356
Spring Street 286
Springer-Verlag New York Inc. 317
SS White 50
St. Vincents Hospital 88,
Stanford Fund, The 262
Staples 101, 292
Star One 330
Star Tribune 92
State of Georgia 365
Steelcase Inc. 332
Stephanie Knopp 237
Stern & Company LLP 282
Stonewall Kitchen 158
Stora Enso Nymölla AB 62
Strake Jesuit College Preparatory 105

Strauss 361
Streamline Communication Ltd. 231, 257
Strobl Baugestibh 290
Subaru 8, 355, 356
Sugen 107
Sun International Hotels Limited 119
Sun Pharmaceutical Industries Ltd. 326
Sunday School Board, The 66
Sunspire 13, 194
Suntrac Radiation Services, Inc. 268
Svenska Spel 347
Swisher International 6
Swissair 345
SWR Television Station Baden-Baden 365
Sydney City Mission 320
Sykes Company, The 188
Sylvia & Cheuk Hung 238
Symantec Singapore Pte Ltd. 208

**T**
Taipei International Poster Invitational Exhibit 82
Taiwan Chinese Poster Design Association 87
Tamalpais Bank 269
Tangram Strategic Design 232
Target Stores 13, 76, 99, 156, 157, 159, 166, 184, 187, 225, 263, 265, 347
Taylor Guitars 127
Taylor Made Golf Co. 126, 151, 152, 183, 299
TCU Art Department 73, 328
TCU Dance Department 75
TechnoGym, USA Corp 150
Tellium 377
Telluride Film Festival 44
Tempo 354
Tetra Pak 53
The Acme Idea Company 278
The American Lawyer 301, 314, 318, 319, 335, 341
The Andy Warhol Museum 22, 44
The Ant Farm 286
The Asia Insurance Co. Ltd 169
The Casino Queen 97, 350, 360
The Coca-Cola Company 85, 181
The EMI Group 120
The Etheridge Company 223
The Fitness Choice 287
The George Gund Foundation 340
The Getty Conservation Institute 223
The Groceria 226
The Hartz Mountain Corporation 197
The Hong Kong Printers Association 141
The Hump Sushi Bar & Restaurant 253, 272
The Ian Potter Museum of Art 297
The Imagination Studios 276
The Independent Film Channel 17
The Institute for Limb Preservation 71
The Jeunes Shop 218
The Keeneland Association 297
The Limited, Inc. 177
The Mann House 54
The Metropolitan Opera 292
The Mills Corporation 296
The Minneapolis Institute of Arts 168
The New Piper Aircraft, Inc. 201
The New York Director's Club 84
The New York Times Company 108
The New York Times Magazine 315
The New Zealand Mountain Safety Council 370
The Progressive Corporation 120, 341, 344
The Quaker Oats Company 188
The Renaissance Handyman 262
The Rockefeller Foundation 105, 341
The Salvation Army Adult Rehabilitation Center 372
The Scotts Company 182
The Stanford Fund 262
The Sunday School Board 66
The Sykes Company 188
The Tractors 172
The Tucson Arts District Partnership 318

The Tussauds Group 261
The Upper Deck Company 49, 51, 92
The Valkyrie Co., Inc. 154
The Vantive Corpration 100
The Washington Times 337
Theatre Department 93
Thomas A. Edison Preservation Foundation 123
Thompson Thrift Development 262
Thomson Financial 314
Tiffany & Co. 74, 87, 157
Tiger Sport 63
Time Life Music 175
Tobacco Associates, Inc.. 60
Tod Bryant Photography 374
Today's Office 373
Todd Haiman Studio 148, 212, 338
Tom Fowler, Inc. 238
Tommy Hilfiger Corporation 106
Tom's of Maine 42
Tonkon Torp 243
Tony Stone 53
Toshiba EID 378
Toyota Marine Sports 8
TOZ (Sara Lee) 176, 294
Tractors, The 172
TranSysoft 281
Traverse City Convention & Visitor's Bureau 263
Tri-State Lottery 361
Tribe Pictures 272, 284
Trickle Up Program 113
Trizec•Hahn 371
Tropical Federal Credit Union 115
Tru Serv Corporation/Taylor Rental Division 350
Trump Hotel & Casino Resorts 115
TTS 291
Tucson Arts District Partnership, The 318
Tussauds Group, The 261
TÜV Süddeutschland Holding AG 112
Two Dimensions 122, 218, 220, 285
Tycoon Magazine/SCG Publishing 303

**U**
U.S. Postal Service 330, 331
Ukulele Design Consultants Pte Ltd. 216
Unicef 371
Unisource 303
United Airlines 19, 21, 28
United Health Services 292
United Nations Office for Project Services 118
Universal Records 175
Universal Studios Florida 241
University Games 197
University of Cincinnati 17
University of Connecticut 67
University of Notre Dame 146
University Press of New England 158, 165
Univision Communications Inc. 121
Upper Deck Company, The 49, 51, 92
Upstate Farms 180, 194
Upstate Litho, Inc. 66
Utopia Marketing 56

**V**
Vail Resorts 85
Valencia Community College 24, 66
Valkyrie Co., Inc., The 154
Valle Redondo S.A. 178
Vancouver Stock Exchange 117
Vantive Corpration, The 100
Vassar College 154
Verilink 102
Vermont Department of Tourism & Marketing 16, 28
Vermont Pure Spring Water 181
VFP Communications Ltd. 72, 318
Viacom Consumer Products 378
VIBE Magazine 335
Victoria's Secret 176
Vin & Sprit 190, 199
Vinomex 191
Virginia Museum of Fine Arts 299
Visio Corporation 110
Vision Recumbents 93
Vista Technologies 55
Visual Marketing Associates 138
VKE 107

Vogue Magazine 206
Voodoo Arts 279
Vulcan Northwest 237

**W**
W.A. Lang 16, 17, 68
Walt Disney Attractions Product Development 247
Walt Disney World Attractions Merchandise 226, 242
Warner Books 163, 164, 166, 167, 168, 169
Warner-Lambert/Rolaids 348
Warner-Lambert Co./Trident Gum 96
Washington City Paper 337
Washington Film Festival 337
Washington Mutual Bank 293
Washington Mutual, Inc. 116
Washington State Fruit Commission/Northwest Cher 85
Washington Times, The 337
Waterman 31
Watson-Guptill Catalog 152
Wausau Papers 133, 136
WDVQ.FM 173
Webcor Builders 275
WellCare Solutions, Inc. 268
Wells Fargo & Company 111
Wells Fargo "innoVisions" 299
Wet Paper BagGraphic Design 69
Wheeler Summer Day Camp 153
when.com 246, 284
Whitehall Robins 5, 19, 183, 357
Whitney Stinger 214
Wimberly Allison Tong & Goo 136
Windstar Cruises 146
WinStar Cinema 89
With-A-Twist 261
Woolworths 180, 216
Workman Publishing 164, 165, 169, 202, 204, 206
Workshop 3000 80
World Boxing Council 234, 316
World Financial Properties 142
World OM Day 288
World Wide Fund For Nature (WWF) 323
WWF Germany, Frankfurt 324, 365
Wyeth-Ayerst Laboratories 302

**X**
Xerox Corporation 108, 273
Xerox De Venezuela 88
Xerox new enterprise co. 268
XL Capital Ltd 116

**Y**
Yamaha Golf Cars 45
Yamato Inc. 66
Yamato Inc. Arjo Wiggins Fine Paper Ltd. 249
Yellow Pages 264
Yes Strategies, Inc. 267
Yoshindo 143
Young & Roehr 245
Young & Rubicam 121, 129
Youth Power/Just Say No 276

**Z**
Zalozba Rokus, D.O.O. 232
Zanders USA 46, 49, 127
Zeum 148, 245, 290
Zippo Manufacturing Company 14, 15, 30, 350
ZVSM 95, 345